In the Shadow of the Garrison State

In the Shadow of the Garrison State

AMERICA'S ANTI-STATISM AND

ITS COLD WAR GRAND STRATEGY

AARON L. FRIEDBERG

PRINCETON UNIVERSITY PRESS

PRINCETON, NEW JERSEY

Library of Congress Cataloging-in-Publication Data

Friedberg, Aaron L., 1956–
In the shadow of the garrison state : America's anti-statism and its Cold War grand
strategy / Aaron L. Friedberg.
p. cm. — (Princeton studies in international history and politics) (Princeton studies in
American politics)
Includes index.
ISBN 0-691-07865-3 (alk. paper) — ISBN 0-691-04890-8 (pbk. alk. paper)
1. Power (Social sciences)   2. State, The.   3. Political science.   I. Title.   II. Series.
III. Series: Princeton studies in American politics
JC330.F74 2000
320.1′01—dc21   99-053043

This book has been composed in Times Roman

The paper used in this publication meets the minimum requirements
of ANSI/NISO Z39.48-1992 (R 1997) (*Permanence of Paper*)

http://pup.princeton.edu

Printed in the United States of America

1   2   3   4   5   6   7   8   9   10

1   2   3   4   5   6   7   8   9   10
(pbk.)

FOR ADRIENNE

CONTENTS

LIST OF FIGURES AND TABLES

FIGURES

LIST OF TABLES

ACKNOWLEDGMENTS

I AM VERY PLEASED to be able to acknowledge the many people and institutions who helped me to complete this book.

First and foremost: to my wife, Adrienne Sirken, who bore with me from beginning to end; and to my two sons, Eli and Gideon, who arrived in the middle and added a dash of chaos, and an incalculable measure of joy, to my life—a thousand, thousand thank yous.

Benjamin Berman, Steven David, John DiIulio, Michael Doyle, John Gaddis, Kurt Guthe, Atul Kohli, Irving Sirken, Ezra Suleiman, and Marc Trachtenberg read the manuscript in whole or in large part and provided many useful comments and suggestions. Alan Brinkley, Richard Betts, Eliot Cohen, Robert Cuff, Robert Gilpin, Samuel Huntington, Jane Katz, Ira Katznelson, and Stephen Rosen also commented on papers in which I developed various aspects of the overall argument. I owe a special debt of thanks to my old friends Steven David and Kurt Guthe for their patience and for their timely words of encouragement. Once again it was Andrew Marshall, with his interest in long-term strategic competition, who inspired me to think through the issues at the heart of this book.

Geoffrey Herrera and Daniel Markey were tireless and resourceful research assistants. Kevin Narizny and Sharon Rudich were extremely helpful in gathering information on a number of important issues. Thanks also to Elizabeth Herron for her expert assistance in the project's final stages. Daniel Markey and Christopher Brest produced the figures and tables.

I wish to thank the librarians and archivists of Princeton University, the National Archives and Records Administration, and the Dwight D. Eisenhower and Harry S. Truman presidential libraries for their invaluable assistance.

I am grateful to the Woodrow Wilson International Center for Scholars of the Smithsonian Institution, where I spent a year getting this project off the ground, and to the Norwegian Nobel Institute, where I spent a delightful Oslo spring bringing it in for a landing. Special thanks to Robert Litwak and Samuel Wells of the Wilson Center and to Geir Lundestad and Odd Arne Westad of the Nobel Institute. Thanks also to Al Bernstein and the National Defense University's Institute for National Strategic Studies. At Princeton I have benefited greatly from my association with the Center of International Studies. My thanks to the Center and to its successive directors: Henry Bienen, John Waterbury, and Michael Doyle.

Seminars at Columbia, Harvard, Johns Hopkins University, the Nitze School of Advanced International Studies, the Norwegian Nobel Institute, Ohio University, Ohio State University, and Yale University provided me with opportunities to clarify my thinking and to receive many helpful comments and suggestions.

Last, but not least, I am extremely grateful to the Lynde and Harry Bradley Foundation, the John M. Olin Foundation, the Smith Richardson Foundation, and the Social Science Research Council for their generous financial support.

In the Shadow of the Garrison State

INTRODUCTION

What follows is a study of the interior dimension of American grand strategy during the Cold War. My goal is to explain the shape and size of the domestic mechanisms through which, over the course of nearly half a century, the United States created the implements of its vast military power.

The argument that I intend to make can be briefly summarized: War, in Charles Tilly's pithy phrase, "made" the modern state. As the technology of warfare evolved, the kingdoms and principalities that crowded the landscape of early modern Europe were forced to assemble larger and more capable militaries in order to survive. But, as Tilly explains, "the building of an effective military machine imposed a heavy burden on the population involved: taxes, conscription, requisitions, and more." In order reliably to carry out these power-creating functions, successful political entities had to develop more efficient tax systems, bureaucracies, and professional armies. The process of creating military power thus tended "to promote territorial consolidation, centralization, differentiation of the instruments of government and monopolization of the means of coercion, all the fundamental state-making processes."[1] War made the state. Or, to put it less elegantly, war and the threat of war required the creation of military power, and, over time, the creation of military power led to the construction of strong, modern states.

The American republic was born while this larger historical process was already well underway and, indeed, it was founded in part out of a reaction against the trend toward ever-greater concentrations of state power (and ever-expanding state capacities for military power creation) taking place on the other side of the Atlantic. If not for its geographical good fortune, the new nation might well have undergone an early, traumatic transformation or, perhaps more likely, it might simply have ceased to exist. Instead, the comparative absence of immediate military threats permitted the United States to survive and thrive during the first century and a half of its existence without developing a central state that was strong in the traditional ways. It was not until the end of the Second World War that a combination of geopolitical and technological developments brought the era of insularity to an end.

In the United States at the middle of the twentieth century, as in other countries earlier in the history of the modern age, the imminent threat of war produced pressures for the permanent construction of a powerful central state. In the American case these pressures came comparatively late in the process of political development; they were new and largely unfamiliar, and they were met

---

[1] Charles Tilly, "Reflections on the History of European State-Making" in Tilly, ed., *The Formation of National States in Western Europe* (Princeton: Princeton University Press, 1975), p. 42.

and, to a degree, counterbalanced, by strong anti-statist influences that were deeply rooted in the circumstances of the nation's founding.

The power-creating mechanisms put in place during the first fifteen years of the Cold War can best be understood as the product of a collision between these two sets of conflicting forces. It is impossible to explain the mechanisms of power creation, the military strategy that they were intended to support, or, more generally, the impact of the Cold War on American society and the American economy without reference to the persistent presence of domestic forces tending to oppose expansions in state power.

Domestic constraints appear also to have contributed to the Cold War's eventual outcome. By preventing some of the worst, most stifling excesses of statism, these countervailing tendencies made it easier for the United States to preserve its economic vitality and technological dynamism, to maintain domestic political support for a protracted strategic competition and to stay the course in that competition better than its supremely statist rival.

ELABORATION

The remainder of this book will be devoted to developing the basic argument sketched out above. Before proceeding I would like to provide preliminary answers to three central questions: What is it, exactly, that I am trying to explain? How do I propose to explain it? And why should the reader prefer the explanation I am offering to others that might be advanced?

Focus

Although I will touch on both sets of issues, I will not be concerned here primarily either with measuring changes in the overall size and internal organization of the federal government or with assessing the effects of over four decades of Cold War mobilization on, for example, American domestic politics, law, education, or culture. I will concentrate my attention not on "the state" alone nor on "society" writ large, but on a cluster of intermediary mechanisms: a parallel set of power-creating institutions that linked the state to society, and permitted it to transform societal resources into military capabilities. Why did these mechanisms take the form they did?

The answer to this question is, I believe, of fundamental importance. As they faced off against each other, the United States and the Soviet Union engaged in what political scientist Kenneth Waltz has called "internal balancing"; both drew heavily on their domestic resources in order to generate ever more military strength. Each hoped in this way to counter, and perhaps to surpass, the other's efforts.[2] Whatever else it may have been, the Cold War was, first and foremost, a sustained competition in power creation.

---

[2] Kenneth N. Waltz, *Theory of International Politics* (Reading, MA: Addison-Wesley, 1979), p. 168.

The mechanisms of power creation were the primary transmission belts through which the pressures of the superpower confrontation made themselves felt in both societies. An adequate appreciation of the domestic effects of the Cold War on the United States (or the Soviet Union) must begin with an examination of these mechanisms. Moreover, as I have already suggested, differences in the power-creating programs of the two sides appear to have had a direct effect on the ultimate outcome of their competition. Understanding the process of power creation may therefore hold the key to explaining the course and conclusion of the Cold War. And understanding the Cold War, in turn, can shed light on an even larger issue: why it is that, over the course of several centuries, liberal democracies have been able to best a series of less liberal, less democratic challengers.

Explanation

The central chapters of this book (chapters 4 through 8) contain detailed examinations of the formation, during the years 1945 to (roughly) 1961, of the five main mechanisms of power creation: those intended to extract money and manpower and those designed to direct national resources toward arms production, military research, and defense-supporting industries. Taken as a whole, this period marked an interval of institutional creation, or "founding." After a decade and a half of flux, the broad outlines of American grand strategy, both its internal and its external aspects, would stay largely fixed for the remainder of the Cold War.

The emergence of stable institutions involves a competition among alternatives, resulting eventually in the selection of a dominant form. In the course of explaining what happened in each power-creating domain, I will therefore need also to offer an account of why certain other things did *not* happen. I will be interested, in other words, in counterfactuals, in paths not taken, as well as in actual outcomes.

There are, of course, an infinite variety of such parallel possibilities, most of them so far-fetched as to be entirely irrelevant to an adequate understanding of actual historical events. I will limit myself here to a consideration of what appear in retrospect to have been the serious contenders; those policies and mechanisms which enjoyed significant support at the time, and which had a real chance of adoption. In every case, as I will show, the main alternatives to what actually emerged would have involved greater societal exertion and a more powerful and intrusive central state. The puzzle I seek to solve, in each instance, is why this did not occur.

In providing an answer I will make reference repeatedly to three sets of explanatory factors: the basic structure of American governmental institutions, the interests and relative strength of various groups (both within the government itself and in society at large), and the content of prevailing ideas, or ideology. Institutions and ideology were, I will argue, of central significance; together they imposed a marked anti-statist bias on the process through which

Cold War power creating mechanisms were built. The fragmented character of the American political system, and in particular the separation of powers between the executive and legislative branches, tended to place considerable obstacles in the way of those who wanted to build stronger, more highly centralized power creating mechanisms. Ideas also acted to shape the struggle over policy among self-interested groups, increasing the influence of those adopting an "anti-statist" stance, while weakening the hand of those whose views could be characterized, fairly or not, as "statist." At the very least, ideas were weapons and, in the ideologically charged atmosphere of the early Cold War, particularly potent ones.

But widely shared and sincerely held beliefs about the proper relationship between state and society, and about the urgent need to limit state power, also exerted an independent influence on the course of events. Ideology was not just a rhetorical cloak concealing selfish interests; it was also a strong source of self-constraint on American government officials. In other places and times, national leaders have tended to be among the most determined state-builders. In the United States, because of the country's unusual history and unique ideological heritage, the highest-ranking political officials have sometimes been the most resolute anti-statists. This is a profoundly important phenomenon, one that cannot simply be explained away with reference to the usual narrow categories of greed or electoral ambition.

A brief word about my own biases: while I have not set out to write a morality tale, I do intend clearly to emphasize the long-term benefits to the health and vitality of the American regime of the anti-statist influences that are so deeply embedded within it. That does not mean, however, that I regard these influences as always and unreservedly positive, or that I intend to treat the postwar advocates of anti-statism as the unvarnished heroes of my story.

Some portion of the anti-statist impulse whose impact I will analyze here was the product of impersonal forces; it was the result of the routine functioning of American political institutions, rather than of the deliberate efforts of any particular contemporary party or group or individual. To the extent that anyone deserves the credit for this, it is the Founding Fathers, not their descendants.

Postwar opposition to the growth of governmental power was also, in some cases, merely a by-product of self-interest, rather than the result of any serious attempt to establish what was best for the country as a whole. As such it was neither contemptible nor especially laudable. Principled postwar anti-statists, meanwhile, were often motivated by other beliefs that I happen to regard as reprehensible or, at best, misguided. Many southern Democrats who favored "states' rights" and a weaker government in Washington were also, not coincidentally, racists; some midwestern Republicans who wanted lower taxes, less federal regulation, and a smaller defense budget were also, as a result, isolationists.

If the most determined postwar anti-statists had had their way, the consequences for the United States, its allies, and, ironically, for the cause of liberty that the opponents of strong government claimed to hold dear would have been serious and perhaps even catastrophic. The world today would not be a better place if, after 1945, the United States had been unwilling to maintain its military might and global presence or to help its allies and former enemies rally and rebuild. On the other hand, in the absence of constraints, the anxiety of the early Cold War could easily have led to deep economic damage, or to radical, and perhaps truly dangerous, changes in American institutions and society. If the thoroughgoing anti-statists were misguided, so too were those of their opponents who, without necessarily intending to, might have transformed the United States into an armed camp. A balance needed to be struck between the necessity for external strength and the desire for domestic freedom. Not everyone saw this clearly at the time; my greatest enthusiasm is reserved for those who did.

Alternatives

There are two main alternatives to the overall explanation that I will offer here. Let me briefly note why I believe my own account to be superior.

Probably the most commonly held view is that the Cold War did, in fact, lead to a monstrous growth in the size and power of the federal government and to the construction of something that might properly be called a "garrison state," or "national security state." This rendering of events is not so much wrong as it is incomplete and disproportionate. There is no question that the American state was bigger and stronger in 1950 than it was in 1930. Given the external pressures, however, it was not nearly as big or as strong as it could have been, nor as many influential people believed at the time that it must become in order to survive. That the American state grew during the early years of the Cold War is important, and it is also obvious, in the sense of being plainly visible. Less obvious, but no less important, is that there were potent restraints on state expansion. It is only by considering what might have been, and by examining the process through which actual outcomes eventually emerged, that we can gain an adequate appreciation of this essential fact.

If the U.S. response to the onset of the Cold War was restrained, some have suggested that the reason may lie not in the character of the American domestic regime, but in the nature of the prevailing military techonology. Perhaps, as Stephen Krasner has written, it was the sheer destructiveness of nuclear weapons that permitted the United States to deter aggression and to defend itself without developing a much stronger and more intrusive central state. Nuclear technology, Krasner notes, "made it possible to create the world's most formidable military force even with a weak government."[3]

Supposing that the United States *did* substitute technology for labor, quality for quantity, it does not follow that this was the only plausible response to the existence of nuclear weapons. In fact, as I will show, there were a number of

---

[3] Stephen D. Krasner, *Defending the National Interest* (Princeton: Princeton Univeristy Press, 1978), p. 67.

alternative courses of action, with considerable logic and powerful constituencies behind them, each of which would have required much higher levels of societal effort and a far stronger state than the approach that was ultimately chosen. The military strategy that the United States eventually adopted, and the domestic power-creating measures undertaken to support it, were matters of choice; they were not somehow dictated by objective, material circumstances or by some inescapable technological reality. Those choices, in turn, were strongly shaped by domestic, anti-statist influences.

One way of illustrating this is to match the American approach to Cold War preparedness against that of its strongly statist Soviet counterpart. A thoroughgoing comparison of the strategies and power-creating programs of the two superpowers is beyond the scope of this book. Nevertheless, as I will note at a number of points, the differences between the two were stark and revealing. The United States and the Soviet Union were very different kinds of countries, and they responded to nuclear weapons in very different ways.

In contemporary academic discourse, anyone who seeks to explain the outcome of the Cold War in terms of unique American characteristics risks being called a "triumphalist." If by this term is meant someone who believes that the United States was destined inevitably to defeat the Soviet Union, or that its eventual victory was a reflection of the inherently superior intelligence of its leaders or the greater intrinsic toughness of its people, then I must reject the label. But if the term refers to someone who not only rejoices in America's Cold War success, but sees in it proof of the practical strengths as well as the moral virtues of the American regime, then I am an unrepentant triumphalist.

CHAPTER ONE

Statism, Anti-Statism, and American Political Development

THE SOURCES AND PERSISTENCE OF AMERICAN ANTI-STATISM

The political philosopher Leo Strauss once described the United States as "the only country in the world which was founded in explicit opposition to Machiavellian principles."[1] Where Machiavelli advised rulers on how to gather up authority into their own hands, the architects of the American republic labored to create a regime in which it would be impossible for even the wiliest and most ambitious prince to achieve the dream of total power. The success of the Founders in this regard owes itself both to the basic structure of the governmental institutions they designed and to the content and continuing appeal of the ideology they promulgated. To borrow a metaphor from modern biology, at the moment of its conception, the new nation had a strong anti-statist strain encoded into its political DNA; one that would reproduce itself and continue to fulfill its protective function in subsequent generations.

Definitions

Like most others who have written on the subject, I begin with Max Weber's definition of the modern state as "an administrative and legal order" that "claims binding authority, not only over [its] citizens . . . but also to a very large extent, over all action taking place in the area of its jurisdiction." The state possesses an "administrative staff," or bureaucracy, and it claims for itself a monopoly over the legitimate use of force within its frontiers. It is "a compulsory association with a territorial basis."[2]

Weber notes that the "organized corporate activity of the administrative staff [is] regulated by legislation," but he clearly distinguishes the legislative function from the executive.[3] Legislatures pass laws. The state is a collection of agencies that act both internally (collecting taxes, enforcing the laws, etc.) and externally (making war, negotiating treaties, and so on). It is, as one scholar has

---

[1] Leo Strauss, *Thoughts on Machiavelli* (Glencoe, IL: Free Press, 1958), p. 13.

[2] Max Weber, "The Fundamental Concepts of Sociology," in Talcott Parsons, ed., *Max Weber: The Theory of Social and Economic Organization* (New York: Oxford University Press, 1950), p. 156. For discussions along similar lines see, among many others, Gianfranco Poggi, *The State: Its Nature, Development, and Prospects* (Stanford, CA: Stanford University Press, 1990), pp. 19–33; Joel S. Migdal, *Strong Societies and Weak States: State-Society Relations and State Capabilities in the Third World* (Princeton: Princeton University Press, 1988), pp. 3–41.

[3] Weber, "Fundamental Concepts."

described it, "an organization, composed of numerous agencies led and coordinated by the state's leadership (executive authority)."[4] Following the spirit of this definition, I will use the term "American state" to refer to the executive branch of the federal (or national) government, including both the office of the president and the various agencies and organizations subordinate to it.[5]

In the American context, the term "state-building" therefore refers to efforts to increase the size and strength of the executive branch.[6] The most relevant measures of state size are numbers of federal employees and the magnitude of the federal budget in relation to the national economy as a whole.[7] State strength or power is more difficult to measure with precision, but I will use these terms to refer to the scope of the economic and societal activities that the federal executive agencies seek to regulate or control, and to their ability to do so successfully. Size and strength are positively related, though not always in a simple, linear fashion. In general, as the American state has grown bigger it has also grown stronger, although not always at the same rate or to the same extent.[8]

---

[4] Migdal, *Strong Societies and Weak States*, p. 19.

[5] For a similar use of the term see Paul P. Van Riper, "The American Administrative State: Wilson and the Founders," in Ralph Clark Chandler, ed., *A Centennial History of the American Administrative State* (New York: Free Press, 1987), pp. 3–36. There are at least three alternative definitions, putting aside for the moment the possibility that the United States simply does not have anything that deserves to be called a "state" in the Weberian sense of the term. Some take a wider view, arguing that "an adequate concept of state" must include the legislative branch. See J. P. Nettl, "The State as a Conceptual Variable," *World Politics* 20, no. 4 (July 1968), pp. 570–71. Others have argued for a narrower definition in which "the American state" consists only of "those institutions and roles that are relatively insulated from particularistic pressures and concerned with general goals (primarily the White House and the State Department and to a lesser extent the Treasury and Defense Departments)." See Stephen D. Krasner, "United States Commercial and Monetary Policy: Unravelling the Paradox of External Strength and Internal Weakness," in Peter J. Katzenstein, ed., *Between Power and Plenty: Foreign Economic Policies of Advanced Industrial States* (Madison: University of Wisconsin Press, 1978), p. 53. Finally, some analysts have used this term to refer to the executive branch bureaucracies, but not to the office of the president. See Louis Galambos, "By Way of Introduction," in Galambos, ed., *The New American State: Bureaucracies and Policies since World War II* (Baltimore: Johns Hopkins Press, 1987), pp. 3–20.

[6] This is the sense in which the term is used by Stephen Skowronek, *Building a New American State: The Expansion of National Administrative Capacities, 1877–1920* (New York: Cambridge University Press, 1982), pp. 3–18.

[7] For discussions and analyses of various indicators see James T. Bennett and Manuel H. Johnson, *The Political Economy of Federal Government Growth, 1959–1978* (College Station, TX: Center for Education and Research in Free Enterprise, 1980); Michael S. Lewis-Beck and Tom W. Rice, "Government Growth in the United States," *Journal of Politics* 47, no. 1 (February 1985), pp. 2–30; William D. Berry and David Lowery, *Understanding United States Government Growth: An Empirical Analysis of the Postwar Era* (New York: Praeger, 1987).

[8] I am less interested here in whether the American state is "weak" or "strong" in comparision to other states, than in the question of how it has grown bigger and stronger over time and, in particular, how its growth has been shaped by the presence of underlying institutional and ideological constraints. The issue of comparative state strength has been discussed at length. See the essays in Katzenstein, *Between Power and Plenty*; Stephen D. Krasner, *Defending the National Interest: Raw Materials Investments and U.S. Foreign Policy* (Princeton: Princeton University Press, 1978); Eric A. Nordlinger, *On the Autonomy of the Democratic State* (Cambridge: Harvard University Press, 1981); Peter B. Evans, Dietrich Rueschemeyer, and Theda Skocpol, eds., *Bringing the State Back In*

"Anti-statism" is the body of ideas and arguments used by those who have opposed efforts to increase the size and strength of the executive branch of the federal government. By "anti-statist influences" I mean to refer both to these ideas and to those features of the original design of American governmental institutions that have tended to inhibit state-building.

Ideas

American animosity toward government is a deep-rooted and long-standing tradition with two main branches. The first and more fundamental of the two embodies a generalized suspicion of power in all its forms and of governmental power in particular. The second consists of a set of ideas regarding the need for strict limits on the government's role in the economy.[9]

THE "ANTIPOWER ETHIC"[10]

The ideologists of the American Revolution were obsessed with power. "They dwelt on it endlessly, almost compulsively," notes Bernard Bailyn. "It is referred to, discussed, dilated on at length and in similar terms," in all of their pamphlets and recorded speeches. The essential attribute of power, in the view of these writers, was its "aggressiveness: its endlessly propulsive tendency to expand itself beyond its legitimate boundaries." This "central thought," they believed, "explained more of politics, past and present, . . . than any other single consideration."[11]

If power was everywhere the hunter, "its natural prey, its necessary victim, was liberty." Power "inhered naturally in government and was the possession and interest of those who controlled government. . . . Liberty, always weak, always defensive . . . inhered naturally in the people and was their peculiar possession and interest."[12] This antinomy between power and liberty, rulers and ruled, state and society, was not unique to a particular situation or to a certain type of regime; it was fundamental and timeless. While breaking with Britain might alleviate the immediate threat to the freedoms of the American colonists, it would not assure them once and for all. Only eternal vigilance could do that.

In moving from Revolution to Confederation to federal Union, Americans created a stronger central government apparatus than the one most had envisioned at the outset, but they did not lose their fear of the state. To the contrary,

---

(Princeton: Princeton University Press, 1985); G. John Ikenberry, David A. Lake, and Michael Mastanduno, eds., *The State and American Foreign Economic Policy* (special issue of *International Organization* 32, no. 1 [Winter 1988]).

[9] For a similar distinction see Ernest R. May, "The Evolving Scope of Government," in Joseph S. Nye, Jr., Philip D. Zelikow, and David C. King, eds., *Why People Don't Trust Government* (Cambridge: Harvard University Press, 1997), pp. 26–27.

[10] The term is Samuel Huntington's. See his *American Politics: The Promise of Disharmony* (Cambridge: Harvard University Press, 1981), p. 33.

[11] Bernard Bailyn, *The Ideological Origins of the American Revolution*, 2nd ed. (Cambridge: Harvard University Press, 1992), p. 56,

[12] Ibid., pp. 57, 59.

the process of debating and ratifying the Constitution served to amplify and to codify these concerns. The advocates of a more powerful federal government were forced repeatedly to explain why the mechanisms that they were proposing would not pose an undue threat to liberty and to accept measures (like a formal Bill of Rights) designed to reduce the danger that such a threat could ever emerge.

Because the fears of the Anti-Federalists were already "deeply rooted in American political culture," writes historian Jack Rakove, the "Federalists . . . had to treat them seriously."[13] Indeed, on a number of crucial issues, the defenders of a stronger union rested their case on the claim that it would actually *reduce* the danger of governmental usurpation of individual freedoms. Thus, in response to those who worried that the proposed Constitution did not explicitly prohibit standing armies, Alexander Hamilton argued that it was under the Articles of Confederation that these "engines of despotism" were actually more likely to arise. In time, Hamilton claimed, the loose Confederacy would inevitably dissolve, and the several states would begin to eye one another with hostility and suspicion. All of the evils so evident in Europe (and of which the Constitution's enemies were, by implication, justifiably afraid) would then come to pass in the New World. Military rivalry would give rise to standing armies and ultimately to a loss of individual freedoms. The reason for this was clear:

> Safety from external danger is the most powerful director of national conduct. Even the ardent love of liberty will, after a time, give way to its dictates. . . . The continual effort and alarm attendant on a state of continual danger will compel nations the most attached to liberty, to resort for repose and security, to institutions which have a tendency to destroy their civil and political rights. To be safe they, at length, become willing to run the risk of being less free.[14]

Whether or not Hamilton was sincere in his expressed concern over standing armies is largely beside the point. What is significant is that his arguments both reflected and lent legitimacy to the very real fears of those whom he was addressing. Even in their efforts to build a stronger state, the Federalists felt compelled to use the rhetoric of anti-statism.

The Founding generation bequeathed to its descendants a "chronic antagonism to the state."[15] Despite the successful construction of a new political sys-

---

[13] Jack N. Rakove, *Original Meanings: Politics and Ideas in the Making of the Constitution* (New York: Knopf, 1996), p. 149. On the importance of the Anti-Federalists in shaping the debate and its ultimate outcome see also Gordon S. Wood, *The Creation of the American Republic, 1776–1787* (New York: Norton, 1993), pp. 519–64; Peter S. Onuf, "Reflections on the Founding: Constitutional Historiography in Bicentennial Perspective," *William and Mary Quarterly* (April 1989), pp. 341–75; Herbert J. Storing, *What the Anti-Federalists Were For* (Chicago: University of Chicago Press, 1981).

[14] Federalist No. 8 ("The Effect of Internal War"), in Edward Meade Earle, ed., *The Federalist* (New York: Modern Library, 1937), p. 42.

[15] Seymour Martin Lipset, *American Exceptionalism: A Double-Edged Sword* (New York: Norton, 1996), p. 39.

tem, "opposition to power, and suspicion of government as the most dangerous embodiment of power," would remain, in Samuel Huntington's words, "the central themes of American political thought."[16] While the extent to which these sentiments are shared and the intensity with which they are expressed have varied over time, they have never disappeared and have reemerged, at intervals, with surprising force. As we shall see, this persistent, deep-seated tradition of suspicion of governmental power has given the opponents of a stronger American state a storehouse of stirring rallying cries with which to mobilize popular support and an armory of potent rhetorical weapons with which to attack their foes.[17]

ECONOMIC LIBERALISM

Historians have been at pains to point out that the first generations of Americans did not embrace laissez-faire as the appropriate basis for government economic policy, either in theory or in practice. The term does not appear in the Constitution, "nor do any even remote synonyms," and for every one of the Founders who "at times echoed some views of Adam Smith . . . many others asserted that he was fundamentally mistaken."[18] Nor does the pattern of early policy betray a principled aversion to any but the most minimal forms of government intervention in the economy. Especially in the early decades of the

---

[16] Huntington, *The Promise of Disharmony*, p. 33.

[17] Popular attitudes toward government can be assessed, albeit indirectly, by the success and failure of competing political parties, programs, and candidates, and, albeit imperfectly, by public opinion polls. For evidence of the persistence of anti-statist attitudes, even at a time of peak popular support for an expanded welfare state see the discussion of a 1964 survey in Lloyd A. Free and Hadley Cantril, *The Political Beliefs of Americans: A Study of Public Opinion* (New York: Simon and Schuster, 1968), pp. 9–40. Free and Cantril found a striking disparity between the willingness of respondents to support particular government programs (urban renewal, federal welfare, and education aid) and their more general ideological predispositions. They concluded that "the liberal trend of policies and programs . . . has little secure underlying foundation in any ideological consensus" (p. 30, 39). Subsequent shifts in public attitudes are traced in Linda M. Bennett and Stephen Earl Bennett, *Living with Leviathan: Americans Coming to Terms with Big Government* (Lawrence: University of Kansas Press, 1990). Although the authors want to argue that traditional hostility to government is fading, much of their evidence seems to suggest the contrary. They present polls which show, for example, that from the 1960s through the 1980s nearly half of those questioned regarded "big government" as "the biggest threat to the country in the future" (p. 36). Writing in the late 1980s, the Bennetts concluded that antigovernment sentiment was on the wane. Nye, Zelikow, and King, *Why People Don't Trust Government*, take the story through the mid-1990s, a period of sharply declining trust in government. Noting the importance of more recent trends (the rise of "postmaterial values") and shorter-term developments (scandals and perceived policy failures), public opinion expert Gary Orren concludes nevertheless that the "traditional antipathy toward government that has been part of American political culture since colonial times" continues to shape public attitudes. See his essay, "Fall From Grace: The Public's Loss of Faith in Government," in Nye, Zelikow, and King, *Why People Don't Trust Government*, pp. 87, 77–107.

[18] William Letwin, "American Economic Policy, 1865–1939," in Peter Mathias and Sidney Pollard, eds., *The Cambridge Economic History of Europe*, Vol. 8, *The Industrial Economies: The Development of Economic and Social Policies* (New York: Cambridge University Press, 1989), pp. 641–42. Elaborating on these themes is Frank Bourgin, *The Great Challenge: The Myth of Laissez-Faire in the Early Republic* (New York: George Braziller, 1989).

nineteenth century, many state governments were heavily involved in regulating industry, enforcing child labor laws, and investing public funds in roads, canals, bridges, and other "internal improvements."[19] While the scope of its activities was considerably narrower, the federal government also intervened in its own way, imposing tariffs that protected the producers of certain commodities and dispensing public lands to private entrepreneurs.[20]

Despite all this, by the closing years of the nineteenth century there had emerged a strong and widely shared presumption in favor of the market over the state, the private sector over the public sector, the efficiencies of "free enterprise" over what turn-of-the-century social theorist Herbert Spencer referred to as the "clumsy mechanisms" of "political schemers."[21] By the 1880s, as English author James Bryce observed, laissez-faire was "the orthodox and accepted doctrine in the sphere both of Federal and State legislation."[22] Writing in 1906, H. G. Wells concluded that, albeit with minor variations, Americans were all adherents of eighteenth-century liberalism, an ideology that aimed to liberate "not only men but property from State control" and that was, in its essence, "anti-State."[23]

This evolution in attitudes, which began in the 1830s and was consolidated after the Civil War, clearly had its roots in changing material conditions. As the economy developed, businessmen had less need of public funds and they grew more concerned about government interference. The emerging American entrepreneurial class therefore underwent what has been described as a "spiritual conversion."[24] They began, writes Arthur Schlesinger, Jr., to "retreat from the Hamiltonian conception of publicly guided private enterprise and to discover belated charm in the Jeffersonian proposition that government was best which governed least."[25] Having done so, they proceeded to erase all memory of their previous dependence on the state and to embrace the myth that America had always been the land of unfettered free enterprise.[26] The fact that subsequent

---

[19] See Oscar Handlin and Mary Handlin, *Commonwealth: A Study of the Role of Government in the American Economy: Massachusetts, 1774–1861* (New York: New York University Press, 1947); Louis Hartz, *Economic Policy and Democratic Thought: Pennsylvania, 1776–1860* (Cambridge: Harvard University Press, 1948).

[20] Ernest May notes that after the dismantling of the Bank of the United States by Andrew Jackson and the defeat by the Jacksonians of Henry Clay's program of internal improvements, the federal government became, in effect, "a passive actor." By the 1830s, there was "no national-level governmental institution (the post office excepted) that was able to play much of a role in American economic life." May, "The Evolving Scope of Government," pp. 33–34.

[21] Quoted in Sidney Fine, *Laissez-Faire and the General Welfare: A Study of Conflict in American Thought, 1865–1901* (Ann Arbor: University of Michigan Press, 1956), p. 35.

[22] Quoted ibid., p. 3.

[23] H. G. Wells, *The Future in America: A Search after Realities* (New York: Harper and Brothers, 1906), pp. 156, 76, 75.

[24] Louis Hartz, *The Liberal Tradition in America* (New York: Harcourt, Brace, 1955), p. 215.

[25] Arthur Schlesinger, Jr., "Affirmative Government and the American Economy," in Schlesinger, *The Cycles of American History* (Boston: Houghton Mifflin, 1986), p. 230.

[26] This erasure of the memory "of the corporate-state co-operation of the pre–Civil War period" has been described as "one of the most vivid examples of collective amnesia in American history."

generations of historians have felt the need to debunk that myth gives ample testimony to its continuing power.

But whatever the realities of history and contemporary policy, why did the *ideal* of the unfettered market and the minimal state gain such acceptance? The relentless propagandizing by business interests may provide a partial explanation. Part of the answer seems to lie also in the fact that economic liberalism harmonized easily with the country's prevailing political anti-statism, while Hamiltonian activism did not. This congruence helps to account for the generalized support of the doctrine of nonintervention, even among those who were not themselves captains of industry.[27]

Popular attitudes toward "big business," and the balance of public and expert opinion regarding the proper economic role of the federal government would seesaw several times after the turn of the twentieth century, but an underlying "hostility to public initiative" and a "general commitment to the view . . . of the natural predominance of private enterprise" would remain. Writing in the 1960s, Andrew Shonfield noted that "many of the simple and certain formulae of [American] popular political debate" seemed to derive from an "extremist version of the private enterprise doctrine" first popularized in the late-nineteenth century. The terms of public discussion implied "a suspicion of public power as such" that struck European observers as "bizarre."[28] If that was less the case at the end of the twentieth century, it was because Europeans had become somewhat more "American" in their thinking about the proper economic role of the state, rather than, as Shonfield expected, the other way around.

Institutions

Building a stronger state involves concentrating power: in the executive/administrative arm of government in relation to its other branches and in government as a whole in relation to its citizens. The American Constitution was meant to make such concentrations of power difficult, if not impossible, to attain. In this sense, at the same time as it established a new state, the Constitution also embodied a profoundly anti-statist doctrine. As its authors intended, the initial design of America's governmental institutions has served as an enduring source of constraint on state-building.

Under the Articles of Confederation, both executive and legislative authority had been granted to the Congress, thereby in effect "establishing . . . parliamentary government without a prime minister."[29] In this scheme, the "United States

---

David Vogel, "Why Businessmen Distrust Their State: The Political Consciousness of American Corporate Executives," *British Journal of Political Science* 8, p. 1 (January 1978), p. 55.

[27] For evidence of the extent of acceptance see Fine, *Laissez-faire and the General Welfare*, pp. 32–164.

[28] Andrew Shonfield, *Modern Capitalism: The Changing Balance of Public and Private Power* (New York: Oxford University Press, 1968), pp. 298–99, 306–7.

[29] Arthur M. Schlesinger, Jr., *The Imperial Presidency* (Boston: Houghton Mifflin, 1973), p. 2.

of America" had a government of sorts, but it (or rather they) did not have a state. By creating the position of president and investing him with "the executive power," the authors of the Constitution planted the seed of a state, but they proceeded simultaneously to surround it with multiple barriers to its subsequent growth.

The president of the United States was not himself a sovereign nor was the office he occupied to be the locus of sovereignty in the new nation. Rejecting the European notion that every political entity must have a center of gravity, "a single, undivided, final power, higher in legal authority than any other power," the Framers proceeded, in effect, to shatter sovereignty and to scatter its pieces throughout their new system.[30] The president would not possess it, but neither would the Congress (as Parliament had done in England since the Glorious Revolution), nor the legislatures of the several states (as had presumably been the case under the Articles of Confederation). In the new regime, sovereignty would belong "in theory to the people and in practice to no one."[31] Deprived of a protective cloak, no individual, and no branch of government could ever proclaim the right to act without restraint. In this abstract but profoundly important way, the authority of both Congress and the president, and the potential power of the American state, was limited from the outset.[32]

Nor was the sovereign power of the people a merely theoretical matter. By creating what they termed a "republican" system of government, the Founders imposed a second layer of protection against an overweening state.[33] The fact that the president and the members of both houses of Congress were to be elected (albeit by different means and with varying degrees of popular participation) meant that the new nation's rulers would be "created by our choice, dependent on our will."[34] At the same time, although the defenders of the Consitution did not stress the point, the fact that the new regime would not be a direct democracy reduced the threat that it might act in the interests of a tyrannous majority.

The president's status as an elected official required to present himself for approval at regular, specified intervals posed an important check on his actions and on those of the executive branch as a whole. Placing the executive power in the hands of one man might seem to elevate him to the status of the king of

[30] Bailyn, *The Ideological Origins of the American Revolution*, p. 198.

[31] James Q. Wilson, *Bureaucracy: What Government Agencies Do and Why They Do It* (New York: Basic Books, 1989), p. 311.

[32] On this issue see Bailyn, *The Ideological Origins of the American Revolution*; Wood, *The Creation of the American Republic, 1776–1787*, pp. 524–36; Forrest McDonald, *Novus Ordo Seclorum: The Intellectual Origins of the Constitution* (Lawrence: University of Kansas Press, 1985), pp. 276–81; Samuel P. Huntington, *Political Order in Changing Societies* (New Haven: Yale University Press, 1968), pp. 98–108.

[33] On the differences between a republic and a pure democracy see Federalist No. 10 ("Numerous Advantages of the Union") in Earle, *The Federalist*, pp. 58–59. On the Founders' novel use of these and other terms see J. G. A. Pocock, "States, Republics, and Empires: The American Founding in Early Modern Perspective," in Terence Ball and J. G. A. Pocock, *Conceptual Change and the Constitution* (Lawrence: University of Kansas Press, 1988), pp. 55–98.

[34] Federalist No. 25 ("The Care of the Common Defense"), in Earle, *The Federalist*, p. 156.

Great Britain, or "the khan of Tartary." Instead, Alexander Hamilton claimed, an elected president, "reeligible" only for as long as "the people of the United States shall think him worthy of their confidence," was in a position more like that of the governor of the state of New York. If he sought to accumulate too much power or if he and his agents acted against the people's wishes, a president, like a governor, could always be turned out at the next election.[35]

As important as electoral accountability in imposing constraints on the president was his constitutionally prescribed relationship to the other two branches of government. By creating a system of "separated institutions *sharing* power," the Framers, in James Madison's words, sought to provide "great security against a gradual concentration of the several powers in the same department."[36] They took particular care to ensure that Congress would have ample means to prevent an undue accumulation of authority in the executive. In extremis Congress could impeach and remove a president. Of greater day-to-day significance was the fact that the Constitution took the essential state-building functions out of the hands of the executive and placed them securely with the legislature. Congress, not the president, would have the power "to lay and collect taxes," borrow and coin money, and "regulate commerce with foreign nations."[37] And within the Congress it was the members of the House of Representatives—who would be subject to biennial direct elections, and who would no sooner have assumed power than they would "be compelled to anticipate the moment when . . . their exercise of it is to be reviewed"—who would have to take primary responsibility for raising revenues.[38]

Along with its regulation of taxation, the Constitution gave Congress control over conscription. Reflecting their belief in the strategic virtues of unity of command, the Framers made the president the "commander in chief" of the army and navy of the United States, and of the state militias, should these ever be called to the nation's defense. But they made certain to give Congress the power "to raise and support armies," "provide and maintain a navy," and to organize, arm, and discipline any nationalized militia units.[39]

The authors of the Constitution knew from their reading of history that wars made states, and it was for this reason that they decided not to give the leader of the American state the authority to make war. As James Madison explained in a letter to Thomas Jefferson: "The constitution supposes, what the History of all [governments] demonstrates, that the [executive] is the branch of power most interested in war, [and] most prone to it. It has accordingly with studied care vested the question of war in the [legislative]."[40] Congress would decide

[35] Federalist No. 69 ("Analysis of Presidential Powers"), in Earle, *The Federalist*, p. 446. Hamilton was here, of course, glossing over the fact that president was to be chosen not by "the people" directly, but by electors appointed by the states.

[36] The first phrase is Richard Neustadt's, from his *Presidential Power: The Politics of Leadership* (New York: John Wiley, 1960), p. 33. The second is from Federalist No. 51 ("On a Just Partition of Power"), in Earle, *The Federalist*, p. 337.

[37] Article I, section 8 of the Constitution, in Earle, *The Federalist*, p. 590.

[38] Federalist No. 57 ("Supposed Dangers"), ibid., p. 372.

[39] Article I, section 8, ibid., p. 590.

[40] Quoted in Schlesinger, *The Imperial Presidency*, p. 5.

when the militia could be called forth "to execute the laws of the Union, suppress insurrections, and repel invasions." And, most important of all, Congress, and not the president, would have the power to declare war.[41]

The potential powers of the new institutions of central government over its citizens were further limited by an assortment of explicit prohibitions scattered throughout the text of the Constitution and concentrated in the Bill of Rights. Neither the president, nor the Congress, nor the president acting with the assent of the Congress could legitimately deprive citizens of their freedom to speak, subject them to unreasonable searches, forbid them a trial by jury, or take from them their right to keep and bear arms. Should the other branches of the federal government seek to violate their freedoms, citizens would have recourse to the judiciary, which would evaluate the actions of its counterparts according to their conformity with the nation's "fundamental law," that is, the will of the people as "declared in the Constitution."[42]

If the powers of the executive were balanced by those of the legislative and judicial branches, the power of the federal government, taken as a whole, was balanced, in part, by that of the states. Compared to the Articles of Confederation, the Constitution shifted the distribution of authority toward the center, but it left the state governments intact and with considerable freedom to act in their own spheres. The states retained what were referred to as the powers of "internal police," which included "not only the definition and punishment of crimes and the administration of justice but also all matters concerning the health, manners, morals, safety, and welfare of the citizenry."[43] Finally, and perhaps most significantly, the states retained their militias. Although these could be placed under federal control by an act of Congress, their continued existence served as "the ultimate counterweight against a despotic concentration of power in the federal government."[44]

The system of government established in 1789, with its combination of fragmented sovereignty, republican rule, dispersed power, written constitutional restrictions, and multiple checks and balances was unlike any the world had ever seen. It was, concludes one observer, "as much an antistate as a state."[45]

STATE-BUILDING UNDER CONSTRAINT

The persistent presence of anti-statist influences, in the form both of prevailing ideas about the proper relationship between state and society and the enduring

[41] Article I, section 8. Earle, *The Federalist*, p. 590.

[42] Federalist No. 78 ("The Judiciary Department"), Earle, *The Federalist*, p. 506.

[43] Indeed, because they were not subject to the Bill of Rights, the states were actually, in certain respects, more powerful than the federal government and could do things (like stifling the press) that it could not. McDonald, *Novus Ordo Seclorum*, p. 288.

[44] Daniel H. Deudney, "The Philadelphian System: Sovereignty, Arms Control, and Balance of Power in the American States-Union, circa 1787–1861," *International Organization* 49, no. 2 (Spring 1995), p. 204.

[45] Ibid., p. 207.

structure of governmental institutions, has not prevented the growth of the American state. But, in six specific ways, these influences have constrained the expansion of the state and shaped the ways in which it has gone forward over time.[46]

The Role of Crises

The American state has not grown steadily over the past two hundred years, but rather in bursts or spurts, with periods of rapid change followed by intervals of comparative stability.[47] The eight critical episodes in this overall process are listed in table 1.1.[48]

Periods of accelerated state-building have generally been preceded either by the anticipation or the actual onset of war, or by a growing sense of impending domestic economic and social crisis. Four of the episodes listed above were triggered by war or its threat, three were associated with perceived domestic crises, and one (the period culminating in the adoption of the Constitution) was brought about by a combination of the two.[49]

---

[46] Thanks in part to their evident resurgence as a force in late-twentieth-century politics, anti-statist influences have begun to receive increasing attention from students of American political development. The lasting tension between anti-statist ideas and American political institutions is the theme of Huntington, *The Promise of Disharmony*. The resistance of the American regime to centralization before and during the Progressive Era is emphasized in Skowronek's *Building a New American State*. Painting a similar picture of the first half of the twentieth century is Barry D. Karl's *The Uneasy State: The United States from 1915 to 1945* (Chicago: University of Chicago Press, 1983). Alan Brinkley describes how anti-statist influences checked the New Deal in *The End of Reform: New Deal Liberalism in Recession and War* (New York: Knopf, 1995). He also points to the wider implications of this insight in his essay "The Problem of American Conservatism," *American Historical Review* 99, no. 2 (April 1994), pp. 409–29. The contention between statist and anti-statist influences must be the axial theme in any comprehensive account of American political development.

[47] For a fascinating comparison of the launching of the New Deal with that of the Great Society, see James T. Patterson, "American Politics: The Bursts of Reform, 1930s-1970s," in Patterson, ed., *Paths to the Present: Interpretive Essays on American History since 1930* (Minneapolis: Burgess Publishing, 1974), pp. 57–101. Patterson argues that the modern welfare state was essentially created during the years 1933–35 and 1964–65.

[48] For another interpretation of the role of crises in the growth of the American state and for the term "critical episodes," see Robert Higgs, *Crisis and Leviathan: Critical Episodes in the Growth of American Government* (New York: Oxford University Press, 1987). Another overview with similar historical scope is Ballard C. Campbell, *The Growth of American Government: Governance from the Cleveland Era to the Present* (Bloomington: Indiana University Press, 1995).

[49] The source of the impetus for state-building in the Civil War, World War I, New Deal, World War II, and early Cold War episodes is clear. On the role of external threats in the first Founding see Frederick W. Marks III, *Independence on Trial: Foreign Affairs and the Making of the Constitution* (Wilmington, DE: Scholarly Resources, 1986). McDonald, *Novus Ordo Seclorum*, pp. 143–83, pays particular attention to the growing fear of internal instability. The sense of social and economic crisis that paved the way for Progressivism is discussed in Robert H. Wiebe, *The Search for Order, 1877–1920* (New York: Hill and Wang, 1968). Anxiety over political instability following the assassination of President Kennedy and over mounting racial unrest provided the backdrop for the launching of the Great Society. See Patterson, "The Bursts of Reform"; Irving Bernstein, *Guns or Butter: The Presidency of Lyndon Johnson* (New York: Oxford University Press, 1996).

TABLE 1.1
Critical Episodes in American State-Building

	War	*Socioeconomic Crisis*
Founding (1776–87)	X	X
Civil War (1861–64)	X	
Progressive Era (1900–14)		X
World War I (1916–19)	X	
New Deal (1933–39)		X
World War II (1941–45)	X	
Early Cold War (1945–60)	X	
Great Society (1964–68)		X

Crises are critical in American political development because the sources of resistance to state-building are so strong. The American political system is, as Walter Dean Burnham has described it, "dedicated to the defeat, except temporarily and under the direct pressure of overwhelming crisis, of any attempt to generate domestic sovereignty."[50] It is only when the threat to national stability or survival appears great that traditional fears of excessive governmental power can be temporarily put aside. And it is at such moments that the multiple institutional obstacles to expanding the scale and scope of executive branch activities are most likely to be lowered, at least for a time.

The willingness of the Congress to pass laws permitting such expansions and to authorize the increases in taxation and expenditure that are usually necessary to sustain them is especially important in this regard. Congress and the executive must come into alignment, however briefly, if major increases in the size and power of the American state are to occur. At such moments, as James Q. Wilson notes, "The Madisonian system is placed in temporary suspense: exceptional majorities propelled by a public mood and led by a skillful policy entrepreneuer take action that might not be possible under ordinary circumstances."[51]

Without a sufficiently intense and galvanizing atmosphere of crisis, attempts at state-building are doomed to fail. In such cases, despite the exertions of aspiring state-builders, the institutional and ideological obstacles in their way will prove immovable. Two recent examples may help to illustrate this pattern.

In the 1980s, claiming that the United States was being "deindustrialized" by

[50] Walter Dean Burnham, *Critical Elections and the Mainsprings of American Politics* (New York: W. W. Norton, 1970), p. 176.

[51] James Q. Wilson, "The Rise of the Bureaucratic State," *Public Interest*, no. 41 (Fall 1975), p. 97. The best discussion of the role of wars in American state-building is Bruce D. Porter, *War and the Rise of the State: The Military Foundations of Modern Politics* (New York: Free Press, 1994), pp. 243–96. On the galvanizing effect of crises in general see, in addition to Higgs, *Crisis and Leviathan*; Matthew A. Crenson and Francis E. Rourke, "By Way of Conclusion: American Bureaucracy since World War II," in Galambos, *The New American State*, p. 141; Marc Allan Eisner, *The State in the American Political Economy* (Englewood Cliffs, NJ: Prentice-Hall, 1995), pp. 30–34; J. Rogers Hollingsworth, "The United States," in Raymond Grew, ed., *Crises of Political Development in Europe and the United States* (Princeton: Princeton University Press, 1978), pp. 163–95.

foreign competitors, congressional Democrats sought to force the implementation of an aggressive national "industrial policy" on an unwilling executive
branch. Advocates called for the creation of new executive agencies, empowered to "pick winners and losers" and to funnel federal support to favored
industries.[52]

Presidents Reagan and Bush opposed these proposals, arguing that they involved undue government interference in the marketplace and that, in any case,
they were unnecessary; the American economy might be evolving under competitive pressures from other countries, but it was not "deindustrializing."[53] Oc-
cupying the institutional and ideological high ground, and having seized the
rhetorical initiative from their opponents, the occupants of the White House
were able to turn aside pressure for change. Support for industrial policy
peaked during the recession of the early 1980s and ebbed thereafter. Ultimately,
as one disappointed analyst would later conclude, "an excess of Madisonian
balance . . . prevented decisive initiatives of any kind in the absence of overwhelming crisis."[54]

In the 1980s, Congress tried to press new powers on an unwilling executive.
In the early 1990s, the institutional roles of advocacy and opposition were reversed, but the eventual outcome was the same. Arguing that the nation faced a
major health care emergency, the Clinton administration sought to win support
for a comprehensive national medical insurance program. Although estimates of
its likely impact differed, there seemed little question that such a program
would have required large increases in federal taxation and spending, and in the
scope of government regulation. The administration's plan was defeated by a
combination of interest group opposition, anti-statist rhetoric, congressional resistance, and the damaging counterargument that there was, in fact, no crisis.[55]

The Filtration of Options

In the American system, leadership of successful attempts at state-building
must come from the executive branch. If their labors are to bear fruit, presidents
must build coalitions of supporters in Congress and in society as a whole.
Constructing a winning coalition requires assembling a program: a reasonably
coherent set of proposals tied together with an underlying rationale and justified

[52] See, for one example among many, the work of two influential industrial policy advocates (and
later Clinton administration officials), Ira Magaziner and Robert Reich, *Minding America's Business*
(New York: Vintage, 1982).

[53] For official refutations of the claim of "deindustrialization" and a brief summary of the admin-
istration's case against industrial policy, see statements by Treasury Secretary Donald T. Regan and
Council of Economic Advisers Chairman Martin Feldstein in Hearings before the Joint Economic
Committee, *The 1984 Economic Report of the President*, 98th Cong., 2d sess. (Washington, DC:
U.S. Government Printing Office, 1984), pp. 24–27, 129.

[54] Otis L. Graham, Jr., *Losing Time: The Industrial Policy Debate* (Cambridge: Harvard University Press, 1992), p. 2.

[55] The best account of this episode is Theda Skocpol, *Boomerang: Clinton's Health Security
Effort and the Turn against Government in U.S. Politics* (New York: Norton, 1996).

in ideological language with reference to overarching American values and beliefs.

Few crises, even wars, are so overwhelming as to permit only one possible avenue of response. Even when the immediate, functional objectives are clear (assembling an army, restoring economic growth), there will invariably be a number of different ways in which they could be attained. The process of responding to a strategic or socioeconomic crisis must therefore begin with the selection, by the president and those around him, of one or a handful of approaches from among a wider array of possibilities. It is here, in the very opening stages of the process of state-building, that underlying anti-statist influences first make themselves felt.

In gravitating toward certain options and away from others, presidents are guided both by their political instincts and by their deeper beliefs. No leader will knowingly choose a path that he regards as impassable, and most will also forgo alternatives that they believe to be morally wrong or not in keeping with what they construe as the nation's basic ideological principles. The preliminary selection of options for state-building therefore involves both anticipation of likely resistance and a measure of self-restraint or self-censorship. These two mechanisms are interrelated and they are not always easy to distinguish from one another, even in retrospect. State-builders who, unconstrained, might harbor truly radical ambitions, may recognize that they risk being branded as "un-American" if they were ever to reveal the full extent of their dreams. Whatever their initial preferences, more prudent, pragmatic leaders are likely to conclude that what the political traffic will bear and what is best for the country are, almost by definition, the same.

While calculations of electoral advantage are never absent, the existence of a dominant societal ideology, as reflected in the deeply held beliefs of top decision makers, can also play a distinct and independent role in the initial filtration of options. Where there is no unique solution to the problem at hand, such beliefs will tend to serve as focal points, drawing decision makers toward certain courses of action and away from others. In these situations, as one study of the role of ideas notes, "political elites may settle upon courses of action on the basis of shared . . . beliefs. Other policies may be ignored."[56]

Ideology thus shapes the contours of the terrain, even if it does not determine the road that will finally be taken; it lays out signposts and warning signals that lead policy makers down certain paths and cause them to avoid or to overlook others. The resulting patterns of convergence and avoidance can be found in a variety of issue areas. Seeking to explain what he refers to as the "silences" in the history of debate over American social welfare policy, Ira Katznelson concludes that "in any given state at a given time," some types of policies "are much more likely to be adopted than others; and some are not even the subject

[56] Judith Goldstein and Robert O. Keohane, "Ideas and Foreign Policy: An Analytical Framework," in Goldstein and Keohane, eds., *Ideas and Foreign Policy: Beliefs, Institutions, and Political Change* (Ithaca: Cornell University Press, 1993), p. 18.

of political discussion and debate."[57] Another comparative study of the economic role of government in postwar advanced industrial countries finds similarly that in the American case, certain options (such as state ownership of most kinds of industrial facilities) do not appear even to have come up. "The story of public ownership in the United States is quickly told," concludes Anthony King, "because for the most part it is a non-story—of proposals that were not made and of things that did not happen."[58] The reason for this, King suggests, is that even in moments of profound crisis and uncertainty political leaders have generally shared the belief that large-scale government ownership of the means of production would be contrary to American economic principles.[59]

Opposition

Efforts to strengthen the American state invariably arouse opposition from an array of groups and individuals. Such opposition is typically rooted in a mix of beliefs and self-interest, with the former often playing a critically important role. Since the days of the Anti-Federalists, a portion of the population has always feared that any increase in the power of the federal government would inevitably threaten individual liberties. As Alan Brinkley notes, many self-styled twentieth-century "conservatives," are, in fact, inheritors of "the anti-statist liberal tradition of nineteenth century America." Their "fear of the state" has inclined them to oppose, as a matter of principle, virtually any departure from past practices that could be characterized as a move toward greater governmental power.[60] Certain policies, like military conscription, have provoked especially intense resistance on ideological grounds, even from those who are not themselves directly affected.

More typical is the opposition that draws strength from a blend of belief and self-concern. The examples are legion: many citizens have opposed the draft both because they objected to the exercise of compulsion by the state and because they did not want to serve, or to send their children to serve, in the armed forces. Many have resisted higher federal taxes because they believed them to be harmful to individual initiative and economic growth, and also because they do not want to surrender an increased fraction of their income to the government. For a century after the Civil War, white southerners touted "states' rights"

[57] Ira Katznelson, "Rethinking the Silences of Social and Economic Policy," *Political Science Quarterly* 101, no. 2 (1986), p. 323.

[58] Anthony King, "Ideas, Institutions, and the Policies of Governments: A Comparative Analysis: Parts I and II," *British Journal of Political Science* 3 (1973), p. 302.

[59] While this has generally been the case, as will be discussed in chapters 2 and 7, the aversion to public ownership was greater in the second half of the twentieth century than in the first. In the postwar period the differences between the United States and virtually every other advanced industrial country on this question have been dramatic. See the striking table in Thomas K. McCraw, "Business and Government: The Origins of the Adversary Relationship," *California Management Review* 26, no. 2 (Winter 1984), p. 34.

[60] Brinkley, "The Problem of American Conservatism," pp. 416–17.

because they believed a loose conception of federalism was in keeping with the intent of the Founders, and because they wanted to preserve the power and privilege they enjoyed on account of race against intrusions from Washington. Members of Congress have often been led, both by their reading of the Constitution and by their desire to avoid losing personal prerogatives, to object to proposals that would enhance the power of the executive branch. During each of the major state-building episodes of this century, congressional Republicans have objected to the state-building efforts of Democratic presidents, both because they believed them to be wrong and dangerous and because they hoped that resistance would yield electoral advantages.

Since the second half of the nineteenth century, the American business community has been a key bastion of resistance to anything savoring of "statism." Individual executives and business organizations have been, as David Vogel points out, "remarkably consistent in [their] opposition to the enactment of any government policies that would centralize economic decision making or strengthen the authority of government over the direction of the business system as a whole."[61] The reasons for this are, again, a mix of pragmatism and principle. Business leaders often fear that government intervention will hurt their own interests, and, on the other hand, they are sometimes willing to abandon their scruples when they think that they will benefit from particular policies. But they are also strongly inclined to believe that, all other things being equal, intervention by the state is morally wrong, economically harmful, politically dangerous, and, at the extreme, that it poses a profound threat to the nation's free enterprise system. The "anti-statist ideology" of American business executives, concludes Vogel, cannot be "dismissed as rhetoric"; it is "sincerely held" and exerts a powerful influence on their positions on a range of political issues.[62]

In the successive struggles over the power of the American state, the opponents of expansion have enjoyed a number of important, though not always decisive, advantages. The first of these, as has already been suggested, is a product of the country's institutional structure. Because of the way decision-making authority is dispersed in the American political system, the advocates of a stronger central state have had to win support (or at least acquiesence) in all three branches of the federal government; their opponents have often been able to block them or to force them to moderate their proposals by exerting a decisive influence in only one branch. The moments at which all the necessary elements come into alignment, and at which truly dramatic increases in state power are therefore possible, have proven to be few in number and short in duration.

The unfolding of the New Deal offers one illustration of the way in which the American system can place multiple obstacles in the path of those who seek dramatic change. In 1933 the Democratic party controlled the White House and,

[61] Vogel, "Why Businessmen Distrust Their State," p. 50.
[62] Ibid., p. 54.

by considerable margins, both houses of Congress. Nevertheless, key elements in President Roosevelt's initial reform package were overturned by a hostile Supreme Court.[63] Later, when the Court became more sympathetic and when he enjoyed continued, though dwindling, congressional majorities, Roosevelt found many of his plans stymied by a shifting coalition of Republicans and conservative Democrats.[64] Whatever their successes in the nation's capital, the New Dealers confronted opposition in the several states, where politics was often marked by "the durable appeal of materialistic, pro-business ideology and . . . stubborn resistance to strong central government, be it in Washington, Albany, or Carson City."[65]

Congress has typically been the locus of struggle between state-builders and anti-statists. Here presidents and their allies push for approval of the laws and appropriations necessary to expand the executive and extend its authority, while their opponents do what they can to stop them. As the New Deal example suggests, a minority opposition party may be able to win over sufficient numbers of the president's own nominal allies to defeat aspects of his program. The rules of procedure in the House and Senate have also at times permitted even very small minorities in one body to block measures that have majority backing. Thus, Woodrow Wilson's 1917 request that he be permitted to arm merchant vessels was approved by the House and then stalled by a handful of "filibustering" Senators. Wilson could denounce his tormentors as a "band of willful men, representing no opinion but their own," but he could not compel them to act. His attempt to increase his own authority and the nation's military power without a formal declaration of war was defeated.[66]

Major episodes of state-building involve competing efforts to win the hearts, minds, and votes of ordinary citizens, as well as the backing of uncommitted members of Congress. In these struggles, the anti-statist forces have tended to hold a rhetorical edge, in addition to their institutional advantages. American history gives them ready access to evocative slogans and potent symbols that ease the task of rallying support. Anti-statists cast themselves as the defenders of liberty, the protectors of the free market, and the keepers of the national tradition of limited government; they easily can, and invariably do, invoke the names and words of the Founders in support of their positions. Their opponents, meanwhile, are portrayed as underminers, if not outright enemies, of freedom and adherents of dangerous, "un-American" doctrines.

In the face of these rhetorical onslaughts, the advocates of state-strengthening

[63] For brief overviews of the Court's role see William E. Leuchtenberg, *Franklin D. Roosevelt and the New Deal, 1932–1940* (New York: Harper and Row, 1963), pp. 143–46; Anthony J. Badger, *The New Deal: The Depression Years, 1933–1940* (London: Macmillan, 1989), pp. 263–68.

[64] For the composition and role of this coalition in the period preceeding the outbreak of the Second World War see James T. Patterson, *Congressional Conservatism and the New Deal* (Lexington: University of Kentucky Press, 1967).

[65] James T. Patterson, *The New Deal and the States: Federalism in Transition* (Princeton: Princeton University Press, 1969), p. 207.

[66] Duane Lockard, *The Perverted Priorities of American Politics* (New York: Macmillian, 1971), p. 136.

have taken one of two tacks. On the one hand, they have argued from necessity, tacitly acknowledging the seriousness of their opponents' concerns but claiming that certain sacrifices and compromises are nonetheless essential to preserve the Republic. This approach (followed to varying degrees by Abraham Lincoln, Woodrow Wilson, and Franklin Roosevelt) may prove persuasive for a time, but it is inherently self-limiting; emergency justifications are acceptable only for as long as an emergency is generally agreed to be underway.

The need to counter the warnings and objections of their opponents has led American state-builders to use the language of supreme emergency, even when the nation is not at war. In the 1930s, as William Leuchtenberg has pointed out, "the New Dealers resorted to the analogue of war, because in America the sense of community is weak, the distrust of the state strong." Despite some initial successes, this technique proved "treacherous" and "inadequate," and its application delayed the effort to "find a way to organize collective action save in war or its surrogate."[67] Some students of American history maintain that at the end of the twentieth century, this dilemma has yet to be resolved. Michael Sherry argues, for example, that the persistent need of modern presidents to make "an end-run around antistatism" is reflected in their repeated declarations of "war"; on poverty, drugs, crime, and disease.[68]

Anti-statists claim to be upholders of liberty; when they are not operating in a full emergency mode, state-builders typically present themselves as the defenders of equality and, ultimately, of democracy. Thus, at the turn of the century, Herbert Croly urged Progressives to fulfill the "promise of American life" by using "Hamiltonian" means (i.e., strong and efficient government) to achieve "Jeffersonian" ends (i.e., a truly equitable society).[69] Croly and the Progressives believed that as corporations grew larger and more powerful, a stronger state would be needed to defend the interests of ordinary citizens. Following this line of reasoning, Theodore Roosevelt promised to put an end "to the impotence which springs from the overdivision of governmental powers," in order to protect "men, women, and children . . . [from] the tyrannies of minorities."[70] Defenders of the New Deal and the Great Society programs of the 1960s asserted, similarly, that a stronger and more active federal government was needed to ensure greater national economic, social, and political equality.

While it has proven potent at times, the strategy of appealing to the ideal of equality to justify a stronger state has also had important limitations. Popular backing for government action designed to right a particular wrong or solve a

---

[67] William E. Leuchtenberg, "The New Deal and the Analogue of War," in John Braeman, Robert H. Brenner, and Everett Walters, eds., *Change and Continuity in Twentieth-Century America* (Columbus: Ohio State University Press, 1964), pp. 142–43.

[68] Michael S. Sherry, *In the Shadow of War: The United States since the 1930s* (New Haven: Yale University Press, 1995), p. 504.

[69] See the discussion of Hamilton and Jefferson in Herbert Croly, *The Promise of American Life* (New York: Macmillan, 1909), pp. 27–51.

[70] Martin J. Sklar, *The Corporate Reconstruction of American Capitalism, 1890–1916* (New York: Cambridge University Press, 1988), p. 353.

particular problem has not translated itself automatically into acceptance of the need for permanent increases in governmental power. Despite the fears of some of the Founders, the American people have never shown much enthusiasm for economic "leveling," in part because of the sacrifices of liberty that pursuing this goal would entail. While majorities have sometimes supported the imposition of restrictions on the freedoms of the wealthy, there has been markedly less support for state-imposed limitations on the many designed to assist the less-fortunate few. Liberty, and not equality, has usually emerged as the more potent value in the American pantheon of virtues.

Patterns of Settlement[71]

Contests over governmental power eventually reach at least a temporary resting point. Depending on the strength of the contending forces, the equilibrium position arrived at after an interval of struggle may be thought of as lying closer to either the statist or the anti-statist end of a notional spectrum of possibilities.

The resolution of the Progressive Era debate over how best to respond to the emergence of large-scale industrial enterprise provides an illustration of this process. At the turn of the twentieth century, and despite considerable resistance, the federal government did move away from its previous posture of virtual noninterference with business. To the dismay of some critics, both at the time and since, it did not proceed all the way to a truly "statist resolution"—in other words, toward a vigorous, sustained, and purposeful effort to determine the course of the nation's industrial evolution, perhaps including widespread government ownership of the means of production.[72]

"Instead of a statist route," writes historian Martin Sklar, "a broad pro-regulatory consensus defined the common ground" of the turn-of-the-century debate over national economic policy. Within this "corporate liberal" consensus there were differences between those, like Theodore Roosevelt, who were willing to consider a higher degree of state involvement in the economy and those, like Woodrow Wilson and, at the other end of the continuum, William Howard Taft, who were markedly less so. Ultimately, policy settled closer to the Wilson-Taft end of an already truncated range of options. The federal government would intervene to break up monopolies and to regulate some businesses (like the railroads) that operated across state lines, but it would not take on a larger role in planning, funding, and directing national economic development. The reason

---

[71] I have borrowed this phrase from Robert Griffith, who uses it to describe the overall outcome of various struggles over post-World War II economic and social policy. See Robert Griffith, "Forging America's Postwar Order: Domestic Politics and Political Economy in the Age of Truman," in Michael J. Lacey, ed., *The Truman Presidency* (New York: Cambridge University Press, 1989), p. 68.

[72] Sklar, *The Corporate Reconstruction of American Capitalism*, p. 433. The best known critique from the left of Progressivism's alleged failings is Gabriel Kolko, *The Triumph of Conservatism: A Reinterpretation of American History, 1900–1916* (New York: Free Press, 1963). Kolko argues that the Progressives did not go nearly far enough. For the polar opposite view see Higgs, *Crisis and Leviathan*, pp. 77–122.

for this outcome, according to Sklar, was "the prevalent antistatism of all major classes and strata" in American society and their consequent indifference, or active resistance, to proposals for truly radical enhancements in governmental power.[73]

Lines of settlement may shift once or more in the course of a single state-building episode. In wartime, with national survival often at stake, the direction of movement has generally been toward the increased exercise of central governmental power. Here, external events tend to strengthen the hand of the statebuilders and to weaken their opponents. In periods of economic and social crisis, however, where the impetus for state-strengthening is usually weaker at the outset and more difficult to sustain over time, the opposite trend has been more typical. In these cases, early bursts of activity are often followed by mounting opposition, and at least a partial reversal of course.

Acutely aware of the resistance they are likely to encounter, American presidents have tried initially to fight wars with the minimum possible level of domestic coercion. Thus, for two years the Lincoln administration sought to avoid creating a "coercive bureaucratic apparatus," by conducting the Civil War with an all-volunteer force comprised of regular army and state militia units. It was not until 1863 that the insatiable demands of the battlefield forced the adoption of national conscription.[74] Similarly, it was only the collapse of an essentially voluntary system for mobilizing industrial production at the end of 1917 that led Woodrow Wilson to seek the creation of federal agencies with the authority to regulate and control the economy.[75] Despite initial hesitation and substantial resistance, war broke down traditional barriers and pushed the nation toward acceptance of a bigger and more powerful state.

The essential story of the New Deal, on the other hand, is of a movement *away* from more overtly statist solutions to the problem of economic depression. Ambitious (and desperate) schemes for widespread, permanent central government planning and control soon gave way to less obtrusive measures.[76] In

---

[73] Farmers, small businessmen, and even organized labor, groups that might have been expected to have "pro-statist proclivities" quickly "succumbed to the much stronger antistatist tradition of American political culture." Sklar, *The Corporate Reconstruction of American Capitalism*, pp. 34–40, 434. For an overview see Eisner, *The State in the American Political Economy*, pp. 98–124. Placing these developments in a wider perspective are Wiebe, *The Search for Order*; and Morton Keller, *Regulating a New Economy: Public Policy and Economic Change in America, 1900–1933* (Cambridge: Harvard University Press, 1990).

[74] Harold M. Human, *A More Perfect Union: The Impact of the Civil War and Reconstruction on the Constitution* (New York: Alfred Knopf, 1973), p. 216. For an interesting comparison of "war mobilization and state formation" in the Confederacy and the Union see Richard Franklin Bensel, *Yankee Leviathan: The Origins of Central State Authority in America, 1859–1877* (New York: Cambridge University Press, 1990), pp. 94–237.

[75] For overviews, see Ronald Schaffer, *America in the Great War* (New York: Oxford University Press, 1991), pp. 31–63; David Kennedy, *Over Here: The First World War and American Society* (New York: Oxford University Press, 1980), pp. 93–143; Robert Cuff, *The War Industries Board: Business-Government Relations during World War I* (Baltimore: Johns Hopkins University Press, 1973).

[76] This is the theme of Alan Brinkley's incisive essay "The New Deal and the Idea of the State,"

part this movement was a reflection of the public response to fluctuating conditions. As the economy seemed to improve, writes historian Barry Karl, "the sense of emergency diminished [and] the fear of strong national government increased." Mounting resistance to concentrations of power in the executive branch was due also to a reassertion of institutional balance. During the first few years of the Depression, Congress had been willing to grant the president an unusual degree of autonomy, but enthusiasm for delegation faded as time wore on.[77] Perhaps most important, the shift in congressional and public attitudes was a reflection of the growing feeling that, with the 1936 electoral sweep, the "court-packing scheme" of 1937, and the introduction of ambitious new proposals for reorganizing the executive branch and increasing its authority, the second Roosevelt administration was in danger of overreaching itself.[78] Despite the existence of an urgent national crisis, moves toward a stronger state generated a powerful counterreaction, and this helped to push policy back in an anti-statist direction.[79]

The creation of a pattern of settlement involves the convergence, through a process of debate, political conflict, and eventual compromise, on a set of responses to a foreign or domestic challenge.[80] These packages of institutions and policies are the product of many conflicting influences, but they exhibit certain common characteristics. Taken together, they reveal a strong and persistent national tendency to rely on private over public actors, inducements over authoritative commands, and decentralization over centralization of control. Thus, the preferred American solution to the challenges of monopoly and depression has been the regulation and stimulation of private enterprise, not its nationalization, and the characteristic American response to the demands of modern warfare has been to turn to corporations for armaments, not to government arsenals. In peacetime and even in war, the federal government has typically sought first to shape the behavior of individuals and groups indirectly, through the use of exhortation, tax incentives, procurement contracts, and transfer payments, rather than to resort to the direct application of coercive power. And, on those occasions when Congress has agreed to expand the authority of the executive branch, it has usually preferred to scatter responsibility for the performance of

---

in Steve Fraser and Gary Gerstle, eds., *The Rise and Fall of the New Deal Order, 1930–80* (Princeton: Princeton University Press, 1989), pp. 85–121.

[77] Karl, *The Uneasy State*, p. 120. As Karl points out, "If emergency and economic crisis were going to be the new way of life, then Congress was determined to find its own way of dealing with them" (p. 169).

[78] See Brinkley, *The End of Reform*, pp. 3–136. Also Arthur A. Ekirch, Jr., *Ideologies and Utopias: The Impact of the New Deal on American Thought* (Chicago: Quadrangle Books, 1969), pp. 177–207; Karl, *The Uneasy State*, pp. 111–81.

[79] The evolution of economic policy is traced by Ellis W. Hawley, *The New Deal and the Problem of Monopoly: A Study in Economic Ambivalence* (Princeton: Princeton University Press, 1966).

[80] Robert Griffith describes the postwar order as "the product of struggle" fought on ten distinct fronts: fiscal, monetary, and tax policy, labor relations, anti-trust, natural resources policy, housing and urban development, social security and health care, and the politics of culture. See Griffith, "Forging America's Postwar Order," p. 68.

new tasks among a variety of agencies, resisting the argument that administrative efficiency requires centralization and retaining its own capacity for oversight and control. Such outcomes have been more in keeping with prevailing beliefs, and more acceptable to the various institutions and societal groups that had the capacity to block or approve them, than the most likely alternatives. In the United States, anti-statist influences have been evident even, and perhaps especially, during episodes of state-building.

Ratchets and Rollbacks

Students of the growth of the modern state note that "in war, what goes up seldom comes down."[81] Once undertaken, emergency increases in the size of central government bureaucracies, the bulk of the revenues they extract, and the range of activities they seek to control are rarely completely reversed. In the aftermath of mobilization, citizens grow accustomed to paying higher taxes and accepting a greater degree of government interference in their day-to-day existence. Having been promised a better life as an inducement for their willing participation in war, they come to expect an array of peacetime benefits from the state. Bureaucrats and politicians, for their part, have an interest in preserving existing tax and spending programs, and often in expanding them. Growth is therefore self-perpetuating; a mechanism is at work that prevents the state, once enlarged, from shrinking back to its previous dimensions.[82]

The situation prevailing after the Second World War will be discussed more fully in subsequent chapters. Prior to 1945, however, the war-related "ratchet effect" at work in the United States was relatively weak. The dramatic increases in the scale and scope of the federal government that occurred during the Civil War and World War One were followed by sharp contractions.[83] Within a few years of the end of both wars, the number of men in the armed forces and the number of civilian government employees had both fallen away dramatically.[84]

[81] Bruce D. Porter, *War and the Rise of the State: The Military Foundations of Modern Politics* (New York: Free Press, 1994), p. 14.

[82] In addition to Porter, *War and the Rise of the State*, the workings of the war-driven "ratchet effect" are discussed in Alan T. Peacock and Jack Wiseman, *The Growth of Public Expenditure in the United Kingdom* (Princeton: Princeton University Press, 1961); Bruce D. Porter, "Parkinson's Law Revisited: War and the Growth of American Government," *Public Interest* no. 60 (Summer 1980), pp. 50–68; Robert Higgs has extended this notion to include the aftermaths of social and economic, as well as military, crises. See Higgs, *Crisis and Leviathan*, pp. 3–34.

[83] Although wartime increases in state power were not as great, and the subsequent reaction was somewhat delayed, the post-1800 collapse of the Federalist party and its program were also, in part, products of a postwar retrenchment.

[84] The regular U.S. Army went from a force of some 16,000 officers and enlisted men to around 1 million during the Civil War, before falling back to roughly 25,000 men in the mid-1870s. The figures for the First World War are approximately 100,000 in 1914, 2.4 million in 1918, and back down to between 130,000 and 140,000 by the early 1920s. The federal government had 36,000 paid civilian employees in 1861, 51,000 in 1871. The great majority in both periods worked for the postal service and most did not live in Washington, D.C. The comparable figures for the early-twentieth century are 400,000 civilian employees in 1914, 850,000 in 1918, and back down to

In the case of the First World War the cutbacks were so precipitous that many former federal employees were left stranded in Washington without the money even to buy a train ticket home.[85] Although they did not return entirely to pre-war levels, the magnitude of federal tax revenues and of total government expenditures also dropped sharply.[86]

These observable changes were accompanied by others less easily measured, but no less significant. Strong wartime presidents, who had gathered considerable authority into their own hands, were replaced, in the 1860s and 1870s and in the 1920s, by far weaker ones. The interbranch balance of power shifted sharply away from the executive toward the Congress and, especially in the decades following the Civil War, away from Washington and toward the states. "From the war years there emerged not a Bismarckian state but rather . . . a system of government dominated by localism and laissez-faire."[87] With the collapse of Reconstruction, writes James McPherson, "the positive liberty of centralized power gave way to the negative liberty of decentralized federalism."[88] Progressive Democrats who hoped to build a permanently stronger state after World War One, adapting "wartime structures to the tasks of . . . peacetime management," also saw their hopes dashed.[89]

The "rollback effect" evident in these postwar periods is a product of the same institutional and ideological forces at work within the various state-building episodes. The centrifugal tendencies that are built into the American constitutional design tended to reassert themselves when the galvanizing energy of a crisis started to subside. Congress and the courts may have fallen into alignment with the executive while a war was underway, but the three branches were more likely to pull in different directions, the states were less likely to accept federal dictates, and citizens were less likely to defer to government at any level once peace had been restored. Some societal groups and geographical regions clearly benefited from mobilization, and especially from the increased government expenditures that went with it, but many others were eager to shake

---

under 550,000 by the early 1920s. See tables in United States Bureau of the Census, *The Statistical History of the United States: Colonial Times to the Present* (Washington, DC: U.S. Government Printing Office, 1976), pp. 1102–3, 1141–42. See also the discussion in Wilson, "The Rise of the Bureaucratic State."

[85] Karl, *The Uneasy State*, p. 46.

[86] In each case, the bulk of the new, continuing postwar expenditures also went to veterans' benefits and debt repayment, rather than for new, other than war-related government programs. See the figures in the Census Bureau's *Statistical History*, pp. 1114–15.

[87] Morton Keller, *Affairs of State: Public Life in Late Nineteenth-Century America* (Cambridge: Harvard University Press, 1977), p. 121.

[88] James McPherson, "Liberty and Power in the Second American Revolution," in McPherson, *Abraham Lincoln and the Second American Revolution* (New York: Oxford University Press, 1991), p. 152. Eric Foner notes similarly that although the war created a temporarily more powerful national state, the "countervailing tendencies" of "localism, laissez-faire, and racism" soon "reasserted themselves." Foner, *A Short History of Reconstruction, 1863–1877* (New York: Harper and Row, 1990), p. 15.

[89] Ellis W. Hawley, *The Great War and the Search for a Modern Order: A History of the American People and Their Institutions, 1917–1933* (New York: St. Martin's, 1979), p. 45.

off the burden of wartime taxes and restrictive regulations. With the return to business as usual, these individuals and groups were freer to express their wishes and to pursue their particular interests.

Last, but not least, the very act of strengthening the state produced an intellectual backlash. What was tolerable in an emergency became repellent in its wake, as assorted critics, commentators, and prophets attacked the deviations of the recent past and called the American people back to their fundamental faith in liberty. Thus, the hitherto unprecedented expansion in the activities of the federal government that accompanied the Civil War was followed not by a new era of statism, but by the full flowering of laissez-faire. In the aftermath of the First World War, writes Ellis Hawley, "traditional fears of big government reasserted themselves" and "antistatism" flourished. The "postwar assault on government" was accompanied by recurrent appeals "to America's tradition of economic individualism."[90] It would take another profound crisis to shake this tradition to its core.

The "Uneasy State"

The character of America's institutions and the content of its reigning ideology together have a final, paradoxical effect on the course of national political development. New executive branch agencies, programs, and functions that survive an immediate, postcrisis rollback will tend to become "locked in" and will be very difficult thereafter to abolish. As James Q. Wilson explains, this is because the same "regime of separated powers" that makes it so difficult to enact new programs or create new agencies also "works to protect agencies, once created, from unwelcome change." Abolishing existing agencies or forcing major changes in their functioning requires "new legislation that must overcome the same hurdles as the original law."[91]

Some of the appendages to the state that sprout in a crisis may live on, but the persistence of underlying anti-statist attitudes ensures that they will eventually be subject to impassioned efforts to cut them back or to excise them altogether. Each of the two major post-1945 episodes of state-building, the first stimulated by the onset of the Cold War, the second featuring the launching of the Great Society, was followed in short order by an attempt to undo its accomplishments. In the late 1960s and early 1970s, some Americans tried to dismantle the "warfare state"; in the 1980s and 1990s, others set their sights on the "welfare state." Despite sharp differences in tone and direction, these countermovements shared a common, anti-statist thrust and drew energy from similar ideological sources.

Biographer Joseph J. Ellis notes that the "antigovernment ethos" that Thomas Jefferson did so much to promulgate continues to exert a powerful influence on American political discourse. The result, writes Ellis, is that in the United

---

[90] Ibid., pp. 47–48, 52.
[91] Wilson, "The Rise of the Bureaucratic State," p. 93.

States, "unlike any other nation-state in the modern world, the very idea of government power is stigmatized" and its proponents are always "on the defensive."[92] No matter how big and strong it grows, the American state is destined always to be uneasy.[93]

[92] Joseph J. Ellis, *American Sphinx: The Character of Thomas Jefferson* (New York: Knopf, 1997), p. 296.

[93] This is the implicit theme of Barry Karl's *The Uneasy State* and the explicit argument of Samuel Huntington's *The Promise of Disharmony*.

CHAPTER TWO

The Cold War Founding

IN THE SPAN of only two decades the United States was engulfed in three waves of crisis as depression, world war, and cold war followed each other in rapid succession. The onset of each emergency produced a powerful impetus toward state-building. To a degree, the effect of these sequential crises was undeniably cumulative. Institutions put in place to deal with one challenge were adapted to the next, and inhibitions to expansions in governmental power, once lowered, were never fully restored.

It is often assumed that by the late 1940s, the combined effects of recurrent crises and of repeated assaults by determined state-builders had simply overwhelmed the traditional sources of opposition to a stronger central government. The end of the Second World War and the start of the Cold War are therefore widely thought to have marked the dawn of a new era of ascendant statism; an era characterized by the emergence of what Robert Higgs ominously describes as "Big Government . . . powerful, highly arbitrary, activist [and] virtually unchecked by the constitutional limitations of checks and balances."[1] "Everywhere," writes Bruce Porter of the early postwar years, "Hamilton's vision of government was triumphant, Jefferson's in full retreat."[2]

While they are not entirely false, these accounts are incomplete in one crucial respect. The impulse toward statism was clearly strong in the immediate postwar period, and its effects were wide-ranging and important. But there were also other, opposing forces at work. At the same time as they produced pressures for a stronger central state, each of the waves of crisis that broke over the nation in the 1930s and 1940s generated its own anti-statist undertow. The critical opening years of the superpower rivalry were therefore characterized by an unusually intense current of *resistance* to statism, as well as a strategically induced push for a permanent expansion in governmental power. The American response to the onset of the Cold War was the product of a clash between these two contradictory impulses. In this chapter I will outline the factors contributing to the strength of each, before turning, in chapter 3, to describing what emerged from their collision.

---

[1] Robert Higgs, *Crisis and Leviathan: Critical Episodes in the Growth of American Government* (New York: Oxford University Press, 1987), p. 233.

[2] Bruce D. Porter, *War and the Rise of the State: The Military Foundations of Modern Politics* (New York: Free Press, 1994), p. 286.

CHANGED STRATEGIC CIRCUMSTANCES

Insularity

The Founders hoped that what George Washington referred to in his Farewell Address as America's "detached and distant situation" would permit it to forgo the necessity and to avoid the dangers of building a strong central state.[3] As Alexander Hamilton pointed out, it was just such a "peculiar felicity of situation" that had permitted the English to preserve their liberties for so long. Had Britain "been situated on the continent, and . . . compelled . . . by that situation, to make her military establishments at home coextensive with those of the other great powers of Europe, she, like them, would in all probability" have become "a victim of the absolute power of a single man."[4]

If they acted wisely, by ratifying the Constitution, building a navy to patrol their coasts, and accepting the need for a small but expansible army to secure their frontiers, the American people, like their British forebears, might "for ages enjoy an advantage similar to that of an insulated situation." "Europe is at a great distance from us," Hamilton observed, and the colonial outposts of the European powers were already too weak to pose a real threat. "Extensive military establishments cannot, in this position, be necessary to our security."[5]

The United States soon achieved the position of virtual insularity and greatly enhanced security toward which Hamilton had pointed, and its people quickly proceeded to go farther than he might have wished in reaping the rewards. With the signing of the Treaty of Ghent in 1814 and the conclusion of hostilities with England, the possibility of any serious land attack on American territory became increasingly remote. By the early decades of the nineteenth century, the British had begun to accommodate themselves to the loss of their former colonies and to withdraw to Canada. Meanwhile, the French and Spanish had been bought out or expelled from their holdings in North America. A weak, independent Mexico posed no real danger, and the Native American tribes, with whom the colonists had long engaged in bloody skirmishes, were in the process of being pacified, decimated, or driven steadily to the West.

Nor were there significant naval threats. Once the Napoleonic Wars had ended and Britain was firmly in command of the seas, no other European power could use its fleet without British permission to strike at America's shores. As relations between Washington and London began to improve, the prospect of any further harassment by the Royal Navy seemed also to diminish.[6] The American navy quickly fell into disrepair, and while state militias remained potent in

---

[3] Felix Gilbert, *The Beginnings of American Foreign Policy: To The Farewell Address* (New York: Harper and Row, 1965), p. 145.

[4] Federalist No. 8 ("The Effect of Internal War") in Edward Meade Earle, ed., *The Federalist* (New York: Modern Library, 1937), p. 40.

[5] Ibid. Hamilton's views on the army and navy are spelled out in Federalist No. 24 ("The Powers Necessary to the Common Defence Further Considered"), in Earle, *The Federalist*, pp. 147–52.

[6] See Walter Lippmann, *U.S. Foreign Policy: Shield of the Republic* (Boston: Little, Brown, 1943).

many places, the size and quality of the regular army dwindled. By the 1830s Alexis de Tocqueville could fairly conclude that "the Americans have no neighbors and consequently no great wars, financial crises, invasions or conquests to fear; they need neither heavy taxes, nor a numerous army, nor great generals."[7] In the decades ahead, the greatest threat to the security of the United States would come from within.

America's strategic insularity was preserved for more than a century. Despite the expansion into the Pacific at the end of the nineteenth century, military threats to U.S. overseas possessions remained remote. Given the state of military technology, the prospect of attacks on home territory was even more distant. At the turn of the century some strategists began to argue that what happened in Europe and Asia could have important implications for American interests and, eventually, for the nation's security. But, even after the First World War, this remained a minority view. Most Americans believed that the United States had intervened in Europe not to prevent a hostile power from gaining preponderance there, but to make the world safe for democracy. With the dissolution of the liberal internationalist dream in the 1920s and 1930s, engagement in world affairs seemed once again to be more optional than mandatory, and the accoutrements of world power appeared as a costly and dangerous luxury, rather than a burdensome necessity.

The End of Insularity: Technology

The Second World War accelerated the growth both of American material power and, ironically, of an accompanying sense of insecurity. By the end of the war there was widespread agreement among strategic planners, political leaders, and the public at large that the era of invulnerability had ended. The single most important and most easily recognizable reason for the change was the rapid advance of military technology.

At the outset of the war, as for most of the preceeding century and a half, America's enemies had no means of striking at it directly and with great force. The nation's land frontiers remained secure, and its coastlines were well protected by a substantial fleet. Despite the addition of a third dimension to modern warfare, aircraft ranges were sufficiently short and the destructive power of available explosive payloads sufficiently small so as to pose no real danger to American territory. Shocking as it undoubtedly was, the Japanese attack on Pearl Harbor was an unrepeatable stunt; it could be carried out only with great exertion against an outpost that was extended, exposed, and inadequately prepared.

By 1945 things had changed or, more precisely, they seemed about to change. Propeller-driven aircraft had increased considerably in range and size, and the ability of massed bombers to do terrible damage, even with old-fashioned chemical explosives, had been clearly demonstrated over Germany and Japan.

[7] Alexis de Tocqueville, *Democracy in America* (New York: Anchor Books, 1969), p. 278.

Jet engines, introduced into combat in the waning months of the war, promised greater speeds and potentially longer ranges. Ballistic missiles too had made their first appearance, and the difference between hurling explosives over the English Channel, as the Nazis had done, and sending them across continents seemed, to most observers, to be merely a matter of degree.[8]

Most significant of all, of course, was the introduction by the United States of the atomic bomb, and the virtually instantaneous recognition that if they had not already done so, others would soon be able to build similar weapons. If these devices could be married with the improved methods of delivery, the possibilities were truly terrifying. At the end of the war the chief of staff of the Army Air Force summed the matter up in the new anodyne language of systems analysis: "Very long-range rockets were not a serious threat before the atomic bomb because . . . the cost of destroying a square mile" of enemy territory using conventional explosives was "comparable with, if not larger than, the damage done to the enemy." With atomic warheads, however, "the total product" would be far more efficient, "for the destructive effect would exceed the total cost by a large factor."[9]

One month after Japan's surrender, in its first top-secret attempt to formulate a strategy for the postwar period, the Joint Chiefs of Staff warned:

> Any nation, which in the future may attempt to dominate the world, may be expected to make her major effort against the United States and before we can mobilize our forces and productive capacity. The power, range and prospective development of modern weapons are such as to favor such an attack. As a result, there will be a marked reduction in the degree of invulnerability to ready attack that has been provided in the past by our geographical position.[10]

Speaking in October 1945, President Truman expressed in public a view that was already fast on its way to becoming conventional wisdom: "Our geographical security is now gone," he told the Congress. "Never again can we count on the luxury of time with which to arm ourselves. In any future war, the heart of the United States would be the enemy's first target."[11]

As relations with the Soviet Union deteriorated, this prediction was repeated many times, with increasing urgency. "Our old allies of time and space—our

[8] Early postwar assessments of the impact of technology on American security will be discussed more fully in chapter 8, below.

[9] H. H. Arnold, "Air Force in the Atomic Age," in Dexter Masters and Katharine Way, eds., *One World or None* (New York: McGraw Hill, 1946), p. 30.

[10] SWNCC 282, "Basis for the Formulation of a U.S. Military Policy," September 19, 1945, in Thomas H. Etzold and John Lewis Gaddis, eds., *Containment: Documents on American Policy and Strategy, 1945–1950* (New York: Columbia University Press, 1978), p. 41.

[11] Harry S. Truman, "Address before a Joint Session of the Congress on Universal Military Training," October 23, 1945, in *Public Papers of the Presidents of the United States (1945)* (Washington, DC: U.S. Government Printing Office, 1961), p. 405. The emergence and crystallization of these anxieties is a central theme in Michael Sherry, *Preparing for the Next War: American Plans for Postwar Defense, 1941–1945* (New Haven: Yale University Press, 1977), especially pp. 191–238.

vast oceanic and polar frontiers—have . . . fallen before the headlong advances of science," warned one official publication in 1947.[12] Within a decade, another report cautioned, "The signal for the start of a war against us will . . . be a large-scale, long-distance onslaught with atomic explosives, against our principal centers of population and production."[13]

The Soviet detonation of an atomic bomb in 1949 fed these fears, as did the subsequent testing of a thermonuclear device in 1953 and indications in 1954 that the Russians were getting ready to deploy a force of intercontinental-range jet bombers. Anxiety reached its apogee in 1957 with the successful launch of the first earth-orbiting *Sputnik*. The debate over the strategic implications of these developments will be discussed in chapter 3. For now the point is simply to recall that, for Americans, the rapid advance of science helped to transform the opening years of the Cold War into a waking nightmare of evaporating security and a mounting sense of physical vulnerability.[14]

The End of Insularity: Geopolitics

Somewhat less spectacular, and less obvious in their immediate implications, were the shifts in the global balance of power brought on by the Second World War. During the opening stages of that conflict, as in the First World War, the United States had been able to rely on other powers to fend off the initial assaults of expansionist authoritarian regimes. From 1914 to 1917 and, again, from 1939 to 1941, the United States had been given time in which to mobilize its resources and to build up its armed forces. In 1945, with the European democracies devastated or exhausted, there was no assurance of a similar breathing space between the onset of war and the beginning of American involvement.[15]

The weakening of America's allies and former enemies and the strengthening, despite terrible losses, of its erstwhile Soviet ally raised a troubling prospect. Whether through subversion or invasion, the Soviets might be able quickly to extend their control across all of Eurasia, filling the power vacuums in Western Europe and Northeast Asia and gaining control, in the process, of vast human, natural, and industrial resources. As George Kennan, director of the State Department's Policy Planning Staff, explained, there were "only five centers of industrial and military power in the world which are important to us from the standpoint of national security." Of these, four (the United States,

[12] War Department, *National Security Program: Universal Military Training* (Washington, DC: War Department, 1947), p. 1.

[13] President's Advisory Commission on Universal Military Training, *A Program for National Security* (Washington, DC: U.S. Government Printing Office, 1947), p. 8.

[14] These developments and their impact on American strategic thought are well covered in a number of works. See Lawrence Freedman, *The Evolution of Nuclear Strategy* (New York: St. Martin's, 1981); Fred Kaplan, *The Wizards of Armageddon* (New York: Touchstone, 1983); McGeorge Bundy, *Danger and Survival: Choices about the Bomb in the First Fifty Years* (New York: Random House, 1988).

[15] Sherry, *Preparing for the Next War*, p. 200.

Britain, the Rhine Valley, and Japan) were in friendly hands, and only one, the Soviet Union, was not. If one or more of these centers changed hands, the balance of world power would shift sharply against the United States.[16] For this reason, concluded a secret 1948 planning document, "Soviet domination of the potential power of Eurasia, whether achieved by armed aggression or by . . . subversive means, would be strategically and politically unacceptable to the United States."[17] In the new postwar world, the United States had a vital interest not only in protecting its own territory from attack, but in preventing certain key regions from falling under hostile control.

As with perceptions of direct vulnerability, this extended conception of American interests, and of the threats to them, percolated rapidly into public view. Melvyn Leffler has shown that by the late 1940s, "the highest civilian officials in the United States shared this geopolitical perspective." Thus, in 1949, Secretary of State Dean Acheson explained that the "loss of Western Europe or of important parts of Asia or the Middle East" would result in "a transfer of potential from West to East, which . . . might have the gravest consequences in the long run." And President Truman made identical, and even more explicit, arguments in a January 1951 address to Congress:

> If Western Europe were to fall to Soviet Russia it would double the Soviet supply of coal and triple the Soviet supply of steel. If the free nations of Asia and Africa should fall to Soviet Russia, we would lose the sources of many of our most vital raw materials. . . . And Soviet command of the manpower of the free nations of Europe and Asia would confront us with military forces which we could never hope to equal.[18]

With memories of the Second World War still fresh, the notion that a hostile power or coalition might be able to achieve rapid conquests, accumulate resources, deprive the United States of markets and allies, isolate it diplomatically and geographically, and perhaps eventually bring it to its knees did not seem in the least far-fetched. It would take more than a decade to achieve a stable domestic consensus on exactly how this danger could best be met.[19] Still, by the

---

[16] Regarding Kennan's views on this issue see John Lewis Gaddis, *Strategies of Containment: A Critical Appraisal of Postwar American National Security Policy* (New York: Oxford University Press, 1982), pp. 30–31; George F. Kennan, *Memoirs, 1925–1950* (Boston: Little, Brown, 1967), p. 359.

[17] NSC 20/4, "U.S. Objectives with Respect ot the USSR to Counter Soviet Threats to U.S. Security," November 23, 1948, in Etzold and Gaddis, *Containment*, p. 208.

[18] Acheson and Truman are both quoted and the antecedents to their formulations are discussed in Melvyn P. Leffler, *A Preponderance of Power: National Security, the Truman Administration, and the Cold War* (Stanford, CA: Stanford University Press, 1992), pp. 10–13. See also Leffler, "The American Conception of National Security and the Beginnings of the Cold War, 1945–1948," *American Historical Review* 89 (1984), pp. 346–81.

[19] At first, a willingness to maintain temporary occupation forces and to provide economic assistance seemed to be what was required. By 1949, the ante in Europe had been raised to include the formation of a formal alliance, the North Atlantic Treaty Organization. With the outbreak of the Korean War, the United States committed itself to placing large ground, naval, and air forces in Europe and Asia. Over the next decade, and despite some efforts to pull back, it became clear that a substantial American forward-based presence was, for all intents and purposes, permanent. On the

end of the war there was a growing belief that in the future America's security would depend on who controlled the Eurasian periphery.

The nation's strategic frontiers now began not at the water's edge, but on their opposite shore. Changing geopolitical conceptions of American interests reinforced the effects of evolving military technology. The insularity on which the nation's security had traditionally depended, and on which, as Alexander Hamilton pointed out, its unique domestic political arrangements had originally rested, was now gone.

POSTWAR ANTI-STATISM

As the Cold War began, the United States thus found itself exposed, for the first time in its history, to that great stimulus to state-building: the perceived presence of a continuing imminent threat of war. At the same time, the late 1940s and early 1950s were marked by an intensification of the anti-statist influences in American political life. This was partly a matter of historical timing, as the forces of opposition stirred up by the New Deal and the Second World War collided with yet another attempt to enhance governmental power. As in all previous state-building episodes, the push for a stronger state also generated its own unique opposition.

The anti-statist current in postwar politics was at its peak in the first, critical years of the Cold War, the period extending from the surrender of the Axis powers to the end of the 1950s. This current fed from four closely interrelated sources, each of which had its distinct tributaries.

Congressional Counterpressures

For at least a decade, beginning with the off-year elections of 1942 and ending with the 1952 presidential campaign, Congress acted as a brake on all efforts to increase the power of the executive branch.[20] In the second half of the 1950s, and especially after 1958, the polarities were reversed, and an increasingly ac-

---

evolution of U.S. interests and the expansion of American commitments see, in addition to Gaddis, *Strategies of Containment*, and Leffler, *Preponderance of Power*; Robert A. Pollard, *Economic Security and the Origins of the Cold War, 1945–1950* (New York: Columbia University Press, 1985); Ernest R. May, "Cold War and Defense," in Keith Nelson and Ronald G. Haycock, *The Cold War and Defense* (New York: Praeger, 1990), pp. 7–73; Robert Jervis, "The Impact of the Korean War on the Cold War," *Journal of Conflict Resolution* 24, no. 4 (December 1980), pp. 563–92. On the disruptive and ultimately abortive efforts of the Eisenhower administration to "redeploy" U.S. forces from Europe and give the Europeans greater control over nuclear weapons in their place, see Marc Trachtenberg, *A Constructed Peace: The Making of the European Settlement, 1945–1963* (Princeton: Princeton University Press, 1999).

[20] In fact, this tendency was visible as early as 1938, and it continued, on a few specific issues, into the first years of the Eisenhower administration. On the later stages of the New Deal, see James T. Patterson, *Congressional Conservatism and the New Deal: The Growth of the Conservative Coalition in Congress, 1933–1939* (Lexington: University of Kentucky Press, 1967).

tivist Congress sought to encourage a reluctant president to do more, rather than less. But during the Cold War's first, formative decade, Congress was the principal source of opposition to expansions in executive power. The reasons for this resistance were a mix of partisan politics, policy disputes between liberal presidents and bipartisan conservative congressional coalitions, and the time-honored interbranch struggle over institutional prerogatives.

PARTISAN POLITICS

Having been brought to the brink of electoral extinction during the first years of the Great Depression, the Republican party began in the late 1930s to reassert itself and to rebuild a portion of its strength. Republican presidential candidates were strikingly unsuccessful in their efforts to unseat Franklin Roosevelt. But the party's congressional wing fared much better in its attempts to regain a dominant influence in the House and Senate. Republican candidates did especially well in off-year elections in which they did not have to run against a ticket headed by an overwhelmingly popular president. Republicans made sharp gains in 1938 and 1942, and, if only briefly, finally succeeded in 1946 in recapturing control of both houses of Congress (see fig. 2.1).

Albeit with some variations by issue and regional background, congressional Republicans tended to be strong, indeed bitter, opponents, first of Roosevelt and then of his successor, Harry Truman. That Republicans should object to the proposals of Democratic presidents comes as no surprise, but the ferocity of their opposition is noteworthy. Beginning with the Depression and the New Deal, many Republicans appear genuinely to have believed not merely that the Democrats were mistaken about the details of particular policies, but that they were fundamentally misguided and that, whether inadvertently or by deliberate design, they were placing the country on a profoundly dangerous course.

Some of the deeper intellectual currents that lay behind this fear will be discussed at greater length below. The essence of the Republican critique was clear enough: rising taxes, expanding expenditures, a ballooning federal bureaucracy, and increasing government regulations and controls were tilting the balance of national power toward Washington, and within Washington toward the executive branch. This twofold centralizing trend was undermining the foundations of the nation's economic system; if permitted to proceed unchecked it would eventually result in a loss of political as well as economic freedoms. Once lost, these liberties might never be regained.

From the 1930s onward, Republicans believed that they were locked in a life-and-death struggle for the future of the nation. With only a brief and, even then, partial hiatus during the opening stages of American involvement in the Second World War, they saw their role as being to block and, where possible, to turn back the "drift toward 'statism.'"[21] Once the war had ended, Republicans

---

[21] The phrase is from a 1949 entry in Dwight Eisenhower's diary. Quoted in Robert Griffith, "Dwight D. Eisenhower and the Corporate Commonwealth," *American Historical Review* 87, no. 1 (February 1982), p. 92. Republican attitudes during the 1930s are well surveyed in Patterson,

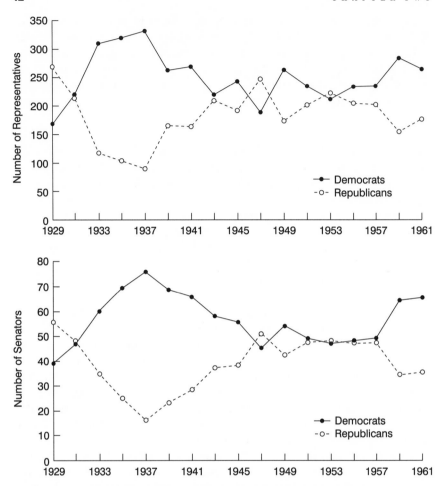

Figure 2.1. The Narrowing Balance of Partisan Power: House and Senate

redoubled their efforts, believing that the historic contest of which they saw themselves a part was about to reach a crucial turning point. The urgency, intensity, and apparent pervasiveness of these sentiments is conveyed in a letter that Dwight Eisenhower wrote to his brother Edgar in 1956, explaining his original decision to run for president:

Congressional Conservatism. See also Alan Brinkley, *The End of Reform: The New Deal in Recession and War* (New York: Knopf, 1995); Barry D. Karl, *The Uneasy State* (Chicago: University of Chicago Press, 1983). On the role of partisan politics during the war years, see John Morton Blum, *V Was for Victory: Politics and American Culture during World War II* (San Diego: Harcourt Brace Jovanovich, 1976); Richard Polenberg, *War and Society: The United States, 1941–1945* (New York: J. B. Lippincott, 1972).

In 1948, '49, '50, '51 and early '52, many hundreds of people were urging me to go into politics. Scores of different reasons were advanced as to why I should do so, but in general they all boiled down to something as follows: "The country is going socialistic so rapidly that, unless Republicans can get in immediately and defeat this trend, our country is gone. Four more years of New Dealism and there will be no turning back. This is our last chance."[22]

While there is no reason to doubt the sincerity of these sentiments, there were clearly other, less lofty impulses at work as well. By the end of the Second World War, the Republicans had been in the minority in Congress for over a decade; in 1948 it would be twenty years since a Republican candidate had been elected to the presidency. Whatever their other motives, Republicans were desperately eager to regain power and increasingly frustrated by their difficulties in doing so. They hoped through relentless criticism and opposition to turn voters away from the Democratic party and to fan any signs of popular dissatisfaction with that party's policies. By blocking, derailing, and dismantling presidential initatives on all fronts and by accusing the Democrats of inclining perilously toward "centralization," "socialization," and "statism," the Republicans aimed to discredit their opponents and to regain control of Congress and the White House. To party loyalists, saving the country and regaining political power were one and the same goal.

THE CONSERVATIVE COALITION

Republicans were not the only ones who objected to what they perceived to be a dangerous growth in federal power. Democrats from southern states had at first been strong supporters of the New Deal and of the dollars and patronage that it brought with it, but they soon became uneasy. Following the court-packing controversy of 1937, southern Democrats began, with increasing frequency, to oppose their party's president.[23] This tendency continued throughout the Second World War and intensified in the late 1940s and early 1950s.

From the turn of the twentieth century to the coming of the New Deal, the Democrats had been a predominately southern political party. Despite the nationwide electoral sweeps of 1932 and 1936, southerners still comprised a substantial fraction of congressional Democrats, and their relative weight increased even further when the party suffered setbacks, as it did in 1942 and again in 1946. Democrats in other parts of the country continued to be vulnerable at the polls in a way that their colleagues from the "solid South" simply were not. Thus, after the 1942 debacle, representatives of fifteen southern and border states occupied over half the Democratic seats in both the House (120 of 222) and the Senate (29 of 57).[24] Throughout the Roosevelt and Truman years, southerners never made up fewer than 40 percent of the Democrats in Congress.[25]

[22] Griffith, "Dwight D. Eisenhower and the Corporate Commonwealth," p. 99.

[23] Patterson, *Congressional Conservatism*, p. 97.

[24] Polenberg, *War and Society*, p. 192.

[25] Ira Katznelson, Kim Geiger, and Daniel Kryder, "Limiting Liberalism: The Southern Veto in

Even when their party controlled the legislative branch, southern Democrats, when they chose to do so, could help to block presidential proposals by voting with the Republicans. During periods of Democratic domination, the safe seats and considerable seniority of many southerners also permitted them to exert influence through their control of key committee chairmanships.[26] When the Republicans held majorities in Congress, Democratic support was also critically important to them in their efforts to oppose the programs of a Democratic president (as in 1946–48) or to support the policies of a Republican (as in 1953–54).[27]

Southern Democrats did not necessarily share the conservative Republicans' ideological animus to "big government," and their partisan political calculations were obviously more complex. Most southerners in Congress had no objection in principle to government spending programs that brought federal dollars to their districts, and despite their displeasure with Roosevelt and Truman, most had no wish to see a Republican elected president. But their desire to preserve their region's racial order led many of them into opposition to presidential initiatives and into alignment with the Republicans on a variety of issues.

The intensity of this opposition and the frequency of these alignments tended to grow along with evidence of a nascent federal commitment to overturning at least the more egregious manifestations of racial injustice. In the 1930s and early 1940s, the New Dealers had tried to step lightly around all such questions. But their caution did not prevent what historian Alan Brinkley has described as a "growing (if premature) suspicion" among white southerners that "the national Democratic party was becoming closely tied to the interests of African Americans."[28] By the late 1940s, with President Truman's 1946 appointment of a special committee on civil rights, his subsequent signing of an executive order desegregating the armed forces, and the inclusion of a civil rights plank in the 1948 party platform, suspicion had hardened into certainty.[29]

Southern Democrats in Congress consistently used their power to try to block civil rights legislation. During and after the war, white southerners also became more leery of any measures that seemed likely to increase the ability of the

---

Congress, 1933–1950," *Political Science Quarterly* 108, no. 2 (1993), pp. 284–85. Katznelson and his colleagues use a slightly more restrictive definition of the "South" than does Polenberg, including only thirteen states to his fifteen.

[26] From 1933 to 1952 "southern Democrats commanded 48 percent of the chairmanships and ranking minority positions in the Senate, and 51 percent in the House." Ibid., p. 285. See also V. O. Key, Jr., *Southern Politics in State and Nation* (New York: Knopf, 1949), pp. 345–46.

[27] On the period 1946–48, see the discussion in Susan M. Hartmann, *Truman and the 80th Congress* (Columbia: University of Missouri Press, 1971). The role of southern Democrats in 1953–54 is discussed in Gary W. Reichard, *The Reaffirmation of Republicanism* (Knoxville: University of Tennessee Press, 1975), pp. 181–217.

[28] Brinkley, *The End of Reform*, p. 143.

[29] See Robert J. Donovan, *Conflict and Crisis: The Presidency of Harry S. Truman, 1945–1948* (New York: Norton, 1977), pp. 332–37; Barton J. Bernstein and Allen J. Matusow, eds., *The Truman Administration: A Documentary History* (New York: Harper Colophon, 1966), pp. 95–114; Alonzo L. Hamby, *Beyond the New Deal: Harry S. Truman and American Liberalism* (New York: Columbia University Press, 1973), pp. 188–90, 209–39.

federal government, or of any other outside force, to intervene in their affairs. Thus a majority of southern Democrats joined with Republicans in opposing strong national labor unions. Albeit in lesser numbers, in the postwar period they also cast crucial votes against presidential initiatives on housing, education, taxes, scientific research, economic planning, and military manpower policy.[30]

INSTITUTIONAL PREROGATIVES

A final factor contributing to congressional resistance to postwar state-building was a sense of diminished institutional prerogatives and damaged institutional pride. At the start of the New Deal and again at the beginning of the war, Congress had acceded to marked increases in the size and authority of the executive branch. But in both cases, acquiescence in a crisis had been followed quickly by resentment, regret, and efforts to recapture at least a portion of the power that had been given up.

This tendency was especially marked after 1942, as the nation threw itself into a total war effort and the ideological balance in the Congress shifted sharply to the right. Republicans and conservative (mostly southern) Democrats were joined together, writes Richard Polenberg, "not only by a mutual desire to protect states' rights, regulate labor unions and curb welfare spending, but also by a shared resentment over the mammoth wartime expansion of executive authority and the corresponding erosion of legislative influence." Under the circumstances it was not surprising that many members of Congress from both parties sought to "reassert their prerogatives," primarily by conducting investigations of the war effort and attacking the domestic programs that were now the neglected and vulnerable stepchildren of "Dr. New Deal."[31]

In all, concludes Barry Karl, "the war enabled Congress to continue something it had already begun in 1937: recouping the powers that the Depression emergency had given to the president." Congress gradually "cut down the authority of the president, limiting it effectively to the wartime emergency programs and removing from his control the New Deal domestic programs that still existed."[32] Perhaps the most spectacular example of this wartime counterattack

[30] On the impact of the conservative coalition see Hartmann, *Truman and the 80th Congress*, pp. 134–35, 156–57; Alonzo L. Hamby, *Man of the People: A Life of Harry S. Truman* (New York: Oxford University Press, 1995), pp. 361–86, 488–508; Edwin Amenta and Theda Skocpol, "Redefining the New Deal: World War II and the Development of Social Provision in the United States," in Margaret Weir, Ann Shola Orloff, and Theda Skocpol, eds., *The Politics of Social Policy in the United States* (Princeton: Princeton University Press, 1988), pp. 81–122. Katznelson and his colleagues have shown that with the single exception of labor policy, there was no solid conservative coalition uniting Republicans and southern Democrats. Before, during, and after the Second World War, many Southern Democrats continued to vote with their northern colleagues and against the majority of Republicans on a variety of economic and social welfare issues. But Democratic cohesion tended to decline over time, while the incidence of southerners aligning with Republicans on these issues increased. These results are summarized in a table in Katznelson, Geiger, and Kryder, "Limiting Liberalism," p. 300.

[31] Polenberg, *War and Society*, p. 193.

[32] Karl, *Uneasy State*, pp. 216–17.

on executive power was the 1943 elimination of funding for the president's National Resources Planning Board (NRPB), an agency then engaged in preparing an ambitious postwar domestic reform agenda. Congressional conservatives did not like the substance of what the NRPB was doing, but beyond this, they were eager to do whatever they could to cut the presidency down to size.[33]

As soon as the war ended, Congress launched a multipronged counteroffensive against presidential power and prerogatives. The motives behind this movement were partly partisan and ideological; Republicans and conservative Democrats who disapproved of the policies of the most recent occupants of the White House were its principal supporters. But even some liberals were uneasy with the disproportionate growth in executive authority that had taken place during the preceding years of economic crisis and wartime mobilization. There was a widespread sense that the balance of institutional power had shifted too far toward the presidency and that it needed now to be brought back into a more equitable alignment.[34]

Some of the elements in the postwar assault on the presidency were more symbolic than substantive. Thus, in one of its first acts, the Republican-dominated Eightieth Congress quickly adopted what would eventually become the Twenty-Second Amendment to the Constitution, limiting presidents to two terms in office.[35] Other measures had more serious and immediate effects. The 1946 Legislative Reorganization Act restructured the committees of both houses of Congress so that they could better oversee key executive branch agencies, increased their budgets to permit the hiring of permanent staff, and gave many of them new powers to subpoena witnesses. These changes were followed by what one author has termed an "investigation explosion."[36]

[33] Philip W. Warken, *A History of the National Resources Planning Board, 1933–1943* (New York: Garland Publishing, 1979), p. 242. See also the discussion in Marion Clawson, *New Deal Planning: The National Resources Planning Board* (Baltimore: Johns Hopkins University Press, 1981), pp. 225–41; Otis L. Graham, Jr., *Toward a Planned Society: From Roosevelt to Nixon* (New York: Oxford University Press, 1976), pp. 1–68; John W. Jeffries, "The 'New' New Deal: FDR and American Liberalism, 1937–1945," *Political Science Quarterly* 105, no. 3 (1990), pp. 397–418. The role of antiplanning sentiment in shaping postwar defense industrial policy will be discussed in chapter 6.

[34] My analysis here draws heavily on an essay by Gary W. Reichard, "The Presidency Triumphant: Congressional-Executive Relations, 1945–1960," in Robert H. Bremner and Gary W. Reichard, eds., *Reshaping America: Society and Institutions, 1945–1960* (Columbus: Ohio State University Press, 1982), pp. 343–68. See also the discussion of postwar congressional attitudes in William E. Pemberton, *Bureaucratic Politics: Executive Reorganization during the Truman Administration* (Columbia: University of Missouri Press, 1979), pp. 13–20.

[35] Reichard, "The Presidency Triumphant," p. 346. Even this measure received some bipartisan support, with roughly one-third of the Democrats in both houses voting in favor. Gary W. Reichard, *Politics as Usual: The Age of Truman and Eisenhower* (Arlington Heights, IL: Harlan Davidson, 1988), p. 29.

[36] Reichard, "The Presidency Triumphant," pp. 345–47. Between 1789 and 1925 Congress conducted a total of 285 investigations. In 1950–51 the number was 236 and in 1951–52, 215. On the "investigation explosion" see Joseph P. Harris, *Congressional Control of Administration* (Washington, DC: Brookings Institution, 1964), pp. 263–64. Ernest S. Griffith, *Congress: Its Contemporary Role* (New York: New York University Press, 1956), pp. 25–42.

The energy from this blast was directed primarily against the executive branch. In the late 1940s and early 1950s, self-appointed congressional watchdogs, proclaiming themselves the defenders of the people's interests against a corrupt and treasonous bureaucratic elite, harried and harassed the executive agencies, accusing them of harboring Communists and forcing the adoption of governmentwide loyalty and security programs. Far from being an indication of the newfound strength of the American state, the anticommunist witch hunts of the early Cold War period were a telling indication of its continuing weakness.[37]

In addition to reorganizing itself, Congress sought to play a key role in the postwar restructuring of the executive branch. At the start of the New Deal and again after Pearl Harbor, the House and Senate had given the president broad, temporary powers to rearrange the executive agencies as he saw fit. At the end of the war, Congress refused President Truman's request for a permanent grant of authority, and instead reasserted its right to approve any proposed reorganization plans. In 1947 House and Senate Republicans also worked to create a Commission on the Organization of the Executive Branch of the Government and arranged for it to be headed by conservative former president Herbert Hoover.[38] Two years later Congress passed a law stipulating that any presidential reorganization plan could be set aside by a majority vote in either the House or the Senate. During Truman's second term, Congress used this "legislative veto" to block twelve of a total of forty-one executive reorganization proposals, including some that were intended to implement the recommendations of the Hoover Commission. Among the schemes rejected were a plan for further unifying the Defense Department and two proposals for the creation of a new Department of Health, Education, and Welfare.[39] With the Cold War underway, Congress could not and did not seek entirely to prevent the growth of the executive branch; it did retain a keen interest, and an important say, in determining exactly where and how it would expand.

---

[37] As one observer notes, "McCarthyism was a movement whose animosity was directed against the idea of an assertive federal government." Rhodri Jefferys-Jones, "1945, 1984: Government Power in Concept and Practice since World War II," in Jefferys-Jones and Bruce Collins, eds., *The Growth of Federal Power in American History* (Dekalb: Northern Illinois University Press, 1983), p. 116. On the anti-statist aspect of McCarthyism see also the discussion in Edward A. Shils, *The Torment of Secrecy: The Background and Consequences of American Security Policies* (Glencoe, IL: Free Press, 1956), pp. 112–19.

[38] On the origins and activities of this commission see Peri E. Arnold, "The First Hoover Commission and the Managerial Presidency," *Journal of Politics* 38, no. 1 (February 1976), pp. 46–70. Also Arnold, *Making the Managerial Presidency: Comprehensive Reorganization Planning, 1905–1980* (Princeton: Princeton University Press, 1986), pp. 118–59. Arnold argues that Hoover's own commitment to orthodox, hierarchical conceptions of organizational efficiency and Truman's surprising reelection victory in 1948 combined to produce a result very different, and far more accepting of presidential power, from what the Commission's creators originally intended. See also Pemberton, *Bureaucratic Politics*, pp. 64–124.

[39] On the "legislative veto" and its relation to executive reorganization see Harris, *Congressional Control of Administration*, pp. 206–10; also Louis Fisher, *The Constitution between Friends: Congress, the President, and the Law* (New York: St. Martin's, 1978), pp. 100–103.

The Mobilization of Business

Reinforcing and, to a degree, motivating congressional resistance to statism was the renewed postwar influence of American business. In the 1930s, as the Depression reached its depths, America's industrial captains had found themselves bearing much of the blame for the nation's troubles. Long accustomed to public respect bordering on veneration, businessmen were subjected instead to ample doses of scorn and abuse. The lurid fantasies of impending expropriation and intense fears of homegrown socialism (or fascism) that marked the business response to the New Deal were, at least in part, a direct emotional reaction to this sudden loss of status.

The Second World War restored the public standing and much of the earlier self-confidence of American businessmen, but it did not alleviate all their anxieties. Once blamed for cutting wages and putting people out of work, the nation's corporate executives and the capitalist—or, as they preferred, "free enterprise"—economic system that they represented were now credited with having orchestrated the miracle of industrial mobilization that had won the war. "The capitalism that had been damned as bankrupt just a few years before," notes Robert Collins, "was now celebrated for its prodigious feats of production."[40] Government's substantial role in organizing and funding this awe-inspiring exercise was glossed over or conveniently forgotten. Instead, it was the state that took the blame for the less pleasant aspects of the wartime experience. The consensus view was that "free enterprise . . . produced the guns, while government, for its restrictive part, rationed the butter."[41]

Despite this seeming reversal of fortunes, American businessmen entered the postwar era shaken by the Depression and fearful of what lay ahead.[42] Business leaders worried that the end of the war would clear the way for a renewed assault on their position by the radical reformers whom they believed still to be lurking in Washington. Preventing this from occurring seemed to require an ongoing political mobilization of great scope, intensity, and sophistication.

The diverse array of business groups and individual corporations that sought to influence policy in the aftermath of the Second World War had a range of preferences and goals, but they shared a common suspicion of the federal government and a desire sharply to circumscribe its power. One exhaustive postwar study of the attitudes of American businessmen concluded that they tended to regard government as "inherently evil" and "inherently dangerous." Most accepted that minimal government action was necessary to enforce "the rules of competition and contract," but believed that the state was ultimately sterile; it could not create anything useful in the way that businessmen produced wealth and individuals generated ideas. In the absence of market discipline, govern-

[40] Robert M. Collins, *The Business Response to Keynes, 1929–1964* (New York: Columbia University Press, 1981), p. 81.

[41] Blum, *V Was for Victory*, p. 116.

[42] Robert Griffith, "The Selling of America: The Advertising Council and American Politics, 1942–1960," *Business History Review* 57 (Autumn 1983), p. 388.

mental "extravagance, inefficiency, and waste" were inevitable. Yet, perversely, government had a marked tendency to grow in size, to expand its powers, and to encroach increasingly on individual liberties. By the late 1940s, adherents of the "American business creed" believed that their society stood "on the edge of [a] fateful line" between capitalist freedom and statist slavery. One false move, one further step in the wrong direction, and the nation might forever lose its traditional freedoms.[43]

In addition to these shared general attitudes toward government, American businessmen agreed also on a range of more specific policy issues. State ownership of plants and production facilities was indistinguishable from socialism and so was to be avoided at all costs.[44] Even if it did not involve direct government takeovers of industry, national economic planning was anathema because it would lead to a loss of autonomy for business and a concentration of political and economic power in the hands of faceless bureaucrats. And, even if they went forward piecemeal, without any explicit attempt at central planning, the cumulative weight of government economic controls and regulations was likely to produce the same dangerous results.[45]

Business leaders were similarly united in their general desire for lower taxes, opposition to prolonged federal budget deficits, and skepticism about all forms of government spending. High taxes suppressed individual and corporate initiative, fueled government waste, and beyond a certain point could undermine the principle of private property and put excessive political power in the hands of the state. Perpetually unbalanced budgets were a symptom of governmental indiscipline and a leading cause of inflation. In addition to being inefficient by their very nature, federal spending programs also led either to higher taxes or bigger deficits.[46]

[43] Francis X. Sutton, Seymour E. Harris, Carl Kaysen, and James Tobin, *The American Business Creed* (Cambridge: Harvard University Press, 1956), pp. 186, 192, 194–95, 205.

[44] Anxiety over nationalization was heightened by the wave of government takeovers in Europe after the war. See the discussion in Andrew Shonfield, *Modern Capitalism: The Changing Balance of Public and Private Power* (London: Oxford University Press, 1965), pp. 71–238; Peter Hall, *Governing the Economy: The Politics of State Intervention in Britain and France* (New York: Oxford University Press, 1986), pp. 48–61, 138–91.

[45] On the evils of regulation in particular see Sutton et al., *The American Business Creed*, p. 215. Business attitudes are further summarized in Marver H. Bernstein, "Political Ideas of Selected American Business Journals," *Public Opinion Quarterly* 17 (Summer 1953), pp. 258–67.

[46] The main divisions within the business community involved the specifics of fiscal policy. Traditional laissez-faire conservatives, like those whose views were represented by the National Association of Manufacturers, favored continuously balanced budgets at the lowest possible levels of taxation and expenditure. Other business executives accepted that New Deal social welfare programs could not easily be done away with, and they recognized that with the onset of the Cold War, it might not be possible to cut defense spending back to pre-war levels. Organizations like the Committee on Economic Development were also willing to see the federal government run temporarily unbalanced budgets as a way of smoothing out the business cycle. As important as they may have seemed at the time, the debates on these issues were far less significant than the broader underlying agreement within the business community about the need to limit the role of the federal government in the nation's economy. These differences are analyzed in Collins, *The Business Re-*

Robert Griffith has described the postwar political mobilization of business as being of such scope and variety as to "defy generalization." Individual firms, industry associations (like the American Medical Association and the National Association of Electric Companies), "peak" associations (like the National Association of Manufacturers [NAM] and the U.S. Chamber of Commerce), and other nationwide groups (like the Committee on Economic Development and the Business Advisory Council) lobbied the Congress and the executive branch on behalf of particular policies and in opposition to others; some also supported candidates whose views reflected their own.[47]

Alongside these more traditional campaign-financing and issue-specific lobbying efforts, firms and business groups also devoted extraordinary resources to "selling free enterprise" and warning against the menace of an encroaching state. After the Second World War, one study found that ordinary advertisements devoted "more space to the merits of the [free enterprise] system, and relatively less space to expounding the virtues of particular products."[48] In addition, various national organizations sponsored public relations campaigns with closely related ideological themes. One NAM leaflet described the American Revolution as a rebellion against "'government planners' in London." Between 1948 and 1950, the Advertising Council distributed over 1.5 million somewhat subtler pamphlets that explained how political freedom had produced the economic "Miracle of America."[49]

Free enterprise was good; too much government was not only bad for the economy, it was a profound threat to traditional American liberties. By the early 1950s, American businesses were devoting over $100 million each year to conveying these basic messages. The results, writes Griffith, were inescapable: "The detritus of these campaigns lay scattered about America's cultural landscape in books, articles and pamphlets, in motion pictures, on billboards and posters, on radio and television, on car cards in buses, trains, and trolleys, even in comic books and on matchbook covers."[50]

Intellectual Trends

Outpourings of enthusiasm for limited government and free markets as well as expressions of hostility toward planning, centralization, and statism were not confined to the covers of matchbooks. To the contrary, the simplistic and self-serving effusions of business and its boosters were only the most visible and

---

sponse to Keynes, and Herbert Stein, *The Fiscal Revolution in America* (Washington, DC: American Enterprise Institute, 1990). Postwar fiscal policy will be discussed at length in chapter 4.

[47] Robert Griffith, "Forging America's Postwar Order: Domestic Politics and Political Economy in the Age of Truman," in Michael J. Lacey, *The Truman Presidency* (New York: Cambridge University Press, 1991), pp. 63, 67.

[48] Sutton et al., *The American Business Creed*, p. 297.

[49] Robert Griffith, "The Selling of America: The Advertising Council and American Politics, 1942–1960," *Business History Review* 57, no. 3 (Autumn 1983), pp. 402–3.

[50] Ibid.

superficial manifestations of a much broader, and considerably deeper, intellectual current. As the Second World War ended and the Cold War began, a remarkable array of philosophers, natural and social scientists, legal scholars, columnists, pundits, and novelists expressed similar concerns over what appeared to them to be a dangerous and perhaps unstoppable movement toward an ever more powerful state.

A review of these writings reveals four closely connected variations on this one basic theme.

ECONOMIC PLANNING AND THE ROAD TO SERFDOM

Much postwar rhetoric regarding the dangers of excessive state control of the economy can be traced to a single source. First published in England in 1944, Friedrich Hayek's *The Road to Serfdom* had its greatest impact in the United States. Hayek asserted simply that any attempt by government to plan and direct economic activity would end up undermining capitalism and destroying individual liberty. Once politicians had identified a seemingly unobjectionable, even laudable, collective aim (such as protecting individual welfare or promoting social equality), they would use it to justify the exercise of state power to "organize the whole of society and all its resources." The success of this enterprise would soon necessitate the denial of the existence of any "autonomous spheres in which the interests of individuals are supreme." In pursuit of its noble goals, the state would be led to intrude into every aspect of social and economic life; eventually it would concentrate all power in its own hands. No matter how benign their intentions, the advocates of "democratic socialism" and the "planned economy" were leading their societies in the same direction as the supporters of communism and fascism. All forms of collectivism, regardless of their initial ideological coloration, would issue eventually in totalitarianism.[51]

Hayek's words were music to the ears of businessmen and anti–New Deal conservatives, for they provided "one of the first academic justifications for their hostility to government intervention that they had seen in almost a generation."[52] Beyond simply confirming such people in their opinions, however, *The Road to Serfdom* armed them with compelling formulations and high-powered intellectual ammunition. The oft-repeated claim that centralizers were leading America down a slippery slope to slavery was drawn directly from Hayek.

Somewhat more surprising was the broader public response. Hayek's book quickly became a best-seller in the United States, it was excerpted in the *Reader's Digest*, and in the crowning symbol of mass-market success, it was soon offered as a Book of the Month Club selection.[53] These achievements were

---

[51] Friedrich A. Hayek, *The Road to Serfdom* (Chicago: University of Chicago Press, 1944), p. 56. The origins and evolution of Hayek's ideas and the placement of this book in the larger body of his work are discussed in Norman P. Barry, *Hayek's Social and Economic Philosophy* (London: Macmillan, 1979). See also Norman Barry, John Burton, Hannes H. Gissurarson, et al., *Hayek's "Serfdom" Revisited* (London: Institute of Economic Affairs, 1984).

[52] Karl, *The Uneasy State*, p. 215.

[53] Over one million copies of the condensed version of Hayek's book were eventually distributed

not unrelated to the book's appeal to business groups, some of which purchased and distributed it to customers and the general public. But Hayek seems also to have struck a genuinely responsive chord among ordinary citizens concerned about the shape of the postwar world. After the New Deal and the war, the question of the appropriate role of government in American society was very much alive. With the struggle against fascism ending and recognition of the true character of the Soviet regime beginning to grow, totalitarianism was no longer a mere abstraction. Beyond this, as Alan Brinkley has pointed out, Hayek tapped a "powerful strain of Jeffersonian anti-statism in American political culture that a decade of the New Deal had done relatively little to eliminate."[54]

Most striking of all was the reaction to Hayek's book among American liberals, many of whom had at one time believed that central government planning was essential to the nation's economic and social well-being. The implication that the New Dealers had been paving the path to perdition was met, of course, with outrage. But even Hayek's harshest critics seemed to share his fear of totalitarianism and to accept his view of the dangers of excessive government interventionism and overly ambitious central planning. "Running through liberal criticism of the book was a strongly defensive tone," notes Brinkley, "an effort to assure a suspicious world that New Dealers, too, were, concerned about the dangers of statism."[55] The "horror of poverty" that had motivated many liberals and social democrats before the war had given way, by the mid-1940s, to the "horror of statist tyranny." Anxiety over this prospect was as real on the left side of the American political spectrum as it was on the right. In all, concludes one survey of postwar opinion, "the most interesting thing about *Serfdom*'s reception was the degree of consensus that it revealed."[56]

NEOCONSTITUTIONALISM

If the experience of the 1930s caused many intellectuals to question the virtues of the American system of government, the triumphs of the 1940s led to a widespread renewal of faith. Liberal democracy had proven its ability both to provide for the needs of its people and to defeat its enemies on the field of battle. Despite these successes, some experts worried that nearly two decades of continual crisis had begun to warp the nation's political institutions; others warned that still greater distortions might lie ahead. The immediate postwar period was thus marked both by a celebration of the virtues of the American Constitution, and of constitutionalism and limited government more generally, as well as by a deep anxiety about their future.[57]

---

through the Book-of-the-Month Club. John Burton, "Introduction," in Barry et al., *Hayek's "Serfdom" Revisited*, p. xi.

[54] Brinkley, *The End of Reform*, p. 160.

[55] Ibid., p. 159.

[56] Theodore Rosenof, "Freedom, Planning, and Totalitarianism: The Reception of F. A. Hayek's *Road to Serfdom*," *Canadian Review of American Studies* 5, no. 2 (Fall 1974), pp. 160–61.

[57] For an overview, see Herman Belz, "Changing Conceptions of Constitutionalism in the Era of World War II and the Cold War," *Journal of American History* 59, no. 3 (December 1972), pp.

This concern is best captured in the writings of Princeton professor Edward S. Corwin. In a penetrating series of lectures delivered within months of the war's close, Corwin sought to assess its impact on the theory and practice of American constitutionalism. Taken together, Corwin argued, the war and the depression that preceded it had resulted in a greatly increased "concentration of power in the hands, first, of the National Government; secondly, in the hands of the President and administrative agencies." The three traditional sources of constraint on federal and presidential power—federalism, the courts, and "a certain interpretation of the doctrine of the separation of power"—had all been badly eroded by the events of the 1930s and 1940s. Primarily as the result of a series of judicial decisions, the traditional "Constitution of Rights" had now been transformed into what Corwin labeled a "Constitution of Powers." Given the lingering effects of legal precedent, these changes could not be quickly reversed.[58]

Although guarded in his assessment of what lay ahead, Corwin was nevertheless clearly troubled by the direction of events. How, in particular, he asked, could "liberty against government" be preserved in a system in which the checks on executive power had been severely weakened? "Our principal reliance for this purpose," Corwin concluded, "must be a better organization of the relationship of President and Congress." The powers of initiative and administration that Congress had recently delegated to the president could not now easily be recalled. Nevertheless, increased congressional assertiveness could at least "constitute something of a guarantee that important legislation will always represent a widespread opinion that it was needed and meritorious, and conversely that projects which do not have that support will fail." Beyond that, "the survival among us of constitutional government and the humane values it was meant to conserve" might depend on uncontrollable events, on the absence of still more severe crises that would further tilt the balance of governmental power toward the presidency. Such good fortune, Corwin concluded gloomily, did not seem likely.[59]

ATOMIC ANXIETIES

The successful detonation of the atomic bomb aroused two distinct fears in the United States. The first and more obvious worry was that the nation had suddenly been rendered vulnerable to devastating external attack. The second, subtler concern was that in order to meet this new threat, the American people might be forced to surrender their traditional freedoms.

As they began to reflect on the political and social effects of the atom, as well as its strategic implications, an array of observers was drawn quickly to

---

640–69. Conveying some of the anxiety of the period are Thomas K. Finletter, *Can Representative Government Do the Job?* (New York: Reynal and Hitchcock, 1945); Clinton L. Rossiter, *Constitutional Dictatorship: Crisis Government in the Modern Democracies* (Princeton: Princeton University Press, 1948).

[58] Edward S. Corwin, *Total War and the Constitution* (New York: Knopf, 1947), pp. 172, 180.

[59] Ibid., p. 180–81.

very similar conclusions: unless they were brought under some kind of international control, the forces released at Hiroshima would lead inevitably to an unprecedented centralization of domestic political power.[60] "Atomic energy looms as a giant new force propelling us towards the organization of society from the center," concluded the director for social sciences at the Rockefeller Foundation at the end of 1945.[61] "This new source of energy must . . . increase enormously the power of the state over the citizen," wrote a professor of international relations.[62] "I warn you," intoned political scientist Charles Merriam in March of 1946, "that greater concentrations of power than ever before are on their way. . . . Unless the greatest care is taken . . . human liberty may be lost . . . in the toils of a concentrated dictatorship such as has never been seen before."[63] While their source was new, writes historian Paul Boyer, these fears had "deep historical resonance in American social thought."[64]

Numerous influences were presumed to be leading to the same troubling result. Nobel Prize winning physicist Harold Urey, a key figure in the Manhattan Project, worried that keeping the terrible secret of the atom would require a continuation and expansion of wartime security measures "backed by the most drastic penalties" for those who disobeyed. An obsessive concern for secrecy would have wider political implications. Deprived of vital information about the nature of the threats confronting their country, and even about the state of their own defenses, the American people would have to "trust men in Washington with important decisions previously made through their elected representatives." Effective power would be concentrated not only in Washington, and not merely in the executive branch, but in the hands of the military. The necessity of preparing to respond immediately to atomic attack would further reinforce these tendencies, resulting eventually in a transfer of "the right to declare war from Congress to a single man." Under these conditions "men on horseback would rapidly appear on the public scene," and American democracy would soon decay into a form of military dictatorship.[65]

---

[60] One intriguing, if partial, dissent from this widely held view is contained in William L. Borden, *There Will Be No Time: The Revolution in Strategy* (New York: Macmillan, 1946), pp. 200–217. Weighing the comparative strengths and weaknesses of democracies and totalitarian dictatorships in an age of atomic weapons, Borden concluded that because of the increasing importance of technology and the diminishing relevance of total societal mobilization, democracies might actually have an edge. But he worried that the ability of dictatorships to strike the first blow might nullify these advantages.

[61] Joseph H. Willits, "Social Adustments to Atomic Energy," *Proceedings of the American Philosophical Society* 90, no. 1 (January 1946), p. 51.

[62] E. L. Woodward, "How Can We Prevent Atomic War?" *New York Times Magazine,* January 13, 1946, p. 40.

[63] Charles E. Merriam, "World Community and the Atom," *Christian Century,* March 6, 1946, p. 298.

[64] Paul Boyer, *By the Bomb's Early Light: American Thought and Culture at the Dawn of the Atomic Age* (Chapel Hill: University of North Carolina Press, 1994), p. 142. His discussion of the early reaction of social scientists and commentators to the detonation of the atomic bomb led me to many of the references cited here (see pp. 141–65).

[65] Harold C. Urey, "How Does It All Add Up?" in Masters and Way, *One World or None,* p. 58.

In order to prevent enemy agents from smuggling atomic explosives into the United States, the federal government would have to be granted virtually unlimited domestic police powers. "Immensely increased internal-security measures will be needed," cautioned the journalists Joseph and Stewart Alsop. Indeed, "the Constitution itself will need to be reinterpreted to make us free from search and seizure only when the agents of the security police are not carrying their Geiger counters."[66] Meeting the threat of atomic sabotage would also require that the nation's borders be effectively sealed and commerce tightly controlled. "Practically all forms of international trade would eventually be carefully overseen by the government," concluded a 1948 report, with licenses issued by the State Department "only to those businesses who pass the most rigid sort of patriotic tests."[67] The postwar era might therefore be marked not by a rebirth of free trade, but by the beginning of a new age of mercantilism.

Reducing the vulnerability of American cities and industry to atomic air attack would require "the redistribution of population, the decentralization of our cities, the dispersal of our industries."[68] Great urban centers would have to be effectively depopulated and their inhabitants relocated, willingly or otherwise, to rural areas and to smaller towns and villages. Some portion of the nation's citizens and critical elements of its productive machinery might even have to be buried underground. Planning such an enterprise and carrying it to fruition over the objections of individuals, firms, industries, states, and perhaps whole regions of the country would require granting the central government virtually unlimited powers.

Preparing for atomic attack would also require organizing and training the entire civilian population of the United States. "Every citizen must be ready for the time when all our great cities will be reduced to radioactive shards . . . when tens of millions of dead will await burial [and] tens of millions of casualties will need care and hospitalization." Preparing for this eventuality would require the American people, "women as well as men," to accept a system of compulsory universal training and service.[69] For a nation with a long history of ambivalence about conscription of any kind, this was a deeply disturbing prospect.

As terrible as atomic warfare would undoubtedly be, a prolonged period of preparation for it might be almost as bad. In an essay published in the March 1947 issue of the journal *Air Affairs*, author Lewis Mumford sketched out a series of scenarios intended to illuminate the "social effects of atomic war." In the first three, war breaks out after increasing periods of time have elapsed and

[66] Joseph Alsop and Stewart Alsop, "Your Flesh *Should* Creep," *Saturday Evening Post*, July 13, 1946, p. 49.

[67] Ryland W. Crary, Hubert M. Evans, Albert Gotlieb, and Israel Light, *The Challenge of Atomic Energy* (New York: Teachers' College, Columbia University, 1948), pp. 38–39.

[68] Norman Cousins and Thomas K. Finletter, "A Beginning for Sanity," *Saturday Review* , June 15, 1946, p. 5. Efforts to promote the dispersal of industry will be discussed in chapter 6.

[69] Alsop and Alsop, "Your Flesh *Should* Creep," p. 49. The attempt to impose universal military training will be discussed in chapter 5.

the number of atomic weapons (and the number of countries possessing them) has grown. The results are predictably grim, culminating in the third case in fatalities and in genetic and environmental damage sufficient to annihilate the human race.[70]

In Mumford's fourth scenario, "atomic war does not break out at all," but it remains "for at least a century . . . a growing threat." Various trends are now "carried to their logical conclusions." Populations are forceably scattered or driven underground. "Taxes continue to rise to a point that nullifies financial success." Eventually, "all the earlier advocates of free enterprise become eager for state ownership and flock into government, where power and privilege are now concentrated." Vast sectors of the economy are nationalized and "the Constitution of every country is altered, where necessary, so as to give complete control to the military caste." All forms of expression are brought under "centralized control." Research, development, and education at all levels are geared to meeting the needs of "atomic warfare and its accessory arts." Perpetual fear of annihilation leads to "purposeless sexual promiscuity . . . narcotic indulgence," and outbreaks of paranoia, claustrophobia, and sadistic violence. While "not a single life has been lost in atomic warfare," by the scenario's end, civilization has, nevertheless, been "fatally destroyed."[71]

ORWELL, LASWELL, AND THE GARRISON STATE

In Mumford's dystopic vision, the awesome might of atomic weapons was the essential force driving the world toward spiritual, if not physical, destruction. For others, the danger lay less in the particulars of military technology than in the brutal, grinding process of a protracted struggle for power and security. The experience of the Second World War showed that even a few years of large-scale mobilization could have significant state-strengthening effects. High levels of military preparation, sustained over many years, would undoubtedly have an even greater cumulative impact. As the wartime alliance between East and West unraveled, many observers feared that even if they were not attacked and defeated outright, the liberal democracies would come in time to resemble their new communist rivals. For the United States, no less than its smaller, weaker allies, liberty might be the price of survival.

George Orwell's *1984* made this case with telling force. In Orwell's story, which appeared in 1949, thirty-five years of confrontation and warfare have reduced England (now "Airstrip One," an outpost of a U.S.-led oceanic empire) to a hellish totalitarianism. Wars, real and imagined, have cleared the way for the concentration of all authority in the hands of a tiny ruling elite. Orwell's book was a condemnation of statism in general and an indictment of communism in particular; it was also a warning of the domestic dangers involved in confronting the Soviet Union. This point was not lost on American readers. The message of Orwell's work, concluded one reviewer, was that "maintaining the

---

[70] Lewis Mumford, "Social Effects," *Air Affairs* 1, no. 3 (March 1947), pp. 370–77. This essay is discussed at length in Boyer, *By the Bomb's Early Light*, pp. 284–87.

[71] Mumford, "Social Effects," pp. 377–81.

delicate balance between . . . freedom and security is the critical problem of our age."[72] Like Hayek's book before it, *1984* quickly became a best-seller in the United States.

Orwell may have been influenced in his thinking by Mumford; both owed something to the speculations of a less widely known writer.[73] As early as 1937, again in 1941, and in a series of influential postwar essays, political scientist Harold Lasswell developed the argument that under conditions of continual crisis and perpetual preparedness for total war, every aspect of life would eventually come under state control. While the changes would be greatest for those countries like the United States that started out with "a minimum of state-ism," all nations would be compelled to conform, or face destruction at the hands of their enemies. Over time, Lasswell feared, there would be a general, evolutionary movement "towards a world of 'garrison states' "[74]

In these strange and terrible new political organisms, authority would be "dictatorial, governmentalized, centralized, integrated."[75] With the state under constant threat, all power would flow to the "specialists on violence," the soldiers, the security policemen, and their civilian assistants. The principal preoccupations of the ruling elite would be maintaining morale and domestic order (through the use of terror, propaganda, and mind-altering drugs) and managing the economy so as to generate the maximum military capabilities. Economic growth would be stimulated, civilian consumption held to a bare minimum, and every available resource directed to sustaining the mass production of armaments at permanently high levels. All scientific effort too would be aimed at "multiplying gadgets specialized to acts of violence."[76]

Orwell gained lasting literary fame, but it was Lasswell's language that exerted the more obvious and immediate influence on postwar debate. By the late

[72] Robert Hatch, "George Orwell's Paradise Lost," *New Republic* 121, no. 5, issue 1809, August 1, 1949, p. 24.

[73] In the summer of 1947, as he was preparing to write *1984*, Orwell laid out three alternative scenarios for the future that closely resembled Mumford's. He pronounced the third of these, a protracted stalemate between the United States and the USSR to be "the worst possibility of all." It would lead to the division of the world into two or three vast superstates and to a "crushing out of liberty" that "would exceed anything that the world has yet seen." See Orwell's essay "Toward European Unity," in Sonia Orwell and Ian Angus, eds., *Collected Essays, Journals, and Letters of George Orwell*, vol. 4 (New York: Harcourt Brace Jovanovich, 1968), p. 371. For an essay describing some of the parallels, if not the actual connections, between the thought of these two contemporaries see Hayward R. Alker, Jr., "An Orwellian Lasswell for Today," in Robert L. Savage, James Combs, Dan Nimmo, *The Orwellian Moment: Hindsight and Foresight in the Post-1984 World* (Fayetteville: University of Arkansas Press, 1989), pp. 131–55.

[74] Harold Lasswell, "The Universal Peril: Perpetual Crisis and the Garrison-Prison State," in Lyman Bryson, Louis Finkelstein, and R. M. MacIver, eds., *Perspectives on a Troubled Decade: Science, Philosophy, and Religion, 1939–1949* (New York: Harper, 1950), p. 325. The earliest formulation of these ideas is contained in Lasswell, "The Garrison State versus the Civilian State," *China Quarterly* vol. 2 (Fall 1937), pp. 643–49.

[75] Harold Lasswell, "The Garrison State," *American Journal of Sociology* 46 (July 1940—May 1941), p. 455.

[76] Harold Lasswell, "The Garrison State and Specialists on Violence," in Lasswell, *The Analysis of Political Behavior* (London: Kegan, Paul, Trench, Trubner, 1947), pp. 153–55.

1940s and early 1950s, the term "garrison state," with all the connotations that it carried, had become commonplace. Lasswell's phrase was "adhered to by intellectuals and alluded to by mass media"; it found its way into editorials, pamphlets, presidential speeches, and top secret government deliberations.[77] "The pressure for security can lead us along a dangerous road," cautioned a 1949 statement by a conservative business group, one "that ends in . . . a garrison-police state."[78] If the United States failed to defend its friends and was forced to face communism alone, warned President Truman in 1952, it would have "to become a garrison state, and to impose upon [itself] a system of centralized regimentation unlike anything we have ever known."[79] As subsequent chapters will show, the term also became a staple part of Dwight Eisenhower's rhetoric, appearing with great regularity in both his public statements and his most closely guarded conversations with top national security advisers.

To a remarkable degree, Lasswell had succeeded in capturing and crystallizing the underlying anxiety of his day. What was at stake was not merely the physical survival of the United States, but its very soul. As they began to face up to the necessity of confronting and containing the Soviet Union, Americans worried deeply about the price they would have to pay. And as they contemplated their newfound enemy, many feared they saw the image of what their own country could all too easily become.

Popular Attitudes

From the mid-1940s to the late 1950s the American people were in a distinctly conservative frame of mind. To judge from opinion polls and election results, the public was skeptical of and resistant to sharp shifts and sudden departures in policy, regardless of direction or purpose. Thus, while most people did not want to see the federal government grow in size or expand its responsibilities, few supported efforts to cut it all the way back to its pre-war dimensions. At home as well as abroad, the American people supported "containment," but were wary of "rollback." These attitudes helped to constrain the growth of government, whether for purposes of providing welfare or preparing for the next war.

World War Two brought more Americans than ever before into direct contact with the federal government, whether as taxpayers, draftees, suppliers of goods and services, or clippers of ration coupons. The results, not surprisingly, were frustration, irritation, and the rapid evaporation of whatever enthusiasm for a more powerful central state remained from the early days of the New Deal. The wartime Office of Price Administration (OPA), which, in addition to regulating prices, set wages, rationed scarce goods, and issued regulations governing ev-

[77] Samuel P. Huntington, *The Soldier and the State* (New York: Vintage, 1957), p. 347.

[78] Commitee for Economic Development, *National Security and Our Individual Freedom* (New York: Committee for Economic Development, 1949), p. 4.

[79] "Special Message to the Congress on the Mutual Security Program," March 6, 1952, in Harry S. Truman, *Public Papers of the Presidents of the United States, 1952–1953* (Washington, DC: U.S. Government Printing Office, 1966), p. 189.

erything from the design of civilian clothing to the amount of fat that could be included on various cuts of meat, was a lightning rod for popular discontent. Described as the "the most intrusive federal bureaucracy ever created in America," the OPA became both "a target for all the frustrations and disappointments of people unaccustomed to regimentation and control" and a symbol of all that was wrong with an overly powerful and intrusive government.[80]

By the end of the war, the majority of Americans may not have been acquainted with the theoretical arguments of Friedrich Hayek or familiar with the term "statism," or even opposed in principle to the temporary continuation of some government price controls (preferably on the things they bought rather than those they sold).[81] But as one newspaper editorial put it, they "were tired of being pushed around and being told what to do" and weary of "Washington's remote control over their daily lives." Tapping these sentiments, the Republican party rode to sweeping electoral success in 1946 on the simple slogan "Had Enough?"[82]

Despite this initial sharp shift and a general move to the right in American politics that would persist well into the 1950s, popular animosity toward government would not prove to be quite as deep or as broad as Republicans had hoped.[83] Harry Truman was able narrowly to win re-election in 1948, in part because he convinced voters that if they controlled both the executive and the legislative branches, the Republicans would proceed to demolish all existing New Deal programs. Most Americans clearly did not want to go that far.[84]

At the same time, as the subsequent failure of most of Truman's ambitious Fair Deal agenda suggests, there was relatively little support for further dramatic growth in the domestic role of the federal government. Public opinion

[80] Brinkley, *The End of Reform,* p. 147. See also Karl, *The Uneasy State,* p. 220; William L. O'Neill, *A Democracy at War: America's Fight at Home and Abroad in World War II* (New York: Free Press, 1993), pp. 248–49.

[81] Only 13 percent of the respondents in an October 1949 poll could define the term "statism," and fully 68 percent did not know the meaning of the word. American Institute of Public Opinion poll cited in *Public Opinion Quarterly* 14, no. 1 (Spring 1950), p. 189. In the immediate aftermath of the war, majorities of those polled favored continuation of price controls and, if the two had to go together, of wage controls as well. By the end of 1946, however, support for controls had dwindled and more people favored dropping price restrictions on most items than continuing them. See results of Survey #343-K, Questions 9a-c (August 1945); Survey #357-T, Questions 6a-c (October 1945); Survey #378-K, Question 9 (October 1946); and Survey #385-T, Question 9 (December 1946) in *The Gallup Poll,* vol. 1, *1935–1948* (New York: Random House, 1972), pp. 522, 535, 602–3, 614–15.

[82] Editorial from a postelection issue of the *Washington Daily News,* quoted in Joseph C. Goulden, *The Best Years: 1945–1950* (New York: Atheneum, 1976), p. 229.

[83] Brian Girvin, *The Right in the Twentieth Century: Conservatism and Democracy* (London: Pinter, 1994), p. 159.

[84] Alonzo Hamby describes the election as failing to produce "a mandate for anything beyond a continuation of the status quo—the logical response to Truman's 'don't let them take it away from you' appeal." Hamby, *Man of the People,* pp. 466, 439–66. For similar interpretations see William L. O'Neill, *American High: The Years of Confidence, 1945–1960* (New York: Free Press, 1986), pp. 84–105; Robert J. Donovan, *Conflict and Crisis: The Presidency of Harry S. Truman, 1945–1948* (New York: Norton, 1977), pp. 395–439.

polls found no enthusiasm for a national health insurance scheme, for example.[85] Where there appeared to be substantial support, in principle, for new programs (like federal housing), much of it melted away when people were asked if they would be willing to pay higher taxes to fund them.[86] Even after the congressionally imposed tax cuts of 1948 and before the increases that accompanied the Korean War, growing numbers of citizens complained that their tax burden was too high, few supported further rate hikes to pay for new programs, and many believed, to the contrary, that the size and cost of the federal government should be reduced. In the early 1950s, with taxes and spending up, these sentiments grew even stronger.[87]

The election of Dwight Eisenhower in 1952 confirmed the general public preference for a "retention without expansion of the New Deal."[88] Eisenhower was strongly opposed, on philosophical grounds, to most forms of federal intervention in society and the economy, and other things equal, he would probably have preferred to dismantle many of the domestic programs he had inherited. But the new president recognized too that by the time he took office, these programs had acquired substantial constituencies that would be difficult and dangerous to confront. As he wrote in 1954, any party that tried "to abolish social security, unemployment insurance, and eliminate labor laws and farm programs" risked political suicide.[89] Ever the realist, Eisenhower committed himself to reducing the government's domestic profile where possible and avoiding major new endeavors. At least until the closing years of the 1950s, his position seemed to accord well with the preferences of a majority of Americans.[90]

The public's cautious acceptance of a limited welfare state was matched by its wary embrace of an expanded warfare state. As the Cold War got underway, there was growing recognition that the United States needed to build up and sustain its military power. But there was also a deep reluctance, and sometimes an outright refusal, to accept the domestic consequences of maintaining such a posture. The American people wanted a stronger military but were reluctant to pay higher taxes, remained ambivalent about accepting conscription, and

[85] For indications of weak public support for an increased government role in the provision of health care, see Survey #437-K, Question #14 (April 1949) and Survey #438-K, Question #5a (April 1949) in *The Gallup Poll*, vol. 2, *1949–1958* (New York: Random House, 1972), p. 802.

[86] Thus, 69 percent of those questioned in one poll supported federal funds for low-rent housing, but only 46 percent said that they would be "willing to pay higher taxes to do this," while 40 percent admitted they were unwilling to shoulder the burden. Survey #433-K, Questions #4a and 4c (January 1949), ibid., p. 781.

[87] Postwar public opinion regarding taxes will be discussed in chapter 4.

[88] Bernard Sternsher, "Reflections on Politics, Policy, and Ideology," in Bremner and Reichard, *Reshaping America*, p. 379.

[89] Letter to Edgar Eisenhower, November 8, 1954, quoted in Girvin, *The Right in the Twentieth Century*, p. 162. For a succinct summary of Eisenhower's views see Fred I. Greenstein, *The Hidden Hand: Eisenhower as Leader* (New York: Basic Books, 1982), pp. 46–54.

[90] For an interpretation of the period as a whole see Charles C. Alexander, *Holding the Line: The Eisenhower Era, 1952–1961* (Bloomington: Indiana University Press, 1975).

showed a strong preference for defense strategies that promised to impose in peacetime the lowest possible human and financial burdens. Americans were anxious about the vulnerability of their homes, cities, and industries to atomic attack, but drew back from the governmental intrusions and social dislocations that accompanied serious efforts to reduce it. They accepted the need to devote a greater portion of the nation's industrial and scientific resources to the production of military power, but were leery of mechanisms for doing so that involved direct government ownership, explicit economic planning, or what appeared to be undue government control of any kind over the private sector. In short, the American people wanted a state that was strong enough to defend them against their foreign enemies but not strong enough to threaten their domestic liberties. These were not unreasonable desires; the question was whether they were compatible.

CHAPTER THREE

The American Strategic Synthesis

BALDWIN'S DILEMMA

In an influential 1947 survey of strategic issues, *New York Times* military correspondent Hanson Baldwin sought to sum up what he considered to be the essence of the problem confronting the United States. Despite the fond hopes of
many in his country, it now seemed clear to Baldwin that the defeat of the Axis
powers would not bring the dawning of a new age of perpetual peace. War was
still a possibility, and thanks largely to the advance of technology, the next war
would be truly "total"; it would demand an even fuller mobilization and a more
efficient utilization of national resources than the one just past. But "total war
means total effort, and the peacetime preparations for it must be as comprehensive . . . as the execution of it." As a result, "the effects of total war transcend
the period of hostilities; they wrench and distort and twist the body politic and
the body economic . . . *prior* to war," as well as during and after. The United
States had no choice but to prepare for the next, truly total war. The question
was whether it could do so "without becoming a 'garrison state' and destroying
the very qualities and virtues and principles we originally set about to save."
This, Baldwin concluded, "is the grand dilemma . . . of our age."[1]

Although it would take more than a decade of intense debate and struggle,
the United States did eventually succeed in generating a stable, workable, and,
as events would ultimately prove, successful solution to Baldwin's dilemma.
That solution had two interrelated components: on the one hand, an outward-
directed military strategy and force posture sufficient to deter the Soviet Union
and to defend American interests; on the other, a set of inward-directed power-
creating mechanisms that generated the military capabilities needed to support
U.S. strategy without doing grievous harm to American institutions or values.

In this chapter I will examine how the internal and external elements of the
Cold War strategic synthesis fit together and describe how domestic constraints
on state-building shaped the evolution of American military strategy. Subsequent
chapters will be devoted to a fuller analysis of the mechanisms of power creation.

THE CREATION OF MILITARY POWER

States create military power by acting on the societies and economies over
which they rule.[2] Using their authority and, where necessary, their coercive

---

[1] Hanson W. Baldwin, *The Price of Power* (New York: Harper, 1947), pp. 18–20.

[2] For stylistic reasons I will use "society" here interchangeably with the more cumbersome "soci-

power, states transform some portion of the resources within their domain into the implements of armed force. Doing this requires the construction of a set of intermediary mechanisms connecting the state to society. These power-creating mechanisms are of two types: some *extract* societal resources (principally money and manpower); others *direct* their flow toward activities that will increase the state's actual or potential military power (i.e., the production of weapons, the manufacture of materials and equipment essential to the assembly of arms and the conduct of warfare, and the pursuit of technological innovations with potential strategic significance) (see fig. 3.1).[3]

The shape of a state's power-creating mechanisms will be determined by both international and domestic forces. In response to perceived external threats, states devise military strategies and seek to build the armed forces necessary to implement them.[4] Producing and sustaining those forces, in turn, will require the construction of appropriate power-creating mechanisms. As figure 3.2 suggests, threats drive strategy, and strategy, in turn, shapes power creation.

But states do not simply act on societies; societies also act upon states. Both

---

ety and the economy" to refer to the sum total of the human, natural, productive, and financial resources that lie within the territory over which a state exerts its control.

[3] Historically, the extractive activities of states have tended to increase in scale (as they developed more complex and reliable systems of taxation and conscription), while their directive efforts have expanded in scope (focusing first on the manufacture of arms, then widening to include the cultivation of supporting industries, and finally the pursuit of technological innovation). On the early mechanisms of revenue raising see Douglass C. North and Robert Paul Thomas, *The Rise of the Western World: A New Economic History* (New York: Cambridge University Press, 1973). On the subsequent expansion in taxes and tax collecting systems see Joseph A. Schumpeter, "The Crisis of the Tax State," in Alan T. Peacock, Wolfgang Stolper, Ralph Turvey, and Elizabeth Henderson, eds., *International Economic Papers*, vol. 4 (New York: Macmillan, 1954), pp. 8–16; and Gabriel Ardant, "Financial Policy and Economic Infrastructure of Modern States and Nations," in Charles Tilly, ed., *The Formation of National States in Western Europe* (Princeton: Princeton University Press, 1975), pp. 164–242. On the development of systems of military service see Otto Hintze, "Military Organization and the Organization of the State," in Felix Gilbert, ed., *The Historical Essays of Otto Hintze* (New York: Oxford University Press, 1975), pp. 178–215. Regarding the production of armaments see Carlo M. Cipolla, *Guns, Sails, and Empires: Technological Innovation and the Early Phases of European Expansion, 1400–1700* (New York: Minerva Press, 1965); William H. McNeill, *The Pursuit of Power: Technology, Armed Force, and Society since A.D. 1000* (Chicago: University of Chicago Press, 1982). For some examples of state policies toward defense supporting industries before the Industrial Revolution see Robert G. Albion, *Forests and Sea Power: The Timber Problem of the Royal Navy, 1652–1862* (Cambridge: Harvard University Press, 1926); and John U. Nef, *Industry and Government in France and England, 1540–1640* (Ithaca: Cornell University Press, 1957). On the military motives for subsequent state support of industrialization see Gautum Sen, *The Military Origins of Industrialization and International Trade* (New York: St. Martin's, 1984). Regarding state support for "strategic" technologies see, in addition to McNeill, *The Pursuit of Power*: Martin van Crevald, *Technology and War* (New York: Free Press, 1989); Maurice Pearton, *Diplomacy, War and Technology since 1830* (Lawrence: University Press of Kansas, 1984).

[4] Threats are a function of the political relationships between the state and its counterparts, the character of available military technology, and geography. Threats are more likely to be perceived as great if a state has antagonistic relations with one or more of its counterparts and if, through some combination of proximity and power projection capacity, they have the means to attack it.

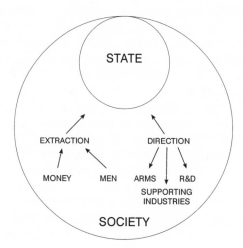

Figure 3.1. The Dimensions of Power
Creation

the extent of a state's extractive and directive efforts and the form of the mechanisms with which they are undertaken will also be influenced by pressures originating within society. A state's susceptibility to such pressures will depend on the character of the larger domestic political regime in which it is embedded: on the structure of basic governmental institutions, the content of the prevailing ideology, and the identity, organization, and strength of the various individuals and societal groups whose interests will be affected by the process of power creation. The activities of these individuals and groups, opposing some state actions and favoring others, will exert an influence on the process of power creation, and through it they may also have an impact on a state's selection of military strategy (see fig. 3.3).

The extent to which societal pressures shape power creation and strategy will depend on both the character of the external environment and the nature of the domestic regime. In wartime, when threats are pressing, societal factors will tend to dwindle in importance as the power of the state and the urgency of its needs grow greater. As different types of regimes struggle to survive, the differences in their power-creating activities will diminish, as all converge towards a more statist norm.

In periods of comparative peace, on the other hand, the intensity of external

Figure 3.2. External Determinants of Power Creation

Figure 3.3. Internal Determinants of Strategy

pressures will diminish and the weight of internal factors will increase. It is under these conditions that variations in the power-creating activities and military strategies of different kinds of regimes are most likely to emerge. To take the ideal-typical extremes: in a totalitarian system, closed hierarchical political institutions, centralizing ideologies, and the atomization of civil society all combine to enhance the power of the state. Totalitarian states are therefore more likely to be able to pursue ambitious force postures and strategies and extensive power-creating programs, even when they are not at war.

In liberal democratic regimes, on the other hand, with representative governments, institutionalized protections for individual rights, ideologies that emphasize personal liberty, and varied, vibrant civil societies, the state will be exposed to an array of conflicting societal pressures. Some groups may favor more defense spending or more spending on particular kinds of weapons, for example, but others are certain to oppose higher taxes or the conscription of military manpower. Whatever the net result, the intensity of the opposition to the state's power-creating activities will be greater in a liberal democratic regime than in a totalitarian one, and will be greatest of all in a liberal democracy that is not at war.

Taken together, a state's external military strategy and its internal program of power creation are not only opposite sides of the same coin; they are also mutually determining elements in what historian Alan Milward has called a "strategic synthesis"[5] (see fig. 3.4).

Milward argues that even in wartime, states rarely come close to exploiting for military purposes their maximum national economic potential. This is due largely to the "political difficulties" and "social resistance" that are encountered as the degree of mobilization increases.[6] Recognizing these constraints, Milward suggests, a state's leaders should adjust their foreign policy goals and their military strategy to achieve what he terms a "correct strategic synthesis." Attaining this balance permits the state to preserve its security and achieve its external aims without, at the same time, changing "society and the political system so much that it is no longer the same as the one originally to be defended."[7]

Milward's formulation suggests that states will necessarily be able to find the

[5] See Alan S. Milward, *War, Economy, and Society, 1939–1945* (Berkeley: University of California Press, 1979), pp. 18–54.

[6] Ibid., pp. 20–21.

[7] Ibid., p. 21.

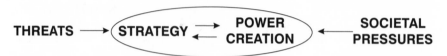

Figure 3.4. Strategic Synthesis

ideal synthesis, that perfect blend of strategy and power creation that will make "exactly those demands on the economy which are sufficient to achieve the strategic purpose."[8] But other equilibriums are conceivable and, especially in the absence of war, some could prove sustainable over long periods of time. Internal constraints may prevent a state from doing enough to prepare itself for war, a failing that can be definitively revealed only once conflict has broken out. On the other hand, over a sufficiently lengthy interval, excessive military exertions can damage a nation's economy and lead to an unintended and undesired transformation of its society and political system. Because of their sensitivity to constraints, liberal democratic regimes are more likely to fall victim to the first failing. Less subject to internal checks, totalitarian regimes are more prone to the second.

THE AMERICAN STRATEGIC SYNTHESIS

Alternative Syntheses

After fifteen years of uncertainty and turmoil, the United States had arrived by the early 1960s at a strategic synthesis that combined a moderate, compromise military strategy of "flexible response" with a power-creating program of constrained extraction, limited directive scope, and a heavy reliance on private institutions to design and build weapons and to conduct scientific research. Despite some comparatively minor alterations, both the inward- and the outward-looking elements of this synthesis would stay fixed for the next quarter century.[9]

The equilibrium point embodied in the American Cold War strategic synthesis was not the only one conceivable, either in retrospect or, more importantly, at the time that it was taking shape. Table 3.1 summarizes the range of alternatives that were either seriously considered or actually adopted, before the United States finally settled on a lasting, stable combination of strategy, forces, and power-creating mechanisms.

Each of the syntheses displayed here embodies a different mix of internal and

---

[8] Ibid.

[9] All the elements in the power creating portion of the synthesis were in place by the late 1950s. The Kennedy administration made the final substantive modification to U.S. military strategy. The largest single subsequent change in power creation came in the early 1970s, with the abandonment of the use of conscription to extract manpower and the shift to an all-volunteer force. The last serious effort to change American military strategy came in the early 1980s.

TABLE 3.1
Alternative Syntheses

	Mobilization	Minimum Deterrence	Massive Retaliation	Flexible Response	Stalemate	Full Warfighting
Strategy	build on warning	nuclear retaliation	nuclear attack on warning	respond first at level of attack, then escalate	fight and win full conventional war	fight and win all-arms (conventional and nuclear) war
Forces	minimal standing	modest atomic air forces; minimal conventional	large nuclear offensive and air defense; minimal conventional	moderate conventional and nuclear	large conventional and moderate nuclear	large conventional and nuclear
Power creation Extraction	low spending; low manpower (plus training for expansion)	low/moderate spending; low manpower (no training)	moderate spending; low manpower (no training)	moderate/high spending; moderate manpower (no training)	high spending; high manpower (plus training)	very high spending; high manpower (plus training)
Direction	arsenals; industrial mobilization planning	industry; no planning	industry; no planning	industry; little/no planning	arsenals; industry; extensive planning	arsenals; industry; extensive planning (plus protection against nuclear attack)

Low ——————— Level of effort ——————→ High

external elements. Overall, the level of societal exertion (or, conversely, the extent of the state's extractive and directive endeavors) needed to sustain each synthesis increases in moving from left ("mobilization") to right ("full warfighting").

Mobilization called for the United States to maintain inexpensive, skeleton forces-in-being, equipped with weapons manufactured mainly in government arsenals and backed by preparations for rapid expansion. In the event of crisis or war, previously trained reservists would be called to active duty and private industry would implement plans to gear up for military mass production.

Minimum deterrence would have downgraded preparations for mobilization of industry and manpower, abandoned government arsenals, and placed virtually exclusive reliance on a modest number of privately manufactured, atomic-equipped long-range aircraft, ready to deliver their weapons at a moment's notice if the Soviet Union attacked the United States or its allies. The hope was that the mere existence of such a force would deter aggression, but would defeat it quickly if deterrence failed. Other nonnuclear ground, naval, and air force units would have been maintained at very low levels.

Massive retaliation was, in effect, a greatly expanded version of minimum deterrence. Nuclear offensive forces would be built up; with the exception of air defenses for the continental United States, all other forms of capability would be held to a minimum. Large numbers of atomic and thermonuclear weapons, carried by an array of delivery vehicles (including long- and short-range aircraft, missiles, and even artillery shells), would be deployed in the United States and around the Eurasian periphery. At the slightest hint of impending aggression (and, if possible, before it had actually begun in earnest), these weapons would be unleashed against the armed forces and urban industrial centers of the Soviet Union and its allies. The aim of U.S. strategy would be to destroy Soviet nuclear forces, decimate the enemy's conventional capabilities, and demolish a good portion of the communist world's productive capacity in as short a period as possible. War would be over in hours or, at most, days; preparations for mobilization of industry and manpower were therefore unnecessary and wasteful.

Nuclear stalemate rested on the belief that, at some point the nuclear arsenals of the two superpowers would be so large and so diverse as to make it impossible for either to disarm the other, even with a surprise first strike. Large-scale use of nuclear weapons by one side would then bring extremely damaging retaliation from its opponent. This would not necessarily mean, however, that war was impossible, and, in fact, certain forms of conflict might actually become more likely once true strategic parity had arrived. Believing that the United States would not risk devastation to stop it, the Soviets and their allies might be tempted to undertake less-than-all-out aggression. It was even conceivable, at the extreme, that the superpowers could fight an extended global war using only conventional means, with nuclear weapons held in a menacing, but mutually neutralizing, reserve. To prepare for these contingencies, the United States would need to maintain a balanced array of very large conventional and nuclear forces. Because a future war could be both intense and protracted, preparations for mobilization of manpower and industry would also be essential.

Full warfighting proceeded from the assumption that even if it involved large exchanges of nuclear weapons, the next war would not be over quickly, and its outcome would not be determined by nuclear weapons alone. Initial massive strikes might be followed by an extended period in which both sides struggled to rebuild their industries and reconstitute their conventional air, naval, and ground forces, eventually bringing them to bear on a global scale in order to achieve a final decision. A full warfighting posture would demand large standing forces of all kinds and extensive preparations for the protection of population and industry against nuclear attack, and for their subsequent mobilization.

As its placement in table 3.1 suggests, *flexible response* required greater exertion than massive retaliation, minimum deterrence, or mobilization, but less than nuclear stalemate or full warfighting. Under this synthesis, the United States would field sufficient conventional (and tactical nuclear) forces to deal with at least some types of limited aggression without resorting to unrestricted use of nuclear weapons. But it would not invest in the types of forces or in the mobilization measures necessary to conduct an all-out conventional war, still less an unlimited nuclear and conventional conflict.

The Search for a Stable Synthesis

Figure 3.5 traces the unfolding of the search for a stable strategic synthesis that began in the immediate aftermath of the Second World War and came to rest finally in the early 1960s. Prior to the Second World War the United States had relied on a mobilization-based synthesis. After the war, the United States did not return to such a posture, but it also failed initially to adopt a coherent alternative.[10] In the late 1940s, planners envisioned World War Three as a protracted, all-arms struggle, and many military officers and civilian officials urged acquisition of the forces and power creating mechanisms necessary to execute a full warfighting strategy. In practice, however, the United States seemed by the end of the decade to be drifting toward minimum deterrence and a heavy reliance on atomic air power.[11]

[10] For helpful overviews of the interwar period see Eliot A. Cohen, "The Strategy of Innocence? The United States, 1920–1945," in Williamson Murray, MacGregor Knox, and Alvin Bernstein, eds., *The Making of Strategy: Rulers, States, and War* (New York: Cambridge University Press, 1994), pp. 428–65; Allan R. Millet and Peter Maslowski, *For the Common Defense: A Military History of the United States of America* (New York: Free Press, 1994), pp. 380–412; Russell F. Weigley, *The American Way of War: A History of United States Military Strategy and Policy* (Bloomington: Indiana University Press, 1973), pp. 233–65. The arguments of the advocates of a return to a heavy emphasis on mobilization and those of their opponents are well treated in Michael Sherry, *Preparing for the Next War: American Plans for Postwar Defense, 1941–1945* (New Haven: Yale University Press, 1977).

[11] The evolution of offical thinking and warplanning during this period is now well covered in a number of sources. See Ernest R. May, John D. Steinbruner, and Thomas Wolfe, *History of the*

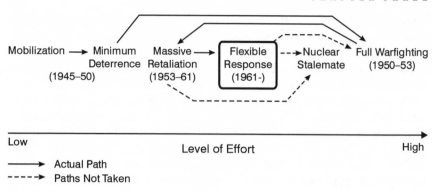

Figure 3.5. The Search for a Stable Synthesis

The sudden onset of war in Korea permitted what would turn out to be a short-lived lurch toward a full warfighting synthesis. Beginning in June 1950, the Truman administration took significant steps to make the United States ready for a protracted, all-out, all-arms clash with the Soviet Union and its allies. Defense budgets, tax rates, and conventional and nuclear force levels were drastically increased, with the expectation that all would remain high even after the war in Asia was finished. President Truman urged the adoption of a universal military training system, arguing that only this plan could provide the vast reserves of trained manpower that would be required to replace battlefield casualties in a future world war and to help stabilize a home front ravaged by Soviet atomic bombs. Because the next war was not expected to end quickly, industrial mobilization would retain its critical importance. For this reason, the administration also launched an extensive and aggressive industrial planning program designed to promote expansion of productive capacity in arms and war-supporting industries, and to reduce vulnerability to aerial attack by encouraging the geographical dispersal of factories.[12]

Strategic Arms Competition, 1945–1972 (Washington, DC: Office of the Secretary of Defense Historical Office, 1981), pp. 1–81; James F. Schnabel, *The History of the Joint Chiefs of Staff: The Joint Chiefs of Staff and National Policy*, vol. 1, *1945–1947* (Wilmington, DE: Michael Glazier, 1979); Kenneth W. Condit, *The History of the Joint Chiefs of Staff: The Joint Chiefs of Staff and National Policy*, vol. 2, 1947–1949 (Wilmington, DE: Michael Glazier, 1979); Steven L. Rearden, *History of the Office of the Secretary of Defense*, vol. 1, *The Formative Years, 1947–1950* (Washington, DC: Office of the Secretary of Defense Historical Office, 1984); Steven T. Ross, *American War Plans, 1945–1950* (New York: Garland, 1988); Ernest R. May, "Cold War and Defense," in Keith Neilson and Ronald G. Haycock, eds., *The Cold War and Defense* (New York: Praeger, 1990), pp. 7–73; Samuel R. Williamson, Jr., and Steven L. Rearden, *The Origins of U.S. Nuclear Strategy, 1945–1953* (New York: St. Martin's, 1993).

[12] In contrast to the periods before and after the Korean War, the evolution of long-range strategic thinking and planning during the period of this conflict has received comparatively less attention from scholars. See Walter S. Pool, *The History of the Joint Chiefs of Staff: The Joint Chiefs of Staff and National Policy*, vol. 4, *1950–1952* (Wilmington, DE: Michael Glazier, 1980); May, Steinbruner, and Wolfe, *History of the Strategic Arms Competition*, pp. 104–52; Doris M. Condit, *History of the Office of the Secretary of Defense*, volume 2, *The Test of War, 1950–1953* (Washington,

The Eisenhower administration initiated a sharp reversal in strategic direction. Budgets, taxes, manpower levels, and conventional forces were cut, universal military training abandoned, and greater emphasis placed on nuclear offensive capabilities. The industrial planning apparatus inherited from the Truman era was quickly dismantled, and the military was instructed to concentrate on preparing for a short, all-out war. During his two terms in office, President Eisenhower resolutely denied that the growth in Soviet striking power was leading to a nuclear stalemate, and thus to the necessity for an American conventional buildup and for a revitalization of preparations for mobilization.[13]

The Kennedy administration accepted the thrust of the argument that Eisenhower had rejected, but it did not embrace all of the apparent implications. Endorsing the logic of the critics of massive retaliation, Kennedy and his advisers declared their intention to create a range of military options short of resort to all-out thermonuclear strikes. In pursuit of enhanced flexibility they initiated an expansion in U.S. conventional (as well as nuclear) capabilities. Bigger nonnuclear ground, sea, and air forces would make it easier for the United States to respond to limited aggression by the Soviet Union or its various clients around the Eurasian periphery. A conventional buildup was also designed to increase the ability of the United States and its NATO allies to hold out against at least the initial stages of a Soviet-led thrust into Western Europe without resorting to the widespread use of nuclear weapons. Having moved a considerable distance away from the posture adopted by his predecessor, however, Kennedy still stopped well short of embracing the possibility of a protracted conventional war between the superpowers. The implications for power creation of this shift in military strategy were therefore more a matter of degree than kind. The incidence of extraction of money and manpower did grow in the early 1960s, albeit fractionally and temporarily, as force levels were increased. But the scope and form of the government's directive activities did not change

DC: U.S. Government Printing Office, 1988); Haejong Lee, "The Political Economy of Rearmament: Truman's 1953 Military Budget in Historical Perspective" (paper presented to the American Political Science Association convention, 1995).

[13] Regarding the initial shifts in Eisenhower administration policy see Glenn H. Snyder, "The 'New Look' of 1953," in Warner R. Schilling, Paul Y. Hammond, and Glenn H. Snyder, *Strategy, Politics, and Defense Budgets* (New York: Columbia University Press, 1962), pp. 379–524; John Lewis Gaddis, *Strategies of Containment: A Critical Appraisal of Postwar American National Security Poicy* (New York: Oxford University Press, 1982), pp. 127–97; Robert J. Watson, *History of the Joint Chiefs of Staff: The Joint Chiefs of Staff and National Policy,* vol. 5, *1953–1954* (Washington, DC: U.S. Government Printing Office, 1986). Regarding warplans, see David Alan Rosenberg, "'A Smoking Radiating Ruin at the End of Two Hours': Documents on American Plans for Nuclear War with the Soviet Union, 1954–1955," *International Security* 6, no. 3 (Winter 1981/82), pp. 3–38; Rosenberg, "Toward Armageddon: The Foundations of United States Nuclear Strategy, 1945–1961" (Ph.D. dissertation, University of Chicago, 1983), pp. 184–300. See also the essays in Marc Trachtenberg, *History and Strategy* (Princeton: Princeton University Press, 1991); and Trachtenberg, *A Constructed Peace: The Making of the European Settlement, 1945–1963* (Princeton: Princeton University Press, 1999).

and, in particular, there was no movement back toward a defense-driven national industrial policy.[14]

Over the course of the next twenty-five years, the synthesis embodied in flexible response would prove to be remarkably resilient. The last serious attempt to move the United States away from this equilibrium point came in the early 1980s, when the Reagan administration reopened discussion of stalemate and full warfighting. Despite some changes in planning assumptions and force levels, the administration did not follow through on the domestic-power creating measures that would have been necessary to support a major shift in strategy. Reagan expanded defense budgets but he proved unwilling to raise taxes, to impose conscription in order to acquire more manpower, or to involve the federal government in any kind of overt industrial mobilization planning. The end result was an awkward amalgam of increased spending on arms and research, modestly expanded force levels, and the eventual abandonment of any pretense of major strategic innovation. Flexible response would endure until the Cold War had run its course.[15]

Explaining the Pattern

The pattern of search and eventual settlement displayed in figure 3.5 can best be understood not as the *result* of some comprehensive, rational exercise in national strategic planning, but as a *resultant*: the by-product of a collision between two opposing vectors. The first of these was made up of three elements that together tended to push the United States toward larger armed forces, more ambitious military strategies, more extensive efforts at power creation, and, in general, toward a larger and more powerful state. Arrayed against these tendencies was a vector comprised of the various anti-statist influences discussed in chapter 2.

The broad geopolitical and technological trends evident at the end of the Second World War have already been briefly surveyed. Changes in Soviet long-range striking power, actual and anticipated, played an especially important role

[14] The definitive account of the Kennedy administration's defense policies has yet to be written. The best overview is Gaddis, *Strategies of Containment*, pp. 198–273. The logic underlying Kennedy's policies is laid out in Maxwell D. Taylor, *The Uncertain Trumpet* (New York: Harper and Brothers, 1960); and William W. Kaufmann, *The McNamara Strategy* (New York: Harper and Row, 1964). See also chapter 8 of Trachtenberg, *A Constructed Peace*; Jane E. Stromseth, *The Origins of Flexible Response: NATO's Debate over Strategy in the 1960s* (London: Macmillan, 1988); and John S. Duffield, *Power Rules: The Evolution of NATO's Conventional Force Posture* (Stanford, CA: Stanford, University Press, 1995).

[15] For the thinking underpinning the defense policies of the first Reagan administration see W. Scott Thompson, ed., *National Security in the 1980s: From Weakness to Strength* (San Francisco: Institute for Contemporary Studies, 1980). For a helpful overview see Samuel P. Huntington, "The Defense Policy of the Reagan Administration, 1981–1982," in Fred I. Greenstein, ed., *The Reagan Presidency: An Early Assessment* (Baltimore: Johns Hopkins University Press, 1983), pp. 82–116. See also Richard Halloran, *To Arm a Nation: Rebuilding America's Endangered Defenses* (New York: Macmillan, 1986); Daniel Wirls, *Buildup: The Politics of Defense in the Reagan Era* (Ithaca: Cornell University Press, 1992).

in driving the American search for a satisfactory synthesis and in undermining support, successively, for mobilization, minimum deterrence, and massive retaliation. A growing appreciation of the impact of atomic weapons on the likely pace and destructiveness of any future conflict helped make a return to mobilization far less likely at the end of the Second World War. On the other hand, doubts about the war-winning capacity, and hence the deterrent effect, of a relatively small U.S. arsenal of atomic bombs prevented the formal adoption of a pure, minimum deterrent policy in the late 1940s. Starting in the mid-1950s, intimations of a dawning era of rough thermonuclear parity eroded the position of those who argued for continued reliance on the threat of massive retaliation.

Intragovernmental politics, the self-interested pursuit of more money, and greater responsibilities by various state agencies provided an additional impetus to strategic expansion. Having grown beyond their wildest dreams during the Second World War, none of the armed services relished a return to the shriveled budgets and puny force postures (or the diminished opportunities for professional advancement) of the pre-war era. It was in part for this reason that no branch of the military (with the partial exception of the Army ground forces, whose leaders regarded sharp cutbacks in their peacetime structure as inevitable in any case) favored a return to reliance on mobilization. On the other hand, while they pleased the newly independent Air Force, both minimum deterrence and massive retaliation gave short shrift to the Army, Navy, and Marines, as well as to the civilian-controlled industrial mobilization agencies that grew up in the late 1940s and early 1950s. Albeit with varying degrees of success, these participants in the strategy-making process raised strong objection to policies that they perceived to be contrary not only to the national interest, but to their own. The search for a stable synthesis was thus influenced by bureaucratic pressures, as well as by disinterested intellectual debate.

Support for greater strategic exertions and, in particular, for increased defense expenditures came finally from a number of influential groups in American society. Provided that they received a share of the benefits and retained an important measure of autonomy, academic scientists, engineers, and arms-building industrialists (especially the makers of airplanes, missiles, munitions, electronics equipment, and ships) tended to favor more rather than less spending on research, development, and weapons procurement.

Taken together, and unopposed, these factors should have pushed the United States farther and faster toward bigger armed forces, more ambitious military strategies, and more extensive power-creating programs. There was certainly no compelling strategic reason why the United States should have stopped short of preparing for even the biggest and most brutal forms of warfare. To the contrary, either stalemate or full warfighting would have been more coherent and, in any event, more clearly in keeping with traditional modes of military thought than was flexible response. Adequate preparations for an extended large-scale conventional conflict or for an unrestricted all-out war were, at the very least, a form of insurance against contingencies that were far from inconceivable. By demonstrating its willingness to wage war across the entire spectrum of conflict, the United States might also have appeared to strengthen its deterrent posture. Flexible response, on the other hand, imposed an arbitrary and somewhat ambiguous ceiling on the extent of American preparations for limited warfare, and it did not provide much guidance on what to do if flexibility failed and the United States found itself in an all-out war with the Soviet Union. Flexible response represented a compromise rather than a unique, elegant, or obviously dominant solution to the strategic problems confronting the United States.

Strategic logic aside, the combination of bureaucratic logrolling and societal interest-group pressures could easily have resulted in the adoption of a more ambitious synthesis. If big, balanced forces and large budgets for weapons and research were good, then still bigger forces and even larger budgets would, presumably, have been better. Left to their own devices, the public and private collaborators in the "military-industrial complex" would no doubt have consumed an even greater portion of the nation's resources.

But, as subsequent chapters will show, there were other, countervailing forces at work. Popular hostility, congressional resistance, and, in the 1950s, presidential objections to higher taxes kept defense budgets lower than they would otherwise have been. Postwar fears of "regimentation" and the mobilization of societal groups opposed to compulsion by the state discouraged a wary Congress from granting executive branch demands for universal peacetime conscription. Ideological and interest-based objections to extensive, overt government economic planning effectively scuttled attempts to implement a comprehensive program of targeted assistance to defense supporting industries, and rendered ineffective government efforts to shape the geographical distribution of the nation's industrial base designed to render it less vulnerable to nuclear attack.

In addition to limiting the *extent* of the federal government's extractive and directive efforts, anti-statist influences also helped determine the *form* of the mechanisms of direction. Appeals from industry, pressure from Congress, and an increasingly widespread belief in the superior efficiency and intrinsic virtue of the private sector combined to move the armed services away from their traditional heavy dependence on federally owned arsenals and shipyards for the design and production of weapons and toward a virtually exclusive dependence on commercial arms suppliers. The same preference for private over public actors, coupled with a desire to minimize extraction and the prevailing postwar suspicion of centralization and excessive government economic intervention, had an impact on the scale, scope, and administrative structure of the U.S. defense research and development program.

Ideologically rooted, interest-driven, and institutionally amplified anti-statist influences thus acted to constrict, constrain, and mold the federal government's efforts at power creation. In the process, they also eased the United States away from the more ambitious military strategies and peacetime force structures and toward those that were less demanding. Objections to the levels of extraction necessary to sustain a full warfighting synthesis and to the scope of the directive activities that it would have required prevented its adoption in the late

1940s and moved the United States toward minimum deterrence. The Korean War lowered the obstacles to power creation for a time, but their reassertion forced the abandonment of a warfighting strategy even before the Asian emergency had fully run its course. It was Eisenhower's desperate eagerness to limit the size and authority of the American state, and not his strategic convictions alone, that caused him to embrace massive retaliation, to force it on a reluctant military establishment, and to hold to it even in the face of growing doubts about its adequacy. John Kennedy was less imbued with anti-statist beliefs than his predecessor, but despite its initial strategic ambitions, his administration too was forced to act under considerable domestic constraints. Limits on spending and a desire to avoid the inefficiencies of industrial planning helped to prevent the move to flexible response from being more radical and far-reaching than it actually was. In the early 1980s it was not crystalline strategic rationality but the ideological inhibitions of the Reagan administration, combined with societal resistance to increased extraction and expanded direction, that prevented a sharp shift toward stalemate or full warfighting.

At its end, as in the beginning, anti-statist influences played a critically important role in shaping how the United States conducted a protracted military competition with the Soviet Union. Had these countervailing influences been significantly weaker or absent altogether, the American strategic synthesis, the postwar role of the American state, the impact of the superpower confrontation on the nation's economy and society, and perhaps even the eventual outcome of the Cold War itself would all have been significantly different.

POSTSCRIPT: THE SOVIET STRATEGIC SYNTHESIS

The simplest way of understanding the Soviet strategic synthesis is to imagine how the United States might have acted in the absence of anti-statist influences. The Soviet Union lacked all such countervailing tendencies; there were no powerful independent societal interests. To the contrary, the few influential groupings in the Soviet system were, in essence, state actors; all benefited from its growth.[16] Communist ideology and the structure of Soviet political institutions combined to elevate the state and to permit, indeed to encourage, a strategically stimulated metastasis in its internal powers. As a result, during most of the Cold War, the Soviet Union pursued a more ambitious military strategy than the United States, and it undertook a far more extensive program of power creation.

The only possible source of constraint in the Soviet system was at the very top. In the early 1960s and again in the late 1980s, the nation's political leaders did try briefly to apply the brakes and to impose some change in strategic direction. So strong were the opposing forces, however, that the results were

---

[16] This was clearly true of the military and security services and the industrial planning ministries. Although nominally separate, the members of the Party apparatus were, in fact, the controllers of the state.

catastrophic, both for the personalities involved and, ultimately, for the Soviet state.

Figure 3.6 displays the evolution of the Soviet strategic synthesis. In essence, the Soviets settled early on a full warfighting approach and then stuck with it, with only minor deviations, for most of the duration of the Cold War.[17]

As the Second World War ended, Soviet planners began to prepare for a possible confrontation with the United States. From the start they recognized that a new war would involve the use of atomic weapons. For a combination of strategic and domestic political reasons, Soviet spokesmen in the early postwar period tended to downplay the importance of such devices, but they did not, as Western observers sometimes claimed, ignore them.[18] In fact, as historian David Holloway notes, in the late 1940s and early 1950s, "There was a striking similarity between Soviet and American assessments of a future war." The next world war would begin with atomic exchanges, but these would be followed immediately by huge conventional battles. The Soviet Union therefore needed to invest in air defenses, atomic bombs, and the long-range aircraft and missiles necessary to deliver them. But it also required a substantial navy, capable of cutting the sea lanes to North America, and large ground forces, ready to advance rapidly into Europe and the Middle East "to prevent the United States from using those regions as a springboard." In anticipation of such campaigns, between 1948 and 1953 the armed forces were doubled in size, from 2.8 to 5.7 million men.[19]

Stalin's death, the development of thermonuclear explosives, and the accumulation of stockpiles of both smaller battlefield weapons and their longer-range and generally larger-yield counterparts led to a reexamination of the prevailing strategic synthesis. The result was more a shift in emphasis than a fundamental change in direction. The extraordinary destructiveness of modern weapons increased their relative importance, enhanced the significance of the

---

[17] The point here is not that top Soviet political and military leaders necessarily believed at any given moment that they could "fight and win a nuclear war," but rather that they generally agreed they *ought* to be able to do so and tried to prepare themselves accordingly. For opposing views on what the Soviet leadership believed see Richard Pipes, "Why the Soviet Union Thinks It Could Fight and Win a Nuclear War," *Commentary* 64, no. 1 (July 1977), pp. 21–34; Robert L. Arnett, "Soviet Attitudes towards Nuclear War: Do They Really Think They Can Win?" *Journal of Strategic Studies* 2, no. 2 (September 1979), pp. 172–91.

[18] In a period when they lagged behind the United States in developing and deploying atomic weapons, the Soviets presumably wanted to reassure their own people and to discourage the Americans. Having left the Soviet Union vulnerable to a near-fatal attack in 1941, Stalin was also understandably eager to avoid any discussion of the subject of surprise. He therefore insisted that, as in the past, future wars would be decided by "permanently operating factors" such as "the stability of the rear," military morale, and organizational ability, rather than by the adoption of specific stratagems or technologies. See the discussion in Herbert Dinerstein, *War and the Soviet Union: Nuclear Weapons and the Revolution in Soviet Military and Political Thinking* (New York: Praeger, 1962), pp. 1–27; Thomas W. Wolfe, *Soviet Power and Europe, 1945–1970* (Baltimore: Johns Hopkins University Press, 1970), pp. 32–69.

[19] David Holloway, *Stalin and the Bomb: The Soviet Union and Atomic Energy, 1939–1956* (New Haven: Yale University Press, 1994), pp. 251, 239, 224–52.

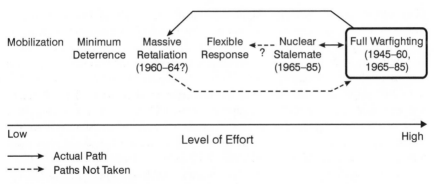

Figure 3.6. The Soviet Strategic Synthesis

opening stages of a future conflict, and raised the potential value of preemptive attack. But war would still be a massive combined-arms affair. Conventional as well as nuclear forces would play an essential role in determining the outcome, and the ability rapidly to mobilize industry and manpower would continue to be of critical importance. As one authoritative Western analysis put it in the late 1950s:

> Soviet leaders and planners have not succumbed to the kind of defeatism that argues that the destruction will be so great as to make it pointless to prosecute a major war in the most vigorous and effective way. The basis of Soviet doctrine is that war would be a calamity indeed, but that its most awful consequences can be reduced by the creation . . . of a differentiated force ready for every contingency.[20]

The costs of creating such a force were very high, and indeed, as American power grew, potentially limitless. In an attempt to put some sort of ceiling on the burdens of power creation and to free up scarce human and financial resources for other, nonmilitary purposes, Nikita Khrushchev sought in the late 1950s to shift Soviet strategy away from warfighting and toward something that more closely resembled massive retaliation. Khrushchev backed cuts in military personnel and a relative increase in attention to developing nuclear capabilities. In 1960 he began to make the case publicly for far-reaching changes in strategy. Following the lead of some of his American counterparts, Khrushchev argued that a future world war would likely be short and that it would be decided by the forces, especially the long-range nuclear missile forces, in existence at the outset. Spending on other forms of capability could safely be reduced.[21]

If "the logic of Khrushchev's preferences had prevailed," writes analyst

[20] Dinerstein, *War and the Soviet Union*, p. 257. Regarding the development of Soviet strategy in this period see also Holloway, *Stalin and the Bomb*, pp. 320–45; and Raymond L. Garthoff, *Soviet Strategy in the Nuclear Age* (New York: Praeger, 1958).

[21] On the background to Khrushchev's initiative, which he describes as aiming at a form of minimum deterrence, see Edward L. Warner III, *The Military in Contemporary Soviet Politics: An Institutional Analysis* (New York: Praeger, 1977), pp. 137–57. The debate over strategy during the early 1960s is detailed in Thomas W. Wolfe, *Soviet Strategy at the Crossroads* (Cambridge: Harvard University Press, 1964).

Thomas Wolfe, the result might have been a "wholesale dismantling of . . . conventional . . . forces. As it turned out, far less radical measures were actually taken." While the ground forces were reduced somewhat in size, they were also outfitted with more modern equipment to improve their mobility and with tactical nuclear weapons to increase their firepower. Tactical air capabilities were also improved.[22] Preparations for mobilization, defense of the homeland, and all-out warfighting continued apace.[23] Khrushchev's attempts to impose a shift in the Soviet strategic synthesis were blocked by resistance from the armed forces and military resentment over his meddling and "hare-brained scheming" would ultimately contribute to his removal from power in 1964.[24]

With Khrushchev gone, the Soviet military was free to get back to the serious, and expensive, business of doing what it had set out to do in the 1950s: building "a force ready for every contingency"; they would continue to do so, essentially uninterrupted, for the next two decades. From the mid-1960s onward, Soviet efforts to make ready for all-out war were augmented by preparations for conflicts in which nuclear weapons might be used in limited ways or perhaps not at all. The Soviet strategic synthesis during this period therefore embodied elements of both full warfighting and nuclear stalemate.[25]

The implications for force planning and power creation were additive and, in sum, staggering. Fighting and winning an all-out nuclear war would require large strategic offensive and defensive forces, as well as extensive measures to protect top leaders and ordinary citizens and to ensure the survival of the productive capacity essential to postwar recovery.[26] Numerous widely dispersed, fast-moving conventional ground armies would be needed to minimize the effects of an enemy use of tactical nuclear weapons. Under the right set of circumstances, the same kinds of forces might be able to destroy the bulk of the

---

[22] Thomas W. Wolfe, *Soviet Military Power and European Security* P-3429 (Santa Monica, CA: RAND Corporation, August 1966), pp. 19–20.

[23] On the continuing importance of industrial and manpower mobilization, see the discussion in the authoritative compendium of Soviet military thought, Marshal V. D. Sokolovsky, ed., *Military Strategy: Soviet Doctrine and Concepts* (New York: Praeger, 1963), pp. 323–38. Changes in Soviet military posture under Khrushchev are discussed at length in Wolfe, *Soviet Power and Europe*, pp. 160–94.

[24] On the military's role in Khrushchev's ouster see Warner, *The Military in Contemporary Soviet Politics*, pp. 52–53; Myron Rush, *Political Succession in the USSR* (New York: Columbia University Press, 1968), pp. 155–64; Michel Tatu, *Power in the Kremlin: From Khrushchev to Kosygin* (New York: Viking, 1968), pp. 419–20.

[25] For analyses of Soviet force posture and doctrine during the late 1960s and early 1970s see John Erickson, *Soviet Military Power* (London: Royal United Services Institute, 1971); Kimberly Marten Zisk, *Engaging the Enemy: Organization Theory and Soviet Military Innovation, 1955–1991* (Princeton: Princeton University Press, 1993), pp. 47–81; Michael MccGwire, *Military Objectives in Soviet Foreign Policy* (Washington, DC: Brookings Institution, 1987), pp. 13–66. According to these accounts, serious Soviet thinking about and preparation for the possibility of a distinct conventional phase in a future war with the United States first became evident in the period 1965–66.

[26] Although its conclusions are overdrawn, William T. Lee and Richard F. Starr, *Soviet Military Policy since World War II* (Stanford, CA: Hoover Institution Press, 1986) contains much useful information on this aspect of Soviet preparations.

enemy's nuclear capabilities before they could be employed while the forces simultaneously smashed his conventional armor and infantry formations. The goal was to be prepared to win a land war as quickly as possible, whether or not nuclear weapons were used. This approach, writes William Odom, was "a quite rational response to the advent of nuclear weapons."[27]

Even if the Americans could be ejected from Eurasia, a war between the superpowers might still drag on. If there had been no nuclear exchanges between the two homelands, "both sides, their military-industrial bases undamaged, would embark on an intense and sustained arms race. . . . If the Soviets were to compete in such a race, they would need to have most of the industrial plants already in place."[28] Vast increases in productive capacity, above and beyond what was necessary to sustain even very large forces-in-being, were therefore essential.[29]

Whatever its flaws or virtues, Soviet strategy had a certain relentless, and very traditional, military logic undergirding it. If war came, the aim was to defeat the enemy's forces, regardless of the level of conflict or the ultimate cost. Whether or not victory, in any meaningful sense of the word, could actually have been achieved is unknowable but also, for present purposes, irrelevant. Soviet military planners did not shrink from confronting the enormous problems that they would face in attempting to defeat the United States and its allies, or from designing the massive forces that they believed would give them the best chance of success. Left to their own devices, American military planners would probably have devised very similar strategies and force postures.

In contrast to the Khrushchevian alternative, the strategic synthesis that solidified with his departure also had the considerable political virtue of satisfying the interests of all branches of the armed forces and of the powerful defense industrial ministries and their associated plants and production facilities. Like its American counterpart, the Soviet synthesis was stable, albeit at a much higher level of societal exertion. The reason for the difference, of course, was that there was no possibility of societal resistance and, at least for the duration of the Brezhnev era, no inclination to impose restraint from on high. As two Western observers would correctly note in the early 1980s: "In an autocratic system like the Soviet Union, . . . an extravagant approach to defense is possible because the populace that bears the real costs has neither the information nor the vote needed to influence the decision process."[30]

But real costs there were and, with the passage of time, they began to accumulate. It was in a desperate effort to reduce these burdens that Mikhail Gor-

---

[27] William E. Odom, *The Collapse of the Soviet Military* (New Haven: Yale University Press, 1998), p. 75. See also Phillip A. Petersen and John G. Hines, "The Conventional Offensive in Soviet Theater Strategy," *Orbis* 27, no. 3 (Fall 1983), pp. 695–740.

[28] MccGwire, *Military Objectives*, p. 58.

[29] Regarding the growth in Soviet military production capacity from the early 1970s onward see Department of Defense, *Soviet Military Power: An Assessment of the Threat, 1988* (Washington, DC: U.S. Government Printing Office, 1988), pp. 36–40.

[30] Petersen and Hines, "Soviet Theater Strategy," p. 731.

bachev, like Khrushchev before him, sought to force a downward shift in the Soviet strategic synthesis: first imposing a change in official doctrine (toward "defensive defense," a stance that bore some resemblance to flexible response), then cutting force levels, and finally attempting to dismantle or convert to civilian purposes at least a portion of the vast military-industrial complex. To revitalize the badly damaged Soviet economy and to reverse some of the effects of the multi-decade military buildup in which his predecessors had indulged, Gorbachev also made a series of steps toward general political and economic liberalization. These initiatives taken together were only modestly successful in achieving their stated aims, but their unintended consequences were nothing short of earth-shattering. Gorbachev's reforms helped set in motion a chain of events that would lead quickly to the collapse of the Soviet Union and the end of the Cold War.[31]

[31] The best account of the central role of military reform in this larger story is Odom, *The Collapse of the Soviet Military.*

Money

THE POLITICAL ECONOMY OF CONSTRAINT

Consequences

In retrospect, what is most remarkable about American defense budgets during the first fifteen years of the Cold War is not how big they were, but how small. Consider the circumstances: in the 1940s and 1950s the memory of the Second World War was still fresh and vivid, and the prospect of another global conflagration did not appear nearly as remote nor as unreal as it would subsequently come to seem. The nation's top political and military leaders all had direct experience of supreme command, and, in striking contrast to their experience of the First World War, the American people had seen for themselves the terrible dangers of unpreparedness. Moreover, as the postwar period opened, the threat to American interests and, indeed, to national survival seemed to be growing rapidly. Ravaged by Nazi invaders, the Soviet Union appeared nevertheless to be proceeding quickly to rebuild its industrial base, modernize its vast conventional forces, and to acquire, in rapid succession, atomic bombs, thermonuclear weapons, and ballistic missiles. Instead of being able to savor the fruits of victory, Americans found themselves increasingly insecure.

How best to meet the threat posed by Soviet power was far from clear. Honest people could, and did, differ wildly in their estimates of the nature, extent, and cost of the defense preparations that would be necessary to deter communist aggression or to defeat it if it came. Especially in the early phases of the superpower confrontation, when experience was limited and war seemed at times to be imminent, there was a strong inclination on the part of military planners to err on the side of caution and to prefer more power and more defense spending to less.

Strategic calculations aside, the Second World War, followed quickly by the move to a posture of permanent peacetime preparedness, created powerful interests inside the federal government and in American society at large. For reasons both sincere and self-serving, the military services, the representatives of arms and defense-related industries, and many members of Congress had a strong predilection for expanding defense budgets and, as revealed repeatedly in public opinion polls, so too did many ordinary citizens.[1]

The upward pressures on military spending in the 1940s and 1950s were therefore considerable; if not for the presence of some counterpressures, bud-

---

[1] See Samuel P. Huntington, *The Common Defense* (New York: Columbia University Press, 1961), pp. 234–51.

gets would have been bigger, the permanent U.S. peacetime force posture would have been larger, and the strategy that those forces were intended to serve would probably have been more ambitious than was, in fact, the case. What seems likely, in particular, is that the United States might have moved during the late 1940s and early 1950s toward more thoroughgoing preparations for fighting, surviving, and winning a war against the Soviet Union, whether fought with or without atomic and thermonuclear weapons. This was certainly the path that traditional military logic seemed to dictate, and it would also have had the not-inconsiderable advantage of satisfying each of the armed services and providing even richer rewards for all of the various private constituencies that stood to gain from increased defense spending.

Early decisions for such a course could well have had far-reaching and long-lasting consequences. If American defense planners and political leaders had committed themselves at the outset of the Cold War to the position that only a full-scale warfighting posture was sufficient to keep the peace and defend the nation, it would have been extremely difficult for their successors to draw away and do less as Soviet power grew. The United States would then have found itself locked onto a path that demanded larger forces, more extensive defense preparations of all kinds, and much bigger budgets. The long-term burdens on the American economy, measured by the share of total national output devoted to defense, would also have been heavier, perhaps considerably so, if such a course had been pursued.

The possibility of an alternative outcome along these lines is more than mere counterfactual speculation detached from any reference to historical reality. In the late 1940s, as we shall see, military planners on several occasions recommended that budgets be expanded by between 100 percent and 300 percent in order to make the United States ready for a future war with the Soviet Union. Throughout the 1950s, even after the substantial buildup that accompanied the Korean War, there were repeated serious proposals that defense spending be increased by as much as 50 percent in real terms. Had these calls been heeded, by the beginning of the 1960s the United States would likely have been devoting upwards of 15 percent of its national output to defense, instead of a rapidly diminishing total of less than 10 percent[2] (see Figs. 4.1 and 4.2).

---

[2] Over the course of the Cold War, the Soviets imposed much heavier burdens on their economy. How much heavier is a matter of ongoing debate. There is little disagreement that after dipping somewhat in the late 1950s, Soviet military expenditures rose steadily in real terms thereafter. According to the most conservative estimates (those prepared in the mid-1980s by the Central Intelligence Agency), in the 1970s and early 1980s the share of Soviet output devoted to the military may have been on the order of 15 to 17 percent. Alternative calculations (which are based on more modest assessments of the overall size of the Soviet economy and include the costs of items such as civil defense, hardening and dispersal of industrial facilities, and the maintenance of excess productive capacity for mobilization purposes) put the figure in the early 1980s at over 20 percent. This would mean that, at that point, the Soviet defense burden was roughly three times as big as the American. For overviews of the controversy regarding the CIA estimates see James H. Noren, "The Controversy over Western Measures of Soviet Defense Expenditures," *Post-Soviet Affairs* 11, no. 3 (1995), pp. 238–76; Daniel M. Berkowitz, Joseph S. Berliner, Paul R. Gregory,

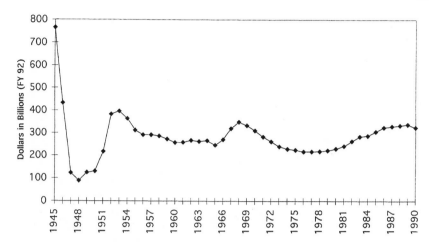

Figure 4.1. National Defense Outlays in Constant Dollars, 1945–1990

Causes

In order to explain the trajectory of American defense expenditures it is necessary to consider not only the forces that propelled them upward during the formative opening acts of the Cold War, but the countervailing influences that helped to restrain their growth. These can be grouped under three headings: politically potent opposition to raising federal taxes along with strong and persistent support for lowering them; the emergence of a conservative consensus on fiscal policy, one that aimed more at promoting macroeconomic stability than at achieving the highest possible growth rates; and a strong aversion to deficit spending.

RESTRAINTS ON TAXES

Hostility to taxation is, of course, a long-standing American tradition, one that precedes and is closed linked with the birth of the Republic. For the Founding generation, taxes were even more a political than an economic concern. The problem was not only that government impositions deprived merchants and farmers of the rightful fruits of their labors, but that they bolstered the strength

Susan J. Linz, and James R. Millar, "An Evaluation of the CIA's Analysis of Soviet Economic Performance, 1970–1990," *Comparative Economic Studies* 35, no. 2 (Summer 1993), pp. 33–57. For a careful and persuasive high-end estimate see David F. Epstein, "The Economic Cost of Soviet Security and Empire," in Henry S. Rowen and Charles Wolf, Jr., *The Impoverished Superpower: Perestroika and the Soviet Military Burden* (San Francisco: Institute for Contemporary Studies, 1990), pp. 127–54. Since the end of the Cold War it has become clear that top Soviet decision makers did not themselves know the exact size of the military budget, still less what fraction of total output it was consuming. Statements by some of Gorbachev's former advisers suggest that they believed the figure might have been somewhere between one-fifth and two-fifths of total output, but thanks to military secrecy, the sheer scope of the military effort, and distorted pricing and accounting practices, they had no real way of knowing. See William Odom, *The Collapse of the Soviet Military* (New Haven: Yale University Press, 1998), pp. 104, 442.

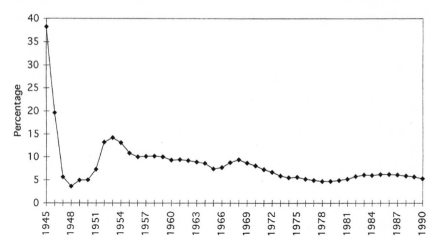

Figure 4.2. National Defense Outlays as Percentage of GDP, 1945–1990

and enhanced the ambitions of the state. Taxes were the meat on which tyrants fed and grew great. Preserving liberty required restricting government's ability to raise revenues, and this meant keeping control over taxation as close to the taxpayer as possible.[3]

The Founders' first efforts to limit the revenue raising powers of the central government were, if anything, too successful. Under the Articles of Confederation, the individual states had a virtual monopoly on taxing power. The purposes for which taxes could be imposed by the "United States in Congress assembled" and the precise form that these could take were both specified in advance, with the clear proviso that any such taxes could be "laid and levied" only "by the authority and direction of the legislatures of the several states."[4] By deliberate design, Congress had neither the "legal authority nor [the] bureaucratic machinery" to enforce its demands for revenues, and it soon encountered grave difficulties in doing so.[5] The near-fatal fiscal weakness of the Confederation was one of the primary factors contributing to its demise.[6]

In theory, at least, the Constitution greatly enhanced the capacity of the new federal government to extract revenues from the general population, but it also installed a number of safeguards and restrictions. Certain forms of taxation were explicitly prohibited (such as duties on exports), and the ability of the government to impose others (such as direct taxes on property and incomes)

[3] On early attitudes regarding taxes and tyranny see Theodore Draper, *A Struggle for Power: The American Revolution* (New York: Vintage Books, 1997).

[4] See Article VIII of the Articles of Confederation, reprinted in Edward C. Smith, ed., *The Constitution of the United States* (New York: Barnes and Noble, 1972), p. 31.

[5] Dall W. Forsythe, *Taxation and Political Change in the Young Nation, 1781–1833* (New York: Columbia University Press, 1977), p. 14.

[6] Because of its inability to tax, wrote Alexander Hamilton, "the government of the Union has gradually dwindled into a state of decay, approaching nearly annihilation." See Federalist No. 30 ("Concerning the General Power of Taxation"), in Edward Meade Earle, ed., *The Federalist* (New York: Modern Library, 1937), p. 183.

was severely constrained.[7] Most important, responsibility for initiating all revenue-raising measures was assigned to the legislative branch, and specifically to
the House of Representatives. The House was the only organ of the new government whose members were directly elected, every two years, and the close
and regular contact that they had with their constitutents was presumed to be a
powerful deterrent to any enthusiasm for taxation.[8]

The evolution of the federal tax system over the next 150 years was driven
primarily by what fiscal historian W. Elliot Brownlee has called "great emergencies" and, in particular, "great wars."[9] Down to 1945, successive crises were
necessary to provoke expansions in the scope and level of federal taxation, and
these were invariably followed by substantial postwar contractions. Throughout
the nineteenth century and into the first decades of the twentieth, federal taxes
remained low, with the great bulk of the revenues generated by customs duties
and excises on commodities. Rates increased dramatically during the Civil War,
and a tax on individual incomes was briefly imposed, but excises were cut
sharply after the war and the income tax was allowed to lapse. The passage of
the Sixteenth Amendment in 1913 made a permanent peacetime income tax
possible, but until the beginning of active American preparation for entry into
the First World War individual tax rates remained low, and only the wealthiest
citizens were susceptible. During the war, taxes on individual and corporate
incomes (including a special tax on "excess" profits) rose drastically before
being cut back again substantially in the 1920s.[10]

The Second World War saw another even more dramatic expansion in federal
taxation. Excises and corporate income taxes went up, and a new emergency
excess profits tax was imposed. Individual income tax rates were raised and, in
a marked departure from past practice, the scope of the tax was expanded to
include the great mass of the middle class. Extraction was rendered more efficient (and somewhat less painful) by the institution of pay-as-you-go withholding from workers' paychecks.[11] Taken together, these innovations transformed

[7] Article I, section 9 of the Constitution specified that direct taxes could be imposed only in proportion to the size of a state's population (with slaves counting for three-fifths of a white man). Tax rates
on property (the most likely form of direct taxation at the time) would therefore have been grossly
unequal between states, with large southern landowners paying far less per acre than their northern
counterparts. "This restriction was so inequitable that, for practical purposes, it virtually denied Congress the power to levy direct taxes altogether." Forrest McDonald, *Novus Ordo Seclorum: The Intellectual Origins of the Constitution* (Lawrence: University of Kansas Press, 1985), p. 264.

[8] Article I, section 7, reprinted in Earle, *The Federalist*, p. 589.

[9] W. Elliot Brownlee, *Federal Taxation in America: A Short History* (New York: Cambridge
University Press, 1996), p. 3. Brownlee identifies five great emergencies: the "social crisis that
extended from 1763 down to the formation of the U.S. Constitution," the Civil War, World War
One, the Great Depression, and World War Two (pp. 10, 1–8).

[10] Regarding the overall evolution of U.S. tax policy down to the Second World War see ibid., pp.
9–88. Regarding the income tax in particular see John F. Witte, *The Politics and Development of
the Federal Income Tax* (Madison: University of Wisconsin Press, 1985), pp. 67–109.

[11] For useful summaries see, in addition to Witte, *The Politics and Development of the Federal
Income Tax*, pp. 110–30; Bartholomew H. Sparrow, *From the Outside In: World War II and the
American State* (Princeton: Princeton University Press, 1996), pp. 97–160.

the federal tax system into "an enormously powerful . . . revenue-raising machine."[12] The question as the war ended was what portion of this mighty new engine would be permitted to remain intact.

With more Americans paying higher federal taxes than ever before in the nation's history, it is hardly surprising that the early Cold War years were characterized by a rise in anti-tax sentiment and by the reemergence of some traditional political themes. Public opinion polls taken in the second half of the 1940s found that a growing majority of those questioned considered their taxes to be too high, even after several big cuts; when the possibility of peacetime tax increases was broached during this period, vast majorities were opposed. After rates were raised during the Korean conflict, anti-tax feeling grew even stronger. By the early 1950s, many people favored laws explicitly limiting the federal government's revenue-raising powers.[13]

As the Founders had intended, Congress proved especially sensitive and responsive to these anti-tax sentiments. In the 1940s and again in the 1950s, it was the legislative branch that resisted raising taxes and pushed most strongly for tax cuts, and presidents, with their broader responsibilities and more all-encompassing perspective, who felt obliged to defend existing high tax rates and, on occasion, to ask for even more. These institutionally rooted preferences remained visible, albeit with variations in intensity, when different political parties controlled Capitol Hill and the White House. Harry Truman tried repeatedly to persuade Congress to raise taxes. Dwight Eisenhower did not call for tax hikes, but after the Korean War he felt compelled by his concerns over national security to defend the extension of some existing tax rates against congressional pressure for further reductions.

Whether controlled by Republicans or Democrats, Congress tended to support tax cuts and to resist tax increases, with the House generally more avid on both points than the Senate. Members of both chambers and of both parties were especially leery of approving presidential requests for election year tax increases (as in the first half of 1950, before the Korean War began, and in 1952, despite the fact that it was still underway). Similar calculations contributed, in 1948 and 1954, to especially strong congressional pressure for tax cuts.

Despite some institutionally induced similarities in view, members of the two major political parties did have significant differences over revenue policy, and

---

[12] Herbert Stein, *Presidential Economics: The Making of Economic Policy from Roosevelt to Reagan and Beyond* (Washington, DC: American Enterprise Institute, 1988), p. 68.

[13] In the late 1940s over half of those questioned typically regarded their tax bill as too high; by 1952 the figure had risen to 71 percent. See Survey #392-K, Question #1b (March 1947); Survey #414-K, Question #2b (March 1948), both in *The Gallup Poll*, vol. 1, *1935–1948* (New York: Random House, 1972), pp. 636, 721; Survey #439-K, Question 7c (April 1949), Survey #452-TPS, Question #9b (March 1950), Survey #486-K, Question #3b (March 1952) in *The Gallup Poll*, vol. 2, *1949–1958* (New York: Random House, 1972), pp. 804, 895, and 1046. In 1949 75 percent of those questioned were against a proposed tax hike. Survey #433-K, Question #13a (July 1949) in *The Gallup Poll* 2:831. By the early 1950s majorities favored laws limiting the percentage of a person's income that could be taken in taxes. Survey #489-K, Question #5 (July 1952); Survey #541-K, Question #27 (February 1955) in *The Gallup Poll* 2:1075, 1038.

partisan competition produced additional downward pressure on taxes. Republicans shared the popular animosity to postwar taxes and were quick to capitalize on it. Most regarded taxes as, at best, a necessary evil and, at worst, a deadly threat to future prosperity. Aside from the presumed economic benefits, reducing taxes was also seen as a way to turn back the tides of statism, checking the growth of government, restraining the expansion of the welfare state, and, where possible, forcing the dismantling of programs put in place during the New Deal. As Senator Robert Taft explained in 1947: "The best reason to reduce taxes is to reduce our ideas of the number of dollars the government can properly spend in a year, and thereby reduce inflated ideas of the proper scope of bureaucratic authority."[14] Although popular support for existing social programs turned out to be greater than Taft and some of his colleagues had anticipated, opposition to taxes did prove to be a potent political tactic. In the late 1940s and early 1950s, Republicans attacked the Democrats as the party of high taxes and, in 1946, 1950, and 1952, this charge brought substantial electoral dividends.

In the late 1940s many Democrats, including President Truman, favored retaining or raising taxes on corporations and those in upper-income brackets in order to pay for expanded social welfare programs. Democrats hoped that supporting such redistributive measures as they had done during the New Deal, would be good for their party as well as for the country. In contrast to the 1930s, however, many more people were now paying income taxes, and with the return to prosperity, incomes were rapidly rising. In these new conditions, the prospect of higher taxes for some seemed to threaten higher taxes for all. The electoral benefits of calling for rate hikes and the dangers of appearing to support higher peacetime taxes, regardless of who was supposed to pay them, quickly became apparent. By the 1950s Democrats, taking a page from the Republican book, had abandoned the practice of advocating tax hikes of any sort, concentrating instead on calling for tax cuts to benefit workers and the middle class.

After the Second World War and again following the Korean War, members of both major political parties favored immediate tax relief for those whom they regarded as their core constituents. Democrats gave precedence to cutting excise taxes (which fell disproportionately on those with lower and middle incomes) and shrinking the lower brackets of the income tax. Republicans were especially eager to reduce impositions on corporate profits and incomes and to lighten the load borne by middle- and upper-income taxpayers. The making of postwar tax policy therefore involved trade-offs in which both parties won concessions for "their" voters, and the tax burdens borne by all groups were reduced. As one observer has written, after 1945, "it is as if there were a continuous force operating like gravity to push tax legislation in the direction of tax reduction, a force that [could] . . . really be overcome only by the abnormal revenue demands of severe national crisis."[15]

---

[14] A. E. Holmans, *United States Fiscal Policy, 1945–1959: Its Contribution to Economic Stability* (London: Oxford University Press, 1961), p. 68.

[15] Witte, *The Politics and Development of the Federal Income Tax*, p. 175.

But even severe crises did not bring a permanent suspension to the laws of fiscal gravity. At the start of wartime emergencies, Democrats were more inclined than Republicans to support higher taxes on corporations and on those in upper personal-income brackets. After 1942, the sheer numbers of middle-income taxpayers (and potential voters) made Republicans as well as Democrats wary of raising their rates. Instead, Republicans leaned toward higher excise taxes and, if necessary, a national sales tax, measures that Democrats opposed as regressive. Even in war, the political parties were vigilant in defending the interests of their supporters and in limiting, or blocking outright, efforts by the other side to impose greater burdens on them. During both the Korean and the Second World Wars, therefore, initial rapid increases in all varieties of taxation were followed quickly by stalemate.

The overall pattern of tax policy during the 1940s and 1950s can be briefly summarized: efforts to increase taxes in the absence of open warfare failed. Such increases occurred only once fighting was underway, and even then they did not go nearly as far as executive branch officials believed to be essential. In postwar periods (after 1945 and again after 1952), tax rates were cut, usually more than the president would have preferred, albeit not all the way back to pre-war levels.

There was a fiscal "ratchet effect" at work in the United States during this period, but it had some unusual characteristics. Thanks to the intensity of American resistance to taxation, the ratchet was difficult to raise, even in wartime; it tended to slip backward signficantly as soon as the pressure for increases was removed, and, having slipped, it became immovable upward while remaining susceptible to further downward movement.

Table 4.1 summarizes the evolution of the federal tax structure between the Revenue Act of 1945 and the Revenue Act of 1954, the last major change in tax policy until the Kennedy tax cuts of 1964.

THE LIMITS TO "GROWTHSMANSHIP"

The revenues available to the United States government during the early postwar period depended on the overall level of national economic activity, as well as on the structure of the federal tax system. When growth was strong, incomes, profits, and transactions of all kinds increased considerably in volume, and so too did tax revenues; when the economy slumped, revenues did as well. By taking steps to minimize recessions, economic policy makers could therefore, without increasing rates or adding new taxes, ensure themselves of generally rising revenues. If they wished quickly and substantially to increase the yield of the existing tax structure, however, they would have had to pursue more aggressive fiscal policies, increasing government spending or cutting taxes as needed in order deliberately to accelerate the rate of economic expansion. Although the doctrine of "growthsmanship" had its advocates in the late 1940s, it would not be adopted as a guide for policy until the early 1960s.[16]

---

[16] I have borrowed this label from Robert M. Collins, "The Emergence of Economic Growths-

TABLE 4.1
Structure of the Federal Tax System, 1945–1954

	1945	1948	1950[a]	1951	1953	1954
Personal	cut	cut[b]	raised	—	cut	—
Corporate	cut	—	raised	raised	extended	retained[c]
Excises	retained	retained	retained	—	extended	some cut[d]
Excess profit	eliminated	—	—	imposed	extended	eliminated

[a]Start of Korean War buildup
[b]Over presidential veto
[c]With significant provisions for relief
[d]Over presidential objections

For most of the twenty years that followed the end of the Second World War, the federal government contented itself instead with the more modest goal of smoothing out fluctuations in the generally rising trend of national economic activity. Growth was desired and encouraged, but rather than aiming at a particular level of total output, or a specific rate of expansion, executive branch officials were concerned primarily with preventing excesses of inflation and unemployment. They hoped to be able to do this primarily by permitting the normal functioning of tax and spending programs to produce small, temporary, countercyclical imbalances in the federal budget. The main differences between the doctrines of growthsmanship and "commercial Keynesianism"[17] are summarized in table 4.2.

Commercial Keynesianism was born of the opposition between those on the left side of the postwar political spectrum, who favored growthsmanship, and those on the right, many of whom tended initially to advocate a return to fiscal orthodoxy. As figure 4.3 suggests, however, growthsmanship was itself a de-

TABLE 4.2
Alternative Doctrines: Growthsmanship versus Commercial Keynesianism

	Growthsmanship	*Commercial Keynesianism*
Goal	Full employment	Stability
Means	Active fiscal policy	Automatic stabilizers
Budgets	Deficits run as needed	Balance over business cycle
Government role	Primary and active	Secondary and passive

manship in the United States: Federal Policy and Economic Knowledge in the Truman Years," in Mary O. Furner and Barry Supple, eds., *The State and Economic Knowledge: The British and American Experiences* (New York: Cambridge University Press, 1990), pp. 138–70.

[17] The author of this term appears to be Robert Lekachman, *The Age of Keynes* (New York: Random House, 1966), p. 287.

Planning ⟶ Growthsmanship ⟶ **Commercial Keynesianism** ⟵ Fiscal Orthodoxy

Figure 4.3. The Postwar Convergence on Commercial Keynesianism

scendant of earlier and even more ambitious conceptions of government's appropriate role in the economy.[18]

In the depths of the Great Depression, some economists had become convinced that the United States was approaching a condition of economic "maturity." With the closing of the frontier and the apparent slowing of technological progress, the long era of rapid, easy growth that had characterized much of the nation's history seemed finally to be coming to a close. Further advances would now depend heavily not on the unfettered workings of the market, but on increased government planning, regulation, and intervention. As progress slowed and profits dwindled, only a strong and farsighted state would have the power to break up cartels along with the resources to sustain minimal levels of investment and growth.[19]

By the late 1930s these ideas and the efforts made to implement them had already come under ferocious attack from those who feared their statist implications. War thinned the ranks of planning enthusiasts still further, and it increased the number and strengthened the convictions of those who opposed them. The prodigies of production achieved after 1941 diminished fears that the American economy had reached its limits, even if they did not dispel concern over what would happen once the war had ended. For those who had been attracted to the ideal of planned economic rationality, the reality of a centrally managed wartime economy, with all its inefficiencies and corruption, was also a rude shock.[20]

As the war approached its end, most New Dealers had abandoned detailed state economic planning in favor of aggressive Keynesian demand manage-

---

[18] These are essentially the positions identified in Stein, *Presidential Economics*, pp. 71–75. Stein uses the labels "reformers and planners," "strict and exclusive Keynesians," "conservative macroeconomists," and "conventional conservatives."

[19] See Alan Brinkley, "The New Deal and the Idea of the State," in Steve Fraser and Gary Gerstle, eds., *The Rise and Fall of the New Deal Order, 1930–1980* (Princeton: Princeton University Press, 1989) p. 99. For more on the reasoning that underlay the thinking of the "planners," see Theodore Rosenof, *Patterns of Political Economy in America: The Failure to Develop a Democratic Left Synthesis, 1933–1950* (New York: Garland, 1983).

[20] The fact that much of the responsibility for economic management came to rest in the hands of businessmen temporarily on leave from their private careers rather than with a selfless band of professional civil servants contributed to liberal disillusionment. For many liberals the functioning of the wartime planning agencies "served not as an inspiration but as an alarming indication of what government management of the economy could become: a mechanism by which members of the corporate world could take over the regulatory process and turn it to their own advantage." Brinkley, "The New Deal and the Idea of the State," p. 103. On the general liberal disillusionment with planning see also Alan Brinkley, *The End of Reform: New Deal Liberalism in Recession and War* (New York: Knopf, 1995), pp. 175–200.

ment, or growthsmanship. Underlying this approach was the belief that although the federal government did not have the responsiblity or the need to manage every aspect of the nation's economy, it did have an obligation to ensure an overall level of national economic activity sufficient to prevent unemployment. By 1945 liberals had begun to converge on the maintenance of full employment as the government's essential economic goal and on adjustments in fiscal policy as the primary means for attaining it.[21]

The liberal vision for the postwar economy was given concrete form in the proposed Full Employment Act, introduced by congressional Democrats early in 1945. The bill called for executive branch planners to prepare an annual National Production and Employment Budget, which would contain estimates of the total size of the labor force for the coming year, the magnitude of the gross national product necessary to employ it, and the volume of public and private investment and consumption required to produce the desired level of GNP. The sum total of public and private spending needed to sustain full employment would then be compared to the actual amount anticipated in the coming year. When a gap between the two was projected, policies would be proposed to eliminate it. Most important, if anticipated demand were too low, the president would be required to put forward a program designed to raise it, if need be by increasing federal spending or cutting taxes in order to produce a stimulative budget deficit.[22]

Opponents of the Full Employment Act objected both to the ends it sought and the means it proposed to meet them. The promise of a guaranteed job, they claimed, would sap worker initiative and undermine the productivity of the American economy. Federal efforts to promote maximum employment would drive up wages and could put some employers out of business. If the proposed bill were enacted, the government would be launched on an endless program of public works and compensatory spending, deficits would become routine, debt would deepen, inflation would skyrocket, business confidence and private investment would plummet, and growth would eventually slow.[23]

Critics also warned that, albeit in a subtle way, the pursuit of full employ-

---

[21] On the rise of "fiscalism" see also Ira Katznelson and Bruce Pietrykowski, "Rebuilding the American State: Evidence from the 1940s," *Studies in American Political Development*, no. 5 (Fall 1991), pp. 301–39.

[22] The terms of Senate bill S.380 are contained in Hearings before a Subcommittee of the Senate Committee on Banking and Currency, *Full Employment Act of 1945*, 79th Cong., 1st sess. (Washington, DC: U.S. Government Printing Office, 1945), pp. 6–9.

[23] The debate over the Full Employment Act and the various criticisms of it are discussed ibid., pp. 77–112. Stephen K. Bailey, *Congress Makes a Law: The Story behind the Employment Act of 1946* (New York: Columbia University Press, 1950) is still the classic treatment of this episode. See also the discussion in Herbert Stein, *The Fiscal Revolution in America* (Washington, DC: American Enterprise Institute, 1990), pp. 197–204; and Brinkley, *The End of Reform*, pp. 227–64. For an excellent overview and an illuminating cross-national comparison see Margaret Weir, "Ideas and Politics: The Acceptance of Keynesianism in Britain and the United States," in Peter A. Hall, ed., *The Political Power of Economic Ideas: Keynesianism across Nations* (Princeton: Princeton University Press, 1989), pp. 53–86.

ment would shift the balance of economic decision-making power toward the state and away from private actors. Despite what its proponents claimed, the Full Employment Act did not provide "an effective 'middle way' between a heavily statist solution to the problems of the economy and a return to the kind of unmediated private enterprise that had produced the Great Depression."[24] To the contrary, declared a statement by the majority of the House Expenditures Committee: "It is either private enterprise or statism."[25] "We might get full employment under that bill, all right" warned the president of the U.S. Chamber of Congress, "but in the process we'd lose our democracy and have a regimented state."[26]

Despite the experience of the Great Depression, some congressional conservatives and the representatives of a number of large business organizations would have preferred to see a return to traditional fiscal orthodoxy, without federal goals, targets, or responsibilities of any kind, and with budgets balanced annually at the lowest possible level of spending and taxation. More moderate and prudent business leaders and politicians recognized, however, that there were dangers to appearing indifferent to unemployment, as well as real advantages to establishing a permanent, if circumscribed, federal role in promoting economic stability. But how best to move away from orthodoxy without setting off down the slippery slope to "serfdom"?

In the course of the debate over full employment, conservative converts to Keynesian economics began to propound a more cautious and limited form of demand management, one in which adjustments would largely be achieved automatically, through the routine operation of existing tax and spending programs, rather than through dramatic departures in government policy on either front. As economic growth accelerated, the progressive federal tax system would soak up more revenues, the budget would begin to show a surplus, aggregate demand would fall and inflationary pressures would be eased. If growth slowed, tax revenues would fall while payments from federal unemployment programs increased, the budget would tilt toward a deficit, aggregate demand would increase, and the recession's duration would be minimized. While it might fall briefly out of balance during periods of recession or excessively rapid growth, the federal budget would tend to balance over the course of the business cycle. More active measures might be needed on occasion, but the beauty of the system of "automatic stabilizers" was precisely that it promised to minimize the need for overly active, interventionist government economic policies.[27]

[24] Brinkley, *The End of Reform*, p. 262. Placing the Full Employment Bill in the larger context of the Truman administration's policies is Alonzo L. Hamby, *Beyond the New Deal: Harry S. Truman and American Liberalism* (New York: Columbia University Press, 1973), pp. 53–85.

[25] Quoted in Bailey, *Congress Makes a Law,* p. 171.

[26] Eric Johnston quoted in Robert M. Collins, *The Business Response to Keynes, 1929–1964* (New York: Columbia University Press, 1981), p. 102.

[27] Regarding these automatic or "built-in" stabilizers see Wilfred Lewis, Jr., *Federal Fiscal Policy in the Postwar Recessions* (Washington, DC: Brookings Institution, 1962), pp. 1–90. See also Stein, *Fiscal Revolution.*

The ultimate outcome of the battle over the Full Employment Act, and over postwar economic doctrine more generally, was a compromise, albeit one clearly weighted toward the "right wing of the Keynesian spectrum."[28] The bill eventually signed into law in 1946 bore some resemblance to the original, but it had been stripped of its most potent provisions. The more modestly titled Employment Act of 1946 acknowledged a federal obligation to promote "maximum" employment (along with "production" and, significant for its anti-inflationary connotations, "purchasing power"), but it did not prescribe any particular policies for achieving these goals. In place of a specific and detailed national budget, the president was now required only to transmit an Economic Report surveying conditions and trends along with reviewing government programs. Instead of transforming the Bureau of the Budget into a powerful center for national economic planning, the law created a new Council of Economic Advisers with minimal staff, uncertain responsibilities, and no clear, permanent source of bureaucratic authority.[29]

Although it did not preclude the possibility of growthsmanship, the postwar debate over economic policy led in practice to an emphasis on stability and to a primary reliance on the automatic tools of commercial Keynesianism. Neither the Truman nor the Eisenhower administration was willing deliberately to run substantial sustained deficits in the hopes of accelerating economic growth. Both abjured long-range economic navigation in favor of short-term corrective steering and, with the exception of the Korean War years, both tolerated only limited, temporary doses of deficit spending as necessary to offset downturns in the business cycle.

The conservative economic doctrine that prevailed during the 1940s and 1950s had important implications for the trajectory of federal spending and, in particular, for defense spending. Had growthsmanship, instead of commercial Keynesianism, been embraced in the opening years of the Cold War, the United States economy might have grown for a time more rapidly (although the rate of inflation might also have been higher), tax receipts would have increased more quickly, even without higher tax rates, and the nation would have found it easier to spend more on defense.

CONSTRAINTS ON DEFICITS

The government's reluctance to engage in deficit spending, whatever its effects on the growth rate and on the future availability of resources, also imposed a more immediate limitation on government expenditures. In the absence of a powerful inhibition against them, unbalanced budgets might have provided a

---

[28] Collins, *The Business Response to Keynes*, p. 16.
[29] The act is reprinted in Council of Economic Advisers, *First Annual Report to the President* (Washington, DC: U.S. Government Printing Office, December 1946), pp. 22–26. Regarding the origins of the Council of Economic Advisers see Edward S. Flash, Jr., *Economic Advice and Presidential Leadership: The Council of Economic Advisers* (New York: Columbia University Press, 1965), pp. 1–17.

tempting escape route for officials caught between the yields of a rigid tax system and mounting demands for ever-larger military and social welfare programs. Instead, political leaders of both parties were united in their opposition to routine deficit spending and in their evident reverence for the principle of a balanced federal budget.

Presidents Truman and Eisenhower shared an oft-expressed ardor for balanced budgets and an abhorence of deficits that, in the eyes of their detractors, seemed at times to border on unreason. This shared preoccupation with matching revenues to expenditures has sometimes been dismissed as the product of a lack of sophistication. Both Truman and Eisenhower started out as small-town boys of modest means who, in later life, prided themselves on knowing the meaning of hard work and the value of a dollar. Neither was greatly enamored of economists or of economic theory. Each used, and appears to have taken seriously, the homely comparision between family and nation to make the point that the United States had to learn to "live within its means."

While their language was sometimes quaint, the two presidents' attachment to balanced budgets was far from simpleminded. As leaders of the nation and of their respective parties, Truman and Eisenhower were deeply concerned with political symbolism. For Truman, eliminating deficits and beginning to pay down the nation's debts were worthy acts of effective, responsible government. After an unbroken string of deficits that began during the Great Depression, balancing the budget was also a way of demonstrating the Democratic party's ability to manage the country in normal times, and a potent proof against Republican charges of fiscal irresponsibility.

For Eisenhower and other conservatives, the ideal of a balanced budget was a tool for enforcing fiscal restraint, but it was also the premier symbol of a state that was limited, as well as merely effective. In this view, the deficits that the nation had run in the 1930s and 1940s were evidence both of profligacy and of the unchecked advance of big government. Given the constraints on taxation, a government that lived within its means would necessarily be restricted in its ability to undertake new and potentially dangerous domestic interventions. For Eisenhower, as for Thomas Jefferson before him, "a balanced national budget signified a popular willingness and ability to limit the purpose and size of the federal government, to restrain its influence in the economy, to protect states' rights, to maintain the Constitution's balance of powers, and to promote republican virtue."[30] In calling for balanced budgets, Eisenhower was deploying a symbol that had a deep resonance and a specific anti-statist significance in American political culture.

Symbolism aside, the reluctance of postwar presidents to indulge in deficit spending also reflected concern over the more direct economic and political consequences of such a practice. However inadequate their formal economic educations, both Truman and Eisenhower were sufficiently well tutored to realize that government spending unmatched by revenues could fuel inflation. Al-

[30] James D. Savage, *Balanced Budgets and American Politics* (Ithaca: Cornell University Press, 1988), p. 5.

beit for slightly different reasons, this was something that both feared and sought to guard against.

The first years of American participation in the Second World War had shown that rapidly rising prices could be extremely unpopular, especially with the ordinary middle-class citizens who would feel them first and most heavily.[31] In addition, as the war ended there was widespread anxiety among economists and politicans of all stripes that the United States would repeat the experience of the 1920s. Then, as Commerce Secretary Henry Wallace warned in 1945, a brief period of "soaring" postwar inflation had been "followed by a sudden sharp smash in prices." In the 1950s, as in the 1920s, inflation could easily give way to depression.[32] Indeed, cautioned President Truman in 1946, because the pressures at work were "many times stronger than those which caused the inflation after World War I," there was a real danger that they could bring a "much more serious" crash.[33]

Fear that deficit-fed inflation would be unpopular and that it could contribute to economic and, perhaps, also to social and political instability influenced President Truman's behavior throughout his time in office, and it persisted in some circles well into the 1950s. As time passed and the likelihood of another depression seemed to dwindle, this concern gradually took on a different form. Especially during the Eisenhower years, inflation came to be regarded as a long-term, secular problem capable of doing considerable damage even if it did not provoke an immediate catastrophe. Steadily rising prices, Eisenhower and his advisers feared, would diminish the willingness of ordinary people to "keep . . . saving their money and . . . indulg[ing] in long term investment," thereby limiting the prospects for future growth.[34] Rejecting the view that a little inflation might be the acceptable price of healthy expansion, Eisenhower declared in 1959: "I believe that economic growth in the long run cannot be soundly brought about except with stability in your price structure."[35] In addition to its impact on the domestic economy, inflation would also harm the nation's strategic position, driving up the cost of arms, weakening the dollar, and eroding the interlocking trade and alliance systems on which it was substantially based.[36]

---

[31] For an overview of the wartime experience with inflation see Harold G. Vatter, *The U.S. Economy in World War II* (New York: Columbia University Press, 1985), pp. 89–112.

[32] Wallace's book *Sixty Million Jobs*, quoted in Hearings before a Subcommittee of the Senate Committee on Banking and Currency, *Full Employment Act of 1945*, p. 984. The prevalence of the early postwar concern over inflation is discussed in Robert Stanley Herren, "Wage-Price Policy during the Truman Administration: A Postwar Problem and the Search for Its Solution" (Ph.D. dissertation, Duke University, Department of Economics, 1974); also Craufurd D. Goodwin and R. Stanley Herren, "The Truman Years," in Goodwin, ed., *Exhortation and Controls: The Search for a Wage-Price Policy, 1945–1971* (Washington, DC: Brookings Institution, 1975), pp. 15–19.

[33] "Radio Report to the American People on the Status of the Reconversion Program," January 3, 1946, in Harry S. Truman, *Public Papers of the Presidents of the United States, 1946* (Washington, DC: U.S. Government Printing Office, 1962), p. 5 (hereafter *PPP 1946*).

[34] Eisenhower quoted in Brian Girvin, *The Right in the Twentieth Century: Conservatism and Democracy* (London: Pinter, 1994), p. 172.

[35] Quoted in Raymond J. Saulnier, *Constructive Years: The U.S. Economy under Eisenhower* (Lanham, MD: University Press of America, 1991), p. 16.

[36] Regarding these concerns, which were greatest toward the end of Eisenhower's second term,

Eisenhower and his economic advisers viewed inflation as yet another unfortunate side effect of the metastasis of the modern state; containing one would require curbing the other. Given his judgment that inflation was the nation's fundamental, underlying economic problem and "most of the time the current and overt problem," Eisenhower's commitment to balanced budgets was not indicative of primitive, pre-Keynesian thinking or crude economic moralism. It was instead, as Herbert Stein points out, "consistent with, indeed required by, modern fiscal policy."[37]

As bad as inflation might be, the cures for it were even worse. If prices spiraled upward, higher taxes would be necessary to absorb excess demand. If taxes could not be raised to adequate levels or with sufficient speed, the government might be forced to resort to the imposition of wage and price controls. Here again, as they struggled to keep budgets balanced, postwar political leaders were haunted, and inspired in their efforts, by recent experience.

Economic controls had been quite effective during the Second World War, but they had also been universally unpopular. By the end of the war, virtually every sector of society felt aggrieved by the way in which wages and prices were being administered, and, not surprisingly, all of them blamed the government for their troubles. Workers wanted higher pay and chafed at any increase in the cost of food and consumer products. Farmers and manufacturers wanted higher prices for their goods and resented any upward increment in the cost of labor or the price of materials that they needed for production. Consumers were frustrated by shortages, tired of rationing, and, in general, fed up with government intrusion into all aspects of their daily economic existence. Sensitive to popular opinion and responsive to interest group pressures, Congress prevented President Truman from preserving a working control system after Japan's surrender and blocked his efforts to reimpose controls when inflation reared its head again in 1947 and 1948.[38]

Opposition to controls derived in part from calculations of immediate pecuniary interest, but the prospect of government-administered wages and prices also aroused a deeper anxiety. A state capable of directing the flow of scarce materials, determining workers' wages, and setting the cost of virtually every important product and commodity in the national economy would have to be endowed with enormous capacities for oversight, administration, and enforcement. Tilting the balance of power toward the state in this way might be

---

see Iwan W. Morgan, *Eisenhower versus the Spenders* (London: Pinter, 1990), pp. 128–32; also John W. Sloan, *Eisenhower and the Management of Prosperity* (Lawrence: University of Kansas Press, 1991), pp. 116–29.

[37] Stein, *The Fiscal Revolution in America*, p. 283.

[38] On the initial postwar struggles over controls see Jack Stokes Ballard, *The Shock of Peace: Military and Economic Demobilization after World War II* (Washington, DC: University Press of America, 1983), pp. 155–92; Darrel Cady, "The Truman Administration's Reconversion Policies, 1945–1947" (Ph.D. dissertation, University of Kansas, Department of History, 1974), pp. 75–102, 136–73; Herren, "Wage-Price Policy during the Truman Administration," pp. 37–78; Goodwin and Herren, "The Truman Years," pp. 9–69.

essential in a crisis, and, provided it was promptly corrected, such a shift need not necessarily produce lasting ill effects. In a protracted Cold War, however, there was a real risk of doing deep and perhaps irreversible damage. A quasi-permanent structure of economic controls would weaken Congress and magnify the power of the executive branch; it would contribute to the regimentation of society and, over time, to the effective destruction of the American free enterprise system.[39] Like a powerful narcotic, controls could "prove habit forming and develop a spirit of acceptance of authority over larger and larger areas of life and weaken the reliance of the people on free bargaining."[40]

Lurking behind imbalanced budgets was the terrifying specter of the "garrison state." Habitual indulgence in deficits would lead to inflation, inflation could lead to the imposition of controls, and controls could result in a progressive loss of domestic freedoms. The more fervent the acceptance of this syllogism, the more determined the efforts to avoid deficit spending. What was at stake in the battle to balance the budget was not merely some abstract ideal of fiscal responsibility, but the very future of the nation.

Cases

The remainder of this chapter will trace the process through which a constrained tax structure and prevailing beliefs about fiscal policy combined to limit defense spending and to shape American strategy during the opening years of the Cold War. This story can be briefly summarized.

Between September 1945 and June 1950 the downward political pressure on taxation was overwhelming. Congress twice cut tax rates (in 1945 and again, over a presidential veto, in 1948) and three times refused presidential requests to raise them in peacetime (in 1948, 1949, and early 1950). Given President Truman's fear of deficit-driven inflation (and his consequent wariness of growthsmanship), the revenues generated by this politically constricted tax structure set a firm upper limit on spending for defense and foreign policy. Truman's desire to preserve, and if possible marginally to expand, existing though still comparatively small federal social welfare programs further reduced the funds available for national security. Despite two crisis-related efforts to push it significantly higher (in the aftermath of the Czech takeover in the spring of 1948 and following the discovery of a Soviet atomic bomb test at the end of 1949), an effective ceiling on defense expenditures was maintained down to the outbreak of the Korean War. Fiscal constraint was the single most important factor pushing the United States toward a strategy of minimum deterrence during this period.

---

[39] The term "regimentation" was used frequently in discussions of controls. See, for example, the contrast between "free enterprise" and "regimentation" in an April 9, 1948, memo from Edwin Nourse, Chairman of the Council of Economic Advisers, quoted in Nourse, *Economics in the Public Service* (New York: Harcourt, Brace, 1953), p. 488.

[40] Edwin G. Nourse, "What Effect Will Armament Spending Have on the Business Outlook?" *U.S. News and World Report*, December 10, 1948, p. 46.

Korea brought a temporary and short-lived lessening of resistance to taxation, an expansion in the tax structure, and a consequent explosion in federal revenues. Despite the best efforts of the Truman administration, the war also resulted in greatly expanded federal budget deficits and at least the tacit adoption of a form of military Keynesianism. An increased flow of funds made possible the abandonment of pure atomic deterrence and a shift toward the balanced force posture needed to support a genuine warfighting strategy. Even before the Korean War ended, however, the reemergence of constraints on taxation had begun to call into question the ability of the United States to sustain such a strategy over the long haul.

The Eisenhower years saw a return to the political economy of constraint, albeit at a higher level of available revenues, thanks both to the growth of the American economy and the retention of some wartime taxes. Tax rates were quickly reduced, though not, in every case, all the way back to pre-war levels. Eisenhower was as eager as Truman had been to force down deficits and head off inflation. Although prepared to be flexible, he was also less committed to social spending than his predecessor, and far less tempted by the prospect that federal fiscal policy could be used to accelerate economic growth. In order to hold down defense spending, Eisenhower forced the military to abandon balanced forces and warfighting and to accept a strategy of massive retaliation. In the mid-1950s and again at the time of the Sputnik crisis, he resisted demands that spending be greatly increased and strategy overhauled in order to respond to the growth of Soviet military power.

The advent of the Kennedy administration brought changed fiscal assumptions, a loosening of perceived constraints on government spending, an accompanying expansion in defense budgets, and a shift in strategy away from massive retaliation and toward flexible response. Neither the relaxation of old constraints nor the change in strategy was as dramatic as it has sometimes been made to seem, however. Moreover, the 1960s also saw the beginnings of the emergence of a powerful new source of downward pressure on defense spending, in the form of greatly expanded social welfare programs. These developments will be briefly discussed in the closing section of this chapter.

ABORTIVE REARMAMENT (1948–1949)

From the close of the Second World War to the outbreak of the war in Korea, the Truman administration found itself caught in an increasingly painful dilemma. On the one hand, deteriorating relations with the Soviet Union made it impossible to cut military spending as far or as fast as had originally been hoped. To the contrary, as the Cold War deepened, there were mounting demands from the military services and the State Department for substantial increases in spending on arms and foreign aid. At the same time, from the public and from Congress came calls for the alleviation of tax burdens and the abandonment of any remnants of the wartime system of wage and price controls. The combination of upward pressure on expenditures with downward pressure on revenues (and controls) raised the prospect of substantial budget deficits and galloping inflation.

In the late 1940s it was this danger, with all of its immediate and potentially disastrous domestic implications, rather than the more remote specter of overseas communist expansionism, that proved to be most compelling. Despite increasingly urgent appeals from his national security advisers, President Truman imposed strict limits on defense expenditures. However desirable a bigger military buildup might have seemed from the strategic point of view, without higher taxes it was simply infeasible. And without war, as events would prove, higher taxes were a political impossibility.

With the final defeat of the Axis powers, the American public was eager to rid itself of wartime taxes, controls, ration cards, and all the other intrusive paraphernalia of a heavily mobilized, centrally planned economy. The Truman administration's efforts to preserve a partial, transitional wage and price control system wound up antagonizing labor, farmers, and, ultimately, urban consumers, weakening the New Deal coalition and contributing to widespread Republican victories in the 1946 elections.[41] Recognizing that the new Congress would soon dismantle what remained of wartime controls, President Truman acknowledged defeat and, soon after the election, ordered their "immediate abandonment."[42]

Taxes too were under attack. Within weeks of the Japanese surrender, President Truman proposed and Congress quickly approved substantial cuts in corporate and personal income tax rates.[43] Insofar as the Congress and, in particular, the Republicans, were concerned, this was merely a small first step. Republican candidates in the 1946 campaign promised further deep, sweeping tax cuts. When a new Congress convened in January 1947, the Republican majority made tax reduction its first order of business. Twice in the course of the year Congress passed tax cutting bills, the president vetoed them, and with a substantial number of Democrats voting against their party's leader, his vetoes were barely sustained. Finally, with another election looming, in the spring of

---

[41] On the Truman administration's efforts to preserve controls in 1945–46 and the disastrous political consequences, see Goodwin and Herren, "The Truman Years," pp. 9–35; Cady, "The Truman Administration's Reconversion Policies," pp. 136–73; Herren, "Wage-Price Policy during the Truman Administration," pp. 37–53; "Inflation and Politics, 1945–1946," in Barton J. Bernstein and Allen J. Matusow, *The Truman Administration: A Documentary History* (New York: Harper, 1968), pp. 46–85.

[42] See "Statement by the President upon Terminating Price and Wage Controls," November 9, 1946, *PPP 1946*, pp. 475–77.

[43] The Revenue Act of 1945, enacted in November, repealed the excess-profits tax, reduced corporate taxes from 40 to 38 percent, and cut personal taxes in all income brackets. The bill did not, however, do anything to reduce wartime excise taxes. See E. Cary Brown, "Federal Fiscal Policy in the Postwar Period," in Ralph E. Freeman, *Postwar Economic Trends in the United States* (New York: Harper, 1960), pp. 149–51; Randolph E. Paul, *Taxation in the United States* (Boston: Little, Brown, 1954), pp. 393–453.

1948 Congress succeeded in overriding the president and pushed through a further sizable reduction in the personal income tax.[44]

These cuts could not have come at a worse time. With inflationary pressures still substantial and with controls effectively eliminated, the Council of Economic Advisers had warned the president in December 1947 that "the only important restraint upon continued advance of prices will be found in the creation of the largest possible government surplus."[45] Surpluses were expected to be forthcoming, but only if the administration succeeded in holding the line on taxes and was able to go forward with further planned reductions in spending and, in particular, with cuts in the defense budget. Military expenditures had fallen off precipitously since the end of the war, but American forces remained scattered around the globe and, as relations with the Soviet Union cooled, it was not clear how quickly they could be brought home. Nevertheless, in fiscal year 1948 President Truman had given the armed services far less than they had originally hoped to receive, and he planned in the coming year to make further reductions.[46] Critical here, as the Bureau of the Budget acknowledged, was the assumption that "international events" would not "give rise to any pronounced change in present policies."[47]

In the opening months of 1948, just as Congress was making ready to cut taxes, this crucial assumption was overturned. The coup that brought commu-

---

[44] Paul, *Taxation in the United States*, pp. 453–501; Holmans, *United States Fiscal Policy*, pp. 56–101; Susan M. Hartmann, *Truman and the 80th Congress* (Columbia: University of Missouri Press, 1971), pp. 71–101; R. Alton Lee, "The Truman-80th Congress Struggle over Tax Policy," *Historian* 33, no. 1 (November 1970), pp. 68–82.

[45] Letter from Edwin Nourse, Leon Keyserling, and John Clark to the President, December 13, 1947. Harry S. Truman Library (HSTL), Papers of Edwin G. Nourse, Box 4, Daily Diary. See, in a similar vein, the statement on proposed tax cuts by Treasury Secretary John W. Snyder before the Senate Finance Committee, April 22, 1947. HSTL, Papers of John W. Snyder, Box 9, Congress (National). Also "Tax Policy and Inflation," December 19, 1947. HSTL, Papers of James E. Webb, Box 19, Bureau of the Budget: Tax Policy.

[46] At the end of 1946 military planners had proposed budgets of $14–15 billion for fiscal year 1948. Such expenditures, warned Budget Bureau Director James Webb, would make substantial tax cuts impossible for the foreseeable future and so "would invite irresistable popular antagonism and would result in more drastic budgetary cuts than could be justified." "Comments on the Size of the Military Defense Budget," October 8, 1946. HSTL, Webb Papers, Box 15, Bureau of the Budget, Federal Budget 1948 (1 of 2). In fact, in fiscal year 1948, the armed services received $10.5 billion. In his budget message for the 1949 fiscal year, delivered just before the onset of the Czech crisis, the president proposed a budget of just over $10 billion. See Warner R. Schilling, "The Politics of National Defense: Fiscal 1950," in Warner R. Schilling, Paul Y. Hammond, and Glenn H. Snyder, eds., *Strategy, Politics, and Defense Budgets* (New York: Columbia University Press, 1962), p. 29; "Annual Budget Message to the Congress, Fiscal Year 1949," January 12, 1948. *Public Papers of the Presidents of the United States: Harry S. Truman (1948)* (Washington, DC: U.S. Government Printing Office, 1964), pp. 26–29 (hereafter *PPP 1948*). In the fall of 1946 Truman had told Webb that he hoped defense spending could eventually be cut to a maintenance level of around $6 billion. Robert J. Donovan, *Conflict and Crisis: The Presidency of Harry S. Truman, 1945–1948* (New York: Norton, 1977), p. 261.

[47] "Preview of the 1949 Budget," May 21, 1947, HSTL, Webb Papers, Box 16, Bureau of the Budget, Subject File Federal Budget, 1949 (1 of 2).

nists to power in Czechoslovakia in late February and the "war scare" that followed led to an immediate scramble to add dollars to the defense budget, and, over the course of the spring and summer of 1948, to a more considered review of the nation's strategy and force posture.[48]

The president's economic advisers were quick to realize the dangers of boosting spending while simultaneously cutting taxes. If such a course were attempted, warned the staff of the Budget Bureau in March 1948, the alternatives would likely be "either inflation or price control over a wide area."[49] In the view of the Council of Economic Advisers, even *discussing* the possibility of greatly increased defense budgets would create "additional [inflationary] pressures." Under such conditions it might be wise from the start to "set aside . . . free market practices . . . and substitute a rather comprehensive set of controls."[50] If taxes were cut and spending raised substantially *without* imposing controls, the result would be to "turn loose or aggravate forces of inflation which are dangerous to our continued prosperity."[51]

Truman was in a bind. With an election approaching and Congress in an antitax mood, there was little prospect in the short run of regaining lost revenues. Renewed controls would also be unpopular, and in any case, Congress was unlikely to authorize them. But unchecked inflation could mean economic disaster and a political catastrophe for the president and his party even worse than the one they had suffered only two years before. Under the circumstances, Truman's only option seemed to be to hold down any increase in defense spending so as to minimize its inflationary effects while at the same time positioning himself to blame Congress if prices did, nevertheless, begin to spiral upward.

In March 1948 the president authorized a $3 billion supplement to the fiscal year 1949 budget request for $10 billion for defense purposes. In July, fully aware that his requests were unlikely to be granted, he asked Congress to reapply the wartime excess profits tax and to authorize the reimposition of a variety of controls.[52] When the Eightieth Congress refused his appeals for more reve-

---

[48] On the Czech crisis and its aftermath see Melvyn P. Leffler, *A Preponderance of Power: National Security, the Truman Administration, and the Cold War* (Stanford, CA: Stanford University Press, 1992), pp. 204–13. Walter Millis, ed., *The Forrestal Diaries* (New York: Viking, 1951), pp. 382–421. For the view that the entire crisis was cooked up by American military and industrial interests to justify increased defense spending see Frank Kofsky, *Harry S. Truman and the War Scare of 1948* (New York: St. Martin's, 1995).

[49] Memo from W. F. Schaub and Arthur Smithies to Webb, March 23, 1948, quoted in Goodwin and Herren, "The Truman Years," p. 54.

[50] Nourse, Keyserling, and Clark to Truman, March 24, 1948, HSTL, President's Secretary's Files (PSF), Box 143, Subject—Agencies, Council of Economic Advisers.

[51] Nourse, Keyserling, and Clark to Truman, March 24, 1948 HSTL, Papers of John D. Clark, Box 2, Letters and Memoranda to the President, 1948–49.

[52] See "Special Message: The President's Midyear Economic Report to the Congress," July 30, 1948, *PPP 1948*, pp. 424–28. The Council of Economic Advisers would have preferred to see individual income tax rates restored but, recognizing that "the determination of Congress to reduce personal income taxes" meant that this was "probably impossible . . . at this time," they proposed trying to reimpose the excess profits tax. For the economic, and some of the political, reasoning

nues and new regulatory authority, Truman denounced it for failing "to protect us from the inflationary dangers which threaten our prosperity," but he pressed ahead with his expanded defense program.[53]

The $3 billion supplement was a compromise, though one much closer to the president's preferences than to those of the military. Truman had originally intended to authorize only $1.5 billion in additional spending; the armed services had initially suggested a $9 billion supplement, an amount that would have nearly doubled the size of the original defense budget. Guided by the calculations of his Budget Bureau director, James Webb, Truman concluded that $3 billion was the maximum that could be added without creating immediate deficits and strong inflationary pressures. Even so, the president worried that if the money was spent in ways that created substantial future commitments, a $3 billion supplement would push defense budgets significantly higher than $13 billion in the years ahead. Given the existing structure of the tax system, and even assuming that favorable economic conditions produced maximum revenues, there was no question but that such expenditures would produce deficits of several billion dollars. "We would then be in a position," the president told Secretary of Defense James Forrestal and the service chiefs, "where even with full employment, business good, and the tax rates still at a very high level, we would be required to resort to large-scale deficit financing." This was unacceptable. Truman authorized the $3 billion supplement, but he also imposed a strict ceiling of $15 billion on any future defense expenditures (including $600 million for expanded strategic stockpiles), ordered the services not to undertake programs that might cause this figure to be exceeded, and requested a subsequent review to see if the ceiling could not be lowered.[54]

---

underlying these proposals, see Council of Economic Advisers, "The Government's Anti-Inflation Program," July 19, 1948, HSTL, Keyserling Papers, Box 2, Report File, 1946–53. Despite his public support for controls, there is evidence that Truman was leery of them. In a letter to Edwin Nourse, chairman of the Council of Economic Advisers, he warned that if the military were allowed "to overstep the bounds from an economic standpoint domestically" the country would be forced "to go back to a war footing—that is not what we want." Truman to Nourse, March 25, 1948, HSTL, Nourse Papers, Box 4. Daily Diary.

[53] "Statement by the President upon Signing Resolution 'To Aid in Protecting the Nation's Economy against Inflationary Pressures,'" August 16, 1948, *PPP 1948*, pp. 449–50.

[54] The best account of the formulation of the FY 1949 supplemental budget is Steven L. Rearden, *History of the Office of the Secretary of Defense*, vol. 1, *The Formative Years, 1947–1950* (Washington, DC: U.S. Government Printing Office, 1984), pp. 309–30. See also Kenneth W. Condit, *The History of the Joint Chiefs of Staff*, vol. 2, *The Joint Chiefs of Staff and National Policy, 1947–1949* (Wilmington, DE: Michael Glazier, 1979), pp. 191–214. Schilling, "The Politics of National Defense," pp. 28–47. The quotation is from a directive read by the president to the Joint Chiefs, the service secretaries, and the Secretary of Defense at a White House meeting on May 13, 1948. Portions of this directive are quoted in Millis, *The Forrestal Diaries*, pp. 435–39. Some of the president's economic advisers worried that even this program would take the nation perilously close to conditions that might produce runaway inflation. Anything more would certainly lead in the words of the Chairman of the Council of Economic Advisers, to "deficit financing, mounting taxation, and extensive economic controls." See the text of a speech to the alumni association of the Illinois Institute of Technology, "Economic Stabilization in a Troubled World," May 19, 1948. HSTL, Nourse Papers, Box 9, Speeches and Addresses, 1946–48.

As the spring crisis cooled, the military began for the first time a serious examination of the forces that would be needed to fight and win a war with the Soviet Union. Instructed by the Secretary of Defense to base their estimates "on military considerations alone," the services at first compiled a wish list with a staggering $30 billion price tag. Under considerable pressure from Forrestal, this figure was eventually reduced to roughly $23 billion. At his insistence the services also prepared a budget of close to $17 billion and designed a third force structure to fit within the president's $14.4 billion ceiling.[55]

The difficulty with both of these smaller estimates, in the view of the military planners, was that if the Soviets invaded Western Europe, the United States would be unable to conduct early operations on a scale sufficient to provide any realistic hope of victory. The smallest budget, in particular, would provide for forces incapable of doing much more than launching retaliatory air strikes from bases in Great Britain. If these did not cause an immediate collapse of Soviet power, the war would quickly be lost. The president's budget would commit the United States to a pure deterrent strategy, in other words, but it was inadequate to fund preparations for extended warfighting.[56]

Arguing that the armed forces were too greedy but that the president's ceiling was too low, Forrestal subsequently tried to nudge Truman upward toward his own happy median figure of $16.9 billion for fiscal year 1950. The president refused to budge. "The 14.4 billion budget is the one we will adopt," he told Forrestal curtly.[57] As the demoralized Secretary of Defense reported to a friend, Truman was "determined not to spend more than we take in in taxes. He is a hard-money man if ever I saw one."[58]

Neither the president's success in holding down the fiscal year 1950 defense budget nor his surprising election victory in November 1948 did much to alleviate the underlying fiscal problem with which he was faced. Toward the end of the year, Truman's economic advisers began to warn him again of the potential for serious inflation.[59] Even with federal spending held to projected levels, the

[55] On the construction of these estimates see Rearden, *The Formative Years*, pp. 335–51; K. Condit, *The Joint Chiefs of Staff and National Policy*, pp. 215–53; Schilling, "The Politics of National Defense," pp. 155–98.

[56] On military planning during this period see Steven T. Ross, *American War Plans, 1945–1950* (New York: Garland, 1988), pp. 79–101. A contemporary article, apparently based on leaks, compares the forces that could be purchased with differing amounts of money, and the strategies each was capable of supporting. "The Arms We Need," *Fortune* 38, no. 6, December 1948, pp. 77–82, 208–9. See also Joseph Alsop and Stuart Alsop, "If War Comes," *Saturday Evening Post*, September 11, 1948, pp. 15–17, 178, 180, 182–83.

[57] See Forrestal to Truman, December 1, 1948; Truman to Webb, December 2, 1948, HSTL, PSF, Box 150, Budget, Miscellaneous, 1945–53, Folder 2.

[58] See a letter from Forrestal to Walter G. Andrews, outgoing chairman of te House Armed Services Committee, December 13, 1948, in Millis, *The Forrestal Diaries*, pp. 536–37. This episode, and its shattering effects on Forrestal, are described in Townsend Hoopes and Douglas Brinkley, *Driven Patriot: The Life and Times of James Forrestal* (New York: Vantage, 1993), pp. 415–21.

[59] "Statement of the Chairman of the Council of Economic Advisers at Meeting of the Cabinet Committee on Anti-Inflation," December 16, 1948, HSTL, Nourse Papers, Box 5, Daily Diary.

reduced taxes voted into effect by Congress meant that deficits were likely, and this could only contribute to a strong upward push on prices.[60] To reduce inflationary pressure, Truman's advisers believed that taxes would have to be restored to levels sufficient to balance the budget and preferably to permit a surplus.[61]

Emboldened by his newfound political strength, in January 1949 Truman asked Congress to raise taxes by a total of $4 billion.[62] Most of the new revenue was to have come from increased taxes on corporations and the wealthy.[63] On the spending side, defense would be held at the level already determined, aid for European recovery would remain constant, and appropriations for an assortment of housing, health, education, and social welfare programs would be modestly increased (by under $1 billion).[64]

Neither the spending nor the revenue raising portions of the president's proposal met with any warmth on Capitol Hill. Despite Democratic gains, both houses of Congress continued to be dominated by coalitions of Republicans and the generally more conservative southern Democrats.[65] Truman's new program of higher taxes and expanded social welfare spending was regarded as "distinctly Left-of-Center."[66] The right-of-center Congress refused to act on it.

Unanticipated economic developments now intervened to force down defense spending. By the spring of 1949 evidence of an impending recession had begun to accumulate. As growth slowed, tax revenues would decline and, if nothing else changed, deficits would rise. The evident unwillingness of Congress to raise taxes (and, to the contrary, the likelihood that it would attempt to cut them still further) was already pointing toward a bigger deficit, even under conditions of full employment. If a moderate decline in economic activity occurred, the budget gap would widen still further. Truman's economic advisers were suffi-

[60] "Balancing the Budget," November 6, 1948. HSTL, Papers of Frederick J. Lawton, Box 5, Budget, National, FY 1950. The 1948 congressional tax cut was estimated by the Treasury to have cost close to $4 billion in lost revenues, a figure that would have been even greater if economic growth had been slower. See an internal memorandum to Treasury Secretary John Snyder, "Budget Revenue Estimates," December 21, 1948, HSTL, Snyder Papers, Box 3, Authorization—Budget (general).

[61] See a memo from the CEA to the president, "Anti-Inflation Program," December 7, 1948, HSTL, Papers of Leon Keyserling, Box 2, Report File, 1946–53.

[62] "Annual Budget Message to the Congress: Fiscal Year 1950," January 10, 1949, in *Public Papers of the Presidents of the United States: Harry S. Truman (1949)* (Washington, DC: U.S. Government Printing Office, 1964), p. 45 (hereafter *PPP 1949*).

[63] Regarding the possible magnitude and precise form of possible tax increases, see the internal deliberations of the Treasury Department in late 1948 as recorded in HSTL, Papers of L. Laszlo Ecker-Racz, Box 1, 1949 Tax Program. Also "Annual Message to the Congress on the State of the Union," January 5, 1949. *PPP 1949*, p. 4.

[64] See "Annual Budget Message to the Congress," *PPP 1949*, pp. 50–95.

[65] Regarding the composition and attitudes of the Eighty-first Congress see Alonzo L. Hamby, *Man of the People: A Life of Harry S. Truman* (New York: Oxford University Press, 1995), pp. 490–98. Also Robert J. Donovan, *Tumultuous Years: The Presidency of Harry S. Truman, 1949–1953* (New York: Norton, 1982), pp. 22–24.

[66] Holmans, *United States Fiscal Policy*, p. 104.

ciently imbued with Keynesian principles not to insist that revenues be made to match expenditures in the midst of a recession and, indeed, they recognized that a modest deficit could contribute to a more rapid recovery. But with inflation still believed to be the nation's primary underlying problem, they feared that the deficits now looming were simply too large to be healthy.[67]

Seeking to stimulate the economy without triggering a new round of inflation, Budget Bureau Director Frank Pace therefore recommended that the president back away from his proposed tax increases, while at the same time reducing expenditures by between $2 and $4 billion. Such changes would preserve a gap between revenues and expenditures in the short run, thereby easing the nation's economy toward recovery. As growth returned and revenues increased, a leaner spending program would make it easier in the long run to balance the budget, even if Congress could not be persuaded to raise taxes. The only question that remained was where spending should be cut.[68]

The answer was not long in coming. On July 1, 1949, Truman once again summoned his top economic and military advisers to the White House and read to them from a prepared statement. Unless there was "an unexpected expansion in national income," it now appeared inevitable that, for at least the next two years, there would be "a deficit so large that firm measures should be taken to reduce it." With military and foreign aid programs consuming half of the federal budget, and with veterans' benefits and interest payments taking up another third, it was "evident" that "adjustments downward must be made in the . . . national security programs." Accordingly, the president ordered the Defense Department to lower its planned spending limit by roughly $2 billion and to "fix a restrictive ceiling of $13 billion" on all future military expenditures. Barring an unanticipated worsening of the international situation, this new ceiling was to be permanent and would provide the framework for all planning of forces and strategy.[69]

Whether because they had become hardened to the realities of their situation or because they had feared something even more drastic, the military did not offer any significant resistance to these new restrictions.[70] The president's deci-

---

[67] See "Budget Projections, 1950–1954," May 6, 1949, in HSTL, PSF, Box 150, Subject, Agencies—Bureau of the Budget, Budget Projections, 1950–1954; Frank Pace (Budget Bureau Director) to Truman, "Budget Alternatives for 1951" (mid-May 1949?).

[68] Because controllable domestic programs were so small and because the government was deeply committed to supporting European recovery, Pace recommended that the president lower the ceiling on defense expenditures from $15 billion to $13 billion. Pace to Truman, "Basic Policies with Respect to 1951 Budget Ceilings," (June 1949?), HSTL, PSF, Box 150, Subject, Agencies, Bureau of the Budget—Budget FY 1951.

[69] "Statement of the President before the National Security Council of the National Military Establishment, the Joint Chiefs of Staff, the Chairman of the Council of Economic Advisers, the Economic Cooperation Administrator, and the Director of the Bureau of the Budget," July 1, 1949, HSTL, PSF, Box 150, Subject, Agencies, Bureau of the Budget—Budget FY 1951. On the events leading up to this meeting see Rearden, *History of the Office of the Secretary of Defense* 1:361–76; Condit, *History of the Joint Chiefs of Staff* 2:257–73.

[70] At the end of his description of the July 1 meeting, Frederick Lawton notes, "The remarkable

sion did, however, give rise to an important and revealing dispute among his economic experts. Following the July 1 meeting, Truman directed the Council of Economic Advisers to consider the overall effects of his proposed budget.[71]

The response of CEA Chairman Edwin Nourse to these queries was characteristically cautious and dour. Nourse, whose views hovered somewhere between the emerging commercial Keynesian consensus and traditional fiscal orthodoxy, argued that the nation had reached the limit of what it could afford to spend on defense. Additional expenditures were out of the question, and deeper cuts would be prudent. Provided that taxes remained unchanged and the economy recovered quickly, the planned defense program would not prevent an eventual return to balanced budgets. In the meantime, small, diminishing deficits were acceptable, although there was a real danger that the appearance "that the Government was accepting deficits as a way of life" would demoralize business, reduce investment, and slow growth. If taxes were cut, however, or if the recovery to full employment was slow, a barely tolerable situation would quickly become impossible. Nor were these far-fetched contingencies. "There is," Nourse observed, "a strong and growing resistance to 'war taxes in peacetime.'" Congress might well cut taxes further, plunging the federal budget deeper into deficit and sending inflation soaring. As parsimonious as it was, the president's program might not be sustainable. Increases in defense spending and foreign aid, on the other hand, would require either higher taxes (which "the temper of Congress and the country" appeared to rule out) or, most likely, bigger deficits.[72]

Nourse's CEA colleagues John Clark and Leon Keyserling, the leading administration advocate of growthsmanship, took a much more relaxed and expansive view. In a dissenting memorandum to the president they argued not only that a $13 billion defense budget was acceptable, but that, if need be, even more money could be spent without doing the nation any grievous harm. If Congress cut taxes again, some change in policy might be necessary. In the

thing was that there was no critical comment of any sort, and no complaint that the job couldn't be done within the dollar figures." For an account of this meeting see Frederick Lawton, "Meeting with the President on 1951 Budget Ceilings for National Defense and Foreign Aid," July 1, 1949, HSTL, Papers of Frederick Lawton, Box 6, Bureau of the Budget, General, Meetings with the President. At a meeting with the Joint Chiefs in late June, Secretary of Defense Louis Johnson had said that he expected congressional pressure to cut military appropriations to $10 billion in FY 1951, and perhaps even to $7.5 billion in FY 1952. Rearden, *The Formative Years*, p. 371.

[71] See Truman to Nourse, [July 5, 1949?], HSTL, Keyserling Papers, Box 3, Report File 1946–53, 1951 Budget Study.

[72] Nourse to Truman, August 26, 1949, HSTL, Nourse Papers, Box 6, Daily Diary. See also his bitter accounts of his confrontations with Keyserling in two memorandums for the record, dated August 22 and 26, 1949, ibid. Nourse also expressed his views more formally in a memorandum to the National Security Council, "Domestic Impact of Budget Ceilings for the Fiscal Year 1951," September 30, 1949, in United States Department of State, *Foreign Relations of the United States, 1949* (Washington, DC: U.S. Government Printing Office, 1974), pp. 394–96 (hereafter *FRUS 1949*). See also his more guarded public comments in a CBS radio broadcast, "Economic Implications of Military Preparedness," August 24, 1949, HSTL, PSF, Box 143, Subject, Agencies, Council of Economic Advisers.

meantime, there was every reason to expect that the projected spending over revenues would contribute to a rapid recovery and to a situation in which "with expanding business activity and increasing employment enlarging the tax base, the deficit . . . would soon be overtaken." In general, "our economy can sustain—in fact must be subjected to policies which *make it able to sustain*—such military outlays as are vital" to the preservation of peace and security.[73]

Although Keyserling and Clark did not spell it out, the direction of their reasoning was clear enough. Growth would provide the escape from what Nourse had portrayed as a tragic dilemma. And among the policies to which the economy might have to be "subjected" in order to get it to grow fast enough were deliberate federal budget deficits. When the nation's economy was growing at less than its full potential, such deficits would eventually be self-correcting, and additional increments of government expenditure could be, in effect, self-financing.

This dispute was one in a series of increasingly bitter and open disagreements that culminated at the end of 1949 in Nourse's resignation and, some months later, in Keyserling's ascension to the chairmanship of the CEA. Nourse may have lost the bureaucratic battle but, in the short run at least, he won the war over policy. The $13 billion ceiling on defense spending still stood, and down to the outbreak of the Korean War and despite a concerted effort by Keyserling and others to persuade him to do so, the president would show little inclination to lift it.

NSC 68 (1950)

Truman's reaffirmation of the $13 billion ceiling in the summer of 1949 was followed almost immediately by a series of troubling events and by a concerted, sustained effort within the government to persuade him of the need for bigger defense budgets. The broad outlines of this story are familiar and need only be summarized here: In September 1949 the United States received definitive evidence of a successful Soviet atomic bomb test. One month later, Chinese Communist forces declared victory over their Nationalist opponents. In November the Atomic Energy Commission briefed the president on the possibility of producing a new fusion "super" weapon many times more powerful than the atomic bomb. At the end of January 1950, in light of all these developments, Truman ordered a special committee to review American national strategy. After two months of intense, secretive deliberation, in April the committee presented its report, designated NSC 68, to the National Security Council.[74]

NSC 68 was, in essence, a battering ram with which its authors hoped to

[73] Keyserling and Clark to Truman, August 26, 1949. HSTL, Keyserling Papers, Box 2, Report File, 1946–53.

[74] The best brief overview of the origins of NSC 68 is Ernest R. May, "NSC 68: The Theory and Politics of Strategy," in May, ed., *American Cold War Strategy: Interpreting NSC 68* (Boston: Bedford Books, 1993), pp. 1–19.

shatter the existing budget ceiling. Later described by Dean Acheson as a device with which "to bludgeon the mass mind of 'top government,'" the report was, in fact, "aimed at only one person: Harry Truman."[75] While it contained no specific cost estimates or recommendations for new programs, the paper's purpose was clearly to convince the president that an increasingly menacing world required major increases in spending on defense and foreign military assistance. Prudent enough not to reveal their preferences at the outset, the principal authors of NSC 68 appear nevertheless to have agreed among themselves that the situation demanded a roughly 300 percent increase in security expenditures.[76] Upon receiving their report, Truman responded immediately that he was "particularly anxious" to have "a clearer indication of the programs which are envisaged . . . including estimates of the probable cost of such programs."[77] This request led in May to the formation of an ad hoc committee of the National Security Council and to the initiation within the Defense Department of a detailed force-planning exercise. Scheduled for completion in the fall, the attempt to translate general arguments for rearmament into a specific set of plans and programs was overtaken in June by the onset of the Korean war. NSC 68 was adopted as a formal expression of U.S. policy in September 1950 and, over the next two years, security spending would rise more rapidly than even its drafters had anticipated.

Precisely what would have happened to NSC 68 and, more importantly, to the defense budget in the absence of the Korean crisis is a question that continues to stir debate among historians.[78] A definitive answer is, of course, im-

---

[75] Dean Acheson, *Present at the Creation: My Years in the State Department* (New York: Norton, 1969), p. 374. Alonzo L. Hamby, *Man of the People: A Life of Harry S. Truman* (New York: Oxford University Press, 1995), p. 527.

[76] There is some confusion on the precise magnitude of the buildup that the authors of NSC 68 had in mind, due in part to their own uncertainty and circumspection at the time and in part to the question of whether, in retrospective discussions, they are talking about defense alone or defense and foreign assistance combined. In 1950 the United States planned to spend $13 billion on its own armed forces and roughly $4 billion on foreign assistance, of which around 75 percent was for economic aid and the rest for military assistance. Paul Nitze, the principal author of NSC 68, has said that he envisioned a "defense budget" of around $40 billion. Acheson put the cost of "the sort of rearmament and rehabilitation-of-forces program that we recommended, at the rate we thought necessary" at "about fifty billion dollars per annum." These figures are not inconsistent, assuming that Nitze's figure does not include increases for foreign assistance. Paul H. Nitze, *From Hiroshima to Glasnost: At the Center of Decision* (New York: Grove Weidenfeld, 1989), pp. 96–97. Acheson, *Present at the Creation*, p. 377.

[77] Truman to James Lay, Executive Secretary of the National Security Council, August 12, 1950, United States Department of State, *Foreign Relations of the United States, 1950*, vol. 1 (Washington, DC: U.S. Government Printing Office, 1977), p. 235 (hereafter *FRUS 1950*).

[78] For a range of opinion on this question, from those who think the defense budget would have remained substantially unchanged to those who believe major increases were in the offing, even without Korea, see: Melvyn P. Leffler, *A Preponderance of Power: National Security, the Truman Administration, and the Cold War* (Stanford, CA: Stanford University Press, 1992), pp. 355–60; David Callahan, *Dangerous Capabilities: Paul Nitze and the Cold War* (New York: HarperCollins, 1990), pp. 120–23; Hamby, *Man of the People*, pp. 527–29; Robert A. Pollard, *Economic Security and the Origins of the Cold War, 1945–1950* (New York: Columbia University Press, 1985), p. 240;

possible. By the spring of 1950 an impressive coalition in favor of increased spending had formed within the executive branch. This grouping gained strength and credibility from the fact that it was led not by the uniformed military, who were always susceptible to charges of alarmism and special plead-ing, but by top civilian officials in the State Department and the White House. In previous budget battles the armed services had proved to be no match for the guardians of fiscal responsibility. Now it was the "mice in the Budget Bureau," as Dean Acheson contemptuously labeled them, who found themselves isolated and outnumbered.[79]

It is certainly conceivable that even without Korea, the advocates of smaller defense budgets, including most notably the president himself, would have found themselves "trapped" and compelled to change course.[80] But what of the intellectual, ideological, institutional, and interest-based constraints on in-creased extraction and expanded defense spending that had been so much in evidence only a few months before? How, exactly, were those constraints to be overcome and an increase in defense spending financed?

Reflecting its bureaucratic origins, and perhaps also the uncertainties of its principal authors, NSC 68 contained not one, but two distinct and seemingly contradictory ways of dealing with this issue. On the one hand, as is most often remembered, the body of the document asserted that economic growth could provide an all-but-painless solution to the nation's problems. If the United States could achieve "a substantial absolute increase in output," it would be able to fund a major military buildup "without suffering a decline in its real standard of living . . . because the required resources could be obtained by siphoning off a part of the annual increment in the gross national product."[81] On the other hand, in its conclusions, NSC 68 called for "sacrifice," noted that a "concerted build-up . . . will be costly and will involve significant domestic financial and economic adjustments," and pointed to the likelihood that it would have to be paid for by a "reduction of Federal expenditures for purposes other than defense and foreign assistance" and, finally, by "increased taxes."[82] Any judgment about plausible alternative trajectories for defense spending in the early 1950s would need to depend on an assessment of the obstacles confront-ing each of these courses of action.

On the critical question of what specific policies would be needed to achieve a higher growth rate, NSC 68 had surprisingly little to say beyond the tantaliz-

---

Samuel Wells, "Sounding the Tocsin: NSC 68 and the Soviet Threat," *International Security* 4, no. 2 (Fall 1979), pp. 116–58; May, "NSC 68," p. 15; Benjamin Fordham, *Building the Cold War Consensus: The Political Economy of U.S. National Security Policy, 1949–1951* (Ann Arbor: University of Michigan Press, 1998).

[79] Acheson, *Present at the Creation*, p. 377.

[80] May, "NSC 68," p. 14.

[81] NSC 68, April 4, 1950, in *FRUS 1950*, p. 258.

[82] The call for sacrifice comes in the last sentence of the report. The recommendations for spend-ing cuts and higher taxes are items 11 and 12 in a 12-point "comprehensive and decisive program to win peace and frustrate the Kremlin design." Ibid., pp. 292, 285.

ing observation that accelerated growth "would permit, *and might itself be aided by* a build-up of the economic and military strength of the United States and the free world."[83] In other words, if they were not entirely offset by higher taxes, increased defense expenditures would add to aggregate demand and help to fuel economic expansion; properly managed, the buildup could be made to pay for itself.

Extraordinary powers of perception are not necessary to detect in these arguments the fine hand of Leon Keyserling.[84] Since displacing Edwin Nourse at the helm of the Council of Economic Advisers in late 1949, Keyserling had pushed hard to put growth at the center of the Truman administration's economic agenda. In articles, speeches, offical reports, and internal memorandums he sang the praises of "the $300 billion economy," and as evidenced by Truman's 1950 economic report (which Keyserling, in typically immodest fashion, first wrote and then cited approvingly), his rhetoric had an obvious appeal to the president.[85]

In the more public formulations of his agenda for economic growth, Keyserling was clearer about ends than about the means with which he proposed to attain them. "Coordination of national economic policy" would certainly be required, though not "central planning," still less "economic statism."[86] Though the market would do most of the work, Keyserling argued that "many public programs" (including aid for education and health care, anti-trust regulation, help for small business, and, in some cases, "public investment in fundamental resource development") were "essential . . . to promote private industrial expansion." Finally, while balanced budgets were "desirable," what was "even more vital" was to avoid "hysteria in our thinking about the budget." In the event of another world war or great depression, "talk about 'budget balance' would be trivia." In recessions, such as those the nation had experienced in 1949, temporary deficits could help to speed recovery. In general, Keyserling concluded, "the surest route to a balanced budget [is] to follow those policies which maximize . . . our prospects for economic growth."[87]

In private, though still cautious and circumspect, Keyserling was somewhat

---

[83] Ibid., p. 258 (emphasis added).

[84] On Keyserling's indirect role in the drafting of NSC 68 see Flash, *Economic Advice*, p. 38.

[85] For Truman's invocation of the $300 billion goal, which he argued could be achieved in five years, see "Annual Message to the Congress: The President's Economic Report," January 6, 1950, in *Public Papers of the Presidents of the United States: Harry S. Truman (1950)* (Washington, DC: U.S. Government Printing Office, 1965), p. 23 (hereafter *PPP 1950*). Regarding the appeal of Keyserling's ideas to Truman see Hamby, *Man of the People*, pp. 500–501.

[86] On the distinction between coordinated policy and central planning, see the Fourth Annual Report to the President by the Council of Economic Advisers, *Business and Government* (Washington, DC: U.S. Government Printing Office, December 1949), p. 23. On the evils of "statism" see a speech by Keyserling at the New School, "The New Truman Administration—Will Its Policies and Planning Lead Us toward State Socialism?" January 18, 1949, in HSTL, Keyserling Papers, Box 18, vol. 5, Articles and Speeches.

[87] Leon H. Keyserling, "Planning for a $300 Billion Economy," *New York Times Magazine*, June 18, 1950, pp. 25–26.

more open about the role of federal fiscal policy in stimulating, and perhaps also in sustaining and accelerating, economic expansion. In the winter of 1949 and the spring of 1950, when the question before the president was how to deal with a budget that remained stubbornly out of balance, Keyserling urged leniency and patience. Equity considerations (and the possibility of electoral gain) might dictate the closing of some loopholes and perhaps also the elimination or reduction of certain excise taxes, but, Keyserling argued, substantial increases in individual and corporate taxes aimed at bringing the budget more quickly into balance were unnecessary, undesirable, and, in all likelihood, politically infeasible. With a recovery underway, revenues would soon begin to rise and the budget would begin to come back into balance. Neither major tax increases nor reductions in planned expenditures were required.[88]

Keyserling was here advocating toleration of relatively small deficits for comparatively limited periods of time with the prospect of balanced budgets, and even substantial surpluses, looming just over the horizon. Whatever his initial misgivings, Truman proved willing in the second half of 1949 to accept this advice. When the moment of truth arrived and the first postwar recession loomed, Truman embraced the emerging commercial Keynesian consensus and permitted the budget to slip temporarily into the red. Whether in the early 1950s he would have been willing to go much further—deliberately running up even bigger deficits by boosting defense spending without raising taxes to match and then sustaining those deficits for a number of years in the hopes of stimulating still faster growth and still more revenues—is another question altogether.

There are reasons to doubt it. To begin with, there is no evidence that Truman had abandoned his fundamental view that protracted deficits were not only dangerous, but positively immoral. As historian Alonzo Hamby points out, although the president was "flexible enough about his belief in a balanced budget to accept a deficit during the 1949 recession . . . he felt far greater pride in the surpluses he had run previously."[89] The careful, defensive way in which Truman justified even the limited deficits that he felt compelled to accept in 1949 and 1950, his eagerness not to take credit for their role in resuscitating the economy but to blame them on ill-advised Republican tax cuts, and his subsequent determination to fund the Korean War on a pay-as-you-go basis all suggest a continuing attachment to the traditional verities of "responsible" public finance.

Even if Truman had become convinced of the desirability of larger deficits, he would have had good reason to be concerned about the response of Congress. In 1949, when it first became clear that the budget was heading out of balance, Republicans and conservative Democrats had responded by pressing

---

[88] See a memo from Keyserling and Clark to Truman, "The Tax Program," December 21, 1949, in HSTL, Clark Papers, Box 2, Letters and Memoranda to the President, 1948–49. Also a memo from Keyserling to Charles Murphy, "Legislative Recommendations Concerning Fiscal Policy and Taxes," December 17, 1949, HSTL, Keyserling Papers, Box 8, Staff.

[89] See "Hamby's Commentary," in May, *American Cold War Strategy*, pp. 153–54.

for deep cuts in government spending.[90] If Truman sought now to boost defense expenditures without significantly raising taxes, he would have to face the likelihood of renewed congressional attacks, most likely on foreign economic assistance and domestic social welfare spending.

There was, finally, the threat of inflation. Keyserling sought to soothe the president's anxieties on this score, arguing that because "unused human and industrial resources were still so large," there was "little danger," at least in the short run, that modest deficits would trigger an upward spiral in prices.[91] What an accelerated military buildup and the prospect of significantly larger and more sustained deficits might do to the economy was unclear. As Hamby points out, fear of inflation and memories of what it had done to his party only four years before were "indelibly etched" in Truman's mind.[92] Some of Truman's advisers may have been willing to accept bigger deficits and the risk of renewed inflation as the price of rapidly expanding American power, but at least in the first half of 1950, the president himself "displayed no such disposition."[93]

What of the bitter pill of tax hikes and social spending cuts? Truman had already demonstrated his desire to increase domestic expenditures, albeit to still comparatively modest levels, and his determination if at all possible to avoid reductions in existing programs. In 1949 he had preferred lowering the ceiling on defense spending to trimming the already sparse domestic portions of the federal budget. There is nothing in Truman's initial reactions to NSC 68 to suggest that its arguments had changed his preferences. To the contrary, his wary response seems to have been due largely to concern over its implications for his domestic program.[94]

Supposing that Truman had been willing or, more plausibly, had somehow been compelled by circumstances to cancel the Fair Deal and cut social spending to the bone, he still would not have been able to free sufficient resources to fund the kind of military program that his strategic advisers had in mind. In fiscal year 1951 the president was proposing to spend an extra $1.3 billion on programs for social welfare, health, housing and community development, education and general research, and natural resource development. The sum total for these programs, which included many relatively uncontroversial items, was only around $6.6 billion. Adding expenditures for agriculture, transportation, and communication (the other major "controllable" items in the budget, as compared to veterans' benefits, interest on the national debt, and the cost of government operations) would bring the total to something over $10 billion.[95] Plaus-

[90] At that time, congressional conservatives threatened to cut all federal spending by 5 to 10 percent in order to achieve an immediate balanced budget. See Holmans, *United States Fiscal Policy*, pp. 115–17.

[91] See a letter from Keyserling and Clark to Lawton, April 28, 1950, HSTL, Keyserling Papers, Box 8, Staff.

[92] See "Hamby's Commentary," in May, ed., *American Cold War Strategy*, pp. 153–54.

[93] Leffler, *A Preponderance of Power*, p. 358.

[94] See May, "NSC 68," p. 14; Hamby, *Man of the People*, p. 528.

[95] See the breakdown in "Annual Budget Message," *PPP 1950*, p. 55.

MONEY **113**

ible reductions in all of these programs put together would have paid for only a fraction of a $30 to $40 billion buildup.[96]

In the end, a major military expansion would almost certainly have required substantially higher taxes. This was something that even Keyserling, with his relentless optimism about the growth potential of the American economy and the revenue-raising capacities of the existing tax system, was prepared at times to admit.[97] Keyserling saw no particular economic problem with raising taxes, especially as faster growth increased profits and incomes, but he was acutely sensitive to the possible political difficulties of doing so.[98] Truman too had no principled objection to recommending higher taxes, especially on corporations and the wealthy, but by the middle of 1950 he already had ample evidence of the resistance that any such proposal would face.

In January 1949 the newly reelected president had tried and failed to raise taxes. One year later, with an off-year election coming up, Truman tried again, this time requesting a more modest package of changes aimed at generating a total of $1 billion in additional revenues.[99] This proposal fared little better. After almost six months of deliberation, the House Ways and Means Committee appeared ready to report a bill that would have produced a net *loss* in revenue, an outcome that the president had already labeled unacceptable and declared he would veto.[100] On May 31, 1950, an internal Treasury Department analysis of

[96] *FRUS 1950*, p. 285.

[97] Keyserling objected to NSC 68's blunt appeal for higher taxes, but he did not entirely rule out the possibility that they might be necessary. Responding to a formal request for CEA comments, one of Keyserling's deputies, at his direction, suggested that the call for spending cuts and tax increases be changed to a recommendation for "a general program designed to promote the full utilization of the United States potential for economic growth." This phrasing would "avoid pre-judgment." Stimulating growth might require "some selective increases" in nondefense expenditures. "It might also be found that certain tax concessions, as well as tax increases, might be an important element in such a general program." A big buildup might require a somewhat heavier tax burden, but it was important to disabuse Congress and the public of the notion that "increased defense must mean equivalently lowered living standards, higher taxes, and a proliferation of controls." Hamilton Q. Dearborn to James Lay, "Comments on NSC 68," May 8, 1950. *FRUS 1950*, p. 310.

[98] See, for example, his December 1949 memos on tax policy, cited above.

[99] The president's plan called for some cuts in excises, closing of certain loopholes, and increases in estate, gift, and corporate income taxes. "Special Message to the Congress on Tax Policy," January 23, 1950, *PPP 1950*, pp. 120–28. The internal deliberations leading up to these proposals are detailed in HSTL, Ecker-Racz Papers, Box 1, 1950 Tax Program, vol. 1.

[100] Members of both parties agreed easily to reduce some excise taxes, but Republicans balked at raising corporate taxes to make up the difference. The Democratic members of the House Ways and Means Committee were finally able, on a party-line vote, to force approval of a corporate tax hike, thereby converting a revenue losing bill to one that was close to being "revenue neutral." As of June 22 the proposed legislation was still expected to lose about $170 million in the coming fiscal year. See "Summary of Estimated Revenue Effect of Tax Changes Adopted by the Ways and Means Committee as of June 22, 1950," HSTL, Snyder Papers, Box 31, Taxes, Folder 1. This bill was expected to encounter difficulty in the House as a whole and in the Senate. See John D. Morris, "Rise of $500,000,000 in Corporation Tax Gains House Favor," *New York Times*, June 16, 1950, p. 1; Morris, "Corporation Taxes to Rise $433,000,000 under House Bill," *New York Times*, June 18, 1950, p. 1; Morris, "Corporation Levy Made Big Tax Issue," *New York Times*, June 25, 1950, p. 35. Also Holmans, *United States Fiscal Policy*, pp. 124–27.

congressional action to date suggested that "there was increasing acceptance of the idea that there might be no tax legislation this year."[101] On June 19, one week before the start of fighting in Korea, Treasury Secretary John Snyder expressed serious doubts about "the possibility of [raising] additional revenues from new taxes prior to the next presidential election barring some major emergency."[102]

If the Korean War had not broken out, Truman might still have tried to use NSC 68–style rhetoric to create a "virtual emergency," stirring public anxiety and perhaps lessening congressional resistance to higher taxes.[103] While some of his security advisers may have favored it, Truman had good reason, given his other concerns, to be cautious of such an approach. Calling for a sudden increase in defense spending in the absence of an obvious crisis might have seemed tantamount to an admission that his previous policies for dealing with the communist threat had been misguided and inadequate. Any proposal for substantially higher taxes would also inevitably have provoked a renewed conservative assault on the president's domestic program. As Keyserling had warned him, if asked to raise taxes the "Dixiecrat-Republican coalition" would prefer instead to cut spending; foreign aid would come under fire and new public assistance and education programs would "encounter much greater resistance."[104] An atmosphere of intensified crisis would have made it that much more difficult to justify spending for "nonessential" purposes.

We cannot know if a war *scare* would have been sufficient to squeeze a tax hike out of Congress. We do know that Truman, having read NSC 68, was reluctant to use it to achieve this goal. In the event, the president did not invoke new external threats, and it does not appear, prior to June 1950, that he stood any chance of getting substantial new revenues for an ambitious military buildup. What seems more likely is that in the early 1950s, defense spending and spending on foreign military assistance would have risen by the nontrivial but still comparatively modest sum of several billions of dollars. The additional resources would have come not from higher taxes, or dramatically increased deficits, or drastic cuts in social spending, but from the revenues generated by a continuing domestic recovery and by planned reductions in spending on foreign economic assistance.[105] In an alternative world, one in which North Korea had

---

[101] L. Laszlo Ecker-Racz, "Status of the Tax Program," May 31, 1950, HSTL, Ecker-Racz Papers, Box 1, 1950 Tax Program, Vol. 1.

[102] Frederick Lawton to Truman, "Present Fiscal and Economic Outlook Affecting the Establishment of 1952 Fiscal Year Budget Ceilings," June 19, 1950, HSTL, PSF, Subject, Agencies—Bureau of the Budget, Budget FY 1952–53.

[103] Some consideration was given to doing this, either in the summer or the fall of 1950. See a memorandum from Lay to the ad hoc committee on NSC 68, "Initial Questions Confronting the Committee," April 28, 1950, *FRUS 1950*, pp. 293–96.

[104] Keyserling to Murphy, "Legislative Recommendations."

[105] This was the course of action advocated by the Bureau of the Budget, which noted that "a moderate increase in security expenditures, partially or wholly offset by the prospective decline in ECA [Economic Cooperation Administration], can be undertaken without serious economic consequences." See a memo by William Schaub of the Bureau of the Budget staff to James Lay, "Com-

not invaded the South, a 30 percent increase in military expenditures was plausible; a 300 percent increase was not.

THE KOREAN WAR (1950–1952)

The Korean War is typically viewed as marking a decisive turning point in the history of the Cold War and, in particular, in the evolution of American defense spending. The outbreak of fighting on the Korean peninsula and the fear that it would be followed shortly by the onset of a third world war, shattered previously existing constraints and permitted defense budgets to soar. With the old barriers removed, expenditures and forces grew dramatically and did not, once the fighting had ended, shrink to anything resembling their earlier dimensions. The war was the event that turned the crank and ratcheted the American military effort to levels far higher than would otherwise have been attained.[106]

This account is accurate, as far as it goes. While the Korean War certainly weakened the constraints on defense spending, it did not do so completely or permanently. In fact, on closer inspection, what is most remarkable about the events that followed the North Korean invasion is just how brief the opening for an accelerated buildup actually was, and how quickly the forces opposing higher expenditures reasserted themselves. Within a matter of months, opposition to financial extraction began to mount, and by the end of 1951, military planners had been forced to revise downward their expectations of the kinds of forces they could expect to maintain on a permanent basis once the fighting had ended. Without Korea, those forces and the budgets needed to pay for them would have been far smaller. But even with American soldiers fighting and dying, and even at a time when the possibility of a wider war seemed very real and the probability that it would involve terrible destruction to the United States seemed to be growing, there was strong downward pressure on defense expenditures. During the war, as before and after, the reluctance of Congress to raise taxes was the critical factor in this process.[107]

---

ments of the Bureau of the Budget," May 8, 1950, *FRUS 1950*, p. 305. Some weeks earlier the Budget Bureau had estimated that the completion of planned economic aid programs could free up as much as $3 billion by 1953. Lawton, "Current Issues." Truman encouraged the Bureau of the Budget in its approach, telling Lawton at a White House meeting that "we were to continue to raise any questions that we had on this program and that it definitely was not as large in scope as some of the people seemed to think." See "Memorandum for the Record," May 23, 1950, HSTL, Lawton Papers, Box 6, Bureau of the Budget, General VI, Meetings with the President.

[106] For the best brief overview of the war's importance see Robert Jervis, "The Impact of the Korean War on the Cold War," *Journal of Conflict Resolution* 24, no. 4 (December 1980), pp. 563–92.

[107] The relative lack of scholarly attention to the internal aspects of the Korean War has only recently begun to be remedied. See the work of Paul G. Pierpaoli, "The Price of Peace: The Korean War Mobilization and Cold War Rearmament, 1950–1953" (Ph.D. dissertation, Ohio State University, Department of History, 1995); and Haejong Lee, "The Political Economy of Rearmament: Truman's 1953 Military Budget in Historical Perspective" (paper presented to the American Political Science Association convention, 1995).

Taxes

The efforts of the Truman administration to raise revenues to fight the Korean War and fund a greatly accelerated military buildup unfolded in four stages, with resistance growing at each until, by the fourth, it had become insurmountable. On the eve of war it had appeared likely that Congress would defy the president's earlier request for an extra $1 billion in revenues and would, instead, cut taxes by a net total of several tens of millions of dollars. Within three months of the North Korean attack the Truman administration had requested and Congress had readily approved a substantial across-the-board rate hike that added close to $5 billion in annual revenues. Before the war began, Congress had been eager to cut excise taxes, willing to plug some loopholes, and sharply divided on the desirability of raising corporate tax rates. Higher personal income taxes were not even on the menu of possible options. In the initial heat of crisis, the House and Senate agreed quickly to retain the loophole-closing provisions of the old bill and to eliminate the proposed excise tax reductions (thereby leaving most excises at World War II levels), while at the same time raising taxes on corporate and personal incomes to where they had stood in 1945.[108]

Despite its sweeping character, the Revenue Act of 1950 was acknowledged at the outset to be a stopgap measure, necessary to help cover the initial costs of war and to dampen inflationary pressures, but insufficient by itself to meet the larger needs that lay ahead.[109] As its next step, the Truman administration planned once again, as it had during the crisis of March 1948, to propose a reimposition of the World War II tax on "excess" corporate profits. Anticipating that such a measure would stir strong opposition from business and congressional conservatives (who regarded it as "socialistic"), the administration decided, despite the urgings of some liberal Democrats, to delay its request until after an interim tax bill had been approved and the mid-term elections had passed.[110]

---

[108] For accounts of these events see Holmans, *United States Fiscal Policy*, pp. 135–40; Witte, *The Politics and Development of the Federal Income Tax*, pp. 137–39; Brown, "Federal Fiscal Policy," pp. 159–60. A very helpful summary of the entire Korean War tax story is contained in a memorandum by Treasury Department official L. Laszlo Ecker-Racz, "Taxation for Defense," December 1952, HSTL, Ecker-Racz Papers, Box 7, Taxation for Defense; on the Revenue Act of 1950, see pp. 3–9. For a summary of the act's provisions see "The Revenue Act of 1950," December 20, 1950, HSTL, Ecker-Racz Papers, Box 1, 1950 Tax Program, Vol. 2.

[109] See a memorandum from Treasury Secretary John Snyder to the president, "Immediate Need for Stop-Gap Tax Legislation," July 24, 1950, HSTL, Ecker-Racz Papers, Box 7, Taxation for Defense. Also Truman's letter of transmittal, "Letter to the Chairman, Senate Committee on Finance on the Need for an Increase in Taxes," July 25, 1950, *PPP 1950*, pp. 545–47. For the early stages of the evolution of administration thinking on taxes see "Memorandum on the Emergency Tax Program," September 20, 1950; "Tax Programming for 1951," September 26, 1950; "Considerations Affecting the Next Revenue Program," October 13, 1950; "A Tax Program to Support the Policy of Containment," October 19, 1950. HSTL, Ecker-Racz Papers, Box 4, 1951 Tax Program, Vol. 1.

[110] For internal deliberations on the pros and cons of an excess profits tax see "The Character and Scope of an Excess Profits Tax for the 1950s," October 25, 1950; "Arguments of Representatives of

President Truman asked Congress for an excess profits tax in mid-November, less than one week after the election decreased the Democratic margin in the House by twenty-eight seats and in the Senate by five, and less than two weeks before the Chinese entered the war on the side of North Korea.[111] Despite the expected protests from business groups, this measure was quickly approved in December by a lame-duck session of Congress. "For many members," as one contemporary account notes, ". . . the chief appeal of the excess profits tax lay in its name." With the war and the economy heating up, men being drafted, and ordinary citizens being asked to bear greater tax burdens, it had become difficult for Congress "to resist the cry to draft 'war-swollen' profits of industry."[112]

Without the sudden worsening of the strategic situation it is unlikely that the new tax would have been passed with such extraordinary dispatch; whether it would have been approved at all by the new and more conservative Eighty-second Congress must remain uncertain. On January 3, 1951, as his first official act of the new year, President Truman signed the Excess Profits Tax Act of 1950 into law, commending Congress for its speedy response but promising that there were "more and much heavier taxes" yet to come.[113] In all, the new measure (which combined a levy on excess profits with a further modest increase in the regular corporate income tax rate) was expected to generate an additional $4 billion in annual revenues.[114]

The enactment of the excess profits tax marked the apogee of executive-congressional cooperation on fiscal policy and the end of a period of extraordinarily rapid expansion in federal revenue-raising capacity. Having obtained two tax hikes (and an extra $9 billion in revenues) in less than six months, the Truman administration now tried for a third increase. In February 1951, stressing that a balanced budget, "pay as we go" approach to mobilization was vital "to keep the Government's finances on a sound footing . . . distribute the cost

---

the Business Committee on Emergency Corporate Taxation and Rebuttal," October 30, 1950; "A Recommended Excess Profits Tax Program," October 30, 1950, all in HSTL, Ecker-Racz Papers, Box 3, Excess Profits Tax, Vol. 1.

[111] The election results reduced the Democrats to a 235 to 199 margin in the House and a 49 to 47 edge in the Senate. On the 1950 elections see Ronald J. Caridi, *The Korean War and American Politics: The Republican Party as a Case Study* (Philadelphia: University of Pennsylvania Press, 1968), pp. 79–107.

[112] See the discussion of the passage of the Excess Profits Act of 1950 in Stephen K. Bailey and Howard D. Samuel, *Congress at Work* (New York: Henry Holt, 1952), 340, 337–56. For the administration's case for the new tax see "Statement of Secretary Snyder before the Senate Committee on Finance," December 4, 1950. HSTL, Ecker-Racz Papers, Box 3, Excess Profits Tax, Vol. 2.

[113] "Statement by the President upon Signing the Excess Profits Tax of 1950," January 3, 1951, *Public Papers of the Presidents of the United States: Harry S. Truman (1951)* (Washington, DC: U.S. Government Printing Office, 1965), p. 1 (hereafter *PPP 1951*).

[114] On the passage of this provision see Ecker-Racz, "Taxation for Defense," pp. 10–13. For a sense of the controversy that it provoked see Hearings before the House Ways and Means Committee, *Excess Profits Tax on Corporations, 1950*, 81st Cong., 2d sess. (Washington, DC: U.S. Government Printing Office, 1950); Hearings before the Senate Finance Committee, *Excess Profits Tax on Corporations, 1950*, 81st Cong., 2d sess. (Washington, DC: U.S. Government Printing Office, 1950).

of defense fairly . . . [and] to help prevent inflation," Truman asked Congress for an additional $10 billion. Of this total, $4 billion was to come from higher personal income taxes, $3 billion from corporate income taxes, and another $3 billion from higher excises.[115] This so-called quickie increase (which would have been the largest ever in the nation's history, exceeding even the yield of the Revenue Act of 1942) was to be followed later in the year by a supplemental request for an additional $6.5 billion.[116]

Truman's recommendation encountered immediate, intense opposition on Capitol Hill and in the country at large. Congressional Republicans attacked the president's program on ideological grounds, calling it "a socialistic plan in the name of defense," warning that it revealed the ambitions of the "hardcore Socialist planners within the Truman administration," and demanding that domestic spending be cut before taxes were raised.[117] Business groups opposed higher taxes on corporations and individuals with higher incomes, and argued instead for the adoption of a national sales tax. Labor unions and farm organizations were fearful of inflation and sympathetic to the administration's appeals for higher taxes and balanced budgets, but most were hostile to excises and other consumption taxes. In general, by the summer of 1951, there was evidence of mounting public opposition to higher taxes of any kind, and even some concern in the Treasury Department that a proposed constitutional amendment capping the income tax could gain sufficient nationwide support to pass, thereby "crippl[ing] the power of the Federal government to finance its activities."[118]

After nine months of deliberation, Congress did eventually pass a bill that raised each major category of taxes, albeit by significantly less than the president had asked. In sum, the Revenue Act of 1951 gave Truman roughly $5 billion, half of what he had initially requested and less than one-third of his total planned tax package for 1951. With the war dragging on, patriotic fervor cooling, partisan sentiment intensifying, and every significant interest group mobilized "to block a drastic increase in those taxes most unacceptable to it,"

[115] See "Special Message to the Congress Recommending a 'Pay as We Go' Tax Program," February 2, 1951, *PPP 1951*, pp. 134–38.

[116] John D. Morris, "Truman to Seek 10 Billions in New Taxes Immediately," *New York Times*, February 1, 1951, p. 1; Morris, "Truman Submits His Plan For 10 Billion Tax Rise Now," *New York Times*, February 3, 1951, p. 1. For the rationale behind these proposals and their sequencing see Walter Heller to L. L. Ecker-Racz, "Some general considerations bearing on the nature and timing of the first part of the 1951 tax program," January 21, 1951; "Statement of Secretary Snyder before the Committee on Ways and Means of the House of Representatives," February 5, 1951; Memorandum from Snyder to Robert Doughton (Chairman of the House Ways and Means Committee), "The Dangers in Delaying the 1951 Tax Legislation," February 10, 1951, all in HSTL, Ecker-Racz Papers, Box 4, 1951 Tax Program, Vol. 1.

[117] The first statement is from the Republican National Committee, the second from Representative Dan Reed. See Holmans, *United States Fiscal Policy*, p. 154; and Witte, *The Politics and Development of the Federal Income Tax*, p. 141.

[118] See a memorandum from Ecker-Racz to Snyder, "Renewed Drive for Constitutional Amendment Limiting Federal Tax Rates," August 22, 1951, HSTL, Ecker-Racz Papers, Box 4, 1951 Tax Program Vol. 1.

the search for revenues had gone as far as it could and had now reached an impasse.[119]

"The basic [political] limitations as they relate to tax policy have emerged fairly clearly," observed a Treasury Department analyst at the end of 1951. "The public, at least at the beginning of 1952, will have no great inclination to accept additional burdens." Congress would "not be receptive to recommendations for heavy additional taxes," and any such requests would now "be carefully scrutinized from the viewpoint of their impact on the election."[120] Congressional Democrats were especially eager to put some distance between themselves and their president. Having sponsored three tax-raising measures in eighteen months, the chairman of the Senate Finance Committee declared that he would not do so again in any situation "short of an all-out war or war crisis."[121] "So far as tax policy is concerned, Congress has simply run out of gas," declared the *New York Times*.[122] "President Truman may ask for more new taxes again next year but the Congressional reception to such a request is likely to be cold."[123]

This prediction turned out to be correct on both counts. Warning that still higher expenditures and potentially enormous budget deficits loomed ahead, the president urged Congress in January 1952 at least to make up for its failings of the preceding year by approving the second half of his original $10 billion request. This proposal for another $5 billion in taxes met with open hostility from Republicans and with active indifference from most Democrats. Without the support necessary to proceed, the administration quietly abandoned its request.[124]

Controls

Running parallel to the struggle over taxes and following a similar trajectory was the battle between Congress and the president over how best to limit inflation during the defense buildup. Fearing that extensive economic controls

[119] Holmans, *United States Fiscal Policy*, p. 190.

[120] See a memorandum by the Tax Advisory Staff of the Secretary, "Issues in the Development of a Tax Program for 1952," December 12, 1951, HSTL, Ecker-Racz Papers, Box 6, Tax Programs 1952.

[121] John Morris, "George for Making Tax Rise Final One," *New York Times*, September 30, 1951, p. 40.

[122] Edward Collins, "Economics and Finance," *New York Times*, October 15, 1951, p. 34.

[123] "More Taxes—and Deficit," *New York Times*, October 14, 1951, sec. 4, p. 2.

[124] For the president's request see "Annual Budget Message to the Congress: Fiscal Year 1953," January 21, 1952, *Public Papers of the Presidents of the United States: Harry S. Truman (1952–53)* (Washington, DC: U.S. Government Printing Office, 1966, p. 66–67 (hereafter *PPP 1952–53*). The reasoning behind it is laid out in a memorandum from the CEA to the president entitled "Suggested Tax Policy for the Economic Report of the President," December 17, 1951, HSTL, Papers of Roy Blough, Box 10, CEA/November-December 1951. Regarding the congressional reaction see John D. Morris, "Rebuff to Truman on Tax Rise Seen," *New York Times* January 9, 1951, p. 23; Morris, "Congress Is Cold to Tax Rise Plea," *New York Times* January 17, 1952, p. 16; Clayton Knowles, "Wary on Tax Rise, Congress Receives New Budget Today," *New York Times*, January 21, 1952, p. 1; C. P. Trussell, "Tax Rise Opposed," *New York Times*, January 22, 1952, p. 1.

would be unpopular and hoping that they would prove unnecessary, Truman was initially reluctant to request their imposition.[125] In the opening months of the war, administration policy reflected Leon Keyserling's view that the best antidote to inflation was to increase output by encouraging a rapid expansion in productive capacity while restricting aggregate demand by raising taxes. Wage and price controls might ultimately prove necessary, Keyserling advised, but a "preoccupation" with them "should not divert public attention from the truth that production, and still more production, is the greatest of all the non-secret weapons in the arsenal of American democracy."[126]

In wartime, as in the period of crisis that preceded it, Keyserling offered the hope that a major expansion in American power could be achieved without substantial economic pain or significant political risk. Despite its obvious appeal, this vision was not, in the end, entirely persuasive. With no early end to the fighting in sight and with inflation and public anxiety over it both increasing, President Truman decided at the end of the summer of 1950 to ask Congress for standby authority to control wages and prices, although once it was in place he made no immediate move to exercise it.[127] It was only after the launching of the Chinese counteroffensive in December that the administration declared a national emergency and took steps to implement a wide-ranging system of controls.[128]

The efforts of the executive branch to administer wages and prices were plagued from the outset by controversy and opposition. As with taxes, objections to controls sprang from a variety of sources. Conservatives warned that controls embodied a stark contradiction of free market principles and cautioned that their implementation would, in the words of Senator John Bricker, vest "in the President more arbitrary power over the lives of the American people than

[125] According to Edward Flash, "the reasons for omitting controls involved recognition of political realities and convictions as to the needs of the moment. . . . The OPA of World War II had lost none of its immediate postwar unpopularity; the hangover of antipathy to anything resembling its resurrection was strong." Flash, *Economic Advice*, p. 42.

[126] See Keyserling's remarks to the Herald Tribune Forum, "Production: America's Great Non-Secret Weapon," October 23, 1950; also "Output, Not Controls—Key Weapon in Crisis!" *Commercial and Financial Chronicle* 172, no. 4968, December 14, 1950, HSTL, Keyserling Papers, Box 18, Vol. 5—Articles, Speeches. See also, more generally, Samuel T. Robino, Jr., "Leon H. Keyserling and the Struggle against Inflation" (master's thesis, University of Missouri at Columbia, August 1992), pp. 43–70.

[127] The president continued to hope that wage and price increases could be limited largely through patriotic appeals, and by Keyserling's program of capacity expansion and tax increases, rather than through direct administrative controls. See "Radio and Television Address to the American People Following the Signing of the Defense Production Act," September 9, 1950, in *PPP 1950*, pp. 626–31. See also a memorandum from the Council of Economic Advisers to Truman, "Special Report on Economic Trends and Policies," September 26, 1950, HSTL, Keyserling Papers, Box 3, Report File 1946–53.

[128] See "Radio and Television Report to the American People on the National Emergency," December 15, 1950, *PPP 1950*, pp. 741–46. Also Fifth Annual Report to the President by the Council of Economic Advisers, *The Economics of National Defense* (Washington, DC: U.S. Government Printing Office, 1950).

any other legislation past or present."[129] Despite these misgivings, most members of Congress preferred initially to grant the president the authority he requested rather than run the risk of being blamed for an ensuing outburst of inflation if they refused. In September 1950 Congress passed the Defense Production Act in part because "a vote for Administration emergency powers served to demonstrate to the electorate that Congress had done its job."[130]

As inflationary pressures appeared to ease and the strategic situation stabilized, principled arguments against controls resurfaced. In 1951 Congress refused the president's request for enhanced control authority and renewed the Defense Production Act only after substantially diluting its powers. As one observer notes, "Many congressmen and senators believed that economic controls were no longer warranted, arguing that their continuation would lead to 'socialism,' excessive economic regimentation, and even dictatorship."[131]

Whatever their ideological predispositions, members of Congress were also susceptible to appeals from constituents who believed themselves to have been harmed by the imposition of controls and, in particular, by restrictions on the prices they could charge. Here the representatives of manufacturing industries, retailers, and livestock producers proved to be particularly effective. In revising the Defense Production Act, Congress passed numerous amendments intended to protect the interests of these and other groups. In the summer of 1952, with yet another election in sight, Congress gave vent to popular frustration with controls by making sharp cuts in appropriations for the administering agencies. The net effect of these changes was first to weaken and then, as the Truman administration neared its end, effectively to eviscerate the system of wage and price controls.[132]

"Stretch Out" and Cut Back

Mounting popular and congressional resistance to taxes and controls compelled the Truman administration to lower its sights and to accept the necessity of a slower and, in the end, a smaller military buildup.[133]

Within weeks of the start of the Korean War, the Joint Chiefs of Staff had

---

[129] Quoted in Caridi, *The Korean War and American Politics*, p. 67.

[130] James A. Durham, "Congressional Response to Administrative Regulation: The 1951 and 1952 Price Control Amendments," *Yale Law Journal* 62, no. 1 (December 1952), p. 2.

[131] Pierpaoli, "The Price of Peace," p. 175.

[132] The struggle over controls is discussed at length ibid., pp. 71–117, 171–231, 246–251, 283–323. On the various congressional restrictions of the administration's control powers see Durham, "Congressional Response," pp. 1–53. See also Herren, "Wage-Price Policy," pp. 118–53; Goodwin and Herren, "The Truman Years," pp. 69–93; Flash, *Economic Advice*, pp. 39–99. One contemporary observer concluded that "the failure to curb inflation after the outbreak of the Korean War was not the result of uncontrollable economic pressures. . . . It was primarily a political failure, to which farmers, labor, business, the President and Congress all contributed." Samuel Lubell, *The Future of American Politics* (New York: Harper, 1952), p. 248.

[133] These events are also analyzed in Lee, "The Political Economy of Rearmament," especially pp. 32–38.

begun to sketch the outlines of the forces they believed would be necessary, both to win that limited conflict and to prepare for the possibility of a much wider conflagration. The planners at first aimed to complete the construction of a full warfighting force by 1954, the date identified in NSC 68 as the "year of maximum danger." Assuming that they could be assembled quickly enough to deter Soviet aggression in that critical year, U.S. and allied forces would then have to be sustained indefinitely at a high level of readiness. The price tag for the initial buildup (which included capital investments in new bases, production facilities, and weapons) would be enormous; the subsequent annual costs of maintaining and upgrading the new force, while more difficult to estimate, would also be extremely high.

Following China's intervention in Korea, U.S. planners upped the ante by urging that the scheduled buildup be completed in two years instead of four. The "year of maximum danger" had now, in effect, been moved back from 1954 to 1952. During the spring and summer of 1951, the military planners took another step, expanding the size of the permanent force that they deemed essential to preserving the nation's security.[134] Finally, in the fall, the Joint Chiefs indicated that substantial additional sums, spread out over several years, would be needed for foreign military assistance and to build up the stocks of weapons and ammunition that would be needed to bring the United States and its allies to a state of full war readiness.[135]

With the president's third tax request stalled, and with the congressional assault on controls intensifying, by the end of the summer of 1951 it had become obvious that the demands of the armed services could be met only with the greatest difficulty. If spending rose fast enough to meet the military's timetable, and if revenues failed to keep pace, the budget deficit would grow alarmingly, and inflationary pressure would mount. Without sufficiently powerful control mechanisms in place, prices would soar and economic (and political) catastrophe would loom.

In the fall of 1951, with decisions about the coming fiscal year still pending, a series of Budget Bureau papers laid out the problem in grim detail. It now appeared that security expenditures would not peak in fiscal year 1953, as had been assumed, but would continue to rise into the mid-1950s. At the same time,

---

[134] The best account of the Korean War planning process is contained in Doris M. Condit, *History of the Office of the Secretary of Defense*, vol. 2, *The Test of War, 1950–1953* (Washington, DC: U.S. Government Printing Office, 1988), pp. 223–305. In July 1950 the Joint Chiefs of Staff had at first recommended a permanent force of 11 Army divisions, 52 Air Force combat wings, 911 ships, and 2.1 million men under arms. By September the figures had risen to 17 divisions, 61 wings, 1,028 ships, and 2.8 million men. In December the figures stood at 18 divisions, 95 wings, 1,161 ships, and 3 million men, all to be ready by June 1952 instead of June 1954. In June 1951 the Army asked for an additional 3 divisions (to a total of 21), the Air Force for another 43 wings (for a total of 138), and the Navy demanded another 30 ships. Total manpower for this force was estimated at close to 4 million men. It was assumed that the United States would have to maintain these forces until at least 1957. See ibid pp. 239 and 278. For another account of these events see Rearden, "NSC 68," pp. 248–389.

[135] D. Condit, *The Test of War* 2:270–71.

there were growing signs of "unwillingness" on the part "of the public, industry, labor, and parts of the Government to accept the sacrifices and take the
steps necessary to accomplish the security program objectives in the time periods designated." Congress had already weakened economic controls and was
unlikely to give the president all he had asked in the way of taxes, and "prospects for additional tax increases next year—a Presidential election year—are
negligible." The result was "an extremely unbalanced Budget outlook," with
deficits projected to rise sharply and stay high for at least the next three years.[136]

Under these circumstances, the administration had three broad choices. If it
continued with planned expenditures, it would either have to try again to raise
taxes and impose tighter controls or simply accept "the calculated economic
risk involved" in running deeply unbalanced budgets. Alternatively, the executive branch could reexamine its spending programs, looking in particular at the
planned timing of the current buildup and the "planned size of military forces
. . . which should be maintained indefinitely under present conditions."[137]

Later Budget Bureau analyses arrived at somewhat different estimates of the
size and timing of the impending deficits, but their fundamental conclusions
remained the same: barring some unanticipated change in the public's willingness to sacrifice, the military buildup would have to be stretched out and, in all
likelihood, scaled back. On October 16, five days after the House and Senate
had agreed to give the president a mere $5 billion in new taxes, a Budget
Bureau memorandum summed up the situation in the following words:

> The magnitude of the budget deficits already in prospect, and the fact that they will
> continue well beyond fiscal 1954, raise the question of whether we can maintain the
> proposed higher levels of security programs. To do so might require a continuation of
> economic restraints and taxes incompatible with what the public would support over
> many years in a situation short of all-out war.[138]

Such views were not, of course, universally shared. The armed forces continued to press to keep the buildup on track, whatever the cost, and Leon Keyserling reminded the president yet again that "a serious deficiency in the military
strength of the free world . . . would be infinitely more dangerous . . . than a
sizable deficit in the Federal budget."[139] But Truman's familiar anxieties on this
subject were beginning to reassert themselves.[140] Substantial deficits might be

[136] "The Budget Outlook and Budget Policy for Fiscal Year 1953," September 13, 1951, HSTL,
Ecker-Racz Papers, Box 6, Tax Program 1952.

[137] Ibid.

[138] "Budgetary Implications of Major National Security Programs," October 16, 1951, HSTL,
PSF, Box 151, Subject, Agencies—Bureau of the Budget, Budget FY 1953. This paper estimated
that even without major increases in foreign military assistance and war reserves, budget deficits
would grow from $6 billion in fiscal year 1952 to $10 billion and $12 billion in the next two fiscal
years. If the proposed new programs were undertaken, deficits would rise from $7 billion to $13
billion to $23 billion.

[139] See a personal letter from Keyserling to Truman, November 2, 1951, *FRUS 1951*, pp. 251–52.

[140] See, for example, his comments at the 105th meeting of the National Security Council, October 18, 1951, HSTL, PSF, Box 220, NSC Meetings—1951.

unavoidable, but Truman was unwilling to take the "calculated risk" of simply allowing them to grow unchecked. Warning that excessive expenditures could wreck the American economy and give the Soviet Union "the fruits of a hot war without having to fight it," the president ordered the defense buildup slowed in late December, and set a new ceiling on all national security programs for the coming fiscal year.[141] Despite deep cuts in planned expenditures, the overall federal budget deficit was still projected at over $14 billion. To help narrow this gap, in January 1952 Truman made his ill-fated request for another $5 billion in taxes.[142]

The "stretch-out" decision of late 1951 relieved some immediate budgetary pressure, but it left the largest strategic and fiscal questions unresolved. Although compelled to accept a later completion date than they would have preferred, military planners were still intent on constructing a very large, balanced, and permanent force of air, naval, and ground units capable of fighting and winning a protracted, all-out war with the Soviet Union. The annual costs of maintaining and upgrading this force were still unclear, but they were certain to be high. To make matters worse, during his final year in office, President Truman received a series of disturbing reports about the projected growth in enemy air power. As the Soviets increased their capacity to strike directly at the United States with atomic and thermonuclear weapons, sizable additional sums would have to be spent on early warning and air defense networks, and on passive measures to protect population and industry.[143] At the end of 1952, the upper limit on the price tag for a permanent Cold War defense posture was not yet in sight.

THE NEW LOOK (1953–1954)

Truman's Legacy

The Truman administration bequeathed a fivefold legacy, and an impending fiscal crisis, to its successor. As illustrated in table 4.3, the United States was

---

[141] D. Condit, *The Test of War* 2:276. The armed services had wanted $64 billion for themselves in FY 1953 and $14 billion more for military assistance. Another $5 to $10 billion would be required to pay for military public works and an accelerated atomic energy program. Instead of the upwards of $80 billion that had been requested for national security programs, Truman agreed to $60 billion, of which some $48 billion was to go to the services. The Joint Chiefs regarded these appropriations as dangerously low, and warned that they would delay the achievement of full readiness until 1956 (pp. 274–83).

[142] Congress, as we have seen, rejected his request, choosing instead to reduce funding for the services by an equivalent amount. For the administration's budget request and its analysis of the fiscal situation see "Annual Budget Message to the Congress: Fiscal Year 1953," January 21, 1952, *PPP 1952–53*, pp. 63–117.

[143] See, for example, the discussions surrounding NSC 135, "Reappraisal of United States Objectives and Strategy for National Security," which extended from the summer into the fall of 1952. *Foreign Relations of the United States, 1952–1954*, vol. 2, pt. 1 (Washington, DC: U.S. Government Printing Office, 1984), pp. 56–165 (hereafter *FRUS 1952–54*).

TABLE 4.3
The Truman Buildup

	June 1950	*December 1952*	*Planned*
Army divisions	10	20	21
Navy ships	618	1,116	1,200
Marine divisions	2	3	3
USAF wings	48	98	143
Manpower	1.45 million	3.5 million	3.6 million

Sources: Figures for June 1950 from Doris M. Condit, *History of the Office of the Secretary of Defense,* vol. 2, *The Test of War, 1950–1953* (Washington, DC: U.S. Government Printing Office, 1988), p. 238. Other figures from Robert J. Watson, *History of the Joint Chiefs of Staff,* vol. 5, *The Joint Chiefs of Staff and National Policy, 1953–1954* (Washington, DC: U.S. Government Printing Office, 1986), pp. 59–60.

far stronger in December 1952 than it had been in June 1950, and it was scheduled to grow stronger still in the months and years ahead.

This new strength had not come cheaply, nor would it be inexpensive to maintain. Truman's second legacy was a greatly expanded annual bill for national security programs. In 1950, the United States government had been contemplating defense budgets of around $13 billion a year. In his final budget message, President Truman estimated the cost of sustaining his planned long-term force posture to be "in the neighborhood of 35 to 40 billion dollars annually."[144] Foreign military and economic assistance as well as the costs of an expanded atomic energy infrastructure would add billions more in security-related expenses. Even without allowing for major new programs for the defense of the continental United States, the outgoing administration projected that by the middle of the decade, the total annual bill for national security programs would stand at around $60 billion.[145]

In addition to bigger forces and higher costs, Truman passed on to his suc-

[144] See "Annual Budget Message to the Congress: Fiscal Year 1954," January 9, 1953, *PPP 1952–53*, pp. 1134–35. The fact that the Eisenhower administration would subsequently spend this much to maintain a considerably smaller force suggests that Truman's estimates were overly optimistic. In 1956 the Eisenhower administration spent $36 billion for a force that had 3 fewer Army divisions, roughly 230 fewer ships, 13 fewer air wings, and 800,000 fewer men under arms. See Robert J. Watson, *History of the Joint Chiefs of Staff,* vol. 5, *The Joint Chiefs of Staff and National Policy, 1953–1954* (Washington, DC: U.S. Government Printing Office, 1986), pp. 82–86. Both Truman and Eisenhower at various points underestimated the effects of inflation and of technological development on annual defense budgets.

[145] See "Analysis of Proposals to Reduce Budget Expenditures in 1954 and 1955," September 1952, and "Budget Expenditures and Proposals to Reduce Them," October 1, 1952, HSTL, Lawton Papers, Box 4, Bureau of the Budget, General IV/Revised Estimates for Receipts and Expenditures. This figure still includes some one-time investments, over and above the projected $35–40 billion maintenance costs for the U.S. armed forces. It also includes charges for the construction of atomic energy facilities and for the reconstruction and rearmament of U.S. allies that presumably would have tended to diminish with the passage of time.

cessor a greatly augmented stream of federal tax revenues. As a result of increased tax rates and the economic expansion that had been stimulated in part by wartime government spending, total federal revenues nearly doubled, in constant dollar terms, between the beginning of 1950 and the end of 1952.[146] Measured in current dollars, in fiscal year 1950 federal budget receipts (tax revenues minus refunds and appropriations to the Social Security trust fund) stood at $37 billion; in fiscal year 1952 the figure was $62 billion, and it was projected to rise to $68 billion in fiscal year 1953.[147]

Impressive as they were, these sums barely covered the costs of national security programs, and they fell well short of the total for all government expenditures. Truman's fourth legacy, therefore, was a substantial and immediate budgetary gap for the coming fiscal year.[148]

Eisenhower's final inheritance from Truman was a ticking fiscal time bomb. As an expression of its reluctance to approve any permanent increase in taxes, the Congress had insisted on a specific termination date for each of the revenue-raising measures that it had passed in 1950 and 1951. In June 1953 the excess profits tax was set to expire. Six months later, individual income tax rates would revert to their pre-emergency levels, and three months after that, both corporate income tax rates and excises would follow suit. As these provisions went into effect, total federal tax receipts would fall off sharply.[149]

As they prepared to hand over power to the Republicans, Truman's budget analysts offered a candid appraisal of the problems that they would be passing along with it. By fiscal year 1955, assuming no worsening of international tensions or provision for any major new programs, total federal expenditures would stand at $80 billion. Of this, $60 billion would go to national security, over $11 billion would be required to meet the irreducible costs of veterans' benefits and interest on the national debt, and $9 billion would remain for all other federal programs. On the other side of the ledger, meanwhile, the enactment of scheduled tax cuts was expected to reduce federal budget receipts to around $62 billion. This figure was based on the optimistic assumption that there would be "generally favorable economic conditions." If growth slowed, revenues would fall further and, instead of $18 billion, the deficit would yawn even wider.[150]

---

[146] In the first quarter of 1950, total federal taxes less transfer payments had stood at $34 billion at 1947 prices. In the first quarter of 1953 the figure was $66 billion. See the table in Brown, "Federal Fiscal Policy," pp. 142–43.

[147] See tables in the annual budget messages for FY 1951 and 1953 in *PPP 1951*, p. 67, and *PPP 1952–53*, p. 1133.

[148] Deficits were projected at $6 billion in FY 1953 and $10 billion in FY 1954. *PPP 1952–53*, p. 1129.

[149] *PPP 1952–53*, p. 1132. For a detailed analysis of the problems in store for the new administration, see a memorandum by the Tax Advisory Staff of the Treasury Department, "Tax Issues in 1953," December 15, 1952, HSTL, Ecker-Racz Papers, Box 7, Taxation for Defense.

[150] See "Analysis of Proposals to Reduce Budget Expenditures in 1954 and 1955."

Eisenhower's Preferences

When he took office at the beginning of 1953, Dwight Eisenhower found himself confronted with alternatives similar to those that had faced his predecessor before the Korean War began. In order to meet the professed needs of the armed services and their allies in the national security establishment, the president either would have to accept a large and continuing budget deficit or would have to maintain and, most likely, raise taxes. Given the comparatively small size and the particular character of the programs involved, feasible cuts in non-defense spending could not do much to ease this situation. If he wanted balanced budgets and lower taxes, on the other hand, the president would have no choice but to cut back on planned defense expenditures and to forgo programs widely deemed essential to the preservation of the nation's security. In order to understand why Eisenhower preferred this final course of action, it is necessary to examine both his beliefs and the political situation with which he found himself confronted upon assuming office.

To a far greater extent than Truman, Eisenhower was personally responsible for shaping his administration's national security strategy. Throughout his eight years in office, he used his immense authority as a former military commander to guide the formulation and implementation of U.S. defense policy and, above all, to restrain the growth in defense expenditures. After a review of the history of the period and a considerations of all of the pressures for bigger budgets, it seems fair to conclude that no other American leader could have been as successful in achieving this goal.

Eisenhower's commitment to holding down defense spending was a logical outgrowth of his essentially anti-statist philosophy of political economy. Although he would prove ultimately to be more pragmatic and flexible than some of his Republican contemporaries, by the time he was elected president, Eisenhower had come to share the critique of big government, planning, centralization, and regimentation that had emerged in response to the experience of the New Deal and the Second World War. He was, as one of his top economic advisers would later describe him, "deeply opposed . . . to any form of statism" and committed, in particular, to reducing government intervention in the nation's economy.[151] Policies that tended in the opposite direction would, he believed, "lead to statism and, therefore, slavery."[152]

These underlying concerns pointed directly to a set of specific policy preferences. Like Truman, Eisenhower was deeply committed to balancing the federal budget. Unlike his predecessor, however, Eisenhower preferred balance at the lowest possible levels of spending and taxation. Where for Truman the obliga-

---

[151] Raymond J. Saulnier, *Constructive Years: The U.S. Economy Under Eisenhower* (Lanham, MD: University Press of America, 1991), p. 2.

[152] See the entry for January 14, 1949, in Robert H. Ferrell, ed., *The Eisenhower Diaries* (New York: W. W. Norton, 1981), p. 153.

tion to match federal revenues and expenditures was, at times, a burdensome constraint and an obstacle to undertaking desirable new programs, for Eisenhower it was a tool useful in imposing restraint on others and in helping to fend off appeals for spending that he was already inclined, on principle, to oppose.

Eisenhower, like Truman before him, came around to the modern view that temporary deficits were acceptable and might at times even be necessary to lift the economy out of a recession. But he was never tempted by the advocates of aggressive Keynesian growthsmanship, nor did he include any in the inner councils of his administration. The idea of the federal government playing a central guiding role in managing the nation's economy and determining the trajectory of its development was anathema to Eisenhower. Like Truman, he also feared that using large protracted deficits to stimulate growth would end up by fueling inflation. Where his predecessor had shown some inclination to impose economic controls, however, and had begun to shy away from them only after learning how unpopular they could be, Eisenhower was fundamentally opposed to federal regulation of wages and prices, and he made the abolition of all remaining wartime controls one of his first official acts as president. Controls, Eisenhower believed, would greatly enhance the powers of the government, paving the way for "regimentation" and, perhaps, for dictatorship.[153]

The new president's views on spending and taxation were also derived from his basic anti-statist principles. Where Truman had no fundamental objection to either, Eisenhower regarded both as, at best, necessary evils. Although some forms of federal social spending might be justifiable or at the very least, politically prudent, the general tendency of such programs was to sap individual initiative, diminish individual freedom, and to disturb and distort the nation's free market economy. Because of the communist threat, high levels of defense spending were unavoidable, but such spending too drew scarce resources away from the more productive uses to which they would otherwise be put by the unencumbered workings of the market. In all, if Eisenhower could not entirely reverse the trend of the previous twenty years toward ever greater federal expenditures, then at least, as he put it, he could make it his mission gradually to bend down the government cost curve.[154]

Eisenhower came into office convinced that taxes were already far too high and was determined to lower them as quickly as possible.[155] Excessive taxation

---

[153] On Eisenhower's decision to lift controls see R. Scott Gordon, "The Eisenhower Administration: The Doctrine of Shared Responsibility," in Goodwin, *Exhortation and Controls*, pp. 95–113. Also Sherman Adams, *Firsthand Report: The Story of the Eisenhower Administration* (Westport, CT: Greenwood Press, 1961), pp. 157–58; Robert J. Donovan, *Eisenhower: The Inside Story* (New York: Harper, 1956), pp. 30–32.

[154] This is an image that Eisenhower acquired from Herbert Hoover. See Saulnier, *Constructive Years*, p. 23.

[155] His views on this subject were influenced by the writings of the economist Colin Clark, who, in a number of widely cited articles in the late forties and early fifties, advanced the claim that there were natural limits to the fiscal burdens that any modern economy could endure without experiencing ruinous inflation. Clark claimed that once taxes consumed more than around 25 percent of a nation's gross national product, popular resistance to taxation would force governments to resort to

destroyed "private incentives and initiative and the production that comes from it." The "objective of tax reduction" was, as he told reporters at his first presidential press conference, "an absolutely essential one, and must be attained in its proper order."[156] Tax cuts were inevitable, and insofar as Eisenhower and all of his top advisers were concerned, further tax increases were out of the question. All that remained to be determined was the "proper order" for reductions.

On this point, Eisenhower found himself under considerable pressure from his ideological allies in the Congress. Having spent the better part of two decades protesting the fiscal policies of Democratic presidents, Republicans were eager to use their newfound power to cut federal taxes. At the very least, the leaders of the new Republican congressional majority were determined to see that the rate increases imposed during the Korean emergency were rolled back as quickly as possible. For such powerful figures as Representative Daniel Reed, chairman of the House Ways and Means Committee, immediate tax cuts were the first order of business. Even before Eisenhower had been sworn into office, Reed introduced legislation calling for speeding up the scheduled expiration date of some wartime taxes.[157]

While he shared the goal of lower taxes and, in general, of reduced federal expenditures, Eisenhower reversed the priorities of many of his Republican colleagues. Cutting taxes immediately, before "we can determine the extent to which expenditures can be reduced," would, he believed, be unwise and, because it risked deeper deficits and accelerating inflation, potentially dangerous. "Reduction of taxes will be justified only as we show we can succeed in bringing the budget under control," Eisenhower informed the Congress in his first State of the Union Address. "As the budget is balanced and inflation checked, the tax burden that today stifles initiative can and must be eased."[158]

Eisenhower found his fellow Republicans exasperating at times, and regarded their inclination to put tax reductions before spending cuts as irresponsible political posturing. "I spend my life trying to cut expenditures, balance budgets,

---

the inflationary practice of printing money. He advanced this argument first in scholarly journals and then in the popular press and before congressional committees. See Colin Clark, "Public Finance and Changes in the Value of Money," *Economic Journal* 55 (December 1945), pp. 371–89; "The Danger Point in Taxes," *Harper's Magazine*, December 1950, pp. 67–69. One of his top economic advisers notes that Eisenhower "frequently pointed out (correctly)" that the United States had passed the critical 25 percent "danger point." Saulnier, *Constructive Years*, p. 22.

[156] "The President's News Conference," February 17, 1953, *Public Papers of the Presidents of the United States: Dwight D. Eisenhower (1953)* (Washington, DC: U.S. Government Printing Office, 1960), p. 47 (hereafter *PPP 1953*).

[157] Regarding congressional pressure for tax cuts during the first year of the Eisenhower administration see Gary W. Reichard, *The Reaffirmation of Republicanism: Eisenhower and the Eighty-third Congress* (Knoxville: University of Tennessee Press, 1975), pp. 97–118. Also Stephen E. Ambrose, *Eisenhower*, vol. 2, *The President* (New York: Touchstone, 1984), pp. 85–87. Iwan W. Morgan, *Eisenhower versus the Spenders* (London: Pinter, 1990), pp. 50–60; Holmans, *United States Fiscal Policy*, pp. 204–15.

[158] "Annual Message to the Congress on the State of the Union," February 2, 1953, *PPP 1953*, p. 21.

and then get at the *popular* business of lowering taxes," he wrote to an old Army friend.[159] As compared to those of his predecessor, however, the new president's differences with the legislative branch were matters of degree and timing, not of fundamental purpose. Congressional pressure for tax cuts merely reinforced Eisenhower's own predilections, impelling him in directions in which he was already inclined to go, albeit at times somewhat faster than he might have preferred.

Eisenhower's Choice

The essential changes in American strategy and force planning undertaken following the "New Look" at national security policy in 1953 are well known. By the end of the year, under the president's direct and firm guidance, the Joint Chiefs of Staff and the National Security Council had agreed to long-range force goals that were significantly lower than those in place at the end of the Truman administration and had adopted an accompanying strategic rationale. Ground and naval forces were to be cut back and consolidated to a significant degree in a mobile strategic reserve based in the continental United States. To deter communist aggression with smaller conventional forces, increased emphasis would be placed on maintaining "adequate offensive retaliatory strength" in the form of a "massive atomic capability." After briefly embracing warfighting, the United States was now shifting toward a strategy of massive retaliation (see table 4.4).[160]

These changes were driven by the need to "meet the Soviet threat to U.S. security" without "seriously weakening the U.S. economy or undermining our fundamental values and institutions" and, more specifically, by the administration's desire to bring long-term expenditures into balance with the expected yield of a diminished and reformed tax structure.[161] Major shifts in tax policy were considered by administration officials to be economically essential as well as politically desirable. "Tax rates are so high and the structure of the tax system so bad," warned the Treasury Department and the Bureau of the Budget, "that normal economic incentives for long-term growth are seriously restricted."[162]

---

[159] Eisenhower to Brigadier General B. F. Caffey. Quoted in Saulnier, *Productive Years*, p. 46.

[160] See NSC 162/2, "Basic National Security Policy," October 30, 1953, *FRUS 1952–1954*, pp. 591, 577–96. This document represents the culmination of a national strategic planning process that began shortly after the new administration took office and included the so-called Solarium studies conducted during the summer of 1953. Its evolution can be traced on pp. 258–576. Regarding the military planning exercise that accompanied and contributed to this larger effort see Watson, *History of the Joint Chiefs of Staff*, pp. 1–37. See also Glenn H. Snyder, "The 'New Look' of 1953," in Schilling, Hammond, and Snyder, *Strategy, Politics, and Defense Budgets*, pp. 383–524; Gaddis, *Strategies of Containment*, pp. 127–63.

[161] These two broad goals are identified in the preamble to NSC 162/2 as the primary aims of U.S. security policy. *FRUS 1952–54*, p. 578.

[162] This sentence was eventually dropped from the official policy guidance statement because some officials regarded it as overly pessimistic. See a preliminary draft of NSC 162/2, "Review of Basic National Security Policy," September 30, 1953, ibid., pp. 491–514.

TABLE 4.4
Truman's and Eisenhower's Long-Term Force Goals

	Truman January 1953	Eisenhower November 1953
Army divisions	21	14
Navy ships	1,200	1,030
Marine divisions	3	3
Air Force wings	143	137
Manpower	3.6 million	2.8 million

Sources: Watson, *History of the Joint Chiefs of Staff* 5:60 and 30.

The estimated annual cost of Eisenhower's planned permanent defense posture, which he hoped to have in place by 1956, was roughly $33 billion. This figure (which was estimated first and used as a ceiling within which military planning then went forward) was derived by what came to be referred to as the "remainder method."[163] If the economy stayed healthy, if all the Korean War tax increases were allowed to lapse, and if the new administration received congressional approval for its own planned tax reform package, by 1956 federal budget receipts were expected to stand at around $60 billion. If "relatively uncontrollable" nonsecurity expenditures were projected to around $14 billion and "controllable programs" could presumably be squeezed down to under $6 billion (from close to $8 billion at the end of the Truman administration), roughly $40 billion would be left for national security programs. Subtracting another $5 to $6 billion for foreign military assistance and $2 billion for atomic energy left approximately $33 billion for the military services.[164]

Eisenhower was ultimately more successful in reducing the size of the U.S. armed forces than in cutting their cost, and largely as a result, he was unable to achieve all that he had hoped in the way of tax reductions. After fending off demands for an immediate rollback, in the spring of 1953 the president's difficulties in obtaining quick spending cuts and his overriding desire to achieve a balanced budget compelled him to ask Congress to extend some wartime taxes. This request was met with a mix of anger and disappointment by many Repub-

---

[163] See Snyder, "The 'New Look' of 1953," pp. 440–43.

[164] These figures and assumptions are contained in a memorandum to Eisenhower from the Bureau of the Budget, "A Report to the President on the Budgetary Situation and Outlook," September 28, 1953, reproduced on microfilm in Research Collections in American Politics, *President Dwight D. Eisenhower's Office Files*, pt. 1, *Eisenhower Administration Series* (Bethesda, MD: University Publications of America, 1990), reel 10, starting at frame 0302 (hereafter DDE OF 10, 0302). Similar calculations were used to shape the work of a special ad hoc Joint Chiefs of Staff committee set up in October 1953 to plan a force around the concepts embodied in NSC 162/2. See Watson, *History of the Joint Chiefs of Staff* 5:28–32. The $33 billion long-term target appears to have emerged in rough form as early as March 1953. See the summary of a report to the NSC by seven civilian consultants, "Condensed Statement of Proposed Policies and Programs" (March 31, 1953?), *FRUS 1952–54* , pp. 281–90.

licans, but in the end, they had little choice but to accept the administration's promise of eventual cuts and far-reaching tax reforms.[165]

Rates were reduced in 1954, but not in every case by as much as they had been raised during the Korean emergency. Just as in wartime the political process had resulted in a rough distribution of burdens, so also the benefits of peace were spread across all sectors of society. By the end of the year virtually everyone had received some relief. Increases in individual income tax rates (the one element in the Korean revenue-raising program that Eisenhower had not attempted to extend) were allowed to lapse, as planned, at the beginning of 1954. Having delayed lifting the excess profits tax for six months, Eisenhower permitted it to expire at the same time, to the great relief of corporate executives and congressional conservatives. After first resisting Democratic pressure for a rollback in excise taxes, the president agreed later in the year to reduce some levies but insisted on keeping others at wartime rates. Corporate income taxes were kept at the levels to which they had been raised in 1950 and 1951, but the pain of this move was eased by the Internal Revenue Act of 1954, which offered considerable tax breaks to the business community and investors.[166]

After the dramatic shifts of 1953–54, both the federal tax structure and the broad outlines of American strategy tended to stabilize. The combination of a postwar recession, which caused revenues to fall, and continuing difficulties in bringing defense costs down (and in squeezing the water out of nondefense programs) meant that deficits were slow to disappear. To keep the problem from worsening, Eisenhower asked Congress in 1954 and again in 1955 to extend existing excise and corporate income tax rates for one more year.[167] As a recov-

[165] See "Special Message to the Congress Recommending Tax Legislation," May 20, 1953, *PPP 1953*, pp. 318–26. Regarding the congressional reaction to the administration's plans see the minutes of two meetings with legislative leaders, April 30, 1953, and May 19, 1953. Reproduced on microfilm in Research Collections in American Politics, *President Eisenhower's Meetings with Legislative Leaders, 1953–1961* (Bethesda, MD: University Publications of America, 1986), reel 1, beginning at frame 0252 and 0243 (hereafter DDE MLL 1, 0252 and 0243).

[166] For overviews of early Eisenhower tax policy see Dan Throop Smith, "Two Years of Republican Tax Policy: An Economic Appraisal," *National Tax Journal* 8, no. 1 (March 1955), pp. 2–11; Holmans, *United States Fiscal Policy*, pp. 204–42; Morgan, *Eisenhower versus the Spenders*, pp. 21–38; Saulnier, *Constructive Years*, pp. 44–48; Ronald F. King, *Money, Time, and Politics: Investment Tax Subsidies and American Democracy* (New Haven: Yale University Press, 1993), pp. 135–50. Regarding the 1954 Tax Reform Act in particular see Witte, *Politics and Development of the Federal Income Tax*, pp. 146–53; Eugene Neil Feingold, "The Internal Revenue Act of 1954: Policy and Politics" (Ph.D. dissertation, Princeton University, Politics Department, 1960).

[167] See "Radio and Television Address to the American People on the Tax Program," March 15, 1954, in *Public Papers of the Presidents of the United States: Dwight D. Eisenhower (1954)* (Washington, DC: U.S. Government Printing Office, 1960), pp. 313–18; "Annual Budget Message to the Congress: Fiscal Year 1956," January 17, 1955, *Public Papers of the Presidents of the United States: Dwight D. Eisenhower (1955)* (Washington, DC: U.S. Government Printing Office, 1959), pp. 97–99. The administration's continuing difficulties in matching expenditures to revenues meant both that further tax cuts were repeatedly deferred and that there was continuing downward pressure on defense spending. See a series of memos from the Bureau of the Budget: "The Fiscal and Budgetary Outlook," May 10, 1954, DDE OF 17, 0189; "Review of the 1955 Budget," September 8, 1954, DDE OF 17, 0082; "Report on the Current Budgetary Situation and Outlook," November

ery got underway, tax revenues increased and began, finally, to outpace expenditures. With economic growth accelerating, however, Eisenhower became increasingly concerned about inflation and so remained reluctant to cut taxes.[168] Ultimately, despite recurrent calls for further reductions, existing rates would be extended repeatedly throughout the remainder of the decade. For ten years after 1954 the structure of the nation's tax system remained essentially unchanged.

Just as strategic concerns helped to limit tax reductions after 1954, so fiscal considerations effectively blocked any major shifts in strategy. As soon as it was articulated, the new policy of "massive retaliation" came under attack as inflexible, incredible, and potentially dangerous. Critics in and out of government warned that as Soviet capabilities grew, a "nuclear stalemate" would develop and the probability of a limited, and perhaps even non-nuclear, war between the superpowers would increase. It followed that the United States might need more of the very conventional capabilities that Eisenhower had begun so vigorously to cut. The problem, of course, was that building (or rebuilding) large ground and naval forces would mean expanding defense budgets, raising taxes, and, if inflation reignited, putting in place economic controls.

In June 1954 the National Security Council debated the proposition that

> in the face of possible nuclear balance in 1956–59, there is serious question whether the United States, while maintaining maximum strategic nuclear capability, can continue to place major reliance thereon as a means of waging general war. Consequently, the United States should undertake to increase the forces and mobilization potential which [it] . . . would need to wage war effectively without strategic use of nuclear weapons.[169]

If this view prevailed, explained Joint Chiefs of Staff Chairman Arthur Radford, the United States would have to undertake "a great increase in conventional forces." An impending nuclear stalemate could therefore upset the delicate balance between strategic and fiscal necessities that the administration had only recently managed to strike. Eisenhower rejected such arguments with barely suppressed rage. If the NSC believed that a massive new buildup was necessary, he concluded angrily, "we might just as well stop any further talk about preserving a sound U.S. economy and proceed to transform ourselves forthwith into a garrison state."[170]

30, 1954, DDE OF 7, 0838; "Review of the 1956 Budget," October 18, 1955, DDE OF 17, 0288. See also John D. Morris, "President Asks 65.5 Billion Budget; Deficit 2.9 Despite 5 Billion Cut," *New York Times*, January 22, 1954, p. 1; William M. Blair, "U.S. Predicts Rise in Budget Deficit Despite Arms Cut," *New York Times*, September 15, 1954, p. 1.

[168] See "Annual Message to the Congress on the State of the Union," January 5, 1956, *Public Papers of the Presidents of the United States: Dwight D. Eisenhower (1956)* (Washington, DC: U.S. Government Printing Office, 1958), pp. 12–13 (hereafter *PPP 1956*).

[169] NSC 5422, "Tentative Guidelines under NSC 162/2 for FY 1956," June 14, 1954, *FRUS 1952–54*, p. 657. Regarding the efforts of the Army and Navy to win approval for major increases in 1954 see Watson, *History of the Joint Chiefs of Staff* 5:74–87.

[170] Minutes of 204th National Security Council Meeting, June 24, 1954, *FRUS 1952–54*, p. 689.

THE SPUTNIK CRISIS (1957–1958)

Neither the pressure for increased defense expenditures nor the president's concern about the likely consequences of acceding to it diminished as the 1950s wore on. The form that this pressure took and the direction from which it came did shift, however, and, most importantly, its intensity grew with the passage of time. By the latter part of the decade there was a substantial body of opinion which held that the United States could, and should, increase its military budget by as much as 50 percent in real terms.

In the midfifties, calls for more spending came primarily from the armed services themselves and took the form of appeals for expanded conventional capabilities. His dominance over the generals established and his position reinforced by the prevailing fiscal climate, Eisenhower was able to dismiss these demands with comparative ease. In the second half of the decade, and especially after the Sputnik crisis of late 1957, the pressure for greatly expanded defense budgets came more from outside the executive branch than from within it: from opinion makers, expert committees, and the Democratic majority in Congress. Instead of simply demanding more World War Two–style ground, naval, and air forces, these critics also urged the acceleration and expansion of ballistic missile programs and the initiation of vast new efforts to defend American territory and citizens against bomber and missile attack. Although it too would largely be turned aside, this second wave of criticism posed a much more serious challenge to the administration's preferred strategic and fiscal policies.

Security expenditures touched bottom in 1954 (fiscal year 1955), and then despite plans for another year of cuts to be followed by a leveling off, they began to climb back upward. The reasons for this unanticipated increase were, first, inflation, which drove up the price of existing programs, and, second, the mounting cost of an accelerating technological competition with the Soviet Union. In 1955 and 1956, well before Sputnik, signs of Soviet progress in developing intercontinental range bombers and ballistic missiles had already resulted in greater American expenditures on bombers, missile development, intelligence systems, and early warning networks. Although he had hoped to see defense expenditures declining toward a steady state, Eisenhower felt constrained to request more money in fiscal year 1956 and again in fiscal year 1957. In December 1956 he authorized a new ceiling of $39 billion for planning purposes for the coming fiscal year, roughly $6 billion more than the level-off cost originally anticipated under the New Look. In an unusual addendum to the minutes of the National Security Council meeting at which this figure was discussed, Eisenhower also noted for the record that for the remainder of his term in office, "except in the event of some unforeseen critical emergency," he would never ask for more money from Congress.[171]

---

[171] See "Memorandum of Discussion at the 307th Meeting of the National Security Council," December 21, 1956, *Foreign Relations of the United States, 1955–1957*, vol. 19, *National Security Policy* (Washington, DC: U.S. Government Printing Office, 1990), p. 394 (hereafter *FRUS 1955–57*).

Eisenhower's discomfort at seeing defense costs creep up was eased somewhat by the fact that with the economy booming, tax revenues were also rising rapidly. The end result was that despite increasing outlays, the federal government was actually running a net budget surplus. Still, there was a strong feeling that things could not continue as they were going. If costs continued to rise, if Congress cut taxes, or if the economy stumbled, deficits would return with a vengeance. Given the administration's preoccupation with inflation, this was a deeply troubling prospect.

"What was making possible the balancing of the budget in FY 1956 and 1957," Secretary of the Treasury George Humphrey informed the National Security Council in January 1956, "was not a reduction in expenditure but an increase in the Treasury's income. We are guessing . . . that this increase will continue in the future," but, whether for political or economic reasons, he acknowledged that it might not.[172] Later in the year, Budget Bureau director Percival Brundage warned Eisenhower that if the most recent additions to the defense budget were taken into account, "the present trend of expenditures will make it unlikely that the budget can be balanced . . . without a further postponement of tax reductions and in all probability the imposition of additional taxes."[173] In order to avoid "the effort to increase taxes that would otherwise be required," Eisenhower pleaded with Secretary of Defense Charles Wilson to do whatever was necessary to stay within budgetary guidelines.[174] By the summer of 1957, the administration was giving serious consideration to withdrawing a substantial portion of U.S. ground and naval forces based in Europe and the Far East in order to shift scarce dollars into strategic offensive and continental defense programs. If inflation continued to drive up costs, defense planners cautioned, a fixed budget ceiling would necessitate even greater cutbacks in the near future.[175]

It was against this backdrop that the Sputnik crisis exploded in the fall of 1957. In early October and, one month later, at the beginning of November, the Soviets succeeded in launching two earth orbiting satellites. The implication of these feats was unmistakable: a country that could loft several hundred pounds of scientific equipment (and, in the second instance, a small dog) into orbit

[172] "Memorandum of Discussion at the 272d Meeting of the National Security Council," January 12, 1956, *FRUS 1955–57*, p. 181.

[173] Brundage to Eisenhower, April 3, 1956, DDE OF 8, 0042. See also a detailed memorandum from Brundage, "Budget policy—the next four budgets," May 23, 1956, DDE OF 7, 0643.

[174] "Memorandum of a Conference with the President," June 27, 1957, *FRUS 1955–57*, pp. 531–32.

[175] See "Memorandum from the President's Special Assistant for National Security Affairs (Cutler) to the President," July 1, 1957; "Memorandum from the Chairman of the Joint Chiefs of Staff (Radford) to the President's Special Assistant for National Security Affairs (Cutler)," July 3, 1957; "Memorandum from the President's Special Assistant for National Security Affairs (Cutler) to the President," July 5, 1957; "Memorandum from the Secretary of Defense (Wilson) to the President," July 10, 1957; "Memorandum of a Conference with the President," July 10, 1957; "Memorandum from the Chairman of the Joint Chiefs of Staff (Radford) to the Secretary of Defense (Wilson)," July 16, 1957; "Memorandum of Discussion at the 331st Meeting of the National Security Council," July 18, 1957; "Memorandum of Discussion at the 332d Meeting of the National Security Council," July 25, 1957, all in *FRUS 1955–57*, pp. 533–35, 538–65.

would soon be able to drop thermonuclear warheads at any point on the surface of the globe. Earlier in the year, the president had appointed a special committee to explore the possibility that increasing Soviet intercontinental strike capabilities might require a massive new American investment in civil defense programs. On November 7, four days after the second Sputnik, the Security Resources Panel of the Science Advisory Committee (generally referred to the as the Gaither Committee, after its director, Ford Foundation board chairman Rowan Gaither) made a formal report of its findings.[176]

Ranging beyond its original charter to consider the entire U.S. defense posture, the Gaither Committee made two interlocking sets of recommendations. At the very least, the United States should spend an extra $19 billion over the next five years to ensure that its own offensive nuclear forces could survive a Soviet surprise attack and to increase the capacity of its conventional forces to fight limited wars. In addition, albeit at a slightly lower level of priority, another $5 billion per year should be devoted to protecting the civilian population against bomber and ballistic missile attack. Most of this money would go to fund a nationwide system of fallout shelters. In all, the Gaither Committee recommended a total of $44 billion in new expenditures between fiscal years 1959 and 1963.[177]

The cost of the first package of programs was estimated to be "barely within the estimated receipts from existing taxes" for the first three years, and more comfortably affordable thereafter, assuming high growth rates and no tax cuts. If full employment were sustained, the program would have "some inflationary effects," which would have to be offset with credit and monetary restrictions. Funding both packages together, meanwhile, would necessitate "an increase in taxes . . . substantial economies in other government expenditures, and other curbs on inflation," presumably including wage and price controls as well as tighter money. The committee's experts calculated that adoption of all of their proposals would raise the share of U.S. GNP devoted to national security from around 10 percent to under 14 percent. Such an allocation of resources was, they concluded, "well within our economic capabilities."[178]

The outline of these recommendations soon found its way into the popular press. Over the course of the following months, the Gaither Committee's essential economic message was also echoed in a number of less specific, less official, but more visible reports. "We can afford what we have to afford," declared a study by the moderate conservative Committee of Economic Development. "The risk that defense spending of 10 to 15 per cent of the gross national product, or if necessary even more, will ruin the American way of life is slight indeed." The key issues were political, not economic: whether the "the Ameri-

[176] On the origins of this report see Morton H. Halperin, "The Gaither Committee and the Policy Process," *World Politics* 13, no. 3 (April 1961), pp. 360–84.

[177] See the text of NSC 5724, "Report to the President by the Security Resources Panel of the ODM Science Advisory Committee on Deterrence and Survival in the Nuclear Age," November 7, 1957, *FRUS 1955–57*, pp. 638–61.

[178] Ibid, p. 648.

can public is willing to let itself be taxed sufficiently" to fund an accelerated buildup and, if not, whether the nation's leaders could persuade the public to change its collective mind.[179]

Eisenhower's response to all of this unsolicited advice, and to the very real and serious political pressures that went with it, was both shrewd and stubborn. The president gave some ground, eventually authorizing increases in defense spending (primarily for ballistic missiles and strategic readiness) and, outside the immediate military realm, for education, scientific research, and space exploration. Some of this spending he regarded as useful, if not essential, but much of it was intended primarily "to stabilize public opinion" and to head off demands for even greater outlays.[180] Compared to the sums being urged on him from all quarters, the additional amounts that the president was ultimately willing to spend turned out to be quite paltry. Forced to violate his earlier pledge to hold military budgets below $39 billion, Eisenhower did not do so by very much. Spending on the armed services rose to just over that amount in fiscal year 1958 and then to roughly $41.5 billion in fiscal year 1959 and fiscal year 1960.[181] Instead of increasing as a share of GNP, defense spending actually declined between the onset of the Sputnik crisis and the end of the decade.[182]

Much bigger budgets, and certainly anything approaching those outlined in the Gaither report were, in Eisenhower's view, unnecessary to ensure American security. Worse still, he was convinced that they would have lasting harmful

[179] See "A Statement on National Policy by Research and Policy Committee of the Committee for Economic Development," in *The Problem of National Security: Some Economic and Administrative Aspects* (New York: Committee for Economic Development, July 1958), pp. 27, 24. See also James F. Brownlee, *The Defense We Can Afford* (New York: Committee for Economic Development, 1958). In 1958 two reports sponsored by the Rockefellers explored the possibility that defense spending might have to rise to around 12 percent of GNP. See "Report II—International Security: The Military Aspect" and "Report IV—The Challenge to America: Its Economic and Social Aspects," both reprinted in Rockefeller Brothers Fund, *Prospect for America* (New York: Doubleday, 1961), pp. 93–155 and 251–333. In the spring of 1957 the liberal National Planning Association had published a study outlining the implications for tax policy of raising defense to 11.5 percent, 13.1 percent, and over 15 percent of GNP. Like the Gaither Committee, the NPA report concluded that boosting defense spending back to Korean War levels would require significantly higher taxes. See Gerhard Colm and Manuel Helzner, "General Economic Feasibility of National Security Programs," March 20, 1957, reprinted in Hearings before the Subcommittee on Fiscal Policy of the Joint Economic Committee, *Federal Expenditure Policy for Economic Growth and Stability*, 85th Cong., 1st sess. (Washington, DC: U.S. Government Printing Office, 1958), pp. 356–61. Drawing on these and other studies, the well-known RAND analyst Bernard Brodie concluded that the United States could easily raise defense spending "from 10 per cent to perhaps 13 or 14 per cent of our growing GNP." "The hurdles though considerable are almost entirely political," a reflection of the fact that "it is difficult in a democracy to raise taxes." Bernard Brodie, *Strategy in the Missile Age* (Princeton: Princeton University Press, 1959), pp. 377, 373.

[180] See a remark by Eisenhower to Secretary of Defense McElroy recorded in "Memorandum of a Conference with the President," December 5, 1957, *FRUS 1955–57*, p. 703. See also Rodger A. Payne, "Public Opinion and Foreign Threats: Eisenhower's Response to Sputnik," *Armed Forces and Society* 21, no. 1 (Fall 1994), pp. 89–112.

[181] For a detailed accounting see Robert A. Divine, *The Sputnik Challenge: Eisenhower's Response to the Soviet Satellite* (New York: Oxford University Press, 1993).

[182] Gaddis, *Strategies of Containment*, p. 185.

effects on the nation's economy. This conclusion was based both on the president's long-standing beliefs about fiscal policy and on his reading of the contemporary political climate. Though he had not yet been able to lower them by as much as he had hoped, Eisenhower continued to believe that taxes were far too high, and he remained eager to cut them. For him, the existing rate structure represented a ceiling and not a floor.[183] If Congress followed the path of fiscal responsibility, and increased taxes to cover substantial new expenditures, the result would be to further sap incentives for work and productive investment. If, on the other hand, it proved easier to boost spending than to raise revenues, the end result of the Sputnik panic would be deeper deficits, inflationary pressures even more intense than those the nation had already been experiencing, and the possibility of renewed economic controls.

These dangers were clearly uppermost in Eisenhower's mind. His first reaction to the Gaither Committee report was to ask if its authors were proposing an immediate move to a controlled economy. "After all," he noted with frustration, "this Administration had gotten rid of controls . . . as soon as it came into office because of its conviction that in the absence of controls the American economy would develop more rapidly. Are we now to advocate the re-introduction of controls?"[184]

Early analyses of the committee's recommendations did nothing to relieve the president's anxieties. Studies by the Treasury Department and the Council of Economic Advisers suggested that the Gaither panel had overestimated tax receipts and underestimated the cost in coming years of other government programs. If balanced budgets were to be preserved, even adoption of the more modest package of programs outlined in the report would therefore require some increase in taxes.[185] With economic growth clearly slowing down at the end of 1957, revenue projections fell even further, and the likelihood of at least temporary deficits increased.[186]

For all the tough talk about sacrifice that came in the wake of the Sputniks, there were no serious proposals for higher taxes emanating from Capitol Hill. Confronted in November 1957 with reports of impending congressional pressure for stepped-up missile development, Eisenhower asked "with a smile . . . which of the two parties was likely to propose a big tax increase in order to mount a crash program."[187] The answer was obvious; everyone wanted more

[183] Holmans, *United States Fiscal Policy*, p. 261.

[184] "Memorandum of Discussion at the 343d Meeting of the National Security Council," November 7, 1957, in *FRUS 1955–57*, p. 632.

[185] See the Treasury Department's contribution to NSC 5724/1, "Comments and Recommendations on Report to the President by the Security Resources Panel of the ODM Science Advisory Committee," December 16, 1957, DDEL, White House Office Files, Office of the Special Assistant for National Security Affairs, Box 75.

[186] See the remarks of CEA chairman Raymond Saulnier in "Memorandum of Discussion at the 345th Meeting of the National Security Council," November 14, 1957, *FRUS 1955–57*, p. 685. Also a memo from Saulnier to Eisenhower, "Projection of Budget Receipts and Expenditures through the Fiscal Year 1962," April 21, 1958, DDE OF 26, 0257.

[187] "Memorandum of Discussion at the 346th Meeting of the National Security Council," November 22, 1957, *FRUS 1955–57*, pp. 693–94.

military capability, but no one was eager to impose the taxes that would be necessary to pay for it. To the contrary, with the recession deepening and another campaign season underway, the tide began quickly to flow in the opposite direction. Some of Eisenhower's advisers were willing to consider the possibility of modest, short-term tax reductions as a way of speeding the recovery, but the president rejected the idea, fearing that Congress would convert small, temporary cuts into big, permanent ones.[188] If taxes came down and defense spending shot up the recession might be shortened, but the nation would be saddled with deep, structural deficits that could "hurt us badly in the future."[189]

Historians have praised Eisenhower for keeping his head when all around were losing theirs; for standing firm in the face of nearly irresistible pressures to launch an unnecessary military buildup, thereby "sav[ing] his country untold billions of dollars."[190] Eisenhower is unquestionably the key figure in the story of the American response to Sputnik. Had he been a person of lesser political stature or markedly different beliefs, defense budgets would doubtless have been bigger by the end of the 1950s. How much bigger is difficult to say, but prevailing congressional attitudes toward taxation and, indeed, the entire history of Cold War fiscal policy to that point suggest that the president was not the only obstacle to a 50 percent real increase in defense spending.

Pursuing such a path would have meant requesting higher taxes and that, in turn, would have provoked precisely the kind of resistance that Harry Truman had encountered before and during the Korean War. Without an actual shooting war, the intensity of political support for higher taxes would probably have been less, and its half-life would surely have been even shorter, than in 1950–51. Assuming that Eisenhower had thrown all of his weight behind it, and that a majority in Congress had been willing to go along and had been able to agree on the details, an increase in taxes might have permitted an upward shift in the long-term trajectory of defense spending. If experience was any guide, however, the extent of the increase would probably have been less than the president's request, and any upward movement in spending paid for by higher taxes would have been followed quickly by mounting pressure for reconsideration and retrenchment. Whatever else he may have accomplished, Eisenhower spared his country the necessity of such an exercise.

THE KENNEDY BUILDUP (1961–1963)

The Democratic critique of Republican policy during the 1960 presidential campaign had two central strands. First, it was charged, Eisenhower's "failure

---

[188] Morgan, *Eisenhower versus the Spenders*, p. 119. Regarding the struggle over how best to respond to the recession see also Lewis, *Federal Fiscal Policy in the Postwar Recessions*, pp. 188–235; Stein, *The Fiscal Revolution*, pp. 319–45.

[189] See "The President's News Conference of March 26, 1958," in *Public Papers of the Presidents of the United States: Dwight D. Eisenhower (1958)* (Washington, DC: U.S. Government Printing Office, 1959), pp. 234–35.

[190] Ambrose, *Eisenhower*, p. 435. Reaching a similar conclusion is Gaddis, *Strategies of Containment*, pp. 185–88.

to understand the ABC's of modern fiscal theory" and, in particular, his obsession with balancing the budget and restraining government spending had condemned the United States to a far lower growth rate than was desirable and achievable. At the same time, the outgoing president's "excessive attention to the budget" was alleged to have resulted in a serious weakening of the nation's defenses.[191] Eisenhower's tightfistedness had led both to a "missile gap" and to a dangerous over-reliance on nuclear weapons and a slighting of conventional capabilities. Candidate, and then president, John Kennedy promised both to "get the country moving again" economically, and, through the expenditure of more dollars on defense, to stiffen its sagging military posture.

During its abbreviated span the Kennedy administration did, indeed, undertake major departures in both fiscal and strategic policy. The relaxation of old strictures against deficit spending and the embrace of growthsmanship contributed to a loosening of the perceived constraints on defense expenditures and a major enhancement of American military capabilities. Between fiscal year 1961 (Eisenhower's last budget) and fiscal year 1964 (Kennedy's last), spending on the armed forces rose by roughly 15 percent in current dollar terms (from $43 billion to $49 billion), and capabilities, measured in combat-ready divisions, fighter wings, ballistic missiles, ships, submarines, and men under arms, all increased. These changes were accompanied by a shift in military strategy away from the threat of prompt nuclear retaliation and toward the promise of a "flexible" and, where possible, a nonnuclear response to communist aggression.[192]

As significant as they undoubtedly were, the innovations of the Kennedy years were less substantial and less revolutionary than they were made to seem at the time, and than they have sometimes been made to seem in retrospect. Certainly when compared to the large, prolonged increases being urged at the end of the 1950s, the expansion in defense spending and military capabilities undertaken in the early 1960s was actually quite limited both in scope and duration. While defense spending grew during the Kennedy years, the economy grew more quickly and the defense share of national output continued to decline. After three years of real growth, by fiscal year 1964 the augmentation of American military power had effectively run its course. In fiscal year 1965, the last before the escalation of the war in Vietnam, defense spending was actually cut by roughly 10 percent. If not for Vietnam there is good reason to believe that U.S. defense spending and force structure would have leveled off at roughly where they stood in 1964. The trends toward a declining defense share of GNP and of total federal spending that were already visible at this point, and that became evident again as the war wound down, would then have continued without interruption.

Why was the Kennedy buildup not even larger and more sustained than it turned out ultimately to be?

[191] For a summary statement of the Democratic critique see Seymour Harris, *The Economics of the Political Parties* (New York: Macmillian, 1962), pp. 145, 169.

[192] The best account of these shifts and their larger implications is Gaddis, *Strategies of Containment*, pp. 198–236.

Evolving Conceptions of Sufficiency

John Kennedy came into office promising to enhance American military power in all of its forms and committed to doing so "without being bound by arbitrary budget ceilings."[193] In its public statements and internal planning documents, the new administration declared its intention to expand U.S. strategic offensive and defensive forces so as to be better able "to deter or deal with a direct nuclear assault against the U.S. or other vital areas," and "in the event of war to . . . minimize damage to the U.S. and its allies." Greatly enhanced civil defense programs would also contribute to this latter goal. Expanded conventional or "general purpose" forces would assist in "frustrat[ing], without using nuclear weapons, major non-nuclear assault by Sino-Soviet forces." At the same time, the United States would increase its ability to "support friendly peoples against Communist efforts to undermine their governments . . . through subversive, paramilitary and guerrilla operations."[194] By enhancing U.S. capabilities at every level, the Kennedy administration planned to increase its options and to move away from its predecessor's alleged excessive reliance on the threat of "massive retaliation" and toward a strategy of "flexible response."[195]

Within two years, administration spokesmen had begun to back away from their earlier formulations and to define their objectives in far more limited and modest terms. In 1961, Kennedy had made much of his intention to build a vast nationwide network of underground shelters, thereby correcting a major deficiency of the Eisenhower years and providing protection for "millions of people against the hazards of radioactive fallout in the event of large-scale nuclear attack."[196] By the end of 1962 these plans had effectively been abandoned.[197] Early in 1962 Secretary of Defense Robert McNamara outlined a strategy for using U.S. nuclear forces to disable their Soviet counterparts, thereby "limit[ing] damage done to ourselves and our allies."[198] One year later, McNamara had begun publicly to raise questions about whether the United States—no matter how extensive its own offensive forces, bomber and missile defenses, and civil defense preparations, and no matter what strategy it

[193] "Special Message to the Congress on the Defense Budget," March 28, 1961, *Public Papers of the Presidents of the United States: John F. Kennedy (1961)* (Washington, D.C.: U.S. Government Printing Office, 1962), pp. 230–31. (hereafter *PPP 1961*).

[194] See Draft Paper Prepared by the Policy Planning Council, "Basic National Security Policy," June 22, 1962, in *Foreign Relations of the United States, 1961–1963*, vol. 2, *National Security Policy* (Washington, DC: U.S. Government Printing Office, 1996), pp. 310, 317, 309–28.

[195] The best summary statement of initial administration reasoning is still William W. Kaufmann, *The McNamara Strategy* (New York: Harper and Row, 1964), pp. 1–101.

[196] "Special Message to the Congress on Urgent National Needs," May 25, 1961, *PPP 1961*, pp. 402–3.

[197] See Fred Kaplan, *The Wizards of Armageddon* (New York: Simon and Schuster, 1983), pp. 307–14.

[198] Quoted in Aaron L. Friedberg, "The Evolution of U.S. Strategic 'Doctrine,' 1945 to 1981," in Samuel P. Huntington, ed., *The Strategic Imperative: New Policies for American Security* (Cambridge, MA: Ballinger, 1982), p. 68.

employed—would be able to limit damage from a concerted Soviet nuclear attack.[199]

As regards general purpose forces, the logic of the administration's desire for options had seemed at times to be pushing it toward seeking the capacity to meet even the very largest communist conventional attack without having to make use of nuclear weapons. By the end of 1963 McNamara was telling audiences both that the United States and its allies were much closer in conventional strength to the Soviets than had previously been assumed, and that he had no intention of recommending the construction of forces "adequate to turn back without nuclear weapons an all-out surprise non-nuclear attack."[200]

The reasons for these downward adjustments in strategic aims are mixed and complex. In part they are a product of events, of the evolving external environment, and of changing views within the Kennedy administration about what was necessary to defend the United States and to preserve its interests. Thus, for example, the Cuban missile crisis of October 1962 seems to have contributed to an erosion in the belief of top U.S. civilian officals that damage could truly be kept limited in a nuclear war. The subsequent acceleration in Soviet strategic nuclear weapons programs (which reflected a very different reading of the lessons of the crisis) tended to reinforce these beliefs and to further weaken support for investments in civil defense or in additional increments of offensive or strategic defensive capabilitiy. Similarly, the recognition that America's allies in Europe were reluctant to undertake a major buildup of general purpose forces and nervous that too much talk about conventional defense would weaken deterrence contributed to shifts in declared U.S. strategy.[201]

Whatever the strategic logic underlying it, however, each of the various changes, redefinitions, and clarifications that occurred between 1961 and 1964 also had the effect of justifying the imposition of some limits on security expenditures. This was not a fortuitous coincidence. Once it rejected the absolute strategic precepts and the "arbitrary" budget ceilings of its predecessor, the Kennedy administration soon found that it had opened the door for vastly expanded funding requests from the armed services.[202] If a little flexibility and a

[199] Ibid., pp. 70–71.

[200] See his speech of November 1963 before the Economic Club of New York, quoted in Kaufmann, *The McNamara Strategy*, p. 309. Regarding the administration's changing assessment of the balance of conventional forces in Europe see Alain C. Enthoven and K. Wayne Smith, *How Much Is Enough?: Shaping the Defense Program, 1961–1969* (New York: Harper Colophon, 1972), pp. 117–64. Regarding the downward adjustment of the administration's aims for European conventional forces see John S. Duffield, *Power Rules: The Evolution of NATO's Conventional Force Posture* (Stanford, CA: Stanford University Press, 1995), pp. 151–93.

[201] These issues are discussed at length in Jane Stromseth, *The Origins of Flexible Response: NATO's Debate over Strategy in the 1960s* (London: Macmillan, 1988).

[202] For an early indication of this problem see a memorandum from McNamara to Kennedy, "Recommended Department of Defense FY 63 Budget and 1963–67 Program," October 6, 1961, reproduced on microfilm in Research Collections in American Politics, *President John F. Kennedy's Office Files, 1961–1963* (Bethesda, MD: University Publications of America, 1989), pt. 3: Departments and Agencies File, reel 11, beginning at frame 00918 (hereafter JFK OF 3/11, 00918). Here

few additional options were good, surely more would be better. Worse yet, as Soviet strength continued to grow there appeared to be no obvious, logical resting point for the American defense buildup. The pursuit of nuclear damage limitation, for example, gave "the Services, and particularly the Air Force, . . . a basis for requesting virtually open-ended strategic weapon programs."[203] By contrast, the notion that the goal of American policy should be to deter attack primarily by promising the second strike—"assured destruction" of the Soviet Union—had the virtue of helping to set some finite limits on the size and cost of U.S. strategic forces. As he struggled to gain control of the military budget and of the armed forces, Secretary of Defense McNamara was especially eager to devise formulations that would justify the imposition of such limits. The downward revision of strategic goals was therefore motivated in large part by a desire to put a lid on defense spending.

The Persistence of Old Fiscal Constraints

Despite its declared intention to increase American power without regard to arbitrary fiscal limitations, the Kennedy administration continued to operate under both self-imposed and congressionally reinforced constraints on spending and on the extent of its willingness and ability to run budget deficits. Largely because of the evolving views of the president and his top advisers, these constraints were less powerful than those at work in the 1950s, and they tended to grow weaker with the passage of time, but they were very much in evidence during the critical formative years of the Kennedy buildup.

While some of the economists he brought with him to Washington would have liked to see a more rapid departure from past orthodoxy, the president himself was extremely cautious. During his first year in office, having won a narrow victory over an opponent who warned that Kennedy's economic policies would bankrupt the nation, the president was particularly reluctant to be viewed as engaging in anything that smacked of fiscal irresponsibility. Quick to see the need for a fiscal stimulus to boost the economy out of the recession he had inherited from his predecessor, Kennedy was nevertheless careful to avoid policies that might appear to risk large, sustained deficits. Thus, while the Council of Economic Advisers urged him in March 1961 deliberately to unbalance the budget by as much as $10 billion, the president was unwilling to go nearly this far.[204] Instead of proposing a temporary income tax cut (as the CEA preferred) or initiating large new public works programs (as economist John Kenneth Galbraith and some labor leaders were urging), Kennedy chose to accelerate and expand a handful of existing defense and non-defense programs (thereby adding

---

McNamara reveals that the services were asking for an average of $15 billion more each year (or a total of $74 billion over five years) than he wanted to give them.

[203] Desmond Ball, *Deja Vu: The Return to Counterforce in the Nixon Administration* (Santa Monica: California Seminar on Arms Control and Foreign Policy, 1974), p. 70.

[204] See a memo from the Council of Economic Advisers to Kennedy, "A Second Look at Economic Policy in 1961," March 17, 1961, JFK OF 3/7, 00469.

around $5 billion to the federal budget) and to suggest a small, revenue-neutral tax reform package. These comparatively modest proposals were accompanied by an oath of fealty to the commercial Keynesian principle of balancing the budget "over the business cycle," running deficits only "in years of recession" and returning to surpluses "in years of prosperity."[205] Even if he had been inclined at this point to go further, this was all that Kennedy believed the political traffic would bear.[206]

The alternative to running much bigger deficits in order to fund a larger military buildup was, of course, to impose higher taxes. Kennedy was certainly aware of the likely political obstacles to following such a course, and there is no evidence that he considered proposing a permanent tax increase. Nevertheless, at the height of the Berlin crisis in July 1961, the president did come close to requesting a one-year tax hike to pay for an extra $3.5 billion in emergency military expenditures. Kennedy apparently believed that a temporary tax increase would spread the burdens of a partial mobilization across the entire population while dampening inflationary pressures and helping to further demonstrate his commitment to fiscal responsibility.[207] His economic advisers responded with horror, claiming that raising taxes would "choke off full recovery" and encourage those fiscal Neanderthals in the Congress who insisted that every increase in spending had to be matched by higher revenues.[208] At the last moment the president was persuaded to drop his tax hike proposal and to accept the resulting additional fiscal stimulus. But the price of this concession was a public declaration that the budget for fiscal year 1963 would be "strictly in balance" and a promise to hold deficits to "a safe level" by applying continual downward pressure on all federal expenditures, including those for national defense.[209]

Nor were these assurances purely rhetorical. In January 1962 Secretary of Defense McNamara informed the Congress that he had stripped some $13 billion from the requests of the armed forces.[210] In all, military spending grew far

---

[205] "Special Message to the Congress on Budget and Fiscal Policy," March 24, 1961, *PPP 1961*, p. 221. Administration policy during this period is summarized in Lewis, *Federal Fiscal Policy*, pp. 245–75. See also Flash, *Economic Advice* pp. 173–218.

[206] Kennedy's political aides and subsequent biographers have claimed that his early objections to large deficits were, as one of them has has put it, "political and not intellectual." His economic advisers do not seem as certain and date the president's conversion to "modern economics" somewhat later. See Arthur M. Schlesinger, Jr., *A Thousand Days: John F. Kennedy in the White House* (Greenwich, CT: Fawcett, 1965), pp. 578–79; Theodore C. Sorenson, *Kennedy* (New York: Bantam, 1966), pp. 444–47; Walter W. Heller, *New Dimensions of Political Economy* (New York: Norton, 1967), pp. 29–31.

[207] Flash, *Economic Advice*, p. 202.

[208] See two memorandums from Walter Heller, chairman of the Council of Economic Advisers, to Kennedy, "The Proposed Tax Increases," July 21, 1961, JFK OF, pt. 2: Staff Memoranda, reel 3, frame 00554 (hereafter 2/3, 00554); and "Check List of Considerations Bearing on Tax Increase Decision," July 23, 1961, JFK OF 3/7, 00856.

[209] "Radio and Television Report to the American People on the Berlin Crisis," July 25, 1961, *PPP 1961*, p. 537. Regarding the abortive tax hike see Sorensen, *Kennedy*, pp. 447–49; Heller, *New Dimensions*, pp. 32–33.

[210] See "Annual Report of the Secretary of Defense," in *Department of Defense Annual Report for Fiscal Year 1962* (Washington, DC: U.S. Government Printing Office, 1963), pp. 31–32.

less rapidly in fiscal year 1963 than in the previous year.[211] One year later, Budget Bureau director Kermit Gordon promised the House Ways and Means Committee that the United States was approaching "a new plateau of readiness" and that, as a result, defense expenditures would tend to grow even more slowly in the future than in the recent past.[212]

During his final two years in office, Kennedy became progressively less concerned with balancing the annual budget and with appearing to adhere to the canons of fiscal orthodoxy. Under the tutelage of his advisers, the president came around to the view that the true aim of government policy should be to close the gap between actual and potential national output, raising production to the levels necessary to sustain full employment, rather than simply to smooth out minor fluctuations in economic performance. Doing this would require a substantial, sustained stimulus instead of a relatively small dose of counter-cyclical fiscal medicine.[213]

In the long run, raising the growth rate promised to enrich the nation and to free the hand of policy makers by generating more resources for every conceivable purpose. In the short run, however, there were political limits to the form and extent of the stimulus that could be applied and some additional constraints on government spending. Ironically therefore, the transition to growthsmanship actually provided an extra downward push on defense expenditures.

As they considered their options in 1962 and 1963, the president's closest economic advisers soon came to the conclusion that the best and most feasible way of adding to aggregate demand was to cut taxes rather than to try for further dramatic increases in government spending. A permanent reduction in tax rates would ease what Kennedy's economists had come to refer to as "fiscal drag," the tendency of the tax system to generate revenues faster than the economy and the federal budget were expanding, thereby limiting demand and restraining growth. Although it faced some resistance from conservatives, who would have preferred to begin by cutting expenditures and balancing the budget, the idea of reducing taxes had an obvious appeal to business leaders and to politicians of all stripes. Boosting spending was a far more controversial proposition. Congress had already shown its reluctance to fund major new social programs, and after the increases of 1961 and 1962, enthusiasm for further

---

[211] Outlays and obligational authority grew by 8.5 percent and 7.5 percent, respectively, in FY 1962. The equivalent figures for FY 1963 were 1.9 percent and 0.2 percent. See Office of the Comptroller, Department of Defense, *National Defense Budget* (Washington, DC: Office of the Comptroller, 1990), pp. 107, 67.

[212] See mimeo of "Statement of Kermit Gordon, Director of the Bureau of the Budget before the Ways and Means Committee of the House of Representatives on the President's Tax Program," February 18, 1963, JFK OF 3/5, 00163.

[213] The best statement of these arguments comes from their main proponent in the administration, CEA chairman Walter Heller. See Heller, *New Dimension of Political Economy*, especially pp. 58–116; also Stein, *Fiscal Revolution*, pp. 395–402. The distinction between merely dealing with temporary slowdowns and overcoming the problem of chronic "sluggishness" is made clearly in an initial overview of economic issues prepared for the incoming administration in January 1961 by Paul Samuelson. See "Economic Frontiers" in Joseph E. Stiglitz, ed., *The Collected Scientific Papers of Paul A. Samuelson*, vol. 2 (Cambridge: MIT Press, 1966), pp. 1478–92.

expansions in defense spending was also on the wane. (In 1962 and again in 1964 Congress approved a defense budget smaller than the one recommended by the administration.) As Walter Heller observed in a December 1962 memorandum for the president entitled "Recap of Issues on Tax Cuts (and the Galbraithian Alternative)":

> An expansion of spending would bring all of the charges of "fiscal irresponsibility" that attach to tax cuts—after all, deficits would be practically the same either way. But on top of this would be all of the opposition to expansion of government, to overcentralization, to a "power grab."[214]

The size of the fiscal stimulus was also determined in part by political considerations. Some economists urged the president to aim for a deficit as big as $15 billion by fiscal year 1964, but his closest aides argued that he should not, under any circumstances, exceed the record of $12.4 billion set by Eisenhower in fiscal year 1959.[215] If he did not spill more red ink than his notoriously parsimonious predecessor, they reasoned, Kennedy would have a better chance of defending his proposals against charges of recklessness. The significance of this consideration is suggested by the fact that "in subsequent explanations of his program Kennedy returned again and again to the idea that he was going to incur a smaller deficit in his positive effort to sustain economic growth than Eisenhower had incurred as a consequence of failure to avoid recession."[216] In the end, Kennedy decided on $13.5 billion in tax cuts, partially offset by reforms that would bring in an additional $3.5 billion in revenues. To avoid going over the magical $12.4 billion deficit limit, these cuts were to be phased in over a period of several years.[217]

In order to hold down the deficit and win support for a tax cut from skeptical congressional conservatives, Kennedy and, after his assassination, Lyndon Johnson also took significant steps to limit government spending. Both men were convinced that without some show of fiscal restraint, their proposals for tax reduction would be defeated and their hope of stimulating more rapid economic growth would be lost. With an eye to influencing congressional opinion, Kennedy originally intended to hold his fiscal year 1965 budget request below the landmark figure of $100 billion. Once he assumed office, Johnson decided to go even further, ordering federal agencies to squeeze their budgets to under

---

[214] Heller to Kennedy, "Recap of Issues on Tax Cuts (and the Galbraithian Alternative)" December 16, 1962, JFK OF 2/3, 00579. On tax cuts versus spending see also Stein, *Fiscal Revolution*, pp. 407–21. Regarding business attitudes see Collins, *The Business Response to Keynes*, pp. 173–95.

[215] Compare a memorandum to the president from Paul A. Samuelson and Robert M. Solow, "Desirable Tax Policy for 1963," November 15, 1962, JFK OF 3/25, 00943, with one from Theodore Sorenson, "Tax Cut," July 12, 1962, JFK OF 3/25, 00355.

[216] Stein, *The Fiscal Revolution in America*, p. 435. Also noting the significance of the $12.4 billion limit is Flash, *Economic Advice*, p. 265.

[217] King, *Money, Time, and Politics*, p. 185. The delicate politics of the tax cut are analyzed in James L. Sundquist, *Politics and Policy: The Eisenhower, Kennedy, and Johnson Years* (Washington, DC: Brookings Institution, 1968), pp. 40–56.

$98 billion and imploring the military, in particular, to "protect your country's purse."[218] In keeping with the new president's wishes, the fiscal year 1965 defense budget actually called for outlays lower than in the previous year, the first such reduction in a decade.[219] By the beginning of 1964, at the latest, the Kennedy buildup had clearly come to a close.

The Emergence of New Constraints

The midsixties mark the beginning of a profound shift in the composition of the federal budget and the emergence of an entirely new and increasingly potent source of constraint on defense spending. These developments were temporarily obscured and partially delayed by the escalation of the war in Vietnam. But even before the dramatic expansion in the U.S. role there, the direction of events had already become clear.

It was the persistence of conservative congressional opposition rather than any fundamental objection from the executive branch that held down the growth of nondefense expenditures in the early 1960s. During his three years in office, President Kennedy had made some cautious, tentative steps toward increasing these portions of the federal budget, and at the time of his assassination, he seemed poised to do more. Further movement would probably have had to await the conclusion of the 1964 elections, but there can be little doubt about the priorities of a second Kennedy administration. As Walter Heller wrote the president in December 1962:

> Our cities need renewal, our colleges and universities have no place for the flood of students about to inundate them, our mass transport system is in a sad state, our mental health facilities a disgrace, our parks and playgrounds inadequate, housing for many groups unsatisfactory.[220]

Fortunately, in a few years time there would be ample resources to tackle all of these problems and more. Once the tax cut was passed and fully implmented, economic growth would accelerate and, even at reduced tax rates, federal revenues would begin to expand.

> In the not-too-long run, the tax cut route is likely to bring us closer to our government program goals than an immediate attempt to push the budget up. . . . a vigorous economy, stimulated by tax cuts, will provide a broader economic base and an atmosphere of prosperity and flushness in which government programs can vie much more successfully for their fair share of a bigger pie.[221]

[218] See Irving Bernstein, *Guns or Butter: The Presidency of Lyndon Johnson* (New York: Oxford University Press, 1996), pp. 33–34, 27–42. See also Stein, *The Fiscal Revolution in America*, pp. 440–53; Sundquist, *Politics and Policy*, pp. 40–53; Sorensen, *Kennedy*, p. 482.

[219] Dennis S. Ippolito, *Uncertain Legacies: Federal Budget Policy from Roosevelt through Reagan* (Charlottesville: University Press of Virginia, 1990), p. 111.

[220] Heller, "Recap of Issues on Tax Cuts."

[221] Ibid.

As Heller would later describe it, by the latter half of the decade, with GNP expanding by 4 to 4.5 percent a year, the essential problem facing economic policymakers would be how best to dispose of "the $7 to $8 billion a year of added Federal revenues automatically generated by normal economic growth." With defense spending having leveled off, the "pleasant choices" would include further tax cuts for lower-income citizens and major new social spending programs. By the spring of 1963 Heller had begun to sketch the outlines for "an attack on poverty."[222] Over the next two years Lyndon Johnson would use the flood of sentiment unleashed by Kennedy's killing and the considerable momentum of his own election victory to step up the timetable of reform and initiate an unprecedented array of social spending programs. These measures, as economist Herbert Stein points out, "were launched in an atmosphere still colored by the notion of the fiscal dividend."[223]

In the happy world that Heller imagined, expanding social programs would not necessarily have to compete for funds with defense. Indeed, depending on how the nation's economic managers chose to divide the fiscal dividend, both defense and nondefense spending might be able to grow simultaneously, and all without higher taxes or deeply unbalanced budgets. In the real world, things turned out rather differently. For a variety of reasons (including increases in longevity, inflation, and the progressive liberalization of eligibility requirements and benefits), the cost of the new social welfare programs grew far more rapidly than anyone had anticipated. Meanwhile, the nation's economy grew much more slowly than Heller had hoped, and although inflation drove up tax revenues, they tended not to increase as rapidly as expenditures. The result, evident by the early 1970s, was a situation in which nondefense programs had begun to compete with, and increasingly to squeeze out, defense spending.[224]

[222] Heller, *New Dimensions of Political Economy*, pp. 105, 20.

[223] Stein, *Presidential Economics*, p. 115. On the origin and subsequent growth of these new social welfare programs see Bernstein, *Guns or Butter*; Irwin Unger, *The Best of Intentions: The Triumphs and Failures of the Great Society under Kennedy, Johnson, and Nixon* (New York: Doubleday, 1996); Gareth Davies, *From Opportunity to Entitlement: The Transformation and Decline of Great Society Liberalism* (Lawrence: University of Kansas Press, 1996).

[224] Stein, *Presidential Economics*, pp. 114–22. Ippolito, *Uncertain Legacies*, pp. 93–227.

CHAPTER FIVE

Manpower

CONSCRIPTION IN AMERICA, 1776–1945

Of all the activities of the modern state, none is so immediate or dramatic in its impact on the lives of ordinary citizens as the extraction of manpower. When it compels young men to undertake military service, the state removes them from their homes and families (peaceably if possible, by force if necessary), subjects them to long periods of often brutal training, and sends them off to fight and, if need be, to die. More even than the power to tax, the power to conscript is truly the power to destroy. How, if at all, can its exercise be justified in a polity committed to the preservation of individual freedom?

Americans have answered this question in two very different ways. In theory, and at the level of political rhetoric, the desire for individual liberty has been counterbalanced by the demands of societal equity. Successive generations have accordingly proclaimed their adherence to the principle that all male citizens share an obligation to participate in military service. In practice, however, the exercise of compulsion has been avoided whenever possible, and reliance has been placed instead on voluntarism.

These two opposing tendencies have been evident since the founding of the Republic. After the Revolution, the newly formed state governments retained the authority claimed by their colonial forebears to require all able-bodied men to serve in local militias. Prior to 1776, however, this obligation was enforced in most places with diminishing frequency and, although revived during the war, it began soon after to evaporate.[1]

Subsequent Federalist schemes for unifying, standardizing, and centralizing the militias and for strengthening requirements for service were defeated or rendered harmless by a Congress suspicious of standing armies and fearful of tyranny. Thus, in 1792, Congress passed the Uniform Militia Act, requiring "every free, able-bodied, white male citizen" between the ages of eighteen and

---

[1] On the origins of American military institutions, with particular reference to early attitudes toward compulsion, see Walter Millis, *Arms and Men: A Study of American Military History* (New York: Mentor, 1958), pp. 11–63; Richard H. Kohn, *Eagle and Sword: The Federalists and the Creation of the Military Establishment in America, 1783–1802* (New York: Free Press, 1975); Lawrence Delbert Cress, *Citizens in Arms: The Army and the Militia in American Society to the War of 1812* (Chapel Hill: University of North Carolina Press, 1982); Louis Morton, "The Origins of American Military Policy," *Military Affairs* 22 (Summer 1958), pp. 75–82; Leon Friedman, "Conscription and the Constitution: The Original Understanding," in Martin Anderson, ed., *The Military Draft: Selected Readings on Conscription* (Stanford, CA: Hoover Institution Press, 1982), pp. 231–96; Denis Sinclair Philipps, "The American People and Compulsory Military Service" (Ph.D. dissertation, New York University, Department of Government, 1955), pp. 1–191.

forty-five to enroll in a state militia. But the law "contained no . . . procedure for enforcing national guidelines." If a state chose not to comply, the federal government was "impotent to intercede."[2] America's armed forces soon came to consist in peacetime of a small, regular federal Army composed entirely of volunteers backed by an assortment of state militias that were themselves manned increasingly on a voluntary basis.[3]

Even in war, the American people proved extremely reluctant to accept compulsory military service. During the War of 1812 a poorly organized and ill-equipped amalgam of professionals and assorted militia forces came close to defeat at the hands of the British. Yet despite the danger, Congress refused to grant President James Monroe's request that he be authorized to draft men into the regular Army. During the debate over conscription, many members questioned whether such action could ever be justified. "Where is it written in the Constitution," asked Congressman Daniel Webster, "in what article or section is it contained, that you may take children from their parents, [and] parents from their children, [and] compel them to fight the battles of any war, in which the folly or the wickedness of Government may engage it?"[4] The eventual American victory helped to bolster confidence in the inherent superiority of volunteer "citizen soldiers." Thirty years later, during the war with Mexico, the United States once again relied on volunteers to do its fighting. By the middle of the nineteenth century, in war as in peace, voluntarism had been enshrined as "the embodiment of the true American military tradition."[5] In *Democracy in America* Alexis de Tocqueville would observe that: "In America conscription is unknown. . . . Compulsory recruitment is . . . contrary to the conceptions and alien to the habits of the people of the United States."[6]

The increasing industrialization of warfare and the accompanying expansion in its scope did eventually force the nation, at moments of great danger, to resort to conscription. In 1863, two years after the onset of the Civil War and one year after the South had adopted a more extensive measure of its own, the federal government finally instituted a draft. In part because of its limited, inequitable application, this measure aroused intense controversy and triggered

---

[2] Kohn, *Eagle and Sword*, p. 135.

[3] In the 1830s and 1840s one state after another either abolished compulsory militia service or passed laws eliminating provisions for enforcement. See John K. Mahon, *History of the Militia and the National Guard* (New York: Macmillan, 1983), p. 83. On the "degeneration of the militia," see also William H. Riker, *Soldiers of the States: The Role of the National Guard in American Democracy* (Washington, DC: Public Affairs Press, 1957), pp. 21–40.

[4] Daniel Webster, "An Unpublished Speech," in Anderson, *The Military Draft*, p. 639.

[5] Russell Weigley, "Introduction," in John O'Sullivan and Allan M. Meckler, eds., *The Draft and Its Enemies: A Documentary History* (Urbana: University of Illinois Press, 1974), p. xvii.

[6] Alexis de Tocqueville, *Democracy in America*, bk. 1 (Garden City, NY: Anchor Books, 1969), p. 222. For a useful overview of manpower policy in the Revolutionary War, the War of 1812, and the war with Mexico see Marvin A. Kreidberg and Merton G. Henry, *History of Military Mobilization in the United States Army, 1775–1945* (Washington, DC: U.S. Government Printing Office, 1955), pp. 1–82.

some of the worst riots in American history. With the North's victory, the federal draft came quickly to a halt.[7]

For the next fifty years, while virtually all of the world's great powers adopted universal conscription to build large standing armies and vast trained reserves, the United States (along with Great Britain, the other insular liberal democratic power) continued to rely on voluntarism. Even on the eve of American entry into the First World War, proposals for the adoption of European-style mass mandatory peacetime training failed to gain widespread support.[8]

Owing in part to a deliberate effort to avoid the mistakes of the Civil War, the draft imposed during the First World War generated more soldiers and less controversy than its predecessor. The Selective Service System put into place in 1917 was deliberately designed to minimize the appearance of both compulsion and inequality, and to reduce popular and congressional anxieties about militarism and the exercise of excessive governmental power. The hiring of substitutes, a practice that had been the cause of much bitterness during the Civil War, was strictly forbidden. Those called were referred to as "selectees" or "servicemen" rather than "conscripts" or "draftees"; they were, in Woodrow Wilson's words, "selected from a nation which has volunteered in mass."[9] The processes of registration and induction were administered through a decentralized system of local civilian boards, rather than run from Washington by uniformed military officers. The numbers of men drafted (and the portion of those eligible who were, in fact, called) was much higher than during the Civil War, thereby alleviating concerns about inequality. Last, but by no means least, conscription was clearly presented as a temporary emergency measure, as, indeed, it proved to be. On the day the war ended, the draft ceased and "troop trains turned around and took draftees home."[10] The Army's plans for a permanent peacetime system of universal military training were abandoned almost as quickly.

In September 1940, with most of continental Europe under Nazi domination and a German descent on Britain expected to begin at any moment, Congress agreed, after considerable debate, to permit the reimposition of a draft. Because the United States was not yet at war, this measure was perceived to be, and was in fact, something new in American history. On the other hand, what critics

---

[7] See Kreidberg and Henry, *History of Military Mobilization*, pp. 83–140. Also John Whiteclay Chambers II, *To Raise an Army: The Draft Comes to Modern America* (New York: Free Press, 1987), pp. 41–71. For an interesting comparison of the mobilization efforts of the North and South see Richard Franklin Bensel, *Yankee Leviathan: The Origins of Central State Authority in America, 1859–1877* (New York: Cambridge University Press, 1990), pp. 94–237.

[8] The worldwide trend toward universal conscription is described in Michael Howard, "The Armed Forces," in F. H. Hinsley, *The New Cambridge Modern History of Europe*, vol. 9, *Material Progress and World-Wide Problems, 1870–1898* (Cambridge: Cambridge University Press, 1979), pp. 204–42.

[9] Chambers, *To Raise and Army*, p. 182; Wilson's speech on draft registration is reprinted in part in O'Sullivan and Meckler, *The Draft and Its Enemies*, p. 128.

[10] Chambers, *To Raise an Army*, p. 239.

denounced as "peacetime conscription" was being imposed during a period of intense crisis and imminent danger. Even the most ardent isolationists could not deny that the threats to the nation's security were large and growing rapidly. The 1940 draft law also contained a number of special provisions that helped to ease its adoption. Draftees could be used only to defend the Western Hemisphere and U.S. overseas possessions, and they could be compelled to serve for only one year. When, in the fall of 1941, the Roosevelt administration requested that the term of service for newly trained men be extended for the duration of the emergency, Congress balked. A compromise measure lengthening tours to eighteen months (thus avoiding, or at least delaying, the effective dismantlement of much of the force that had begun to be assembled during the previous year) passed the House of Representatives by the famously narrow margin of a single vote. It was only the Japanese attack on Pearl Harbor several months later that transformed the draft from "a transitory and experimental tool" with an uncertain future to a great engine of mass military mobilization.[11] As it had during the First World War, the Selective Service System provided the military with a large and steady stream of men between 1941 and 1945, as many as half a million a month during the early stages of the war, and a total of 10 million by the time it had reached its end.[12]

The Pattern of Cold War Conscription

By the middle of the twentieth century the United States had arrived at a "military format," a set of institutions and policies for the extraction of manpower that combined voluntarism in peace with massive, temporary, and near-universal conscription in war.[13] The onset of the Cold War raised profound doubts about the continuing adequacy of these arrangements. Rather than simply fielding small forces at home, the United States was now committed to maintaining large and seemingly permanent garrisons in foreign countries. And instead of assuming that they would have several years in which to mobilize mass armies for a third world war, American military planners found themselves called upon to prepare both for the sudden outbreak of another total global conflict and for the possibility of repeated, scattered "small wars." Under these circumstances, the traditional American distaste for conscription in anything less than a supreme emergency had come to many to seem archaic at best and a threat to national survival at worst. The confrontation with the Soviet Union thus raised the tension between the demands of the common defense and the desire for maximum individual liberty to a level unprecedented in American history, and

---

[11] George Q. Flynn, *The Draft, 1940–1973* (Wichita: University of Kansas Press, 1993), p. 52; on the passage of the 1940 law see pp. 9–52. Also J. Garry Clifford and Samuel R. Spencer, Jr., *The First Peacetime Draft* (Wichita: University of Kansas Press, 1986).

[12] Clifford and Spencer, *The First Peacetime Draft*, p. 231.

[13] The term "military format" is borrowed from Samuel E. Finer, "State and Nation-Building in Europe: The Role of the Military," in Charles Tilly, ed., *The Formation of National States in Western Europe* (Princeton: Princeton University Press, 1975), p. 90.

in doing so, it opened in the most fundamental form the question of the appropriate extent of the power of the state over the lives of its citizens.

At the end of the Second World War the United States had open to it essentially three broad choices of military format, each embodying a different degree of compulsion. At one extreme were plans for universal service that would have extracted some measure of participation from virtually every male (and eventually, in some schemes, every female) citizen. At the opposite end of the spectrum was a system that relied entirely on patriotic and financial inducements to draw volunteers into military service. Lying in between these two extremes was some form of limited conscription, with compulsion applied in varying quantities to produce a mixed force of draftees and volunteers.

As figure 5.1 suggests, the evolution of the nation's military format over the course of the Cold War described a distinct downward trajectory. While it would certainly have been equitable, universal conscription would also have required an unprecedented peacetime exercise of extractive power. For this reason, a universal training system of the type urgently advocated in the late 1940s and early 1950s by the nation's top military and political leaders aroused strong opposition from an assortment of societal groups. Congressional sensitivity to interest group pressures, the susceptibility of many members to ideological arguments against conscription, and an extreme wariness among elected officials about imposing additional burdens on their constituents combined to kill universal training.

Given the political obstacles to universal conscription, the United States was headed back in the late 1940s to its traditional peacetime practice of relying entirely on volunteers. It was only the crises of 1948 and, in particular, the onset of the Korean War that made possible the imposition of a limited draft. Limited conscription involved a narrower exercise of government power; it was also, as a result, highly inequitable, and a combination of demographic and strategic factors made it more so with the passage of time. Such a system was tolerable for a while under the special circumstances prevailing in the 1950s, but it could not remain so for long; even before the escalation of the war in Vietnam, limited conscription had begun to come under serious challenge.

Vietnam delayed the demise of the draft while simultaneously sealing its fate. The war heightened concerns about the inevitable inequities of "selective service." It also reawakened deep-seated and widespread misgivings about any exercise of compulsion by the state. With the collapse of popular and elite support for limited conscription, the United States returned, finally, to an all-volunteer force. Reliance on volunteers in any but the most extreme national emergency satisfied the preference for liberty, as it had in earlier periods, without offending in any obvious way against the desire for equality.

Analysts of Cold War manpower policy have tended to focus on only the middle portion of this story: on the postwar adoption of a limited draft. Some have described this as the product of a national "transvaluation of values,"[14] a

---

[14] Richard Gilliam, "The Peacetime Draft: Voluntarism to Coercion," in Martin Anderson, ed.,

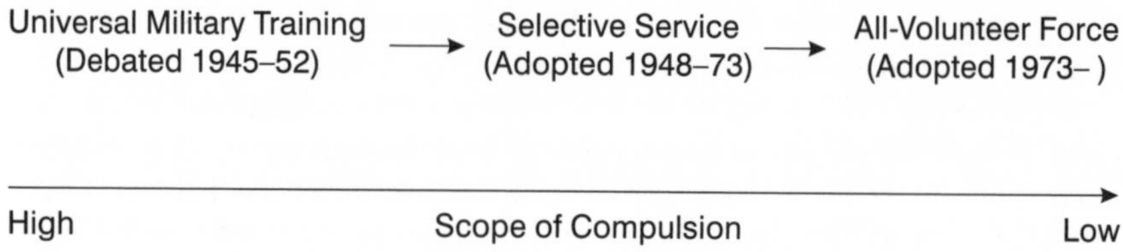

Universal Military Training	Selective Service	All-Volunteer Force
(Debated 1945–52) →	(Adopted 1948–73) →	(Adopted 1973–)

High   Scope of Compulsion   Low

Figure 5.1. Alternative Military Formats

panicked sacrifice of freedom on the altar of security and even, in one formulation, "the triumph of facist sentiment"[15] over American liberalism. The imposition of any form of conscription in the absence of a large-scale war for national
survival certainly represented a significant departure from past practices, and it
is not unreasonable to view it as marking at least a temporary and partial victory of the desire for security over the love of liberty. Viewed more closely and
seen in its entirety, however, the period of the Cold War appears as an ongoing
struggle between these contending impulses, one in which traditional preferences continued to exert a powerful influence on events, and from which they
eventually emerged triumphant. Placed in its proper perspective, the resort to a
peacetime draft appears not as a trend but as a detour; it involved a temporary
departure from dominant national traditions rather than a lasting transvaluation
of national values.[16]

REJECTING UNIVERSAL CONSCRIPTION

For the better part of a decade following the close of the Second World War, the
United States struggled to devise a military format that would be both strategi-

---

The Military Draft: Selected Readings on Conscription (Stanford, CA: Hoover Institution Press,
1982), p. 99.

[15] Robert Higgs, *Crisis and Leviathan: Critical Episodes in the Growth of American Government*
(New York: Oxford University Press, 1987), p. 241.

[16] By way of comparison, the Soviet Union maintained a system of universal conscription from
1918 until the end of the Cold War. With relatively few exceptions, young men were drafted at age
eighteen or nineteen and required to serve for several years in the regular armed forces. This
interval of active duty was preceded by mandatory basic training for pre-draft-age secondary school
students and followed by an extended period of enrollment in the reserves. As the United States cut
back and then eliminated the use of conscription in the late 1960s and early 1970s, the Soviets
moved in the opposite direction. With the size of the eligible cohort increasing due to demographic
trends, Soviet manpower policies were adjusted to ensure that virtually all young men continued to
receive training and to serve in the regular forces. The Soviet approach to the extraction of manpower permitted the maintenance of the world's largest standing forces (rising from 3.6 million in
1960 to 6 million in 1985) and vast ready reserves (on the order of 25 million men by the 1980s).
These force levels were consistent with the requirements of Soviet strategy for fighting a nuclear or
large-scale conventional war. See Ellen Jones, *Red Army and Society: A Sociology of the Soviet
Military* (Boston: Allen and Unwin, 1985), pp. 31–78; William Odom, *The Collapse of the Soviet
Military* (New Haven: Yale University Press, 1998), pp. 38–48, figures cited from pp. 38–39.

cally adequate and domestically acceptable. It was only with the close of the Korean War that this period of uncertainty and instability came to an end and the institutional arrangements that were to persist for the next two decades became firmly established. The process through which this temporary equilibrium point was reached can be separated into two distinct but closely interrelated and chronologically overlapping developments. The first of these (the rejection of universal military training) will be discussed in this section and the second (the adoption of a limited draft) in the section below.

The Case for Universal Military Training (UMT)

In the early years of the Cold War the American state might well have armed itself with powers of compulsion far more extensive than those it was eventually able to obtain. Indeed, if matters had rested entirely in the hands of the highest ranking executive branch officials, there can be little doubt that this is precisely what would have occurred. Between 1945 and 1952, these men made repeated attempts to gain acceptance for what was, in effect, a form of universal peacetime conscription. The defeat of their efforts was due to the continuing presence of important ideological and institutional constraints on the extractive powers of the American state, even during a period when it was arguably at the very apex of its authority. By effectively eliminating from serious consideration the most extensive and intrusive military format, this outcome also served to constrict the boundaries within which all subsequent debates on the subject would occur. At the outset of the Cold War universal conscription was a distinct possibility; by the early 1950s this was no longer the case.

Well before the surrender of the Axis powers, top U.S. military and political leaders had committed themselves to the adoption of a permanent peacetime program of universal military training. In 1943 the Joint Chiefs of Staff agreed that such a program would be central to any future policy for national defense.[17] One year later, in a War Department circular laying down guidelines for postwar planning, Army Chief of Staff General George C. Marshall identified the passage of a law mandating universal training as "the essential foundation of an effective national military organization."[18] At the conclusion of the war in Europe, Marshall declared that if the nation failed to adopt universal military training, it would be because it had chosen "to ignore completely the tragedies of the past and present which we are seeking to avoid for the future."[19]

These views were endorsed, publicly and in private, both during the war and

[17] Michael S. Sherry, *Preparing for the Next War: American Plans for Postwar Defense, 1941–1945* (New Haven: Yale University Press, 1977), p. 59.

[18] War Department Circular 347, "Military Establishment—General Principles of National Military Policy to Govern Preparation of Post-War Plans," August 25, 1944, p. 4, reproduced in Harry S. Truman Library (HSTL), Offical File (OF) 109, Box 498, Universal Military Training.

[19] General of the Army George C. Marshall, "Biennial Report of the Chief of Staff of the United States Army to the Secretary of War, July 1, 1943, to June 30, 1945," in Walter Millis, ed., *The War Reports of General of the Army George C. Marshall, General of the Army H. H. Arnold, Fleet Admiral Ernest J. King* (Philadelphia: J. B. Lippincott Co., 1947), p. 294.

after, by influential civilian officials (including, among others, the Secretaries of State, War, and the Navy), as well as by uniformed military officers.[20] Beginning in 1945 UMT received repeated public presidental endorsements. In his last State of the Union address, Franklin Roosevelt declared that "we must have universal military training after this war."[21] Harry Truman took a similar stance; less than three months after the surrender of Japan, he appeared before a joint session of Congress to urge it to adopt UMT at the earliest possible moment.[22] During his seven years in office, Truman pushed for universal training with what one historian terms "remarkable persistence,"[23] ultimately requesting its adoption by Congress on seventeen separate occasions.[24]

While their details varied, all the postwar proposals for UMT shared certain essential features and, at base, a common rationale. Each of the plans put forward from 1945 onward would have required that upon reaching a specified age, all young men who satisfied minimal physical and intellectual requirements be compelled to undergo a period of basic military training, followed by a number of years of reserve duty. Depending on the stringency of the standards for induction, such a system would have touched the life of virtually every male citizen, extracting from the general population between three-quarters of a million and close to one million new trainees annually.[25] After only a few years of operation, UMT would have generated a huge pool of ready reservists.

Perhaps the greatest irony of the postwar debate over UMT is the fact that its proponents were attempting to avoid precisely the kind of opposition that their

[20] For an overview of the opinions of various Cabinet officers on this issue see their September 1945 memorandums to the president in HSTL, President's Secretary's Files (PSF), Box 146, Subject File—Agencies, Military Training. For a concise statement of the public case for UMT see a brief article by then Assistant Secretary of State John J. McCloy, "Plan of the Armed Services for Universal Military Training," *Annals of the American Academy of Political and Social Science* 241 (September 1945), pp. 26–34.

[21] Quoted in a memo from Secretary of War Henry Stimson to President Truman, May 30, 1945, HSTL, OF 109, Box 498, Universal Military Training.

[22] See "Address before a Joint Session of the Congress on Universal Military Training," October 23, 1945, in *Public Papers of the Presidents of the United States: Harry S. Truman (1945)* (Washington, DC: U.S. Government Printing Office, 1961), pp. 404–13 (hereafter *ppp 1945*). For the background to the drafting of this message see memorandums contained in HSTL, Papers of George M. Elsey, Box 89, Folder 1, Public Statements Notes, Subject File—National Defense—UMT.

[23] Russell Weigley, *The American Way of War: A History of United States Military Strategy and Policy* (Bloomington: Indiana University Press, 1973), p. 370.

[24] John M. Swomley, Jr., "A Study of the Universal Military Training Campaign, 1944–1952" (Ph.D. dissertation, University of Colorado, Boulder, Political Science Dept., 1959), p. 434.

[25] In 1945 Secretary of War Robert Patterson estimated that UMT would draw roughly 700,000 men each year. See Samuel A. Tower, "House Foes Delay Training Hearings," *New York Times*, November 9, 1945. In 1947 manpower planners calculated that over the next several years approximately 1 million young men would reach the age of eighteen each year. Of this number it was assumed that 50,000 would be too physically or mentally handicapped to be suitable for service, another 100,000 to 150,000 would volunteer for the armed forces, and the remainder, somewhere between 750,000 and 950,000 men, would be compelled to undergo military training. See Report of the President's Advisory Commission on Universal Training, *A Program for National Security* (Washington, DC: U.S. Government Printing Office, 1947), pp. 52–53.

proposals ultimately did so much to provoke. General Marshall and his allies believed that the United States would have no choice but to keep up its military strength once the Second World War was over, but they were also convinced that the American people would never agree to the maintenance of large permanent armed forces. This aversion to standing armies, they believed, went back to the founding of the Republic, and it was assumed to be a product of a fear of militarism, a desire to avoid excessive expenditures, and, most important, an abhorrence of peacetime conscription.[26]

Bridging the gap between strategic necessity and domestic constraint would require the creation of a two-tiered military system. On the one hand, once peace had been restored, the regular armed forces would have to be reduced to the minimum possible size and be made up entirely of volunteers. At the same time, graduates of a universal training program would be organized into reserves "capable of furnishing, in time of emergency, the required number of units effectively organized for rapid mobilization, expansion, and deployment."[27] Because it did not involve compulsory service in the regular armed forces, its supporters maintained that universal training could not be considered a form of conscription. Participants in UMT would be "citizens in training" rather than conscripts or draftees.[28] The combination of small volunteer regular forces and large trained reserves would therefore allow the United States to maintain a substantial military capability without resort to peacetime conscription.

The fundamental purpose of universal training was visibly and effectively to increase U.S. preparedness for the sudden onset of another global war and, in the process, to reduce the likelihood that it would ever occur. In contrast to the American people's rejection of similar proposals after World War One, their willingness to submit in peacetime to compulsory military training would, it was argued, give clear evidence of their determination to resist future aggression. In the 1930s, according to Acting Secretary of State Joseph Grew, American reluctance to bear the burdens of a strong national defense, symbolized by the rejection of peacetime training, had "invited contempt" and increased the odds of aggression.[29] By contrast, in 1945, the willingness of the American people to "stand a year of training to perform the primary duty of citizens, namely to defend their country," would, in the words of Secretary of War Henry Stimson, "have a tremendous effect upon our . . . neighbors, both friendly and unfriendly."[30] "The basic purpose of universal military training," according to the War Department's planners, was to "encourage the other world powers to

---

[26] Regarding the presumed popular resistance to large standing forces see, for example, the discussion in Marshall's, "Third Biennial Report," in Millis, *War Reports*, pp. 289–300.

[27] Memorandum from George C. Marshall to Harry S. Truman, "Basis for a Post-War Army," May 5, 1945, HSTL, OF 109, Box 498, Universal Military Training.

[28] Truman, "Address before a Joint Session of Congress," *PPP 1945*, p. 407.

[29] Acting Secretary of State Joseph C. Grew in Hearings before the House Select Committee on Postwar Military Policy *Universal Military Training*, 79th Cong., 1st sess. (Washington, DC: U.S. Government Printing Office, 1945), p. 3.

[30] Henry L. Stimson, "Statement by the Secretary of War at the Cabinet Meeting September 7, 1945, in re Military Training," HSTL, PSF, Box 146, Subject File—Agencies, Military Training.

believe that the United States is not only desirous but is prepared to enforce its determination to outlaw aggression. . . . The governments and military staffs of foreign powers must be, impressed with our determination to enforce our national policy."[31] Failure to adopt this essential measure could have dire consequences. "If you decide to repeat the policies of the past," General Marshall warned Congress in 1945, "it means that your lack of readiness would . . . encourage the very thing you wish so earnestly to avoid."[32]

Potential deterrent effects aside, the advocates of UMT believed that if war came, advanced preparations would have serious and substantial military benefits. Armed with a vast supply of ready reservists, the United States would be able to multiply its fighting power virtually overnight, rather than after months or even years of painstaking mobilization and training. This was critically important because in the next war, speed of response would be essential to national survival. The weakening of the other democratic powers and the evolution of technology meant that World War Three would likely begin with massive attacks on the continental United States.[33] In the event of a surprise attack, especially one involving the use of atomic weapons, Secretary of War Robert Patterson advised the Congress that "universal military training would insure, as no other method would, that trained men would be near at hand to alleviate the effects of the initial attack." A vast reserve of "trained men, armed with the most powerful weapons," would also be ready rapidly to attack the enemy's homeland and his advanced bases, carrying "the war to the enemy more quickly than he can bring it to us." "Without such preparedness," Patterson concluded, "annihilation may be our lot."[34]

Toward the end of the Second World War the dominant strategic principle of the new era was summed up in a simple formula by General Dwight D. Eisenhower, then the Supreme Commander of the Allied Expeditionary Force in Europe: "In a serious war the quicker the maximum potential can be converted into tactical power the surer the victory and the less the cost."[35] Without UMT, Eisenhower and most other military experts agreed, a suitably rapid conversion from potential to actual power would be impossible.

Explaining Defeat

Believing it to be essential to the nation's security, executive branch officials undertook four successive campaigns (in 1945, 1947, 1948, and 1951) aimed at

---

[31] War Department, "Notes on Universal Military Training," (September 1945?), HSTL, PSF, Box 146, Subject File—Agencies, Military Training.

[32] Army Chief of Staff General George C. Marshall in House Select Committee, *Universal Military Training*, p. 571.

[33] The impact of these changes on postwar American strategic thought is discussed in chapter 2.

[34] See statement of Secretary of War Robert P. Patterson in Hearings before the House Committee on Military Affairs, *Universal Military Training* 79th Cong., 1st sess. (Washington, DC: U.S. Government Printing Office, 1946), p. 5.

[35] Letter to Representative Clifton Woodrum, June 2, 1945, in House Select Committee, *Universal Military Training*, p. 487.

gaining public and congressional approval for universal military training. Each of these efforts received open personal support from the president; all were backed by the testimony of respected military experts and, from outside the government, by powerful veterans' organizations. All were eventually defeated. Although in 1951 the Congress did finally accept the *principle* of universal training, no program was ever adopted for putting that principle into practice. How can this outcome best be explained?

STRATEGIC RATIONALITY?

The push for universal training has generally been portrayed in accounts of the early Cold War as an atavistic response to radically transformed circumstances. With the advent of nuclear weapons and ballistic missiles, the importance of mass armies and the extractive mechanisms necessary for their creation had, presumably, been sharply diminished. A nuclear war would be over quickly, and its outcome would be determined by the forces (especially the air forces) available at its outset, rather than by any that could be mobilized once fighting was underway. This retrospective judgment of its value leads easily to the conclusion that UMT's defeat was simply a matter of good strategic sense triumphing over backward-looking military parochialism.[36]

There are at least two difficulties with this view. First, it is not at all clear that at the time of its defeat, universal training was nearly so irrelevant as it has sometimes been made to seem. Moreover, even if UMT *was*, by some objective standard, ill-suited to the needs of the nuclear age, unless we can show that it was widely acknowledged at the time, this fact alone would not necessarily explain its rejection. Indeed, an examination of the struggle over universal training reveals that its demise had much more to do with anxiety over its domestic political consequences and its potential impact on American society than it did with any collective evolution in the thinking of military planners about the implications of atomic weapons. The final burial of UMT in the early 1950s *preceded* by several years a shift in official strategy that minimized the importance of the kind of capabilities that it promised to provide. UMT had ceased for reasons of practical politics to be a viable policy well before it was abandoned by military planners as undesirable.

For virtually the entire period during which universal training was under serious consideration (and certainly at the time of the first three failed campaigns for its adoption in 1945, 1947, and 1948) there was no chance of the United States delivering an atomic "knockout blow" against the Soviet Union, and no prospect that it would soon be able to do so. Workable thermonuclear weapons and an era of "nuclear plenty" had not yet arrived and were by no means assured. By the mid-1950s things had begun to change, but in the late

---

[36] See, for example, Samuel Huntington, *The Common Defense: Strategic Programs in National Politics* (New York: Columbia University Press, 1961), pp. 29, 436; Gregg Herken, *The Winning Weapon: The Atomic Bomb in the Cold War, 1945–1950* (New York: Vintage, 1982), p. 247; Russell F. Weigley, *History of the United States Army* (New York: Macmillan, 1967), pp. 496–500; and Millis, *Arms and Men*, pp. 307–9, 320–22.

1940s the American atomic arsenal was simply too small to be decisive, and the Soviet arsenal was smaller still.[37]

If it had broken out at this time, World War Three might have begun in the air, but as General Marshall explained in 1948, it would have ended up "in the mud and on the ground."[38] Marshall's assessment was bolstered in 1949 and 1950 by two highly classified analyses which concluded that, despite its lead in atomic capabilities, the United States would not be able for some time to deliver a quick and decisive aerial attack on the Soviet Union.[39] As the findings of these studies implied, atomic exchanges would in all likelihood have been followed by prolonged struggles for bases, then by vast land battles, and finally by the conquest and occupation of enemy territory. In such a monumental struggle, the ability quickly to mobilize large trained forces for the stabilization of the home front and the conduct of offensive operations could well have been decisive.

Whether or not it was realistic, this vision of World War Three as a protracted slugging match continued to dominate official U.S. strategic thinking and formal American military planning well into the 1950s. In 1947 the Joint Chiefs of Staff informed President Truman that if war came during the next decade, American "external manpower requirements" would be "at least on the order of those of World War II" and that, in addition, "internal requirements" would make "far greater demands in the event of future war" than they had in the previous two. For these reasons, the Chiefs emphasized "the overriding importance . . . of having trained forces quickly available," and they urged the rapid adoption of universal training.[40]

The war plans of the day also reflected the assumption that another struggle for global military preponderance would be long, and that it would require the commitment to battle of vast armies and navies. In documents prepared before and immediately following the outbreak of fighting in Korea, the Joint Chiefs of Staff anticipated that a future world war would unfold in four phases, last at least four years (and possibly more), and require the eventual mobilization of a sixteen hundred ship navy and more than seventy infantry and armored divi-

---

[37] The United States had only around fifty atomic bombs in 1948, but close to three hundred by the end of 1950. The Soviets apparently had only fifty in 1952. See David Alan Rosenberg, "U.S. Nuclear Stockpile, 1945 to 1950," *Bulletin of the Atomic Scientists* (May 1982), pp. 25–30; John Lewis Gaddis, *We Now Know: Rethinking Cold War History* (Oxford: Clarendon Press, 1997), p. 103.

[38] Statement by Secretary of State George C. Marshall in Hearings before the Senate Armed Services Committee, *Universal Military Training* 80th Cong., 2d sess. (Washington, DC: U.S. Government Printing Office, 1948), p. 21.

[39] For the text of the 1949 Harmon Report see "Evaluation of Effect on Soviet War Effort Resulting from the Strategic Air Offensive," in Thomas H. Etzold and John Lewis Gaddis, eds., *Containment: Documents on American Policy and Strategy, 1945–1950* (New York: Columbia University Press, 1978), pp. 360–64. On the origins of this document and the subsequent Hull Report see also the essay "The Nuclearization of NATO and U.S.-West European Relations," in Marc Trachtenberg, *History and Strategy* (Princeton: Princeton University Press, 1991), especially pp. 153–60.

[40] Letter from Harry S. Truman to Dr. Karl T. Compton, January 17, 1947, HSTL PSF, Box 146, Subject File, Agencies—Military Training.

sions, plus assorted smaller units.[41] It was only in 1953 and 1954, with the advent of the Eisenhower administration, that the presumed length of a future war and estimated requirements for conventional forces began to be reduced.[42] Until then, the official position continued to be that the next war would be protracted, that its outcome would turn on the use of conventional as well as atomic weapons, and that the chances of the United States winning it would be considerably enhanced by the adoption of universal military training. "The push-button era of warfare has certainly not yet arrived," warned Secretary of Defense James Forrestal, "and may be many years in the future." In the meantime it was crucial for the United States to maintain "a properly balanced military establishment," comprised "not only [of] adequate air power but strong land and sea forces as well." For the purpose of generating these forces, universal training was indispensable.[43]

Although there were dissenters from this view, in the late 1940s they were in a distinct minority. Civilian strategists like *New York Times* military correspondent Hanson Baldwin argued in his columns that UMT was not militarily essential and that, in fact, it would "starve . . . more important aspects of national defense" (including "air power, missiles, new weapons, [and] sea power") while it created at the same time "the shadow of security without its substance," encouraging the development of a "Maginot Line . . . psychology."[44] If it wished to avoid war, the United States should emphasis "readiness potential" (especially atomic air forces-in-being) over the "mobilization potential" embodied in UMT.[45] Baldwin's arguments anticipated many aspects of what would later become the conventional critique of universal training, but at the time, his opinions were not widely shared and, indeed, were repudiated by his own newspaper.[46]

---

[41] See the documents reproduced in *Budgets and Strategy: The Road to Offtackle* and *Blueprint for Rearmament: Reaper*, vols. 12 and 15 of Steven T. Ross and David Alan Rosenberg, eds., *America's Plans for War against the Soviet Union, 1945–1950* (New York: Garland, 1989–90). The evolution of American planning during this period is well summarized in Samuel R. Williamson, Jr., and Steven L. Rearden, *The Origins of U.S. Nuclear Strategy, 1945–1953* (New York: St. Martin's, 1993). For a detailed discussion of the Army's plans, in particular, see John Michael Kendall, "An Inflexible Response: United States Army Manpower Mobilization Policies, 1945–1957" (Ph.D dissertation, Duke University, Department of History, 1982), pp. 43–156.

[42] The early stages of this process are discussed in Robert J. Watson, *History of the Joint Chiefs of Staff*, vol. 5, *The Joint Chiefs of Staff and National Policy, 1953–1954* (Washington, DC: JCS Historical Division, 1986), pp. 150–62. Changing assumptions about the duration of a future war will be discussed at greater length in chapter 6.

[43] Letter from James Forrestal to Owen J. Roberts, Chairman of the National Security Committee, January 23, 1948, HSTL, John H. Ohly Papers. Forrestal's views and language reflect the conclusions of the 1947 Presidential Advisory Commission on Universal Training, *A Program for National Security*, pp. 12–19.

[44] See Hanson W. Baldwin, "UMT's Value Weighed," *New York Times*, May 4, 1947, p. 24. Baldwin was consistently skeptical of UMT. See, for example, his earlier critique of Marshall's final war report, "For the Future Defense," *New York Times*, October 10, 1945, p. 1.

[45] See Hanson Baldwin, *The Price of Power* (New York: Harper, 1947), pp. 277–78.

[46] On its editorial pages the *Times* continued to call for UMT and to criticize its opponents. See,

In 1945, 1947, and 1951–52 the strategic arguments against UMT played virtually no role in determining its fate. On each of these occasions the nation's military leaders were united in their public support of the measure, and there was no authoritative challenge to the claim that it was essential to the nation's defense. In each case UMT was openly defeated or effectively derailed for reasons that had little or nothing to do with strategy.

The events of 1948 provide only a partial exception to this pattern. In that year the combination of a perceived worsening in relations with the Soviets and the continuing efforts of the Truman administration to hold down defense spending caused disputes between the armed services to boil over into public view. When pressed by Congress, representatives of the newly independent Air Force acknowledged that they would prefer to see scarce dollars spent on more aircraft rather than on a training program whose primary purpose was to provide reserves for the ground forces. This rather unsurprising admission (which involved a statement of budget priorities rather than the presentation of a fully articulated alternative strategic vision) was seized upon by the administration's opponents and contributed to the defeat of its third campaign for UMT. A plausible strategic argument that universal training was unnecessary (or at least less important and less pressing than other measures) was useful to those who were already inclined to oppose it for entirely different reasons. But enthusiasm for air power was the *result* and not the cause of a deep, underlying distaste for peacetime conscription.[47]

SOCIETAL RESISTANCE AND THE STRUGGLE FOR LEGITIMACY

From the mid-1940s onward, the suggestion of anything even remotely resembling universal peacetime conscription aroused sustained vocal opposition from an assortment of labor, education, farm, church, left-wing, and pacifist groups. The members of these organizations were motivated by a mix of self-interest and deeply held beliefs.[48] Although they differed in many respects, all shared a

---

for example, "General Marshall's Report," *New York Times*, October 10, 1945, p. 20; and "Unfinished Business," *New York Times*, July 29, 1947, p. 20.

[47] The comparative unimportance of strategic arguments in the first campaign for UMT is evident in Michael Sherry's account. See Sherry, *Preparing for the Next War*, pp. 58–90. One historian notes that in 1947, "issues of military strategy . . . had little visible impact on congressional treatment of UMT." James M. Gerhardt, *The Draft and Public Policy: Issues in Military Manpower Procurement, 1945–1970* (Columbus: Ohio State University Press, 1971), p. 71. For two accounts of the events of 1948 see Townsend Hoopes and Douglas Brinkley, *Driven Patriot: The Life and Times of James Forrestal* (New York: Vintage, 1992), pp. 365–83; Frank Kofsky, *Harry S. Truman and the War Scare of 1948* (New York: St. Martin's, 1993), pp. 195–213. By contrast to 1948, in 1951–52 there was no open interservice dispute about UMT and comparatively little discussion of its strategic merits. See the account in Gerhardt, *The Draft and Public Policy*, pp. 169–87.

[48] The material interests of professional educators, farmers, and unionists are easiest to discern. Colleges and universities relied on a steady flow of high school graduates, a stream that would be interrupted, and perhaps thinned, by an intervening period of mandatory military training. Farmers depended on the labor of their sons. Having just come through a war in which the federal government had contemplated drafting laborers and assigning them to work in particular industries, union leaders were understandably leery of any kind of universal obligation to the state. The concerns of other groups were somewhat more abstract. Church leaders feared for the souls of the young.

common abhorrence of compulsion by the state, and while they sometimes couched their objections in strategic or economic terms, it was this theme, expressed in a thousand different ways, that was central to all of their arguments.

The enemies of UMT were able to exert an influence on events out of proportion to their actual numbers. This was a result, first of all, of their ability to deploy arguments that resonated with widely held American beliefs about the appropriate limits of state power. In the battle of ideas, UMT's opponents were therefore successful in casting doubt not merely on its utility, but on its very legitimacy. Universal mandatory military service in peacetime would, they claimed, disrupt the education of the nation's youth and expose them at a tender age to the evils of drinking, gambling, and prostitution; it would take young men away from their farms at harvest and fatally undermine the principle of free labor. Over time, compulsory training would expose virtually the entire adult male population to militaristic propaganda, thereby altering the character of American foreign policy and, ultimately, society. Widespread compulsion, in the absence of a clear and present danger to national survival, represented an excessive imposition on the liberties of a free people; it was, in the end, dangerous, evil, and un-American.[49]

These assertions moved the debate over UMT away from the technical issues on which government manpower planning experts might otherwise have had a decisive advantage and toward broad philosophical questions on which they could not claim a monopoly of wisdom. By attacking the legitimacy of universal training, its enemies were able to gain the rhetorical initiative, an advantage that they never subsequently surrendered. From the very outset of the debate, the advocates of UMT were forced onto the defensive, and the more they tried to justify their preferred policy in terms of American history and ideology, the more they tended to undermine their own position.

Supporters of universal training claimed that in addition to being necessary, it was also fully in keeping with America's democratic principles and, in particular, with its egalitarian ideals. "Equality of obligation . . . is the essence of democracy," proclaimed one offical report. "We therefore recommend that the principle of universality be extended to the maximum practical extent."[50] While a compulsory training program would require those called to surrender a certain fraction of their personal freedom, it had the considerable advantage of demanding the same sacrifice from all who were eligible. Indeed, as its supporters rightly pointed out, no other military format could possibly be as fair. In emphasizing its universality, however, UMT's advocates also managed to call attention, albeit inadvertently, to its extraordinary scope. This was a program that

---

Pacifists worried about militarism at home and war abroad. The left objected to any measures that might bring the United States closer to confrontation with the Soviet Union.

[49] For a concise summary of the views of these groups see Swomley, "A Study of the Universal Military Training Campaign," pp. 254–85. All of the main arguments against UMT were advanced during the first campaign for its adoption and simply repeated thereafter. The flavor of the debate is best captured in the 1945 hearings conducted by the House Select Committee on Postwar Military Policy, cited above in n. 29.

[50] *A Program for National Security*, p. 42.

would, as they proudly proclaimed, touch every man (and perhaps eventually every woman) in the country, and not only in wartime, but for an indefinite period of uneasy peace.[51] Underlining these facts made it that much more difficult to deny that UMT represented what one skeptic termed a "drastic, almost revolutionary" departure from the policies of the recent past.[52]

In part for this reason, UMT's backers were especially eager to refute the charge that their program was historically as well as philosophically "un-American." To the contrary, they claimed, it was the maintenance of large *permanent* armies that the American people had always regarded with repugnance. By preparing a large pool of ready reservists, training would allow the nation to preserve its security without abandoning its traditional preference for small peacetime forces.[53] The idea that all American citizens had a duty to participate in the defense of their community was, moreover, one that had a long and honorable past. In their quest for legitimacy, the authors of postwar training proposals harkened back to the Militia Act of 1792 and even to the colonial statutes that preceded it.[54] George Marshall invoked George Washington's proposals for a program of peacetime training, and Harry Truman conducted his own research into Thomas Jefferson's views on the subject.[55]

These exercises in creative historiography may have helped to establish the distant antecedants of UMT, but they also served to heighten awareness of just how different it was from anything in living memory. After all, despite an early proclamation of allegiance to the principle of universal service, there was no denying that previous generations of Americans had, with the exception of a few brief intervals, continued to worship what the exasperated author of one government sponsored study referred to as "the false gods of voluntarism."[56] After briefly adopting conscription in times of emergency, the United States had each time "reverted to the same misconceived military policy," abandoning compulsion in favor of a reliance on volunteers.[57] Pondering the nation's history

---

[51] In addition to recommending training of some kind for virtually every man in the country (with the sole exception of "those unfortunately handicapped persons who could make no material contribution of any kind"), the Compton Commission also urged "consideration of the advisability of establishing a program for women." Ibid.

[52] Willard Waller, "A Sociologist Looks at Conscription," *Annals of the American Academy of Political and Social Science* 241 (September 1945), p. 95.

[53] See, for example, the arguments by General Marshall in his 1945 "Third Biennial Report," in Millis, *War Reports*, pp. 289–300 and in his congressional testimony of that year before the House Select Committee on Postwar Military Policy, *Universal Military Training*, pp. 567–78.

[54] In 1947 the federal government published a four-volume compilation of all "enactments of compulsion" from 1607 to 1918. See U.S. Selective Service System, *Backgrounds of Selective Service*, vols. 1–4 (New York: Arno Press, 1979).

[55] Marshall, "Third Biennial Report," pp. 291–92. Letters from Harry S. Truman to Lieutenant Colonel W. J. Morton (the librarian of the U.S. Military Academy at West Point), October 11, 1946; Truman to Secretary of War Robert Patterson, October 9, 1946; and Patterson to Truman, October 16, 1946, all contained in HSTL, PSF, Box 146, Subject File—Agencies, Military Training.

[56] *Backgrounds of Selective Service* 1:81.

[57] Ibid., p. 68.

led to what were, at best, some rather mixed conclusions about just how "American" universal mandatory peacetime service truly was.

While emphasizing its strategic essentiality, egalitarian character, and historical roots, UMT's supporters also tried to downplay the extent to which their program would infringe on individual liberties. This involved a mix of hairsplitting and disingenuousness that had an effect precisely opposite to the one intended. The authors of the War Department's early postwar plans tried to persuade Congress and the public that despite all appearances, what they were proposing did not really involve anything that could properly be called "conscription." As Brigadier General John Palmer explained in 1945:

> Conscription, according to the definition in our standard dictionaries, is a "compulsory enlistment or enrollment for military or naval *service.*" . . . Our young men should be called to the colors for *training* only. . . . They are not to be subject . . . to military *service.*[58]

The difference between *training* and *service* was what would separate the American brand of compulsion from its European and Asian counterparts. As important as it may have been to defense planners (and dictionary authors), this distinction seems for the most part to have been lost on the larger audience. To most people, conscription was still conscription, even if it involved only a year or six months of dull and grueling training in the United States, instead of two or three years of potentially dangerous overseas military service. As James Forrestal explained, trying to draw a sharp line between the two forms of mandatory duty involved "straining at a gnat. . . . When a man's son is inducted into the service he is taken away from home, and to the parent there just isn't any distinction between Universal Training and Selective Service."[59]

Similarly, the claim that compulsory service (or training) was really no different from mandatory jury duty, or tax payment, or school attendance did not win many converts.[60] Even some advocates of UMT found the argument that it was simply another form of education (which was also, after all, being imposed on minors who had no "legal right of choice") to be "strange" and even "fascist . . . in character."[61]

The final, and in many ways the most self-defeating, tactic employed by UMT's supporters was their attempt to justify it in other than strictly military terms. This was a mistake that representatives of the armed forces had been prudent enough to avoid, but which their civilian counterparts made repeatedly

---

[58] See the testimony of Brigadier General John McA. Palmer in *Universal Military Training* (1945), p. 492 (emphasis added). This point was echoed repeatedly by Marshall and others.

[59] Memorandum from James Forrestal to John Steelman, August 11, 1948. HSTL, OF 109, Box 498, Universal Military Training.

[60] See, for example, the statement by Joseph Grew, at that time the National Vice Chairman of the National Security Committee, in the 1948 hearings, *Universal Military Training*, p. 130.

[61] See the critique of an American Legion pamphlet making these arguments in Edward A. Fitzpatrick, *Universal Military Training* (New York: McGraw-Hill, 1945), pp. 240–41.

and with great, if ill-advised, enthusiasm.[62] President Truman went so far in 1946 as to have the word *military* dropped from the name of his Advisory Commission on Universal Training because, as he put it, "the military phase is incidental to what I have in mind."[63] The purpose of such a program, Truman told his commissioners, was to give

> our young people a background in the disciplinary approach of getting along with one another, informing them of their physical make-up, and what it means to take care of this temple which God gave us. If we get that instilled into them, and then instill into them a responsibility which begins in the township, in the city ward, the first thing you know we will have sold our Republic to the coming generations as Madison and Hamilton and Jefferson sold it in the first place.[64]

Stressing the civic benefits of training was intended to make it more palatable to a general public wary of statism, militarism, and compulsion. But Truman's vision of UMT as a nationwide physical fitness, personal hygiene, and high school civics class rolled into one inspired more ridicule and hostility than it did support. It was one thing to argue that compulsion was an unavoidable evil made necessary by external threats to the nation's freedom, quite another to assert that it was a positive good. The image of the state as an all-wise molder of bodies, minds, and souls was a direct affront to American liberal preferences and traditions. And the seemingly casual admission that recruits would receive political indoctrination (or "instruction in the meaning and obligations of citizenship") as well as military preparation did nothing to dispel the faint odor of totalitarianism that lingered over all proposals for universal training.[65]

---

[62] On the military's sensitivity to charges that it was seeking, through training, to inculcate militarism see Sherry, *Preparing for the Next War*, pp. 69–73. Truman received sharply conflicting advice on this issue, and he seems himself to have been of two minds. While members of the White House staff pushed hard for "a universal training program which contribute[s] to national security through non-military training," as well as to military preparation, the Secretary of Defense warned that "an unrealistic non-military plan . . . would raise extraneous questions that might seriously confuse the basic issue." See a confidential staff memorandum entitled "Universal Training—Background, Present Status, and Principal Issues," sent to the Secretary of State on January 28, 1948, and a memorandum from Forrestal to Truman dated January 10, 1948, both in HSTL, PSF, Box 146, Subject File—Agencies, Military Training. Throughout the UMT controversy, Truman expressed enthusiasm for a program that would improve the moral and physical well-being of the nation's youth as well as increasing their readiness for war. In 1946, for example, he told the president of Princeton University that he was "very anxious to work out a Universal Training plan that will first and foremost, give us an adequate defense set-up; second, that will contribute to the physical fitness of our young men. In fact, I think, this is probably just as important as an adequate defense program." Letter from Truman to Harold W. Dodds, December 3, 1946, HSTL, PSF, Box 146, Subject File—Agencies Military Training.

[63] Robert David Ward, "The Movement for Universal Military Training in the United States, 1942–1952" (Ph.D. dissertation, University of North Carolina, Department of History, 1957), p. 230.

[64] Harry S. Truman, *Memoirs: Years of Trial and Hope*, vol. 2 (New York: Doubleday, 1956), p. 54.

[65] *A Program for National Security*, p. 61.

CONGRESSIONAL UNCERTAINTY AND INACTION

As they considered how best to respond to administration requests for UMT, members of Congress found themselves confronted by conflicting pressures. Executive branch assertions that universal training was essential to the nation's security could not be lightly dismissed, especially in a period of deepening international uncertainty and tension. Official arguments were echoed by the spokesmen of several large and powerful veterans' organizations, and if opinion polls were to be believed, they appeared to have gained broad public acceptance.[66] Balanced against this were the activities of a comparatively small but evidently dedicated and determined coalition of opponents.

In the absence of sustained public opposition, the pressures for UMT would probably have proved overwhelming. Instead, as has already been suggested, the running debate over universal training raised lasting questions about its legitimacy. Philosophical arguments aside, the very existence of an organized, vocal anticonscription movement also served to suggest that UMT might not be quite as popular, and a vote for it might not be as free of political danger, as appeared at first glance to be the case. Public opposition to universal training therefore helped to bolster the resolve of those in Congress who were already inclined, for a variety of reasons, to vote against it, while at the same time inducing doubt and hesitation in many who might otherwise have been neutral or favorably disposed.

While Democrats were generally more supportive than Republicans, opposition to universal training was not merely a matter of partisan politics. Each of the Truman administration's campaigns won backing from a number of Republicans (including some influential members of the various military affairs committees), and each was opposed by some Democrats. Nevertheless, the strongest and most consistent congressional opposition to UMT came from the Republican party, and in particular from its conservative midwestern wing. It was in this part of the country that principled anticompulsion arguments struck their most responsive chord, and here too that the various agricultural groups opposed to UMT had their greatest clout. Senator Robert Taft of Ohio, the leading Republican opponent of universal training, spoke for many when he warned that its adoption would transform the United States into a "militaristic and totalitarian country."[67] Massive peacetime conscription was "contrary to the whole concept of American liberty. . . . It is hard to think of any more drastic limitation of personal freedom," Taft declared, "than to permit the state to take boys from their homes, their education, or their chosen occupations and subject them for a year to the arbitrary direction of some military officer, and indoctrination courses prepared by some ideological bureau of the War Department."[68] Univer-

[66] According to the Gallup Poll, between 1942 and 1956 support for UMT never dipped below 60 percent and, at the peak of the controversy (between 1945 and 1950), it averaged close to 75 percent. Swomley, "A Study of the Universal Military Training Campaign," p. 287.

[67] Quoted in Caroline Thomas Harnsberger, *A Man of Courage: Robert A. Taft* (New York: Wilcox and Follett, 1952), pp. 204–16.

[68] Quoted in Lynn Eden, "Capitalist Conflict and the State: The Making of United States Military Policy in 1948," in Charles Bright and Susan Harding, eds., *Statemaking and Social Movements:*

sal peacetime conscription was "un-American," Taft told his colleagues and his constituents, and it deserved to be defeated.[69]

Where conservative Republicans worried most about state-directed compulsion, some southern Democrats were more troubled by UMT's egalitarian aspect. Despite their general enthusiasm for military preparedness, many in the solidly Democratic South feared that a truly universal training program would promote "race mixing" and undermine segregation. Especially after 1948, as it became clear that the Truman administration was serious about promoting civil rights and desegregating the armed forces, southern support for UMT tended to waver. Thus, while many of the societal groups opposing universal conscription came from the liberal and even radical end of the political spectrum, they found allies among the most conservative, even reactionary, elements in the country and in Congress. On the issue of mandatory military training, pacifists and labor leaders made common cause with racists and anti-statist conservatives. As would happen again in the 1970s, opposition to conscription helped forge an odd alliance of left and right.[70]

Many members of Congress who lacked either strong philosophical or clear-cut electoral reasons for voting against UMT appear nevertheless to have been impressed by the fervor of those who lobbied against it. The outpouring of opposition that accompanied each effort to pass UMT suggested that the nation-wide polls proclaiming its popularity could be wrong (as they had been in the presidential election of 1948) or, at the very least, that they might not accurately reflect the climate of opinion in particular states and districts. This seeming discontinuity between what they were themselves experiencing and what they were reading in the newspapers caused many representatives and senators to disregard the public opinion polls and to rely more directly on their own views and political instincts.[71] The result was a striking and, to some, an exasperating disjuncture between polling data and congressional behavior. "If public opinion polls are any criterion," declared a *New York Times* editorial in 1945, then the Congress was "so far behind the people on the question of universal military training that it is no contest."[72] Two years later, the *Times* would again bemoan the strange reluctance of Congress to act, despite the fact that 73 per-

---

Essays in History and Theory (Ann Arbor: University of Michigan Press, 1984), p. 245. For more on Taft's views see Robert A. Taft, *A Foreign Policy for Americans* (New York: Doubleday, 1951), pp. 66–73; also Russell Kirk and James McClellan, *The Political Principles of Robert A. Taft* (New York: Fleet Press, 1967).

[69] "Taft Calls the Training Measure Obsolete, Wasteful, Un-American," *New York Times*, June 27, 1947, p. 1.

[70] On southern ambivalence about UMT see the analysis in Swomley, "A Study of the Universal Military Training Campaign," pp. 394–433; also Ward, "The Movement for Universal Training," p. 461. Southern votes in the House of Representatives were critical in derailing the last serious effort to establish a universal training program in 1952.

[71] Swomley, "A Study of the Universal Military Training Campaign," pp. 290. George Gallup would later cite UMT as an example of an issue on which public opinion polls had failed to sway Congress, quoted ibid., p. 291.

[72] "Congress and the People," *New York Times* November 27, 1945, p. 22.

cent of those holding strong opinions on the subject were apparently in favor of UMT.[73] As one frustrated supporter of training observed, the activities of an "organized, highly vocal minority" had apparently been quite successful in causing "many congressmen [to] believe that the country does not want universal military training although every poll ever taken shows a large pro majority."[74]

Whatever the latest polls might show, members of Congress had to be concerned that public support for UMT was wide rather than deep, and that it might therefore be prone to rapid evaporation.[75] Once a program was in place there was a danger that it could prove to be a good deal less popular in practice than it had seemed in the abstract, perhaps even provoking a backlash against those who had voted for it. Many legislators seemed to sense that support for UMT by those answering a pollster's question would not necessarily translate itself into "support for the program when it involved sending relatives and friends to a year of military training."[76]

Even if the polls were right and most Americans were truly willing to accept universal training, there was little reason to think that they would do so with great enthusiasm or that they would be deeply disappointed if it were not adopted. With the exception of the members of some veteran's groups, support for UMT from the public at large was more passive than active. UMT's opponents, on the other hand, were clearly highly motivated; they cared deeply about the issue of compulsion in peacetime, and there was good reason to expect that they would seek to punish those who ignored their wishes. The obvious intensity with which they held their opinions gave added weight to the opinions of those who opposed universal training. As they considered their options, many in Congress apparently came to the conclusion that they would lose more votes than they might win by coming out clearly in favor of universal training.[77]

Congress was quick to detect the dangers that lurked behind a seemingly popular program like UMT. Indications of this sensitivity can be found in the fact that the House, where every member faced reelection every two years, tended consistently to be less supportive of training than did the Senate. The eagerness of UMT's enemies to delay decision in off years and to force consideration when elections loomed indicates a similar assessment that whatever the other evidence might suggest, support for universal peacetime conscription could turn out to be a very risky proposition.[78]

[73] "Taboo," *New York Times*, July 23, 1947, p. 22.

[74] Worthington Thompson (executive secretary, Citizens Committee for Military Training of Young Men, Inc.) to General Harry Vaughn, August 19, 1946. HSTL, OF 109, Box 498, Universal Military Training.

[75] For the claim that as early as 1945 public support for UMT was "widespread, but soft," see Sherry, *Preparing for the Next War*, p. 75.

[76] Perry McCoy Smith, *The Air Force Plans for Peace, 1943–1945* (Baltimore: Johns Hopkins University Press, 1970), p. 96.

[77] Clyde E. Jacobs and John F. Gallagher, *The Selective Service Act: A Case Study of the Governmental Process* (New York: Dodd, Mead, 1967), pp. 28–29.

[78] For contemporary analyses bolstering these conclusions see, for example these articles from the

The net effect of the various pressures for and against UMT is manifest in the pattern of congressional behavior. Rather than reject administration proposals openly, Congress repeatedly sought opportunities to avoid making a decision. By sidestepping the issue and then delaying implementation, Congress succeeded eventually in killing UMT.

In 1945, despite urgent appeals for a quick decision, a Democratically controlled Congress permitted hearings on UMT to drag on for months without the matter ever being brought to a vote. Fearing that popular approval of universal training would begin to dwindle once peace had been declared, its supporters sought a decision before the close of hostilities. War and Navy Department officials testified vigorously and unanimously in favor of UMT. Confronted by an expert consensus on the strategic necessity of training, critics concentrated on the threat it allegedly posed to "the nation's freedoms [and] political traditions," and they "accused the military of trying to railroad the nation into UMT while the war was still on."[79] Faced with evidence of popular resistance to the administration's plans and with an election year looming, neither Republicans nor Democrats were eager to act. After having failed to move before the surrender of Japan, the House Democratic leadership in October 1945 declined to comment on President Truman's urgent request for passage of a training bill.[80] In the same month a straw poll of senators found twenty-five in favor, nineteen opposed, and forty "undecided and in no hurry to make up their minds."[81] This reluctance to act continued into the following year and, by the end of 1946, the first campaign for UMT had ended "not in defeat, but in inanimate suspension."[82]

In 1947 and 1948 the Truman administration redoubled its efforts to obtain early passage of a training bill. A commission of outside experts was appointed to generate public support for UMT, and various steps, both rhetorical and concrete, were taken to reduce anxiety about its extensive, compulsory, and potentially militaristic character. Among other things, the proposed term of service for trainees was shortened from one year to six months, and it was announced that any program would be overseen by a special civilian commission rather than operate under direct military control.[83]

New York Times: "House Foes Delay Training Hearings," November 9, 1945, p. 9; "1945 House Vote on Training Fades," November 18, 1945, p. 33; "UMT Bill Action Sought in House," May 9, 1947, p. 11; "Training Law Is Unlikely This Session, in Capital View," June 3, 1947, p. 1; "Training Measure May Be Postponed," June 22, 1947, p. 19; "Senate Uncertain over Draft, UMT," March 21, 1948, p. 23; "Congress Hostile to UMT But Draft Is Firmly Backed," April 4, 1948, p. 1.

[79] Sherry, *Preparing for the Next War*, p. 83.

[80] Swomley, "A Study of the Universal Military Training Campaign," p. 405.

[81] Ward, "The Movement for Universal Training," p. 131.

[82] Gerhardt, *The Draft and Public Policy*, p. 38; the events of 1945–46 are well covered on pp. 3–38; and in Ward, "The Movement for Universal Training," pp. 99–200.

[83] For the recommendations of the Compton Commission see *A Program for National Security*, pp. 40–95. Also "Training of All Youth at 18 Is Urged by Truman Board, Seeing War Peril after 1955," *New York Times*, June 21, 1947, p. 1. The idea of a special UMT commission dates back to the end of 1944, when the Bureau of the Budget advised President Roosevelt, in effect, that the matter was too important to be left to the generals. See Harold D. Smith (Director, Bureau of the

By 1947, following the midterm elections of the previous year, both houses of Congress were in Republican hands. Although the administration's new proposals did receive endorsement from major figures in both parties, key Republicans in both the House and Senate remained deeply and unalterably opposed to UMT, and they used their enhanced influence to delay bringing the matter to a vote. Public hearings were extended to permit a full airing of all possible objections to the proposed training plan. When the House Armed Services Committee finally did report favorably an administration-sponsored bill in the summer of 1947, the Republican chairman of the Rules Committee refused to permit it to be brought to the floor for debate, and once again the matter was put off into an election year.[84]

In 1948, as we have seen, congressional opponents used hearings on the administration's defense program to expose and then to exploit divisions within the military about the priority that should be attached to universal training. Many who were already declared enemies of UMT seized on new strategic arguments against it and evidence of intramilitary disputes over its value to bolster their preferred positions. Senator Taft, who had long framed his objections to universal conscription in broad philosophical terms, now "shifted his attack to new ground, promoting air power as the principal means of defense and an alternative to UMT."[85] Others, both Republicans and Democrats, also embraced air power because it gave them a way of opposing or ignoring the administration's proposed manpower policies without appearing weak or irresponsible on defense. A bigger Air Force cost money, but its functioning did not depend on universal conscription, and this, rather than any thoughtful consideration of its true strategic value, was the main source of its appeal on both sides of the aisle. Presented with another opportunity to avoid decision, Congress in the spring of 1948 once again refused to act on UMT.[86]

Three years later, with war underway in Korea and both the House and Senate back safely in Democratic hands, the Truman administration made one last attempt to force its proposals through Congress. Past disputes among military experts were put aside as representatives of all the armed services came forward dutifully to testify that a universal training program was now essential to na-

---

Budget), Memorandum for the President, "Universal Military Training," December 29, 1944. HSTL, Papers of James E. Webb, Box 20, BoB Subject File—UMT. (Webb's papers contain much useful information on the deliberations of the Compton Commission.)

[84] Both Senator Chan Gurney, Chairman of the Senate Armed Services Committee, and Walter Andrews, Chairman of the House Armed Services Committee were favorably disposed to UMT. But Gurney had less influence with his colleagues than Taft, whose strong public denunciations of UMT helped keep Senate Republicans in line. In the House, Andrews (a moderate Republican from New Jersey) found his efforts to push UMT blocked by Rules Committee Chairman Leo Allen (R., Ill.). On the parliamentary maneuvering that led up to the 1948 defeat of UMT see Jacobs and Gallagher, *The Selective Service Act*, pp. 29–42; also Ward, "The Movement for Universal Military Training," pp. 201–65.

[85] Gerhardt, *The Draft and Public Policy*, p. 92.

[86] On the events of 1948 see ibid., pp. 58–127; also Eden, "Capitalist Conflict and the State."

tional survival.[87] In 1951 Congress finally passed legislation declaring a universal obligation for all male citizens to undergo a period of military training, but it delayed implementation of an actual program until the details could be studied by yet another independent commission. This group was quickly constituted, and within a matter of months it had made its predictably positive report.[88] By 1952, however, with the Korean emergency diminishing in intensity and another election fast approaching, congressional enthusiasm for UMT, always limited, had already begun to cool. Public hearings brought forth the usual stream of objections to universal conscription, an idea that seemed to have gained few new friends while losing none of its old enemies. Uneasy about pressing ahead, a coalition of House Republicans and Democrats voted to recommit the bill that would finally have launched universal training, and the Senate then refused to take any further action.[89] Early in 1952, before the election of Dwight Eisenhower, the adoption of the New Look, and a clear shift in national strategy away from warfighting and toward massive retaliation, universal military training was effectively dead, killed by a national aversion to compulsion that remained potent even in the depths of the early Cold War.

SELECTING "SELECTIVE SERVICE"

How, given this demonstrable distaste for conscription, did the United States come nevertheless to adopt a limited draft? The answer to this question can be summed up under three headings: crisis, indirection, and compromise. If not for the unanticipated events of 1948 and 1950 there is strong reason to believe that contrary to the advice of the nation's top military and political leaders and despite their best efforts, by the early 1950s the American armed forces would have been manned on an entirely voluntary basis. The decision to rely instead on limited conscription, with all of its potential problems, appears more clear-

[87] See the testimony contained in Hearings before the Senate Armed Services Committee, *Universal Military Training* 81st Cong., 2nd sess. (Washington, DC: U.S. Government Printing Office, 1950); and Hearings before the House Armed Services Committee, *Universal Military Training* 82d Cong., 1st sess. (Washington, DC: U.S. Government Printing Office, 1951).

[88] See National Security Training Commission, *Universal Military Training* (Washington, DC: U.S. Government Printing Office, 1951); also in the *New York Times*, October 29, 1951, see "U.M.T. Report Asks 6 Months' Training for Youths at 18," p. 1, and "Quick Action Asked on U.M.T. Program," p. 20. For a contemporary critique that sums up most of the counterarguments see a 1952 pamphlet by the National Council against Conscription, "The Facts *Behind* the Report," reprinted in John Whiteclay Chambers II, ed., *Draftees or Volunteers: A Documentary History of the Debate over Military Conscription in the United States, 1878–1973* (New York: Garland Press, 1975), pp. 409–17.

[89] The motion to recommit received the votes of 83 percent of House Republicans and 38 percent of Democrats, roughly half of whom were from the South. See the discussion in Swomley, "A Study of the Universal Military Training Campaign," pp. 394–443. As one editorial writer complained, what the House had done was "to kill the universal military training program by indirection. This may be good politics in an election year, but it is a malodorous way to do business." "Funds for U.M.T. Study," *New York Times*, June 22, 1952, sec. 4, p. 8.

cut in retrospect than it was at the time. In fact, no such decision was ever openly and explicitly made. Albeit with dwindling certainty as to how long it would truly be necessary, in 1948, 1950, and 1951 the draft was presented by its supporters as a temporary measure that would soon be replaced with something more satisfactory. Instead of embracing selective service, the nation might more accurately be said to have backed into it. While this outcome did not result from a clear and explicit weighing of all the available alternatives, it did represent a compromise of sorts. Neither the advocates of universal conscription nor the proponents of complete voluntarism were entirely satisfied with the draft. For the first group it was a less-than-ideal means of meeting immediate needs; for the second it was the lesser of two evils. No conscription might have been preferable to limited conscription, but limited conscription was certainly preferable to universal conscription.

As the Second World War drew to a close, American military planners were eager to end the draft and to make the transition to their preferred peacetime format of a small standing volunteer force, backed by reservists supplied through a system of universal training. The Selective Service Act of 1940 had originally been set to expire in May 1945, but delays in ending the fighting and then in reaching a final postwar settlement, coupled with lack of progress in gaining congressional approval for UMT, led to two one-year extensions. These were obtained in exchange for firm assurances from the executive branch that the continuation of conscription was intended solely as a stopgap measure. Congress also made a number of changes in the law that tended to soften some of its harsher aspects. Although men could still be drafted, the term of their service was limited to no more than eighteen months, fathers and those under the age of nineteen were deferred, and military planners promised to use the draft only to fill whatever gap remained between needs and voluntary enlistments. "We do not recommend conscription as a long-range military policy for this Nation," the Secretary of War reassured members of Congress in 1946. "We do not recommend it."[90]

In March 1947 the draft was finally allowed to lapse.[91] A second campaign for UMT was launched, combined with serious efforts to put the regular armed forces on a completely voluntary basis.[92] After a year of continued congressional foot-dragging on universal training, declining enlistments, and worsening relations with the Soviet Union, the United States found itself facing a situation

[90] Secretary of War Robert Patterson in Hearings before the House Committee on Military Affairs, *Extension of the Selective Training and Service Act*, 79th Cong., 2d sess. (Washington, DC: U.S. Government Printing Office, 1946), p. 27; Gerhardt, *The Draft and Public Policy*, pp. 43–57.

[91] Despite the risk of some short-term personnel shortages, this decision reflected what the Secretary of War described as "our earnest desire to place our Regular Army on an entirely volunteer basis at the earliest possible moment." Robert Patterson to Harry S. Truman, January 31, 1947. HSTL, White House Central Files, Confidential Files, Box 32, Subject File—1945–53, Selective Service.

[92] On this episode see John Alger, "The Objective Was a Volunteer Army," *U.S. Naval Institute Proceedings* 96, no. 2 (1970), pp. 62–68; and Rocco M. Paone, "The Last Volunteer Army, 1946–1948," *Military Review* (December 1969), pp. 9–17.

in which, according to Secretary of State Marshall, it was "playing with fire while [having] nothing with which to put it out."[93] The nation's foreign policy was bringing it increasingly into confrontation with the Soviet Union, but its military policy was barely capable of supplying the forces with which to man existing positions, still less to fight a full-scale war.

By the end of 1947 monthly volunteer recruitments were falling well short of established targets, and at the same time, the Joint Chiefs of Staff were pressing for an expansion in the size of U.S. forces-in-being.[94] The Joint Chiefs' estimates of "available military strength balanced against present and possible commitments" revealed significant shortfalls in both Army and Navy manpower. If war came quickly, there would not be sufficient forces to implement existing emergency plans.[95] Despite mounting difficulties, there was no prospect at the beginning of 1948 of an imminent return to limited conscription. President Truman regarded the draft as a "political headache" because of the inevitable inequities involved in its application, and he feared that its renewal would interfere with implementation of UMT and give the Republicans an issue they could exploit in the coming campaign.[96] Without some dramatic event it is unlikely, given the prevailing attitudes on both sides, that the president would have sought or the Congress would have approved a reinstitution of the draft.

In late February 1948 communists seized control of Czechoslovakia, and in early March, General Lucius Clay, U.S. military governor in Germany, sent a cable to Washington warning that a clash with the Soviet Union might now be imminent. Faced with what appeared to be a sudden increase in the probability of war, the Truman administration sought to bring the nation's capabilities and commitments into better balance by increasing American military power. To bolster the U.S. capacity to fight a future world war, the White House moved first to reinvigorate its efforts to obtain passage of UMT. It was only several days later, at the urging of the Joint Chiefs of Staff, that President Truman also decided to request "temporary reenactment of selective service legislation" in order to satisfy immediate manpower needs. A renewed draft was necessary, Truman told Congress, "until the solid foundation of universal training can be established. Selective service can then be terminated and the regular forces may then be maintained on a voluntary basis."[97]

---

[93] See Forrestal's summary of a February 12, 1948 meeting of the National Security Council in Walter Millis, ed., *The Forrestal Diaries* (New York: Viking Press, 1951), p. 373.

[94] Kenneth W. Condit, *The Joint Chiefs of Staff and National Policy*, vol. 2: *1947–1949* (Wilmington, DE: Michael Glazier, 1979), pp. 188–93. Gus C. Lee and Geoffrey Y. Parker, *Ending the Draft: The Story of the All Volunteer Force* (Alexandria, VA: Human Resources Research Organization, 1977), p. 16.

[95] See the account of a February 18, 1948 briefing at the White House by Major General Alfred Gruenther in Millis, *Forrestal Diaries*, pp. 374–77.

[96] George Q. Flynn, *The Draft, 1940–1973* (Lawrence: University of Kansas Press, 1993), pp. 98–102.

[97] "Special Message to the Congress on the Threat to the Freedom of Europe," March 17, 1948, *Public Papers of the Presidents of the United States: Harry S. Truman (1948)* (Washington, DC: U.S. Government Printing Office, 1964), pp. 185–86. The Czech coup occurred on February 24. On

MANPOWER   **175**

The administration had intended the draft and UMT as a package, rather than as alternatives. By requesting both at once, however, it gave Congress a way of meeting the needs of the moment without committing itself to a potentially unpopular long-term policy. The path to reactivation of the Selective Service System was cleared by the acquiescence and even, in some cases, the "reluctant endorsements" of some of the most vociferous opponents of conscription.[98] In the spring of 1948 a number of education, labor, and farm leaders who remained strongly opposed to UMT were willing to accept a return to the draft (provided that it was clearly of limited scope and finite duration) precisely because it presented an alternative to universal conscription.[99]

The combination of an immediate need and an apparently acceptable short-term means of satisfying it eased the way for reenactment of the draft. Presented with the opportunity of chosing between temporary limited conscription and a permanent universal alternative, Congress did not hesitate for long. By summer the draft was renewed and UMT had once again been buried. Even so, the decision to reactivate Selective Service was hedged about with conditions. Where the executive branch wanted a five-year authorization to draft men for up to twenty-four months of service, Congress agreed to only two years of authority and twenty-one-month tours.[100] As historian James Gerhardt points out, "Selective Service was promoted by the Administration as a temporary measure, and Congress' action in limiting the life of the act . . . indicates it was accepted in the same spirit."[101] In the hopes that conscription could still be avoided, the House also required a ninety-day delay in enacting the new law to provide an opportunity for increased voluntary enlistments.[102]

March 2 the Secretaries of State (Marshall) and Defense (Forrestal) agreed to renew "the drive for UMT." Clay's telegram arrived on March 5. At a meeting in Key West on March 12 the Joint Chiefs of Staff concluded that in order to prepare to execute existing war plans, it was "now necessary to ask immediately for a restoration of Selective Service." See Millis, *Forrestal Diaries*, pp. 387–97. Also Walter Millis, Harvey C. Mansfield, and Harold Stein, *Arms and the State: Civil-Military Elements in National Policy* (New York: Twentieth Century Fund, 1958), pp. 210–13. Truman's request for draft renewal came as something of a surprise on Capitol Hill, where, on the eve of his speech, news accounts referred to a "moral certainty . . . that [the president] would not ask for a revival of selective service." "Martin's Warning," *New York Times*, March 17, 1948, p. 1. For the background to these decisions see Melvyn P. Leffler, *A Preponderance of Power: National Security, the Truman Administration, and the Cold War* (Stanford, CA: Stanford University Press, 1992), p. 203–13.

[98] Lee and Parker, *Ending the Draft*, p. 18.

[99] See, for example, the statements by Herbert W. Voorhees, of the American Farm Bureau Federation; William Dameron of the International Association of Machinists; Dr. Ralph Himstead, American Association of University Professors; George F. Zook, President of the American Council on Education, in Hearings before the Senate Armed Services Committee, *Universal Military Training* (1948), pp. 138–44, 861–65, 881–86, 891–902.

[100] See "Comparison of Administration's Proposal for Manpower Legislation with the Provisions of the Selective Service Act of 1948 as Finally Passed by the Senate and House, June 21, 1948," HSTL, PSF, Box 136; General File—Selective Service System.

[101] Gerhardt, *The Draft and Public Policy*, p. 119.

[102] Gilliam, "The Peacetime Draft," p. 109. See also Robert H. Rankin, "A History of Selective Service," *U.S. Naval Institute Proceedings* (October 1951), pp. 1073–81.

With the passing of the immediate emergency and a subsequent lowering of planned force levels, the new draft authority quickly lapsed into disuse. After only three months of callups (during which a total of only thirty thousand men were inducted), no more were issued.[103] From February 1949 until June 1950 inductions were suspended altogether and there was no expectation that they would be renewed in the foreseeable future. As the authorization for limited conscription approached its scheduled termination in 1950, administration spokesmen requested a three-year extension, but they promised that they had "no intention . . . of exercising the provisions of the Selective Service Act in the near future, or for that matter in peacetime in general."[104]

Even with these assurances there was serious doubt about whether a new draft law would be approved. With no one actually being drafted, Congress moved to make deep cuts in funding for the Selective Service System.[105] By the summer of 1949, it was widely assumed that "unless an unforeseen emergency develops," the peacetime draft would expire on June 24, 1950.[106] Toward the end of 1949 the State Department expressed considerable anxiety that a termination of the draft "might be regarded as inconsistent with our policies under the North Atlantic Treaty . . . and as a weakening of our resolve to maintain the strength of the free world."[107] Despite this danger, the Secretary of the Army was forced to conclude that "from all present indications . . . the proposal for extending Selective Service has but little chance for success."[108] There was ample reason to think so. Upon learning of the administration's proposed three-year extension of the existing draft law, Carl Vinson, powerful Democratic chairman of the House Armed Services Committee, told reporters that there was "'no justification' for a draft extension on military or other grounds."[109]

As Congress began to consider the matter more closely it became increasingly clear that if an extension were granted, it would be only with the imposition of tight new restrictions on the president's power to order conscription. After months of discussion, and with literally hours left to go before the expiration of the 1948 authority, a new bill had still not been signed into law. Both houses of Congress favored preserving "the administrative structure of the [Se-

---

[103] Selective Service System, *Outline of Historical Background of Selective Service* (Washington, DC: U.S. Government Printing Office, 1961), pp. 17–18.

[104] Statement by General Omar N. Bradley, Chairman, Joint Chiefs of Staff, Hearings before the House Committee on Armed Services, *Selective Service Act Extension* 81st Cong., 2d sess. (Washington, DC: U.S. Government Printing Office, 1950), p. 5159. See also the statement by the Secretary of the Army, Gordon Gray, on p. 5127.

[105] See "House Fund Cut Would Kill Draft System, Hershey Says," *New York Times*, April 28, 1949, p. 1; "Hershey Appeals for Draft Funds," *New York Times*, May 21, 1949, p. 5.

[106] "Army Manpower Draft Expected to End in June," *New York Times*, August 5, 1949, p. 3.

[107] James Webb (Acting Secretary of State) to Louis Johnson (Secretary of Defense), November 15, 1949. HSTL, PSF, Box 136, General File—Selective Service System.

[108] Gordon Gray to Louis Johnson, December 9, 1949, HSTL, OF, Box 845 (1949–50), Conscription.

[109] "Johnson Requests Draft's Extension as 'Essential' Step," *New York Times*, December 18, 1949, p. 1.

lective Service] system without giving the President much power to use it."[110] The House version of a renewal bill would have forbidden any return to conscription without a congressionally approved declaration of national emergency; the Senate was moving toward similar restrictions, and there were signs that the president would accept considerable constraints on his freedom to use the draft rather than face a complete loss of extractive authority.[111] On June 23 the old law expired and Congress gave itself an additional fifteen days in which to act. On June 24 the Korean War began. Three days later the House and Senate agreed to extend the existing draft authority essentially unchanged from its previous form.[112]

But for Korea it is quite likely that by the beginning of the 1950s, the United States would have completed the transition to an entirely voluntary military format. Congress had already beaten back three separate attempts to gain approval of universal training and showed no signs of changing its mind. If a new draft law had been passed in the summer of 1950, it would almost certainly have prohibited the use of even limited conscription in situations short of a declared national emergency. In the absence of war, the United States would have entered the new decade with standing forces made up entirely of volunteers and without any provision for compulsory manpower training. Instead, with American soldiers fighting and dying in Korea, Congress quickly passed a one-year renewal of the draft and agreed to reexamine UMT.

In the heat of war and under considerable pressure from the executive branch, Congress agreed initially to make sweeping changes in the nation's military format. In 1951 presidential induction authority was extended for four years, the longest such extension since the Second World War, although still considerably less than the permanent authorization requested by the Defense Department.[113] As signified in its title, the Universal Military Training and Service Act of 1951 also declared an all-inclusive obligation for young men to participate in the nation's defense, and it took the first steps toward creating a

[110] Gilliam, "The Peacetime Draft," p. 110.

[111] On the various alternative restrictions being considered before the outbreak of the Korean War see Chambers, *Draftees or Volunteers*, p. 368. Also "Draft's Extension Delayed in Senate; Pentagon Worried," *New York Times*, June 20, 1950, p. 1. The Defense Department and the White House staff were initially divided on what limitations to accept. In a memorandum to the president, National Security Resources Board Chairman John Steelman criticized "representatives of the Defense Department" for their willingness to accept a provision requiring a joint resolution of Congress before draft authority could be exercised. "Status of Selective Service Legislation," (January 1950?) HSTL, PSF, Box 136, General File—Selective Service System. The Defense Department later suggested that the president be required to seek prior congressional approval except in the event of a sudden emergency. See "Defense Chiefs Offer Compromise On Selective Service to Congress," *New York Times*, January 26, 1950, p. 10. With the deadline approaching, Chairman of the Joint Chiefs Omar Bradley indicated that the administration would be willing to accept the requirement of congressional authorization of any new use of the draft as the price of keeping the Selective Service System in operation. "'Cold War' Outlook Bad, Says Bradley," *New York Times*, May 3, 1950, p. 6.

[112] Selective Service System, *Outline of Historical Background*, pp. 18–19.

[113] Gerhardt, *The Draft and Public Policy*, p. 221.

National Security Training Corps in which every male citizen would be required to serve once the Korean conflict had ended.

Unanticipated events strengthened the hand of those who favored compulsion and weakened the opposition of those who opposed it. But even the shock of war was not sufficient to eliminate that resistance altogether. As in 1948, the opponents of conscription chose to concentrate their fire on its more extensive manifestations. While they acknowledged that a draft might be necessary to meet the needs of the present emergency, the various anticonscription organizations continued their relentless criticism of universal training.[114] However distasteful it might be, wrote the president of one such group, "Selective Service is infinitely preferable to UMT."[115] Once again, a limited draft, authorized for a finite duration, appeared as the lesser of two evils.

The pattern of congressional action reveals a similar hierarchy of preferences. Having declared the principle of universality, Congress refused to approve a program that would make it a reality. At the end of the Korean War the draft remained in place, but UMT had effectively disappeared from view.[116] After eight years of debate and instability, the United States had finally arrived at the military format it was to maintain for the next two decades. But this outcome, "evolved . . . rather than . . . ever being officially declared";[117] it emerged from a collision between external imperatives and internal constraints, rather than from deliberate pursuit.

THE "QUIET TRIUMPH" OF A "LIBERAL DRAFT"[118]

The Institutionalization of Conscription

Given the turmoil surrounding its adoption, it is striking that by the mid-1950s, the draft had apparently come to be accepted as "an established principle of peacetime American life."[119] In contrast to the earlier, tumultuous debates over manpower policy, by the middle of Eisenhower's first term in office congressional approval of conscription had become largely a matter of routine. As

[114] See, for example, the statement by John Swomley, Director of the National Council against Conscription, in Hearings before the Preparedness Subcommittee of the Senate Armed Services Committee in *Universal Military Training and Service Act of 1951*, 82d Cong., 1st sess. (Washington, DC: U.S.Government Printing Office, 1951), pp. 936–43.

[115] James G. Patton, president of the National Farmers Union, to Senator Robert Taft, February 9, 1951; quoted in Flynn, *The Draft*, p. 124.

[116] Allan R. Millett and Peter Maslowski, *For the Common Defense: A Military History of the United States of America* (New York: Free Press, 1984), p. 493.

[117] Lee and Parker, *Ending the Draft*, p. 22.

[118] These phrases are borrowed, respectively, from Gerhardt, *The Draft and Public Policy*, p. 189, and Eliot Cohen, *Citizens and Soldiers: The Dilemmas of Military Service* (Ithaca: Cornell University Press, 1985), p. 184.

[119] Walter Millis, *Individual Freedom and the Common Defense* (New York: Fund for the Republic, 1957), p. 13.

required by the Universal Military Training and Service Act of 1951, Congress renewed its authorization of the Selective Service System at four-year intervals (in 1955, 1959, and again in 1963), but it did so by wide margins and with dwindling discussion. Public opinion polls also seemed to indicate strong and consistent support for conscription. From the midfifties to the midsixties, approval for continuation of the draft (or, in some surveys, opposition to its abolition) ran at well over 60 percent of those questioned.[120] Finally, in perhaps the most meaningful measure of legitimacy, from Korea to Vietnam there was virtually no resistance to the draft from those called upon to serve. Public protests were unheard of and attempts at evasion by inductees exceedingly rare.

To all outward appearances, then, after a shaky start the draft would seem at long last to have struck sturdy roots in American political soil. As one study describes it, following the Korean War, "the institution used for conscription achieved a state of equilibrium that held for over two decades."[121] From the beginning, however, this equilibrium was less sturdy and less stable than it appeared. The legitimacy of the draft, its acceptance by both elites and the general public, rested on foundations that were subject to erosion and sudden collapse. Because it fell on some but not others, limited conscription imposed less of a burden on society as a whole, but for the same reason it was inherently unfair. This societal sacrifice of equity for liberty was acceptable only under certain rather narrow conditions. Limited conscription aroused little opposition so long as the number of those drafted remained relatively small, the uses to which they were put retained broad public approval, those who preferred to avoid service could do so with relative ease, and the inevitable inequity of the selection process did not receive undue attention. If one of these parameters changed, support for the draft would weaken; if all of them changed at once it would disappear altogether.

The Pillars of Stability

DECLINING IMPOSITIONS

Aside from the fact that the United States was at peace, the single most important reason for widespread popular acceptance of the draft during the 1950s and into the 1960s was "the simple fact that few young men were being drafted."[122] The burden of conscription was not only comparatively light, it tended also to diminish with time. Between 1953 and 1961 the absolute number of men inducted each year fell more or less steadily from over 560,000 to roughly

---

[120] See, for example, Survey #548-K, Question #19 (July 1955); Survey #571-K (October 1956), both in *The Gallup Poll*, vol. 2, *1949–1958* (New York: Random House, 1972), p. 1344, 1448–49; Survey #730-K, Questions #11a, #3, #10a (July 1966), in *The Gallup Poll*, vol. 3, *1959–1971* (New York: Random House, 1972), pp. 2016–17.

[121] Gary L. Wamsley, *Selective Service and a Changing America: A Study of Organizational-Environmental Relationships* (Columbus, OH: Charles E. Merrill, 1969), p. 41.

[122] Flynn, *The Draft*, p. 169.

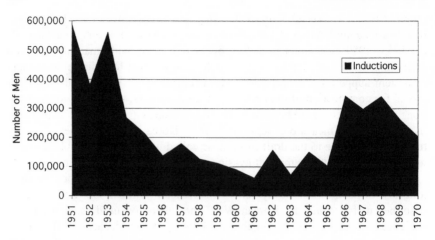

Figure 5.2. A Limited Draft: Total Annual Inductions

61,000. Over the same period, draftees went from comprising over half to just under 10 percent of the strength of the active duty armed forces (see fig. 5.2).[123]

More significant from a political point of view, the portion of those eligible for service who actually ended up being drafted in any given year also declined sharply. In 1953 just under 6 percent of a total of 9.5 million registrants between the ages of eighteen and twenty-six were drafted. By 1961 less than 0.5 percent of the over 14 million men between those ages suffered a similar fate. From the end of the Korean War to the beginning of the escalation in Vietnam, the odds that a young man reaching draft age would ever have to do military service tended to diminish markedly (see fig. 5.3).

The causes of this declining reliance on the draft were mixed. With the end of the Korean War and the advent of the New Look, the American armed forces were cut considerably in size. President Eisenhower's policy of increasing reliance on air power and nuclear weapons was designed to conserve manpower as well as money and, indeed, it succeeded better at the first goal than at the second. From the early fifties to the early sixties the overall size of the U.S. military fell by almost 1 million men, with the Army (always the most manpower-intensive service and, after Korea, the only one to continue using draftees) taking well over half of the total cuts.[124] The move to smaller standing forces and the shift away from any meaningful preparations for mobilization and protracted warfighting meant that there was less reason to continue drafting and training a large portion of the male population.

[123] See Hearings before the House Armed Services Committee, *Review of the Administration and Operation of the Selective Service System*, 89th Cong., 2d sess. (Washington, DC: U.S. Government Printing Office, 1966), p. 10001.

[124] Kevin N. Lewis, *Historical U.S. Force Structure Trends: A Primer*, P-7582 (Santa Monica: RAND Corp., 1989), pp. 20–33. On the successive cuts in manpower during the Eisenhower years see Huntington, *The Common Defense*, pp. 64–112.

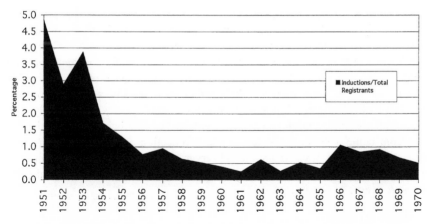

Figure 5.3. The Declining Incidence of Conscription: Inductions as Percentage of Total Registrants

As the number of inductees declined, the size of the pool from which they were selected expanded at an accelerating pace. By the late 1950s the number of men of draftable age grew by an average of 770,000 each year, as compared to an average increase of 450,000 per year during the first half of the decade.[125] With the coming of age of the first products of the postwar baby boom in the early 1960s, the size of the eligible cohort increased even more rapidly. During the Eisenhower years the combination of demographic shifts and force size reductions drove down the burdens imposed by the draft with particular speed. But even with the adoption of flexible response in the early 1960s and the accompanying modest expansions in conventional forces and draft callups, demographic trends were sufficiently powerful to prevent a sharp upsurge in the incidence of conscription.

The draft was used as little as it was during the post-Korean period in large part because the nation's military and political leaders made a deliberate effort to minimize their reliance on compulsion. Since volunteers were assumed to be better motivated, the armed services preferred them to conscripts, even if some fraction of them were, in fact, draft induced.[126] The Navy, Air Force, and Marines regarded the draft as a useful goad to enlistment rather than a direct source of manpower. Having given up on the idea of universal training, the Army was also content to use conscription as sparingly as possible.

This restraint had obvious political benefits as well. The smaller the number of inductees, the fewer who were likely to object to government manpower

[125] Gerhardt, *The Draft and Public Policy*, p. 228.

[126] Choosing to serve gave those who did so some say in the service and specialties to which they were assigned, a measure of choice that would be lost if a young man were to be drafted. By some estimates, during this period as many as a third of all volunteer enlisted men joined up rather than risk induction. See the results of a 1964 survey in *Review of the Administration and Operation of the Selective Service System*, p. 10038.

policies for anything other than reasons of abstract principle. The use of the draft largely as, in President Eisenhower's phrase, a "stimulant" to voluntarism also helped to reduce at least the appearance of excessive coercion.[127] It therefore tended to reinforce the perception that even in its deadly confrontation with communism, the United States was remaining as true to its ideals as possible and resisting the temptation to take on the worst attributes of its opponent. Limited Cold War conscription was, in Eliot Cohen's words, "a typically 'liberal' draft—that is, a minimal draft for the purpose of inducing men to enlist."[128] Far from being a fluke, this outcome was a reflection of deeply rooted American preferences. It was, as another observer has described it, an attempt "to avoid a complete break with the American past and to preserve some alternatives to overt state conscription."[129]

GENEROUS DEFERMENTS

From the end of the Korean War onward, the Selective Service System found itself confronted by an embarrassment of riches, with the supply of eligible manpower far outstripping the military's demands. In order to simplify the process of choosing small numbers of draftees from among the multitude of potential candidates, the managers of the nation's manpower program began to exclude whole subgroups of the population from consideration for induction. During the Korean conflict many college students were granted deferments on the grounds that, as one official put it, "if America is to have a chance of winning an all-out war with Russia it must plan on the most effective use of its brainpower, for in manpower it is greatly outnumbered."[130] After the war this policy was continued, with the result that large numbers of college graduates were able not only to defer military service but ultimately to avoid it altogether. Similar reasoning also led to the exclusion of all those with particular kinds of technical training or occupational specialties that were deemed essential to the nation's security and well-being. Scientists and engineers received special treatment on these grounds, but so did doctors, dentists, and agricultural workers. Raising mental and physical standards for induction was another way in which a sizable fraction of those who had registered for the draft could be eliminated from consideration. To further drain the overflowing manpower pool, deferments were granted on the basis of age and personal status. Beginning in the midfifties, fathers and those over the age of twenty-six were effectively excused

---

[127] Flynn, *The Draft*, p. 162.

[128] Cohen, *Citizens and Soldiers*, p. 184.

[129] Gilliam, "The Peacetime Draft," p. 109.

[130] J. F. Victory of the National Advisory Committee on Aeronautics to Lewis Hershey, Director of the Selective Service System, July 27, 1950, quoted in George Q. Flynn, "The Draft and College Deferments during the Korean War," *Historian* vol. 50, no. 3 (May 1988), p. 378. See also Donald D. Stewart, "The Dilemma of Deferment," *Journal of Higher Education* 24, no. 4 (April 1953), pp. 186–90.

from involuntary service. In 1963, with the flood of excess males still growing, a similar privilege was extended, in practice, to all married men.[131]

The cumulative effect of all these decisions was to shrink the circle of those who were truly susceptible to conscription. In 1961, for example, a total of over 24 million men were registered for the draft. Out of this number close to 10 million were twenty-six years of age or older and hence ineligible to be called. Of the remaining 14 million men between the ages of eighteen and a half and twenty-six, 11.5 million were granted deferments of one kind or another, leaving only 2.3 million available for service. Of these, in the year in question, only 61,000 actually were drafted.[132]

Aside from narrowing the field for selection, the increasingly generous deferment policies put into place in the 1950s and early 1960s served two less obvious but ultimately even more important political purposes. By rationalizing the exclusion of substantial portions of the population, a formal system of deferments went some distance toward justifying the inequality of the draft. After having first been reluctant to view their function as anything other than simple procurement, Selective Service officials by the late fifties had embraced their expanded role as the "storekeepers of the nation's manpower," and were quite open in proclaiming their intention to use deferments to "channel" men toward occupations deemed critical to the nation's security.[133]

In a more subtle way, a liberal deferment policy also served as a safety valve, relieving societal pressure that might otherwise have built up for the abandonment of limited conscription. By satisfying the demands for preferential treatment of various groups or, in some cases, preemptively granting blanket exemptions, the Selective Service System was able to insulate itself from organized and politically effective protest. In this way, for example, opposition from scientific, educational, and agricultural groups was defused before it had even had the chance to build.[134]

---

[131] For more on the deferments policies of the 1950s and early 1960s see George Q. Flynn, *Lewis B. Hershey, Mr. Selective Service* (Chapel Hill: University of North Carolina Press, 1985), pp. 190–215; Flynn, *The Draft*, pp. 134–65. Gerhardt, *The Draft and Public Policy*, pp. 227–42; Harry A. Marmion, "A Critique of Selective Service with Emphasis on Student Deferment," in Sol Tax, ed., *The Draft: A Handbook of Facts and Alternatives* (Chicago: University of Chicago Press, 1967), pp. 54–61; Marmion, "Historical Background of Selective Service in the United States," in Roger W. Little, ed., *Selective Service and American Society* (New York: Russell Sage, 1969), pp. 35–52.

[132] See Selective Service System, *Annual Report of the Selective Service System, 1961* (Washington, DC: U.S. Government Printing Office, 1961), pp. 58–63.

[133] See Selective Service System, *Annual Report of the Selective Service System, 1957* (Washington, DC: U.S. Government Printing Office, 1957), pp. 61–62. Special treatment was easier to justify in some cases than in others. The argument that the country needed more nuclear physicists or electrical engineers was plausible on its face, but even where the links to defense were less obvious, government spokesmen showed surprising rhetorical creativity. Thus, the exemption of fathers from the draft was justified on the grounds that it "strengthen[ed] the Nation's civilian economy" and even, by encouraging marriage, "foster[ed] the family life of the Nation." Gerhardt, *The Draft and Public Policy*, p. 233.

[134] This is the basic argument of Flynn, *The Draft*, pp. 134–65.

The combination of high mental and physical standards with generous occupational and education deferments meant that during the era of stability, those most likely to serve came from the middle and lower-middle classes. The typical draftee in this period was neither very rich nor very poor, neither highly educated nor entirely uneducated.[135] The members of this middle slice of the nation's population were not only most vulnerable to conscription, they were also least inclined to object to it. More-educated and better-off young men of draft age were substantially more likely to perceive the process of selection as unfair. By contrast, those who were most susceptible to selection (blue-collar and nonprofessional white-collar workers with, at most, a high school education) were also most likely to regard the system as equitable in its operations and were therefore, presumably, least inclined to object when called.[136] As long as this harmonious pattern could be preserved, the draft was unlikely to face strong popular opposition.

THE ILLUSION OF EQUITY

As limited conscription became more limited and less equitable, government officials invested ever greater energy in maintaining an illusion of fairness. This sensitivity to appearances (first made manifest in the misleading title of the 1951 draft law) suggests an awareness of the potential fragility of public support for any use of compulsion that was not truly universal. Throughout the 1950s, the leaders of the Selective Service System continued to proclaim that in one way or another, every young man, regardless of education or income, was making a contribution to the defense of the nation. The fact that some did their part by attending college and then joining the ranks of a well-paying profession while others did two years of compulsory service in the Army was downplayed or ignored. "The strength of the Selective Service System is its uniformity," proclaimed Congressman Carl Vinson in 1955. "It applies to everybody equally and alike. As long as we keep that as the fundamental basis, we are on sound ground."[137]

By the late 1950s government spokesmen were using ever more tortured formulations to describe the workings of a system that was, in fact, increasingly selective in its impositions. In preparation for the 1959 draft renewal hearings the Defense Department commissioned a study on the incidence of the draft which concluded that virtually no young man who had received a I-A rating and was "qualified and available for service will be in a position to escape his

---

[135] In the years 1955–65 high school graduates were most likely to serve, followed by those with either incomplete secondary or partial college educations and, last, by college graduates and those with little or no education. Neil D. Fligstein, "Who Served in the Military, 1940–1973," *Armed Forces and Society* 6, no. 2 (1980), p. 305.

[136] For a national survey conducted in 1966 see Wamsley, *Selective Service and a Changing America*, pp. 178–79. The results of a 1964 survey of men ages sixteen through 34 and a 1966 survey of Wisconsin residents are reported in James W. Davis, Jr., and Kenneth M. Dolbeare, *Little Groups of Neighbors: The Selective Service System* (Chicago: Markham, 1968), pp. 162–63, 167–69.

[137] Quoted in Gerhardt, *The Draft and Public Policy*, p. 243.

military service obligation."[138] This statement was correct, but it was really no more than an elaborately inverted way of admitting that only those unfortunate enough to be without any one of a very long list of possible excuses (fatherhood, mental or physical disabilities, occupational or educational deferments, etc.) had reason to fear being drafted.

The claim that military service was a nearly universal experience also helped to bolster the legitimacy of the draft. If virtually every young man of a certain age could be shown to have done his duty, then there could be little cause for complaint from those few who were compelled to serve. Thus, in 1959 the Defense Department published statistics showing that as of June 1958 close to 70 percent of all those reaching twenty-six years of age (plus or minus six months) were participating in or had completed some form of military service.[139] The apparently casual choice of base date was, in fact, critical in determining the results of these calculations. Those who were twenty-six by the summer of 1958 had been eighteen in the summer of 1950, just old enough to be drafted or to volunteer for service in the Korean War. The apparently high incidence of service in the late 1950s was largely an echo of that earlier emergency. Similar estimates in 1962, 1964, and 1966 would show a rapid falling away in the portion of twenty-six year olds with any kind of military experience.[140] The percentage of those who had been drafted was, of course, smaller still.

Some of the public opinion polls cited earlier as providing evidence of popular enthusiasm for the draft seem, on closer examination, to suggest that at least some of this support was contingent on the assumption of universality. One 1955 Gallup poll found, for example, that when asked to choose between two options, 74 percent of those questioned favored drafting "all able-bodied young men for 18 months" while only 16 percent favored drafting "some men for two years and excus[ing] others."[141] Claims of "universal service" notwithstanding, the results of American manpower policy in the 1950s and early 1960s could be described far more accurately by the second statement than by the first. The fraction of the general population that supported the draft in the belief that it was truly universal is not clear from these results. Given the rhetoric to which they were continually exposed, however, ordinary citizens could certainly have been excused for making such a mistake.

Erosion

With the passage of time it became increasingly difficult to sustain even the illusion of equity. By the late 1950s some observers were beginning to express anxiety over the legitimacy of a system that imposed the burden of military

[138] House Armed Services Committee, *Universal Military Training and Service Act Extension* 84th Cong., 1st sess. (Washington, DC: U.S. Government Printing Office, 1959), p. 29.
[139] Ibid., pp. 32–33.
[140] See the table in *Review of the Administration and Operation of the Selective Service System,* p. 10005.
[141] Survey #548-K, Question #19 (July 1955), *The Gallup Poll* 2:1344.

service on a dwindling portion of the nation's population. In 1958 an independent study warned (accurately, as events would prove) that "no compulsory system which is not universal and non-discriminatory can long survive in a free society." The report's author recommended that serious consideration be given to placing the armed forces on an entirely voluntary basis.[142] While they were not yet willing seriously to entertain such a radical alternative, some government officials were also concerned about the continued viability of ever more limited conscription. Reviewing existing policies in anticipation of the forthcoming congressional debate on renewal, the Office of Civil and Defense Mobilization advised in 1958 that "if the draft continues as is, equity problems which can be serious politically as well as philosophically are bound to arise."[143]

Despite these misgivings, the Eisenhower administration was unwilling to do anything that might invite serious congressional review of the Selective Service System. According to historian George Flynn, this attitude reflected a suspicion that if the subject were reopened, "traditional American opposition to coercion might lead to dumping the entire idea of conscription."[144] Whatever its other shortcomings, the draft was still considered useful as a spur to enlistments. Doing away with it (or even talking about doing so) might lead to a sharp drop in the number of volunteers. In order to avoid this danger, the Eisenhower administration in its waning years did not offer any substantial proposals for draft reform, and it did its best to squelch serious debate over the possibility of doing away with limited conscription.[145]

But ignoring the problem did not make it go away. By the early 1960s the gathering effects of the baby boom were inescapable. Expressing concern over the unfairness of the existing system (and voicing a private preference for an eventual return to voluntarism), President Kennedy ordered a review of the draft in September 1963.[146] The next year, despite the fact that Selective Service had just been renewed with little debate, there were signs of growing discontent with the status quo. In 1964 the subject was raised in Congress as often as it had been in all of the preceding ten years. Bills calling for reform were introduced, including one that would have abolished the draft before the next scheduled renewal vote in 1967. Republican presidential candidate Barry Goldwater denounced the draft as unnecessary and declared his intention to abolish it "as soon as possible."[147] President Lyndon Johnson quickly announced a comprehensive review of the nation's manpower policies and a detailed examination of

---

[142] John Graham, *The Universal Military Obligation* (New York: Fund for the Republic, 1958), pp. 8–9.

[143] Memorandum by J. Roy Price, October 21, 1958, quoted in Flynn, *The Draft*, p. 163.

[144] Ibid., p. 164.

[145] In 1957 a Defense Department advisory commission on military pay concluded that if salaries were increased, the military might be able to draw enough volunteers to permit abolition of the draft. Although it did make some adjustments in pay scales, the Eisenhower administration rejected the idea of doing away with the draft on the grounds that an all-volunteer force would be too expensive. See Gerhardt, *The Draft and Public Policy*, pp. 215–16, 246–47.

[146] This study ultimately recommended only very minor alterations in existing practices. Flynn, *Lewis B. Hershey*, pp. 225–26.

[147] Gerhardt, *The Draft and Public Policy*, p. 286.

the prospects for an all-volunteer force. Johnson's motives were clearly tactical, but the fact that he felt the need to respond at all indicates that he already sensed an erosion in public support for the draft.[148]

"Had it not been for the Vietnam War," writes sociologist David Segal, "conscription might have been phased out in the United States a decade earlier than it was."[149] Questions of timing aside, the larger point remains: by the early 1960s the United States was well on its way to abandoning the draft. As the baby boom generation came of age and the Selective Service System became ever more selective, it became increasingly difficult to defend from accusations of inequity. The greater the attention focused on the actual operations of the system, the more likely the erosion of its legitimacy. After slightly over a decade, the brief interval of equilibrium was coming to a close. The incongruity between America's values and the functioning of its institutions of conscription could not be indefinitely sustained.

The Death of the Draft and the Return to Voluntarism

The escalation of American involvement in Southeast Asia struck simultaneously at each of the pillars on which acceptance of limited conscription had come to rest during the 1950s. Instead of a mere handful, substantial numbers of men were soon being drafted into the armed forces. Many of the old deferment "safety valves" were shut off or appreciably constricted, thereby provoking anxiety and hostility among those who had previously been protected. Despite its increased use, however, the draft continued to be highly selective and thus highly inequitable; although many were called, many more were passed over. And in contrast to the years since Korea, now those selected were being asked to risk their lives in an increasingly unpopular war.

These changes led quickly to antidraft protests, a national debate over the legitimacy of limited or, indeed, *any* form of conscription, the collapse of public support for Selective Service, and the emergence of an all-volunteer force. By subjecting the institutions of conscription to increased stress, Vietnam revealed their underlying weakness.

Escalation and Opposition

In July 1965 President Johnson decided to increase substantially the American military role in South Vietnam. Draft calls increased dramatically in 1965 and 1966 (more than tripling from 100,000 to over 300,000) and stayed high for the remainder of the decade before declining again in the early seventies.[150]

[148] Flynn, *Lewis B. Hershey*, pp. 226–27.

[149] David R. Segal, *Recruiting for Uncle Sam: Citizenship and Military Manpower Policy* (Lawrence: University Press of Kansas, 1989), p. 34.

[150] Because he wished to avoid putting the nation on a full war footing, Johnson decided that the necessary expansion in U.S. forces would be accomplished through the use of the draft, rather than the mobilization of existing reserve units. See Larry Berman, *Planning a Tragedy: The American-*

As the military's demand for manpower mounted, deferments were tightened. In 1965 married men lost their protected status. Rather than passing over virtually all college students, in 1966 the Selective Service System began administering a standardized test to determine which ones would continue to be eligible (by virtue of their high scores) for exemption from the draft.[151] In 1967 college students were granted a blanket deferment for as long as they remained in school, but most deferments for graduate education were canceled.[152]

The combined effect of all these changes was to increase the incidence of conscription. By one estimate, within two years of the onset of escalation the probability of induction for all young men had tripled. The change in climate was felt most acutely by the nation's college students, who had grown accustomed, as a group, to substantial immunity from the draft. Despite the fact that they continued to find ways of avoiding conscription and ultimately served at lower rates, it was these students, rather than their less privileged, more compliant, but more vulnerable contemporaries, who were most active in protesting government policy.[153]

Stepped-up fighting and rising draft calls led to "teach-ins" and debates on college campuses, to "stop the draft" rallies of growing size and vehemence, and eventually to scattered attacks on the outposts of the Selective Service System.[154] These more dramatic public expressions of opposition were accompanied by increasingly widespread individual efforts to evade or resist the draft.[155]

---

ization of the War in Vietnam (New York: Norton, 1982), pp. 125–26. Twenty years after the fact Johnson's decision still rankled some military officers. See John D. Stuckey and Joseph H. Pistorius, "Mobilization for the Vietnam War: A Political and Military Catastrophe," *Parameters* 15, no. 1 (Spring 1985), pp. 26–38.

[151] This was a practice that had begun during the Korean War and had been abandoned in the early sixties. Flynn, *Lewis B. Hershey*, p. 241.

[152] Timothy B. Clark, Joseph Foote, David Fouquet, et al., *U.S. Draft Policy and Its Impact* (Washington, DC: Congressional Quarterly Press, 1969), p. 5.

[153] By one estimate, between 1965 and 1970 the probability of a college graduate's being drafted doubled. Flynn, *The Draft*, p. 171. Nevertheless, during the entire Vietnam War, college graduates were almost 20 percent less likely to serve in the military than those with fewer years of education. Fligstein, "Who Served in the Military," p. 305. On the relationship between increased draft calls and the expansion of the anti-war movement see Michael Useem, *Conscription, Protest, and Social Conflict: The Life and Death of a Draft Resistance Movement* (New York: Wiley, 1973), pp. 80, 136–37. Also, Charles DeBenedetti and Charles Chatfield, *An American Ordeal: The Antiwar Movement of the Vietnam War* (Syracuse: Syracuse University Press, 1990), pp. 165–67. On the central role played by college students in the anti-war movement see Melvin Small, "The Impact of the Antiwar Movement on Lyndon Johnson, 1965–1968: A Preliminary Report," *Peace and Change* 10, no. 1 (Spring 1984), pp. 1–22.

[154] One study counts a total of fifteen attacks on Selective Service offices between 1968 and 1971. Stephen M. Kohn, *Jailed for Peace: The History of American Draft Law Violators, 1658–1985* (Westport, CT: Greenwood Press, 1986), p. 83.

[155] Many young men (especially the wealthier and better educated) went to great lengths to obtain physical, mental, or occupational deferments or to appeal their classification as eligible for service by local draft boards. Some violated the law by failing to register or by going "underground" or fleeing the country when called. Others sought status as conscientious objectors, and a small number, having exhausted all other remedies, chose to refuse induction and go to prison. The most

Coping with all of this passive and active resistance undoubtedly imposed costs on the Selective Service System, the Justice Department, and the courts, but it never came close to derailing the draft or disrupting the flow of manpower into the armed forces.[156] The mechanisms of extraction continued to deliver ample quantities of men, both volunteers and conscripts, to fight the war in Southeast Asia. As the American role in the fighting dwindled after 1970, the task became that much easier.[157]

Despite its evident failure to bring down "the system," the antidraft movement had a broader and deeper effect than was immediately apparent. As in the 1940s, the most vocal opponents of conscription were in a distinct minority and their broader political agendas were not widely shared. Like their predecessors, however, the opponents of the draft succeeded in calling attention to the special dilemmas that compulsion posed for a liberal society and in mobilizing arguments that had a wider resonance. It was precisely the appeal to "American values," to the virtues of fairness and personal freedom, rather than any radical critique of American society that eventually won support among political elites and ordinary citizens. After having receded for a time, questions about the fairness of limited conscription and, indeed, about the acceptability of *any* form of state compulsion, had now been brought back to center stage.

The Critique of Inequity

Prior to 1965 discontent with the draft had centered on the fact that it was selecting an ever smaller fraction of an expanding manpower pool. Escalation and stepped-up inductions alleviated this problem, but only to a limited degree and in a narrow, purely statistical sense. After 1965, the number of inductees

---

complete account of all of these forms of draft avoidance, evasion, and resistance is Lawrence M. Baskir and William A. Strauss, *Chance and Circumstance: The Draft, the War, and the Vietnam Generation* (New York: Knopf, 1978). The authors estimate that out of a total of close to 27 million men who were eligible for the draft during the Vietnam era, 8.7 million enlisted and 2.2 million were drafted. Of the remaining 16 million, 15.4 million were legally deferred, exempted, or disqualified, and the remaining 570,000 were "apparent draft offenders." Out of this number, 360,000 either never registered for the draft and were never prosecuted or committed other undetected violations of the selective service laws. Of the remaining 210,000 "accused draft offenders," 198,000 had their cases dropped, 3,000 became fugitives, and only 8,750 were ever convicted of draft law violations. Of these only 3,250 were imprisoned. Ibid., p. 5. In short, most draft resistance was passive rather than active. See also Useem, *Conscription, Protest, and Social Conflict,* pp. 125–33.

[156] For claims to the contrary see Kohn, *Jailed for Peace,* pp. 73–99. Also DeBenedetti and Chatfield, *An American Ordeal,* pp. 183, 309. For a more balanced assessment see Tom Wells, *The War Within: America's Battle over Vietnam* (Berkeley: University of California Press, 1994), pp. 267–70.

[157] One study concludes, somewhat reluctantly, that antidraft protests "failed to make much of a dent in the supply of cannon fodder available for shipment to Vietnam. . . . And, save for scattered locations, the courts . . . remained unclogged." Wells, *The War Within,* p. 268. For a similar conclusion see also Myra MacPherson, *Long Time Passing: Vietnam and the Haunted Generation* (New York: Doubleday, 1984), p. 94.

grew significantly in absolute terms, and despite the effects of the baby boom, the percentage of eligible men drafted also rose significantly. But even with the war going at full throttle, the fraction of all those between the ages of eighteen and twenty-six who were compelled to perform military service remained extremely low. The incidence of conscription increased to levels that had not been seen since the mid-1950s, but with callups smaller and the population bigger, it never approached the levels attained during the Korean War.

More significant than these statistical shifts, of course, was the fact that in contrast to the post-Korean period, draftees were now being killed.[158] What was at stake was not just the likelihood that some young men rather than others would have their lives disrupted and their careers delayed, but the certainty that some would live while others died. Vietnam transformed the issue of equity from a slowly simmering controversy into a roiling national debate.

The discussion of fairness focused first on procedures and then, as the war dragged on, on the more fundamental issue of outcomes. Critics pointed out that the welter of regulations governing deferments coupled with the Selective Service System's reliance on over four thousand local boards to make decisions about draft eligibility led inevitably to an uneven application of the rules. A man who could be declared fit for service by one board might easily be granted a deferment by another.[159]

As the war intensified and the number of American casualties grew, a second and even more telling critique began to emerge. Not only was the Selective Service System capricious in its operations; it appeared also to be guilty of systematic bias. Critics charged that the draft was sending disproportionately large numbers of poor (and especially poor black) men to fight and die in Vietnam. Whether class was more important than race in determining a man's fortunes, and whether the outcome of the entire process was the result of some deliberate conspiracy or merely the "product of numerous smaller decisions manifest in the complex system of exemptions, deferments, and induction priorities," mattered relatively little.[160] What counted, from the point of view of practical politics, was the deepening impression of inequity, reinforced by a steady stream of academic studies and news reports.[161]

---

[158] Flynn, *The Draft*, p. 167.

[159] On the origins of the decentralized system See Wamsley, *Selective Service and a Changing America*, pp. 13–102. For critiques of its workings during the Vietnam era see also Davis and Dolbeare, *Little Groups of Neighbors*; Gary L. Wamsley, "Decision-Making in Local Boards: A Case Study," in Little, *Selective Service and American Society*, pp. 83–108.

[160] Michael Useem, "Conscription and Class," *Society* 18, no. 3 (March/April 1981), p. 30.

[161] As sociologist Morris Janowitz notes, "University-based charges of the unrepresentativeness of casualties became a central note of political dissensus and popular agitation." Morris Janowitz, *The Last Half-Century: Societal Change and Politics in America* (Chicago: University of Chicago Press, 1978), p. 198. For various efforts to sort out the statistics see, in addition to Fligstein, "Who Served in the Military"; Maurice Zeitlin, Kenneth Lutterman, and James Russell, "Death in Vietnam: Class, Poverty, and the Risks of War," *Politics and Society* 3 (Spring 1973), pp. 313–28; Gilbert Badillo and David Curry, "The Social Incidence of Vietnam Casualties: Social Class or Race?" *Armed Forces and Society* 2, no. 3 (Spring 1976), pp. 397–406. For the argument that "class was far more important than race in determining the overall social composition of American forces," see Chris-

Before the full force of Vietnam had even been felt, some public figures (including President Johnson) had already given tacit acknowledgment that there might be difficulties with the draft. As protests against it mounted, official declarations of concern became blunter, more frequent, and more anguished. In contrast to the 1950s, when great energy had been invested in persuading the public of the fundamental fairness of limited conscription, now government officials joined in describing its failings. In the spring of 1966 Secretary of Defense Robert McNamara gave a speech in which he termed the fact that "the Selective Service System draws on only a minority of eligible young men . . . an inequity."[162] Several months later President Johnson referred publicly to the draft as a "crazy quilt system" that was in need of reform.[163] In a special message to Congress in March 1967 the president warned that "the danger of inequity" was "embedded" in the nation's changing demographic profile, and he acknowledged a growing concern "in the Executive Branch, in Congress, in the Nation generally . . . [that] the System might have drifted from the original concept of equity." This concern had "deepened as young men were called to the field of combat."[164] To address the issue of fairness, Johnson appointed yet another study commission. Its report, made public in 1967, was pointedly entitled *In Pursuit of Equity: Who Serves When Not All Serve?*[165] Later that same year, although it made few substantive alterations, Congress changed the title of the law authorizing conscription from the Universal Military Training and Service Act to the Military Selective Service Act.[166] Albeit in a small and seemingly insignificant way, this change too was an acknowledgment that the illusion of universality and equity could no longer be sustained.

The comments of high-ranking government officials from the mid-1960s onward suggest an increasing discomfort with the inequities of limited conscription, and were rooted both in a concern over the possible political implications and, at least in some cases, in a genuine feeling that the system was profoundly flawed and unfair. These authoritative statements also tended to confirm the validity of criticisms emanating from college campuses and, although it is impossible to measure their precise impact, they cannot help but have contributed to growing doubts about the legitimacy of the draft among the public at large.

If the draft was unfair, it could either be reformed or abandoned. If it was abandoned, it could be replaced either with some form of universal service or with an entirely volunteer force. Proposals for universal service, in turn, came

tian G. Appy, *Working Class War: American Combat Soldiers and Vietnam* (Chapel Hill: University of North Carolina Press, 1993), p. 22.

[162] Robert S. McNamara, "Voluntary Service for All Youth," speech of May 19, 1966, reprinted in Chambers, *Draftees or Volunteers*, pp. 552, 542–53.

[163] Flynn, *Lewis B. Hershey*, p. 242.

[164] See the text of Johnson's message on Selective Service, March 6, 1967, reprinted in Clark et al., *U.S. Draft Policy*, p. 40.

[165] Report of the National Advisory Commission on Selective Service, *In Pursuit of Equity: Who Serves When Not All Serve?* (Washington, DC: U.S. Government Printing Office, 1967).

[166] Clark et al., *U.S. Draft Policy*, p. 21.

in left- and right-wing variants. Some liberals agreed with Secretary of Defense McNamara that all young men should be required to choose between two years of military service or an equivalent period "in the Peace Corps or in some other volunteer developmental work at home or abroad."[167] A few conservatives countered by proposing the implementation, at long last, of a genuinely universal program of military training.[168] While either of these plans might have dealt effectively with the issue of equity, both were attacked on the familiar grounds that they would lead to an unnecessary and undesirable expansion in the government's powers of compulsion.[169]

The idea of universal service lingered on for some time, but for all practical purposes discussion of how best to deal with the inequities of selective service was reduced quickly to a debate between the advocates of voluntarism and the proponents of procedural reform. Each of the major changes in the Selective Service System instituted after 1965 was part of an overall effort to respond to growing accusations of inequity. Toward this end, most deferments had been suspended by the early 1970s, the autonomy of local boards had been sharply reduced, and a national lottery, intended to make the selection of inductees as random and uniform as possible, had been introduced.[170]

As useful as they may have been in defusing immediate criticism, marginal reforms did nothing to change the single most important characteristic of the draft. No matter how even-handed and objective the methods of selection, the burden of mandatory service imposed by any system of limited conscription would always be unequal. The issue now was whether the country would, or indeed *should*, continue to tolerate such a system. Candidate Richard Nixon gave one clear answer on the eve of the 1968 presidential election:

> [A] system of compulsory service that arbitrarily selects some and not others simply cannot be squared with our whole concept of liberty, justice and equality under law. . . . It's not so much the way they're selected that's wrong, as it is the *fact* of selection. . . . The only way to stop the inequities is to stop using the system.[171]

---

[167] See McNamara's mistitled speech, "Voluntary Service for all Youth," p. 552. For other proposals along these lines see George Walton, *Let's End the Draft Mess* (New York: David McKay, 1967); Terrence Cullinan, "The Courage to Compel," *Forensic Quarterly* 42, nos. 1–3 (May 1968), pp. 211–24. Also Margaret Mead, "A National Service System as a Solution to a Variety of Problems," in Tax, *The Draft*, pp. 99–109.

[168] See Dwight D. Eisenhower, "This Country *Needs* Universal Military Training," *Reader's Digest*, September 1966, pp. 49–55.

[169] Like the proposals themselves, criticisms on these grounds came from both left and right. See articles by, respectively, a noted libertarian polemicist and two members of the Citizens' Crusade against Poverty. Ayn Rand, "The Wreckage of Consensus," in Anderson, *The Military Draft*, pp. 171–80; and Richard W. Boone and Norman G. Kurland, "Freedom, National Security, and the Elimination of Poverty: Is Compulsory Service Necessary?" in Tax, *The Draft*, pp. 265–79.

[170] On the implementation of these changes see Curtis W. Tarr, *By the Numbers: The Reform of the Selective Service System, 1970–1972* (Washington, DC: National Defense University Press, 1981).

[171] Richard M. Nixon, "The All-Volunteer Armed Forces," an address given over the CBS Radio Network, October 17, 1968, reprinted in Chambers, *Draftees or Volunteers*, p. 573–74.

The Assault on Compulsion

The thrust of Nixon's case against the draft placed him in some rather unusual company. As they had done two decades earlier, many on the left wing of the American political spectrum had begun by the late 1960s to challenge the "subordination of the individual to the state" inherent in *any* system of compulsion.[172] "Conscription is confiscation," wrote the leaders of the National Council to Repeal the Draft.[173] The "primary defect of the draft," wrote another critic, was not "inequality of treatment" but the fact that "a man who is compelled to enter the Army feels a loss of freedom." In the final analysis, "the issue is freedom, rather than equality under compulsion."[174]

Closer to Nixon's ideological home, right-wing libertarians were starting to make very similar assertions. "Of all the statist violations of individual rights in a mixed economy," wrote Ayn Rand in 1967,

> the military draft is the worst. . . . It negates man's fundamental right—the right to life—and establishes the fundamental principle of statism: that a man's life belongs to the state. . . . Once that principle is accepted, the rest is only a matter of time.

Instead of leaving it to "the extreme *left*—the Vietniks and Peaceniks" who had first raised the issue, it was conservatives, the "alleged defenders of freedom and capitalism, who should be opposing the draft."[175]

Led by economist Milton Friedman, a number of capitalism's most ardent defenders in the late 1960s had already begun to move in precisely this direction. Friedman and his associates did not denounce the draft in principle, and, for the most part, they built their critique of it on cool reasoning rather than heated rhetoric. Conscription was a "tax-in-kind," extracted by the state (in collaboration with a majority of society) from an unfortunate few. Slightly higher money taxes on the population as a whole would permit the military to pay enough to attract a sufficient number of genuine volunteers. Determining the precise levels of payment necessary to build a voluntary force of a given size under varying conditions of unemployment was a matter of estimating the price elasticity of supply for military labor.[176]

Underlying the technical jargon and the technocratic stance was a powerful normative concern.[177] Voluntarism was not only more efficient than conscription, it was also morally superior. Conscription was involuntary servitude. Such an imposition on individual freedom, if it could ever be tolerated, was accept-

---

[172] John M. Swomley, Jr., "Twenty-five Years of Conscription," in Chambers, *Draftees or Volunteers*, p. 474.

[173] Thomas Reeves and Karl Hess, *The End of the Draft* (New York: Random House, 1970), p. 21

[174] John M. Swomley, Jr., "Why the Draft Should Go," in Anderson, *The Military Draft*, p. 582.

[175] Rand, "The Wreckage of Consensus," pp. 172, and 177.

[176] See Walter Y. Oi, "The Costs and Implications of an All-Volunteer Force," in Tax, *The Draft*, pp. 221–51.

[177] James Burk, "Debating the Draft in America," *Armed Forces and Society* 15, no. 3 (Spring 1989), p. 442.

able only under conditions of supreme national emergency. The abandonment of taxes-in-kind had been "one of the greatest advances in human freedom." In adopting the draft, wrote Friedman, the United States had "reverted to a barbarous custom. It is past time that we regain our heritage."[178]

Historian James Burk notes that "the resort to 'free market' economic ideology was politically crucial at this juncture." The libertarian economists made an analytically elegant case for the feasibility of an all-volunteer force. More important, as Burk suggests, they "supplied a doctrine that accommodated the radical promotion of the rights of individual conscience within politically traditional terms."[179] The notion that any measure of compulsion was inherently undesirable and that the draft should therefore be abolished rather than merely reformed was no longer the exclusive province of the left. Voluntarism was now an idea that could be embraced by conservative members of Congress and presidential candidates.[180] What appeared at first to be a proposal favored by only an odd coalition of the extreme left and the far right was rapidly gaining support from the political mainstream and, increasingly, from the general public.

Dismantling the Draft

Conscription was "more of a political issue in 1968 than . . . in any general election since 1864."[181] With the Democratic party taking a cautious, lukewarm stance in favor of draft reform, candidate Richard Nixon saw an opportunity to outflank the opposition, winning over some antidraft, anti-war voters who might not otherwise have supported him. The prospect of alienating those who still favored the draft does not appear to have worried Nixon a great deal, perhaps because, if recent trends were any indication, many of them could be assumed to be on the verge of changing their minds.[182] Support for continued conscription was soft and getting softer all the time. As in the 1940s, opposing compulsion seemed the better bet in American politics.[183]

---

[178] Milton Friedman, "Why Not a Voluntary Army?" in Tax, *The Draft*, p. 207. For an early statement of the conservative case against conscription see also Bruce K. Chapman, "Politics and Conscription: A Proposal to Replace the Draft," in Tax, *The Draft*, pp. 208–20. Also Chapman, "Why Not Abolish the Draft?" *National Review* 19, no. 11 (March 21, 1967), pp. 303–5.

[179] Burk, "Debating the Draft," p. 442.

[180] See, for example, a book by a group of Republican congressmen: Robert Stafford, Frank J. Horton, Richard S. Schweiker, et al., *How to End the Draft: The Case for an All-Volunteer Army* (Washington, DC: National Press, 1967).

[181] James A. Huston, "Selective Service as a Political Issue," *Current History* 55, no. 326 (October 1968), p. 218.

[182] The polls showed that support for the draft had dropped off considerably since the escalation of the war in Vietnam, from a "rally round the flag" high of 90 percent in December 1965, to 79 percent in August 1966, to 58 percent in February 1967. Still, as the election approached, a bare majority of Americans (53 percent in May 1968) continued to favor the existing system. These are the results of a repeated Harris poll survey conducted over a period of six years. See the table in Useem, *Conscription, Protest, and Social Conflict*, p. 115.

[183] On the genesis of Nixon's decision to call for an end to the draft (and the role of Martin Anderson, a young Friedmanite on his staff), see Donald Smith, "The Volunteer Army," *Atlantic*

Nixon's public advocacy of an all-volunteer force set in motion a chain of events that would complete the delegitimation of the draft. The only alternative to voluntarism, he declared near the close of the campaign, was "never-ending compulsion in a society consecrated to freedom. . . . I say it's time we looked to our consciences. Let's show our commitment to freedom by preparing to assure our young people theirs."[184] This proclamation was followed in the immediate aftermath of the election, by the formation of a presidential commission charged not with reviewing the options, as so many earlier groups had already done, but with developing "a comprehensive plan for eliminating conscription."[185]

Within a year the so-called Gates Commission issued a report that built a moral as well as a practical case for voluntarism. Virtually all of the arguments against limited conscription that had been developed over the preceding five years (and most of those against compulsion more generally) were now interwoven with impressive numerical tables and mathematical formulas. The draft was an unfair, "discriminatory," and "regressive" tax, a "hidden tax," a "tax-in-kind." It was also "a relatively recent phenomenon" that did not accord well with "the nation's legal and political traditions" and whose continued application "undermine[d] respect for government." By contrast, a return to voluntarism would "strengthen our freedoms, remove an inequity," and "enhance [the] dignity" of the armed forces. An all-volunteer force would minimize "government interference with the freedom of the individual."[186] In addition, as President Nixon explained, "by upholding the cause of freedom without conscription," the United States would demonstrate "in one more area the superiority of a society based upon belief in the dignity of man over a society based on the supremacy of the State."[187]

With the authoritative presentation of a clear alternative, remaining public support for the draft quickly evaporated.[188] On June 30, 1973, after twenty-five

---

Monthly 234, no. 1 (July 1974), pp. 8–9. Also Robert Griffith, Jr., "About Face? The U.S. Army and the Draft," *Armed Forces and Society* 12, no. 1 (Fall 1985), pp. 119–23; and Lee and Parker, *Ending the Draft*, p. 29.

[184] See Nixon, "The All-Volunteer Armed Forces," in Chambers, *Draftees or Volunteers*, pp. 576, 578.

[185] "Statement by the President," March 27, 1969, in The President's Commission on an All-Volunteer Armed Force, *Report of the President's Commission on an All-Volunteer Armed Force* (Washington, DC: U.S. Government Printing Office, 1970), p. vii.

[186] Ibid., pp. 5–33.

[187] "Nixon's Message on the Draft, 1970," reprinted in O'Sullivan and Meckler, *The Draft and Its Enemies*, p. 278.

[188] At the time of Nixon's innaugural only 32 percent of those interviewed in one poll expressed approval of the idea of replacing conscription with an all-volunteer force. In the early spring of 1969 another survey reported that support had grown to 38 percent. See Flynn, *Lewis B. Hershey*, pp. 273–74. In less than a year, by January 1970, a majority of those questioned (52 percent) favored "a volunteer army as a substitute for the present draft lottery system." See "Poll Says Most Americans Favor All-Volunteer Army," *New York Times*, January 27, 1970, p. 40. By the summer of 1970, following the release of the Gates Commission report, 71 percent of respondents supported such a shift. Flynn, *Lewis B. Hershey*, p. 284. By 1973, one nationwide survey found citizens

years and despite considerable misgivings on the part of the military, the United States ended its experiment with limited peacetime conscription.[189]

POSTSCRIPT: THE RESILIENCE OF VOLUNTARISM

The launching of the All-Volunteer Force was followed, in short order, by sharp shifts in the demographic and strategic conditions that had eased its adoption. Yet despite frequent complaints that the All-Volunteer Force was not providing adequately for the nation's defense, the United States did not change its military format. Once conscription had been abandoned, a combination of domestic political pressures and ideological constraints prevented its reimposition. In contrast to conditions in the post-Korean War era, the equilibrium that prevailed after Vietnam proved to be highly stable; it was much easier for the United States to proceed down the scale of compulsion than it was to move back up.

By the early 1980s, as the baby boom generation aged, the size of the pool of possible military volunteers began to shrink.[190] Just as the supply of potential recruits was set to dwindle, however, the demand for military manpower started to rise. The collapse of détente in the second half of the 1970s led to calls for larger U.S. forces-in-being to bolster deterrence.[191] The continuing growth in

---

supporting the all-volunteer force by a two-to-one margin over the draft. See Jerald G. Bachman, John D. Blair, and David R. Segal, *The All-Volunteer Force: A Study of Ideology in the Military* (Ann Arbor: University of Michigan Press, 1977), p. 33.

[189] For slightly varying accounts of the military's attitudes toward the all-volunteer force, see Flynn, *The Draft*, pp. 266–71; and Griffith, "About Face?" pp. 120–29. For a sense of contemporary anxiety on the subject see, for example, Brig. Gen. Lynn D. Smith, "An All-Volunteer Army: Real Future Possibility or Impractical Dream?" *Army* (April 1969), pp. 22–31; Lieut. Leon Preston Brooks, "Vital Interests and Volunteer Forces," *U.S. Naval Institute Proceedings* (January 1971), pp. 18–23; David Syrett and Richard H. Kohn, "The Dangers of an All-Volunteer Army," *Military Review*, June 1972, pp. 70–74. More upbeat is Col. Selwyn P. Rogers, Jr., "An All-Volunteer Force," *Military Review*, Summer 1970, pp. 89–95.

[190] See the analysis in William P. Snyder, "Military Personnel-Procurement Policies—Trends—Context," in John B. Keeley, *The All-Volunteer Force and American Society* (Charlottesville: University Press of Virginia, 1978), pp. 1–38. See also Richard W. Hunter, "An Analysis of the All-Volunteer Armed Forces—Past and Future," in Robert K. Fullinwider, ed., *Conscripts and Volunteers: Military Requirements, Social Justice, and the All-Volunteer Force* (Totowa, NJ: Rowman and Allanheld, 1983), pp. 23–45. In addition to concerns about a decline in the quantity of available recruits, there were also worries, based on early experience with the all-volunteer force, about their quality. For slightly varying interpretations of the evidence regarding the quality of the early all-volunteer force see Morris Janowitz and Charles C. Moskos, Jr., "Five Years of the All-Volunteer Force, 1973–1978," *Armed Forces and Society* 5, no. 2 (February 1979), pp. 171–218; Richard V. L. Cooper, "The All-Volunteer Force: Status and Prospects of the Active Forces," in Andrew J. Goodpaster, ed., *Toward a Consensus on Military Service* (New York: Pergamon Press, 1982), pp. 76–112; Martin Binkin, *America's Volunteer Military: Progress and Prospects* (Washington, DC: Brookings Institution, 1984

[191] Critics claimed that U.S. standing forces had been allowed to shrink to dangerously low levels in part to accommodate the rather disappointing capacity of the all-volunteer force to generate sufficient numbers of capable volunteers at an acceptable cost. One study pointed out, for example, that, between 1973 and 1978, "the capacity of the armed services to meet their numerical goals has

Soviet strategic nuclear capabilities seemed also to increase the likelihood of a large and possibly protracted conventional conflict between the superpowers. In such a contingency, the United States would have to place heavy reliance on its reserve forces; since the return to voluntarism, however, these had diminished considerably in size and quality. By the end of the 1970s it had become increasingly common for military strategists to conclude that the ability of the United States to fight a large conventional war in Europe or Southwest Asia had "been significantly reduced as a result of the decision to adopt an All-Volunteer Force."[192]

Despite a virtual consensus among experts that a return to the draft was strategically necessary, and in spite of at least some evidence that the public might be willing to go along, the nation's political leaders proved extremely reluctant to take such a step.[193] Following the Soviet invasion of Afghanistan in December 1979, President Jimmy Carter asked Congress for the authority to begin once again to register nineteen and twenty year olds for the draft, but he did not go so far as to request the power actually to resume inductions. On the contrary, Carter was quick to offer assurances that he had no immediate intention of resorting to conscription. This pledge may have diluted the image of toughness that the president hoped to convey, but it also helped ease congressional approval of his request. After lengthy debate and against significant resistance from both Republicans and Democrats, in the summer of 1980 registration was finally approved.[194]

---

in large part been the result of a downward recasting of manpower objectives." Janowitz and Moskos, "Five Years of the All-Volunteer Force," p. 179. By 1979 the U.S. active duty force stood at 2,049,000 men, down almost half a million men from the force levels maintained before Vietnam and from the 2.5-million-man force promised by the Gates Commission.

[192] Kenneth J. Coffey, *Manpower For Military Mobilization* (Washington, DC: American Enterprise Insitute, 1978), p. 1. Also Coffey, *Strategic Implications of the All-Volunteer Force* (Chapel Hill: University of North Carolina Press, 1979). Somewhat more measured, but still pessimistic, is William J. Taylor, Jr., "U.S. Security Requirements: Missions, Manpower, Readiness, Mobilization, and Projection of Forces," in Goodpaster, *Toward a Consensus on Military Service*, pp. 52–75. For more on the reserve issue see Arthur L. Moxon, "U.S. Reserve Force: The Achilles' Heel fo the All-Volunteer Force?" in Franklin D. Margiotta, James Brown, and Michael J. Collins, eds., *Changing U.S. Military Manpower Realities* (Boulder, CO: Westview Press, 1983), pp. 39–65. Also John B Keeley, "United States Reserve Forces: A High-Cost. Low-Return Investment in National Security," in Keeley, *The All-Volunteer Force and American Society*, pp. 166–82; and John Turley, "Mobilization Manpower: A Credible Force or an Empty Promise?" *Military Review* (August 1981), pp. 2–12.

[193] For examples of calls for a renewed draft see James L. Lacy, "The Case for Conscription," in Brent Scowcroft, ed., *Military Service in the United States* (Englewood Cliffs, NJ: Prentice-Hall, 1982), pp. 195–219; Eliot Cohen, "Why We Need a Draft," *Commentary* (April 1982), pp. 34–40. One 1981 survey found 65 percent of those over the age of fifty favoring a resumption of the draft, but only 46 percent of those between eighteen and twenty-nine in favor. Goodpaster, *Toward a Consensus on Military Service*, p. 305. Also citing opinion polls is Lt. Col. Henry J. Sage, "The Drift toward the Draft," *U.S. Naval Institute Proceedings* (June 1979), pp. 44.

[194] On this episode see Bertram M. Gross, "The Drive to Revive the Draft," *Nation* 229, no. 12 (October 20, 1979), p. 1; Dick Kirschten, "The Flap over Draft Registration—Only the Public Seems to Like It," *National Journal* 12, no. 16 (April 19, 1980), p. 645; Bernard D. Rostker,

In the presidential campaign that followed, Ronald Reagan attacked his opponent both for letting down the nation's defenses and for seeking to bolster them by taking steps to restore the draft. In keeping with his broad ideological preferences, Reagan promised that if elected, he would improve the All-Volunteer Force, thereby increasing American power abroad without enhancing the extractive capacities of the American state at home. Once in office, the new administration proceeded, through increased pay and stepped-up efforts at recruitment, to breathe new life into the All-Volunteer Force. Aided by rising unemployment and by a prudent scaling back in initial plans for much larger standing forces, the Reagan administration was able in the early 1980s to match the demand for military manpower to the supply of volunteers. As the sense of imminent crisis dwindled, so too did any possibility of a return to the draft. Once buried, limited conscription would not be disinterred for the remainder of the Cold War.[195]

"Selective Service Program Overview and Results of the 1980 Registration," in William J. Taylor, Jr., Eric T. Olson, and Richard A. Schrader, *Defense Manpower Planning: Issues for the 1980s* (New York: Pergamon Press, 1982), pp. 179–93; Martin Anderson, ed., *Registration and the Draft* (Stanford, CA: Hoover Institution, 1982); Herbert C. Puscheck, "Selective Service Registration: Success or Failure?" *Armed Forces and Society* 10, no. 1 (Fall 1983), pp. 5–25; James B. Jacobs and Dennis McNamara, "Selective Service without a Draft," *Armed Forces and Society* 10, no. 3 (Spring 1984), pp. 361–79. The substance of the administration's recommendations is contained in House Committee on Armed Services, *Presidential Recommendations for Selective Service Reform*, 96th Cong., 2d sess. (Washington, DC: U.S. Government Printing Office, 1980).

[195] Reagan's top adviser on domestic affairs was Martin Anderson, the man who had first persuaded Richard Nixon to embrace the all-volunteer force. On the administration's early manpower decisions see Caspar W. Weinberger, *Military Manpower Task Force: A Report to the President on the Status and Prospects of the All-Volunteer Force* (Washington, DC: U.S. Government Printing Office, November 1982); Secretary of Defense Caspar W. Weinberger, *Annual Report to the Congress, Fiscal Year 1983* (Washington, DC: U.S. Government Printing Office, 1982), pp. III-161–81; also Robert B. Pirie, Jr., "Military Manpower in Current U.S. Strategic Planning," in Gregory D. Foster, Alan Ned Sabrosky, and William J. Taylor, Jr., *The Strategic Dimension of Military Manpower* (Cambridge, MA: Ballinger, 1987), pp. 53–63.

Supporting Industries

WHY NO INDUSTRIAL POLICY IN AMERICA?

This is the story of a dog that did not bark. Following the close of the Second World War the federal government might have developed an approach for dealing with defense supporting industries that was highly centralized in institutional structure, broad in directive scope, and reliant on potent, intrusive policy instruments. The Cold War could have given rise to a single executive branch agency, charged with setting production targets in hundreds of supporting industries (from steel, to cement, to sulfuric acid) and possessed of the power to use direct subsidies, tax incentives, and protective tariffs, among other tools, to sculpt the nation's industrial base in order to make it ready for war. This agency might also have been authorized to fund the construction, where necessary, of government-owned production facilities and to use its powers to promote the dispersal of privately owned plants and factories so as to render them less vulnerable to nuclear attack.

As improbable as it may appear in retrospect, such an outcome was a very real possibility in the late 1940s and early 1950s. Eager to apply the lessons of the recent world war and fearful that another was imminent, many American strategists were convinced of the need for a strong, active, permanent industrial planning system. After several years of largely ineffectual efforts, they found an opportunity in the Korean War to put their ideas into practice. As that conflict drew to a close, most of the elements just described were actually in place.

Yet within a few years, the institutions of central industrial planning had shriveled to insignificance, and the implements with which they had once been armed had largely been discarded. What emerged instead, and what persisted thereafter, was a pattern of weak or nonexistent central institutions and a heavy reliance on procurement as the preferred instrument of defense industrial policy. To the extent that it helped the broad array of supporting industries for reasons of national security from the late 1950s onwards, the federal government did so primarily by buying their products or, more typically, by buying weapons and other defense systems into which those products were incorporated.

The demise of defense industrial policy is often portrayed as a logical, inevitable response to the advent of nuclear weapons. As with the rejection of universal military training, however, this outcome too was at least as much a product of domestic anti-statist influences.

In the initial postwar period, official U.S. war planning was based on the expectation that a future conflict with the Soviet Union would be long and that its successful conduct would require large-scale industrial mobilization. Despite this belief, it was only while the Korean War was actually in progress that active preparations for such a contingency were undertaken. Until the early 1950s, military strategy and domestic preparations for power creation simply did not match up.

The subsequent shift toward massive retaliation under the Eisenhower administration, and the accompanying assumption that the next war would be over quickly, diminished the importance of emergency war production and justified decreased government efforts to shape the wider national industrial base. However, the change in planning assumptions was itself partly a reflection of the desire of top officials to do away with the apparatus of defense industrial policy. The intensity and importance of this desire is suggested also by the fact that the federal government at the same time effectively abandoned efforts to promote industrial dispersal. Dispersal continued to appear prudent to many observers, and in any event, the government remained formally committed to its achievement, despite shifts in military strategy. Whatever the arguments in its favor, however, such a policy faced insurmountable domestic obstacles.

That interest in an active defense industrial policy diminished when military strategy changed in the early 1950s does not explain why the pattern of policy did not shift substantially when strategy changed again in the early 1960s and, once more, in the early 1980s. A lack of attention to industrial planning followed logically from the view that a future war would be over in hours or days, before mobilization could have any effect. But as assumptions about the likely length and character of warfare evolved (with the advent of flexible response in the Kennedy administration and, twenty years later, a renewed belief in the possibility of truly protracted superpower conflict) the nation's defense industrial policy did not.

If strategy alone cannot do so, what *does* account for the absence of strong defense industrial planning institutions, and for the almost exclusive reliance on procurement as the preferred tool for assisting defense supporting industries?

Planning was a fighting word in the 1940s and 1950s; its mere mention, even when linked to the phrase *national security*, provoked protests from many politicians, business executives, and intellectuals. The widespread animosity to statism that characterized the early-postwar period thus played a critical role in blocking the creation of new, powerful government industrial planning institutions, regardless of their apparent strategic importance. (A resurgence of such sentiments played a similar role in the early 1980s.)

In addition to its ideological foundations, opposition to planning and to an authoritative, centrally directed defense industrial policy was also consistent with the interests of most industrialists and many members of Congress. Corporate executives might have been willing to accept federal assistance, but they were deeply suspicious of any arrangements for extending it that threatened to interfere with their freedom to make decisions about such vital matters as productive capacity and plant location. Congressmembers were eager to win federal help for firms in their states and districts, and for that reason were reluctant to agree to the creation of executive branch agencies that might be insulated from their influence. Fear that a federal industrial planning agency might, for strategic reasons, encourage the development of certain parts of the country over others helped to make Congress additionally wary.

Especially in the absence of strong central institutions, interest groups might have been able to capture the instruments of defense industrial policy and turn them to their advantage. Indeed, throughout the Cold War, supporting industries (backed by their congressional allies) regularly sought government assistance on national security grounds. For the most part, however, these pressures did not produce the desired results. In a few instances, where the views of industry and executive branch officials converged, assistance was offered, but in most cases industry's advances were deflected with partial concessions or fended off altogether.

Ideology was the primary source of this executive branch aversion to extending preferential treatment to particular firms and sectors. In the 1950s (and again in the 1980s) top officials from the president on down were convinced of the virtues of freely functioning markets and were reluctant to intervene, regardless of possible short-term political gains and despite appeals to the needs of national security. While subsidies and tariffs appeared dubious, the notion of government helping an industry or a particular firm by buying its products did not. To the contrary, such transactions were generally regarded as merely another form of market exchange, albeit one between private sellers and a large and powerful public buyer. This understanding helped to legitimize procurement as the primary instrument of government policy toward defense-supporting industries.

In an essay on the antecedents of American industrial policy historian Thomas McGraw observes that

> except in time of war, [the American] system has never lent itself to coherent state direction. Only palpable external threats have overcome the nation's powerful commitment to individual freedom of choice. For any economy, industrial policy tends to diminish such freedom and to increase coercion; and Americans have accepted extensive coercion only in the face of an enemy.[1]

McCraw is right, but as this chapter will show, he does not go far enough. *Even* in the face of an enemy, and to a remarkable degree even in wartime, the American system has proven itself to be highly resistant to centralized industrial planning.[2]

---

[1] Thomas K. McCraw, "Mercantilism and the Market: Antecedents of American Industrial Policy," in Claude E. Barfield and William A. Schambra, eds., *The Politics of Industrial Policy* (Washington, DC: American Enterprise Institute, 1986), pp. 56–57.

[2] Precisely the opposite could be said of the Soviet Union, which retained in peacetime what has been aptly described as a "permanent war economy." During the Cold War, the entire Soviet economy was subject to a highly centralized industrial planning system that gave top priority to the needs of the military. Indeed, to a considerable degree, there was no distinct civilian industrial sector. Enterprises involved primarily in the production of arms and military equipment (which were grouped together into a handful of large ministries and operated under the direct control of a

202

THE LESSONS OF THE PAST

American strategists believed that they had learned very similar lessons from the nation's experience in the two world wars. Both conflicts confirmed the supreme importance of industrial production in modern warfare. Both demonstrated that even for a country with as much productive capacity and potential as the United States, the transition from normal peacetime activity to a full war footing would not be easy, automatic, or necessarily very rapid. And, in both cases, effective utilization of the nation's vast resources ultimately required the creation of strong central government institutions with extraordinary directive powers. The initial fumbling and delays that plagued American mobilization in the two world wars drove home the importance of advance planning and preparation, and raised serious questions about the proper peacetime economic role of the state in an era of total warfare.

Prior to the U.S. entry into World War One virtually no plans had been made for mobilizing the nation's productive resources.[3] "America had at her disposal a vast economic potential, but not the institutions or plans for its conversion into military strength."[4] According to historian Louis Hunter, the roots of this situation lay deep in "the nature of [American] national development and experience—especially the tradition of assertive individualism, and the general hostility toward Government interference with business."[5]

---

single Military-Industrial Commission) also produced some goods for civilian consumption. On the other hand, many nominally "civilian" enterprises in sectors such as metals, chemicals, electrical equipment, and machine tools (what are referred to in this chapter as "defense supporting industries") provided most of their output to the arms producers. Virtually any facility whose productive capacity might be useful for military purposes was also subject to the direction of state defense industrial planners. Plants were required to maintain "mobilization kits" containing stockpiles of the tools and raw materials that would be needed for quick conversion to defense production. Through much of the Cold War, decisions about plant location were also influenced by efforts to reduce vulnerability to nuclear attack. Regarding the organization and functioning of the Soviet defense industrial planning system see Julian Cooper, *The Soviet Defence Industry: Conversion and Reform* (London: Royal Institute of International Affairs, 1991), pp. 1–29; Clifford G. Gaddy, *The Price of the Past: Russia's Struggle with the Legacy of a Militarized Economy* (Washington, DC: Brookings Institution, 1997), 9–46; William Odom, *The Collapse of the Soviet Military* (New Haven: Yale University Press, 1998), pp. 49–64. Industrial mobilization measures are discussed in David F. Epstein, "The Economic Cost of Security and Empire," in Henry S. Rowen and Charles Wolf, Jr., *The Impoverished Superpower: Perestroika and the Soviet Military Burden* (San Francisco: Institute for Contemporary Studies, 1990), pp. 133–37; and Michael Checinski, "The Mobilization Aspect of the Soviet Economy as a Factor in Preparedness for War," in Robert L. Pfaltzgraff, Jr., and Uri Ra'anan, eds., *The U.S. Defense Mobilization Infrastructure: Problems and Priorities* (Medford, MA: Archon Books, 1983), pp. 143–57.

[3] Louis Hunter, *Economic Mobilization Planning and National Security, 1947–1953* (Washington, DC: Industrial College of the Armed Forces, 1954), pp. 5–6. For a review of what planning there was see Marvin A. Kreidberg and Merton G. Henry, *History of Military Mobilization in the United States Army, 1775–1945* (Washington, DC: U.S. Government Printing Office, 1955), pp. 214–40.

[4] Gerd Hardach, *The First World War, 1914–1918* (Berkeley: University of California Press, 1977), p. 96.

[5] Hunter, *Economic Mobilization Planning*, p. 6.

Initial attempts to satisfy the emergency needs of the armed services involved little more than an extension of peacetime procurement practices, with a multitude of military supply bureaus each trying to buy what it needed on the open market.[6] This led quickly to inflation, shortages, a crisis in war production, and, ultimately, the creation of the War Industries Board (WIB), a quasi-governmental organization charged with responsibility for coordinating military demands with industrial supply. Reflecting American sensibilities and the government's limited administrative capabilities, the WIB was staffed primarily by "dollar-a-year men" on loan from business, and it operated under an "ideology of voluntarism" in which "education, cooperation among civilian volunteers, widespread consultation among private groups, and a general spirit of patriotism" were supposed to take the place of "manipulation and dictation."[7] Heralded as "America's answer to the bureacratic statism of Europe, the ultimate vindication of the liberal tradition," the Board nevertheless involved a substantial, if temporary, increase in central control over the economy.[8] Under the direction of the WIB, American war production accelerated, although it did not reach its peak until the fighting in Europe had already ended.[9]

Military planners spent the twenty years after World War One preparing to avoid the mistakes of their predecessors. Organizations were established to train Army and Navy officers in the arcane details of industrial mobilization, to ensure that the services had made detailed advanced estimates of their likely re-

---

[6] On the pre-war relationship of the Army to industry see Daniel R. Beaver, "The Problem of American Military Supply, 1890–1920," in Benjamin F. Cooling, *War, Business, and American Society* (Port Washington, NY: Kennikat Press, 1977), pp. 73–92. On the Navy see Benjamin F. Cooling, *Gray Steel and Blue Water Navy: The Formative Years of America's Military-Industrial Complex* (Hamden, CT: Archon Books, 1979).

[7] See Robert D. Cuff, "Herbert Hoover, the Ideology of Voluntarism, and War Organization during the Great War," *Journal of American History* 64, no. 2 (September 1977), pp. 358, 358–372.

[8] Stephen Skowronek, *Building a New American State: The Expansion of National Administrative Capacities, 1877–1920* (New York: Cambridge University Press, 1982), p. 236.

[9] No American tanks saw service in Europe and U.S.- made guns and aircraft were not available until after the war was over. The main American contribution to the Allied war effort was in the manufacture of ammunition. Hardach, *The First World War*, pp. 98–99. For overviews see Bernard Baruch, *American Industry in the War: A Report of the War Industries Board* (New York: Prentice-Hall, 1941); Ronald Schaffer, *America in the Great War: The Rise of the War Welfare State* (New York: Oxford University Press, 1991), pp. 31–63; Robert Higgs, *Crisis and Leviathan: Critical Episodes in the Growth of American Government* (New York: Oxford University Press, 1987), pp. 123–58; Paul A. C. Koistinen, "The 'Industrial-Military Complex' in Historical Perspective: World War I," *Business History Review* 41 (Winter 1967), pp. 378–403; David Kennedy, *Over Here: The First World War and American Society* (New York: Oxford University Press, 1980), pp. 93–143. On the workings of the War Industries Board see the writings of Robert Cuff, *The War Industries Board: Business-Government Relations during World War I* (Baltimore: Johns Hopkins University Press, 1973); "Woodrow Wilson and Business-Government Relations during World War I," *Review of Politics* 31, no. 3 (July 1969), pp. 385–407; "Bernard Baruch: Symbol and Myth in Industrial Mobilization," *Business History Review* 43, no. 2 (Summer 1969), pp. 115–33; "Business, the State, and World War I: The American Experience," in J. L. Granatstein and R. D. Cuff, eds., *War and Society in North America* (Toronto: Thomas Nelson, 1971), pp. 1–19; see also Robert F. Himmelberg, "The War Industries Board and the Antitrust Question in November 1918," *Journal of American History* 52, no. 1 (June 1965), pp. 59–74.

quirements in a future war, and to provide for the coordination of these diverse demands on industry. Beginning in the early 1920s, increasingly detailed Industrial Mobilization Plans were prepared on a regular basis. These documents, drawn up in collaboration with industry representatives, laid out the military's vision of how a future mobilization should proceed and how it ought to be organized. The purpose of the plans and of the activity surrounding their preparation was to make ready for the speediest possible transformation of the nation's raw economic resources into the implements of military power.[10]

Interwar planning for industrial mobilization involved virtually no active intervention by the federal government in the workings of the civilian economy. Until shortly before the outbreak of the Second World War, few attempts were made to encourage or, through the actual expenditure of federal funds, to induce industry to expand capacity or undertake other investments that would better prepare it for conversion to war production. Its passive and generally unobtrusive quality notwithstanding, the military's planning for another great mobilization did arouse considerable anxiety and opposition. Spokesmen for labor and agriculture objected that they had been excluded from the planning process and warned that a too-cozy relationship between industry and the military would lead to collusion, war profiteering, and a repeat of the inefficiencies and excesses of the First World War.[11] Some industry representatives, for their part, worried that the New Dealers in Washington were preparing not only for war, but for a "golden opportunity to do away with the profit system and the Constitution at one fell swoop."[12]

As war drew closer, the suspicions of both left and right helped to prevent an early and smooth mobilization of American industrial potential. Fearful that it would be captured by business interests, President Roosevelt's closest advisers warned him against creating a single mobilization agency on the model of the War Industries Board, as the military had suggested, and instead encouraged his inclination to disperse authority among an assortment of ad hoc agencies and boards. The results were predictably chaotic.[13]

Prior to Pearl Harbor, sporadic government efforts to promote plant expan-

---

[10] For overviews of interwar industrial mobilization planning see Hunter, *Economic Mobilization Planning*, pp. 7–18; Kreidberg and Henry, *History of Military Mobilization*, pp. 493–540; Harold W. Thatcher, *Planning Industrial Mobilization, 1920–1940* (Washington, DC: Quartermaster Corps Historical Studies, 1943); Paul A. C. Koistinen, *The Hammer and the Sword: Labor, the Military, and Industrial Mobilization, 1920–1945* (New York: Arno Press, 1979), pp. 1–77; Peter Mansfield Abramo, "The Economic and Military Potential of the United States: Industrial Mobilization Planning, 1919–1945" (Ph.D. dissertation, Temple University, August 1995).

[11] See the discussion in Hunter, *Economic Mobilization Planning*, pp. 14–15; also Albert A. Blum, "Roosevelt, the M-Day Plans, and the Military-Industrial Complex," *Military Affairs* 36, no. 2 (April 1972), pp. 44–46; and Blum, "Birth and Death of the M-Day Plan," in Harold Stein, ed., *American Civil-Military Decisions* (University: University of Alabama Press, 1963), pp. 61–96.

[12] Editorial in the April 22, 1939, edition of *Iron Age* (the journal of the iron and steel industry), quoted in Roland N. Stromberg, "American Business and the Approach of War, 1935–1941," *Journal of Economic History* 13, no. 1 (Winter 1953), p. 69.

[13] See the discussion in Blum, "Birth and Death of the M-Day Plan."

sion and initial conversion measures were also met with suspicion and resistance from industry. Still reeling from the effects of the Depression, many business executives feared being saddled with excess capacity should war somehow be avoided. The all-important producers of steel and aluminum "fought government attempts to force enlargement of their facitilies," and automobile manufacturers simply refused to accept any contracts that would force them to modify existing plant and equipment.[14] In the period leading up to American entry into the war, the federal government generally lacked the means, legal or economic, to compel them to do otherwise.

Even after December 1941 the twin processes of extending state control over all aspects of the economy and concentrating authority into a relatively small number of hands faced greater political and ideological obstacles in the United States than in any of the other combatants.[15] It was not until the middle of 1943, after almost a year and a half of active American participation in the war, that a stable institutional structure was finally in place and the mobilization could proceed without further substantial disruptions.[16]

In all, historian Alan Brinkley notes, the United States "approached the task of organizing the economy for war in a way that suggested a degree of anti-statism." As in World War One, the agencies eventually created to manage the productive effort were temporary and staffed largely by businessmen, many of whom "were implacably hostile to anything that smacked of centralized planning and considered it their mission not only to expedite war mobilization but to resist any attempt to make the war an occasion for the permanent expansion of the state."[17] Accordingly, as the Army's official history would later describe it, every effort was made to conduct the emergency mobilization "with a minimum of government supervision by harnessing the profit motive within the general framework of the existing economic and industrial system."[18]

After some hesitation, America's productive machinery slipped into gear, and

---

[14] See Barton J. Bernstein, "The Automobile Industry and the Coming of the Second World War," *Southwestern Social Science Quarterly* 47, no. 1 (June 1966), p. 22; Also Bruce Catton, *The War Lords of Washington* (New York: Harcourt Brace, 1948), pp. 40–50.

[15] Alan S. Milward, *War, Economy, and Society 1939–1945* (Berkeley: University of California Press, 1977), p. 112.

[16] After 1943 the Office of War Mobilization played the role of umpire between the demands of the military procurement agencies and an organization representing civilian production needs. The director of the OWM (later the Office of War Mobilization and Reconversion) reported directly to the president. See Samuel P. Huntington, *The Soldier and the State: The Theory and Politics of Civil-Military Relations* (New York: Vintage Books, 1957), pp. 337–44. On the struggles over organization see Donald M. Nelson, *Arsenal of Democracy: The Story of American War Production* (New York: Harcourt, Brace, 1946); Eliot Janeway, *The Struggle for Survival* (New Haven: Yale University Press, 1951); H. M. Somers, *Presidential Agency: OWMR, the Office of War Mobilization and Reconversion* (Cambridge: Harvard University Press, 1950).

[17] Alan Brinkley, "The New Deal and the Idea of the State," in Steve Fraser and Gary Gerstle, eds., *The Rise and Fall of the New Deal Order, 1930–1980* (Princeton: Princeton University Press, 1989), p. 103.

[18] R. Elbertson Smith, *The Army and Economic Mobilization* (Washington, DC: U.S. Government Printing Offiice, 1958), p. 456–57.

the nation's factories began to turn out vast quantities of arms, ammunition, and other military supplies. Given the length of the struggle, the contribution of American industry ultimately proved to be decisive, both in arming the nation's own forces and in providing desperately needed supplies to U.S. allies.[19]

PLANNING FOR THE NEXT WAR (1945–1950)

The Dissolution of Space and Time

The conduct and ultimate conclusion of the Second World War gave rise both to self-congratulation and to self-doubt. On the one hand, the war left little question as to the awesome productive power of the American economy. On the other, the process of mobilization, especially in its earlier stages, was widely perceived to have been a mess, if not a near disaster. After the war Bernard Baruch, former head of the War Industries Board and the self-styled "godfather" of interwar mobilization planning, claimed: "Our failure to mobilize properly, and in time, cost us billions of dollars. But infinitely more important, it added months to the conflict and names to the casualty lists."[20] How could similar delays be avoided in the future?

By the close of the war in the Pacific a handful of experts had begun to argue that industrial mobilization was all but obsolete. Within weeks of the bombing of Hiroshima and Nagasaki, Vannevar Bush, director of the Office of Scientific Research and Development, warned a group of military planners that an "atomic war would be over so quickly that the crippling of a nation's industry

---

[19] For helpful overviews which place central importance on industrial production in determining the outcome of the war see Paul Kennedy, *The Rise and Fall of the Great Powers: Economic Change and Military Conflict from 1500 to 2000* (New York: Random House, 1987), pp. 275–357; also John Ellis, *Brute Force: Allied Strategy and Tactics in the Second World War* (New York: Viking, 1990). For an overview of the American mobilization see Harold G. Vatter, *The U.S. Economy in World War II* (New York: Columbia University Press, 1985). Extremely detailed official accounts of the administration of the war production effort can be found in Bureau of the Budget, *The United States at War* (Washington, DC: U.S. Government Printing Office, 1946); and Civilian Production Administration, *Industrial Mobilization for War*, vol. 1, *Program and Administration* (New York: Greenwood Press, 1969). On the conduct of the mobilization by the various branches of the armed services see Smith, *The Army and Economic Mobilization*; Robert H. Connery, *The Navy and the Industrial Mobilization in World War II* (Princeton: Princeton University Press, 1951); Irving Brinton Holley, Jr., *Buying Aircraft: Materiel Procurement for the Army Air Forces* (Washington, DC: U.S. Government Printing Office, 1964). For critical analyses of the entire wartime experience see Gregory Hooks, *Forging the Military-Industrial Complex: World War II's Battle of the Potomac* (Chicago: University of Illinois Press, 1991); Paul A. C. Koistinen, "Warfare and Power Relations in America: Mobilizing the World War II Economy," and Robert D. Cuff, "Commentary," both in James Titus, ed., *The Home Front and War in the Twentieth Century: The American Experience in Comparative Perspective* (Washington, DC: Office of Air Force History, 1984), pp. 91–118. See also Joe R. Feagin and Kelly Riddell, "The State, Capitalism, and World War II: The U.S. Case," *Armed Forces and Society* 17, no. 1 (Fall 1990), pp. 53–79.

[20] Quoted in Harry Yoshpe, "Bernard M. Baruch: Civilian Godfather of the Military M-Day Plan," *Military Affairs* 29 (Spring 1965), p. 13.

would have no effect on the outcome."[21] Several months later General Leslie Groves, the head of the Manhattan Project, told an audience of mobilization specialists that the weapon he had helped to create would soon put them out of a job: "We do not know what would happen in an atomic war," Groves admitted, "but we visualize it as one in which the decision will be reached before great forces . . . could be mobilized and put into the field. . . . The war . . . is going to be fought largely with the initial stockpile of military equipment, augmented by very minor production of essential items. . . . We cannot count on industrial mobilization as we thought of it before."[22]

The dominant view in the late 1940s, however, was precisely the opposite. Far from diminishing the role of mobilization, advances in airpower and atomic weaponry (combined with the weakening of America's democratic allies) were believed, in fact, to have increased its importance.[23] If another war came, the United States would be involved from the first day. The nation would now have to stand ready at a moment's notice to expand drastically production of arms and military equipment. And it would need to be able to do so even after having been struck first by a surprise enemy attack. In the next war, wrote one pair of authors in the *Harvard Business Review*: "Victory will be achieved by the nation that can best protect its industrial potential at the outset of hostilities and strike back speedily and vigorously with an expanding volume of planes and air missiles. . . . American industry must be able to discount the effects of an initial attack and still be in position to accelerate output to required peak levels immediately after the onset of hostilities."[24]

Precisely what this would require in the way of peacetime measures was unclear, but the implications were ominous. Official documents called for preparations for "an instantaneous transition from peace to war,"[25] for "plans and preparations for the mobilization of manpower, resources and industry," and the "maintenance of industries essential to the national war effort so designed and

---

[21] From an August 22, 1945, briefing to the Joint Planning Staff, quoted in James F. Schnabel, *The Joint Chiefs of Staff and National Policy,* vol. 1, *1945–1947* (Wilmington, DE: Michael Glazier, 1979), p. 139.

[22] Lecture by Gen. Leslie Groves (January 10, 1946), "The Atomic Bomb," *Lectures Delivered at the Industrial College of the Armed Forces (January–June 1946)*, vol. 22, pt. 1 (Washington, DC: Industrial College of the Armed Forces, 1946), p. 15.

[23] For a fuller discussion of these developments, see chapter 2.

[24] Sidney M. Robbins and Thomas E. Murphy, "Industrial Preparedness," *Harvard Business Review* 26, no. 3 (May 1948), pp. 329–30. For a sampling of contemporary commentary on the continuing importance of industrial mobilization see Gen. J. Lawton Collins, "The Core of Security: Science, Industry, and the Armed Forces United," *Ordnance* (July–August 1949), pp. 19–20; Lt. Col. Carl T. Schmidt, "An Introduction to the Economics of Mobilization," *Military Review* 29, no. 7 (October 1949), pp. 25–29; William S. Friedman, "Industrial Mobilization Planning—A must for Security," *Air Force* (October 1949), pp. 24–27, 47; Committee on National Defense, *A Blueprint for Industrial Preparedness* (Washington, DC: Chamber of Commerce of the United States, 1949).

[25] From Annex 82 of the 1947 Mobilization Plan. Reprinted in Federal Emergency Management Agency, *Resource Management: A Historical Perspective* (Washington, DC: FEMA, May 1989), p. D-5.

located as to give maximum insurance against destruction by enemy attack."[26] In the new era of cold war, it seemed, the American people would have to accept what they had never before been willing to tolerate in peacetime, and had tolerated only grudgingly in time of war: a central government endowed with the authority to shape the composition and even the geographical distribution of the nation's industrial base.

The National Security Resources Board

The National Security Act of 1947 laid the foundations of the institutional apparatus with which the United States was to conduct its half of the Cold War. In addition to unifying the armed services into a single department with a civilian defense secretary (known first as the National Military Establishment, later the Department of Defense), the act called into existence three organizations at the highest levels of government charged with the overall "coordination [of] national security": the National Security Council (NSC), the Central Intelligence Agency (CIA), and the National Security Resources Board (NSRB).[27]

Although its purpose was somewhat vaguely stated ("to advise the President concerning the coordination of military, industrial, and civilian mobilization"),[28] the NSRB was, in the words of its principal architect, "potentially one of the most influential units of the President's staff." This "high-ranking civilian body was conceived of as providing the basis for a kind of economic and social general staff, comparable in position and prestige" to the NSC, the CIA, or the National Military Establishment.[29] Despite these lofty ambitions, however, the Board never became anything more than an ineffectual advisory appendage to the Executive Office of the President, with little authority and no access to powerful policy instruments. Of the institutions created by the National Security Act, only the National Security Resources Board would encounter impassable ideological and political obstacles and cease to exist before the Cold War had reached its conclusion.

From its inception the NSRB's primary purpose was to reduce to an absolute minimum the interval that would separate the initiation of a crisis from the achievement of full-tilt economic mobilization. Toward this end the Board was given responsibility for advising the president on a wide array of issues, includ-

---

[26] State-War-Navy Coordinating Committee, September 19, 1945, "Basis for the Formulation of a U.S. Military Policy," in Thomas H. Etzold and John Lewis Gaddis, eds., *Containment: Documents on American Policy and Strategy, 1945–1950* (New York: Columbia University Press, 1978), p. 44.

[27] On the origins and subsequent revisions of the 1947 act see Paul Y. Hammond, *Organizing for Defense: The American Military Establishment in the Twentieth Century* (Princeton: Princeton University Press, 1961), pp. 186–370.

[28] For the text of the NSRB's charter see Harry Yoshpe, *The National Security Resources Board: A Case Study in Peacetime Mobilization Planning* (Washington, DC: Executive Office of the President, 1953), pp. 8–9.

[29] Report by Ferdinand Eberstadt to Arthur M. Hill, June 4, 1948, Harry S. Truman Library (HSTL), President's Secretary's Files (PSF), Box 147, Subject File, Agencies, NSRB.

ing the preparation of plans for industrial mobilization, emergency economic stabilization, and the wartime organization and operations of the federal government. Whether the Board itself was to have any operational responsibilities and, if so, how it was to go about discharging them were subjects of debate. Some of its supporters pictured the NSRB as a wartime mobilization agency-in-waiting, ready to spring into action at a moment's notice. Others believed that it should confine itself to long-range planning, leaving the task of actual implementation to an entity that would be created when the need arose.[30]

During its first few months of operation, there was little talk of giving the NSRB extensive peacetime responsibilities. This began to change during the European crises of the spring of 1948. Believing that the probability of war was increasing with every passing day, members of the Board, backed by a number of influential outside supporters, pressed President Truman to greatly expand the agency's powers. In April 1948, NSRB Chairman Arthur Hill warned the president that in contrast to the period before the outbreak of the Second World War, the United States was now faced with "greatly reduced margins of time and of resources." Like most of his contemporaries, Hill believed that the United States would "not again be given the opportunity to prepare for war after hostilities [had] begun." Moreover, if war came suddenly and soon, it would fall not on a nation in depression, but on an economy already operating at close to full productive capacity. Runaway inflation, shortages, and deadly mobilization delays would be the inevitable results.[31]

To avoid these dangers, Hill urged Truman to request immediate congressional authorization to impose wage and price controls, to allocate scarce materials and resources to the needs of national security, and to reenact wartime legislation authorizing a federal agency "to create and finance Government corporations with power to deal in materials, equipment, and facilities, and to lend money for purposes relating to the national security programs." Experience had taught that all of these functions would have to be integrated and coordinated by "a central agency . . . designated by the President." According to Hill, the "legislative history of the National Security Act . . . and the preponderance of opinion of leading authorities" suggested that this agency should be the NSRB.[32]

---

[30] For the varying views on the NSRB's role see Yoshpe, *The National Security Resources Board*, p. 20. See also Edward H. Hobbs, *Behind the President: A Study of Executive Office Agencies* (Washington, DC: Public Affairs Press, 1954), pp. 156–59; and William Y. Elliott, *Mobilization Planning and National Security* (Washington, DC: Library of Congress Legislative Reference Service, 1950), pp. 52–79. For more on the origins of the NSRB see Hunter, *Economic Mobilization Planning*, pp. 20–45; Robert Cuff, "Ferdinand Eberstadt, National Security Resources Board, and the Search for Integrated Mobilization Planning, 1947–1948," *Public Historian* 7, no. 4 (Fall 1985), pp. 39–42. Jeffery M. Dorwart, *Eberstadt and Forrestal: A National Security Partnership, 1901–1949* (College Station: Texas A & M University Press, 1991), pp. 105–7, 131–48.

[31] Arthur M. Hill, "A Recommendation to the President by the National Security Resources Board on Steps and Measures Essential to the Fulfillment of the National Security Program (NSRB-R-7)," April 30, 1948, HSTL, PSF, Box 147, Subject File, Agencies, NSRB.

[32] *Ibid.* Hill's thinking reflected that of Ferdinand Eberstadt. See Cuff, "Ferdinand Eberstadt," p. 49; Yoshpe, *The National Security Resources Board*, p. 25–26. Among those lobbying the president

Had these recommendations been accepted, the NSRB would have been transformed into an extremely powerful agency, possessed not only of the responsibility for conducting long-range planning, but of the authority and ability to intervene actively in the nation's peacetime economy. This did not happen. Instead, the Board's bid to become the administrative hub of a wide-ranging national defense industrial policy was rejected, and in no uncertain terms, by President Truman himself. "I do not intend," Truman wrote Hill, "to vest in the National Security Resources Board any responsibilities for coordination of the national security programs of the Government which require the exercise of directive authority over any department or agency, or which imply a final power of decision resting with the Board." The Board should stick to its "statutory duty" of "producing information and advice upon which Presidential action may be taken."[33]

Truman's decision reflected the preferences of his more trusted, and more liberal, advisers in the Bureau of the Budget, the Council of Economic Advisers, and in the Department of Commerce. If the NSRB's authority was enhanced, they warned, their own agencies and, ultimately, the president himself might lose control over economic policy to an organization whose staff would inevitably be dominated by "dollar-a-year" businessmen.[34] At the same time, there was also the risk that by boosting the visibility of the Board, the president might actually provoke Congress into abolishing it, as it had the Office of War Mobilization and Reconversion in 1946 and the similarly named National Resources Planning Board in 1943. The latter had been attacked as an instrument of creeping socialism or, at the very least, as a tool with which the executive branch could increase its capacity for independent action and extend state control over the nation's economy. "Had Congress been aware that NSRB not only contained holdover personnel from the New Deal's National Resources Planning Board, but also pursued similar studies of the country's natural resources," writes Robert Cuff, "the board might not have escaped scrutiny." Indeed, "given the fierce hostility to 'planning' and 'big government' evident in postwar political debate, it is remarkable that the agency survived at all." Facing an election, and with anti-statist sentiment running high, the Truman administration "felt compelled to keep a cautionary eye on the 'centralizers' within . . . its own ranks."[35]

---

was Bernard Baruch. For the latter's views during this period see Jordan A. Schwarz, *The Speculator: Bernard Baruch in Washington, 1917–1965* (Chapel Hill: University of North Carolina Press, 1981), pp. 508–21.

[33] Truman to Hill, May 24, 1948, quoted in Hunter, *Economic Mobilization Planning*, p. 76.

[34] Dorwart, *Eberstadt and Forrestal*, p. 162; Yoshpe, *The National Security Resources Board*, p. 26. For the official reaction of the Commerce Department see William Foster (acting Commerce secretary) to Arthur Hill, April 29, 1948, HSTL, PSF, Box 147, Subject File, Agencies, NSRB.

[35] Robert Cuff, "From the Controlled Materials Plan to the Defense Materials System, 1942–1953," *Military Affairs* 51, no. 1 (January 1987), p. 3.

Paper Planning for War

Lacking the authority to act, the NSRB confined itself to an unintrusive, and hence uncontroversial, form of paper planning for economic mobilization. In the period before the outbreak of the Korean War, the Board's staff spent most of its time drafting and redrafting standby emergency legislation and preparing what were referred to as "resource/requirement balance sheets." As one NSRB official explained it:

> We have defined economic mobilization planning as the process of estimating the requirements or needs of war [both military and civilian]; of appraising the resources or means which would be available for meeting those needs; of measuring deficiencies revealed by the comparison of needs with means; and of determining the steps necessary to balance needs with means.[36]

Among the steps that might have to be taken to bring resources and requirements into balance were "measures designed to increase inadequate resources and capacities vitally essential for mobilization, including increases in power generation, in the capacity to produce basic metals, in the development of new sources of mineral supply, in fuel production, [and] in transport capacity." Because "two or more years are required to provide many of the essential facilities necessary for the support of an adequate war production program," some of these steps would have to be taken well before the beginning of the next war.[37]

But here the Board lacked the ability to do anything to correct the problems it had identified. Having pinpointed potential bottlenecks, it could do little more than exhort businessmen to invest in what might turn out to be excess productive capacity should a national emergency fail to arise. As one Board official put it rather plaintively: "We are dropping [the problem] in the lap of the businessman and are saying: 'Will you come through for us?'"[38]

The response from the private sector was markedly unenthusiastic. As before the Second World War, business executives were concerned about overinvestment, but there were also broader political issues at stake. Industry leaders feared that government efforts to shape their decisions through exhortation might give way eventually to more forceful and intrusive measures, and they worried that the appeal to military necessity masked other, broader ambitions. These fears were not entirely without foundation. In the late 1940s, some Truman administration officials believed that for reasons of welfare as well as

[36] Ralph J. Watkins, Director, Office of Plans and Programs, National Security Resources Board, "Some Aspects of Industrial Mobilization Planning," October 22, 1948, National Archives and Records Administration (NA), Washington, DC, Record Group (RG) 304, Entry 31, Box 102, F1-1 (hereafter NA RG 304/31/102/F1-1), p. 17.

[37] National Security Resources Board, "Essential Areas of Action for the Mobilization of Resources in the Event of War," November 1949, NA RG 304/31/76/C2–13, pp. i–ii.

[38] George Felton, Director, Office of Production, quoted in "Some Aspects of Industrial Mobilization Planning," NA RG 304/31/102/F1-1, p. 55.

security, partial nationalization of certain industries might be necessary to ensure adequate supplies of key materials at suitably low prices. Thus, at the end of 1948, the Assistant Secretary of the Interior argued publicly that the federal government should provide low-cost loans to encourage an expansion of steel production capacity, and that it should construct its own plants if industry executives refused to go along. President Truman echoed this suggestion in his 1949 State of the Union address, then backed away in the face of criticism from Congress and industry alike. Federal bureaucrats might believe that more steel production capacity was in the nation's best interest, but they had means of neither creating it nor of inducing others to do so. This episode fed fears of statism at the same time as it revealed "the incredibly barren arsenal of public tools" then available to erstwhile government industrial planners.[39]

Dispersal

Unlike all of the other major combatants, the United States remained immune throughout the Second World War from serious aerial assault. The massive U.S. industrial mobilization effort was so successful, in part, because it was able to go forward unmolested. American strategists did not expect to be so fortunate the next time around. Throughout the early years of the Cold War they worried obsessively about the effects of enemy bombardment on the nation's standing forces, its people, and its capacity to manufacture additional increments of military power.

In the late 1940s it was widely assumed that the most effective way to offset the destructive power of aerially delivered atomic weapons would be through the dispersal of population and industry. Civilian experts put forward plans for the creation of "satellite," "doughnut," and "rodlike" cities that would spread people and factories over wider areas and render them less vulnerable to attack.[40] Far from being rejected as outlandish and impractical, dispersal and its possible benefits received attention at the highest levels of government. Among the other duties enumerated in the 1947 National Security Act, the National Security Resources Board was given specific responsibility for overseeing "the strategic relocation of industries . . . and economic activities, the continuous operation of which is essential to the Nation's security."[41]

---

[39] Paul A. Tiffany, *The Decline of American Steel: How Management, Labor, and Government Went Wrong* (New York: Oxford University Press, 1988), p. 62. See also Marvin Barloon, "The Question of Steel Capacity," *Harvard Business Review* 27, no. 2 (March 1949), pp. 209–36. Nationalization of key industries was very much in vogue in the late 1940s in Britain and France. See Peter Hall, *Governing the Economy: The Politics of State Intervention in Britain and France* (New York: Oxford University Press, 1986), pp. 70–71, 139–40.

[40] See, for example, Ansley J. Coale, *The Problem of Reducing Vulnerability to Atomic Bombs* (Princeton: Princeton University Press, 1947); Hanson W. Baldwin, *The Price of Power* (New York: Harper, 1947), 252–65; Ralph E. Lapp, *Must We Hide?* (Cambridge, MA: Addison-Wesley, 1949), pp. 157–68; B. H. Liddell Hart, *Defence of the West* (New York: William Morrow, 1950), pp. 89–90.

[41] Yoshpe, *The National Security Resources Board*, p. 9.

Programs to promote industrial dispersal continued from the late 1940s until the late 1950s. From the beginning, however, all such efforts were constricted and restrained by a single overarching fact. Any serious attempt to alter the geographical distribution of the nation's industries would have required an enormous increase in the powers of the federal government, measured both by its ability to dictate to private business and by its capacity to resist entreaties from city, state, and regional interests. As one contemporary observer warned, a meaningful, mandatory decentralization program would "require the endowment of government with powers of compulsion so enormous that the 'garrison state' would no longer be a figure of speech."[42] Whatever the strategic virtues of dispersal, resistance to any such expansion in governmental power proved in the end to be overwhelming.

The constraints on dispersal were at least partially self-imposed. Even dedicated dispersal enthusiasts balked at the thought of endowing the federal government with the authority simply to tell businessmen where they could and could not build plants. Most recognized, in any case, that such an arrangement was politically impossible. "The job of dispersion is one that industry must assume," acknowledged one official publication. "Ours being a democratic Nation dedicated to the principles of free enterprise, the Government can neither dictate nor finance such a large-scale change in industrial pattern."[43]

Instead of compelling dispersal, the federal government in the late 1940s took steps to induce it through exhortation. Official publications explained the dangers of concentration and sought to persuade businessmen that they would have a better chance of surviving an atomic attack if they located their facilities at least three miles away from other potential targets. "Draw a three-mile radius circle about the periphery of your present facilities," instructed a helpful 1948 NSRB brochure. "Then . . . list everything within this circle which you believe would be of interest to the strategic planner of a potential enemy. . . . As a result of your investigation, you should be able to conclude . . . whether all of your facilities should be relocated . . . whether part of your facilities should be relocated, or whether no further expansion should be attempted in the present area."[44]

Even these fairly mild suggestions provoked misunderstanding and a storm of controversy. In 1949 there were rumors, triggered by an Air Force decision to have its new B-47 bomber built at a Boeing plant in Wichita, Kansas, rather than one in Seattle, that the government now regarded entire areas of the country as irretrievably vulnerable and was planning a wholesale transfer of critical industries. NSRB headquarters in Washington was bombarded with inquiries from local governments, chambers of commerce, and from the congressional representatives of regions fearing evacuation (primarily on the East and West

[42] Baldwin, *The Price of Power*, p. 253.

[43] National Security Resources Board, *National Security Factors in Industrial Location* (Washington, DC: NSRB, 1948), p. 12.

[44] Ibid., pp. 7–8.

coasts) and from those (primarily in the Mid- and Southwest) that hoped to benefit.[45]

To alleviate these concerns the Board issued statements explaining that it was concerned only with the dispersal of industry *within* a given region rather than with its distribution *among* regions.[46] In 1950 Board planners, recognizing that very little relocation of old factories was taking place, decided to further narrow their focus to encouraging the intraregional dispersal of *new* productive facilities.[47]

INDICATIVE INDUSTRIAL PLANNING (1950–1953)

The Korean conflict marked a major discontinuity in the course of the Cold War. Between 1950 and 1953, as previous chapters have described, the level of overall U.S. defense spending, the size of the American armed forces, and the character of the nation's overseas commitments all changed dramatically and permanently. During this period the federal government also instituted a system of indicative industrial planning under which it sought actively to influence the structure of the American economy so as to improve its ability to support a massive, sustained war production effort. That system was intended to be permanent, rather than simply being an emergency measure, yet, in contrast to the other, longer-lasting legacies of Korea, this one did not live out the decade.

Strategic Rationale

Like the increases in defense expenditure and force posture that it accompanied, the industrial planning system that took shape after the invasion of South Korea reflected the logic of NSC 68. The authors of that document had argued that while an immediate Soviet attack on the West was unlikely, the probability of aggression would grow with the passage of time. If nothing was done to alter current trends, by 1954, at the latest, the relative strength of the Soviet Union would have increased to the point where its leaders might feel able to risk war with the United States. In order to push this date as far forward into the future as possible, the United States and its allies would have to undertake a concerted effort to expand both their forces-in-being and the capacity rapidly to transform their superior economic potential into actual military power.[48]

The Korean mobilization was conducted with these twin goals in mind. "Our dual aim is strength in being and capacity to mobilize," declared one statement

---

[45] See letters contained in NSRB Central Files, July 1949–April 1953, NA RG 304/31/93/E4-10. One enterprising town adopted as its slogan: "If you would escape ATOM bombs, locate in Yale, Michigan."

[46] See statement by NSRB Chairman John Steelman, October 7, 1949, NA RG 304/31/93/E4-8.

[47] See "Proposed Outline of a Program for Strategic Relocation-Dispersion of Industries, Services, Government and Economic Activities," April 24, 1950, and "The Space Factor in National Security (preliminary draft), July 14, 1950, NA RG 304/31/93/E4-8.

[48] NSC 68 is discussed at length in Chapter 4.

of official policy.[49] With the militarization of containment, American troops were being stationed at permanent bases throughout Europe and Asia, as well as doing the bulk of the fighting in Korea. To equip these forces and to contribute to the rapid rearmament of U.S. allies around the world, current output of military end items was to be increased. To guard against the possiblity of rapid escalation to total global war, stockpiles of critical materials were to be assembled and arms production capacity enlarged beyond what was needed to satisfy expanded immediate needs. A greatly augmented productive base was a necessary domestic concomitant of the shift in strategy from deterrence to warfighting.[50]

Accompanying the growth in weapons production, large additional increments in output would be sought in a wide variety of supporting industries. Greater capacity in basic industries would make it possible to sustain a rapid military buildup without severe cutbacks in production of civilian goods, and in the event of all-out war, it would leave the nation that much better prepared for total mobilization.[51] In all, the program set in motion during the first months of the Korean War was intended to bring the country to a state of greatly enhanced readiness by the end of 1953, just in time for the arrival of the year of maximum danger.[52]

Institutional Mechanisms

The Korean emergency led to the final eclipse of the NSRB and the creation of a far more powerful central planning institution. At the end of 1950, following China's unexpected entry into the war, President Truman declared a national emergency and announced the establishment within the Executive Office of the President of an Office of Defense Mobilization (ODM). What had appeared precipitate and politically risky before the crisis began now seemed simply prudent. ODM's formation aroused no opposition in Congress or from elsewhere in the executive branch. Its director was to be "an Assistant President for mobilization," with the authority "to direct, control, and coordinate all mobilization activities of the Executive Branch of the Government." His respon-

[49] Director of Defense Mobilization, Second Quarterly Report to the President, *Meeting Defense Goals* (Washington, DC: Office of Defense Mobilization, July 1951), p. 3.

[50] Early estimates set production capacity targets of 50,000 planes and 35,000 tanks per year, and 18,000 jet engines per month. Director of Defense Mobilization, First Quarterly Report to the President, *Building America's Might* (Washington, DC: Office of Defense Mobilization, April 1951), p. 1.

[51] See Director of Defense Mobilization, Fourth Quarterly Report to the President, *The Battle for Production* (Washington, DC: Office of Defense Mobilization, January 1952), p. 1.

[52] See W. Glenn Campbell, ed., *Economics of Mobilization and War* (Homewood, Ill.: Richard Irwin, 1952), p. 6; also "Getting Ready for Big War: Plan for Industry Mobilization," *U.S. News and World Report*, February 16, 1951, pp. 13–14. "We'll Be 'Mighty within Three Years': An Interview with Charles E. Wilson, Director, Office of Defense Mobilization," *U.S. News and World Report*, March 23, 1951, pp. 30–35; Office of Defense Mobilization, *The Story of Defense Mobilization: How the United States Is Building Its Might in Order to Avert a Third World War* (Washington, DC: U.S. Government Printing Office, 1951).

sibilities were to be discharged with the assistance of a manpower administrator, an Economic Stabilization agency (in charge of wage and price controls) and a Defense Production Administration responsible for both short- and long-range production planning. To assist him in coordinating the activities of the rest of the government, the ODM director was made chairman of a Defense Mobilization Board, which included twelve agency heads, six of cabinet rank.[53]

Policy Instruments

War gave teeth to the mobilization planning process begun by the NSRB. Instead of simply identifying potential short- and long-run production problems, the Office of Defense Mobilization had the authority to administer an array of programs designed to overcome them by altering the structure of the American economy. Both the nature of the instruments ODM had at its disposal for accomplishing this objective and the manner in which they could be applied were still constrained in important ways by a mix of ideological concerns and interest group pressures. Nevertheless, the "arsenal of public tools" was not nearly so barren at the end of the Korean crisis as it had been when the war began.

At the heart of the new industrial planning system was a set of "resource/requirement" calculations very much like those that had been done in the late 1940s. Civilian planners estimated maximum demand for a range of materials and products (usually in an all-out war with the Soviet Union beginning in 1954 or 1955) and compared it to projected domestic supplies. Where gaps were found to exist, numerical production targets or "expansion goals" were set. By 1953, 255 such goals had been specified, ranging from tons of steel, cement, aluminum, iron ore, and copper, to barrels of petroleum, sulfuric acid, and formaldehyde, to kilowatts of electric power and numbers of aircraft engines, wood chippers, antifriction bearings, precision screws, steam turbines, metal fasteners, machine tools, gears, propellors, and presses.[54]

Once production targets had been set, the only question that remained was how best to reach them. During the Second World War the federal government

---

[53] On the structure and functions of ODM see Hobbs, *Behind the President*, pp. 192–97. The NSRB lingered on until the end of the war, but it played an increasingly minor role both in overseeing current operations and in planning for the future. On the demise of the NSRB see Yoshpe, *The National Security Resources Board*, pp. 37–71.

[54] In part because of difficulties in obtaining calculations of their needs from military planners (who were themselves undecided on the likely dimensions of a future war), many of these figures were little more than guesstimates. Many goals were also published before routine procedures for calculating them had been put into place. On the evolution of the planning process see a brief and skeptical memo prepared for the Bureau of the Budget, "Metamorphosis of the 'Mobilization Base'" (early 1953?), NA RG 51/51.26/25/96. For more detailed overviews see Bureau of the Budget, "Mobilization Base," September 17, 1953, NA RG 51/51.26/24/96; Director of Defense Mobilization, Sixth Quarterly Report to the President, *Defense Mobilization—The Shield against Aggression* (Washington, DC: Office of Defense Mobilization, July 1952), pp. 15–22. And Defense Production Administration, *Industrial Growth: Expansion under the Mobilization Program* (Washington, DC: DPA, May 1952).

had financed fully two-thirds of the total industrial expansion. Slightly over one-half of the government's investment involved direct expenditures by the military services on arms-building arsenals and shipyards. The other half took the form of government investment in supporting industries where the extent of civilian needs after the war was uncertain and private business was therefore reluctant to provide sufficient funds for expansion. Operating through the Defense Plant Corporation (a subsidiary of the Depression-era Reconstruction Finance Corporation), the federal government paid for the construction of aluminum, magnesium, synthetic rubber, machine tool, and aviation fuel factories, leased them to commercial operators and, in most cases, sold them off at bargain prices once the war was over.[55]

In 1950, in contrast to 1941, American strategic planners believed themselves to be at the beginning of a confrontation of potentially limitless duration. If 1954 came and went without total war against the Soviet Union, the United States would still have to maintain a high level of readiness. State ownership of the means of production and other extraordinary interventions in the civilian economy might be acceptable in a short-term emergency, but in a protracted "twilight struggle" of unforeseeable length they ran the risk of undermining the foundations of the nation's economic system, perhaps even transforming it over time into a replica of its competitor. For this reason the architects of the Korean mobilization decided early on that it would be

> desirable that [the necessary] expansion be undertaken to the maximum possible extent by private business within the framework of the competitive enterprise system. . . . The objective of the whole operation is to get expansion of productive capacity, to get it quickly, in the areas of the economy in which it is needed, and to get it by encouraging business to take the initiative with a minimum of Government intervention and assistance.[56]

Especially in defense-supporting industries, direct federal investment was to be held to an absolute minimum.

This ideologically rooted inclination was strongly reinforced by Congress, which also gave voice to industry concerns about possible competition from government. In the summer of 1950 the House and Senate passed the Defense Production Act, granting the president most of the powers he had requested to manage the buildup, but denying his request that the federal government be authorized to construct nonarsenal production facilities, should the need arise.[57]

---

[55] See Gerald T. White, "Financing Industrial Expansion for War: The Origin of the Defense Plant Corporation Leases," *Journal of Economic History* 9, no. 2 (November 1949), pp. 156–83. The dramatic expansion in federally owned arms production facilities during the war will be discussed in chapter 7.

[56] W. H. Harrison, Defense Production Administrator, to Stuart Symington, Director, NSRB, March 5, 1951, NA RG 304/31/113/F20-8.

[57] "Proposed amendments to the Defense Production Act," November 14, 1951, NA RG 304/31/79/C3-5. For the legislative history of the act see Congressional Service, *United States*

The expansion in supporting industries was to be carried out instead exclusively by the private sector, with government acting, in the words of one official report, to "channel" the flow of corporate investment "into those parts of the economy that most directly support both the current defense program and full mobilization requirements."[58] In part this aim would be accomplished simply by spending more on arms and military equipment, thereby increasing demand for the products of supporting industries and encouraging some measure of private investment in additional productive capacity. Where necessary, expansion would be further encouraged by the use of an assortment of other instruments. The Defense Production Act authorized the executive branch to extend loans, guarantee loans made by private institutions, and make commitments to purchase "metals, minerals, and other raw materials" (all within precisely specified dollar ceilings) as necessary to encourage commercial investment in expansion.[59]

Together with these measures, Congress also agreed to revitalize a special provision in the tax code that had been used to stimulate investment during both World Wars. The so-called rapid tax amortization privilege made it possible for firms to write off a portion of their investment in new facilities in five years instead of the usual twenty, thereby reducing tax liability at a time when, thanks to the defense buildup, earnings were likely to be at a peak.[60] The granting of this privilege quickly became the principal instrument for guiding the Korean era mobilization. After announcing an expansion goal, the Office of Defense Mobilization (or one of the agencies to which it delegated responsibility) would review industry proposals for investment and grant "certificates of necessity" to those most likely to contribute to its attainment. In this way, government could help to steer private capital in directions deemed necessary to national security in a manner that benefited business and did not involve either the appearance of undue coercion or the direct expenditure of tax revenues. Because so many stood to gain, there was considerable

---

Code: 81st Congress, Second Session (1950), vol. 2 (Brooklyn: Edward Thompson, 1950), pp. 3620–59. For the Senate report on the bill see "The Defense Production Act of 1950 (Report no. 2250)," *Senate Reports: Miscellaneous*, vol. 5 81st Cong., 2d sess. (Washington, DC: U.S. Government Printing Office, 1950). See also Hearings before the Senate Committee on Banking and Currency, *Defense Production Act of 1950*, 81st Cong., 2d sess. (Washington, DC: U.S. Government Printing Office, 1950).

[58] Director of Defense Mobilization, *Defense Mobilization*, p. 15.

[59] Congressional Service, *United States Code* 2:3637–38.

[60] For a concise explanation of this provision and an account of its use during the World Wars see a memorandum for Stuart Symington in the NSRB Central Files, "Special Amortization of Emergency Facilities," August 8, 1950, NA RG 304/31/113/F20-6. See also Fifth Intermediate Report of the House Committee on Expenditures in the Executive Departments, *Certificates of Necessity and Government Plant Expansion Loans*, 82d Cong., 1st sess. (Washington, DC: U.S. Government Printing Office, 1951); Joint Committee on Defense Production, *Defense Production Act Progress Report No. 25: Review of Tax-Amortization Program* 83d Cong., 1st sess. (Washington, DC: U.S. Government Printing Office, 1953).

early enthusiasm from industry for the rapid tax amortization program.[61] It was, as one participant in the process described it, a "typically American" way of solving the capacity problem.[62]

Dispersal Revisited

The Korean War provided both a motivation and an opportunity for stepped-up efforts at promoting industrial dispersal. With World War Three suddenly a very real prospect, the vulnerability of American industry became an even more pressing concern. Previous efforts to achieve dispersal through cheerleading and scare-mongering had clearly failed; some more potent inducements would have to be found. As one official put it in the spring of 1951: "If the Government is unwilling to implement its own policy and relies on 'the initiative of private enterprise' it is not establishing a policy but is merely expressing a fond hope." The federal government might not be able to dictate to industry, but it "should be ready to support its policy by offering incentives to industry to locate in the right places and by vetoing locations which manifestly endanger the national security."[63]

The wartime industrial planning system provided some new means for achieving these goals. In August 1951 it was announced that location would be used as one criterion in evaluating requests for rapid tax amortization privileges, with preference given to construction projects located outside heavily congested areas. Increased Soviet striking power and the fact that America's "continued existence as a free nation" depended "largely on [its] industrial capacity" called for the implementation of "new and more positive policies" to promote dispersal.[64] Government spokesmen were careful to specify that the object of the exercise was to scatter new facilities, not to move old ones, and they were at pains to point out that "no region of the country is to be built up at the expense of another." To head off charges of an excessive expansion in federal power, they also sought to shift most of the burden for implementing the

[61] Steel industry executives, for example, lobbied both Congress and the executive branch for a revival of World War Two tax provisions. See a telegram from Benjamin Morrell (president, Jones and Laughlin Steel) to Stuart Symington, August 10, 1950, NA RG 304/31/113/F20-6; also Tiffany, *The Decline of American Steel*, pp. 91–94.

[62] Lt. Comdr. Joseph Z. Reday, "Industrial Mobilization in the U.S.," *U.S. Naval Institute Proceedings* (October 1953), pp. 1065–75. As of the end of 1952 fully half of all the certificates of necessity granted had been issued to the primary metal, chemical, petroleum, transportation equipment, and machinery industries. For a breakdown see Office of Defense Mobilization, *Expansion Progress: Projects under Certificates of Necessity* (Washington, DC: ODM, June 1953), table 4.

[63] Tracy Augur (General Services Administration) to Ramsay Potts (special assistant to the chairman, NSRB), May 23, 1951, NA RG 304/31/96/E4-68. For a critical analysis of government dispersal programs up to this point see Materials Prepared for the Joint Committee on the Economic Report by the Committee Staff, *The Need for Industrial Dispersal*, 82d Cong., 1st sess. (Washington, DC: U.S. Government Printing Office, 1951).

[64] "Statement of Policy on Industrial Dispersion," August 10, 1951, NA RG 304/34/15/E4-67.

new policy down to state and local governments, which, together with business and labor, were to draw up their own dispersion plans.[65]

Despite these precautions, the announcement of a redoubled effort to promote dispersal triggered yet another cycle of protests and clarifications. Residents of both coasts, and especially of the older industrial regions of the Northeast, were especially concerned. Opponents denounced dispersal both for its presumed short-term consequences and for its alleged long-term dangers. According to one New Bedford, Massachusetts, newspaper, the use of tax breaks to promote scattering would compel "the citizens of long-established, industrial areas like New England . . . to underwrite the cost of new industries in other sections." If there was any doubt that the Truman administration was "working toward Socialist control of the economy, the President's dispersal decree . . . should dispel it." The program bore "a strong resemblance to the various blueprints by which the Soviet Union pushes its Communist planning." Striking a similarly apocalyptic chord, Pennsylvania Senator Jack Martin warned that "the advocates of a planned and controlled economy" had taken another step forward in their efforts "to destroy the American system of free enterprise and to place industry under the strangling clutch of bureaucratic regulation."[66]

President Truman responded to these accusations of statism by explaining that the government had no intention of moving plants and labor from one part of the country to another, nor even of telling any company or person where to locate. The new policy "merely encourages the spacing of *new* defense and defense-supporting industries *a few miles apart*." Using financial inducements to achieve this goal was a "common sense program . . . consistent with the American system of competitive free enterprise."[67]

The use of tax breaks may have given the federal government slightly more leverage over the evolution of the nation's industrial geography, but not a great deal. Despite what some planners wished, there were no sanctions to prevent companies from locating in already crowded areas. Moreover, to meet the urgent needs of war, dispersal requirements were often waived for the construction of critical facilities, which could usually be built more quickly, easily, and cheaply in areas that were already heavily developed.[68] The desire of federal bureaucrats to avoid further public criticism or congressional interference seems also to have encouraged leniency. In any event, the Korean War expansion and dispersal program produced what was, at best, a slight and temporary deviation

[65] See National Security Resources Board, *Is Your Plant a Target?* (Washington, DC: NSRB, 1951), p. 3.

[66] Quotes from "Congress Defied," *Standard Times*, August 13, 1951; and *Congressional Record*, August 21, 1951, both contained in a file marked "Industrial Dispersion Newspaper Clippings," HSTL, PSF, Box 147, Subject File, Agencies, NSRB.

[67] "Statement by the President," August 23, 1951, NA RG 304/34/15/E4-10 (emphasis in original). Further clarifying the government's policies was a pamphlet entitled *National Industrial Dispersion Program: A Question and Answer Guide* (Washington, DC: National Security Resources Board, February, 1952).

[68] For complaints on this score see Project East River, *Federal Leadership to Reduce Urban Vulnerability* (New York: Associated Universities, 1952), pp. 5–7.

in overall trends in industrial location. Given the comparatively feeble instruments employed, there was little prospect that it would do anything more.[69]

"Strength for the Long Run"[70]

The wide-ranging defense industrial policy put into place during the Korean conflict and the institutions created for its implementation were intended by their architects and operators to be permanent. As the war and the Truman presidency approached their respective conclusions, administration officials reviewed existing programs and made plans for their refinement and perpetuation. Although some expansion goals had been reached (especially in basic industries like steel and crude petroleum), others remained to be completed.[71] As the pressing needs of the Korean crisis receded, the Office of Defense Mobilization prepared to undertake a renewed effort to estimate full mobilization requirements across the entire spectrum of supporting industries. These calculations were expected to yield new and more tightly focused production targets, but they were also seen as the beginning of an ongoing iterative process. "Periodic reviews of our position," declared the Director of Defense Mobilization at the end of 1952, will permit adjustments in "our programs to accord with changes in our resources, our military weapons, and our strategic planning. The procedure should gain in efficiency and realism with repeated use."[72] Over time, the nation's industrial base could be "expanded and reshaped" as needed "so as to continually increase our potential fighting power."[73]

What was envisioned was "not a one shot program, or a quarterly one, but one which must be pursued slowly and steadily over a long period of time." The task was "in its fullest sense . . . gigantic." As long as the threat of all-out war remained, the federal government would have to take active measures to mold the national economy into "an organized machinery for production which . . . can be marshalled for action in an orderly and disciplined way," and at a moment's notice.[74] "The ability of the nation to throw its great industrial

---

[69] For analyses of the impact of the program see two internal NSRB reports: "Different Classes of Industry in Million Dollar Plants," May 24, 1952, NA RG 304/31/100/E4-74; and "Progress Report to the President," January 17, 1953, NA RG 304/34/15/E4-10. See also Neil P. Hurley, "The Role of Accelerated Tax Amortization in the National Industrial Dispersion Program" (Ph.D. dissertation, Fordham University, 1956).

[70] This is the title of an ODM report. See Director of Defense Mobilization, Fifth Quarterly Report to the President, *Strength for the Long Run* (Washington, DC: Office of Defense Mobilization, April 1952).

[71] Ibid., pp. 14–15.

[72] Director of Defense Mobilization, Eighth Quarterly Report to the President, *The Job Ahead for Defense Mobilization* (Washington, DC: Office of Defense Mobilization, January 1953), p. 28. See also a letter from Henry Fowler, Director of Defense Mobilization to his assistant, Edwin George, asking him to chair an ODM "Mobilization Base Program Committee," October 30, 1952, NA RG 51/51.26/25/96.

[73] Director of Defense Mobilization, *The Job Ahead*, p. 26.

[74] Bureau of the Budget, "Organization for 'Mobilization Base' Activities," July 28, 1952, NA RG 51/51.26/25/96, pp. 1–2.

strength on the scales of war quickly and efficiently" remained essential to deterrence and, if it failed, to victory. "The challenge, therefore," wrote the recently retired Director of Defense Mobilization in 1953, "is to make our mobilization base ready in all important respects for possible use in any full-scale war forced upon us."[75]

Meeting this challenge on an ongoing basis would require, in addition to new analytical techniques, improved administrative arrangements for formulating and coordinating policy within the executive branch, an extension of the Defense Production Act to allow for the continuing use of existing policy instruments and, perhaps, the creation of new and more powerful ones. With the Korean War ending and the defense buildup leveling off, planners expected private industry to become increasingly reluctant to invest in what amounted to standby capacity. For this reason ODM recommended that the federal government ask again for the authority to build facilities for the production of items other than weapons.[76]

THE END OF INDUSTRIAL MOBILIZATION PLANNING (1953–1960)

Instead of building on it, the Eisenhower administration set about to dismantle the foundation left by its predecessor. The period 1953 to 1960 was marked by institutional devolution and policy constriction. By the end of the 1950s the United States had departed from the path on which it appeared to have been traveling, however hesitantly, since the onset of the Cold War. The movement toward broad national planning for supporting industries was checked and a new trend, toward a decentralized industrial policy of procurement, firmly established.

Changes in Strategy

The simplest and most obvious explanation for this development is that it was the result of a shift in strategy, driven, in turn, by the inexorable advance of technology. As the United States and then the Soviet Union began to acquire large numbers of thermonuclear weapons, the potential destructiveness of a future superpower conflict rose sharply. Top U.S. decision makers, starting with

[75] Henry H. Fowler, "The Mobilization Base Concept," *Federal Bar Journal* 13, no. 3 (April–June 1953), p. 148.

[76] See Director of Defense Mobilization, *The Job Ahead*, p. 30. For more on the Truman administration's assessment of the long-term requirements for defense industrial policy see Council of Economic Advisers, *The Economic Report of the President* (Washington, DC: U.S. Government Printing Office, 1952), pp. 1–13, 95–121; Bureau of the Budget, "Production Policy Committee Paper on Providing and Maintaining the Mobilization Base," August 28, 1952, NA RG 51/51.26/24/96; Bureau of the Budget, "Mobilization Base Policy," September 5, 1952, NA RG 51/51.26/25/96; Bureau of the Budget, "Next Steps in Mobilization Base Planning," September 24, 1952, NA RG 51/51.26/25/96; Defense Production Administration, "The Mobilization Readiness Program," 1/7/53 January 7, 1953, NA RG 51/51.26/25/96.

President Eisenhower, soon came to the conclusion that if it was to be won at all, the next world war would have to be won very quickly, with the weapons on hand in its opening moments. American planners began to turn away from preparing for a prolonged global struggle and toward preparations for a single massive strike on the Soviet Union and its satellites. Such an attack, it was hoped, would knock the Soviets out of a war in a matter of hours or, at most, days. If this approach succeeded, industrial mobilization would be unnecessary; if it failed, and the Soviets were able to deliver large numbers of thermonuclear weapons against targets in the United States, industrial mobilization would probably be impossible. Either way, resources expended in preparing for it would most likely turn out to have been wasted.

Internally consistent as it undoubtedly was, and sensible as it may ultimately have been, the adoption of this concept was neither inevitable nor immediate. As has been discussed in previous chapters, the growth of Soviet atomic and thermo-nuclear striking power in the 1950s caused many observers to conclude that a new era of stalemate was about to dawn. "Nuclear plenty" might lead to what Army Chief of Staff Matthew Ridgway described in 1955 as a "mutual cancella-tion of nuclear advantage," resulting either in "mutually limited use" of nuclear weapons or perhaps even "in common refusal to use nuclear weapons at all."[77]

If nuclear weapons were not employed on a massive scale, a future war might not be over quickly and industrial mobilization could well retain its rele-vance. As the Cold War wore on, the initiation of "significant military opera-tions short of general war [i.e., all-out nuclear war]" was, in the view of the Commandant of the Marine Corps, "the increasingly probable enemy course." In such a conflict, "the concept of expansion of our industrial mobilization base after hostilities start is still sound."[78] If the United States permitted its mobiliza-tion capacity to atrophy, it might find that it had little choice but to escalate quickly to all-out thermonuclear war, even if by doing so it risked devastating retaliation. Indeed, as one well-known civilian strategist warned in 1956, the failure to prepare for protracted but limited conflict could turn out to be a deadly self-fulfilling prophecy.[79]

These arguments had a compelling logic of their own, and those advancing them (including representatives of the Army, Marines, and the now-sizable in-dustrial mobilization bureaucracy) were not without influence. Still, over time,

---

[77] See Ridgway's letter of resignation to Secretary of Defense Charles E. Wilson, June 27, 1955, in *Soldier: The Memoirs of Matthew B. Ridgway* (New York: Harpers, 1956), p. 324. The back-ground to this letter and the Army's stuggle against massive retaliation are discussed in A. J. Bacevich, "The Paradox of Professionalism: Eisenhower, Ridgway, and the Challenge to Civilian Control, 1953–1955," *Journal of Military History* 61 (April 1997), pp. 303–34. See also Bacevich, *The Pentomic Era: The U.S. Army between Korea and Vietnam* (Washington, DC: National Defense University Press, 1986). For a full account of the interservice debate on these questions see also Maxwell Taylor, *The Uncertain Trumpet* (New York: Harper and Row, 1959).

[78] See service comments by the Commandant of the Marine Corps and the Chief of Staff of the Army on the draft by the Deputy Director for Logistics, Joint Staff, "Status of the Mobilization Base," July 12, 1956, in the Radford Papers, NA RG 218/4/76.

[79] Klaus Knorr, *The War Potential of Nations* (Princeton: Princeton University Press, 1956), p. 7.

it was the short-war concept that emerged triumphant and that was reflected increasingly in official planning documents. In its first year in office the Eisenhower administration reduced the length of the conflict for which the armed services were required to prepare from five to four years. By the end of 1954 this figure had been cut again to three years.[80] Further, truly substantial reductions did not come until Eisenhower's second term. Early in 1957 the anticipated duration of a general war with the Soviet Union was reduced from three years to six months. At the end of 1959 that number was abandoned in favor of "something shorter" (apparently sixty days).[81] By the end of the decade, the official view was that expressed by one Air Force general: "The post D-Day mobilization concept of war had become obsolete." In a future conflict "there would be no time to mobilize in the traditional sense [and] national resources going into a 'mobilization base' would [therefore] be largely wasted."[82]

The Air Force won out, not because it necessarily had the better of the arguments, but because it had the strong backing of the president and, at his direction, the support of the Secretary of Defense and two successive chairmen of the Joint Chiefs of Staff. But why did Eisenhower feel so strongly on this subject? Interestingly, the president himself never fully accepted the idea that the next war would be over in a matter of days. As he told the National Security Council in 1956: "Those who argued that a future thermonuclear war would be won or lost in a period of thirty days were crazy. A modern war is not going to be won simply by destroying the enemy's cities."[83] While he was skeptical that a superpower war could somehow be kept conventional, the president also did not entirely dismiss the possibility, and he urged that paper planning for "full ground mobilization" be continued.[84]

Putting such plans into practice was another matter. In part the issue was one of direct costs; the United States simply "could not afford to prepare to fight all

[80] Robert J. Watson, *History of the Joint Chiefs of Staff*, vol. 5, *The Joint Chiefs of Staff and National Policy 1953–1954* (Washington, DC: JCS Historical Division, 1986), pp. 150–62.

[81] These changes are discussed in "Implementation of the New Mobilization Base Concept," April 9, 1957, Dwight D. Eisenhower Library (DDEL), Office of the Special Assistant for National Security Affairs (OSANSA), NSC Series, Subject Subseries, Box 5, Mobilization Base, January 1956–April 1959. See also "Memorandum of Meeting with the President," October 1, 1959, and "Memorandum of Meeting with the President," October 14, 1959, both in DDEL, OSANSA, Special Assistant Series, Presidential Subseries, Box 4, Meetings with the President, June-December 1959; and "Discussion at the 449th Meeting of the National Security Council," June 30, 1960, DDEL, Ann Whitman File (AW), National Security Council, Box 12.

[82] Nathan F. Twining, *Neither Liberty nor Safety* (New York: Holt, Rinehart, and Winston, 1966), p. 17. Twining was Chief of Staff of the Air Force from 1953 to 1957 and Chairman of the Joint Chiefs from 1957 to 1960.

[83] "Memorandum of Discussion at the 272d Meeting of the National Security Council," January 12, 1956, in *Foreign Relations of the United States, 1955–1957*, vol. 10, *Foreign Aid and Economic Defense Policy* (Washington, DC: U.S. Government Printing Office, 1989), p. 568 (hereafter *FRUS 1955–57*, 10).

[84] See "Memorandum of Discussion at the 273d Meeting of the National Security Council," January 18, 1956, and "Memorandum of a Conference with the President," May 24, 1956, both in *Foreign Relations of the United States, 1955–1957*, vol. 19, *National Security Policy* (Washington, D.C.: U.S. Government Printing Office, 1990), pp. 182–86 and 311–15.

kinds of wars."[85] As the experience of the Truman administration made plain, preparing to fight protracted, large-scale wars in particular also meant ongoing government industrial planning and continuous economic interventionism. These were things that Eisenhower was determined to avoid as a matter of principle, even if doing so meant running certain strategic risks. Stalemate might not be impossible, but its potential domestic consequences helped to make it unthinkable.

Institutional Devolution

Before the debate over strategic assumptions had been fully joined, the Eisenhower administration had already moved to reverse the trend toward centralization and increased institutional strength that had become evident during the Korean War. The timing of these developments suggests that they reflected an underlying distaste for statism that was, in some measure, independent of and prior to any calculation of the nation's defense needs.

Shortly after taking office, the new administration announced a reorganization of the executive branch that dissolved the NSRB and converted the ODM into a permanent peacetime agency. The new Office of Defense Mobilization seemed to some contemporary observers finally to embody the centralizing vision of Ferdinand Eberstadt, frustrated father of the original National Security Resources Board.[86] But appearances were deceiving. Immediately on its reconstitution, the ODM was instructed by the White House to delegate its functions "to other agencies of Government to the maximum extent possible."[87] ODM's staff and budget were cut, and its new director announced his intention to reduce to a minimum its "direct operating functions."[88] Work on new and more powerful planning techniques (most notably input-output models of the national economy that would have permitted more accurate estimates of wartime needs and peacetime production targets) was also curtailed.[89] Putting aside the recommendations of their predecessors, the Eisenhower administration's defense mobilizers also made no move to seek additional authority for peacetime economic intervention from Congress. In particular, the idea of requesting blanket authorization to build industrial facilities at federal expense was quietly dropped.[90] All of these moves were consistent with a suspicion of planning, centralization, and interventionism, a general desire to avoid increasing the size and power of

[85] "Minutes of the 227th Meeting of the National Security Council," December 3, 1954, *Foreign Relations of the United States, 1952–1954*, vol. 2, *National Security Affairs* pt. 1 (Washington, DC: U.S. Government Printing Office, 1984), p. 804 (hereafter *FRUS 1952–54*, 2).

[86] Hobbs, *Behind the President*, p. 203.

[87] See discussion at Defense Mobilization Board Meeting No. 39, May 14, 1953, NA RG 51/51.26/22/86. See also Defense Mobilization Orders (DMOs) 30, I-8, I-12, and I-13 (dated August 14, 1953 and February 10 and October 1, 1954) delegating aspects of ODM's authority to the Departments of Commerce, Defense, and Interior, NA RG 51/51.26/26/108.

[88] Sterling Green, "Here's Where War Mobilization Stands," *Nation's Business* (May 1954), p. 48.

[89] Cuff, "From the Controlled Materials Plan," p. 5.

[90] See Green, "Here's Where War Mobilization Stands," p. 54.

government, and a resistance to policies that would bring the state into competition with business.

In 1958 ODM was merged with the Federal Civil Defense Agency to form the Office of Civil and Defense Mobilization. The ordering of functions in its title suggested the priorities of this new organization. But the shift in wording simply ratified a change in substance that had been becoming evident for several years. As the presumed length of a future war was reduced, it followed that civilian domestic agencies should concern themselves not with how to wage it, but with how best to survive and recover from its effects.[91] Industrial mobilization was increasingly irrelevant. By the end of the decade there was no longer any single institution with the responsibility and the power to monitor and modulate the composition of the nation's economy. The specter of a centrally administered national defense industrial policy had, for the time being at least, been effectively banished.

Policy Constriction

Over the course of the 1950s, as it encouraged a weakening of central institutions, the Eisenhower administration nevertheless retained a tight grip over the instruments of industrial policy. Even as their use for strategic purposes was being curtailed, these could have been converted into tools for extending benefits to private interests. The administration sought to avoid this by resisting business and congressional pressures and limiting strictly the use of the more intrusive preferential devices for shaping the nation's industrial structure. With a few exceptions, these efforts were quite successful. By the end of the decade, simple procurement for current needs was the primary mechanism through which the federal government acted to influence the fortunes of most supporting industries.

SUBSIDIES

One of the main arguments for using the tax code to encourage selected industrial expansion was that it permitted the achievement of national strategic objectives with less government interference in the economy than did the use of loans, for example, or direct government expenditures on productive facilities. Still, the granting of rapid tax amortization benefits to targeted industries did involve a significant degree of intervention, and this fact aroused opposition from key Eisenhower appointees.

The leading critic of rapid amortization was George Humphrey, a former steel company executive and, from 1953 until 1957, the Secretary of the Treasury. Humphrey argued that rapid write-offs had tangible costs to the government in the form of deferred tax revenues. Even more important, he maintained, the extension of amortization privileges by the federal government was unfair,

---

[91] For an overview of what it describes as the "gradual evolution away from emphasis on industrial expansion," see Report of the Office of Defense Mobilization to the Joint Committee on Defense Production, *Defense Mobilization in a Full Economy* (Washington, DC: ODM, March 14, 1957).

unhealthy, and ultimately dangerous to the American system of free enterprise. Continuation of the system put in place during the Korean War necessarily involved offering "an indirect subsidy to certain businesses, and . . . granting favors to a selected group of taxpayers, [thereby] unfairly discriminating against the remainder."[92] By encouraging investment in certain industries over others, government would distort the natural process of development and create "a hindrance to sound, balanced, vigorous growth of our whole free economy." The use of such instruments was "dangerous" because "artificial stimulants" could "well become artificial controls." Emergency powers retained in peacetime would place undue authority in the hands of the federal government and, in particular, the executive branch. Under the arrangements established during the Korean War, executive agencies could help selected industries and hurt others through indirect means and without congressional oversight. This, Humphrey warned, "is not the American way." If subsidies were to be given to particular industries, they should be offered openly and "through regular channels" in the form of direct payments, authorized by Congress, from the federal treasury.[93]

As soon as it came into office, the Eisenhower administration began a review of existing capacity-expansion targets. At the beginning of 1953, 237 of 255 Korean War production goals remained open; within a year, 150 of these had been closed.[94] By the fall of 1955, 33 of the original goals were still open.[95] In 1956, despite, and in some measure *because* of, pressure for additional privileges from such industries as steel, shipbuilding, and commercial aircraft, the criteria for granting certificates of necessity were significantly tightened. Only those companies producing for the immediate needs of Defense Department and the Atomic Energy Commission would now be considered eligible for rapid tax amortization.[96] By 1957 only 12 goals remained.[97]

As the number of goals diminished and the volume of rejected applications increased, so too did the incidence of complaints of unfair treatment. Industry spokesmen claimed that the government was discriminating between sectors (favoring the manufacturers of railway cars over the makers of trucks, for example) and within sectors, among firms and between regions. These protests led to congressional investigations, pressure for even tighter restrictions designed to minimize the impact of government actions on commercial competition, and an

[92] Quoted in Bureau of the Budget, "Defense Mobilization Board Meeting No. 121," September 20, 1956, NA RG 51/51.26/24/91, p. 1.

[93] Secretary of the Treasury George Humphrey, "Statement before the Subcommittee on Legal and Monetary Affairs of the House Government Operations Committee," July 18, 1955, NA RG 51/51.26/23/88, pp. 1–2.

[94] See Bureau of the Budget, "Comments on Agenda for Defense Mobilization Board Meeting No. 49," January 27, 1954, p. 1, and Office of Defense Mobilization, "Use of Tax Amortization to Achieve Expansion Goals," January 27, 1954, p. 4, both in NA RG 51/51.26/22/86.

[95] Joint Committee on Defense Production, *Fifth Annual Report of the Activites of the Joint Committee on Defense Production*, 84th Cong., 2d sess. (Washington, DC: U.S. Government Printing Office, 1955), p. 3.

[96] Arthur Flemming, Director, Office of Defense Mobilization, "Memorandum for the President," December 22, 1956, DDEL Central File (CF), Office Files (OF), 72H, Box 320.

[97] Office of Defense Mobilization, *Defense Mobilization in a Full Economy*, p. 27.

eventual decision simply to allow the authority for granting rapid write-offs to expire at the end of 1959.[98]

TARIFFS

The Cold War gave an added strategic impetus to postwar American efforts to promote freer international trade. U.S. policy makers were eager to hasten the rebuilding of needed allies and to stave off a new depression that would discredit capitalism and strengthen the appeal of communism. Receptiveness to imports was one important means of achieving this goal.[99]

The prospect of impending war with Russia could also have given rise to a strong opposing tendency: a strategically motivated move toward the protection of industries deemed vital to national defense or, at the very least, an effort on the part of domestic interests to exploit national security concerns for their own benefit. As the 1954 report of one pro-protectionist congressional committee argued:

> Strategic considerations today make it imperative that we maintain going-concern industries in the production of basic materials and manufactured goods essential to our security in the event of war. This automatically requires that those domestic industries which would be displaced by foreign industries enjoying a greater comparative advantage must be protected until the peace of the world is assured and strategic considerations can give way to welfare economics.[100]

Despite periodic pleas from industry spokesmen and some members of Congress, the Eisenhower administration successfully resisted the temptations of defense protectionism. This course of action reflected above all an abiding faith in the virtues of free trade, a faith bolstered by a calculation of the strategic costs and benefits of protecting domestic industries against imports from allied countries. As was true of subsidies, so also in the case of tariffs, the administration's evolving official vision of a future war reinforced its inclination to avoid undue intervention in the nation's economy. But here too, the timing and consistency of the administration's actions suggest that causality did not flow in only one direction. Eisenhower and his top advisers recoiled from the image of a long war in part because of an appreciation of the sorts of economic policies that making ready for it might require.

As it had since 1934, Congress continued in the aftermath of the Second

---

[98] Regarding congressional pressure on the executive branch see "Tax Amortization" file, DDEL CF, OF, Box 763, 148-F; also Hearings before the Senate Committee on Finance, *Rapid Amortization of Emergency Facilities*, 85th Cong., 1st sess. (Washington, DC: U.S. Government Printing Office, 1957).

[99] On the origins and evolution of postwar U.S. commercial policy see Robert Gilpin, *The Political Economy of International Relations* (Princeton: Princeton University Press, 1987), pp. 171–230. Also Robert A. Pollard, *Economic Security and the Origins of the Cold War, 1945–1950* (New York: Columbia University Press, 1985).

[100] Report of the Minerals, Materials, and Fuels Economic Subcommittee of the Senate Committee on Interior and Insular Affairs, "Accessibility of Strategic and Critical Materials to the United States in Time of War and of Our Expanding Economy," quoted in Max Fieser, *Economic Policy and War Potential* (Washington, DC: Public Affairs Press, 1964), pp. v–vi.

World War to grant the president the power to negotiate tariff reduction agreements with foreign governments. In 1954, however, and again in 1955 and 1958, this authority was accompanied by a series of additional stipulations. By the end of the decade, the executive branch had been authorized to restrict imports "whenever danger to our national security results from a weakening of segments of the economy through injury to any industry." Investigations to determine whether such damage was imminent were to be conducted by the chief civilian mobilizer (by 1958 the Director of the OCDM), either at his own initiative or "upon application of an interested party" elsewhere in the government or in industry.[101]

Had the Eisenhower administration been inclined to use them for protective purposes (or merely had been less vigilant in *preventing* them from being employed in this way) these provisions could have resulted in the imposition of restrictions on a wide variety of imports. Instead, from the outset, the administration sought to prevent the claims of national security, narrowly conceived, from interfering with the movement toward freer international trade. The passage of the 1954 Trade Bill and the announcement of a decision to limit imports of Swiss watch movements, in which defense considerations had played a role, were followed by an upsurge of industry interest in the possibility of seeking protection on national security grounds.[102] This trend alarmed executive branch officials, who warned that any further surrender of ground would result in "a wave of applications to the President [from manufacturers] for classification as products needed for projected national defense."[103]

---

[101] The Trade Agreements Extension Act of 1958 quoted in Edward E. Groves, "A Brief History of the 1988 National Security Amendments," *Law and Policy in International Business* 20, no. 3 (1989), p. 591.

[102] By mid-1956 ODM had as many applications for protection pending before it as did the Tariff Commission. See Hearings before the Subcommittee on Foreign Economic Policy of the Joint Economic Committee, *Defense Essentiality and Foreign Economic Policy Case Study: The Watch Industry and Precision Skills*, 84th Cong., 2d sess. (Washington, DC: U.S. Government Printing Office, 1956), p. 2. The 1954 watch decision appears to have been both a special case and a learning experience. Eisenhower inherited the issue from his predecessor and made his decision before procedures had been established for dealing with national security import cases. American watchmakers claimed both that their Swiss competitors were engaging in unfair business practices and that, because domestic watchmakers employed highly skilled workers who would be needed in wartime to manufacture fusing mechanisms, their own survival was essential to U.S. national security. The president's initial decision was based primarily on a finding of economic injury, although "collateral" benefits to the nation's defense industrial base were also cited. After having increased tariffs on certain watch movements in 1954, Eisenhower refused all subsequent appeals for further protection and, as will be noted below, he also declined ever again to accept the national security argument for tariffs on manufactured goods. For an overview of the watch case see Percy W. Bidwell, *What the Tariff Means to American Industries* (New York: Harper, 1956), pp. 88–129. For the reasoning underlying the 1954 decision see a report to the Director of ODM by an Interdepartmental Committee on the Jeweled Watch Industry, *The Essentiality to National Security of the American Jeweled Watch Industry*, June 30, 1954, DDEL CF, Confidential File, Subject Series, Box 98, Trade Agreements and Tariff Matters—Watches (3). On government actions regarding the watch industry throughout the 1950s see the documents contained in the file on "Watches and Watch Movements," (1960?), DDEL CF, OF, Box 806, 49-B-2.

[103] See the memo from a staff member to the chairman of the U.S. Council on Foreign Economic

From 1954 onward the administration sought actively to discourage defense protectionism. Industry petitions were repeatedly rejected, often after long and intentionally frustrating delays.[104] Government officials advised business executives and members of Congress that they had no intention of treating the national security provisions in the trade law as a substitute for routine procedures for requesting protection.[105] Although the drastic foreshortening of war-planning horizons that took place in the late 1950s was not discussed in public, there was frequent reference to "new weapons and strategic concepts" and to their dampening effect on industry claims of essentiality. Changes in strategy simply made it easier for the administration to do what it was already inclined to do for other reasons.[106] By the end of the decade, an internal review could point with pride to "a consistent pattern of denials" of industry petitions and to the fact that "the OCDM . . . has been exemplary in upholding the President's liberal world trade policy."[107] With the exception of one case involving oil, the Eisenhower administration turned down every appeal for protection brought before it on national security grounds.[108]

PREFERENTIAL PROCUREMENT

Since the Great Depression, the federal government had been required by law to grant preference to American producers in the letting of procurement contracts. Under the terms of the so-called Buy American Act of 1933, executive agencies were instructed to purchase from domestic sources, except in cases where their prices were significantly higher (usually 25 percent or more) than those of potential foreign suppliers.[109] Less visible than traditional import duties,

---

Policy, C. Edward Galbreath to Clarence Randall, March 21, 1955, in DDEL Council on Foreign Economic Policy (CFEP), Records, Chron File, Box 5, March 1955.

[104] For an overview see a document prepared by the Committee on Foreign Economic Policy, "Appendix: Review of Section 8 Cases" (1960?), DDEL CFEP, Office of the Chairman, Records, CFEP Paper Series, Box 5.

[105] Statement by ODM Director Gordon Gray in Hearings before the House Committee on Ways and Means, *Renewal of Trade Agreements Act*, 85th Cong., 2d sess. (Washington, DC: U.S. Government Printing Office, 1958), p. 95.

[106] For details of the methods used in reviewing cases see Director of the Office of Civil and Defense Mobilization, *Report to the Congress on the Administration of Section 8 of the Trade Agreements Extension Act of 1958*, February 1, 1959, DDEL White House Office (WHO), Staff Research Group, Records, Box 15, OCDM, 396–600.

[107] See a memorandum for the Director of the CFEP, July 6, 1960, DDEL, CFEP, Records, Office Series, Box 1, CFEP Briefing Papers. For Eisenhower's views on import restrictions and national security see his remarks in "Discussion at the 409th Meeting of the National Security Council," June 4, 1959, DDEL AW, NSC, Box 11.

[108] See Hearings before the House Committee on Ways and Means, *Trade Expansion Act of 1962* 87th Cong., 2d sess. (Washington, DC: U.S. Government Printing Office, 1962), p. 766.

[109] For background see Department of State, "The 'Buy American' Policy: Reasons and Effects," December 15, 1952, DDEL CF, OF, Box 625, 122-M, American Made Goods (Buy American); also a report to the Randall Commission on Foreign Economic Policy by Raymond Vernon, "The Buy American Policy," November 17, 1953, DDEL Commission on Foreign Economic Policy, Box 46, Drafts of Report, Area 4, No. 1.

these restrictions nevertheless amounted, in effect, to a "supertariff" on goods used by the government.[110]

The Eisenhower administration recognized that, in the words of its first Director of Defense Mobilization, "current procurement of supplies and equipment is a major instrument in the preservation of sources of supply and the development of productive capacity," and it was willing to accept the idea that a deviation from low-cost bids might occasionally be necessary to maintain parts of the domestic defense industrial base.[111] But the preservation of a huge, officially sanctioned price differential was clearly inconsistent with the push for freer international trade. In 1954 President Eisenhower requested that the Buy American Act be amended so that foreign bidders could be treated equally, provided that their governments afforded a similar courtesy to American firms. When Congress refused to agree, the president issued an executive order reducing the price advantage given to U.S. companies by a considerable margin.[112] Higher differentials might still be permitted where the needs of national security seemed to require them, but they were to be granted only after careful review by the Office of Defense Mobilization.[113] As with its handling of tariffs, the ODM proved quite wary of setting precedents that might encourage industry to seek special privileges from the government. In the late 1950s, for example, OCDM fended off a series of appeals for special treatment from the makers of electric power generators, in part because it feared similar requests from the machine-tool, heavy earthmoving, and chemical plant industries.[114] In its narrowing of formal procurement preferences, the Eisenhower administration moved about as close to a purely free-market solution as political circumstances would allow.

LOANS AND PURCHASE GUARANTEES

The 1950 Defense Production Act created two special devices for the expansion of capacity in defense supporting industries. Within specified dollar limits, the executive branch was authorized to extend loans (and to guarantee private loans) to companies involved in the manufacture of certain critical items and to make advance commitments to purchase their products. These policy instru-

---

[110] Remarks by Dr. Ralph W. E. Reid at a meeting of the Council on Foreign Economic Policy, April 14, 1960, DDEL CFEP, Office of the Chairman, Records, CFEP Paper Series, Box 3, CFEP 554(2), p. 5.

[111] Director of the Office of Defense Mobilization to the Secretaries of Defense and Commerce and the Chairman of the Atomic Energy Commission, November 15, 1954, DDEL AW Admin, Box 14, Flemming.

[112] From 25 percent to 6 percent in most cases. On the reasoning behind this compromise decision see Minutes of Cabinet Meeting, August 18, 1954, DDEL AW, Cab, Box 3.

[113] See White House Press release, April 7, 1955, DDEL CF, OF, Box 625, 122-M, American Made Goods (Buy American).

[114] See DDEL CFEP, Office of the Chairman, Records, Randall Series, Subject Subseries, Box 4, Electrical Equipment (1–5). For more on the resolution of the generator case see a press release from the Office of Civil and Defense Mobilization, November 18, 1960, DDEL WHO, Staff Research Group, Records, Box 15, OCDM 741.

ments were used during the Korean War to stimulate the production of machine tools and raw materials (especially minerals), and even as strategy changed, they continued to be employed in this way down to the end of the 1950s.

In contrast to tax breaks, tariffs, and procurement preferences, the use of loans and purchase guarantees was constricted slowly and with some difficulty. One reason for this was the perceived special character of the sectors at which they were directed. A shortage of machine tools was generally considered to have been the principal cause of delay in both the World War Two and the Korean mobilizations. Avoiding bottlenecks in some future defense buildup required the maintenance of an industry larger than could be sustained by normal peacetime demand. To achieve this end the government loaned the machine-tool makers money to expand their productive capacity and promised to buy whatever portion of their output could not be sold on the commercial market. These tools were then leased to industry, donated to high school vocational training programs, or placed in stockpiles.[115]

Minerals and raw materials were also widely regarded as different from other industrial products. After the Second World War, "America appeared to have become a 'have-not' nation . . . its self-sufficiency in natural resources at an end."[116] Concern over the possible strategic consequences of this condition led both to an effort to ensure access to foreign sources of raw materials and to increased interest in discovering and exploiting remaining domestic reserves. In pursuit of this second goal, the federal government provided funds for investment in new capacity while creating demand by buying and stockpiling a portion of the resulting production.[117]

The privileged status of minerals and machine tools was given an institutional manifestation in the provisions of the Defense Production Act, which both identified these sectors as especially important and provided mechanisms specifically designed to assist them. In addition, the mining industry benefited from a powerful and concentrated political lobby and from the idiosyncratic beliefs of President Eisenhower. Most mining was done in a handful of western states whose congressional representatives vigorously resisted efforts to curtail stockpiling programs, which tended to keep prices high.[118] As compared to the situation in the case of tax subsidies, for example, these pressures were not offset by countervailing pressures from other regions of the country.

---

[115] On the wartime origin of these programs see Joint Committee on Defense Production, *Defense Production Act Progress Report No. 13: Machine Tools*, 82d Cong., 2d sess. (Washington, DC: U.S. Government Printing Office, 1952). On their implementation see various committee reports, in particular those of the Joint Committee on Defense Production, *Eighth Annual Report of the Activites of the Joint Committee on Defense Production*, 86th Cong., 1st sess. (Washington, DC: U.S. Government Printing Office, 1958), pp. 86–93.

[116] Pollard, *Economic Security*, p. 197. Also Stephen D. Krasner, *Defending the National Interest* (Princeton: Princeton University Press, 1978), pp. 50–51.

[117] For an overview of these programs at mid-decade see Office of Defense Mobilization, "Stockpile Policies and Programs of the U.S. Government," February 26, 1956. In *FRUS 1955–57*, 10:575–89.

[118] The best account of the politics of the stockpiling program is Glenn H. Snyder, *Stockpiling Strategic Materials* (San Francisco: Chandler Publishing, 1966).

Even as he urged cutbacks in most other areas of defense industrial policy, Eisenhower continued to regard stockpiling with special sympathy. When his advisers pointed out that large stockpiles were inconsistent with the assumption of a very short war, the president responded, first, that "the theory of the thirty to sixty day war has nothing whatsoever to back it up" and, second, that in any case, the nation had nothing to lose by "storing up imperishable supplies that it does not . . . produce in sufficient quantity." Due to the continuing depletion of the world's resources, Eisenhower argued, "the time is bound to come when some of these items will begin to mount sharply in price. . . . This is the case where the provisioning of war reserves . . . does not constitute a drain upon the long term resources of the nation."[119]

One final explanation for the persistence of programs designed to help the mineral and machine-tool industries is the character of at least some of the instruments employed. Purchase guarantees and stockpiling could be seen as special forms of procurement. As the federal government bought tanks and planes from industry, so also it purchased tools and materials that it then laid away for emergency use. Such actions appeared less interventionist and more in keeping with the dictates of a free economy than tariffs, targeted tax breaks, or blatantly protectionist procurement preferences. For this reason, too, programs designed to assist the mineral and machine-tool industries continued until well into the 1950s, although by the end of the decade, they had been considerably reduced.[120]

The End of Industrial Dispersal

As the destructiveness of nuclear weapons grew, so too did the seeming urgency of dispersal. Terrible though they were, Hiroshima-style fission bombs could not engulf entire large cities in a single explosion. Fusion weapons, as the first

---

[119] Diary entry for January 11, 1956, DDEL AW, DDE Diary, Box 12, January 1956. For more on Eisenhower's views of stockpiling see Discussion at the 325th Meeting of the NSC, May 27, 1957, DDEL AW, NSC, Box 8; and Discussion at the 330th Meeting of the NSC, July 11, 1957, DDEL AW, NSC, Box 7.

[120] Shortened planning horizons did result in curtailment of mineral and material stockpiling goals, although they were never set below the levels assumed to be necessary for a three-year war. See Special Stockpile Advisory Committee, "Stockpiling for Defense in the Nuclear Age," January 28, 1958, DDEL CFEP, Office of the Chairman, Randall Series, Agency Subseries, Box 3, OCDM (1). Also Snyder, *Stockpiling*, pp. 189–237. By 1960 "technical advances in the missile, airborne, and space vehicle programs, and related changes in . . . strategic concept" were acknowledged to have "presented new problems to the Government in the management of its machine tool mobilization program," raising questions "as to the need for retaining thousands of tools which . . . are not required for current or future foreseeable military programs." Joint Committee on Defense Production, *Tenth Annual Report of the Joint Committee on Defense Production*, 87th Cong., 2d sess. (Washington, DC: U.S. Government Printing Office, 1960), p. 62. By the end of the 1950s industry representatives were complaining that because of cutbacks in government procurement, total demand for machine tools was being allowed to fall to dangerously low levels. See a memorandum from the National Machine Tool Builders Association to Leo Hoegh, Director, OCDM, August 17, 1959, NA RG 51/51.26/15/139.

American test made plain in the fall of 1952, were another story altogether.[121] Given the impending acquisition of H-bombs and ballistic missiles by the Soviet Union, an NSC study concluded that it had become even more important to alter "the metropolitan pattern of America so that it presents fewer concentrated targets for attack."[122] The Soviets did not succeed in detonating their own device until the end of 1955 but as one Office of Defense Mobilization report argued in 1954: given "known increases in Soviet capabilities [the U.S.] should . . . accelerate measures for dispersal to safer areas of important productive capacity."[123] The H-bomb seemed "at last" to have given "dispersal advocates . . . a powerful wedge with which to penetrate the indifference of American industrialists."[124]

It was not to be. As the yield of Soviet weapons grew, the ability of the federal government to compel industrial dispersal diminished. The sharp constriction of the rapid tax amortization program meant that government planners had been deprived of their most potent inducement and were now once again virtually powerless to exert a direct influence on decisions about industrial location. During the Eisenhower years, federal procurement agencies were instructed, where possible, to give contracts to companies with factories in more remote areas.[125] As with the wartime system of tax breaks, however, this provision was often violated in the interests of practicality. The effect on the nation's industrial geography was negligible. After nearly a decade of trying, government programs, a classified 1957 assessment concluded, had been "almost wholly ineffective in promoting dispersion of American industry."[126]

By the end of the 1950s efforts to achieve even the modest goal of local industrial scattering had been effectively abandoned. All that remained of the dispersal program was a "counseling" service to let interested businessmen know if their construction plans would place them in high-risk areas.[127] Dispersal was discarded not because it had come to be universally regarded as a

---

[121] The best account of the development of these new weapons is Richard Rhodes, *Dark Sun: The Making of the Hydrogen Bomb* (New York: Simon and Schuster, 1995).

[122] "Continental Defense (NSC 5408)," February 11, 1954, *FRUS 1952–54*, 2:623.

[123] National Security Planning Board, "Guidelines for Mobilization," October 5, 1954, *FRUS 1952–54*, 2:735.

[124] Hurley, "The Role of Accelerated Tax Amortization," p. 83.

[125] See "Memorandum of Discussion at the 149th Meeting of the National Security Council," June 19, 1953, *FRUS 1952–54*, 2:375; also Hearings before the Joint Committee on Defense Production, *Defense Production Act Progress Report No. 42*, 85th Cong., 2nd sess. (Washington, DC: U.S. Government Printing Office, 1958), pp. 28–44.

[126] Office of Defense Mobilization, "The Mobilization Program: Status on June 30, 1957 (NSC 5720, Part 4)," DDEL OSANSA, NSC Series, Status of Projects Subseries, Box 7, p. 27. For a similar assessment see University of Maryland, Bureau of Business and Economic Research, "Industrial Dispersal," *Studies in Business and Economics* 9, no. 4 (March 1958).

[127] For indications of growing disillusionment with dispersal see Office of Defense Mobilization, "The Mobilization Program: Status on June 30, 1956 (NSC 5611, Part 4)," DDEL OSANSA, NSC Series, Status of Projects Subseries, Box 7, p. 28. And Office of Civil and Defense Mobilization, "The Civil and Defense Mobilization Program: Status on June 30, 1960 (NSC 6013, Part 4)," DDEL OSANSA, NSC Series, Status of Projects Subseries, Box 9, p. 8. Regarding "counseling" see Joint Committee on Defense Production, *Eighth Annual Report*, pp. 194–98.

strategic non sequitor, but because its implementation would have required a domestic transformation more sweeping than most Americans were willing even to contemplate, still less to undertake.[128]

STRATEGIC CHANGE, INDUSTRIAL POLICY CONTINUITY

From 1953 to 1960 American military planners concentrated with increasing single-mindedness on the prospect of a war of unrestrained intensity and limited duration. Albeit with lags in certain areas, U.S. defense industrial policy generally followed this narrowing of focus. Indeed, as has been demonstrated, the desire to constrict the government's more intrusive directive activities was one motive behind the shift in military strategy. After an interval of discontinuity, by the late 1950s the interior and exterior aspects of the American strategic synthesis had come more fully into alignment.

In the early 1960s the emphasis of American strategy changed again, but this time the mechanisms of power creation did not all follow suit. Instead of concentrating narrowly on preparing for a short, total war, military planners were charged from the Kennedy years onwards with contemplating a much wider array of possible contingencies. In the early 1980s the importance of making ready for an extended conventional conflict with the Soviet Union received particular emphasis. Yet despite shifts in strategy that might have seemed to demand it, there was no substantial change in government policy toward defense supporting industries. The reasons, once again, were primarily domestic in origin.

Flexible Response and Industrial Mobilization

With the election of John Kennedy and the coming to power of many who had previously been critics of the Eisenhower administration, more attention began to be paid to the possibility of longer, lesser wars, including wars between the superpowers fought primarily with conventional weapons. The arguments of those who had earlier warned of the implications of a strategic nuclear stalemate were now taken more seriously. Despite this development at the level of doctrine, however, the interior dimension of American strategy remained virtually unchanged. The movement from massive retaliation to flexible response did not result in renewed interest in a wide-ranging defense industrial policy.

Secretary of Defense Robert McNamara was no more eager than his predecessors to incur the domestic costs of preparing for a protracted conventional conflict. In order to avoid the necessity of doing so, McNamara and his advisers

---

[128] In the Soviet Union, by contrast, strategically motivated, state-directed dispersal of industry continued into the 1970s. See Leon Goure, *Civil Defense in the Soviet Union* (Berkeley: University of California Press, 1962); and Goure, *War Survival in Soviet Strategy* (Miami: Center for Advanced International Studies, 1976), pp. 137–43. In the late 1970s the CIA concluded that these programs had been abandoned. See Director of Central Intelligence, *Soviet Civil Defense* (Washington, DC: Central Intelligence Agency, July 1978), p. 10. Recent evidence suggests, however, that efforts at industrial dispersal continued into the 1980s. Gaddy, *The Price of the Past*, p. 40.

chose, in essence, to assume the problem out of existence. A mutual withholding of nuclear weapons by the superpowers might be possible, they argued, but only if both were fighting for limited objectives. If the stakes were raised, the probability of escalation would increase. On the other hand, a war fought for limited ends was unlikely to be either large or long.[129] "If a war of this kind did occur," wrote two key McNamara aides, "we would have time to mobilize our industrial potential and ought to 'win' eventually, just as we did in World War I and World War II, even if we were relatively unprepared at the beginning."[130] In the meantime, preparations for a large, long war such as "the accumulation of raw material stockpiles [and the] . . . construction of new capacities in industries that might 'bottleneck' the expansion of war production" would be wasteful and inefficient.[131]

This line of reasoning was given practical expression following the Berlin Crisis of 1961. From that point onward, all the military services were instructed to prepare for six months of "non-nuclear combat." According to McNamara, "It was assumed that such combat consumption needs as existed after six months could be met from new production, thereby in effect providing support for an indefinite period."[132] How that new production was to be provided was left unresolved.[133]

Defense Industrial Policy Revisited (1980–1984)

THE IMPLICATIONS OF PARITY

Underpinning McNamara's refusal to engage in serious preparations for mobilization was an awareness that despite earlier anxieties about a possible missile gap, the United States continued to enjoy a substantial margin of nuclear superiority. As long as they retained some confidence in their own willingness to escalate to the use of nuclear weapons, American planners could avoid contemplating the prospect of protracted conventional conflict with the Soviet Union. Such a war was implausible because, quite simply, the United States had no

[129] This reasoning is laid out in a paper by Charles Hitch (head of the economics department at RAND and, under McNamara, Assistant Secretary of Defense), "Domestic Economic Policies for National Security," March 1955. In Joint Economic Committee, *Defense Essentiality*, pp. 19–34.

[130] Charles J. Hitch and Roland N. McKean, *The Economics of Defense in the Nuclear Age* (Cambridge: Harvard University Press, 1960), p. 14.

[131] Ibid., pp. 17–18.

[132] Secretary of Defense Robert S. McNamara, "Statement before the Senate Armed Services Committee on the Fiscal Year 1969–73 Defense Program and 1969 Defense Budget," January 22, 1968, in Hearings before the Subcommittee of the Senate Committee on Appropriations, *Department of Defense Appropriations for Fiscal Year 1969*, 90th Cong., 2d session (Washington, DC: U.S. Government Printing Office, 1968), pp. 2734–35.

[133] To the extent that industrial mobilization planning continued during the 1960s, it was directed at preparing for increased production of ammunition and spare parts to meet the needs of a limited peripheral war such as the one the United States would eventually try to fight in Vietnam. Rod Vawter, *Industrial Mobilization: The Relevant History* (Washington, DC: National Defense University Press, 1983), p. 50. See also Theodore J. Panaytoff, *The Department of Defense Industrial Mobilization Production Planning Program in the United States* (Texarkana: U.S. Army Logistics Management Center, 1972).

intention ever of allowing one to develop. It was only with the unquestioned disappearance of the option of escalation that the issue of defense industrial policy would be reopened.

By the early 1970s the Soviet Union had clearly achieved strategic nuclear equivalence with the United States. Both superpowers now had nuclear offensive forces so large and so diverse that even after a massive enemy attack, they could still deliver a crushing retaliatory blow. Whereas in the early 1960s, U.S. leaders might conceivably have been able to contemplate initiating the use of nuclear weapons, ten years later that option had come to seem increasingly unattractive.[134] Nuclear stalemate, anticipated since 1950, had finally arrived.

Although there was considerable initial disagreement about the implications of this new situation, by the late 1970s a growing number of Western strategists had come to accept the sorts of arguments first advanced (and then generally rejected) during the 1950s. Strategic nuclear parity, it was widely claimed, not only enhanced the importance of conventional forces for purposes of deterrence, it also increased the likelihood of a large and protracted conventional war. The mutual cancellation of nuclear advantage meant that, as Secretary of Defense Donald Rumsfeld put it in 1977, "the main burden of deterrence has once again fallen on the conventional forces."[135] Moreover, if deterrence failed, the reluctance of both superpowers to use nuclear weapons might mean that a war between them would remain conventional. Such a struggle could go on for some time. If the United States continued to plan only for a very short war, it ran the risk of discovering that "the enemy could outlast us." Accordingly, it was becoming more important that the United States and its allies "hedge substantially against longer-war eventualities."[136]

Rumsfeld's conclusion was shared not only by those with an obvious interest in its practical implications, but by some presumably more objective observers.[137] Thus, in one widely cited article, British military historian Michael Howard pointed out that under conditions prevailing at the end of the 1970s: "Deterrence works both ways. . . . The prospect of nuclear war is so appalling that we

---

[134] As one analyst describes the situation: "Parity . . . made the danger of deliberate escalation unmistakable rather than just probable." Richard Betts, "Elusive Equivalence," in Samuel P. Huntington, ed., *The Strategic Imperative: New Policies for American Security* (Cambridge, MA: Ballinger, 1982), p. 118.

[135] Secretary of Defense Donald H. Rumsfeld, *Annual Defense Department Report, FY 1978* (Washington, DC: Department of Defense, 1977), p. 85. This view was echoed by, among others, German Chancellor Helmut Schmidt, who argued in a much-publicized 1977 speech that strategic parity made it necessary to redress imbalances at the lower levels of military capability. See David N. Schwartz, *NATO's Nuclear Dilemmas* (Washington, DC: Brookings Institution, 1983), p. 1.

[136] Rumsfeld, *Annual Report*, p. 97.

[137] Among the interested parties were the Army and its industrial suppliers. See Association of the United States Army, *Army Industrial Preparedness: A Primer on What It Takes to Stay until the War Is Over* (Washington, DC: AOUSA, May 1979); and American Defense Preparedness Association, *Defense Readiness–Force Sustainability and Industrial Preparedness: Why We Are Concerned* (Washington, DC: ADPA, August 1980). See also the discussion in David E. Bahr et al., *Long War versus Short War: An Appraisal of Policy* (Washington, DC: Industrial College of the Armed Forces, May 1983).

no less than our adversaries are likely, if war comes, to rely on 'conventional' operational skills and the logistical capacity to support them for as long as possible."[138]

Intensified concern over the possibility of protracted conventional warfare led, logically, to renewed interest in industrial mobilization. As relations with the Soviet Union worsened, various government agencies began once again to examine the question of how best to prepare for substantial and possibly sustained increases in defense production.[139] Despite a lengthening list of studies, by the end of the 1970s outside critics claimed that little had actually been done.[140] In part to counter these complaints, in his 1980 State of the Union address President Jimmy Carter announced a "major effort to establish a coherent and a practical basis for all government mobilization planning." This statement was followed by a Presidential Decision memorandum (PD 57) aimed at, among other objectives, improving the nation's capacity for industrial mobilization.[141] Carter did not remain in power long enough to put these declarations into practice.

When he took office, Ronald Reagan found himself presented with an apparent choice between his two most cherished objectives: strengthening national defense and reducing government economic intervention. The kind of military strategy that had permitted Reagan's Republican predecessor to escape a similar dilemma thirty years before no longer presented itself as an acceptable option. Serious preparations for large, protracted wars appeared necessary, and it seemed that they would require substantial departures from the principles of laissez-faire.

Unlike Eisenhower, Reagan never succeeded in resolving the dilemma confronting his administration in a fully coherent fashion. Because of the high costs, direct and indirect, of preparing for mobilization warfare, declared strategy and actual preparations for its execution diverged sharply. In another sense, however, the outcome of the 1980s was both coherent and fully consistent with

---

[138] Michael Howard, "The Forgotten Dimensions of Strategy," *Foreign Affairs* 57, no. 5 (Summer 1979), p. 986.

[139] Evidence of this renewed interest can be found in studies sponsored by the Arms Control and Disarmament Agency, the Air Force, and the Federal Emergency Management Agency. See J. H. Ott et al., *Problems of Mobilization, Modernization and Arms Control* (Washington, DC: Battelle Laboratories, May 1977); Geneese G. Baumbusch et al., *Defense Industrial Planning for a Surge in Military Demand* (Santa Monica, CA: RAND, September 1978); Leonard Sullivan, et al., *Impact of Enhanced Mobilization Potential on Civil Preparedness Planning* (Washington, DC: System Planning Corporation, June 1979). See also General Accounting Office, *Restructuring Needed of Department of Defense Program for Planning with Private Industry for Mobilization Production Requirements* (Washington, DC: GAO, May 1977).

[140] See, for example, the writings of Fred Ikle, who would later become Undersecretary of Defense for policy in the Reagan administration. Ikle argued that despite the loss of strategic superiority, a continuing preoccupation with "'short war' planning" had led to "a starkly illogical neglect of [U.S.] industrial mobilization capacity." Fred Charles Ikle, "Preparing for Industrial Mobilization: The First Step toward Full Strength," in W. Scott Thompson, ed., *National Security in the 1980s: From Weakness to Strength* (San Francisco: Institute for Contemporary Studies, 1980), p. 64. Also "Can We Mobilize Industry?" *Wall Street Journal* (December 26, 1979).

[141] "Revived Mobilization Planning," *Air Force Magazine* (June 1980), pp. 18–19.

the pattern of the 1950s. Strategy changed, but as regards supporting industries, its interior dimension remained essentially fixed. In the 1980s, as in the 1950s, the United States rejected industrial planning and extensive defense protectionism. Once again, a substantial part of the explanation can be found in the antistatist inclinations of the occupants of the executive branch.

STRATEGIC THEORY VERSUS REALITY

The Reagan administration not only accepted the logical possibility of a protracted conventional war with the Soviet Union; it committed itself to do whatever was necessary to prepare for such a conflict. Secretary of Defense Caspar Weinberger warned publicly that "we cannot count on a war ending within a few months" and declared his intention to "overcome the 'short war' fallacy" by taking steps to "repair our capacity rapidly to expand defense production."[142] Behind closed doors, Weinberger endorsed a secret Defense Guidance document, and the president signed a National Security Decision Directive (NSDD 32), both of which, according to published reports, required preparations for a large, long global conventional war.[143] These were followed shortly by another presidential directive (NSDD 47), which has been described as mandating "the necessary industrial mobilization capability to prosecute a major military conflict."[144]

Despite the urgency of these declarations, according to the head logistician for the Joint Chiefs of Staff it soon became clear that little "and in some cases, nothing" was being done to implement them.[145] Part of the reason was cost. Preparations for protracted conventional warfare required accumulating ammunition reserves and expanding plant capacity so as to be able quickly to manufacture more. Such measures did not demand enhanced peacetime intervention by the government in the civilian economy, but they were expensive.[146] Even in

---

[142] Secretary of Defense Caspar W. Weinberger, *Annual Report to the Congress, FY 1983* (Washington, DC: Department of Defense, February 8, 1982), pp. I-17 and I-13. For further discussion of "industrial responsiveness" see pp. III-191–95. See also an article by the Undersecretary of Defense for Policy, Fred Charles Ikle, "Strategic Principles of the Reagan Administration," *Strategic Review* (Fall 1983), p. 16.

[143] According to one account of the March 1982 Defense Guidance: "Under an assumption of a nuclear standoff between the United States and the Soviet Union, American armed forces were instructed to prepare to fight a prolonged war around the globe with conventional arms." Richard Halloran, *To Arm a Nation: Rebuilding America's Endangered Defenses* (New York: Macmillan, 1986), p. 212. NSDD-32 (signed in May 1982) reportedly "arrived at a strategy for fighting a prolonged conventional war." Richard Halloran, "Reagan as Military Commander," *New York Times Magazine*, March 15, 1984, p. 58. See also the reference in Linton F. Brooks, "Naval Power and National Security: The Case for the Maritime Strategy," *International Security* 11, no. 2 (Fall 1986), p. 61.

[144] Alfred G. Hansen, "General Hansen on Industrial Mobilization," *National Defense* 72, no. 434 (January 1988), p. 51. NSDD-47 was promulgated in July 1982 and is reproduced in Christopher Simpson, ed., *National Security Directives of the Reagan and Bush Administrations: The Declassified History of U.S. Political and Military Policy, 1981–1991* (Boulder, CO: Westview Press, 1995), pp. 158–69.

[145] Hansen, "General Hansen on Industrial Mobilization," p. 51.

[146] The Joint Chiefs estimated in the early 1980s that adequate preparations for a prolonged

an era of rising defense budgets, resources were still limited, and military planners generally preferred buying new weapons to investing in "industrial preparedness."[147]

Discussion of mobilization also reopened the much broader question of the shape and character of the nation's defense industrial policies. A truly protracted conflict might require not only marginal increases in the manufacture of military consumables, but full-scale conversion of industry and the reorientation of the entire national economy toward defense production. Especially in light of the difficulties facing many American manufacturing industries in the early 1980s, serious preparation for these contingencies seemed to point toward a much more interventionist role for the federal government.[148] But this was something to which the new administration was strongly, indeed viscerally, opposed. Seeking to discourage the use of defense arguments to justify calls for protectionism and national economic planning, administration officials were careful to specify that all mobilization preparations should place primary reliance on "market forces for resource allocation" and "avoid interference in commercial areas."[149]

The fear that planning for a long war might open a veritable Pandora's box of appeals for interventionism proved to be amply justified. Intimations of changes in strategy were followed, in short order, by efforts to draw government back into the kind of role that it had all but abandoned in the mid-1950s. Most of the pressures for movement in this direction came from the older manufacturing industries. Their claims of "defense essentiality" and their pleas for help in the face of intensified foreign competition were echoed and amplified by some members of Congress (particularly those from the Northeast and Midwest, where the affected industries were concentrated), and they were received with some sympathy by those parts of the Defense Department bureaucracy with a

---

conventional war would add another 20 percent, or $325 billion, to the Reagan administration's 5-year, $1.5 trillion long-term defense plan. Halloran, *To Arm a Nation,* p. 222.

[147] Hansen, "General Hansen on Industrial Mobilization," p. 51.

[148] In the late 1970s and early 1980s, U.S. manufacturers in a number of defense-related sectors (including steel, machine tools, and semiconductors) were experiencing stiff competition from foreign firms. These difficulties were due in part to long-term shifts in comparative advantage and also, from the start of the Reagan administration, to a rapidly rising dollar. Whatever their source, the troubles of American manufacturers caused some observers to worry that in the words of the head of the Air Force Systems Command, the United States was "sliding . . . toward the status of a second rate industrial power," and that it would soon be unable "to maintain (its) position as a first-rate military power." See Briefing by Gen. Alton Slay in Hearings before the House Committee on Armed Services, *Capability of U.S. Defense Industrial Base,* 96th Cong., 2d sess. (Washington, DC: U.S. Government Printing Office, 1980), pp. 547–48. For other expressions of official anxiety on this score see Report of the Defense Industrial Base Panel of the House Committee on Armed Services, *The Ailing Defense Industrial Base: Unready for Crisis,* 96th Cong., 2d sess. (Washington, DC: U.S. Government Printing Office, 1980); Report of the Defense Science Board 1980 Summer Study Panel, *Industrial Responsiveness* (Washington, DC: Office of the Undersecretary of Defense for Research and Engineering, January 1981).

[149] See the discussion of NSDD-47 in Jack Nunn et al., *National Security Emergency Preparedness Mobilization Policy Review* (Washington: Industrial College of the Armed Forces, February 1990), mimeo, p. 9.

primary responsibility for mobilization. For the most part, however, the White House proved extremely resistant to all such appeals.

REVITALIZED INSTITUTIONS?

Renewed interest in mobilization brought renewed attention to the institutional mechanisms created for its management. In 1981 the Reagan administration formed a new Emergency Mobilization Preparedness Board within the National Security Council to coordinate the mobilization planning activities of all executive agencies.[150] It rejected suggestions that this ad hoc group be converted into something more permanent and powerful, however.[151] Proposals (such as one contained in a study sponsored by the Defense Department's Industrial College of the Armed Forces) that the president "establish a mobilization readiness czar . . . with authority similar to that of the Director of the Office of Defense Mobilization" were met with an equal lack of enthusiasm.[152] Whatever its concerns about mobilization, the administration had no intention of creating within its ranks an authoritative and potentially disruptive advocate of industrial planning and economic interventionism.[153]

EXPANDED LOANS AND SUBSIDIES?

The return to issues of mobilization also brought with it a reawakening of interest in long-dormant instruments of defense industrial policy. In the early 1980s the Reagan administration asked Congress to extend the Defense Production Act and to authorize the granting of small loans to domestic producers and processors of certain critical materials. The response to these requests was alarmingly enthusiastic. Members of the House of Representatives sought to transform the Defense Production Act into the centerpiece of a broad national industrial policy and to endow the executive branch with unsought, and unde-

---

[150] See the statement of Lawrence Brady, assistant secretary for Trade Administration, Department of Commerce in Hearing before the Senate Committee on Banking, Housing, and Urban Affairs, *Reauthorization of the Defense Production Act*, 97th Cong., 2d sess. (Washington, DC: U.S. Government Printing Office, 1982), p. 12.

[151] See John W. Eley, "Management Structures for Industrial Mobilization in the 1980s," in Hardy L. Merritt and Luther F. Carter, eds., *Mobilization and National Defense* (Washington, DC: National Defense University Press, 1985), p. 35–36.

[152] Vawter, *Industrial Mobilization*, p. 98.

[153] Toward the end of the decade there were other proposals for new industrial planning institutions. These met with a similar fate. See Report to the Secretary of Defense by the Undersecretary of Defense (Acquisition), *Bolstering Defense Industrial Competitiveness* (Washington, DC: Department of Defense, July 1988). And Final Report of the Defense Science Board 1988 Summer Study, *The Defense Industrial and Technology Base* (Washington, DC: Department of Defense, October 1988). Both of these reports were instigated by Robert Costello, a former engineer and GM executive and, from 1987 to 1989, Assistant Secretary of Defense for Production and Logistics. For more on the background to these reports see Roderick L. Vawter, *U.S. Industrial Base Dependence/Vulnerability, Phase I: Survey of Literature* (Washington, DC: Mobilization Concepts Development Center, December 1986); Martin Libicki, Jack Nunn, Bill Taylor, *U.S. Industrial Base Dependence/Vulnerability, Phase II: Analysis* (Washington, DC: Mobilization Concepts Development Center, November 1987).

sired, powers.[154] Under the terms of proposed amendments to the act, large sums were to be allocated for loans to small- and medium-sized businesses across the entire spectrum of defense-supporting industrial sectors.[155]

In fending off these proposals, administration spokesmen argued that they would amount to "an enormous bailout program" for domestic industries under pressure from foreign competition, and further, that they would disrupt credit markets by setting "the government up as a privileged competitor to private financial institutions."[156] Offering grants and loans "across the board to failing private sector defense-related industries would be a dangerous and self-defeating policy . . . [that] would fast lead to total government support of a huge portion of the private sector."[157] Instead, the administration proposed to "rely on the marketplace to help our industries become more competitive and to reduce our dependence on foreign source[s]."[158] Rather than protecting or subsidizing the defense-supporting industries, government would simply buy more of their products or, rather, it would buy more of the end items into which their products were incorporated.[159]

RENEWED PROCUREMENT PREFERENCES?

In addition to urging extensive use of grants and loans, Congress also sought to assist beleaguered domestic producers by imposing restrictions on the govern-

[154] Useful background to this debate can be found in Leon N. Karadbil and Roderick L. Vawter, "The Defense Production Act," in Merritt and Carter, *Mobilization and the National Defense*, pp. 37–59.

[155] See the text of H.R. 5540, A Bill to Amend the Defense Production Act of 1950 to Revitalize the Defense Industrial Base of the United States, in Hearing before the House Committee on Banking, Finance, and Urban Affairs, *To Amend the Defense Production Act of 1950*, 97th Cong., 2d sess. (Washington, DC: U.S. Government Printing Office, 1982), pp. 2, 3–17. All but one of the seventeen cosponsors of this bill were from a northeastern or midwestern state. For a sense of the industry appeals that lay behind this proposal, see statements by representatives of the machine tool, steel, shipbuilding, metal casting, and forging industries in Hearing before the Subcommittee on Monetary and Fiscal Policy of the Joint Economic Committee, *Restoring America's Defense Industrial Base*, 97th Cong., 1st sess. (Washington, DC: U.S. Government Printing Office, 1982). For another attempt to accomplish similar ends see the discussion of H.R. 2057 in Hearings before the House Committee on Banking, Finance, and Urban Affairs, *The Defense Industrial Base Revitalization Act*, 98th Cong., 1st sess. (Washington, DC: U.S. Government Printing Office, 1983). Both measures were strongly opposed in the Senate, and neither was ever passed into law.

[156] Statement by Richard E. Donnelly, Director for Industrial Resources, Office of the Undersecretary of Defense for Research and Engineering, in Hearing before the House Committee on Banking, Finance, and Urban Affairs, *To Amend the Defense Production Act of 1950*, pp. 121, 125.

[157] Statement by Assistant Secretary of Commerce for Trade Administration Lawrence J. Brady, in Ibid., p. 428.

[158] Statement by John D. Morgan, Chief Staff Officer, Bureau of Mines, Department of the Interior, in Ibid., p. 26.

[159] Statement by William S. Long, Deputy Undersecretary of Defense for Acquisitions Management, in Ibid., p. 19. In addition to rejecting the authority and funding that the House sought to grant it, the administration imposed tight new restrictions on *any* use of Defense Production Act funds to encourage expansions in industrial capacity. See testimony of Kevin Boland, General Accounting Office, in Hearing before the Senate Committee on Banking, Housing, and Urban Affairs, *Reextension of the Defense Production Act*, 98th Cong., 1st sess. (Washington, DC: U.S. Government Printing Office, 1983), pp. 122–23.

ment's ability to buy from their overseas competitors, even in cases where foreign suppliers could offer equivalent products at lower prices. Beginning in the early 1980s, "buy American" provisions for a variety of manufactured goods (including everything from machine tools to passenger automobiles) were added to annual Defense Department appropriations bills.[160]

In keeping with its overall approach, the Reagan administration opposed broad procurement preferences on classic free market grounds. Restricting competition would raise costs to the Defense Department and thus to taxpayers. Preference, it was pointed out, amounted to a form of backdoor protectionism that, if it had any long-term effect on domestic producers, would likely reduce the incentive for them to become more efficient and more competitive. Finally, "buy American" provisions risked antagonizing U.S. trading partners and provoking retaliatory action.[161] The administration successfully opposed blanket restrictions, and with more mixed results, it argued that the decision to impose procurement preferences should be left in the hands of the executive branch.[162]

HEIGHTENED IMPORT RESTRICTIONS?

The confluence of strategic and economic trends in the early 1980s could have led to a marked increase in defense protectionism. Fearing that imports were eroding essential industries, and preferring not to place reliance on foreign sources for products that would be vital in any future military mobilization, the executive branch might have resorted to tariffs or quotas to preserve domestic suppliers. With only a handful of exceptions, this did not happen. Not only did the administration refrain from raising import barriers for reasons of national security; it sought actively to discourage the use of such arguments by industry.

Under the terms of section 232 of the 1962 Trade Expansion Act, Congress granted the president the authority to investigate claims that imports were endangering the nation's security and gave him the power to impose restrictions in those cases where he believed a threat to exist.[163] In the eighteen years from 1962 to 1980 there were only ten section 232 investigations, only two of which (both involving oil) led to a positive finding of harm. In its first three years in office, by contrast, the Reagan administration had launched five national secu-

[160] For a list of congressionally mandated procurement restrictions see Department of Defense, *The Impact of Buy American Restrictions Affecting Defense Procurement* (Washington, DC: DoD, July 1989), pp. 18–22. This tendency culminated at the end of the decade in attempts to require that *all* Defense Department purchases be made from American sources. See Hearings before the House Comittee on Banking, Finance, and Urban Affairs, *Defense Production Act Amendments of 1989 (H.R. 486)* (Washington, DC: U.S. Government Printing Office, 1989).

[161] For a summary of these arguments and an assessment of the actual effects of the restrictions imposed during the 1980s, see Department of Defense, *The Impact of Buy American Restrictions*, pp. 35–48.

[162] During the 1980s Congress imposed fourteen new procurement restrictions, and the Office of the Secretary of Defense added another four. As compared to the congressionally mandated preferences, these tended to be narrowly focused, limited in duration, and hedged with an assortment of possible exemptions. Ibid., pp. 24–31.

[163] These provisions were a continuation of those first enacted in 1954. See Groves, "A Brief History."

rity import studies, including, for the first time, one initiated at the request of the Department of Defense.[164]

Already faced with a flood of appeals for protection on other nondefense grounds, the administration moved quickly to close off this potential new avenue of appeal. Elaborate procedures were put in place that tended to slow down the review process and to make it more difficult for claimants to prove that whatever injury they had suffered from imports, there would be inadequate domestic supplies of their product in an emergency.[165] These changes had the desired effect, by the mid-1980s, of sharply slowing the flow of national security import cases. As the Cold War peaked and then wound down, the danger of rampant defense protectionism was thus effectively contained.[166]

---

[164] Early in 1982 the Secretary of Defense requested a study of the threat to national security posed by imports of metal fasteners. This apparent flirtation with overt protectionism was not repeated. For a record of cases and decisions see U.S. Department of Commerce, Bureau of Export Administration, Office of Industrial Resource Administration, *Section 232 Investigations: The Effects of Imports on the National Security* (Washington, DC: DoC, July 1989), pp. 19–22.

[165] According to one participant in the process, after the first few section 232 investigations in the early 1980s, analytical assumptions and models used were changed to make it more difficult to build a national security case for import restrictions. See Richard Levine, "Trade vs. National Security: Section 232 Cases," *Comparative Strategy* 7, no. 2 (1988), pp. 134–39.

[166] Of the six investigations involving manufacturing industries conducted between 1981 and 1989, half were simply dismissed. See "Investigation of Imports of Glass-Lined Chemical Processing Equipment," *Federal Register* 47, no. 53, (March 18, 1982), pp. 11746–54; Department of Commerce, *The Effects of Imports of Nuts, Bolts, and Large Screws on the National Security* (Washington, DC: DoC, February 1983); Department of Commerce, *The Effects of Imports of Plastic Injection Molding Machines on the National Security* (Washington, DC: DoC, January 1989). In each of the remaining cases, evidence was found both that imports were substantially to blame for an ongoing erosion in domestic productive capacity and that supply shortages were likely in an emergency. In two of these instances, however, the administration was able to fashion compromises that offered some relief to industry (and to itself) without the use of tariffs and without any formal invocation of the president's authority to grant protection for reasons of national security. In the case of ferroalloys the government sought to keep some domestic firms alive by paying them to process and upgrade materials held in federal stockpiles. See Department of Commerce, *The Effect of Imports of Chromium, Manganese, and Silicon Ferroalloys and Related Materials on the National Security* (Washington, DC: U.S. Government Printing Office, December 1982). Domestic manufacturers of ball bearings were denied tariff protection but subsequently granted a measure of preference in federal procurements. See Department of Commerce, *The Effect of Imports of Anti-Friction Bearings on the National Security* (Washington, DC: DoC, July 1988); also "Presidential Decision: Anti-Friction Bearing Section 232 National Security Import Investigation," *Federal Register* 54, no. 11 (January 18, 1989), p. 1975. Even in the case of machine tools, the single instance in which an investigation did lead to the imposition of import barriers, great care was taken to avoid setting a precedent that could be exploited by future claimants. Instead of raising tariffs, the administration coerced Japan and Taiwan into imposing "voluntary" restraints on exports of certain types of tools to the United States, and, once again, it refused to invoke its powers under section 232 of the Trade Act. See "Statement on the Machine Tool Industry, May 20, 1986," in *Public Papers of Ronald Reagan, 1986* (bk 1) (Washington, DC: U.S. Government Printing Office, 1988), pp. 632–33. The heated internal debate on this issue (which pitted the Defense and Commerce Departments against the free-trading State Department, NSC, Office of Management and Budget, and the Council of Economic Advisers) is recounted in Clyde Prestowitz, *Trading Places* (New York: Basic Books, 1988), pp. 217–49.

Arms

EXPLAINING THE PRIVATIZATION OF U.S. ARMS PRODUCTION

How, during the Cold War, did the American armed forces come to rely on private entities to design, develop, and build their weapons for them? The answer to this question is not nearly so obvious as it might appear to be at first glance.

Alternative Accounts

TRADITION?

Paying private manufacturers to supply public agencies would certainly seem to be a characteristically American way of doing business. Yet prior to 1945, the U.S. military had always taken care to maintain a high degree of self-reliance. From the time of the Revolutionary War, the Army, with its system of arsenals, and the Navy, with its shipyards, had each preserved a substantial in-house capacity for the development, manufacture, and repair of armaments. In peacetime, the services bought routine items like food and uniforms from industry, but they typically designed and built many, and sometimes all, of their own weapons. The armed services turned to commercial suppliers for a significant fraction of their weapons only in war, when the federal arsenals and shipyards were temporarily incapable of meeting the sheer volume of their demands. As familar and natural as it would subsequently come to seem, the postwar shift toward virtually exclusive reliance on commercial arms makers therefore represented a veritable revolution in peacetime procurement practices.

EFFICIENCY?

Surely private producers were more efficient, more cost-effective, and more innovative than their public sector counterparts. This is certainly what the proponents of private production claimed during the formative early years of the Cold War, and there are good reasons, in retrospect, to think that they were right. But the fact of superior efficency does not in itself explain the triumph of the private producers over the arsenals and shipyards. Efficient institutions do not always win out over their less efficient rivals.

If private producers were more efficient after 1945, they probably also were more so before 1939; yet the pre- and postwar patterns of production were very different. Whatever the truth of the matter may have been, during the 1940s and 1950s concrete evidence of the superiority of the private sector was, as we shall see, surprisingly sparse. Private producers' assertions of greater relative efficiency were subject to challenge on factual grounds, and even if accepted, such claims could conceivably have been trumped by appealing to other, non-economic factors. The defenders of the arsenals and shipyards argued that when properly measured, their performance was not significantly different from that of private manufacturers, and they went on to assert that in any case, there were good strategic reasons for maintaining a large and thriving network of public facilities. The failure of these arguments demands an explanation.

INTERESTS?

The turn from public to private arms production is sometimes explained with reference to a shift in the balance of interest group strength brought about by the Second World War. Prior to the war, low peacetime procurement budgets and the tendency of the military services to rely on their own internal sources of supply combined to suppress the growth of a commercial arms industry. Federal facilities, meanwhile, often employed significant numbers of civilian workers and provided sizable indirect economic benefits to the communities in which they were located. The public arms producers could therefore count on substantial political support whenever their livelihoods were threatened; their fledgling private sector rivals, by contrast, were comparatively small, weak, and vulnerable.

The mobilization that began in the late 1930s led to an enormous expansion in both the public and private (and quasi-private) components of the American arms production system. Because of deliberate decisions taken at its very start, however, the wartime military buildup tended to increase the size, importance, and relative political strength of industry at the expense of the arsenals and shipyards. By the war's end, the United States had a large and thriving commercial arms industry. Many of the firms involved in arms production were eager to return to civilian pursuits as soon as the fighting stopped, but others, especially those manufacturing aircraft and ships, faced uncertain peacetime prospects. As the Cold War got underway, and as it became apparent that defense spending would not return to pre-war levels, firms in these industries pressed hard to be sure that they would get their share of the procurement budget and to head off any possible public sector challenge.[1]

This interest-driven account is plausible, but it leaves a number of questions unanswered. First, the decision to rely so heavily on private producers in wartime was not in itself a foregone conclusion. While this had been the prevailing practice in previous wars, in the late 1930s and early 1940s there were some in the United States government (including President Roosevelt) who were willing at least to consider a much larger public sector role in weapons production. The fact that they did not pursue this option would have important implications for the subsequent course of events.

---

[1] For an argument along these lines, and an excellent overview of the evolution of arms production practices, see Harvey M. Sapolsky, "Equipping the Armed Forces," *Armed Forces and Society* 14, no. 1 (Fall 1987), pp. 113–28.

The mere existence at the end of the Second World War of a group of companies interested in remaining in the arms making business also does not in itself explain their ultimate success in being able to do so. Firms with similar desires had existed after the First World War, but they were, for the most part, quickly displaced by their public sector counterparts. Nor was the public sector noticeably weaker in 1945 than it had appeared in 1918. To the contrary, by the end of the Second World War the government-owned and -operated arms production complex had grown greatly in size, economic importance, and potential political influence. As in previous disputes over procurement practices, the federal arsenals and shipyards could once again claim to have tradition and experience on their side. As the war ended, the future balance of public versus private production remained to be determined, and a return to pre-war patterns could hardly be ruled out.

Finally, the attitudes of the private arms makers towards the government cannot be inferred simply from their commercial status. In some sectors (shipbuilding), public and private producers were direct competitors. In others (aircraft assembly), private companies made extensive use of government-owned facilities and equipment. Not all private producers were equally hostile to government participation in the productive process. Yet in every area, there was a marked postwar movement toward thoroughgoing privatization, at times, ironically, against the wishes of major private actors.

The Role of Ideas and Institutions

The postwar privatization of American arms production was the end result of a protracted process of debate and political struggle. The course of that struggle was determined not only by the emergence of powerful interest groups, but by changes in prevailing ideas and in the roles of key governmental institutions.

IDEAS

At the most general ideological level the burgeoning of anti-statist sentiments in the 1940s and 1950s tended to strengthen the hand of the privatizers and to discredit those who advocated anything that savored of socialism. The peak of the Progressive Era and the depths of the Depression had been marked by an increase in public suspicion of "big business" and by a growing willingness, in some intellectual and political circles, to entertain the possibility of at least a measure of public ownership of the means of production. By the end of the war, however, the polarity of popular sympathies had been reversed. As compared to the 1930s, by the mid-1940s the reputation of government had fallen while that of business was on the rise. Whatever enthusiasm there might once have been for a greatly expanded state role in economic management (and, in particular, for the nationalization of key industries) had largely disappeared.

The ideological character of the emerging competition with communism further reinforced these tendencies. In the context of the Cold War, proposals for expanded state ownership of industrial facilities were susceptible to withering attack on ideological grounds. Moving in this direction, it was claimed, would mean traveling a substantial step toward serfdom. Even the continued legitimacy of traditional federally owned facilities like the armories and navy yards was now open to question. In the superheated ideological atmosphere of the time, the possibility of government competition with industry could easily be made to appear not merely as a question of dollars and cents, but as a matter of life and death.

Popular attitudes on the specific issue of arms production mirrored these more general intellectual trends. In the 1920s and 1930s, commercial munitions manufacturers had been widely reviled as "merchants of death," whose greedy machinations helped drag the nation into an unnecessary and ultimately fruitless war. Between the wars, widespread suspicion of industry's motives and fear of its presumed hidden power worked to the benefit of the government-controlled arsenals and shipyards.

The conduct and conclusion of the Second World War, by contrast, cast the private arms makers in a far more favorable light. American industry could now style itself as the "arsenal of democracy," and the prodigious flood of weapons that it produced was widely credited with having saved the world from fascism. On the other hand, the military ordnance bureaus were subject to criticism for having failed to keep pace with advances in technology before the start of the war and, at least in its early stages, for having sent American men into battle with weapons inferior to those of their opponents.

A third and final intellectual development bolstered the trend toward privatization. The rising reputation of business along with the deepening connections between industry and the armed forces that developed during the Second World War encouraged postwar efforts to apply economic reasoning and modern management techniques to the problems of military procurement. In the 1950s there was much discussion of the need to transform the Department of Defense into "a more efficient, economical, and businesslike . . . organization"; in the 1960s, Secretary of Defense McNamara sought to impose rigorous standards of cost-effectiveness on all of the department's activities.[2]

Detailed objective comparisons of the costs and innovative capacities of the public and private arms producers were comparatively few, and they came toward the end of the process of privatization (in the early 1960s), rather than at its beginning (in the late 1940s). Such studies as there were generally supported the claims of industry at the expense of the arsenals. But, whatever the facts might show, the determination of government officials to be "businesslike" was in itself revealing of a growing belief in the inherent superiority of the private sector. By the 1950s, that belief was deep, widespread, and influential, even if the evidence to support it was not.

---

[2] See Commission on Organization of the Executive Branch of Government, *Business Organization of the Department of Defense* (June 1955), p. xxi.

INSTITUTIONS

After the Second World War, as before, Congress continued to play the pivotal, constitutionally mandated role in determining how the nation would support its army and maintain its navy. While the *form* of congressional participation in shaping the procurement process remained constant, the *content* of its contribution was now the opposite of what it once had been. This shift in institutional preferences reflected the changes in interest group strength and ideological emphasis sketched briefly above. Instead of protecting the old-line arsenals and navy yards, as it had done between the wars, Congress became a powerful proponent of private arms production. Now whenever the military services showed signs of doubt or delay, Congress was there to push them farther, faster down the road toward privatization.

Postwar changes in the organization of the executive branch made a final contribution to this process. The creation and gradual strengthening of the Office of the Secretary of Defense moved power away from the military departments and toward central civilian decision makers. Where the pre-war services had enjoyed considerable autonomy in setting procurement procedures, their Cold War counterparts were subject to a far greater degree of oversight and control. Left to follow their organizational traditions and personal predilections, top Army and Navy officers would have been slower to privatize and more inclined to rely on the vast industrial complexes under their direct control. Intervention from their civilian superiors helped to prevent them from doing so.

To sum up: At the end of the Second World War, the United States had an arms production system that combined privately owned and operated facilities with some that were publicly owned and privately operated, and still others that were both owned and operated by the federal government. During the opening years of the Cold War, the public elements in this system came under attack both from Congress and from the top levels of the executive branch. Although the differences were largely a matter of degree, congressional action was more obviously and immediately motivated by a desire to satisfy the demands of industry, while executive decision makers tended to place great emphasis on their desire for efficiency. Throughout the American government and, indeed, throughout American society, there was also a widely shared and ultimately decisive belief that placing primary reliance on the private sector to produce the nation's arms was good for reasons of political principle as well as of practicality.

Under these combined pressures, the public components of the arms production system shrank while the private portions flourished. By the early 1960s the Army, Air Force, and Navy had all come to rely on arms manufactured (and, for the most part, developed) in facilities operated (and, for the most part, owned) by private industry.[3]

While there are some variations, the story of the first fifteen years of the Cold

---

[3] In the Soviet Union, of course, all arms were developed and produced in state-owned and -operated facilities.

War is basically one of convergence toward the norm of privatization. The next three sections will trace this process in each of the postwar service branches.

NAVY

From John Paul Jones to Pearl Harbor

Prior to the Cold War, the United States had a long and storied history of public naval construction. In 1794 Congress authorized the manufacture of six ships to protect America's coasts and commerce. After some deliberation, President George Washington decided that in the interests of cost and quality control, it would be best if these vessels were assembled directly by agents of the federal government, rather than by private builders working under contract. To spread the benefits as widely as possible, Washington also decided to build each vessel in a different port.[4] By the turn of the century, the Navy Department had established six permanent shipyards at Washington, D.C.; Portsmouth, New Hampshire; Norfolk, Virginia; Boston; New York; and Philadelphia. These were to be the "manufactories, repair-shops, and storehouse of the navy." Despite some temporary closures, all six would remain in service for the next 160 years. Over the course of the nineteenth century another facility was added along the Atlantic seaboard (at Charleston, South Carolina) and, with the expansion of the United States across North America, several more were built on the Gulf and West coasts.[5]

From the establishment of the federal shipyards until the 1880s, there was virtually no peacetime construction of naval vessels in private yards.[6] Between the end of the War of 1812 and the start of the Civil War, 97 of a total of 101 naval vessels procured were built in federal facilities. In wartime, however, the pattern was largely reversed. To achieve a rapid buildup in capabilities (and to compensate for the loss of its Norfolk yard to the Confederacy) the U.S. Navy was forced to lean heavily on private industry. From 1861 to 1865, only 25 percent of over two hundred warships added to the federal fleet were assembled in public yards. After the war, naval construction fell off precipitously, and from the mid-1860s to the mid-1880s, the majority of what little new building there was and most of the money spent repairing and upgrading aging Civil War–era vessels went once again to the navy yards.[7]

[4] On the early years of the Navy and its yards see Charles Oscar Paullin, *Paullin's History of Naval Administration, 1775–1911* (Annapolis, MD: U.S. Naval Institute, 1968), pp. 89–158. See also Leonard D. White, *The Federalists: A Study in Administrative History* (New York: Macmillan, 1948), pp. 160–63.

[5] Paullin, *Paullin's History*, p. 112.

[6] John G. B. Hutchins, *The American Maritime Industries and Public Policy, 1789–1914* (Cambridge: Harvard University Press, 1941), p. 456.

[7] For summary statistics on public versus private naval construction see Michael A. Evanchik, "A Transaction Cost Analysis of Defense Contracting" (Ph.D. dissertation, University of Washington, 1989), p. 226. Regarding the Civil War buildup, see Warren D. Renninger, *Government Policy in*

The three decades prior to the outbreak of the First World War marked the first period of substantial and sustained peacetime procurement of naval vessels from commercial suppliers. By the 1880s the Navy's production facilities had endured almost two decades of minimal work and technical stagnation. In the commercial world, meanwhile, the pace of change had been extraordinarily rapid. As the nineteenth century drew to a close, the major European powers were beginning to exploit the products of the "second industrial revolution" to build steam-powered, steel-hulled ships with big, accurate breech-loading guns.

If the U.S. Navy was to field a world class fleet, replacing its motley flotilla of wooden sailing ships and iron monitors with new battleships and cruisers, it had two basic alternatives: either it could modernize its in-house design and manufacturing capabilities (and, in particular, its capacity to make and use the highest quality steel) or it could hire private firms to do the work. Despite resistance to privatization from the Navy's design and construction bureaus, the size of the investment that would have been necessary to maintain a posture of self-reliance helped tip the balance toward increased use of commercial contractors. Beginning with appropriations authorized in 1882 and with subsequent waves of construction extending to the eve of the First World War, most new naval vessels were built by private industry. The navy yards, meanwhile, concentrated most of their efforts on repairing existing ships.[8]

Although the United States got its "New Navy" and the private shipbuilders made money, the deepening relationship between government and industry was not an entirely happy one. With only two (later three) large firms capable of manufacturing the thick, hardened nickel-steel alloy needed to make ships' armor, there was concern in the Navy and in Congress about price-fixing and excess profits. Progressives and populist congressional Democrats were especially vocal in warning of the depredations of the "armor trust," and in calling for the establishment of a government-owned steel plant and a return to greater reliance on the federal shipyards.[9]

Following Woodrow Wilson's election in 1912, these views began to have an impact on policy. In 1914 Navy Secretary Josephus Daniels requested funds to upgrade the shipbuilding capabilities of six government navy yards and ordered that several new vessels be built in them.[10] When his decision aroused the ire of

---

Aid of American Shipbuilding (Philadelphia: University of Pennsylvania, 1911), pp. 35–37. Postwar procurement and repair policy are discussed in Paullin, *Paullin's History,* pp. 335–86.

[8] These developments are treated at length in Frank M. Bennett, *The Steam Navy of the United States* (1896; reprint Westport, CT: 1972). See also George T. Davis, *A Navy Second to None: The Development of Modern American Naval Policy* (New York: Harcourt, Brace, 1940), pp. 86–196; Robert G. Albion, *Makers of Naval Policy, 1798–1947* (Annapolis, MD: Naval Institute Press, 1980), pp. 178–204.

[9] See Dean C. Allard, Jr., "The Influence of the United States Navy upon the American Steel Industry, 1880–1900" (master's thesis, Georgetown University, 1959).

[10] Harvard University, Graduate School of Business Administration, *The Use and Disposition of Ships and Shipyards at the End of World War II: A Report Prepared for the United States Navy Department and the United States Maritime Commission* (Washington, DC: U.S. Government Printing Office, 1945), p. 202.

the commercial shipmakers, Daniels retorted that "in all matters relating to navy yards my duty is to the Government yards as superior to that of the private yards."[11] Even if the Navy did not build all of its own ships, the fact that it was equipped to do so should, he explained in his 1915 annual report, "have a tendency to secure a reduction in the prices quoted by private shipbuilders." In 1916, in response to Daniels's request, Congress also approved construction of a large steel armor production plant. The purpose of this move, as with the revitalization of the navy yards, was not to reestablish a "monopoly by the Government in the manufacture of munitions," but to provide a check on private industry.[12]

During the relatively brief period of American involvement in the First World War, the majority of new naval vessels were once again built in private yards. But the war also provided the occasion for a revitalization of the federal facilities and, perhaps inevitably, it gave rise to new tensions between government and industry. A series of disputes over contracts and ship design reinforced the suspicions of some naval officers regarding the "purely mercenary nature of the private sector."[13] Once the fighting had stopped, the Navy's design and construction bureaus sought to retain their newfound strength, reversing the trend toward privatization of the late-nineteenth century and regaining a portion of their earlier, preponderant peacetime role in warship design and construction.

Naval planners recognized the importance of a healthy commercial shipbuilding industry to any future mobilization. Nevertheless, with resources increasingly constrained by postwar congressional parsimony and, in the 1920s, by the effects of international arms control agreements, the Navy gave first priority to preserving its own productive base. The eventual result, according to one historian, was a military-industrial complex "without an industrial side," except in the subcontracting of parts. From the mid-1920s to the mid-1930s, "a military-industrial complex did not exist," and "the navy held a clear monopoly" in ship design and construction.[14] With government contracts evaporating, several large commercial shipbuilders were forced to go out of business.

The shift toward greater self-reliance was rooted in the Navy's conception of

[11] Quoted in Henry C. Ferrell, Jr., "Regional Rivalries, Congress, and the MIC: The Norfolk and Charleston Navy Yards, 1913–20," in Benjamin Franklin Cooling, ed., *War, Business, and American Society* (Port Washington, NY: Kennikat Press, 1977), p. 64. According to one account, by 1915 Daniels "had plans for reopening and expanding all the Government navy yards, and called for complete utilization of all existing public facilities." He had "equally ambitious plans for establishing public facilities to provide the Navy with armorplate, fuel, and ordnance." John W. Adams, "The Influences Affecting Naval Shipbuilding Legislation, 1910–1916," *Naval War College Review* 22, no. 4 (December 1969), p. 55.

[12] Quoted in Melvin I. Urofsky, "Josephus Daniels and the Armor Trust," *North Carolina Historical Review* 45, no. 3 (July 1968), p. 261.

[13] Gary E. Weir, *Forged in War: The Naval-Industrial Complex and American Submarine Construction, 1940–1961* (Washington, DC: Naval Historical Center, 1993), p. 2. See also Weir, *Building American Submarines, 1914–1940* (Washington, DC: Naval Historical Center, 1991), pp. 47–59.

[14] Allison W. Saville, "The Naval Military-Industrial Complex, 1918–1941," in Cooling, *War, Business, and American Society*, p. 115.

its organizational interests and responsibilities, but it received a powerful additional impetus from Congress. During the 1920s, complaints of private profiteering in the recent war eventually hardened into accusations that the "merchants of death" had actually conspired to cause the conflict, and that they were working hard to push the world toward another cataclysm. In the United States, the big private shipbuilders, in particular, were alleged to be conspiring to sabotage ongoing international efforts to negotiate deep reductions in naval armaments. These charges were followed by a barrage of muckraking books and newspaper articles, and in the mid-1930s, by protracted congressional hearings.[15]

Proposals for the outright nationalization of the munitions industry were widely discussed in the 1930s but, in the end, they did not make much headway.[16] In the prevailing climate of opinion, however, there was substantial congressional support for legislation designed to strengthen the publicly controlled arms producers and to limit procurement from private sources. Thus, in 1934, when Congress voted the first large increases in naval expenditures since the end of the war, it directed that "the first and each succeeding alternate vessel" of every major class of ship and the "main engines, armor, and armament for such vessels" were to be "constructed or manufactured in the Government navy yards, naval stations, naval gun factories, naval ordnance plants, or arsenals of the United States." The so-called Vinson-Trammel Act also stipulated that 10 percent of all naval aircraft and engines were to be publicly constructed, and for good measure it imposed a limit on the profits that private shipbuilders and plane makers could earn in doing business with the Navy.[17]

The trend toward privatization of naval construction that had appeared to be underway before 1914 was thus substantially undone in the years leading up to the Second World War. Between 1931 and 1941 almost half of all new ship tonnage was produced in government yards.[18] During these years, the Navy took care to maintain its role in designing and building a significant fraction of the most important and technologically advanced classes of ships (see fig. 7.1).[19]

---

[15] See John E. Wiltz, *In Search of Peace: The Senate Munitions Inquiry, 1934–1936* (Baton Rouge: Lousiana State University Press, 1963). Also Earl A. Molander, "Historical Antecedents of Military-Industrial Criticism," *Military Affairs* 40, no. 2 (April 1976), pp. 59–63; Paul A. C. Koistinen, ed., *The Military-Industrial Complex: A Historical Perspective* (New York: Praeger, 1980), pp. 47–67. For an influential statement of the case against the arms makers, see Philip Noel-Baker, *The Private Manufacture of Armaments* (London: Victor Gollancz, 1936).

[16] The pressure was sufficiently strong, however, that in 1935 the State Department sent a detailed analysis of the problem to President Roosevelt. Wiltz, *In Search of Peace.* p. 94.

[17] For the text of the bill, see Michael Allen West, "Laying the Legislative Foundation: The House Naval Affairs Committee and the Construction of the Treaty Navy, 1926–1934" (Ph.D. dissertation, Ohio State University, 1980), pp. 542–45. Regarding the connection between the munitions industry hearings and the restrictive provisions of the Vinson-Trammel Act, see Gary E. Weir, "Coming Up to Speed in American Submarine Construction, 1938–1943," *War and Society* 11, no. 2 (October 1993), p. 81.

[18] Figures derived from a table in H. Gerrish Smith and L. C. Brown, "Shipyard Statistics," in F. G. Fassett, Jr., ed., *The Shipbuilding Industry in the United States* (New York: Society of Naval Architects and Marine Engineers, 1948), pp. 199–200.

[19] Saville, "The Naval Military-Industrial Complex," pp. 108–111.

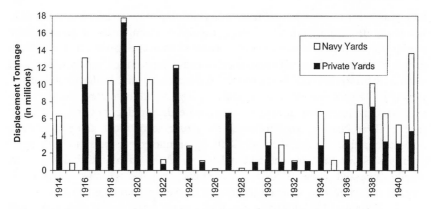

Figure 7.1. Public versus Private Construction of Naval Vessels, 1914–1941

Mobilization

Starting in 1940, the United States made rapid and dramatic additions to its shipbuilding capabilities. Virtually all of this expanded capacity was federally financed, much of it was government owned, and a significant fraction was government operated. In addition to enlarging and improving the existing complex of Navy yards, the government paid for the construction of new shipbuilding facilities, some of which were then leased to industry, while others were operated by private corporations working under contract.[20]

At the time of the attack on Pearl Harbor, there were eight navy yards and twenty-four privately owned shipyards in the United States; by V-J Day another ninety-nine yards had been added. At the war's end, the federal government owned outright an additional twenty contractor operated yards in addition to its major pre-war yards, it was joint owner with industry of twenty more contractor operated facilities, and it owned a significant share of the land and equipment being used in twenty more "private" shipyards.[21] By 1944, according to one

---

[20] All told, roughly one-third of the nation's total wartime investment in shipbuilding went into the Navy yards and one-half went to pay for facilities that were government owned but contractor operated. Less than 10 percent of new capacity was privately financed; the remainder was paid for by the government and leased to industry. For an overview of the wartime expansion in industrial capacity see George Vincent Sweeting, "Building the Arsenal of Democracy: The Government's Role in Expansion of Industrial Capacity, 1940 to 1945" (Ph.D. dissertation, Columbia University, 1994), figures for the shipbuilding program derived from pp. 246–50, 260–61, and 269. See also Robert H. Connery, *The Navy and the Industrial Mobilization in World War II* (Princeton: Princeton University Press, 1951), pp. 344–65; Robert G. Albion and Robert H. Connery, *Forrestal and the Navy* (New York: Columbia University Press, 1962), pp. 59–82; Bartholomew H. Sparrow, *From the Outside In: World War II and the American State* (Princeton: Princeton University Press, 1996), pp. 161–257.

[21] Smith and Brown, "Shipyard Statistics," pp. 163–64. Starting in 1939, the number of building berths, or shipways, capable of manufacturing vessels of over three hundred feet in length had risen from 119 to 614. Of these, at war's end, 49 were in the Navy yards, 349 were in government-

estimate, the dollar value of Navy-owned industrial facilities exceeded the combined assets of General Motors, United States Steel, and American Telephone and Telegraph.[22] At the peak of the wartime mobilization, in the summer of 1943, over 1.7 million civilians were at work in shipbuilding facilities around the country. Of these, over 350,000 were employed directly in the navy yards.[23]

The Navy's role in building the big ships that were the heart of its fighting fleet was even larger than the raw figures would seem to suggest. Most of the activity in the government owned/contractor operated yards, and much in the purely private yards as well, involved the production of large numbers of cargo and transport vessels and of relatively small and simple combatants, such as destroyers, frigates, and mine layers. Major combatants, on the other hand, were built in a handful of private yards and in the traditional navy yards. Three navy yards and three large private yards built the nation's battleships, two navy yards and three private yards assembled aircraft carriers, and two navy yards and six private yards were involved in the construction of cruisers.[24] During the war, there were a total of five prime contractors for submarines: the navy yards at Portsmouth, New Hampshire, and Mare Island, California, and three yards operated by commercial shipbuilding concerns.[25]

By the end of the Second World War, in short, the Navy owned a large and technologically sophisticated array of ship manufacturing facilities. Depending on how much new construction was required once hostilities had ended, some analysts estimated that the Navy might even have sufficient capacity to become completely independent of private producers.[26] This fact, as an influential government-sponsored survey of the shipbuilding industry pointed out in June 1945, raised an obvious question for postwar policy makers: "Should ships for the Navy be built in private yards in peacetime, and, if so, to what extent? The answer to this question," the report concluded with some understatement, "will

---

owned/contractor-operated "emergency yards," and the remaining 216 were in private shipyards. For wartime growth figures see Harvard University, *The Use and Disposition of Ships*, p. 180. Regarding the postwar distribution of shipways, see James W. Culliton, "Economics and Shipbuilding," in Fassett, *The Shipbuilding Business*, p. 12.

[22] Sparrow, *From the Outside In,* p. 162.

[23] Hearings before the Seapower Subcommittee of the House Armed Services Committee, *Current Status of Shipyards*, 93d Cong., 2d sess. (Washington, DC: U.S. Government Printing Office, 1974), p. 27.

[24] See table in Smith and Brown, "Shipyard Statistics," p. 134.

[25] Weir, *Forged in War*, pp. 7–35.

[26] Estimates of likely postwar construction requirements ranged from a low of fifty merchant ships and one Navy vessel per year to a high of seventy-five merchant ships and twenty Navy vessels, the last figure being the number of warships constructed in 1937. The Navy yards alone were deemed capable of carrying out the first program and building 80 percent of the ships in the second without any help from private industry. The Navy yards and the government-owned/contractor-operated (GOCO) "emergency yards" together could build six times the number of ships in the maximum program without contracting out to privately owned and operated facilities. See Harvard University, *The Use and Disposition of Ships*, pp. 186–87.

be important to the owners of many of the private yards because it may mean the difference between staying in business and going out of business."[27]

Privatization

INITIAL PREFERENCES AND ULTIMATE OUTCOMES

The Navy's preferred approach to warship procurement during the opening years of the Cold War was essentially what it had been in the interwar period and, indeed, since 1914. Following the surrender of Japan (and with only a brief interruption during the Korean conflict) the Navy proceeded quickly to sell, lease, or mothball the productive capacity that it had accumulated outside its own yards since 1940.[28] As before the war, the navy yards themselves were to be the main locus for repairs and overhauls. Contracts for new ship construction and for conversion of old vessels to newer types through the addition of modern weapons and equipment were to be distributed between private and public yards. Navy planners would assign contracts, as they saw fit, on a year-by-year basis. As the Chief of the Bureau of Ships explained to Congress in 1953, the Navy sought to "spread [its work] out among what might be called the better shipbuilders, including the naval shipyards, in order to give them a continuity of work, so that they are in a position to keep together their design talents . . . and their production talents."[29] The aim of this policy was to preserve the Navy's core capacities while at the same time to help keep industry healthy, thereby maintaining "a ready additional source of shipbuilding facilities and know-how for the Nation should emergency arise."[30]

The 1950s and early 1960s saw an increasingly intense and politicized struggle over how the Navy should allocate its business between public and com-

---

[27] Ibid., p. 201.

[28] The Navy initially retained twenty-five war-built yards and maintained its facilities in twelve privately owned yards. See James A. Cook, *The Marketing of Surplus War Property* (Washington, DC: Public Affairs Press, 1948), pp. 39–40. By the mid-1950s, the Navy continued to own and operate a total of ten shipyards; it had leased another thirty-two facilities to industry (only twenty-three of which continued in use as shipyards) and retained six more on inactive status. See Report to the Congress by the Commission on Organization of the Executive Branch of the Government, *Report on Real Property Management* (Washington, DC: U.S. Government Printing Office, 1955), p. 67.

[29] Statement by Rear Adm. Homer Wallin, Chief, Bureau of Ships, Hearings before the Subcommittee of the Senate Committee on Appropriations, *Department of Defense Appropriations for 1954*, 83d Cong., 1st sess. (Washington, DC: U.S. Government Printing Office, 1953), p. 1793.

[30] Statement by Rear Adm. Bernard Manseau, Acting Chief, Bureau of Ships, Hearings before the Subcommittee of the Senate Committee on Appropriations, *Department of Defense Appropriations for 1955*, 83d Cong., 2d sess. (Washington, DC: U.S. Government Printing Office, 1954), p. 647. See also statement by Rear Adm. Homer Wallin, Chief, Bureau of Ships, Hearings before the Subcommittee of the Senate Committee on Appropriations, *Department of Defense Appropriations for 1953*, 82d Cong., 2d sess. (Washington, DC: U.S. Government Printing Office, 1952), p. 1171. See also Ellis B. Garner, Jr., "Problems and Prospects of the United States Shipbuilding Industry," *Naval War College Review* 24, no. 2 (October 1971), p. 15.

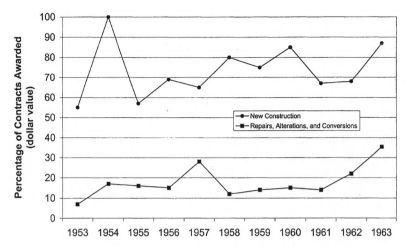

Figure 7.2. The Increasing Dominance of the Private Shipyards, 1953–1963

mercial facilities. The outcome of this controversy was a clear victory for private industry. Over the course of slightly more than a decade, the private shipbuilders were able to corner the market for new construction contracts, and to command an increasing share of the repair and conversion work that had once been almost the exclusive preserve of the public navy yards (see fig. 7.2).[31] How was this victory attained?

PRESSURES FOR PRIVATIZATION

It is important to note at the outset that the shift toward industry was not driven primarily by objective calculations of relative cost. At the end of the Second World War a Harvard Business School study noted the "absence of accounting evidence" to sustain the view that private yards were necessarily cheaper than their public counterparts.[32] It was not until the early 1960s that such comparisons were attempted, and even then there was considerable disagreement over the results. Although the Navy did eventually concede that new ships could probably be built more cheaply in private yards, it never accepted the view that its own facilities were less efficient in every respect than those of private industry. Moreover, as Navy officials explained repeatedly to their critics, there were factors other than cost to be taken into account, including the desire to preserve essential skills in both the public and private sectors while maintaining the broadest possible mobilization base and ensuring the existence of shipyards within easy reach of both the Atlantic and the Pacific fleets.[33] As their cham-

---

[31] See table in Hearings before the Subcommittee of the Senate Committee on Appropriations, *Department of Defense Appropriations for 1964*, 88th Cong., 1st sess. (Washington, DC: U.S. Government Printing Office, 1963), p. 1360.

[32] Harvard University, *The Use and Disposition of Ships*, p. 203.

[33] See the 1953 remarks of Navy Secretary Robert B. Anderson, in Tom Paul Emerich, "The

pions pointed out, the navy yards, unlike their commercial competitors, also could not "decline to accept work" or "be paralyzed by strikes."[34]

Despite the ambiguity of the available evidence on costs, the various arguments that could be marshaled in favor of the public producers, and the clear preference of top naval officers for maintaining a high degree of self-reliance and maximum flexibility in making procurement decisions, the Navy nevertheless found itself forced increasingly into the arms of industry. The proximate source of the pressure for privatization was the Congress, which was responding, in turn, to appeals from business interests and, more generally, to the prevailing ideological climate.

The close of the Second World War found the federal government in possession of a vast portfolio of manufacturing assets, not only in shipbuilding and other directly military fields, but in major supporting industries such as steel, synthetic rubber, and aluminum. Under the watchful eye of Congress and the few large corporations that dominated each of these industries, the executive branch quickly disposed of the great bulk of its holdings in these clearly commercial sectors.[35] Despite the big postwar sell-off, by the early 1950s the federal government as a whole, and the Department of Defense in particular, continued to own (and, in many cases, to operate) a dizzying assortment of what were described as "commercial- and industrial-type facilities." According to one authoritative 1954 survey, the Defense Department owned more than 2,500 such facilities in forty-seven different categories, including clothing, paint, ice cream, and chain manufacturing, bakeries, sawmills, and meat cutting plants, and watch, car, shoe, and tire repair.[36]

The end of the Korean War brought a second wave of agitation for privatization, this one propelled more by the concerns of the many smaller firms in this wide assortment of industries. In 1953 Congress began an extended series of investigations into "government competition with private enterprise" and ordered the formation of a Commission on Organization of the Executive Branch of the Government, to be chaired by former president Herbert Hoover.[37] The so-

---

United States' Shipbuilding Industry and National Policy" (Ph.D. dissertation, Georgetown University, 1955), p. 105.

[34] See remarks of Rear Adm. R. K. James, Chief, Bureau of Ships, quoted in Hearings before the Subcommittee of the Senate Committee on Appropriations, *Department of Defense Appropriations for 1963*, 87th Cong., 2d sess. (Washington, DC: U.S. Government Printing Office, 1962), p. 1574.

[35] See Frederick J. Dobney, "Evolution of a Reconversion Policy: World War II and Surplus War Property Disposal," *Historian* 36 (May 1974), pp. 498–519; Louis Cain and George Neumann, "Planning for Peace: The Surplus Property Act of 1944," *Journal of Economic History* 41, no. 1 (March 1981), pp. 129–35.

[36] See Report to the Congress by the Commission on Organization of the Executive Branch of the Government, *Business Enterprises* (Washington, DC: U.S. Government Printing Office, 1955), p. 1.

[37] The centers of congressional activity on this issue were the Senate Select Committee on Small Business and the House and Senate Committees on Government Operations. The various hearings on the subject are filled with the complaints of small business owners. See, for example, the four volumes of Hearings before a Subcommittee of the House Committee on Government Operations, *Investigation into Commercial and Industrial-Type Activities in the Federal Government*. 83d Cong., 1st sess. (Washington, DC: U.S. Government Printing Office, 1953). The evolution of congressional interest in this subject is traced in a Study Prepared by the Staff of the Senate Committee

called second Hoover Commission highlighted the problem of government ownership and cast the issue in broad historical and ideological perspective. Most government-owned "business-type enterprises" had been established during emergencies and, in particular, during the two world wars and the Depression. Because of the "normal rigidities that are a part of Government," state-owned enterprises lacked the "initiative, ingenuity, [and] inventiveness" that are "the genius of the private enterprise system" and could not be expected to produce the same "excellent results." Nevertheless, because "their personnel and the citizens in the communities where they operate resist termination," many "continue to function long after the original need has passed and even though [their] operation . . . is not in the public interest." To the maximum extent feasible, the Commission concluded, the federal government should divest itself of its "business-type" holdings. "The burden of proof in all instances must be on the Government. Unjustified continuance is a definite injury to the vitality of the whole private enterprise system."[38]

These sentiments found a sympathetic audience in the Eisenhower White House. Budget Bureau Director Rowland Hughes regarded extensive government ownership as unacceptable in "a country which is the citadel and the world's principal exponent of private enterprise and individual initiative."[39] In his first budget message in January 1954, President Eisenhower announced "the beginning of a movement to shift . . . to private enterprise Federal activities which can be more appropriately and efficiently carried on in that way." This was followed, in short order, by a Budget Bureau circular requiring the executive branch agencies to catalog their "commercial-industrial" holdings, selling wherever possible and justifying their actions when they did not.[40]

The possibility that government-owned facilities might be able to perform certain tasks at lower cost than private operators was specifically disallowed as justification for their continued operation. As a 1956 Budget Bureau directive explained, federal facilities did not have to pay taxes, "thereby keeping costs down" and giving them an unfair advantage. More important was the matter of principle: "Above all, the decision whether to continue or discontinue a Government activity solely on an apparent cost basis runs counter to our concept that the Government has ordinarily no right to compete in a private enterprise economy."[41]

For the Defense Department, satisfying the complaints of small business was relatively easy. Within a few years, the armed services had sold off hundreds of the small manufacturing facilities that they had acquired since the start of the Second World War.[42] But the push for privatization, and the ideological lan-

---

on Government Operations, *Government Competition with Private Enterprise*, 88th Cong., 1st sess. (Washington, DC: U.S. Government Printing Office, 1963).

[38] *Business Enterprises*, pp. xi–xiii.

[39] December 7, 1954, speech quoted *ibid.*, p. xviii.

[40] These executive branch actions are discussed in *Government Competition with Private Enterprise*, pp. 316–17.

[41] Budget Bureau memorandum to the president, October 1956, quoted ibid., p. 320.

[42] Ibid., pps. 319, 327.

guage in which it was couched, also raised troubling questions about the legitimacy of the military's larger-scale industrial activities, even those with long traditions. In the context of a worldwide contest with communism, private ownership of the means of production came to be regarded not only as more practical and efficient, but as morally superior to any alternative form of economic organization. If this was the case, however, continued government ownership of arsenals, shipyards, and aircraft factories would be extremely difficult to justify.

The policies of the Navy were especially open to challenge in this regard, for it was the public navy yards that competed most obviously and directly with existing privately owned businesses. As the Hoover Commission noted in 1955, since the end of the war the Navy had exhibited a "tendency . . . to achieve self-sufficiency" in "construction of new vessels and in ship repair and conversions." Navy facilities now employed over half of the nation's shipyard workers, and the "serious competition" that they created was further weakening the private yards. The Commission concluded that continued operation of all of the exising navy yards represented "a destructive intrusion into the private shipbuilding industry of this country," and it recommended further study of "the effect on the private shipbuilding industry of the construction and repair of naval vessels in Government shipyards."[43]

Within a few years of the Hoover Commission report, the shipbuilding industry had begun to lobby Congress to force a change in Navy policy. Traditionally high U.S. labor costs plus the reconstruction and modernization of commercial yards in Japan and Western Europe combined after the Second World War to constrict the overseas market for American-built ships. As the 1950s wore on, domestic manufacturers found themselves ever more dependent on the federal government for their survival. In keeping with its general policy of doing what it could to help the private yards, the Navy's Bureau of Ships assigned them an increasing fraction of its new construction contracts. But strict limitations on overall defense spending, a national military strategy that favored nuclear over conventional forces, and the rising technological complexity and cost of each individual ship meant that there was not a great deal of business to be had. By the end of the decade, with the number and dollar value of new ship orders from the Navy and other customers at a post-Korea low, the industry had arrived at a moment of crisis (see fig. 7.3).[44]

[43] *Business Enterprises*, pp. 10–11.

[44] See the figures in James R. McCaul, "The Shipbuilding Industry in the United States," in Center for Maritime Studies, *Improving the Prospects for United States Shipbuilding* (Glen Cove, NY: Webb Institute for Naval Architecture, 1969), pp. 11–13. For an overview of what he calls the "long-term decline" of the American shipbuilding industry see Clinton H. Whitehurst, Jr., *The U.S. Shipbuilding Industry: Past, Present, and Future* (Annapolis, MD: Naval Institute Press, 1986), pp. 1–31. Also, Clark G. Reynolds, "American Maritime Power since World War II," in Robert A. Kilmarx, ed., *America's Maritime Legacy: A History of the U.S. Merchant Marine and Shipbuilding Industry since Colonial Times* (Boulder, CO: Westview Press, 1979), pp. 215–54; Edward G.

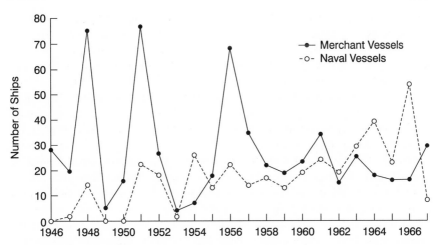

Figure 7.3. Naval and Merchant Vessels Ordered from Private Yards, 1946–1967. (1,000 Gross Tons or Larger)

The major private shipmakers responded to their worsening plight by launching what one Navy officer described bitterly as an "advertising campaign" to "discredit the naval shipyards" and to win for themselves the maximum possible share of ship repair and construction work.[45] The ensuing debate over procurement policy pitted the big shipmakers and the representatives of the states and districts in which their facilities were located against the Navy, the public yard employee unions, and *their* political allies.

Both sides produced figures purporting to prove their superior efficency. When an industry-sponsored study concluded that, in aggregate and on average, the private yards were cheaper than the navy yards, the civilian employees of the Norfolk Naval Shipyard responded with charts and graphs to support their contention, that once "all costs are considered and fair comparisons are made," the public yards appeared in a "surprisingly . . . favorable light."[46]

For its part, the Navy admitted that largely because the private yards were freer to hire and fire employees, "on a straight competitive dollar-for-dollar basis" they might have the advantage in new ship construction.[47] In this area,

Sanders, "The U.S. Shipbuilding Industry: A Case Study in the Economics of Government Procurement" (Ph.D. dissertation, Yale University, 1969).

[45] See a June 2, 1961, speech by Rear Adm. R. K. James, Chief, Bureau of Ships, "The Case for the Naval Shipyards," reprinted in *Department of Defense Appropriations for 1963*, pp. 1628–31.

[46] Study by the certified public accounting firm of Ernst and Ernst quoted by Edwin M. Hood, President, Shipbuilders Council of America and statement by Frank H. Wright, Quarterman's and Leadingmen's Association, Portsmouth, VA, both ibid., pps. 1568, 1577.

[47] See testimony of Rear Adm. R. K. James, Chief, Bureau of Ships, Hearings before a Subcommittee of the House Committee on Appropriations, *Department of Defense Appropriations for 1963*, pt. 4 *Procurement*, 87th Cong., 2d sess. (Washington, DC: U.S. Government Printing Office, 1962), p. 295. In 1961 Admiral James had been willing to admit only that "in the past few years" the cost

the Secretary of the Navy acknowledged to Congress, "perhaps private yards do appear at least to have a greater degree of efficiency in comparision to Government yards, [although] . . . the evidence is not clear."[48] But the Navy was already directing a high percentage of its construction contracts to industry and could not do much more without going out of the shipbuilding business altogether. As regards repairs and conversions, the navy yards were roughly comparable to industry in cost, and they had real, noneconomic advantages, such as their location and proximity to barracks for housing crew members while their ships were being overhauled.[49]

Whatever the merits of their case, the private shipbuilders had a number of raw political advantages. Although neither employed huge numbers of workers, by the early 1960s the private shipyards had roughly 30 percent more civilian employees (and potential voters) than did the navy yards.[50] More important, while there were only 11 major public facilities in nine states, in 1962 the private firms involved in naval construction and repair were divided into 155 facilities distributed among twenty-four states. Almost all the states and many of the congressional districts that housed a federal navy yard also had private shipyards, thereby diluting support for public construction. On the other hand, many states with no navy yards (including New Jersey, Ohio, Maryland, Florida, Illinois, Texas, and Louisiana) had private shipyards eager to obtain Navy business. The representatives of these states tended to be among the strongest supporters of privatization.[51]

Most members of Congress, of course, had no direct stake in shipbuilding. In seeking their support and in attempting to undermine their sympathy for the navy yards, the commercial shipbuilders had a final, decisive advantage. The proponents of privatization were relentless in portraying themselves as the defenders of "free enterprise," and ruthless in painting their opponents as the self-interested beneficiaries of a system that was archaic, if not downright un-American. "The Nation's shipyard complex exists half free and half nationalized, in contradiction to our free, competitive economic system," warned the president of the Shipbuilders Council of America in 1962. "Private enterprise is the cornerstone of our creative economy, and we therefore advocate that a

---

of building new ships had been "generally higher in naval shipyards than in private shipyards." He attributed this in part to the distressed state of the industry and predicted that once conditions improved, prices would rise. See his testimony in Hearings before a Special Subcommittee on Utilization of Naval Shipyard Facilities of the House Armed Services Committee, *Utilization of Naval Shipyard Facilities*, 87th Cong., 1st sess. (Washington, DC: U.S. Government Printing Office, 1961), pp. 2701–2.

[48] Secretary of the Navy Fred Korth, in *Department of Defense Appropriations for 1963*, pt. 4, p. 1558.

[49] Ibid., p. 1556.

[50] In 1961 there were roughly 96,000 civilian workers in the naval shipyards versus 122,000 in the private shipyards. *Current Status of Shipyards*, p. 27.

[51] Lists for FY 1963–65 are contained in Hearings before a Subcommittee of the House Committee on Appropriations, *Department of Defense Appropriations for 1966*, pt. 3, *Secretary of Defense*, 89th Cong., 1st sess. (Washington, DC: U.S. Government Printing Office, 1965), pp. 734–42.

larger share of naval ship work . . . be placed with private shipyards."[52] "I am frankly appalled by the size of the Government-owned naval shipyard complex," thundered Texas Senator John Tower. "It escapes me how this country which is trying to convince the rest of the world of the dangers and defects of Socialist ideologies permits the perpetuation of this gigantic contradiction of the American way of life." The United States should disband its "socialized shipyard facilities," Tower concluded, and reserve "all naval shipwork for private shipyards."[53]

In the face of such rhetoric, the defenders of the navy yards could appeal to tradition, attack industry for its greed and lack of commercial competitiveness, and make the often complex case for their own special capabilities and virtues; but they seemed to recognize that the deck was heavily stacked against them. The "so-called private shipbuilding industry," as one spokesman for the Philadelphia naval shipyard described it with considerable frustration, was, in fact, already heavily dependent on government subsidies. "It is antiquated, unprogressive, and cannot compete" with foreign shipbuilders. Instead of modernizing, industry appealed to the government for help. "Over the years, these cries . . . have caused the Navy to give more and more of its new construction to private shipyards. . . . Having gobbled up the new construction it now wants the repair and conversion work." Despite their evident failings, the private shipbuilders had succeeded brilliantly in gaining the ideological high ground: they presented themselves to Congress as "the representatives of dynamic free enterprise and the defenders of what all good Americans hold dear" and cast the public shipyards as "the 'bad guys.' We are against home, mother, and freedom. They go home with the money."[54]

The accuracy of this summation is indicated by the course of events. In 1962, over the Navy's objections, Congress passed a law requiring that 35 percent of the annual budget for ship conversions and repairs be placed with private industry. This was considerably less than the 75 percent that some industry spokesmen had been demanding, but it still represented a substantial reallocation of resources. In two years the dollar value of industry contracts for repairs and conversions shot up by a factor of four, and the private share of all such work more than doubled, from 14 percent in 1961 to over 35 percent in 1963.[55] Turning a deaf ear to the Navy and the Defense Department, Congress reaffirmed its decision in 1963 and again in 1964.

A congressionally mandated transfusion of federal funds helped to keep industry alive, but only at the expense of the health of the public sector. As

[52] Edwin Hood, in *Department of Defense Appropriations for 1963*, pt. 4, p. 1570–71.

[53] Tower letter to Senator Richard Russell, in *Department of Defense Appropriations for 1964*, pp. 1380–81.

[54] See statement of Lewis Bogdanoff, Vice President of the Joint Committee for Yard Development, Philadelphia Naval Shipyard, ibid., pp. 1382–85.

[55] See table in Hearings before Subcommittee of the Senate Appropriations Committee, *Department of Defense Appropriations for 1965*, pt. 2, 88th Cong., 2d sess. (Washington, DC: U.S. Government Printing Office, 1964), p. 589.

activity in the navy yards diminished, it became more difficult to justify the costs of keeping all of them open. In 1964, Secretary of Defense McNamara ordered a review of the existing naval shipyard complex.[56] The findings of the so-called Shipyard Policy Board provided the basis for a compromise with Congress: the Navy would continue to allocate a high percentage of new construction (on the order of 80 percent annually) to industry and it would close two of its beloved shipyards. In return, Congress would drop its requirement that a fixed portion of repairs and conversions be performed by industry. Recognizing that the public and private sectors could do such work "with essentially equal efficiency" and that the remaining naval shipyards "must be maintained for strategic and operational reasons," the Navy argued that it should once again be free to allocate these contracts as it saw fit.[57]

In 1965 and 1966 the Defense Department instructed the Navy to close both its major fleet repair facility at San Diego and its New York shipyard. In 1967 Congress agreed to lift the repair allocation requirement, but only after the Defense Department had issued a general instruction to all the armed services ordering them to place roughly 30 percent of maintenance work with industry.[58] Within a year the Navy also began to allocate all of its contracts for new construction with commercial shipyards.[59] By the end of the 1960s, for the first time in over half a century, the United States Navy was no longer in the business of building its own warships.

ARMY

Origins of the Arsenal System

By the end of the Second World War the United States Army, like its sister service, had 150 years of accumulated experience in arms manufacturing. As with naval vessels, so also with the implements of land warfare, the federal government tended to rely heavily on its own productive capacities in peacetime, turning to industry on a substantial scale only when the nation was at war.

[56] The composition and mission of the shipyard "study group" is described by Secretary of the Navy Paul Nitze in Hearings before Subcommittee of the Senate Appropriations Committee, *Department of Defense Appropriations for 1965*, pt. 1, *Procurement*, 88th Cong., 2d sess. (Washington, DC: U.S. Government Printing Office, 1964), pps. 525, 579–80. See also Jack Raymond, "McNamara Plans $68 Million Cuts in Installations," *New York Times* (April 25, 1964), p. A1.

[57] Regarding the rationale for yard closures and elimination of the 65 to 35 ratio see testimony of Secretary of the Navy Paul Nitze in Hearings before a Subcommittee of the House Appropriations Committee, *Department of Defense Appropriations for 1966*, pt. 3, *Secretary of Defense*, pp. 728–29. Regarding new ship construction see Rear Adm. W. A. Brockett, Chief, Bureau of Ships, in Hearings before a Subcommittee of the House Appropriations Committee, *Department of Defense Appropriations for 1966*, pt. 2, *Operation and Maintenance*, p. 302.

[58] These events are reviewed in *Current Status of Shipyards*, pp. 1–17.

[59] According to a review by the Naval Ship Systems Command, starting in 1968 "all of the Navy's new construction work" was assigned to industry. Ibid., p. 91. One account dates the shift to decisions taken in 1967. See Clinton H. Whitehurst, Jr., "Is There a Future for Naval Shipyards?" *U.S. Naval Institute Proceedings* (April 1978), pp. 31–32.

In 1794, following a conflict in which American forces had been compelled to use arms captured from the British, imported from France, or purchased in small lots from an assortment of private gunsmiths, Congress authorized the president to establish two national armories.[60] The first of these, located in Springfield, Massachusetts, began production of muskets in 1795; the second, at Harpers Ferry, Virginia, was founded in 1796. Two years later, worried about the possibility of war with France and by the still limited output of the two federal facilities, Congress appropriated funds for the purchase of small arms, ammunition, and artillery pieces from private manufacturers. The contractors often failed to produce weapons that met government specifications, and in many cases did not succeed in producing any weapons at all. Their poor performance led, after the War of 1812, to a further expansion in the government arsenal system, and to the creation of a central Ordnance Department to oversee the activities of both the public and private arms producers. By 1816 there were a total of five federal arsenals in operation, two making small arms (Springfield and Harpers Ferry) and three more (at Watertown, Massachusetts; Watervliet, New York; and Frankford, Pennsylvania) occupied mainly with the manufacture of ammunition.[61]

Over the next three decades the Ordnance Department devoted itself to pursuing the holy grail of interchangeability, developing tools, gauges, and production methods so precise and uniform that all weapons of the same model would be virtually identical, no matter where each had been manufactured. Once its armories had achieved this goal, in the 1840s, the Army became increasingly self-reliant, producing most of the shoulder arms it needed and purchasing relatively small numbers of other weapons (including pistols and artillery pieces) from private concerns. For the remainder of the century, writes one historian, "large scale contracting came to an end, except for a temporary revival during the Civil War."[62]

At the start of that war the federal armories scrambled to increase production while at the same time assisting private contractors in their efforts to convert to the manufacture of standard issue weapons. With the loss of Harpers Ferry, the Springfield Armory became the central site for construction of shoulder arms. Between 1861 and 1865, one-quarter of all such weapons (and over half of all

[60] The term "arsenal" is sometimes used to describe those places where arms are *stored* and "armory" to refer to places where weapons are *manufactured*. I will use the terms interchangeably here to refer to federal arms production facilities.

[61] With the destruction of Harpers Ferry during the Civil War, and the subsequent construction of two more arsenals (Picatinny and Rock Island), by the twentieth century the Army had a total of six.

[62] Felicia J. Deyrup, "Arms Makers of the Connecticut Valley: A Regional Study of the Economic Development of the Small Arms Industry, 1798–1870," *Smith College Studies in History* (1948), p. 117. On the evolution of the private arms makers see Robert A. Howard, "Interchangeable Parts Reexamined: The Private Sector of the American Arms Industry on the Eve of the Civil War," *Technology and Culture* 19, no. 4 (October 1978), pp. 633–49. On relations between government and industry immediately before and during the war see Deyrup, "Arms Makers," pp. 177–208.

standard-issue rifled muskets) were built at Springfield.[63] Private contractors made the rest, along with all of the gunpowder, revolvers, artillery pieces, and other weapons that the government had not manufactured before the war.[64]

After the South's surrender, federal procurement fell precipitously, existing contracts were terminated, and the war-bloated private firearms industry began a long and painful period of contraction. With government storage depots overflowing with Civil War–era weapons, Congress saw little need for additional purchases. Except for a handful of contracts for experimental breech-loading rifles, the Army once again virtually ceased to do business with commercial arms makers. The peacetime pattern first established in the years before the war was thus restored. "To all intents and purposes," writes Merrit Roe Smith, "the government discontinued the contract system and it would not reappear until the eve of World War I."[65]

The Army's ties to industry actually grew even more attenuated at the close of the nineteenth century and the beginning of the twentieth. Where the Navy had turned to the private sector in the 1880s to meet its rapidly increasing demands for steel armor, guns, and ships, the Army, whose needs (and resources) were considerably more modest, created a new in-house capability for cannon construction.[66] After the Spanish-American War (which was short enough to preclude the possibility of major industrial mobilization, but long enough to reveal serious flaws in the Army's weapons and supply system), the Ordnance Department received additional funds. These it applied to developing a new standard rifle, expanding capacity for its production, and, for the first time, building a federal factory for the manufacture of smokeless gunpowder. In the years leading up to the outbreak of the First World War, "government manufacture of small arms as well as most artillery became the general rule, and . . . the art of ordnance-making in America was chiefly contained within the government establishments."[67] The Army "neglected private producers, concentrated on modernizing its own manufacturing facilities," and, until shortly be-

---

[63] See the discussion in Michael S. Raber, "Conservative Innovators, Military Small Arms, and Industrial History at Springfield Armory, 1794–1918," *Industrial Archaeology* 14, no. 1 (1988), pp. 13–15.

[64] James A. Huston, *The Sinews of War: Army Logistics, 1775–1953* (Washington, DC: Office of the Chief of Military History, 1966), p. 178.

[65] Merrit Roe Smith, "Military Arsenals and Industry before World War I," in Cooling, *War, Business, and American Society*, p. 36. On post–Civil War developments see also Deyrup, "Arms Makers," pp. 209–16. For an overview of the industry in the 1880s see a report to the Department of the Interior by Charles H. Fitch, *Report on the Manufacture of Fire-Arms and Ammunition* (Washington, DC: U.S. Government Printing Office, 1882).

[66] In 1887 the Watervliet arsenal, which had previously manufactured gun carriages for commercially built artillery pieces, began construction of cannon. Levin H. Campbell, *The Industry-Ordnance Team* (New York: McGraw-Hill, 1946), p. 38.

[67] Constance M. Green, Harry C. Thomson, and Peter C. Roots, *The Ordnance Department: Planning Munitions for War* (Washington, DC: Office of the Chief of Military History, 1955), p. 19. On the Spanish-American War and its aftermath see also Raber, "Conservative Innovators," pp. 17–19. Regarding the Ordnance Department's failings during the war, and its subsequent development of a new rifle, see William H. Hallahan, *Misfire: The History of How America's Small Arms Have Failed Our Military* (New York: Charles Scribner's Sons, 1994), pp. 233–78.

fore the United States entered the fighting, made no serious preparations for drawing on the nation's industrial resources in the event of mobilization.[68]

True to form, the Army reverted during the 1920s and 1930s to a posture of virtual self-reliance. This was not entirely a matter of choice. Radical postwar budget cuts meant that there were barely enough procurement dollars to keep the arsenals occupied, let alone to offer any sizable contracts to industry.[69] As with the Navy, the Army's inclination to preserve its own productive base in an era of extreme scarcity was reinforced by mounting public hostility toward the private arms makers and by the strength of the allies of the traditional arsenals. Since the 1850s, Congress had periodically enacted legislation encouraging procurement from public sources, and in 1920 it did so again. The so-called Arsenal Act of that year required the Secretary of the Army to have "supplies needed for the Department of the Army made in factories or arsenals owned by the United States, so far as those factories or arsenals can make those supplies on an economical basis."[70]

Although the act's final, crucial phrase was left undefined, the sense was clear enough, as was its impact. Purchases of new arms and ammunition fell to pitifully low levels, and whatever work there was went to the arsenals. Between the early 1920s and the late 1930s, the Army bought only 35 tanks and a total of 126 75- and 105-millimeter guns, all of them built in its own factories. During the 1930s the Frankford Arsenal was the only plant in the United States producing ammunition for military small arms, while the Picatinny arsenal was the only facility capable of manufacturing and loading artillery and mortar shells. Stockpiles of old rifles, and the Ordnance Department's painstakingly slow progress in developing a new one, meant that there were no contracts for small arms until the late 1930s.[71] As the Second World War approached, the United States had virtually no commercial capacity for the manufacture of military munitions.

Mobilization

Large-scale land warfare required production on a truly massive scale. Where the Navy needed dozens or hundreds of ships of various types, the Army de-

[68] Daniel R. Beaver, "The Problem of American Military Supply, 1890–1920," in Cooling, *War, Business, and American Society,* p. 77.

[69] "The meager Ordnance budget in the 1920s and 1930s had barely sufficed to keep the arsenals open and had not permitted placing any substantial small arms orders with private industry." Harry C. Thomson and Lida Mayo, *The Ordnance Department: Procurement and Supply* (Washington, DC: U.S. Government Printing Office, 1960), p. 156. Also, Green, Thomson, and Roots, *Planning Munitions for War,* p. 47.

[70] See *United States Code Annotated: Title 10, Armed Forces* (St. Paul, MN: West Publishing, 1975), p. 379.

[71] Regarding interwar procurement of small arms, ammunition, and tanks see Thomson and Mayo, *Procurement and Supply,* pps. 72, 156, 191, and 224. Figures for artillery pieces are from Green, Thomson, and Roots, *Planning Munitions for War,* p. 47. On artillery ammunition see Campbell, *The Industry-Ordnance Team,* p. 41. On the protracted development of the M1 rifle see Edward C. Ezell, *The Great Rifle Controversy: Search for the Ultimate Infantry Weapon from World War II through Vietnam and Beyond* (Harrisburg, PA: Stackpole Books, 1984), pp. 1–40.

manded tens of thousands of tanks and armored vehicles, hundreds of thousands of artillery pieces and machine guns, millions of rifles, tens of millions of tons of explosives and propellants, and billions of rounds of ammunition.[72]

The system put in place to produce this staggering volume of armaments may be thought of as comprising a set of three concentric circles.[73] At the nucleus of the system were the Army's own arsenals. The six "old-line" facilities that had been in operation since the nineteenth century (Springfield, Watertown, Watervliet, Rock Island, Picatinny, and Frankford) were all expanded, and two new ones (at Huntsville, Alabama, and Joliet, Illinois) were added after 1940. The arsenals built small arms, artillery pieces, and ammunition and did research and development work; they also played a vital early role in transferring production technology and in instructing inexperienced civilians in the lost art of ordnance manufacture. Especially during the "defense period," between the fall of France and the attack on Pearl Harbor, production at the arsenals was critically important, though it ultimately made up only a small fraction of the nation's total output of most military end-items. There were a number of exceptions to this rule. As it had been during the Civil War, the Springfield Armory became the nation's leading manufacturer of rifles, eventually turning out over four thousand M1s per day, for a total of over 3.5 of the 4 million produced during the war.[74] Watervliet Arsenal also held its own, remaining the biggest single wartime producer of cannon.[75]

While large in absolute terms, the War Department's investment in its arsenals represented only a small portion of the total direct expenditure on productive capacity.[76] Bigger and far costlier was the second tier of the arms production complex: the nationwide network of factories built with Army funds and then operated, under varying arrangements, by private firms. In these plants, some assembled on the scale of small cities, the military manufactured virtually all of the explosives and much of the ammunition used during the war.[77] These

---

[72] Total wartime production figures for various items are contained in Thomson and Mayo, *Procurement and Supply.*

[73] I will concentrate here on production of guns, ammunition, explosives, and tanks and motor vehicles. Aircraft will be discussed below. Items other than munitions will not be considered here.

[74] For daily production figures see Stanislaus J. Skarzynski, "The Spirit of the Springfield Armory," *Historical Journal of Massachusetts* 13, no. 2 (1985), p. 142. Slightly different figures for total production are reported in Green, Thomson, and Roots, *Planning Munitions for War*, p. 59; and Campbell, *The Industry-Ordnance Team*, p. 37.

[75] Campbell, *The Industry-Ordnance Team*, p. 42.

[76] Roughly 10 percent of the total national investment in production of guns, ammunition, explosives, and tanks and motor vehicles went to government-owned and -operated facilities, as compared to roughly 30 percent for production of ships. Virtually all munitions manufacturing was carried out by the Army, which supplied ordnance for the Navy as well as for its ground and air forces. See table in Sweeting, "Building the Arsenal of Democracy," p. 249.

[77] See ibid., pp. 262–63. For an overview see Joel Davidson, "Building for War, Preparing for Peace: World War II and the Military-Industrial Complex," in Donald Albrecht, ed., *World War II and the American Dream* (Cambridge: MIT Press, 1995), pp. 186–229. Construction of the GOCOs is also discussed in detail in R. Elberton Smith, *The Army and Economic Mobilization* (Washington, DC: Office of the Chief of Military History, 1959), pp. 476–502; Campbell, *The Industry-Ordnance*

facilities were regarded as extensions to the arsenal system, and in contrast to what had happened after the First World War, the Army planned to retain many of them under its control once the fighting was over.[78]

The third and final tier of the national munitions production system was made up of facilities that were either fully privately owned or publicly financed and leased from the government with the expectation that they would be purchased by industry once the war was over. Not surprisingly, such arrangements were most common in sectors that were believed to have the greatest postwar commercial potential (such as motor vehicles) and virtually nonexistent in fields like explosives manufacturing that appeared to have none.[79] Military planners assumed that virtually all privately owned and leased capacity would be converted to civilian uses as soon as the wartime emergency had passed.

By 1945 the Ordnance Department owned a far-flung empire of 216 production facilities, most of them contractor-operated.[80] These plants, as one historian has pointed out, "represented a quantum leap in munitions production capacity, and gave the armed services a degree of independence and control that military leaders would be loathe to relinquish."[81]

Decline of the Arsenal System

In the first fifteen years after the end of the Second World War, the Army sought to devise a new set of institutional arrangements for the design and manufacture of armaments, one in which industry would continue to be engaged but in which the Ordnance Department and its arsenals would still play the central, dominant role. Like the Navy's attempt to preserve a high degree of autonomy and to dictate the terms of its relationship with industry, this effort also failed. By the mid-1960s the Army too had been forced to accept an arms procurement system that was more heavily privatized than what it would have preferred.

CONSTRICTING THE ORDNANCE EMPIRE

The Army did manage initially to retain ownership of a substantial array of facilities for the mass production of ammunition and explosives. Some of these continued to operate (mostly under the direction of contractors) to supply cur-

---

Team, 101–15. Large numbers of heavy vehicles were also assembled in GOCO facilities. One plant alone, the massive Chrysler-run Detroit Tank Arsenal, produced a quarter of all the light, medium, and heavy tanks built during the war. See the table in Thomson and Mayo, *Procurement and Supply,* p. 242.

[78] Smith, *The Army and Economic Mobilization,* p. 497; Gerald T. White, *Billions for Defense: Government Financing by the Defense Plant Corporation during World War II* (University: University of Alabama Press, 1980), p. 6.

[79] Sweeting, "Building the Arsenal of Democracy," p. 249.

[80] Smith, *The Army and Economic Mobilization,* p. 499.

[81] Davidson, "Building for War," p. 213. See also Gregory Hooks, *Forging the Military-Industrial Complex: World War II's Battle of the Potomac* (Urbana, Ill.: University of Illinois Press, 1991), pp. 132–34.

rent needs; the rest were held in reserve for possible future mobilizations. The Army's standby munitions capacity was activated during the Korean War, more production facilities were built, and in the war's aftermath, the size of the military's industrial reserve increased.[82]

Over the course of the 1950s, however, the number of government-owned factories was sharply reduced. This change was due in part to the aging of production equipment, the tightening of the Army's procurement budget, and changing assumptions about the likely character of a future war. Ideological factors also played a role. Government-owned plants manufacturing ammunition and explosives did not compete with industry in the same way as the Navy's shipyards. The firms that ran most of the Army's factories were quite content with existing arrangements and had no desire to take on the responsibility and expense of owning their own equipment. There were typically no purely private operators from whom the hybrid government-owned, contractor-operated facilities might be said to be taking business. Nevertheless, during the 1950s, the continued existence of an Army-owned production base was regularly criticized as an affront to the principles of private enterprise. The same generalized, ideologically rooted, probusiness, antigovernment sentiments that served to weaken the position of the shipyards also helped to eat away at support for the Army's ordnance empire.

The 1955 Hoover Commission report that urged privatization of naval construction also recommended the sale of as many government-owned munitions factories as possible.[83] Called to testify before Congress, Army officials felt compelled to declare their support for "the basic principle that free-competitive enterprise should be fostered by the Government" and to offer assurances that it was "the policy of the Army to place main reliance on private industry for the production of military materiel." The Army retained the right to set up its own industrial plants, but "only when private enterprise is unable or unwilling to perform the services or provide the products."[84]

Wherever possible, the Army was committed by the second half of the 1950s to closing or selling the facilities it owned and, with the exception of the arsenals themselves, to relying on private industry to operate those that remained. In keeping with this policy, by end of the decade the size of the military's industrial complex had been considerably diminished. In 1954 there were 86

[82] After the Second World War, the armed services had retained 150 plants for permanent use. Of these 47 were involved in the manufacture of ammunition and explosives, 36 of ships and aircraft, and most of the remainder of guns, chemicals, and armored vehicles. Some of these plants were kept in operation but the majority were placed in reserve. Sweeting, "Building the Arsenal of Democracy," pp. 337–38. In 1955 the Hoover Commission found that the Army, Navy, and Air Force together controlled a total of 249 plants, active and reserve, government and commercially operated. *Report on Real Property Management*, pp. 61–62.

[83] Ibid., pp. 75–76.

[84] See statement of Frank H, Higgins, Assistant Secretary of the Army for Logistics, in Hearings before the Subcommittee for Special Investigations of the House Committee on Armed Services, *Utilization of Government-Owned Plants and Facilities*, 85th Cong., 2d sess. (Washington, DC: U.S. Government Printing Office, 1959), pp. 1102–4.

active, government-owned facilities manufacturing explosives, weapons, and chemicals, most of them under the control of the Army, and 28 operated directly by the government.[85] Five years later, the number of active, Army-owned facilities stood at 34, of which 17 were Army-operated.[86]

ASSAULT ON THE ARSENALS

The postwar role that the Army envisioned for its arsenals was essentially the one that it would have preferred for them to have played in the interwar years. As in the 1920s and 1930s, it was expected that Army technicians would generally take the lead in designing new weapons, making prototypes, and devising production techniques for eventual large-scale manufacture by industry. In some cases, the arsenals would set up assembly lines to test their concepts, building batches of new weapons for experimentation or actual field use. By participating in "the entire cycle of production," the Army would hone its engineering skills while at the same time maintaining at least a fraction of the capacity it would need in an emergency.[87] In contrast to the interwar period, however, when bare bones budgets forced a choice between in-house production and outside contracting, the great bulk of military manufacturing would be done by industry. The Army had no desire to sever its ties to the private sector, but it did intend to maintain its position as the preeminent partner in "the Industry-Ordnance team."[88]

Despite the seeming limits to its ambitions, the arsenal system came under devastating public attack in the late 1950s. Critics of the Army in Congress, parts of industry, the other military services, and increasingly, the Office of the Secretary of Defense, accused it of clinging to a system that was functionally inadequate and philosophically inappropriate. The Army sought to defend itself with appeals to tradition and claims of strategic necessity and superior performance, but as with the Navy yards, the advocates of anything remotely resembling public production found themselves on the wrong side of a volatile ideological debate. By the mid-1960s the once-powerful and independent Army Ordnance Department had been effectively organized out of existence, the arsenal system stood relieved of its responsibilities in a number of critical areas, and several of the old-line arsenals were slated for closure.

This process of defeat and retreat unfolded in two stages, the first involving a failed Army bid to master the development of ballistic missiles, the second a

[85] See the table in *Business Enterprises*, p. 14. Although this table does not provide a breakdown, all but a handful of the facilities in these sectors would have been under Army control.

[86] See Hearings before a Subcommittee of the Senate Armed Services Committee, *Military Procurement*, 86th Cong., 1st sess. (Washington, DC: U.S. Government Printing Office, 1959), pp. 666–67. Of the seventeen Army owned and operated facilities, nine were Ordnance arsenals, two were arsenals under the control of the Chemical Corps, and three more were proving grounds.

[87] Maj. Gen. J. B. Medaris, "The Arsenal Philosophy," *Ordnance* (July–August 1959), p. 49.

[88] The phrase, in widespread use in the postwar years, was the title of a 1946 book by the Army's wartime chief of ordnance, Lt. Gen. Levin Campbell. As will be discussed below, as the arsenal system began to come under fire, the Army was forced increasingly to articulate the reasons for its continued existence.

disastrous effort by the arsenals to perform their oldest and most basic task: designing and building a new standard infantry rifle.

Throughout the 1950s, the Army waged a protracted bureaucratic struggle with the Air Force to determine which service would lead the way in developing ballistic missiles and in exploiting the military potential of outer space. The ground forces had gotten off to an early lead in this contest, thanks to their postwar inheritance of the German V-2 rocket team and to the Air Force's initial preoccupation with manned bombers.[89] When confronted with a series of high-level decisions intended to limit its responsibility to so-called tactical or battlefield systems, the Army responded by redefining the scope of the battlefield and pushing ahead with its efforts to build weapons of considerable range and payload. Army theorists maintained that even an intermediate range ballistic missile (IRBM) that could reach as far as fifteen hundred miles was "a field artillery weapon and therefore as logically a development by Army Ordnance as the M1 rifle."[90]

At the end of 1956, having earlier authorized two IRBM projects (the Army's Jupiter and the Air Force's Thor), the Secretary of Defense sought to rein in interservice rivalry by declaring that the ground forces would not be given operational control of any weapon with a range greater than two hundred miles. This decision, and the Sputnik crisis of the following year, brought the issue of missile development into full public view.[91]

As Michael Armacost has pointed out, the Thor-Jupiter controversy of 1957–58 involved "more than simply the jurisdictional question of who would design, produce, and deploy the IRBM." The debate over the comparative virtues of the two missiles quickly blossomed into a contest between the Army's arsenal system, with the significant role that it accorded to public officials, and the Air Force "weapons system manager" concept, in which responsibility for virtually every aspect of design, development, and production rested squarely with pri-

[89] For the Army's view of the story see "What You Should Know about Birds and Bullets: In Ballistics, Army Has the Know-How," *Army* 6, no. 11 (June 1956), pp. 16–21; also "Army 'Firsts' in Missiles and Space," *Military Review* 39, no. 5 (August 1959), pp. 77–81.

[90] See "The IRBM: The Army has the Know-How," *Army* 6, no. 8 (March 1956), p. 13. Also Maj. N. A. Parson, Jr., "The IRBM Artillery-Support Weapon: Answer to the Artilleryman's Dilemma," *Army* 6, no. 8 (March 1956), pp. 14–17; Col. Bradford Butler, Jr., "The Impact of Long-Thrust Atomic Weapons," *Army* 7, no. 8 (March 1957), pp. 27–29; Capt. Patrick W. Powers, "The Pentomic Army's Missile Power: Weapons and Capabilities," *Army* 7, no. 9 (April 1957), pp. 15–17, 56, 58; Powers, "The Pentomic Army's Missile Power: Weapons of the Army Missile Commands," *Army* 7, no. 11 (June 1957), pp. 46–52; Lt. Gen. James M. Gavin, "Why Missiles?" *Army* 8, no. 4 (November 1957), pp. 25–29.

[91] For the Army's perspective see "The Roles and Missions Decisions: Why Did the Ball Bounce as It Did?" *Army* 7, no. 6 (January 1957), pp. 16–17. For an interpretation of events more favorable to the Air Force see David Anderton, "Services Push Missile Programs Hard," *Aviation Week* 66 (February 25, 1957), pp. 98–101; "Army Partisans Challenge Wilson; Denounce IRBM, Aviation Edicts," *Aviation Week* 66 (March 25, 1957), pp. 27–28.

vate industry.[92] This was a dispute that the Army initiated, but that, in the prevailing climate of opinion, it had little chance of winning.

With funding for conventional ground forces tightly constrained by the New Look, Army planners saw ballistic missiles as crucial to institutional survival. When Secretary of Defense Charles E. Wilson issued his restrictive ruling, Army partisans lashed out in frustration and desperation at their principal competitors. The proponents of air power, they pointed out with some justification, had been slow to recognize the significance of ballistic missiles. This oversight, some Army officers suggested darkly, was hardly accidental. The Air Force lacked the kind of independent, in-house expertise that the Army possessed in its arsenals, and as a result, the new service had become a slave to its industrial suppliers. But the manufacturers of airframes and engines who sold planes to the Air Force were heavily invested in technologies that were now on the verge of obsolescence. Not only did these firms lack experience in developing ballistic missiles; until very recently they had had no motivation for doing so. The nation could not afford to place its security in the hands of a small group of short-sighted and self-interested corporations.[93]

Contrasting itself to the Air Force, the Army claimed that it had both a proven postwar track record in building rockets and, in its Redstone Arsenal, a strong institution capable of controlling and directing the further development of this revolutionary technology. The Army's assertions of superiority gained credence when, in the late spring of 1957, after a string of spectacular Air Force failures, the Redstone team succeeded in test firing the first American IRBM.[94] The subsequent ascent of the Soviet Sputniks (and, in early 1958, the U.S. response, in the form of an Army-launched earth-orbiting satellite) forced the Air Force further onto the defensive and threatened to reopen the question of which organization should control the nation's missile and space programs.[95]

Faced with criticism of its weapons development system, the Air Force and its industrial allies unleashed a sharp counterattack. According to a leading aerospace publication, the Army's apparent triumphs were not really the product of better organization, but rather the handiwork of a small cluster of German rocket scientists with dubious pasts.[96] More generally, and contrary to the

[92] Michael H. Armacost, *The Politics of Weapons Innovation: The Thor-Jupiter Controversy* (New York: Columbia University Press, 1969), p. 9.

[93] For a summary of the Army's case against the Air Force see the memoirs of the one-time head of the Army missile program, Maj. Gen. J. B. Medaris, *Countdown for Decision* (New York: G. P. Putnam's Sons, 1960).

[94] "Army Wins Missile Race," *Aviation Week* 66 (June 10, 1957), p. 25.

[95] For indications of growing Air Force and aviation industry anxiety on this score see, for example, "Industry Missile Role Defended," *Aviation Week* 66 (July 8, 1957), p. 30; and Claude Witze, "Army Stages Clutch Fight to Keep IRBM," *Aviation Week* 66 (September 9, 1957), pp. 40–41.

[96] "Wernher von Braun and his able group of former Peenemunde technicians represent virtually the Army's entire technical capability in this field," wrote the editors of *Aviation Week*, and consequently, "the Army brass clings to them almost hysterically for shelter." "Who Really Develops Missiles?" *Aviation Week* 67 (September 23, 1957), p. 21.

claims being made for them, the Army's arsenals actually had "a black record in new weapons development dating back to the Civil War." Nor had other countries profited from resort to similar state-centered design and production systems. The nationalized pre-war French aircraft industry had "completely failed that country in its hour of crisis." Since the war, Britain's aviation industry had been "plagued by a Socialist government that imposed government control" and "disastrously decelerated the once lively pace" of technological progress.[97] In the words of the president of the Aircraft Industries Association, "Government agencies have never been successful aircraft producers, and there is no reason to believe that they can manufacture missiles."[98]

At the heart of the Air Force counteroffensive was the accusation, whether implied or directly stated, that the arsenal system was statist, "socialistic," anti–free enterprise, and hence un-American.[99] Questions of efficacy aside, an arms procurement mechanism that placed primary responsibility in the hands of private industry was therefore preferable, on principled grounds, to one that gave the lead role to public actors. "You can get all kinds of pros and cons on this," explained the Air Force's chief of missile development, "but I think that philosophically it is true that . . . the policy of this country is to have private enterprise do the job for the Government instead of having the Government do the job."[100] The Air Force was acting in harmony with this fundamental precept of American life; the Army, its critics claimed, was not.

The tactic of transforming the contest between Thor and Jupiter into a cosmic rivalry between free enterprise and statism was misleading, to say the least, but it was no less effective for being so. In truth, the differences between the Army and the Air Force development systems were matters of degree rather than kind. The design of both Thor and Jupiter had involved a measure of collaboration between government and industry, and both were to be produced in quantity by industrial contractors. Nevertheless, having been accused of heresy, Army officials soon found themselves called upon to defend their methods to Congress and the public. Where they had once touted the unique advantages of their arsenal-centered procurement system, they were now compelled to downplay the extent to which it differed from its contractor-driven Air Force competitor.

Army partisans were at pains to point out that contrary to what was being suggested, they did not advocate large-scale public production of sophisticated armaments. "Our arsenals are far from manufacturing plants," explained the Secretary of the Army. "They are pilot facilities where teams of experts work

---

[97] "The 'Missile Industry' Myth," *Aviation Week* 67 (September 16, 1957), p. 21.

[98] "Industry Missile Role Defended."

[99] On charges of socialism see Armacost, *The Politics of Weapons Innovation,* p. 156.

[100] See testimony of Maj. Gen. Bernard A. Schriever, Commander, Air Force Ballistic Missile Division, in Hearings before the Preparedness Investigating Subcommittee of the Senate Armed Services Committee, *Inquiry into Satellite and Missile Programs*, 85th Cong., 1st and 2nd sess. (Washington, DC: U.S. Government Printing Office, 1958), p. 1640.

out production systems and check out manufacturing processes."[101] Thus, while it was true that Redstone Arsenal had developed and built the first Jupiters, and while it did have the capacity to make more, the Army promised that it had no intention of using its facilities in this way on a regular basis. "We don't engage in volume production of a weapon," the Army's chief procurement officer reassured Congress.[102] In the case of Jupiter, the prime manufacturing contractor would be the Chrysler Corporation. More generally, as another Army spokesmen pointed out, "We still spend almost all of our tax dollar with industry" with only a small fraction going to pay for work done in-house.[103]

Army officials acknowledged that the Ordnance Corps did a certain portion of the engineering and design work on new weapons in its own facilities, but they explained that this was essential to maintaining control over the subsequent stages of development and production by industry. Such arrangements did not imply that the Army had failed to "appreciate and make full use of the industrial might of the United States."[104] In any case, the procedures used on the Jupiter and earlier Redstone missile programs, in which an arsenal had acted as prime development contractor, were anomalous. Without admitting that they had done anything wrong, Army officials promised, in effect, not to do it again. "It is not the intention of the Army to have the Redstone-Jupiter pattern be that for future Army missiles," wrote the Army's director of research and development. This pattern was "the exception, rather than the Army rule."[105]

As the Thor-Jupiter controversy reached its peak, Army officials ostentatiously announced that their next big missile (the seven-hundred-mile range Pershing) would be developed from the start by industry, rather than beginning life in an arsenal, and they instituted new procedures designed to encourage early commercial participation in future weapons programs.[106] Army spokesmen, in a belated bow to the importance of good public relations and a tacit acknowledgment of their vulnerability, also began to change the language that they used, renaming Redstone the "Army Rocket and Guided Missile Agency" and attempting to substitute anodyne labels like "Army technical centers" or "Ordnance engineering centers" for the now weighted word *arsenal*.[107]

---

[101] Secretary of the Army Wilbur Brucker, quoted in J. H. Hinrichs, "Army Ordnance Arsenals," *Ordnance* (September–October 1958), pp. 21.

[102] Statement by Brig. Gen. Jean Engler, Director of Procurement, Office of Assistant Chief of Staff for Logistics, Department of the Army, in *Utilization of Government-Owned Plants and Facilities*, p. 1116.

[103] Maj. Gen. John B. Medaris, Commanding General, U.S. Army Ordnance Missile Command, in Hearings before a Subcommittee of the House Committee on Government Operations, *Organization and Management of Missile Programs*, 86th Cong., 1st sess. (Washington, DC: U.S. Government Printing Office, 1959), p. 255.

[104] Medaris, "The Arsenal Philosophy," p. 51.

[105] Dr. William H. Martin, "Industry and the Arsenals," *Army* 9, no. 8 (March 1959), p. 29.

[106] Evert Clark, "Army Modifies Arsenal Concept; Pershing Contract Goes to Martin," *Aviation Week* 68 (March 31, 1958), p. 19; "Army and Industry," *Aviation Week* 68 (May 25, 1958), p. 25.

[107] The name "Redstone Arsenal" continued to refer to a geographical location, though not to the

All of this availed the Army but little. It soon became clear not only that the ground forces had failed to regain control of the nation's missile programs, but that their weapons procurement system had been badly discredited and seriously damaged into the bargain. One squadron of Jupiters was eventually manufactured at the Redstone Arsenal, but the program was quickly canceled; with it went the Army's last hopes of playing a role in long-range ballistic missiles.[108] A final effort to recoup by shifting resources from missiles to large space boosters also ended in failure. At the end of 1958, the Army was compelled to surrender control of its contractor-operated Jet Propulsion Laboratory to the newly formed National Aeronautics and Space Administration. One year later, President Eisenhower ordered the prize rocket design team at Redstone transferred to NASA, and the facility itself placed under the command of a former Air Force general.[109] The Army's defeat was total and its humiliation deep. With NASA following the Air Force model, most of the work done at what had once been the Redstone Arsenal was soon being performed by private contractors.[110]

According to H. L. Nieburg, the lesson of the Thor-Jupiter contest and its aftermath was obvious for all to see: an "extensive in-house engineering-management capability was a positive *disadvantage* in mobilizing congressional and public influence to support military missions and budgets."[111] The reason for this was not so much that the government facilities had clearly failed in their mission or that they lacked outside allies (the Army, after all, had Chrysler on its side); rather, they were perceived increasingly to lack legitimacy. Thus, despite its early successes in the ballistic missile field, by the end of the 1950s the

---

missile research unit housed there. The renaming of Redstone was part of a larger reorganization of Army missile programs; see "U.S. Army Ordnance Missile Command," *Military Review* 38, no. 5 (August 1958), pp. 11–19; also Michael E. Baker, *Redstone Arsenal: Yesterday and Today* (Washington, DC: U.S. Government Printing Office, 1993). For changing labels see "U.S. Army Capabilities in the Space Age: A Review of the U.S. Army Technical Services' Performance and Potential," reprinted in Hearings before the House Committee on Science and Astronautics, *Basic Scientific and Astronautic Research in the Department of Defense*, 86th Cong., 1st sess. (Washington, DC: U.S. Government Printing Office, 1959), p. 370; Medaris, "The Arsenal Philosophy," p. 52. Regarding the Army's sensitivity to the "stigma of . . . identification with the arsenal system," see Armacost, *The Politics of Weapons Innovation,* p. 160.

[108] Medaris, *Countdown for Decision,* pp. 183, 231.

[109] For these events see Ford Eastman, "NASA Takes Over Jet Propulsion Lab," *Aviation Week* 69 (December 8, 1958), p. 30; Evert Clark, "NASA Gains Army Missile Team, Saturn," *Aviation Week* 71 (October 26, 1959), p. 28; Hearing before the NASA Authorization Subcommittee of the Senate Committee on Aeronautical and Space Sciences, *Transfer of Von Braun Team to NASA*, 86th Cong., 2d sess. (Washington, DC: U.S. Government Printing Office, 1960); Hearing before the House Committee on Science and Astronautics, *Transfer of the Development Operations Division of the Army Ballistic Missile Agency to the National Aeronautics and Space Administration*, 86th Cong., 2d sess. (Washington, DC: U.S. Government Printing Office, 1960).

[110] H. L. Nieburg, *In the Name of Science* (Chicago: Quadrangle Books, 1970), p. 233. The transfer of these government facilities and their absorption into an increasingly contractor-centered organization is discussed in Robert L. Rosholt, *An Administrative History of NASA, 1958–1963* (Washington, DC: U.S. Government Printing Office, 1966), pp. 44–48, 61–65, 107–23, 350.

[111] Nieburg, *In the Name of Science,* p. 189.

appropriateness of the Army's arsenal system had been called into question, and its survival was very much in doubt.[112]

As the rocket rivalry entered its most intense public phase, a second controversy was just beginning to unfold. In the spring of 1957, twenty-one years after the standardization of the M1 and twelve years after it had begun to work in earnest on a replacement, the Army finally settled on a design for its new standard infantry rifle. The weapon designated the M14 was seen by Army officials as a classic expression of what they were still proud to call their "arsenal philosophy." Designed, developed, and painstakingly tested by government engineers, it was to be manufactured in limited quantities at a pilot line at the Springfield Armory and then turned over to industry for mass production. This approach, as the journal *Ordnance* assured its readers, was the nation's tried and true method for developing new rifles; it had "borne fruit for more than a century."[113]

Almost as soon as it was unveiled, however, the M14 began to draw fire, both from outside the Army and from within its ranks. Critics complained that the new rifle was little more than an incremental improvement over its predecessor. Like the M1, the M14 was essentially a marksman's rifle, accurate and deadly when fired at individual targets over long ranges. The new weapon was also supposed to be capable of unleashing controlled automatic bursts, but its weight and the Ordnance Department's insistence on using large-caliber ammunition made it extremely difficult to handle when used in this way. In this respect at least, the M14 compared unfavorably to its Soviet counterpart, the Kalashnikov AK 47 assault rifle.[114]

With the M14 about to enter volume production, a potential challenger emerged from an unexpected quarter. First tested in 1957, the so-called AR-15 rifle was made largely of plastic and designed to fire a large volume of small caliber bullets; it had "the very characteristics [the] M14 was supposed to have and didn't: true light weight . . . true automatic fire, fully controllable." More

---

[112] For evidence of defensiveness and uncertainty see, in addition to the articles already cited, "How Army's Arsenal System Works," *Armed Forces Management* 6 (October 1959), pp. 15–17; "The Arsenals," *Ordnance* (July–August 1960), pp. 55–57; Maxwell R. Warden, "Arsenals Are Essential," *Ordnance* (November–December 1960), pp. 349–50. For an overview of the contemporary controversy over alternative relationships between the services and their suppliers see Col. Edward N. Hall, "Industry and the Military in the United States," *Air University Quarterly Review* 10, no. 3 (Fall 1958), pp. 26–42.

[113] "Right Arm of the Fighting Man," *Ordnance* (May–June 1959), p. 925. Initial plans called for two commercial contractors to produce thirty-five thousand M14s each, with Springfield manufacturing fifteen thousand. See testimony of Brig. Gen. J. E. Engler, Director of Procurement, Office of the Deputy Chief of Staff, Logistics, in Hearings before the Subcommittee of the House Committee on Appropriations, *Department of Defense Appropriations for 1960*, pt. 5, *Procurement*, 86th Cong., 1st sess. (Washington, DC: U.S. Government Printing Office, 1959), pp. 218–19.

[114] The Army's traditional emphasis on marksmanship and the implications for the design of the M14 are explained in Thomas L. McNaugher, *The M16 Controversies: Military Organizations and Weapons Acquisition* (New York: Praeger, 1984), pp. 15–47.

threatening to the Army than its technical characteristics was the new weapon's lineage. The M14, with all its shortcomings, was the product of over a decade of work by government committees; the AR-15 had been designed in nine months by a lone employee of the Armalite Corporation, a division of Fairchild Engine and Airplane. These differences were emphasized when Colt Firearms, having purchased the production rights to the AR-15, began a national publicity campaign attacking the M14 and the Ordnance Department. The only problem with its rifle, Colt's president claimed, was that "it hadn't been invented by Army arsenal personnel."[115] The import of these comments was plain: private initative and inventiveness were being stifled by self-protective government bureaucrats, and the nation's defenses were suffering as a result.

As interest in a possible alternative grew, the Army rushed to put the M14 into production. The ensuing manufacturing problems, both at Springfield and at the two commercial arms makers chosen as outside contractors, provoked investigations by journalists, Congress, and, most importantly, the new Secretary of Defense.[116] McNamara's examination of the M14 program led him quickly to the conclusion that not only had the Army chosen the wrong rifle, but that its traditional methods for procuring small arms were fundamentally flawed and badly outmoded.

McNamara's business background and deep aversion to inefficiency inclined him from the start to be skeptical of a system that gave government agencies the lead responsibility for designing and building new weapons. What he had heard of the Thor-Jupiter controversy and what he learned of the Army's conduct of its rifle program did nothing to disabuse him of this prejudice. "I think it is a disgrace the way this project was handled," McNamara told the Senate Preparedness Committee in the summer of 1961. "This is a relatively simple job, to build a rifle compared to building a satellite . . . or a missile system." And yet the process of designing a new rifle had taken years to complete, and the move from prototype to mass production was obviously plagued with problems and delays.[117] These comments, writes Thomas McNaugher, "hardly endeared McNamara to the Ordnance Department." On the other hand, "what he found when he examined the M14 did not endear the department to McNamara, either."[118]

Although he was not yet ready to cancel the M14, the Secretary of Defense demanded a new round of tests of alternative rifle designs and he initated a

[115] Hallahan, *Misfire*, pps. 458, 468; see also McNaugher, *The M16 Controversies*, p. 11.

[116] On the "production crises" of 1960–61 see Ezell, *The Great Rifle Controversy*, pp. 139–61. An influential contemporary article on the subject was written by reporter A. J. Glass, "The M-14: Best Army Rifle in World—Or 'a Major Ordnance Blunder'?" *New York Herald Tribune*, June 26, 1961. The Senate Preparedness Committee held hearings on the M14 in the summer of 1961. For a defense of the Ordnance Corps see "The New M14 Rifle," *Ordnance* (January–February 1962), p. 539. The sequence of events is reviewed in House Armed Services Committee, *Report of the Special Subcommittee on the M-16 Rifle Program*, 90th Cong., 1st sess. (Washington, DC: U.S. Government Printing Office, 1967), pp. 5321–35.

[117] Hallahan, *Misfire*, p. 479.

[118] McNaugher, *The M16 Controversies*, p. 107.

major management study of the Army research and development bureaucracy. In the summer of 1962 McNamara unveiled a new organization scheme in which the various technical services (including the Chemical, Ordnance, and Signal Corps) were subsumed into an Army Materiel Command.[119] These reforms had the effect of severely weakening the traditionally independent and powerful Ordnance bureaucracy, placing it firmly under the control of higher authority and easing the way for a further transfer of its responsibilities outward, to the private sector. As McNamara's chief of research explained to Congress, in the past the Army had tended to go "a long way into the production area." Now it was "both desirable and necessary for the Army to go outside to industry to try to get into its developments a little bit of the same drive . . . that has been the case among the aircraft contracts."[120]

In 1963, McNamara ordered the Army to cease procurement of M14s after only one-quarter of a planned 5 million rifles had been manufactured, and he authorized the purchase of the first sizable batch of AR-15s for use by the Air Force and by Army Special Forces units.[121] For the next several years the question of what weapon to adopt as the infantry standard was held in abeyance while the Springfield Armory, now forced to compete against a private arms producer, labored to develop an alternative to the AR-15.[122] The escalation of the war in Vietnam, a conflict in which the range and accuracy of the M14 were virtually useless but for which its rapid fire competitor was ideally suited, finally forced the issue. At the end of 1965 the Army began to buy large numbers of M16s (a "militarized" version of the AR-15) from Colt, eventually issuing them to U.S. forces in Europe as well as Southeast Asia.[123]

By the late 1960s, for the first time in its history, the United States Army was equipped with a standard rifle that had been developed and built entirely by private industry in privately owned facilities. Not only had the arsenals failed to play a role in the procurement of this new weapon, there was mounting evidence that they had sought to delay and even to sabotage it, rigging tests and, in the process of "militarization," imposing some additional requirements that actually made the rifle less reliable. Reports that M16s were jamming frequently

[119] For a comparison of the old and new Army systems see Hearings before a Subcommittee of the House Committee on Government Operations, *Systems Development and Management*, pt. 4, 87th Cong., 2d sess. (Washington, DC: U.S. Government Printing Office, 1962), pp. 1376–81. The link between the M14 controversy and the reorganization is drawn both by McNaugher, *The M16 Controversies*; and Hallahan, *Misfire*, pp. 480–81.

[120] See statement by Harold Brown, Director of Defense Research and Engineering, in Hearings before a Subcommittee of the House Committee on Government Operations, *Systems Development and Management*, pt. 2, 87th Cong., 2d sess. (Washington, DC: U.S. Government Printing Office, 1962), p. 473.

[121] Hallahan, *Misfire*, p. 477; Ezell, *The Great Rifle Controversy*, p. 153; William Beecher, "Choice of Basic Rifle Stirs Pentagon Debate in an Age of Missiles," *Wall Street Journal*, July 2, 1963.

[122] Ezell, *The Great Rifle Controversy*, p. 194.

[123] *Report of the Special Subcommittee on the M-16 Rifle Program*, pp. 5337–42; McNaugher, *The M16 Controversies*, pp. 115–29.

in Vietnam led in the summer of 1967 to an angry congressional investigation into the Army's handling of its small arms programs.[124] These events cleared the way for McNamara to take a final, significant step toward full privatization. At the end of 1967 he ordered the Springfield Armory to close after nearly 192 years of continuous operation.[125] Most of the armory's engineers scattered to other federal jobs or retired and went to work for private industry. Having dominated the field for over a century, the United States government had now given up virtually all of its in-house capacity for the design and manufacture of military small arms.[126]

AIR FORCE

Early Privatization

Prior to 1917 the American armed forces showed little interest and had accumulated no experience in manufacturing military aircraft. The first powered flight took place in 1903, but despite the domestic origin of the new invention, both the Army and the Navy were slow to recognize its potential strategic significance. Thus, when the United States entered the First World War, it had a fledgling aviation industry but no aeronautical equivalent to the system of federal arsenals and shipyards.

The absence of a preexisting government-owned industrial base (and the technological expertise and entrenched procurement bureaucracy to match) eased the way for heavy reliance on commercial aircraft producers. In contrast to ships and rifles, where mobilization had resulted in an expansion of both private- and public-sector facilities, the wartime production of aircraft was almost entirely a private affair. Caught up in a "groundswell of wartime enthusiasm and unrealistic expectations" about the potential of airpower, Congress quickly voted massive appropriations for the procurement from industry of large numbers of airplanes.[127]

From the start, the appeal of airpower depended in part on its presumed commercial source. Mass-produced planes were widely viewed both as decisive weapons and as potent symbols of America's industrial prowess. Popular maga-

---

[124] "The manner in which the Army rifle program has been managed," concluded a report to the House Armed Services committee, "is unbelievable." *Report of the Special Subcommittee on the M-16 Rifle Program*, p. 5371. For the hearings on which this report is based see *Hearings before the Special Subcommittee on the M-16 Rifle Program*, 90th Cong., 1st sess. (Washington, DC: U.S. Government Printing Office, 1967). This episode is discussed in James Fallows, *National Defense* (New York: Random House, 1981), pp. 76–95.

[125] Arms production at Springfield began in 1776, nineteen years before the creation of the first federal arsenal. See Walter D. Mosher, "The Springfield Armory," *Military Review* 51, no. 8 (August 1971), pp. 27–32.

[126] On the decision to close the armory and its aftermath see Ezell, *The Great Rifle Controversy*, pp. 226–28.

[127] Charles J. Gross, "George Owen Squier and the Origins of American Military Aviation," *Journal of Military History* 54, no. 3 (July 1990), p. 295.

zines and congressional debate were filled with images of endless waves of aircraft pouring out of American factories, darkening the skies, and breaking the stalemate in Europe. Aircraft, and privately manufactured aircraft in particular, were the ideal weapons for what historian Michael Sherry has described as "a nation that wanted the fruits of centralized state power without challenge to traditions of decentralized authority and individual autonomy."[128]

There was one significant exception to the general rule of private aircraft production. At the end of 1917 the Navy opened a manufacturing facility at its Philadelphia shipyard, where it proceeded to assemble flying boats for use by the fleet. Because their needs were quite modest compared to those of the Army, Navy officials worried that they might not be able to find commercial suppliers willing to meet them. In addition, Secretary of the Navy Josephus Daniels regarded the Naval Aircraft Factory, like the armor plant he had ordered built the year before, as a valuable source of unbiased information on technology and production costs. Operating its own manufacturing facility would give the Navy both a secure source of supply and a "yardstick" against which to measure the performance of private contractors.[129]

While the Army had a bigger procurement budget, the Navy, between its own plant and a comparative handful of industrial allies, actually managed to put more aircraft in service.[130] Still, the wartime air mobilization effort was widely viewed as a failure and a national disgrace. Despite all the money that had been spent, the promise that American factories would produce vast war-winning fleets of aircraft went unfulfilled. Output was disappointing, many planes were obsolete by the time they were built, and few finished aircraft actually reached American forces in Europe. Even before the fighting had ended, there were ugly allegations of profiteering by an "aircraft trust" and of incompetence, if not downright corruption, on the part of military procurement officers. Congressional suspicion and mistrust of the aircraft manufacturers would persist well into the interwar period.[131]

---

[128] Michael Sherry, *The Rise of American Air Power* (New Haven: Yale University Press, 1987), p. 53. On the symbolic appeal of airpower in the United States see also Jacob Vander Meulen, *The Politics of Aircraft: Building an American Military Industry* (Lawrence: University of Kansas Press, 1991), pp. 12–17. On enthusiasm for airpower as an expression of "liberal militarism" more generally, see David Edgerton, *England and the Aeroplane: An Essay on a Militant and Technological Nation* (London: Macmillan, 1991).

[129] On the origins of the Naval Aircraft Factory, see William F. Trimble, "The Naval Aircraft Factory, the American Aviation Industry, and Government Competition, 1919–1928," *Business History Review* 60, no. 2 (Summer 1986), pp. 175–98; Trimble, *Wings for the Navy: A History of the Naval Aircraft Factory, 1917–1956* (Annapolis, MD: Naval Institute Press, 1990), pp. 1–59; Izetta Winter Robb, "The Navy Builds an Aircraft Factory," in Adrian O. Van Wyen, ed., *Naval Aviation in World War I* (Washington, DC: U.S. Government Printing Office, 1969), pp. 34–37; Elsbeth E. Freudenthal, *The Aviation Business: From Kitty Hawk to Wall Street* (New York: Vanguard Press, 1940), pp. 45, 57–58.

[130] According to one source, the Army managed to provide only 196 aircraft to its frontline forces by Armistice Day, while the Navy delivered 570. Freudenthal, *The Aviation Business,* pp. 57–58.

[131] For the charge that the government got "196 planes for 1 billion dollars," see ibid., pp. 35–61. For the response that the government spent less money and industry produced more planes (albeit

The 1920s and 1930s were marked by close congressional scrutiny and tight regulation of relations between the armed services and the aviation industry, and by periodic threats of expanded public-sector participation in the manufacture of aircraft. In the end, however, the norm of private production was preserved, due in part to the relatively low priority assigned to air power by both the Army and the Navy during much of the interwar period. Neither the top commanders nor the established procurement bureaucracies of either service were primarily concerned with acquiring aircraft. As we have seen, the Army's arsenals concentrated what resources they had on perfecting the implements of land warfare, while the Navy's yards devoted themselves mainly to manufacturing surface ships and submarines. For the Army and, to a somewhat lesser degree, for the Navy as well, initiating large-scale, in-house production of aircraft would have required major investments in plant and equipment. Given the scarcity of available funds and prevailing attitudes about the likely subordinate role of airplanes in a future war, such an undertaking was extremely improbable.[132]

The middle-ranking officers most closely involved in the interwar development of air power also tended to be favorably disposed to industry and sympathetic to its needs. This was, in part, a matter of making a virtue of necessity; the airmen had few allies in their own services, and they knew that if they were to have planes to fly, they would have to rely heavily on industry to provide them. In both services there was also a genuine admiration for the inventiveness and audacity of the private air entrepreneurs and a recognition of the advantages to be gained from a continuing association with them. As one officer explained in the early 1920s, when a congressional committee pressed the Navy to build all its own aircraft, "We want to get the ideas of outside people. . . . We want to make use of outside facilities and outside engineers and inventors."[133] In the 1930s, the ability of the commercial aircraft companies to pay their personnel more than government salary scales would permit helped to further bolster their positions as repositories of knowledge and talent.[134]

Despite persistent suspicion of their business practices, the private plane makers were able to avoid some of the hostility directed at the shipbuilders and the other makers of more traditional munitions. Barely in existence before the war, the aircraft manufacturers could not very well be accused of having started

not in time to see action in Europe), see Howard Mingos, *The Birth of an Industry* (New York: W. B. Conkey, 1930), pp. 1–55; Grover Loening, *Takeoff into Greatness: How American Aviation Grew So Big So Fast* (New York: G. P. Putnam's Sons, 1968), pp. 113–16.

[132] Interwar aircraft procurement policy is discussed at length in Vander Meulen, *The Politics of Aircraft*. See also Edwin H. Rutkowski, *The Politics of Military Aviation Procurement, 1926–1934: A Study in the Political Assertion of Consensual Values* (Columbus: Ohio State University Press, 1966); Irving Brinton Holley, Jr., *Buying Aircraft: Materiel Procurement for the Army Air Forces* (Washington, DC: U.S. Government Printing Office, 1964), pp. 43–150.

[133] Quoted in Trimble, "Naval Aircraft Factory," p. 181.

[134] See the discussion in a Harvard Business School study by Robert Schlaifer and S. D. Heron, *Development of Aircraft Engines and Fuels: Two Studies of Relations between Government and Business* (Elmsford, NY: Maxwell Reprint Co., 1950), pp. 35–39.

it. As in 1917, there was also a sense during the interwar years that airplanes were a different and potentially more benign form of military technology. Even if airpower had failed to live up to its promise during the last war, there was still hope that it might succeed in staving off a future conflict or, if this was not possible, in making sure that it was decided far from the shores of the United States and with a minimal loss of American life.[135]

The expectation that airplanes would someday have far-reaching and beneficial commercial applications also helped to mute congressional and popular animosity toward the aviation industry. It was one thing to advocate government manufacture of products that had no conceivable civilian use or counterpart, another to propose the effective nationalization of an industry that might one day revolutionize the country's transport and communications systems. While there was some talk of nationalization during the early 1930s, the ultimate course of legislative action was quite moderate. The Army Arsenal Act of 1920 was not interpreted as mandating in-house procurement of airplanes, and the 1934 Vinson-Trammel Act that required half of all naval vessels to be built in public yards imposed a more modest target of only 10 percent for naval aircraft.[136]

Last but by no means least, the private plane makers had themselves to thank for their own survival. Energetic, visionary, persuasive, and badly in need of military contracts, the aircraft company executives were acutely aware of the threat posed by the possibility of increased public production. While competing vigorously against one another, the industry's leaders were nevertheless able to make common cause in opposing proposals for expanded government manufacture of aircraft. They organized various associations and organizations to lobby Congress and displayed an early knack for deploying the language of economic liberalism, casting themselves as the exemplars of free enterprise and as underdogs faced with the possibility of unfair competition from the federal government.[137]

Mobilization

The air industry's closest brush with nationalization came after the Munich crisis of 1938. Growing recognition that war might truly be imminent, and that

---

[135] On evolving American attitudes toward airpower see Sherry, *The Rise of American Airpower,* pp. 22–75.

[136] Holley, *Buying Aircraft,* pp. 124–28.

[137] As one manufacturer of seaplanes put it in 1925: "It is pretty hard for an individual to compete with a rich man like the Government." Quoted in Trimble, "Naval Aircraft Factory," p. 189. The activities of the Aeronautical Chamber of Commerce and the Manufacturers Aircraft Association in stimulating popular and congressional support for the industry are discussed in Mingos, *The Birth of an Industry,* pp. 48–95. For an overview of the industry in the late 1930s see William Barclay Harding, *The Aviation Industry* (New York: Charles D. Barney, 1937). See also G. R. Simonson, "The Demand for Aircraft and the Aircraft Industry, 1907–1958," *Journal of Economic History* 20, no. 3 (September 1960), pp. 361–82; Wayne Biddle, *Barons of the Sky* (New York: Simon and Schuster, 1991).

air power would play a critical role in determining its outcome, led to an anxious high-level reexamination of existing procurement policies. At a White House meeting in November, President Roosevelt ordered the War Department to draw up plans for acquiring ten thousand additional aircraft over the next two years. Of this total, one-fifth were to be constructed in two new government-owned factories. Five more assembly plants would also be built by the Works Progress Administration and placed on standby status pending the need for an even more dramatic buildup.[138]

Roosevelt's proposal for what was referred to at the time as a federal "air arsenal" struck terror in the hearts of aviation company executives. "To some," writes historian Irving Holley, the plan "reeked of socialism." At the very least it "spelled trouble in the form of increased competition."[139] These concerns reflected an obvious self-interest, but they also had a wider resonance. By the late 1930s Congress and the public had grown much warier of expansions in federal authority, and serious suggestions that the government take on new responsibilities for manufacturing aircraft were greeted with even greater skepticism than had been the case only a few years before. In 1934, at the peak of the "merchants of death" hearings, industry had been cast as the villian and government as the potential savior of the peace and protector of the public interest. Now, in the eyes of many, the situation was reversed. As one newspaper headline put it: "Nationalization of Entire Aviation Industry Threatened by Left Wingers in Washington."[140]

The final blow to the president's plan was struck by the Army Air Corps itself. Industry spokesmen assured their military customers that they had sufficient capacity to meet increased production targets. If federal funds were diverted from purchasing commercially manufactured aircraft to constructing government plants, however, the consequences would be catastrophic. Faced with the choice between building up their own emergency productive capacity and keeping industry healthy and reasonably happy, Air Corps procurement officers preferred the latter course. Soon after it was advanced, the idea of an air arsenal was quietly dropped. The military turned its attention instead to placing orders with industry, facilitating the export of U.S.-made planes to America's allies overseas, and trying to coax reluctant companies to expand their facilities in anticipation of the nation's eventual entry into the war.[141]

---

[138] For various accounts of this plan see Jeffrey S. Underwood, *The Wings of Democracy: The Influence of Air Power on the Roosevelt Administration, 1933–1941* (College Station: Texas A & M University Press, 1991), pp. 134–37; Holley, *Buying Aircraft*, pp. 169–80; H. H. Arnold, *Global Mission* (New York: Harper and Brothers, 1949), pp. 173–79.

[139] Holley, *Buying Aircraft*, p. 277.

[140] Headline from the *New York Sun* cited ibid., p. 185. Holley indicates the date as November 18, 1939, but it seems likely the year was actually 1938. This would have put the story four days after the White House meeting. The 1938 elections are generally seen as having marked a major turning point in public support for the New Deal. In that year the Democrats lost seventy seats in the House and seven in the Senate. See Alan Brinkley, *The End of Reform: New Deal Liberalism in Recession and War* (New York: Knopf, 1995), pp. 140–43.

[141] Holley, *Buying Aircraft*, p. 178.

The basic decision to rely on private manufacturers was reaffirmed when the world crisis deepened. In May 1940, with France on the verge of collapse, President Roosevelt went before Congress to request funds to buy fifty thousand airplanes and to permit the construction of sufficient capacity to manufacture fifty thousand more each year. The question now was not whether the government should participate directly in the productive process, but what it could do to assist private firms in making the necessary investments in plant and equipment. As the pace of preparations increased, aircraft had thus clearly been placed in a category distinct from ships, guns, or other munitions. Instead of constructing federally owned facilities for their manufacture, the government would continue to rely on industry to build its planes for it.[142]

Despite the worsening international situation, industry executives remained fearful of overbuilding and were reluctant to expand as far or as fast as the military deemed essential. At first, mobilization planners sought to ease the process by getting Congress to lower existing statutory limits on industry profits and revising the tax laws to permit rapid amortization of investments in new manufacturing plants. The aim of these initiatives was to make expansion more appealing to industry and to finance as much of the buildup as possible with private capital. When it became clear that this approach would not be sufficient, planners began to look for ways of channeling federal funds directly into private hands. The institutional mechanism that they devised for this purpose, the so-called Defense Plant Corporation (DPC), was authorized to give firms the money with which to build new facilities and buy necessary equipment. Private operators would then lease their plants from the government, which retained title to them. When the war emergency was over, the lessee would have the option of buying its facility outright. Only plants that were not purchased in this way would revert to the government for continued operation or sale as surplus.[143]

DPC financing was an important way station between purely private and outright government ownership of the means of production; it was devised specifically to minimize fears of statism and to reduce the risk that when the war was over, government would control large chunks of the nation's commercial industrial base. Over the course of the Second World War, a combination of DPC funding and private (usually tax-depreciated) investment provided the great majority of the resources used to expand output in steel, synthetic rubber, mining, machine tools, and, above all, aircraft. Between 1940 and 1945 American airframe and engine manufacturing capacity increased by 4,000 percent; 90 percent of this expansion was financed by the government, roughly three-quarters through the DPC. At the war's end the federal government owned 350

---

[142] The orgins of the fifty-thousand-plane requirement are discussed ibid., pp. 223–46.

[143] The origins of the various methods of financing industrial expansion are discussed at length ibid., pp. 290–329; Sweeting, "Building the Arsenal of Democracy," pp. 91–169; Smith, *The Army and Economic Mobilization*, pp. 437–502. On the DPC in particular see Gerald T. White, "Financing Industrial Expansion for War: The Origins of the Defense Plant Corporation Leases," *Journal of Economic History* 9, no. 2 (November 1949), pp. 156–83; White, *Billions for Defense*; Clifford J. Durr, *The Defense Plant Corporation* (University: University of Alabama Press, 1950).

airframe, engine, and component manufacturing facilities, and DPC-financed plants accounted for over 70 percent of the aviation industry's overall productive capacity.[144]

Reprivatization

The buildup in aircraft manufacturing capacity was essentially complete in 1943; the peak of production came a year later. Victory brought what has been described as "a spectacular expansion in reverse"; orders plummeted, plants closed, and most of the companies that had not been involved in aircraft manufacture before the war left the industry and returned to peacetime pursuits. By the end of 1945 only 16 of a peak 66 major airframe assembly plants remained open. By the end of 1946, fully two-thirds of all the aviation plants built with federal funds during the war had been declared surplus. Most of these were sold and either scrapped or converted to civilian use. A number of other government-owned aircraft manufacturing facilities were placed on inactive reserve status.[145]

Despite the massive sell-off and contrary to what the architects of the buildup had intended, the government continued to own a sizable portion of the nation's aircraft manufacturing capacity. The reasons for this were simple enough. With the prospect for future orders uncertain, most of the major aviation companies did not want to take the risk of purchasing facilities that might never again be used at anything close to full capacity. Military planners, on the other hand, were reluctant simply to scrap the entire portfolio of government-owned factories and equipment. Some of these would no doubt prove invaluable in a future crisis, even if the contractors, for purely commercial reasons, did not want to buy them. Without a government-owned and -operated "air arsenal," the armed forces, and especially the newly independent Air Force, knew that they would have to continue to rely on private operators to build their planes for them. In the immediate aftermath of the war, the planners worried that left to fend for itself, the American aviation industry would wither away altogether.[146]

As it had been during the war, continued government ownership of privately

---

[144] For financing in various sectors see the table in Sweeting, "Building the Arsenal of Democracy," p. 249. Regarding the aircraft industry see White, "Defense Plant Corporation Leases," p. 158; Cook, *The Marketing of Surplus War Property,* pp. 22–23.

[145] See William Glenn Cunningham, "Postwar Developments and the Location of the Aircraft Industry in 1950," in G. R. Simonson, ed., *The History of the American Aircraft Industry* (Cambridge: MIT Press, 1968), pp. 182–85; Cook, *The Marketing of Surplus War Property,* p. 24.

[146] See the discussion in Merton J. Peck and Frederic M. Scherer, *The Weapons Acquisition Process: An Economic Analysis* (Boston: Harvard University Graduate School of Business Administration, 1962), pp. 164–65. The question of how to stimulate sufficient demand for civilian and military aircraft to maintain the industry in peacetime was the subject of two sympathetic postwar reports. Interestingly, neither one addressed the issue of extensive government ownership of plant and equipment. See a Report by the President's Air Policy Commission, *Survival in the Air Age* (Washington, DC: U.S. Government Printing Office, 1948); Report of the Congressional Aviation Policy Board, *National Aviation Policy,* 80th Cong., 2d sess. (Washington, DC: U.S. Government Printing Office, 1948).

operated facilities was a second-best solution. What the industry feared, and had been able thus far to avoid, was nationalization or at least direct competition from government-owned and -operated factories.[147] What the military wanted but had not yet been able to attain was a truly private aviation industry, large and vital enough to meet its current and possible future needs.

The goal of full privatization moved somewhat farther out of reach during the Korean conflict, when the wartime practice of providing public funds to finance emergency expansion was repeated, albeit on a smaller scale. After requiring contractors to use existing facilities to the greatest extent feasible and seeking to induce the maximum possible private investment through tax incentives, the Defense Department did ultimately provide some money for new factories. But the government paid for only 25 percent of the expansion in aircraft manufacturing plants between 1950 and 1953, as compared to over 85 percent in the period 1940 to 1945. The policy of limiting expenditures on new buildings was partially offset by a continued willingness to help pay for machine tools and other production equipment. With the shift toward larger airframes and from propellers to jet engines, such expenditures were considerable. During the Korean War the federal share of outlays for new equipment was roughly 80 percent of the total, slightly less than in World War Two.[148]

Since the early 1940s, emergency federal financing of plant and equipment had generally been regarded as an unavoidable necessity. After Korea, however, the government's considerable portfolio of investments came to be viewed increasingly as an anomaly and an embarrassment, both to the aviation industry and to the Air Force. Over the course of the next decade, pressure for full privatization increased, and the government's role in the productive process, always peripheral, diminished.

Unlike their Army and Navy counterparts, Air Force procurement officers had no in-house productive capabilities to protect. To the contrary, spokesmen for the nation's youngest military service took pride in proclaiming their belief in the virtues of private enterprise and in declaring their independence from burdensome backward arsenals and shipyards.[149] As Air Force officials pressed home their public relations advantage against the other services, they grew more self-conscious about their ongoing role as landlords and property owners, and more determined to jettison their considerable industrial holdings.

---

[147] The possibility of nationalization reared its head again briefly in 1948 when Henry Wallace suggested that "the only way to protect peace and the public interest is for the government to take over all companies making military aircraft." Quoted in Frank Kofsky, *Harry S. Truman and the War Scare of 1948* (New York: St. Martin's Press, 1995), p. 255.

[148] See the discussion and figures in John S. Day, *Subcontracting Policy in the Airframe Industry* (Boston, MA: Harvard University Graduate School of Business Administration, 1956), pp. 42–48; John B. Rae, *Climb to Greatness: The American Aircraft Industry, 1920–1960* (Cambridge: MIT Press, 1968), pp. 197–200.

[149] See, for example, a statement by Dudley Sharp, Assistant Secretary of the Air Force (Materiel), in Hearings before the Subcommittee for Special Investigations of the House Armed Services Committee, *Aircraft Production Costs and Profits*, 84th Cong., 2d sess. (Washington, DC: U.S. Government Printing Office, 1956), p. 2819–23.

Air Force planners had other, more concrete reasons for promoting increased private ownership. Despite the preferential treatment it received during the Eisenhower years, the air arm too had to worry about its budget, and each dollar spent on tools and factories was one that could not be used to buy more planes and missiles. Much of the plant and equipment being maintained, at considerable expense, on standby status was also rapidly becoming obsolete. The move from propellers to jets had already reduced the utility of many older Air Force–owned facilities, and the next leap, from jets to rockets, was expected to have even more far-reaching effects.[150]

In the second half of the 1950s, the Air Force also led the way in adopting procurement policies that more closely matched the evolving national military strategy. Of all the services, it was the Air Force that embraced most fully the view that a future war with the Soviet Union would be brief and enormously destructive, and that it would be fought entirely with weapons already on hand. If this were the case, then there was no point in investing in productive capacity beyond what was necessary to supply current needs. "The older industrial mobilization concepts which required standby war-plant capacity are not adaptable to our current problem of maintaining an adequate force in being," explained one official. "For these reasons the Air Force . . . is actively engaged in [building] a forward looking industrial base which is adjusted to firm weapons program needs, and is privately capitalized to the maximum degree that is possible."[151] What this meant in practice was selling or scrapping more government-owned standby facilities, increasing pressure on industry to buy leased plants and equipment, and refusing, except in unusual cases, to pay for more.[152]

Since the early 1940s, the companies most heavily dependent on government capital were the largest makers of airframes. By the mid-1950s the government owned around 70 percent of the industrial floor space of twelve major aircraft manufacturers, and just over half the floor space of twenty top firms.[153] Albeit with varying degrees of self-professed discomfort, the leaders of the bigger companies tended to believe that a measure of continuing government investment and ownership was inevitable. Testifying before Congress in 1956, some industry executives deplored "the huge investment of Government money" in

---

[150] See G. R. Simonson, "Missiles and Creative Destruction in the American Aircraft Industry, 1956–1961," *Business History Review* 38, no. 3 (Autumn 1964), pp. 302–14.

[151] Dudley Sharp, Assistant Secretary of the Air Force (Materiel), in Hearings bfore the Subcommittee for Special Investigations of the House Armed Service Committee, *Utilization of Government-Owned Plants and Facilities*, 85th Cong., 2d sess. (Washington, DC: U.S. Government Printing Office, 1959), p. 1146.

[152] See Evert Clark, "Industry Faces Increasing Competition: Defense Begins Push to Decrease Use of Government Facilities; Encourage Privately Financed Plants," *Aviation Week* 69 (October 6, 1958), p. 26.

[153] For the first figure see Aircraft Industries Association of America, *Aviation Facts and Figures, 1956* (Washington, DC: Lincoln Press, 1956), p. 9. For the second, see Miguel Angel Reguero, *An Economic Study of the Military Airframe Industry* (Dayton, OH: Department of the Air Force, 1957), pp. 84–86.

aircraft manufacturing facilities and declared their strong belief "in the traditional American free-enterprise system under which each manufacturer owns its own facilities."[154] Others took a more measured tone: "I wonder if the issue is really that of Government ownership versus private enterprise," responded the president of another major company. "I am sure that none of us in industry . . . believe in socialistic or anarchistic concepts."[155]

Whatever their preferred rhetorical strategy, the industry's leaders all pointed with pride to the new investments that their companies had undertaken in recent years and to the generally diminishing share of their plant and equipment that was owned by the federal government. There was widespread agreement also that if the trend toward full privatization were to continue, the military's estimate of what constituted "fair" industry profits would have to change. When government furnished virtually all productive facilities, as it had during the Second World War, profits that were a relatively small fraction of sales still amounted to a very favorable return on company investment. If in their negotiation of peacetime production contracts military procurement officers continued to hold companies to the same level of return on sales while pressing them to invest more of their own funds in new facilities, returns on investment would fall. This, industry executives warned, would make it more difficult for them to raise private capital for new facilities. Government policy therefore linked profits and investments. As one executive told Congress: "[We agree] with the Government's objective of having industry provide more of the facilities needed to accomplish defense work. However, the company can move in this direction only as it is permitted to earn and retain earnings which make investment in facilities economically sound."[156] Industry anxiety on this score mounted in the late 1950s as the pace of technological change again accelerated and as government pressed harder for greater corporate self-reliance.[157]

---

[154] See testimony of Robert Charles, Executive Vice President, McDonnell Aircraft Corporation, in Hearings bfore the Subcommittee for Special Investigations of the House Armed Services Committee, *Aircraft Production Costs and Profits* 84th Cong., 2d sess. (Washington, DC: U.S. Government Printing Office, 1956), p. 2127.

[155] See testimony of John Jay Roberts, Chairman of the Board and President, General Dynamics Corporation in *Aircraft Productionn Costs and Profits*, p. 2578,

[156] See testimony of Clyde Skeen, Company Controller, Boeing Airplane, in *Aircraft Production Costs and Profits*, p. 1806. This issue is discussed in Peck and Scherer, *The Weapons Acquisition Process*, pp. 164–70.

[157] For statements of industry concern see also Aircraft Industries Association of America, *Aviation Facts and Figures, 1958* (Washington, DC: American Aviation Publications, 1958), pp. 10–14; *Aviation Facts and Figures, 1959* (Washington, DC: American Aviation Publications, 1959), pp. 10–12; Claude Witze, "Subcontractors Face Stiffer Competition: Military Anticipates Fewer Primes, Excess Space, as Emphasis Swings from Airframes to Missiles," *Aviation Week* 66 (May 27, 1957), p. 26. The acceleration of the missile/space race did result in a temporary increase in government facility investment, but the general trend was downward. For overall figures for government investment in industry facilities, see *Aerospace Facts and Figures, 1960* (formerly *Aviation Facts and Figures*) (Washington, DC: American Aviation Publications, 1960), p. 15. Regarding the missile programs in particular see Maj. Gen. Bernard Schriever, "The USAF Ballistic Missile Pro-

Congressional opinion on the question of government ownership shifted over time from ambivalent acceptance to growing hostility. The major post-Korea investigation of military procurement policies and aviation industry practices came to the conclusion that "the production of military airframes is, in essence, a Government enterprise." Heavy federal investment in the process was thus a fact of life that it would "not do to bemoan."[158] But this acquiescent attitude did not last for long.

As with the munitions manufacturing GOCOs (but in contrast to the federal shipyards) Air Force–owned, contractor-operated aircraft production facilities could not be said to constitute a simple case of government competition against industry. As was true in other sectors, however, the very idea of government ownership came to be regarded with increasing skepticism in the second half of the 1950s. A deviation from free market principles that was acceptable under conditions of acute emergency became less so as the Cold War stabilized and the nation settled in for what President Eisenhower referred to as "the long pull." Although it drew back from suggesting an immediate sale of all federally owned facilities, the Hoover Commission warned that the aviation industry had become "a 'ward' of the Government." This was "not a healthy condition," and the Commission recommended that it be remedied by permitting higher profits in exchange for an industry commitment to increase investment in plant and equipment. The aim of this policy should be to arrive "at private ownership as an alternative to Government ownership."[159]

Government might not be competing with industry in manufacturing aircraft, but its assistance could give some firms an edge over potential rivals. As it became clear that defense spending (and Air Force spending, in particular) would stay high for the foreseeable future, smaller firms became more eager to get and hold a piece of the market. The increasing importance of missiles and electronics also encouraged companies that had not done so previously to compete with the traditional airframe manufacturers for a share of the aerospace procurement budget. In the late fifties Congress began to hear more frequently from smaller firms, which complained about the advantages enjoyed by their larger cousins and urged the establishment of a level playing field. The cheapest way for the government to do this was not to pay for still more facilities, but to divest itself as fully as possible of its existing holdings.[160] By the end of the decade Air Force officials were reassuring Congress that they were selling off

---

gram," *Air University Quarterly Review* 9, no. 3 (Summer 1957), p. 16; and Brig. Gen. Ben Funk, "Impact of the Ballistic Missile on Industry," *Air University Quarterly Review* 9, no. 3 (Summer 1957), pp. 96–7.

[158] See Subcommittee for Special Investigations of the House Armed Services Committee, *Report on Aircraft Production Costs and Profits*, 84th Cong., 2d sess. (Washington, DC: U.S. Government Printing Office, 1956), p. 3113.

[159] *Real Property Management*, p. 67.

[160] For complaints about government policy see, for example, Hearings before Subcommittee No. 4 of the House Select Committee on Small Business, *The Aircraft Industry*, 85th Cong., 2nd sess. (Washington, DC: U.S. Government Printing Office, 1959).

plant and equipment as quickly as they could, minimizing new investments, and if anything, showing a preference for contractors who supplied their own facilities. "All other things being equal," the Air Force procurement chief testified in 1960, "the man without the Government facility will get the award."[161]

As he would do in other sectors, Robert McNamara pushed the privatization of aerospace production forward faster toward its logical end point. During his first two years in office, the Defense Department sold off 55 of a remaining total of 202 GOCO facilities, including several big aircraft production plants. Like its predecessor, the new administration justified its actions not merely on efficiency grounds, but in ideological terms, as an indication of its "dedication to the preservation and strengthening of a free enterprise economy."[162]

In addition to selling old facilities, McNamara cut new investment to a trickle, declaring that in future it would be held "to the absolute minimum," and he announced policies designed to encourage more private funding of industry expansion. The most important of these initiatives was a change in procurement regulations to permit higher industry profits.[163] "We have encouraged contractors to invest their own resources in industrial facilities," McNamara told the Congress. "We are hopeful that these efforts will . . . contribute to the maintenance of the independence and integrity of the private enterprise system."[164]

As flows of government funds diminished and corporate investment increased, the balance of public versus private ownership of the industry's capital stock shifted. This was a trend that had already been set in motion during the Eisenhower years, but that accelerated during the early 1960s. Reliable industrywide statistics are not available.[165] One study of five top aerospace companies

[161] General Davis, Director of Procurement and Production, Air Materiel Command, quoted in William L. Baldwin, *The Structure of the Defense Market, 1955–1964* (Durham, NC: Duke University Press, 1967), p. 186.

[162] See testimony of Thomas D. Morris, Assistant Secretary of Defense, Installations and Logistics, in *Department of Defense Appropriations for 1964*, pt. 5, *Procurement*, pp. 161, 159–63. Among the facilities sold were the General Dynamics plant in Groton, Connecticut, and a Boeing plant in Renton, Washington. See also the 1963 report *Government Competition with Free Enterprise*, pp. 299–304.

[163] Defense Department directives on profits and facilities policies (issued in 1963 and 1964, respectively) are discussed in Aerospace Industries Association of America, *Aerospace Facts and Figures, 1964* (Los Angeles: Aero Publishers, 1964), pp. 89–92. Evidence of falling industry profits prior to the change in department policy is contained in Arthur D. Little, Inc., *How Sick Is the Defense Industry?* (Cambridge, MA: Arthur D. Little, 1963), pp. 42–58. Figures for public and private investment in new aerospace production equipment are reported in Hearings Before the Subcommittee on Department of Defense of the Senate Committee on Appropriations, *Department of Defense Appropriations, 1965*, pt. 1, *Procurement*, p. 779.

[164] See McNamara's testimony in Hearings before the Subcommittees of the House Committee on Appropriations, *Department of Defense Appropriations for 1968*, pt. 2, *Secretary of Defense*, 90th Cong., 1st sess. (Washington, DC: U.S. Government Printing Office, 1967), p. 466.

[165] One study reports that in the 1950s, the share of government ownership of productive facilities was "about 70 percent, by 1963 it was 55 percent, and by 1976 it was 35 percent." The source of this information is not clear, nor is it obvious if it is meant to refer to the aerospace industry in particular or to all defense-related industries. Jacques S. Gansler, *The Defense Industry* (Cambridge: MIT Press, 1980), p. 292.

found that by 1962, for the first time since the end of the Korean War, the contractors owned a larger portion of their facilities than the government did. In 1964 contractor-owned machine tools exceeded in value those supplied by the Air Force.[166] After a quarter century, and not entirely of its own volition, the aerospace industry was finally beginning once again to approximate its ideal image of itself as a bastion of private ownership and free enterprise.[167]

CONCLUSION: THE CONSEQUENCES OF PRIVATIZATION

Suppose that the various debates and struggles detailed in this chapter had turned out differently. Suppose that the American armed forces, in the wake of the Second World War, had reverted to their traditional peacetime practice of building most of the weapons they needed in federally owned and operated arsenals and shipyards. Would a largely public arms production system have been more efficient than the one that actually took shape? More innovative? Would its existence or, more precisely, would the *absence* of a large private arms manufacturing sector have resulted in defense and foreign policies very different from those the United States actually chose to pursue? That these counterfactual questions cannot all be answered with assurance does not make them any less important to ask.

Cost

The issue of comparative cost is easiest to address. There is no reason, either theoretical or empirical, to believe that government-owned factories would have been more efficient producers of arms than were their private, profit-motivated counterparts. While it did not always do so effectively, the federal government at least had the possibility of keeping costs down by using competition between rival suppliers and contracts that linked profits to efficiency. Simulating these incentives in a system in which both "buyers" and "sellers" were public entities would have been far more difficult.[168]

---

[166] See Francis W. Shepherd, "The Industrial Mobilization Value of Government-Owned Facilities" (Ph.D. dissertation, George Washington University, 1977), pp. 36–37. These figures, drawn from a government-commissioned study, compare the total undepreciated acquisition costs of government versus private investments. Given that most of what the government owned had been purchased in the 1940s and early 1950s, the current market value of its investments in the early 1960s was probably much lower than that of the companies.

[167] Compared to World War II and even Korea, government investment in plant and equipment during the Vietnam War was extremely small, amounting to only $0.8 billion in 1975 dollars, versus $51.8 billion and $23.8 billion, respectively. Ibid., p. 1. At least during the early stages of the war, the majority of these funds went to expand and modernize the munitions manufacturing base. See figures in *Department of Defense Appropriations for 1968*, pt. 2, pp. 604–5.

[168] The two classic discussions of government contracting with private arms producers are John Perry Miller, *Pricing of Military Procurements* (New Haven: Yale University Press, 1949); Frederic Scherer, *The Weapons Acquisition Process: Economic Incentives* (Boston, MA: Harvard University

The available evidence, sparse thought it is, bears out the expectation of superior private-sector cost effectiveness. In the few instances where direct comparisions were made (as was the case, in the early 1960s, in the manufacture of new warships and M14 rifles), private firms consistently gave better value for the taxpayer's dollar. It seems reasonable to conclude therefore that a force equipped with government-built weapons would have cost more, perhaps much more, than one in which the same systems were assembled by industry. All other things being equal, the fiscal burdens of the Cold War would probably have been considerably greater under a system of public manufacturing.

Innovation

In the wake of the controversy over the Army's arsenal system, a number of thoughtful observers noted the absence of a careful and complete comparison of the performance of public and private weapons development organizations. An influential 1963 book on arms procurement policy pointed out: "Specific examples can be brought forth to support virtually any contention about the relative effectiveness of arsenals and private industry [but] a thorough comparative study of [their] average success records . . . has never been made." In the absence of such a study, "no firm conclusions" could be offered.[169] The fact that so many people were so firmly convinced of the superiority of the private sector suggested to economist Carl Kaysen in the early 1960s that the matter was being treated as "an issue of principle rather than a question of balance and emphasis."[170]

Kaysen's assessment of the politics of the situation was certainly correct, even if his enthusiasm for in-house weapons development appears now to have been misplaced. A thorough study of the performance of the arsenal system would probably reveal that the Army's missile program (like the atomic bomb project before it) was the exception that proved the rule; the rifle program was far more typical. When working on an emergency basis, outside normal bureaucratic channels, with ample resources, and a team of highly talented civilian personnel recruited especially for a particular job, government laboratories were capable of making major breakthroughs. Functioning free of competitive pressures, and working on less dramatic, sequential improvements in weapons capability, the in-house facilities were inclined to be plodding and unimaginative.

The Air Force's contractor-centered research and development system had its flaws, but a lack of enthusiasm for innovation was not among them. To the contrary, the primary criticism of the aerospace companies in the late 1950s and early 1960s was that they were overly eager to advance new ideas in the

---

Graduate School of Business Administration, 1964); for a comparison of public versus private production see pp. 385–88.

[169] Ibid., p. 389–90.

[170] Carl Kaysen, "Improving the Efficiency of Military Research and Development," *Public Policy* 12 (1963), p. 273.

294 CHAPTER SEVEN

hopes of gaining an edge on their competitors and winning the government's business.[171] This tendency increased the risk of waste and the desirability of higher-level mechanisms of oversight and control. Given that the United States was engaged in a technological competition with the Soviet Union, however, a strong bias toward innovation also had some very distinct advantages. It is unlikely that a primarily public arms development system would have been more innovative, and hence more effective in international competition, than the largely private system that had come into existence by the early 1960s; it most likely would have been less so.[172]

Impact

What of the impact of the private arms makers on American foreign and defense policy? Assuming for a moment that the United States did indeed need to arm itself against external enemies, would it have done so differently if the federal government had performed this task directly, rather than hiring private entities to do it? Would U.S. defense spending have been higher or lower under such circumstances? Would the United States government have found it easier to compose its differences with the Soviet Union and wind down military expenditures, if not for the fact that a relaxation of tensions would have been costly to its suppliers?

A greatly enlarged network of government laboratories and factories would have given rise to its own expanded cluster of societal supporters. The managers of these federal facilities might have been more constrained than their corporate counterparts in lobbying Congress directly for more money, but their employees and the communities in which they operated need not have been. Even if government-owned arsenals and shipyards assembled weapons, they would also most likely have relied on industrial subcontractors for materials, parts, and tools. These private actors too would have had a direct stake in the well-being of their public sector customers. In a world dominated by government arms makers there would still have been interest-based societal pressures for ever-larger defense budgets.

Public producers might actually have been better situated than their private counterparts to delay or prevent deep reductions in military spending. Even when budgets were tight, contractors could usually be expected to survive by

[171] This is the theme of H. L. Nieburg's book *In the Name of Science* and of many subsequent critiques of the role of the "military-industrial complex" in fueling the "arms race."

[172] The overall performance of the American research and development system over time and in comparison to the Soviet system will be considered in chapter 8. A thorough comparison of the performance of all three U.S. services might well reveal that the Navy, with its mix of strong in-house facilities and strong ties to contractors, had the best track record of all. The Navy's success during the 1950s and early 1960s in developing nuclear propulsion, fleet ballistic missiles, and antisubmarine warfare technologies lends some credence to this speculation. See the discussion of the unique blend of public and private institutions used to develop the Polaris missile in Harvey M. Sapolsky, *The Polaris System Development: Bureaucratic and Programmatic Success in Government* (Cambridge: Harvard University Press, 1972), pp. 61–93.

laying off workers, diversifying, or taking on smaller pieces of larger programs. In the final analysis, in a market economy, the survival of any given company could also not be said to be the responsibility of the federal government. Eliminating an arsenal or shipyard, on the other hand, meant laying off federal employees and dissolving capabilities that might be difficult to reassemble. It was for these reasons that Frederick Scherer concluded in the early 1960s that "political pressures act with greater consistency to insure the survival of government arsenals. It may be difficult . . . to shed a major contractor, but it is even more difficult . . . to close an arsenal or shipyard."[173]

The big American defense firms probably played as small a role in perpetuating the Cold War as they did in starting it. Whatever one's views on this question, however, it is difficult to believe that a large, deeply entrenched public bureaucracy with nowhere to go but out of business would have been a less effective opponent of peace. This is a possibility that the many Cold War critics of the "military-industrial complex," and the occasional advocates of public arms production, do not seem to have considered.

[173] Scherer, *The Weapons Acquisition Process,* p. 388.

CHAPTER EIGHT

Technology

FREE MEN AND MODERN ARMS

In an influential 1949 book, former wartime science czar Vannevar Bush asserted the existence of a connection between the fundamental character of a nation's domestic political regime and its capacity for technological innovation. "The philosophy that men live by," Bush claimed,

> determines the form in which their governments will be molded. Upon the form of their government depends their progress in utilizing the applications of science to raise their standards of living and in building their strength for possible war.[1]

The burden of this chapter is to make the case that Bush was right. As the next four sections will demonstrate, each of the essential structural characteristics of the American Cold War research and development system (its size and strategic importance, its organizational pluralism and lack of bureaucratic centralization, its constrained functional scope, and its reliance on private entities) was strongly influenced by ideological considerations and by the workings of American domestic political institutions. Moreover, as I will suggest in concluding, the structure of the U.S. research and development system and its performance during the Cold War appear to have been strongly linked. The large, open, and loose-limbed American system was well suited for promoting innovation, and it tended over time to outperform its more rigid, closed, and hierarchical Soviet counterpart.[2]

SIZE AND STRATEGIC IMPORTANCE

Over the course of the Cold War, the United States devoted enormous resources to achieving and maintaining an advantage over the Soviet Union in most areas of military technology. Indeed, for nearly half a century, the pursuit of qualitative superiority was a central, persistent feature of the entire American defense effort.

The vigor with which the United States sought technological supremacy reflected the intensity of a set of complementary beliefs about the respective strengths and weaknesses of the U.S. and Soviet (or, more generally, the "free

---

[1] Vannevar Bush, *Modern Arms and Free Men: A Discussion of the Role of Science in Preserving Democracy* (New York: Simon and Schuster, 1949), p. 9.

[2] Differences in the structure and performance of the U.S. and Soviet research and development systems will be discussed in the final section of this chapter.

world" and "totalitarian") systems and about the specific character of the strategic competition between them. From the onset of the Cold War, top American decision makers tended to believe both that it was necessary for their country to seek a technological edge over the Soviet Union and its allies and that such an advantage could be achieved and maintained. These beliefs helped to keep technology at the forefront of American strategy and to sustain a massive four-decade flow of resources into research and development.

What might be called the doctrine of comparative technological advantage clearly served the interests of certain groups in American society. Universities, a cluster of high-technology industries, and the scientists and engineers they employed all benefited in obvious and unambiguous ways from federal largesse, and academics and industrialists were naturally among the most enthusiastic advocates of a substantial research and development effort. For the armed services, endless technological change was a rather more mixed blessing, bringing as it did a steady stream of fresh funding and new weapons as well as regular disruptions to existing patterns of organization and doctrinal thought. It was precisely the desire to avoid such disruptions that had often caused military organizations to cling to existing ways of warfare. The postwar embrace of a policy of perpetual innovation by the armed services helped to overcome these traditional sources of resistance to technological change.

The doctrine of comparative advantage also had a wider resonance with political leaders and with the American public. Because it fit well with other deeply held beliefs (about, among other things, the virtues of freedom, the sanctity of human life, the evils of compulsion, and the advantages of the market system), this set of ideas was remarkably successful as an instrument of persuasion. When acceptance of the precepts of the doctrine was deep and widespread among political elites and the public at large, the pursuit of technological superiority was carried forward with great energy. It was only when those beliefs were called into question (as they were for a time in the 1960s and the early 1970s) that political backing for this endeavor faded and the flow of resources slowed (see figs. 8.1 and 8.2).

Necessity

Before the Second World War had ended and the Cold War began, senior American scientists and top military planners were already agreed that the preservation of a "preeminent position" in weapons technology must be a central goal of peacetime defense policy.[3] Achieving this objective would require a large and continuing research effort. The costs might be high, but the stakes were even

---

[3] See Gen. H. H. Arnold, "Third Report of the Commanding General of the Army Air Forces to the Secretary of War, November 12, 1945," in Walter Millis, ed., *The War Reports of General of the Army George C. Marshall, General of the Army H. H. Arnold, and Fleet Admiral Ernest J. King* (New York: Lippincott, 1947), p. 470. The early emergence of this conviction and its initial implications are analyzed insightfully by Michael S. Sherry, *Preparing for the Next War: American Plans for Postwar Defense, 1941–1945* (New Haven: Yale University Press, 1977), pp. 120–58.

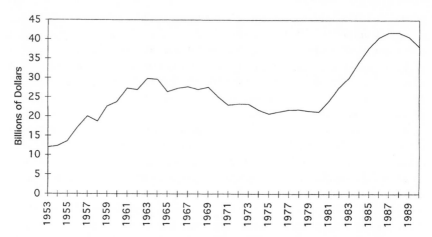

Figure 8.1. Defense Research, Development, Test, and Evaluation (RDT&E) Spending in Constant 1991 Dollars

higher. The "stability and peace" of the new postwar world, declared physicist Arthur Compton, "can not be ensured unless the dominant world power keeps up a vigorous and continued growth of science."[4] It was impossible to be "too strong, or too emphatic," declared Secretary of War Robert Patterson, about the government's interest in "the promotion of scientific research and development for new weapons. We would be . . . blind . . . if we were not alive to that most urgent need."[5]

Initial support for a vigorous postwar military research program was not the result of fear of a particular rival, but reflected instead a number of more general considerations. First, and most obvious, was the recognition that the character of war was being transformed by scientific advance. It was widely acknowledged that technological breakthroughs had been essential to the recent Allied victory. Radar had helped win the Battle of Britain; proximity fused artillery shells had helped turn the tide at the Battle of the Bulge. "Time and again," Vannevar Bush reminded the Congress in October 1945, "the margin which separated victory from disaster was . . . afforded by our scientific and technical advantages."[6] The atomic bombs that brought the war suddenly to a close were only the most recent, and most spectacular, illustrations of the role of science in the conduct of modern warfare.

Despite its stunning achievements, however, the wartime effort to develop and deploy superior weapons had not been a thoroughgoing success, as those who had been most closely associated with it knew. The quality of American

[4] Arthur H. Compton, "What Science Requires of the New World," *Science* 99, no. 2559 (January 14, 1944), p. 25.

[5] Hearings before a Subcommittee of the Senate Committee on Military Affairs, *Hearings on Science Legislation*, 79th Cong., 1st sess. (Washington, DC: U.S. Government Printing Office, 1945), p. 229.

[6] Ibid., p. 199.

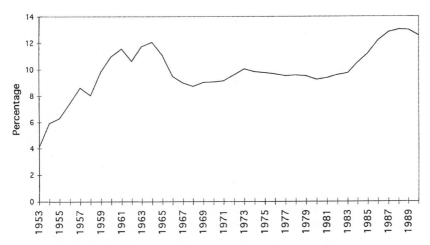

Figure 8.2. RDT&E Spending as Percentage of Total Defense Spending

tanks, aircraft, and artillery never exceeded that of their German counterparts, and by 1945, the Nazis had taken a substantial lead in developing exotic new weapons like jet aircraft and long-range rockets. In terms of the level of sophistication of its basic battlefield forces, the United States started out behind and, in most respects, never caught up.[7] As the war drew to a close, there was widespread agreement that this failure was due in large part to the inadequate funding and insufficient attention that had been devoted to military research during the interwar period.[8] As they were in the areas of industrial mobilization and manpower training, American planners were eager to avoid the mistakes of their pre-war predecessors.

The prevailing belief that the next war would come suddenly and with little warning made continuing peacetime research even more important. "Twice we have just gotten by because we were given time to prepare while others fought," warned Vannevar Bush. "The next time . . . we are not likely to be so

[7] Harold Brown, *Thinking about National Security: Defense and Foreign Policy in a Dangerous World* (Boulder, CO: Westview Press, 1983), pp. 225–26. For a vivid account of the impact of quantity regardless of quality, see John Ellis, *Brute Force: Allied Strategy and Tactics in the Second World War* (New York: Viking, 1990). For a sobering assessment of Germany's technological accomplishments at war's end see Theodore von Karman, *Where We Stand: A Report Prepared for the AAF Scientific Advisory Group* (Dayton, OH: Headquarters Air Materiel Command, 1945).

[8] See, for example, Frank Jewitt, "The Mobilization of Science in National Defense," *Science* 95, no. 2462 (March 6, 1942), pp. 235–41; Rear Adm. J. A. Furer, "Scientific Research and Modern Warfare," *United States Naval Institute Proceedings* 71, no. 3 (March 1945), pp. 259–73. On interwar defense research see A. Hunter Dupree, *Science in the Federal Government: A History of Policies and Activities to 1940* (Cambridge: Harvard University Press, 1957), pp. 331–36, 367–68; Mark S. Watson, *Chief of Staff: Prewar Plans and Preparations* (Washington, DC: Department of the Army, 1950), pp. 15–56; Clarence G. Lasby, "Science and the Military," in David D. van Tassell and Michael G. Hall, eds., *Science and Society in the United States* (Homewood, IL: Dorsey Press, 1966), pp. 251–82.

fortunate."[9] If the United State simply stockpiled old weapons and waited for the next war to begin before it started developing new ones, it would find its forces at a severe, and perhaps decisive, disadvantage. Given the rapid pace of technological advance and the speed and destructiveness of modern weapons, the only solution was "to continually replace the old things with the new creations of the research laboratory and of American inventive genius."[10] Perpetual innovation was an essential element of any policy of peacetime preparedness.

The clear emergence of the Soviet Union as the most likely enemy in any future war added urgency and a clear focus to the discussion of the role of technology in American strategy. From the start of the Cold War, it was widely assumed that the superior extractive capacities of the communist states gave them certain inherent military advantages. Thanks both to the sheer size of the populations and economies under their control and to their ability to tax and conscript virtually without limit, the Soviets and their allies could generate enormous forces in peacetime and even bigger ones, on short notice, in the event of war. Free from democratic constraints, to say nothing of considerations of simple human decency, the leaders of the "slave states" could also afford to use their forces with a reckless disregard for casualties. Unless they were willing to adopt similar domestic powers and battlefield tactics, the nations of the free world would have to offset the advantages of their rivals by substituting firepower for manpower, capital for labor, quality for quantity. Heavy reliance on technology was therefore not an option for the West; given the internal characteristics of the Cold War competitors, it was essential.

This line of argument first began to emerge at the close of the Second World War, and by the beginning of the 1950s it had congealed into strategic dogma. During the war Western observers had been impressed and horrified by the way in which Stalin's armies hurled themselves against the Nazi invaders. Soviet leaders had shown themselves willing to accept massive losses in order to achieve their objectives. As early as November 1945 James Forrestal recorded in his diary the observation that in any future war involving "a combination of Russia and the Asiatic powers the manpower available to such a combination would be so tremendous and the indifference to the loss of life so striking that it would present a very serious problem to this country."[11] Over the next several years this anxiety grew deeper, as the line separating East from West hardened and the obstacles facing a substantial peacetime expansion in U.S. and allied forces became clearer. While the American people rushed to demobilize and resisted plans for universal military training, the Soviets, fresh from their bloody victory over the Germans, appeared to be keeping their enormous armies at the ready. If another war came it seemed inevitable that the United States and its allies would be at a distinct numerical disadvantage.

---

[9] Vannevar Bush, "Science and Security," *Sea Power*, July 1945, p. 35.

[10] Rear Adm. J. A. Furer, "Post-War Military Research," *Science* 100, no. 2604 (November 24, 1944), p. 464.

[11] Diary entry for November 20, 1945, quoted in Walter Millis, ed., *The Forrestal Diaries* (New York: Viking, 1951), p. 108.

Prior to the outbreak of the Korean War, allusions to what Chairman of the Joint Chiefs of Staff General Omar Bradley in a 1949 article termed "the hordes of the East" had already begun to appear in Western strategic debate.[12] After "human waves" of Chinese troops crossed the border into North Korea in December 1950, such references became commonplace. In Europe, as in Asia, it was assumed that a combination of "manpower saturation and complete disregard of human losses . . . [could] be expected as a standard tactic of any Soviet indoctrinated force."[13] Communism had at its disposal a "horde of expendable manpower."[14] But any attempt to "meet the hordes of communism man for man, gun for gun" would be a ruinous mistake.[15] "If war comes," warned Vannevar Bush in a 1952 speech, "we cannot meet hordes with hordes."[16]

The alternative was, of course, to meet superior numbers with superior weaponry. Beginning in the late 1940s this line of reasoning was used to justify the increasing nuclearization of American strategy. In 1948 the combination of rising tensions in Europe and strict constraints on United States defense spending seemed to leave the United States little choice but to rely on long-range atomic air power. With no hope of an immediate and massive conventional buildup, Secretary of Defense Forrestal noted at the time of the Berlin crisis that he was "increasingly impressed by the fact that the only balance that we have against the overwhelming manpower of the Russians, and therefore the chief deterrent to war, is the threat of immediate retaliation with the atomic bomb."[17]

One year later the American atomic monopoly had been shattered and questions were mounting about the ability of the U.S. Air Force to deal a true knockout punch against Russia. Under these circumstances the need to compensate for the "military prostration of our Western European allies" (and presumably also the unwillingness or inability of the United States to close the gap in conventional forces) was offered as an argument for expanding atomic stockpiles and preparing to use atomic weapons wherever "they could be employed more economically than other military measures."[18] Noting that a "determination to have superior military equipment and to base war strategy on its use" was virtually the only aspect of military policy on which all parties were

[12] General Omar Bradley, "This Way Lies Peace," *Saturday Evening Post*, October 15, 1949, p. 168.

[13] Lt. Colonel George B. Pickett, "What Profiteth a Nation?" *Military Review* 34, no. 4 (July 1954), p. 5.

[14] "The Case for Tactical Atomic Weapons," *Army* 6, no. 8 (March 1956), p. 24.

[15] Col. George C. Reinhardt, *American Strategy in the Atomic Age* (Norman: University of Oklahoma Press, 1955), p. 118.

[16] Vannevar Bush, "Organization for Strength," Remarks at Tufts College Centennial Celebration, Medford, MA, October 11, 1952, in (Washington, DC, National War College Library) typescript, p. 3.

[17] From a November 1948 memo "Points for the President," quoted in Millis, *Forrestal Diaries*, p. 538.

[18] "Report to the President by the Special Committee of the National Security Council on the Proposed Acceleration of the Atomic Energy Program," October 10, 1949, Harry S. Truman Library (HSTL), President's Secretary's Files (PSF), Subject File National Security Council, Atomic, Folder Atomic Energy—Expansion of the Atomic Energy Program.

agreed, Forrestal in 1949 declared his intention "to take full advanatge of every possible technological superiority."[19]

The experience of war in Korea further strengthened the conviction that qualitative advantages were essential to the defense of Europe and the survival of the West. Atomic weapons of all sizes would have to be used both to lay waste to the Soviet homeland and to block the advance of Soviet ground forces. Smaller battlefield weapons, in particular, might, in the words of a highly classified report advocating their deployment, "make the difference between victory and defeat in Europe," where NATO forces were assumed to be vastly outnumbered.[20] "Atomic weapons used tactically are the natural armaments of numerically inferior but technologically superior nations," declared one congressional enthusiast in 1951. "They are the natural answer to the armed hordes of the Soviet Union and its satellites . . . They will decisively help to shift the balance of military power toward the free world and against the slave world."[21] Secretary of Defense Robert Lovett's language was slightly more measured, but his reasoning was identical. Making the case for yet another expansion in the atomic energy program in 1952, he asserted that developing still larger stockpiles would

> go far toward providing the free world a means of balancing the superior manpower and the advantage of surprise and initiative held by Communist forces. Military requirements for atomic weapons . . . arise, primarily, from the necessity of meeting Communist aggression by more extensive use of our superior industrial and scientific resources rather than by attempting to match our potential enemy man-for-man.[22]

The Eisenhower administration elevated the substitution of firepower for manpower to the position of key organizing principle of national strategy. Atomic and thermonuclear weapons of every conceivable yield were now unquestionably at the heart of Western defenses, and initial discussions of the necessity of "assuring our lead in non-conventional weapons" or insuring "superior research and development" centered on the need for more and better bombs.[23] Over the course of the 1950s, however, the discussion of technology grew broader and more general. Maintaining across-the-board qualitative supe-

[19] Secretary of Defense James Forrestal, *Second Report of the Secretary of Defense for the Fiscal Year 1949* (Washington, DC: U.S. Government Printing Office, 1950), p. 48.

[20] The 1952 "Vista Report" is quoted in David C. Elliot, "Project Vista and Nuclear Weapons in Europe," *International Security* 11, no. 1 (Summer 1986), p. 169.

[21] "Some Comments on Tactical Atomic Weapons," Memorandum for the Chairman of the Joint Committee on Atomic Energy from J. K. Mansfield, Chief of Special Projects, August 15, 1951, *Foreign Relations of the United States 1951*, vol. 1, *National Security Affairs; Foreign Economic Policy* (Washington, DC: U.S. Government Printing Office, 1979), pp. 158–63.

[22] "Expansion of the Atomic Energy Program," Memorandum for the Executive Secretary, National Security Council, from Secretary of Defense Robert A. Lovett, May 16, 1952, in *Foreign Relations of the United States, 1952–1954*, vol. 2, *National Security Affairs*, pt. 2 (Washington, DC: U.S. Government Printing Office, 1984), p. 935.

[23] See "Basic National Security Policy, NSC 162/2," October 30, 1953, *Foreign Relations of the United States, 1952–1954*, vol. 2, pt. 1, p. 591.

riority was now seen as fundamental to the administration's efforts to hold down the costs of defense and avoid transforming the United States into a garrison state. At the same time, however, the fact that the Soviets were making technical advances of their own meant that the United States would have to work even harder (and spend even more money) just to hold its existing lead. "The cold war," wrote one administration adviser in 1955, "has become, in large measure, a technological race for military advantage."[24]

The widening and the intensification of this race are suggested in two mid-decade reports. A high-powered Technological Capabilities Panel, appointed to consider ways of reducing the danger of surprise attack, ended up by recommending improvements in, among other things, intelligence collection, transoceanic communications, and high-energy jet fuels, as well as the more rapid development of ballistic missiles and nuclear powered aircraft and a more extensive consideration of the ways in which technology could be used to assist in the conduct of "peripheral wars." Because the Soviets would "certainly do everything possible to achieve an advantage by searching for big advances in their weapons technology," the United States had no choice but to do the same.[25]

Toward the end of 1955 another study advised that "achievement and maintenance of technological superiority, both in the short-run and for an indefinite period of years," and in nonnuclear as well as nuclear fields, had become "indispensable elements" of U.S. strategy. The challenge now was not simply to offset great masses of manpower, but to match and surpass the capabilities of large numbers of Soviet tanks and aircraft, some of which were beginning, in certain respects, to outperform their Western counterparts. Given that the Soviets had demonstrated the capacity to achieve "a high and increasing rate of technological advance, particularly in military fields," it was "essential" that the United States "commence with no further delay actions needed to assure long-range technological superiority."[26]

Well before Sputnik, therefore, the Soviets had evolved, in American perceptions, from the mere masters of vast "slave armies" to sophisticated military competitors. Their superior extractive capabilities permitted the communist countries not only to put large numbers of men in uniform, but to equip them with advanced (and steadily improving) arms and equipment. Maintaining an advantage over these forces would require not the acquisition of a single "winning weapon," but the development and deployment of a steady stream of new military systems. For the West, by the mid-1950s, preserving technological su-

[24] David Z. Beckler, Executive Secretary of the Science Advisory Committee, quoted in Daniel J. Kevles, "Cold War and Hot Physics: Science, Security, and the American State, 1945–1956," *Historical Studies in the Physical and Biological Sciences* 20, no. 2 (1990), p. 239.

[25] Report by the Technological Capabilities Panel of the Science Advisory Committee, "Meeting the Threat of Surprise Attack," February 14, 1955, *Foreign Relations of the United States, 1955–1957*, vol. 19, *National Security Policy* (Washington, DC: U.S. Government Printing Office, 1990), pp. 45, 41–56.

[26] Report by the ODM-Defense Working Group, "Achieving and Maintaining U.S. and Free-World Technological Superiority over the U.S.S.R.," December 20, 1955, *Foreign Relations of the United States* 1955–1957, 19:173–77.

premacy had become even more essential and urgent than it had appeared only a few years before.

Feasibility

Fortunately for the United States, the same imbalance in internal characteristics that made technical superiority necessary was also widely believed to make it feasible. The very domestic strength that permitted the totalitarian states to extract human and material resources in such quantities from their own societies also tended, in the long run, to suppress their capacity for innovation. On the other hand—and, again, over time—the apparent domestic weakness of the democracies was actually their greatest source of strength. Free societies, those with democratic political systems and market economies, might have a hard time supporting very large defense forces, but they were better equipped to undertake a race for technological advantage. Although it wavered at times, this belief too was persistent and, along with its counterpart, it provided the intellectual underpinning for a key aspect of American Cold War strategy.

The ultimate superiority of democratic science was the central theme of Vannevar Bush's 1949 study, *Modern Arms and Free Men*. Totalitarian regimes, Bush argued, were rigid, arbitrary, hierarchical, and regimented. As the Nazi failure to build an atomic bomb demonstrated, such regimes were prone to putting "nincompoops with chests full of medals" in charge of "organizations concerning whose affairs they were morons," and they were consequently susceptible to waste, inefficiency, false starts, and disastrous mistakes. At a deeper level, totalitarian states were, by their nature, intolerant of heresy, individual genius, the free movement of peoples and ideas, and the "winnowing of chaff by competition and criticism" on which true scientific progress inevitably rested.[27]

What had been true of the "totalitarians of the right" during the recent war would be true also of their left wing counterparts. The "pyramidal totalitarian regime . . . centered in Moscow is an exceedingly powerful agency for cold war," Bush warned. "It can force its people to enormous sacrifice and thus build great quantities of materials of war. . . . But it is not adapted for effective performance in pioneering fields, either in basic science or in involved and novel applications." This did not mean, however, that the United States could afford to rest on its oars. The communists could "copy and improve," and they could bring to fruition some portion of the great "mass of scarcely developed techniques" remaining from the Second World War. To maintain its lead over the Soviet Union, the United States would therefore have to "continue to break new ground." But "we can do so with our head high," Bush declared, "for we have a system essentially adapted for the purpose." In the long run, the "democratic

[27] Bush, *Modern Arms and Free Men*, pp. 207, 204.

system . . . is not only the best system . . . it is the strongest system in a harsh contest."[28]

Bush's arguments were echoed by other leading advocates of the doctrine of comparative advantage. The nation's unparalleled ability to exploit technology, explained Massachusetts Institute of Technology president Karl Compton in a 1949 speech, was responsible for "the American achievement to which we owe our economic strength and standard of living," namely, the superior productivity of American workers and farmers.

> It is in our tradition, therefore, to follow this policy by providing our soldiers, sailors, and airmen with equipment which will multiply as much as possible their power as fighting men. . . . We must . . . substitute the maximum of mechanical power and technical skill for brute human force if we should again have to fight. . . . We must rely on continual technological progress to keep us secure against any possible competitor.[29]

Confidence in the natural advantages of "free" American science received a series of blows between the late 1940s and the late 1950s. The unexpectedly early detonation of an atomic bomb by the Soviets, and their subsequent successes in building a thermonuclear weapon and launching the first earth-orbiting satellites, caused some questioning of earlier assumptions. The Russians might be more adept at imitation, and even at achieving some technological breakthroughs, than they had at first appeared. Even if this were true, however, it did not follow that the Soviet system was inherently superior or that the American system was in need of a fundamental overhaul. Coolly dismissing those who had begun to doubt, Vannevar Bush told Congress after the first Sputnik launch that Soviet successes in space were the result of an ongoing relaxation in high-level political controls: "When they . . . gave freedom to their scientists, they became good competitors. In that respect, you can say that they copied us."[30]

More typical was the view that Soviet gains were the temporary product, in effect, of brute force, of a concentration of scientific effort that totalitarianism made easier, but that could not be counted on to produce sustained results. "A major industrial power can achieve almost any technological feat it can conceive of," explained Eisenhower's chief science adviser, "provided only that it is willing to concentrate its energies and resources on that goal. But that diver-

---

[28] Ibid., pp. 206, 209, 8. On the issue of democratic versus totalitarian science see also John R. Baker, *Science and the Planned State* (London: Allen and Unwin, 1945).

[29] Karl T. Compton, Address at the Dedication of the Aeroballistics Facility, Naval Ordnance Library, "Science and National Strength: Some Lessons from World War Two," June 27, 1949. (Washington, DC., National War College Library) Mimeo.

[30] Hearings before the Preparedness Investigating Subcommittee of the Senate Armed Services Committee, *Inquiry into Satellite and Missile Programs*, 85th Cong., 1st and 2d sess. (Washington, DC: U.S. Government Printing Office, 1958), p. 63.

sion of energies is a political and not a technological act."[31] The United States might need to concentrate its own energies more than it had been doing, but thanks to the most fundamental attributes of its domestic system, its capacity for innovation still far exceeded that of its rival.

ORGANIZATION

The importance that American leaders attached to maintaining a qualitative edge over the Soviet Union may have made a large-scale research and development effort inevitable. But the intense desire for advantage did not in itself dictate the manner in which that effort would be organized within the federal government. Indeed, given the perceived urgency of stimulating rapid and sustained technological advances, the administrative structure that had emerged by the end of the 1950s must appear somewhat puzzling.

Despite repeated calls for unity of effort and concentration of authority, the system that took shape during the first full decade of the Cold War was characterized above all by its pluralism and decentralization. Federal funding for research flowed from an array of agencies and organizations whose activities were, at best, loosely coordinated with one another. Although there were several attempts to build one, no central institution for the integration of these various research programs was ever established. Far from being the product of a unified national master plan, the federal investment in science and technology represented instead the sum total of the independent activities of an assortment of parallel agencies (including the Atomic Energy Commission, the National Institutes of Health, the National Science Foundation, the three armed services, and, somewhat later, the National Aeronautics and Space Administration), each intent on pursuing its own goals.[32] This system has been variously characterized as "plural and interrelated,"[33] "fragmented and pluralized,"[34] "pluralistic [and] loosely coordinated,"[35] a system of "loose pluralism,"[36] and, less charitably, an

---

[31] James R. Killian, Jr., *Sputnik, Scientists, and Eisenhower: A Memoir of the First Special Assistant to the President for Science and Technology* (Cambridge: MIT Press, 1977), p. 6.

[32] Kenneth Jones, "The Government-Science Complex," in Robert H. Bremner and Gary W. Reichard, eds., *Reshaping America: Society and Institutions, 1945–1960* (Columbus: Ohio University Press, 1982), p. 320.

[33] Frederick Seitz, *Federal Support of Basic Research in Institutions of Higher Learning* (Washington, DC: National Academy of Sciences, 1964), p. 56.

[34] Sanford Lakoff, "The Scientific Establishment and American Pluralism," in Lakoff, ed., *Knowledge and Power: Essays on Science and Government* (New York: Free Press, 1966), p. 377.

[35] Jeffrey Stine, Report Prepared for the Task Force on Science Policy, House Committee on Science and Technology, *A History of Science Policy in the United States, 1940–1985*, 99th Cong. 2d sess. (Washington, DC: U.S. Government Printing Office, 1986), p. 34.

[36] Bruce L. R. Smith, *American Science Policy since World War II* (Washington, DC: Brookings Institution, 1990), p. 15.

"institutional maze."[37] Most of its pieces were in existence by 1950; by the end of the decade, the remainder had fallen into place. From that point onward, the structure of the federal research system would remain essentially static.

The overall pattern of pluralism and decentralization that characterized the entire national research effort was mirrored, at least initially, in the narrower realm of defense-related research. Here too, a set of parallel agencies (the Army, Navy, and Air Force) pursued largely independent research programs. And here too, despite repeated high-level efforts to impose it, there was considerable opposition to centralization. Only under conditions of intense crisis, and even then only in part, could this resistance be overcome.

In the construction of governmental mechanisms for the control of research, as in other arenas of postwar institution building, ideological factors, interest group pressures, and executive-legislative tensions tended to promote the diffusion of power and to discourage its concentration. Those who opposed the creation of strong central agencies for the support and direction of research (whether for reasons of principle, of bureaucratic, professional, or partisan political self-interest, or, as was often the case, of some combination of these elements) were able to mobilize powerful, ideologically resonant arguments in favor of their preferred position. Whatever the exigencies of the Cold War might seem to require, proposals for centralization were always vulnerable to the criticism that they were alien and dangerously statist.

The separation of powers also tended to strengthen the hands of those who preferred a decentralized system. The ability of Congress to modify or block significant proposed changes in the organization of the executive branch and a general postwar congressional reluctance to permit unchecked concentrations of power in the executive helped to slow, modify, and in some cases, to derail efforts to build strong institutions of central control. Even in an area where centralization was widely believed to be critical to national survival, the American regime proved extraordinarily resistant to it.

The Formation of the National Science Foundation

Historians of postwar American science policy regard the years 1945 to 1950 as a critical, formative period. According to one authoritative account, "the mechanisms, rationales, and structures put into place during this period changed only slightly in the years thereafter."[38] The central event in this crucial interval, it is further agreed, was the belated formation of the National Science Foundation (NSF). The delay in creating this agency, writes historian Daniel Kevles, was

---

[37] Carrol Pursell Jr., "Science and Government Agencies," in van Tassell and Hall, *Science and Society in the United States*, pp. 248–49.

[38] Stine, *A History of Science Policy*, p. 25. Similarly, Carrol Pursell concludes that "by the end of the Truman Era the postwar federal science establishment was virtually complete." Pursell, "Science and Government Agencies," p. 246.

"critically important in the evolution of postwar policy for research and development."[39]

Had it been established earlier, along the lines favored by key Democrats, the NSF could well have become a central mechanism for the coordination of the entire national research effort. Congressional opposition, fueled by ideology and partisan political calculation and reinforced by the objections of leading spokesmen for science and industry prevented this from occurring. When it was finally established in 1950, the NSF was consigned to the important but peripheral role of supporting those forms of basic research in which other government agencies could not be persuaded to take an interest. "Instead of dominating the federal science matrix," the NSF "would inherit the remaining unoccupied spaces."[40] It was the failure to create a strong central research agency in the immediate postwar period that guaranteed the pluralistic and decentralized character of the nation's subsequent research effort.[41]

The absence of a strong controlling mechanism at the core of the entire postwar government research system was not due to any lack of interest in building one. As the war drew to a close, plans for the creation of such an entity gained considerable support among liberal members of Congress and, within the executive branch, from the president and his top White House advisers. Had he been able to act independently of the Congress or simply to win its approval, at war's end Harry Truman would have ordered the establishment of a central science agency with broad powers of coordination and control. To Truman and other inheritors of the New Deal legacy it seemed only natural that if the federal government were to take on a new peacetime role as a sponsor of science and technology, its administrative capacities should be enlarged accordingly.

The impulse toward centralization first became evident soon after America's entry into the war. In 1942 Senator Harley Kilgore, an ardent New Dealer from West Virginia and a member of the Committee on Military Affairs, introduced legislation calling for the creation of a "superagency" combining all the government's technical bureaus and "empowered to draft technical personnel and facilities, compel the licensing of patents for war uses, and finance research projects which might contribute to victory."[42] Kilgore's scheme was denounced by leading scientists and industrial researchers as a "radical change of philosophy" that would "regiment research" and confer "totalitarian powers" on the federal

[39] Daniel J. Kevles, *The Physicists: The History of a Scientific Community in Modern America* (New York: Alfred A. Knopf, 1978), p. 360.

[40] Roger L. Geiger, *Research and Relevant Knowledge: American Research Universities since World War II* (New York: Oxford University Press, 1993), p. 19.

[41] Stine, *A History of Science Policy*, p. 34. For similar conclusions see Geiger, *Research and Relevant Knowledge,* p. 18; Jones, "The Government-Science Complex," p. 318; Kevles, *The Physicists,* p. 360.

[42] Daniel J. Kevles, "The National Science Foundation and the Debate over Postwar Research Policy. 1942–1945," *Isis* 68, no. 241 (1977), p. 9.

government.[43] Military officers and Vannevar Bush, in his capacity as director of the Organization for Scientific Research and Development (OSRD), objected also that the implementation of Kilgore's plan would disrupt existing arrangments and delay the development of new weapons.[44]

Rebuffed in his efforts to reshape wartime research, Kilgore began to turn his attention to preparing for the postwar era. In 1943 he authored legislation that would have created a permanent Office of Scientific and Technical Mobilization (OSTM). The aim of this new office was broadly to "develop comprehensive national programs for the maximum use of science and technology in the national interest in periods of peace and war."[45] Among its other powers, the OSTM would have been authorized to conduct its own research, to integrate the research activities of other government agencies into a coordinated national effort, and to provide funds for scientific education and for the support of work on problems of potential medical, military, and commercial importance carried out in nongovernmental institutions.[46]

Some supporters welcomed this plan as marking a turn away from the laissez-faire approach to science, "an important milestone in the recognition of the place science and technology [should] occupy . . . in the structure of the state," and a first step toward "the ultimate creation of a Department of Science and Technology." But the more numerous (and influential) critics attacked it as, in the words of a National Association of Manufacturers report, "the most ambitious project to socialize industrial research ever . . . proposed in the United States Congress."[47] If Kilgore had his way, some experts warned, the federal government would assume permanent command of the nation's technological resources and American scientists would be reduced to little more than "intellectual slaves of the State."[48]

Subsequent versions of Kilgore's plan were softened in response to criticism. Among other changes, Kilgore dropped the original title of the office he had proposed and renamed it the National Science Foundation because a foundation "had the sound of private support."[49] But the essence of his vision remained

---

[43] These comments are contained in the respective statements of Frank Jewett, President of the National Academy of Sciences; Warren Watson, Secretary of the Manufacturing Chemists' Association; and Charles Parsons, Secretary of the American Chemical Society, in Hearing before a Subcommittee of the Senate Committee on Military Affairs, *Technological Mobilization*, 77th Cong., 2d sess. (Washington, DC: U.S. Government Printing Office, 1942), pages 903, 897, 896.

[44] On the defeat of Kilgore's initial proposal and the subsequent evolution of his plans see Kevles, "The National Science Foundation."

[45] Hearing before a Subcommittee of the Senate Committee on Military Affairs, *Scientific and Technical Mobilization*, 78th Cong., 1st sess. (Washington, DC: U.S. Government Printing Office, 1943), p. 2.

[46] Ibid., pp. 1–8.

[47] Statement by chemist Albert Parson Sachs and quote from a National Association of Manufacturers report entitled "Shall Research Be Socialized?" ibid., pp. 225, 309.

[48] National Academy of Sciences President Frank Jewett quoted in Kevles, "The National Science Foundation," p. 11.

[49] Robert Franklin Maddox, "The Politics of World War II Science: Senator Harley M. Kilgore and the Legislative Origins of the National Science Foundation," *West Virginia History* 41, no. 1

unchanged, and by the end of the war, it had been adopted by the Truman administration. In a September 1945 speech outlining his agenda for the postwar world, President Truman called for the establishment of "a single Federal research agency" authorized to "promote and support" research in basic science, social science, medicine and public health, and on "all matters pertaining to the defense and security of the Nation." The new agency would also grant scholarships, "coordinate and control diverse scientific activities now conducted by the several departments and agencies of the Federal Government," and make available to industry "the fruits of research financed by Federal funds." Because the various fields of knowledge were themselves intimately interrelated, the president "urged upon the Congress the desirability of centralizing these functions into a single agency."[50] At the beginning of 1946 Senator Kilgore introduced legislation designed to put this proposal into effect.

The Kilgore-Truman plan quickly ran afoul of interest group and congressional opposition. Leaders of large industrial concerns, many of which had benefited from government-sponsored research during the war, worried that liberalized patent policies would undermine their competitive positions.[51] While virtually all scientists favored continued federal funding of research, many feared undue government interference in their activities. More general concerns about planning, centralization, and statism were also common. To conservatives, an institution along the lines proposed by the administration represented, in the words of one group of Republican Senators, "a clear exposition of the philosophy of centralization and control." Such an agency would bring a "large sector of our national economy . . . under the centralization, control, and supervision of Washington"; it was "a link in the chain to bind us into the totalitarian society of the planned state."[52] Social-scientific research would lead to the perfection of instruments of social control. Those with "conservative political and economic views" were, in the words of historian J. Merton England, "haunted by the specter of a revived New Deal in which science would become a tool for federal planners."[53]

Intellectual leadership of the anti-administration forces was provided by the

---

(1979), p. 30. For a summary of his views at the end of the war see Senator H. M. Kilgore, "Science and the Government," *Science* 102, no. 2660 (December 21, 1945), pp. 630–38. See also Maddox, "Senator Harley M. Kilgore and World War II" (Ph.D. dissertation, University of Kentucky, 1974), especially pp. 61–94, 194–210.

[50] "Special Message to the Congress Presenting a 21-Point Program for the Reconversion Period," September 6, 1945, *Public Papers of the Presidents of the United States: Harry S. Truman (1945)* (Washington, DC: U.S. Government Printing Office, 1961), pp. 293–94.

[51] On business hostility to Kilgore's proposals see Maddox, "The Politics of World War II Science," p. 27. Also Kevles, *The Physicists*, pp. 344–45. For a brief explication of differences over patent policy see a memorandum from J. Donald Kingley to John R. Steelman, "Issues Involved in Proposed Legislation for a National Science Foundation," December 31, 1946, HSTL, Official Files (OF) 681, 192–E, NSF (1945–47).

[52] Quoted in J. Merton England, *A Patron for Pure Science: The National Science Foundation's Formative Years, 1945–1957* (Washington, DC: National Science Foundation, 1983), pp. 47–48.

[53] Ibid., p. 36.

nation's top "scientist-statesmen" and, in particular, by Vannevar Bush. Bush
was a conservative Republican, and his role as director of a powerful wartime
bureaucracy had served only to deepen his anti-statist sentiments. Despite his
cordial relationship with President Franklin Roosevelt, Bush remained profoundly skeptical of the New Deal, hostile to its "centralizing tendencies," and
opposed to what he saw as "dangerous trends counter to traditional American
values."[54]

Bush feared that the creation of an institution along the lines preferred by
Kilgore and Truman would contribute to the general movement toward what he
termed the "detailed regimentation" of American life and, more specifically,
that it would interfere with the conduct of "free science . . . carried on by free
men whose guide is truth."[55] Bush objected both to the breadth of the activities
to be undertaken by the proposed new science agency (especially its support for
the social sciences and its potential for interference with industrial research)
and, even more importantly, to its administrative structure. The centralization of
activities and concentration of decision-making power implicit in a Kilgore-
Truman style agency might "lead to efficiency . . . but it is a kind of autocracy
which holds grave dangers to the full development of science."[56] A high-level
government office, staffed by bureaucrats with little knowledge of science and
responsive to the wishes of equally ignorant politicians, would inevitably distort
the character and diminish the quality of the nation's research effort. Under
such a system, scientists would be subject to powerful pressures to follow the
lead of ill-informed "faddists" and to undertake projects whose real purpose
was not the advancement of knowledge, but the satisfaction of interest group
demands.[57]

Spurred on by Kilgore's initiatives, Bush put forward his own plan for the
administration of postwar science.[58] Like Kilgore, Bush hoped to provide a
steady flow of government resources for research, but he sought to ensure that
the mechanisms for directing it would be placed well beyond the reach of normal political and bureaucratic influences. Instead of creating a new government
bureau of the sort he so abhorred, Bush recommended what one of his assistants delicately referred to as "a new social invention—of government sanction
and support but professional guidance and administration."[59] In place of civil
servants, Bush's proposed National Research Foundation would be run by a
board of "persons not otherwise connected with the Government and not repre-

[54] Nathan Reingold, "Vannevar Bush's New Deal for Research: Or, The Triumph of the Old
Order," *Historical Studies in the Physical and Biological Sciences* 17, no. 2 (1987), p. 302.

[55] Bush, *Modern Arms and Free Men*, p. 248–49.

[56] See his testimony in *Hearings on Science Legislation*, p. 203.

[57] Bush, *Modern Arms and Free Men*, p. 249.

[58] On the origins of Bush's proposals see J. Merton England, "Dr. Bush Writes a Report: 'Sci-
ence-The Endless Frontier,'" *Science* 191 (January 9, 1976), pp. 41–47; England, *A Patron for
Pure Science*, pp. 9–23; Detlev W. Bronk, "The National Science Foundation: Origins, Hopes, and
Aspirations," *Science* 188, no. 4187 (May 2, 1975), pp. 409–14; Vannevar Bush, *Pieces of the
Action* (New York: Morrow, 1970), pp. 63–68.

[59] Kevles, "The National Science Foundation," p. 22.

sentative of any special interest." Once appointed by the president, these men (whom Bush clearly assumed would be scientists) would elect their own chairman and govern their own affairs.[60] Under their management, the Foundation would be authorized to disburse public funds, but it would do so without direct political oversight or interference. Public support without political control— these, in David Dickson's words, were "the terms under which the scientific community was prepared to enter a peacetime contract with the state."[61]

Bush's plan, outlined in his July 1945 pamphlet *Science—The Endless Frontier*, provided the enemies of the Truman-Kilgore approach with an alternative around which to rally, and it contributed substantially to the five-year stalemate that followed. In 1946, thanks in large measure to objections to the plan's allegedly statist features, Congress failed to pass a bill favored by the administration. The next year, with Republicans in control of both the House and Senate, the president vetoed an alternative measure that more closely mirrored Bush's preferences. In Truman's words, the governing mechanism favored by Bush

> would, in effect, vest the determination of vital national policies, the expenditure of large public funds, and the administration of important governmental functions in a group of individuals who would be essentially private citizens. The proposed . . . Foundation would be divorced from control by the people to an extent that implies a distinct lack of faith in democratic processes.[62]

Three more years would elapse before a compromise bill could be passed and signed into law.[63]

Although it was not what either of them had initially hoped for, the National Science Foundation that finally emerged bore a far closer resemblance to Bush's vision than it did to Kilgore's. The new agency would have a presidentially appointed director, as Kilgore and Truman insisted, but the scope of its activities and of its powers was to be sharply circumscribed, more so in fact than even Bush had originally proposed. Instead of supporting every variety of work in either the full spectrum of possible fields (as Kilgore had wished) or merely medical, military, and basic scientific research in the natural sciences (as Bush preferred) the new Foundation was to concentrate on only the last of these categories of activity. By 1950 the possibility of anything broader and more

[60] See Vannevar Bush, *Science: The Endless Frontier*, (Washington, DC: U.S. Government Printing Office, 1945), pp. 28–33.

[61] David Dickson, *The New Politics of Science* (Chicago: University of Chicago Press, 1984), p. 26.

[62] "Memorandum of Disapproval," August 6, 1947, HSTL, OF 681, 192-E, NSF (1945–47). This file contains considerable material on the events leading up to the veto and its immediate aftermath. See also John Walsh, "Truman Era: Formative Years for Federal Science," *Science* 179 (January 19, 1973), p. 263; Don K. Price, "The Deficiencies of the National Science Foundation Bill," *Bulletin of the Atomic Scientists* 3 (1947), pp. 291–94.

[63] A useful summary of the NSF controversy can be found in Nelson W. Polsby, *Political Innovation in America: The Politics of Policy Initiation* (New Haven: Yale University Press, 1984), pp. 35–55. See also Kevles, "The National Science Foundation"; Kevles, *The Physicists*, pp. 356–59; England, *A Patron for Pure Science*, pp. 9–106.

ambitious had been largely overtaken by events. While Congress and the executive deliberated over the shape of the NSF, the armed services (along with the Atomic Energy Commission and, in the medical field, the National Institutes of Health) had taken on themselves the responsibility for supporting virtually all research, basic and applied, that was even remotely related to the completion of their assigned missions. Pluralism was thus effectively guaranteed.[64]

The delay in reaching a compromise, as well as its final terms, also served to limit the possibility that when it did finally emerge, the new institution could play an active role in integrating the activities of other federal agencies. Instead of being a superagency with broad powers of direction and control, the NSF was authorized merely to "evaluate" the programs of other agencies and to "encourage" the formulation of "a national policy for the promotion of basic research."[65] But the Foundation's placement in the federal science system and its late arrival on the scene made even these rather modest goals difficult to achieve. As one observer notes, the idea that a small, independent upstart of an agency could "'evaluate' the work of other, larger agencies with higher ranks in the federal hierarchy was . . . anomalous."[66] Faced with stiff bureaucratic resistance from agencies with bigger budgets and more firmly established ties to Congress, the NSF quickly abandoned any pretense of playing a coordinating role.[67]

While they did not transform its fundamental features, the Sputnik crises of the late 1950s did produce some lesser shifts in the composition of the federal science system. By stimulating the formation of an independent space agency, the Soviet satellite tests simply added another element of diversity to the already pluralistic government research complex. Within a few years of its founding the National Aeronautics and Space Administration had grown into one of the largest sources of federal funding for research and development.[68]

---

[64] For more on these events see Kenneth M. Jones, "Science, Scientists, and Americans: Images of Science and the Formation of Federal Science Policy, 1945–1950" (Ph.D. dissertation, Cornell University, 1975), especially pp. 269–410.

[65] Charles V. Kidd, *American Universities and Federal Research* (Cambridge: Harvard University Press, 1959), pp. 4, 22.

[66] Morgan Sherwood, "Federal Policy for Basic Research: Presidential Staff and the National Science Foundation, 1950–1956," *Journal of American History* 55, no. 3 (December 1968), p. 600.

[67] This was in spite of the efforts of the Bureau of the Budget in the early 1950s to get it to do so. See the discussion in Milton Lomask, *A Minor Miracle: An Informal History of the National Science Foundation* (Washington, DC: NSF, 1976), pp. 91–110. Kevles notes that although "the Foundation was legally authorized to slip an evaluative check rein over agency research programs . . . the defense agencies were determined to resist such judgment." The agency's first director therefore "prudently" decided "to ignore the Foundation's mandate for planning." Kevles, *The Physicists*, pp. 359–60. Even before the passage of the 1950 bill "the theme of coordination . . . attracted near universal opposition from the existing agencies and their allies within and without the Congress . . . They did not want another entity standing between themselves and the president." Reingold, "Vannevar Bush's New Deal for Research," p. 326.

[68] On the origins of NASA see Walter A. McDougall, *The Heavens and the Earth: A Political History of the Space Age* (New York: Basic Books, 1985), pp. 157–75; also Enid Curtis Bok Schoettle, "The Establishment of NASA," in Sanford A. Lakoff, ed., *Knowledge and Power: Essays on Science and Government* (New York: Free Press, 1966), pp. 162–270.

In addition to encouraging still more horizontal expansion, the Sputnik crises also led to two further attempts to add a vertical dimension to the existing system. Expressing his desire for more and better advice on scientific issues, in 1957 President Eisenhower named a Special Assistant for Science and Technology and created a White House–level President's Science Advisory Committee (PSAC).[69] During the first few years of its existence, this group was able to play an important part in overseeing the research activities of the various government agencies, including those of the Department of Defense. But as its first director acknowledged, the PSAC's power was "more charismatic than bureaucratic."[70] Lacking any direct authority of their own, the special assistant and his advisory committee depended entirely for their influence on maintaining an extremely close relationship with the president. When this connection atrophied, as it did after the early 1960s, PSAC quickly become irrelevant.[71]

Sputnik also led to one last push for a strong, Kilgore-style central research agency. In the late 1950s this idea reemerged in the form of a proposal from congressional Democrats for the creation of a cabinet-level Department of Science and Technology.[72] The new department would absorb the functions of all nonmilitary research agencies (including the Atomic Energy Commission) and would have as its primary goal "the co-ordination and centralization" of the "dispersed" federal research effort.[73] Predictably, these suggestions met with overwhelming resistance from scientists who had learned to prosper under pluralism, from the heads of existing agencies threatened with absorption, from congressional Republicans motivated by partisanship and ideology, and from an assortment of "individuals and groups opposed to growth in government across the board."[74] In contrast to the late 1940s, now the notion of a powerful new

[69] On the origins and functioning of PSAC, see the memoirs of its first two directors: Killian, *Sputnik, Scientists, and Eisenhower;* and George B. Kistiakowsky, *A Scientist at the White House: The Private Diary of President Eisenhower's Special Assistant for Science and Technology* (Cambridge: Harvard University Press, 1976).

[70] Killian, *Sputnik, Scientists, and Eisenhower*, p. 116.

[71] President Nixon eventually disbanded PSAC. The more formally institutionalized mechanisms for providing the president with scientific advice (beginning with the Office of Science and Technology first set up by Kennedy) have tended to be even less influential. For an assessment of the difficulties facing PSAC in the mid-1960s see Carl William Fischer, "Scientists and Statesmen: A Profile of the Organization of the President's Science Advisory Committee," in Lakoff, *Knowledge and Power*, pp. 315–58. For an overview of the activities of PSAC and its successors see Gregg Herken, *Cardinal Choices: Presidential Science Advising from the Atomic Bomb to SDI* (New York: Oxford University Press, 1992). On the structure of presidential science advising see James Everett Katz, *Presidential Politics and Science Policy* (New York: Praeger, 1978); also George Rathjens, "Science Advising: Eisenhower to the Present," in Kenneth W. Thompson, ed., *The Presidency and Science Advising*, vol. 8 (Lanham, MD: University Press of America, 1991), p. 37–54.

[72] McDougall describes this as "an updating of the Kilgore notion." *The Heavens and the Earth*, p. 167.

[73] Hubert H. Humphrey, "The Need for a Department of Science," *Annals of the American Academy*, no. 327 (1960), p. 27.

[74] Stine, *History of Science Policy*, p. 45. For a summary of the debate on this issue see Hearings before the Subcommittee on Reorganization and International Organizations of the Senate Committee on Government Operations, *Create a Department of Science and Technology* 86th Cong., 1st sess. (Washington, DC: U.S. Government Printing Office, 1959).

science agency also faced opposition from the White House. The drive for centralization went nowhere. Even the energy provided by an acute crisis was insufficient to overcome the strong underlying tendencies toward decentralization and pluralism.

Military Research

Powerful centrifugal forces were also at work in the narrower realm of military research. Here, as at the overall national level, bureaucratic resistance to centralization was reinforced by congressional reluctance to permit ever greater concentrations of executive power. The combination of these forces was sufficient, between the end of the Second World War and the onset of the Sputnik crisis, to defeat repeated efforts to impose even a modest measure of central control over defense research. It was only under the unique conditions prevailing at the close of the 1950s that some steps toward centralization became feasible.

Having accepted the need for continual innovation, the Army, Navy, and Air Force were each eager in the early postwar period to pursue their own research and development programs. The services were jealous of one another and hostile to any attempts to impose cooperation on them, but their natural preference for autonomy in this and other areas would have availed them little without the help of Congress. While Presidents Truman and Eisenhower sought repeatedly to promote unity of effort by enhancing the authority of the top civilian and military leadership of the new national military establishment, Congress tended to act in ways that slowed or moderated their attempts at reform. Throughout the early Cold War period, albeit with varying degrees of success, the legislative branch "consistently and persistently resisted attempts to centralize the Defense Department."[75] This behavior was a reflection both of a sense of institutional prerogatives and a broader concern about permitting undue concentrations of power.

Many members of Congress feared that by strengthening the hand of the Secretary of Defense and the Chairman of the Joint Chiefs of Staff in relation to the individual armed services, they would be weakening their own capacity to maintain control over defense policy.[76] Some members also worried that bolster-

---

[75] John C. Ries, *The Management of Defense: Organization and Control of the U.S. Armed Services* (Baltimore: Johns Hopkins Press, 1964), p. 211. See also Paul Y. Hammond, *Organizing for Defense: The American Military Establishment in the Twentieth Century* (Princeton: Princeton University Press, 1961). For useful overviews see Vincent Davis, "The Evolution of U.S. Central Defense Management," and William J. Lynn, "The Wars Within: The Joint Military Structure and Its Critics," both in Robert J. Art, Vincent Davis, and Samuel P. Huntington, eds., *Reorganizing America's Defense: Leadership in War and Peace* (New York: Pergamon-Brassey's, 1985), pp. 149–67 and 168–204.

[76] As Robert Art explains: "Congressmen have traditionally seen their ability to influence defense policy enhanced under a decentralized structure and have feared loss of influence under a more centralized one. . . . Therefore, not surprisingly, America's defense establishment has reflected the pluralistic and decentralized nature of America's national governmental system." Robert J. Art, "Introduction: Pentagon Reform in Comparative and Historical Perspective," in Art, Davis, and Huntington, *Reorganizing America's Defense*, p. xiv.

ing the authority of a handful of uniformed officers, especially in the intense atmosphere of the Cold War, could open the door to militarism.[77] Congress therefore tended to act as a buffer, shielding the services from presidential efforts to build up institutions with the power to compel cooperation and coordination. Even a popular, determined, and uniquely authoritative president like Eisenhower had considerable difficulty in achieving these ends. It was only the specter of impending technological inferiority (and the belief that greater central control was necessary in order to stave it off) that made possible real changes in the structure of defense research.

The first plans for a peacetime scientific establishment would have achieved centralization by taking the most important research functions entirely out of the hands of the military. These proposals were the work of civilian scientists eager to preserve both their crucial wartime role and their independence from political or military interference. As an interim step between the dissolution of the OSRD and the creation of a defense branch in a civilian-controlled national research organization, Vannevar Bush and a number of his senior colleagues in 1944 proposed the formation of a Research Board for National Security (RBNS). Housed in the National Academy of Sciences (an independent advisory body created during the Civil War), the new board would be a quasi-private institution authorized to disburse public monies and charged with the responsiblity of complementing "the work of the military's own technical bureaus on the nuts-and-bolts development of military hardware [by exploring] the long-range, fundamental scientific aspects of defense technology."[78] This plan, like Bush's larger scheme for an independent National Research Foundation, was widely (and correctly) seen by critics in Congress and the White House as an attempt to circumvent normal political controls on government expenditures.[79] Although the RBNS was brought briefly into existence, it survived for only a year (during most of which time it was denied government funding) and, at the beginning of 1946, was quietly disbanded.[80]

Having failed to establish a mechanism outside the defense establishment, the advocates of coordination sought to build one within its boundaries and, specifically, within the newly founded Office of the Secretary of Defense (OSD). The 1947 National Security Act that established the Secretary's office also created a Research and Development Board (RDB) to advise him and to assist in the formulation of an integrated research and development program. The RDB (which drew its expertise primarily from part-time committees of

[77] Regarding congressional fears of a "man on horseback" see Ries, *The Management of Defense*, p. 166.

[78] Daniel J. Kevles, "Scientists, the Military, and the Control of Postwar Defense Research: The Case of the Research Board for National Security, 1944–1946," *Technology and Culture* 16, no. 1 (January 1975), p. 27. See also the testimony by Bush, Frank Jewett, and others in Hearings of the House Committee on Military Affairs, *Research and Development*, 79th Cong., 1st sess. (Washington, DC: U.S. Government Printing Office, 1945).

[79] A. Hunter Dupree, "National Security and the Post-War Science Establishment in the United States," *Nature* 323 (September 1986), p. 214.

[80] On this episode see, in addition to Kevles, "Scientists, the Military, and the Control of Postwar Defense Research"; Sherry, *Preparing for the Next War*, pp. 134–58.

civilian technical consultants) was intended, in the words of the first Secretary of Defense, to be "the center in the National Military Establishment of the application of science to war."[81] But the RDB shared the initial frailty of the larger office of which it was a part.[82] Lacking in authority, wracked by interservice rivalries and suspicions, and largely excluded from the most important decisions about technology and strategy, the RDB "came to naught, effective neither in its coordination of military research nor viable as a mechanism for bringing civilian influence to bear on military planning."[83]

Subsequent variations on the same theme fared little better. On taking office, President Eisenhower sought to strengthen the Defense Secretary's hand by, among other things, abolishing the amorphous RDB and creating a new Assistant Secretary of Defense for Research and Development. But the 1953 reforms (which were at the outer limits of what the president could undertake without explicit congressional approval) did little to enhance effective central control of military research. The new Assistant Secretary could offer advice to his boss and seek to encourage coordination among the services, but he lacked the authority to veto or alter their programs.[84] Accomplishing more than this would require congressional authorization for a major augmentation in the powers of the Secretary of Defense, and that, in turn, was unlikely without some substantial shock to the existing system.[85]

[81] James Forrestal, quoted in Daniel J. Kevles, "K_1S_2: Korea, Science, and the State," in Peter Galison and Bruce Hevly, *Big Science: The Growth of Large-Scale Research* (Stanford, CA: Stanford University Press, 1992), p. 317. On the structure and intended mission of the RDB see Edwin A. Speakman, "Research and Development for National Defense," *Proceedings of the I.R.E.* (July 1952), pp. 772–75.

[82] "As an arm of the Secretary of Defense . . . the board reflected the department's bureaucratic weakness." Thomas J. Misa, "Military Needs, Commercial Realities, and the Development of the Transistor, 1948–1958," in Merritt Roe Smith, ed., *Military Enterprise and Technological Change: Perspectives on the American Experience* (Cambridge: MIT Press, 1985), p. 266. "The RDB reflected the problems of the Department which it served, often operating as yet another interservice battleground." Rip Bulkeley, *The Sputniks Crisis and Early United States Space Policy* (Bloomington: Indiana University Press, 1991), p. 30.

[83] Harvey M. Sapolsky, *Science and the Navy: The History of the Office of Naval Research* (Princeton: Princeton University Press, 1990), pp. 34–35. See also Kevles, "K_1S_2," p. 323; Kevles, "Cold War and Hot Physics," pp. 246–49. For more on the problems and failings of the RDB see Don K. Price, *Government and Science: Their Dynamic Relation in American Democracy* (New York: New York University Press, 1954), pp. 145–59. Dissatisfaction with the RDB is a recurrent theme in interviews conducted in 1950–51 by science policy consultant William Golden. See William A. Blanpied, ed., *Impacts of the Early Cold War on the Formulation of U.S. Science Policy: Selected Memoranda of William T. Golden, October 1950–April 1951* (Washington, DC: American Association for the Advancement of Science, 1995).

[84] Herbert F. York and G. Allen Greb, "Military Research and Development: A Postwar History," *Bulletin of the Atomic Scientists* 33 (January 1977), pp. 20–24; also testimony of Deputy Secretary of Defense Donald Quarles, in Hearings Before the Subcommittee of the Senate Committee on Appropriations, *Department of Defense Appropriations for 1959*, 85th Cong., 2d sess. (Washington, DC: U.S. Government Printing Office, 1958), pp. 199–205. For the background to the 1953 reforms see Walter Millis, Harvey C. Mansfield, and Harold Stein, *Arms and the State: Civil-Military Elements in National Policy* (New York: Twentieth Century Fund, 1958), pp. 375–87.

[85] Critics objected both to the substance of the 1953 reforms and to the unilateral way in which they were implemented by the executive. See Hearings before the House Committee on Govern-

Sputnik provided the necessary shock. The apparent inability of the United States to keep pace with the Soviets in developing ballistic missiles was widely interpreted as the result of flaws in the American system for managing defense research and development. With the military-technical competition heating up, decentralization (and the duplication and inefficiency that presumably went with it) were luxuries the United States could no longer afford.[86] "We are faced with an enemy who is able, not only ruthlessly to concentrate his resources, but rapidly to switch from one direction or degree of emphasis to another," warned the Gaither Committee at the end of 1957. The United States, on the other hand, had "lost ability to concentrate resources . . . and to change direction or emphasis with the speed that a rapidly developing international situation and rapidly developing science and technology make necessary." Remedying these shortcomings would require "a decision within the Executive Branch to seek from Congress the amendment of present legislation, which freezes the organization of the Defense Department along lines that may have been appropriate before the evolution of present weapons systems, but which are clearly inappropriate today and may become intolerable in the near future."[87]

President Eisenhower, long convinced of the inadequacies of the existing system and, in particular, of the wastefulness of interservice rivalry, did not need to be persuaded of the need for change. Seizing the opportunity presented by a perceived national emergency, he proposed yet another set of reforms in 1958, aimed at enhancing the authority of the Secretary of Defense and the Chairman of the Joint Chiefs of Staff and giving them the power to formulate and impose a unified military program on the armed services. What was needed, Eisenhower argued, was "full coordination" in the "development, production, and use" of new weapons, and "clear organization and decisive central direction" over the national defense effort as a whole.[88] Particularly important was the creation of a "real boss over research and engineering,"[89] who had the authority to "prevent unwise service competition."[90]

The combination of Eisenhower's personal authority in matters military, the weight of expert opinion, and the prevailing atmosphere of crisis helped to weaken, but did not entirely erase, congressional opposition to institutional re-

---

ment Operations, *Reorganization Plan No. 6 of 1953 (Department of Defense)* 83rd Cong., 1st sess. (Washington, DC: U.S. Government Printing Office, 1953), quote from p. 9.

[86] For recent accounts of the reaction to Sputnik see Robert A. Divine, *The Sputnik Challenge: Eisenhower's Response to the Soviet Satellite* (New York: Oxford University Press, 1993). Also Bulkeley, *The Sputniks Crisis*, pp. 185–214. For one example of contemporary anxiety see Hans J. Morgenthau, "The Decline of America," *New Republic* 137, no. 25 (December 9, 1957), pp. 10–14.

[87] Security Resources Panel of the Science Advisory Committee, *Deterrence and Survival in the Nuclear Age* (Washington, DC: Office of Defense Mobilization, 1957), pp. 8–9.

[88] "Annual Message to the Congress on the State of the Union," January 9, 1958, in *Public Papers of the Presidents of the United States: Dwight D. Eisenhower (1958)* (Washington, DC: U.S. Government Printing Office, 1959), pp. 8–9, (hereafter *PPP 1958*).

[89] Eisenhower to Ann Whitman quoted in Divine, *The Sputnik Challenge*, p. 129.

[90] "Special Message to the Congress on Reorganization of the Defense Establishment," April 3, 1958, *PPP 1958*, p. 284.

form. The case for increased central control over research and development proved especially difficult to resist. Having made much of the need to win the "space race," Eisenhower's Democratic critics could not easily object to measures that appeared to respond directly to their concerns. Nevertheless, influential members of Congress continued to warn that aspects of the president's plan could transform the Secretary of Defense into an all-powerful "czar,"[91] and that strengthening the Joint Chiefs might pave the way for a "Prussian-type supreme command."[92] Of these two fears, the latter tended to be the stronger. Consistent with its worries about militarism, Congress was generally more willing to enhance the power of top civilians than to bolster the position of their uniformed counterparts.

The Defense Reorganization Act of 1958 ultimately passed by Congress did not contain all of the provisions that Eisenhower had requested, but it did authorize the establishment within the Office of the Secretary of Defense of a civilian Director of Defense Research and Engineering (DDR & E).[93] Equivalent in bureaucratic rank to the service secretaries, the new DDR & E had the authority "to approve, modify, or disapprove programs and projects of [the military] departments and other Defense agencies . . . and the right to initiate or support promising programs and projects for research and development."[94] If the Secretary of Defense was prepared to use it, he now had available to him, for the first time, an instrument with which to exert substantial control over the pace and direction of the nation's entire military research effort.

SCOPE

Despite its size, the scope of the American Cold War research program was actually quite narrow. The great bulk of all federal research expenditures (generally on the order of 80–90 percent of each year's budget) went to support so-

[91] Senator Mike Mansfield quoted in Brian R. Duchin, "'The Most Spectacular Legislative Battle of That Year': President Eisenhower and the 1958 Reorganization of the Department of Defense," *Presidential Studies Quarterly* 24, no. 2 (Spring 1994), p. 249.

[92] Congressman Carl Vinson quoted in Divine, *The Sputnik Challenge*, p. 133.

[93] On the battle over the 1958 reforms see ibid., pp. 128–43; Duchin, "1958 Reorganization," pp. 243–62; Lynn, "The Wars Within," pp. 174–81; Ries, *The Management of Defense*, pp. 185–88.

[94] Michael H. Armacost, *The Politics of Weapons Innovation: The Thor-Jupiter Controversy* (New York: Columbia University Press, 1969), pp. 235–36. In addition to the research programs and facilities of the three services, the Director of Defense Research and Engineering also had within his control the resources of the newly created Advanced Research Projects Agency (ARPA). Established initially as a "special projects agency," ARPA became, in effect, the research arm of the DDR&E. Through it the Director could pursue technologies in which the military services could not yet be persuaded to take an interest. On the initial relationship between these two entities see ibid., pp. 226–37; also York and Greb, "Military Research," pp. 24–26; Herbert York, *Race to Oblivion: A Participant's View of the Arms Race* (New York: Simon and Schuster, 1970), pp. 116–20. Regarding ARPA (later DARPA) see Richard J. Barber Associates, *The Advanced Research Project Agency, 1958–1974* (Washington, DC: Barber Associates, December 1975); Jeffrey F. Rayport, *DARPA*, case study #9-390-142, (Boston: Harvard Business School, February 1990).

called applied research and development. These monies were used to pay for the creation and perfection of new devices and techniques intended to assist government agencies in the performance of their respective missions. The remainder of the federal research and development budget was devoted to supporting "basic" scientific research: inquiries aimed at expanding knowledge of fundamental natural processes, without regard to practical utility.[95]

The vast majority of all government spending on research (including a significant portion of basic as well as applied work) was motivated by concerns over national security. Although the portion of federal research and development funds provided by the Department of Defense did fluctuate over time, the balance was taken up by agencies with security-related missions: NASA and the Atomic Energy Commission (later the Department of Energy). Taken together, expenditures on defense, space, and energy-related research generally accounted for upwards of 75 percent of all federal spending on science and technology, with medical research making up most of the remainder (see fig. 8.3).[96]

Whether for good or ill, federally funded research activity undoubtedly had an impact on the process of commercial innovation in the United States and on the development by industry of products intended for sale primarily to private civilian consumers. Insofar as the government was concerned, however, such effects were largely "the indirect and . . . even unintended consequences of policies pursued for other reasons."[97] Over the course of the Cold War, and in marked contrast to many of its allies and commercial competitors, the United States government spent virtually nothing on supporting civilian industrial research *for its own sake*, nor did it create powerful new agencies for that purpose.[98] Although they did appear from time to time on the federal organization table, the institutions established between 1945 and the end of the Cold War for the express purpose of promoting commercial innovation were small, weak, and, in budgetary terms, insignificant.[99] Despite periodic efforts to broaden the

---

[95] See the figures in Congressional Budget Office, *Using Federal R & D to Promote Commercial Innovations* (Washington, DC: Government Printing Office, 1988), p. 34. For an overview of postwar federal investments in research and development see David Mowrey and Nathan Rosenberg, *Technology and the Pursuit of Economic Growth* (New York: Cambridge University Press, 1989), pp. 123–68.

[96] On defense research and development see John A. Alic, Lewis M. Branscomb, Harvey Brooks, et al., *Beyond Spinoff: Military and Commercial Technologies in a Changing World* (Boston: Harvard Business School Press, 1992), p. 98. For the breakdown of federal research by function see the figures in Linda R. Cohen and Roger G. Noll, *The Technology Pork Barrel* (Washington, DC: Brookings Institution, 1991), pp. 32–33.

[97] Alic et al., *Beyond Spinoff*, p. 65.

[98] For comparisons of public spending on industrial research in the United States, France, Germany, Japan, and the United Kingdom, see Alexander H. Flax, "Interdiffusion of Military and Civil Technologies in the United States of America," in Philip Gummett and Judith Reppy, eds., *The Relations between Defence and Civil Technologies* (Boston: Kluwer Academic Publishers, 1987), p. 127.

[99] For an overview of policies and institutions in the United States, Japan, Germany, France, and the United Kingdom see Richard R. Nelson, *High-Technology Policies: A Five-Nation Comparison* (Washington, DC: American Enterprise Institute, 1984). See also Organisation for Economic Co-

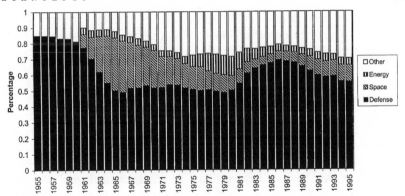

Figure 8.3. A Focused Research Effort: Defense, Space, and Energy Shares of Federal R & D Expenditures. (Note: NSF data for 1955–60 do not include separate figures for space and energy. Most of the former and some of the latter are included under the "Defense" category for this period.)

scope of the government's activities to include direct and deliberate sponsorship of commercial technologies, the overall pattern of expenditures and institutions remained largely unchanged for more than four decades. As with so much else about the Cold War science system, this pattern was set early, in the years immediately following the end of the Second World War.

Forgoing Industrial Research

During the war, despite the best efforts of some eager New Dealers, government-sponsored work on materials and industrial processes remained a poor second cousin to weapons-related research. The military, and most top civilian scientists, regarded industrial research and development as a diversion from their search for war-winning weapons. With a very few exceptions, such as the pursuit of low-cost synthetic rubber, projects of this type were considered unlikely to have much influence on the course of the conflict. State-directed industrial research might not do much good, but the mostly conservative leaders of the wartime science effort feared that it could do real long-term harm. Having crossed over into what had once clearly been a private domain, the government might be unable or unwilling to withdraw once the war was over. If the "starry-eyed New Deal boys" had their way, wartime experiments could blossom into a permanent apparatus for planning and directing all aspects of the nation's technological evolution.[100]

While they seldom said so at the time, this was precisely what many re-

operation and Development, *The Aims and Instruments of Industrial Policy: A Comparative Study* (Ottawa: OECD, 1975), especially pp. 53–65. For a more detailed comparison of the United States and Japan see Daniel I. Okimoto, *Between MITI and the Market: Japanese Industrial Policy for High Technology* (Stanford: Stanford University Press, 1989), pp. 1–111.

[100] Frank Jewitt, quoted in Carroll Pursell, "Science Agencies in World War II: The OSRD and Its Challengers," in Nathan Reingold, ed., *The Sciences in the American Context: New Perspectives* (Washington, DC: Smithsonian Institution Press, 1979), p. 373.

formers had in mind. Democrats like Senator Harley Kilgore, Secretary of Agriculture (and later Vice President) Henry Wallace, and Maury Maverick of the War Production Board (WPB) argued that a major expansion in the scope of the government's technological endeavors was vital to achieving victory. But they also saw ongoing federal sponsorship of commercial research as an instrument for breaking up concentrations of corporate power and permanently "democratizing" the American economy.

New patent laws requiring the immediate release of any innovation funded, even in part, by government agencies, were only a first step. In 1942 a WPB planning committee recommended the immediate formation of a $100 million War Research Development Corporation with "complete authority" to conduct industral research, to "test new industrial processes, to build pilot plants, to construct factories . . . to provide industry with new processes and products" and to "make sure" that these were "extensively used once they were provided." Here was a plan, as one sympathetic observer later commented, that would have "reached straight into the board rooms and the counting houses."[101] With help from Vannevar Bush and Frank Jewett, the proposal was quickly smothered and a far more modestly proportioned Office of Production Research and Development (OPRD) was eventually established instead. Between 1942 and 1945 OPRD would spend roughly $9 million on projects that included the development of more efficient techniques for the mass production of penicillin and alcohol; OSRD, by contrast, expended more than $450 million.[102]

"Small as it was," observes David Hart, "OPRD symbolized an ideal of state-led development of industrial technology that its organizers refused to let die."[103] As the war drew to a close, the advocates of an expanded federal role in commercial research made a renewed push for public acceptance. Failure to act on their earlier proposals, they claimed, had resulted in an increased concentration of control over technology in the hands of a few large corporations.[104] Along with its other undesirable effects, this trend raised the prospects of high unemployment, and perhaps even a renewed depression, once peace was restored. Testifying before the Congress in 1943, Vice President Henry Wallace asserted

---

[101] Bruce Catton, *The War Lords of Washington* (New York: Harcourt, Brace, 1948), p. 132. Catton's book laments at length the failure of the New Dealers' wartime efforts to transform the structure of the American economy.

[102] On the origins of the OPRD see ibid, pp. 123–38; Peter Neushul, "Science, Technology, and the Arsenal of Democracy: Production Research and Development during World War II" (Ph.D. dissertation, University of California at Santa Barbara, 1993), pp. 34–65; Richard B. Henderson, *Maury Maverick: A Political Biography* (Austin: University of Texas Press, 1970), pp. 236–38; David M. Hart, "Competing Conceptions of the Liberal State and the Governance of Technological Innovation in the U.S., 1933–1953" (Ph.D. dissertation, Massachusetts Institute of Technology, 1995), pp. 309–29.

[103] Hart, "Competing Conceptions," p. 340.

[104] Regarding the wartime concentration of federally funded scientific research see Report of the Smaller War Plants Corporation to the Special Senate Committee to Study Problems of American Small Business, *Economic Concentration and World War II*, 79th Cong., 2d sess. (Washington, DC: U.S. Government Printing Office, 1946), pp. 51–53.

that the war had unleashed "a flood of discoveries" that could "open vast industrial frontiers." But he warned that innovation and growth would be stifled if
"research is dominated by a small number of large corporations and cartels." To
prevent this from occurring, Wallace favored using "the catalytic . . . stimulating, power of Government to aid private enterprise to serve the economic needs
of the common man." Among the measures he proposed were a new patent
policy, direct federal funding of some commercially relevant research, and improved mechanisms for the distribution of information about new products and
industrial processes, including any seized from hostile powers during the war.[105]
In 1945, following his demotion to Commerce Secretary, Wallace made these
programs into one of the main planks in his personal platform for ensuring
peacetime prosperity.[106]

At the beginning of 1946 Wallace established an Office of Technical and
Scientific Services inside the Commerce Department and gave it sweeping responsibility for initiating and conducting "research and development work on
such mechanisms, processes and inventions as will advance the technological
productivity of the nation, create new enterprises and additional employment,
and foster and promote the nation's business."[107] But Wallace's dreams could
not be realized without money, and this was something a hostile and suspicious
Congress resolutely refused to supply. Funds for the new office were cut to the
bone, and the need for any expansion in government's role was sharply questioned. Promoting commercial innovation was something at which, as a 1947
House Appropriations Committee report put it, "private research with a profit
motive, has done rather well in the U.S. thus far."[108] In the political climate of
the late 1940s suggestions to the contrary were regarded as dubious, if not
downright dangerous. Postwar proposals for increased government support of
industrial research, concludes David Hart, "foundered on the shoals of Congressional laissez-fairism."[109]

Funding Basic Science

Vannevar Bush shared some of Wallace's concerns about monopoly control of
technology, but not his enthusiasm for a direct government role in promoting
and guiding commercial innovation. Bush believed that far from increasing the
pace of technological progress, changes in the patent laws that Wallace,

[105] Hearings before the Subcommittee on War Mobilization of the Senate Committee on Military
Affairs, *Scientific and Technical Mobilization*, pt. 5, 78th Cong., 1st sess. (Washington, DC: U.S.
Government Printing Office, 1943), pp. 705, 709.

[106] See the discussion "The Federal Government and Technology," in Henry A. Wallace, *Sixty
Million Jobs* (New York: Simon and Schuster, 1945), p. 49.

[107] From the executive order establishing the office, quoted in Hart, "Competing Conceptions,"
p. 355.

[108] Ibid., p. 365.

[109] For a thorough, thoughtful treatment of these events see ibid, pp. 366, 340–79. Also see
Robert K. Stewart, "The Office of Technical Services: A New Deal Idea in the Cold War," *Knowledge* 15, no. 1 (September 1993), pp. 44–77.

Kilgore, and others favored would weaken incentives for new discoveries.[110] Broadening the scope of the federal government's activities to include sponsoring commercial research would virtually guarantee political contamination of the funding process.[111] Where firms and industrial laboratories were engaged in the development of "better products for public consumption," the government should content itself with ensuring fair competition among them.[112]

Direct government involvement in the commerical sphere was undesirable but it was also, in Bush's view, unnecessary. Because of its practical, short-run orientation, private industry could not be relied upon to fund the basic scientific research from which new knowledge, and hence "new products and processes," derived. However, if public agencies took appropriate steps to ensure a strong and steady stream of basic scientific discoveries, private industry, driven by the relentless pursuit of profit, would surely "rise to the challenge of applying new knowledge to new products." The government's responsibilities regarding commercial innovation were therefore critical, but also quite limited. As Bush explained in 1945: "The most important ways in which the Government can promote industrial research are to increase the flow of new scientific knowledge through support of basic research, and to aid in the development of scientific talent." Beyond this, government need do little more than to encourage industry to do its own research by strengthening the existing patent system and adjusting the tax code to favor private research and development expenditures.[113]

What Bush was proposing was a middle course between a complete withdrawal of government support for anything not directly related to the performance of its essential missions and a far more thoroughgoing interventionism along lines proposed by Wallace and Kilgore. Federally financed basic scientific research would prime the pump of technological progress, government agencies would sponsor developments directly relevant to their needs, and private industry would pursue applications with commercial potential. This formulation appealed to most scientists and industrialists, as well as to conservative members of Congress leery of further expansions in the peacetime powers of the state.

Contributing to the general acceptance of Bush's formula in the 1940s and 1950s was a renewed confidence in America's overall economic prospects, and in the technological superiority of American industry. Despite the reformers' fears, the wartime boom did not give way to a postwar crash. Moreover, regardless of how the United States was faring in its military-technical competition

---

[110] See his comments in Vannevar Bush, "The Kilgore Bill," *Science* 98, no. 2557 (December 31, 1943), pp. 573–74.

[111] Kevles, *The Physicists*, pp. 342–48. In the words of one critic, proposals for federal funding of commercial research risked creating "a new 'pork barrel'" which unscrupulous politicians might use to reward old friends and win new ones. John Q. Stewart, "The 'Science Mobilization Bill,'" *Science* 97, no. 2526 (May 28, 1943), pp. 486–87.

[112] Bush, "The Kilgore Bill," p. 576.

[113] Bush's views on the government's role in commerical innovation are laid out in *Science: The Endless Frontier*, pp. 2–3, 5–7, and 13–17.

with the Soviet Union, U.S. firms in most commercial sectors appeared to be surging ahead of their competitors in other capitalist countries. This was, in part, the result of the recent war, which had drained budgets, destroyed laboratories, emptied universities, and prompted the flight to America of top scientists and engineers from around the world. As some observers pointed out, the United States could not expect to remain so far ahead forever. "Our technology is sufficiently advanced and our resources sufficiently adequate so that there is no immediate prospect that we shall fall technologically behind," advised a 1947 report of the President's Scientific Research Board. Nevertheless, "the future is certain to confront us with competition from other national economies of a sort we have not hitherto had to meet. Many of these will be state-directed in the interest of national policies. Many will be supported by . . . the most modern technology. . . . The danger lies in the future."[114] For the time being, all that was required for the United States to retain its overall edge was that the federal government provide generous support for basic scientific research.

One final element in the rationale for the constrained scope of postwar technology policy remained to be put in place. Vannevar Bush and the other architects of postwar science policy had never made any claims about the broader benefits to be derived from applied mission-oriented research. To the extent that these efforts aided the agencies of government in fulfilling their responsibilities (in particular, by safeguarding the nation's security) they would justify themselves. As the Cold War got going in earnest, however, it began to appear that, in a number of instances, federally funded defense (and later space) research was leading to the development of technologies with important commercial applications. Borrowing from the knowledge gained in designing and building similar products for the government, American companies were taking a wide lead in the development of civilian nuclear reactors, commercial jet aircraft, semiconductors, computers, communications satellites, and air traffic control radars. From the first, the precise magnitude of the spillovers or spinoffs from military to civilian sectors was a subject of debate. By the late 1950s and early 1960s, however, the existence of such effects was not seriously in doubt.[115] The system

---

[114] The President's Scientific Research Board, *Science and Public Policy*, vol. 1, *A Program for the Nation* (Washington, DC: U.S. Government Printing Office, August 27, 1947), p. 4.

[115] Frequent assertions about the positive spinoffs from noncommerical research and development began to appear at about the same time as the expansion of the space program. This development coincided with the first expressions of anxiety about the possible harmful effects of massive government research programs on the economy as a whole. Pointing out the existence of spinoffs from defense and space research was therefore one way for its defenders to counter the claims of the critics. For a useful overview of the literature on spinoffs see Jay Stowsky, "From Spin-Off to Spin-On: Redefining the Military's Role in American Technology Development," in Wayne Sandholtz, Michael Borrus, John Zysman, et al., *The Highest Stakes: The Economic Foundations of the Next Security System* (New York: Oxford University Press, 1992), pp. 114–40. Also Gummett and Reppy, *The Relations between Defence and Civilian Technologies*; Alic et al., *Beyond Spinoff*. For an attempt at a broader historical view see Barry Buzan and Gautam Sen, "The Impact of Military Research and Development Priorities on the Evolution of the Civilian Economy in Capitalist

put in place a decade earlier appeared to be working better than its creators anticipated; the possibilities for progress and prosperity seemed truly endless.

MECHANISMS

A fourth and final distinguishing feature of the postwar research system was the way in which it mobilized "private energies on a large scale for public purposes."[116] From the end of the Second World War to the end of the Cold War, roughly three-quarters of the annual government defense research budget was expended in corporate and university laboratories or in facilities owned by the government but operated by private organizations; only the remaining 25 percent went to pay for work done by federal employees in federal laboratories.[117] The great majority of state-sponsored research was thus performed in private institutions that retained their independent identities while working under contract for the government. These arrangements for the conduct of government-funded research were a distinctively American creation (see fig. 8.4).

Birth

The birth date of the contract system can be fixed with unusual precision. In May of 1940 France fell to the Germans, and Britain seemed in imminent danger of following suit. As they had done against Poland only a few months before, the Nazis had once more demonstrated their mastery of the modern battlefield. In the United States, writes historian Hunter Dupree, there was growing fear that "scientific research was the factor which made the panzer divisions invincible." Because of their ability ruthlessly to mobilize and direct "the intellectual resources of their citizenry," the dictatorships seemed to some observers "to possess a terrible and possibly decisive advantage over pluralistic

States," *Review of International Studies* 16, no. 4 (1990), pp. 321–39. For early contemporary views see Robert A. Solo, "Gearing Military R & D to Economic Growth," *Harvard Business Review* 40 (November–December 1962), pp. 49–60; and H. L. Nieburg, *In the Name of Science* (Chicago: Quadrangle Books, 1970).

[116] Bruce L. R. Smith, "Accountability and Independence in the Contract State," in Smith and D. C. Hague, eds., *The Dilemma of Accountability in Modern Government: Independence versus Control* (New York: Macmillan, 1971), p. 14.

[117] As compared to the other varieties of government research and development spending, *defense* research dollars have tended to go more heavily to industry than to universities, but the overall public/private breakdown is still roughly the same. As indicated in figure 8.4, in FY 1990 the breakdown for all kinds of federally funded research was: 25 percent federal labs, 49 percent industry, 18 percent university, and 8 percent university run/federally funded research centers (FFRDC). Alic et al., *Beyond Spinoff*, p. 92. The FY 1984 Defense Department research budget breakdown was: 23 percent in-house, 71 percent industry, 4 percent universities, and 2 percent federal contract research centers. Franklin A. Long and Judith Reppy, "The Decision Process for U.S. Military R&D," in Kosta Tsipis and Penny Janeway, eds., *Review of U.S. Military Research and Development*, 1984 (New York: Pergamon-Brassey's, 1984), p. 7.

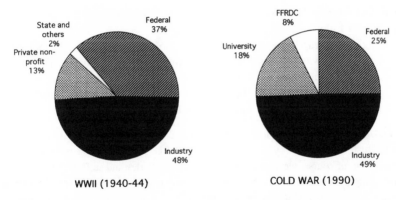

Figure 8.4. The Contract System: Research and Development by Performer

democracies."[118] With American involvement now virtually unavoidable, the urgent question before U.S. decision makers was how best to overcome the apparent disadvantages of their political system in order rapidly to mobilize the nation's scientific resources for war.

The most obvious approach to this problem would have been to follow the precedent set during the First World War: expanding existing Army and Navy laboratories, drafting civilian scientists and engineers and putting them to work under the direction of professional military officers. As Dupree notes, "This direct action was the World War I way of bringing civilian resources into the service of the military."[119] During the interwar years, as we have seen, the armed services came to rely heavily on their own facilities for the development and production of new weapons. By the late 1930s, one leading scientist would later recall, "The Army, the Navy, and the Air Corps each had its own technical divisions, its own laboratories, arsenals and proving grounds." As war approached, "the President might have merely urged [them] to expand their technical departments."[120]

Instead, at its first meeting on July 2, 1940, Roosevelt's National Defense Research Committee decided that, henceforth, a significant portion of all military research would be done in privately owned facilities by private citizens working under contract to the federal government.[121] Over the course of the war emergency both the volume of such extramural work and its fraction of total defense research grew dramatically. Between 1940 and 1944, over 60 percent of all government-sponsored research and development was performed in indus-

---

[118] A. Hunter Dupree, "The Great Instauration of 1940: The Organization of Scientific Research for War," in Gerald Holton, ed., *The Twentieth Century Sciences* (New York: Norton, 1972), p. 448.

[119] Dupree, *Science in the Federal Government*, p. 314.

[120] James B. Conant, "The Mobilization of Science for the War Effort," *American Scientist* 35, no. 2 (April 1947), p. 200.

[121] On the origins of the research contract see Irvin Stewart, *Organizing Scientific Research for War: The Administrative History of the Office of Scientific Research and Development* (Boston: Little, Brown, 1948), pp. 12–13, 191–99.

trial and university laboratories.[122] This wartime experience set the precedent for what was to follow.

The federal research contract, "the single most important institutional invention of the war," was the brainchild of one man: Vannevar Bush.[123] The novelty of Bush's idea and the extent of his responsibility for it is suggested by a passage from the memoirs of James Conant, chemist, Harvard president, and himself a major figure in the wartime mobilization of science:

> I remember exactly when I learned of the new idea. It was during one of my first talks with Bush in my capacity as a member of NDRC. I recall saying something to the effect that, of course, we would have to build laboratories and staff them with government employees. "Not at all," Bush replied. "We will write contracts with universities, research institutes and industrial laboratories." . . . I shall never forget my surprise at hearing about this revolutionary scheme.[124]

Like all social inventions, the success of this revolutionary idea depended on its ability to win widespread acceptance. The appeal of the contract system was due, in no small part, to desperation. In the summer of 1940 time was of the essence, and building new government facilities and finding the best people to staff them would have been a complex, laborious, and costly process. Once the idea had been advanced, mobilizing civilian scientists and engineers in place and making maximum use of existing privately owned facilities appeared obviously to be the quickest and easiest way to accelerate the nation's defense research program.

Drawing on his assessment of the World War One mobilization and, more fundamentally, on his understanding of the requirements of innovation, Bush was also eager to insulate scientists from the stultifying effects of hierarchical, bureaucratic control. By placing a substantial portion of the nation's emergency research effort safely outside the military chain of command, Bush believed that he was increasing the prospects for scientific flexibility and creativity. Finally, the contract system was designed to minimize disruptions to the normal patterns of peacetime life. Bush had no desire to pave the way for a permanent expansion in the size and power of the state. For this reason, even as he participated in an unprecedented exercise of governmental authority, he preferred to adopt "tactics and policies minimizing the impact on the old order."[125] The contract

[122] Of a total of $1.9 billion spent on research in fiscal years 1940 through 1944, $689 million were allocated to government laboratories, $915 billion to industry, and $235 billion to private, nonprofit institutions (mainly universities). See figures contained in Subcommittee on War Mobilization of the Senate Military Affairs Committee, *Legislative Proposals for the Promotion of Science* 79th Cong., 1st sess. (Washington, DC: U.S. Government Printing Office, 1945), pp. 22–25.

[123] Harvey Brooks, "What Is the National Agenda for Science, and How Did It Come About?" *American Scientist* 75 (September-October 1987), p. 511.

[124] James B. Conant, *My Several Lives: Memoirs of a Social Inventor* (New York: Harper and Row, 1970), p. 236. Bush gives a rather more laconic account of the origins of the contract system in his own memoirs. See Vannevar Bush, *Pieces of the Action* (New York: William Morrow, 1970), pp. 38–39.

[125] Reingold, "Vannevar Bush's New Deal," p. 314.

was intended, in Hunter Dupree's words, to be a "nonrevolutionary" device "by which the universities and industrial research laboratories were preserved as institutions even while their social role was temporarily but radically changed." Any other, more direct means of mobilization would have had an even more dramatic and far-reaching impact on the nation's scientific insititutions.[126]

The reasons for the broader appeal of Bush's invention are readily apparent and, in the first instance, firmly rooted in considerations of institutional and individual interest. Despite some initial skepticism, and an irreducible measure of continuing friction with the civilian scientists, the armed forces came quickly to see the virtues of contract research. The use of civilians in nonmilitary settings did not appear at the time to threaten the continued existence of the traditional system of service laboratories and arsenals, but merely to supplement its capabilities. Especially in the many new areas where the armed services lacked experience and technical expertise, the contract mechanism permitted ready access to critically important knowledge and skills.[127]

Insofar as the scientists themselves were concerned, the advantages of the contract system were even more obvious. Instead of having their laboratories emptied of personnel, stripped of equipment, and possibly shut down on government orders, universities and corporations were able to undertake considerable expansions in their existing research facilities, often at taxpayers' expense. And, instead of being drafted, relocated, and placed under the command of military officers, many civilian scientists and engineers could continue to work in familiar settings, in accordance with familiar rules and patterns of authority. Aside from some predictable grumbling about regulations and red tape, research contracts won ready acceptance in industry and academia.[128]

While contracts thus served the material interests of the participating parties, their broader appeal derived from a less tangible, but no less important, source. Even in the midst of a dire national emergency, the contract system maintained a vital measure of separation between the public and private spheres. Arrangements under which the government paid private entities to do research for it "resonated symbolically to the culture of the marketplace"; they were compatible with American ideology in a way that no other means of mobilizing the nation's scientific resources could possibly have been.[129] The image of

---

[126] Dupree, "The Great Instauration," pp. 457, 459. For a similar assessment see George H. Daniels, "Office of Scientific Research and Development (OSRD)," in Donald R. Whitnah, ed., *Government Agencies* (Westport, CT: Greenwood Press, 1983), p. 426–32.

[127] On the military's recognition of the virtues of the contract system see Paul Forman, "Behind Quantum Mechanics: National Security as Basis for Physical Research in the United States, 1940–1960," *Historical Studies in the Physical Sciences* 18, no. 1 (1987), pp. 177–78.

[128] On the wartime embrace of the contract system by industry and academia see Pursell, "Science Agencies in World War II," p. 363. See also S. S. Schweber, "The Mutual Embrace of Science and the Military: ONR and the Growth of Physics in the United States after World War II," and Paul K. Koch, "The Crystallization of a Strategic Alliance: The American Physics Elite and the Military in the 1940s," both in E. Mendelsohn, M. R. Smith, and P. Weingart, eds., *Science, Technology, and the Military*, vol. 12 (Dordrecht: D. Reidel, 1988), pp. 1–45, 87–116.

[129] Larry Owens, "The Struggle to Manage Science in the Second World War: Vannevar Bush and

"free men" putting their heads together to outwit the regimented scientists of the "slave states" was an attractive one, both during the war and after. Whatever its practical merits, the contract system was also America's symbolic answer to what Winston Churchill had rightly called the "perverted science" of totalitarianism.[130]

Maturity

The forces favoring perpetuation of the contract system after the end of the Second World War were even more powerful than those acting at the moment of its inception. In 1940 the contract system was a bold experiment, even a gamble; by 1945 its efficacy had been decisively demonstrated. The detonation of the first atomic bomb eliminated any lingering doubts about the ability of civilian scientists, working outside the confines of traditional defense research establishments, to produce fundamental breakthroughs in military technology. If anything, it was the old network of intramural institutions that now had to justify its continued existence. However unfairly, the Army and Navy laboratories were widely blamed for having failed to prepare the armed forces adequately for the onset of war. And, whatever the wartime achievements of the military researchers, it was their civilian counterparts, operating under new institutional arrangements, who got most of the public credit for winning the battle of the laboratories.[131]

The transition from a hot, total war of limited duration to a protracted cold war also tended to strengthen the practical arguments in favor of the contract system. After the defeat of the Axis powers, patriotic fervor quickly dissipated and most scientists were eager to get back to their own research agendas. With industry and academia once again offering the most obvious avenues for professional advancement, "the necessity of using private careers for public purposes became all the more evident."[132] If the nation's top scientists and engineers were to be kept engaged in defense-related research, contracts would be indispensable.

In 1940 the expectation that, one way or another, the coming war would be

---

the Office of Scientific Research and Development" (University of Massachusetts, Amherst, October 12, 1993), mimeo, p. 5.

[130] On June 18, 1940, Churchill warned the British people that "If we fail, then the whole world, including the United States, including all that we have known and cared for, will sink into the abyss of a new Dark Age made more sinister, and perhaps more protracted, by the lights of perverted science." Winston S. Churchill, "Their Finest Hour," in *Blood, Sweat, and Tears* (New York: G. P. Putnam, 1941), p. 314.

[131] See Clarence H. Danhof, "From Improvisation to Policy," *George Washington Law Review* 31, no. 4 (April 1963), pp. 738–39. Regarding the performance of the pre-war system see General George C. Marshall, "Third Report of the Chief of Staff of the Army," in Walter Millis, ed., *The War Reports of General of the Army George C. Marshall, General of the Army H. H. Arnold, Fleet Admiral Ernest J. King* (Philadelphia: J. B. Lippincott Co., 1947), pp. 259–61.

[132] Price, *Government and Science*, p. 77.

of limited length had helped to focus research on a number of key areas.[133] In 1945, the prospect of a potentially endless military-technical competition made it all the more important that the government remain "in close touch with advancing knowledge and technology" across a wide range of fields, and that it retain the capacity rapidly to shift resources from one area to another.[134] The ability to recruit researchers without regard to civil service regulations or personnel restrictions also made for greater flexibility.[135] The promise of contracts helped to promote competition among researchers, thereby increasing the prospects for innovation.[136] The presumed efficiencies of the private sector also held out the promise of lower costs, a more important consideration in peacetime than in war.[137] Finally, government contracts were clearly seen as a way to build up private research institutions across the country, expanding the ranks of the nation's scientists and engineers, contributing to its long-term scientific strength and its economic welfare, while at the same time better enabling it to stay the course of a qualitative arms race with the Soviet Union.[138]

The likelihood that this race would be a long one helped bolster the case for contracts in other ways as well. If a comparatively brief interval of total war had threatened permanently to upset the balance between state and society, the dangers of a sustained, if partial, mobilization were in many ways even greater. Trying to conduct a large and continuing defense research program with the mechanisms that had existed before the war would have required placing a substantial portion of the nation's scientific resources under direct government control. Greatly expanding the government research complex, or effectively nationalizing academic and industrial research facilities, would have had far-reaching economic and political effects. Movement in this direction would also, of course, have aroused strong objections on ideological grounds. The contract system, as one enthusiast pointed out, provided a means of "pleasing both those who want a small government and those who want big new governmental programs. . . . Given the demand for services and for the continuation of a 'free enterprise' system [it is] probably essential."[139]

All these arguments, practical and ideological, were advanced in the 1940s

[133] See Joel Genuth, "Microwave Radar, the Atomic Bomb, and the Background to U.S. Research Priorities in World War II," *Science Technology and Human Values* 13, nos. 3 and 4 (Summer and Autumn 1988), pp. 276–89; Stanley Goldberg, "Inventing a Climate of Opinion: Vannevar Bush and the Decision to Build the Bomb," *Isis* 83 (1992), pp. 429–52.

[134] Danhof, "From Improvisation to Policy," p. 739.

[135] Price, *Government and Science*, p. 77.

[136] Robert Gilpin, *France in the Era of the Scientific State* (Princeton: Princeton University Press, 1968), p. 135.

[137] Regarding this and other postwar arguments for the contract system see Smith, "Accountability and Independence in the Contract State," pp. 17–19.

[138] For an informative study of the impact of government support on two key private institutions see Stuart W. Leslie, *The Cold War and American Science: The Military-Industrial-Academic Complex at MIT and Stanford* (New York: Columbia University Press, 1993).

[139] Victor K. Heyman, "Government by Contract: Boon or Boner?" *Public Administration Review* 21, no. 2 (1961), p. 61.

and 1950s by those who benefited most directly from a perpetuation of the contract system, as well as by many others who did not. At the end of the war, in contrast to its beginning, there was a substantial established constituency outside of government for continued heavy reliance on extramural research. Interest group pressures helped hold the contract system in place. But it should be pointed out that by 1945, virtually no one had any inclination to get rid of it. In contrast to the intense debates over other aspects of the Cold War research and development system, the means by which research was to be conducted were largely uncontroversial. What Clarence Danhof has called the shift "from improvisation to policy" was accomplished quickly and virtually without challenge.[140]

In the initial postwar period, the executive branch, with an occasional nudge from Congress, moved quickly to consolidate and expand its reliance on private research institutions. As early as 1944 a joint War and Navy Department Committee on Postwar Research had advised that the widespread use of contracts would be essential to maintaining American technological preponderance. Any inclination on the part of the services to go back to their traditional ways of doing business was discouraged by new peacetime procurement regulations, which mandated a continuation of wartime practices for buying research from the private sector, and by edicts from the newly formed Office of the Secretary of Defense, which declared that government-owned laboratories would receive "only those projects that cannot be contracted for with academic or industrial facilities."[141] Even in entirely new and especially sensitive areas, such as the development of atomic energy, strong preference was to be given to the use of research contracts with private institutions. Thus the Atomic Energy Act of 1946 specifically called for a continuation of the wartime practice of using industry and university personnel to operate government-owned nuclear research facilities.[142] The major public studies of postwar science policy were similarly supportive of contracting out for basic research.[143]

[140] On the absence of controversy on this issue see Danhof, "From Improvisation to Policy," p. 739.

[141] The best and most comprehensive treatment of the transition from hot to Cold War is Clarence H. Danhof, *Government Contracting and Technological Change* (Washington, DC: Brookings Institution, 1968), pp. 65, 39–69; On the military in particular see pages 43–56. Regarding the 1947 Armed Services Procurement Act (which made possible the continued purchase of research services without the traditional and cumbersome requirements for advertising and bidding) see James F. Nagle, *A History of Government Contracting* (Washington, DC: George Washington University Press, 1992), pp. 466–72. Also F. Trowbridge vom Baur, "Fifty Years of Government Contract Law," *Federal Bar Journal* 29 (1970), pp. 328–32.

[142] According to one study, "Contracting with private organizations for the management, staffing, and operation of government-owned plants and laboratories was the principal . . . means of retaining a degree of normalcy and freedom in the evolving system of nuclear science and industry," especially in light of the extraordinary powers granted government by the act. Harold Orlans, *Contracting for Atoms* (Washington, DC: Brookings Institution, 1967), p. 6. See also Morgan Thomas, *Atomic Energy and Congress* (Ann Arbor: University of Michigan Press, 1956); Richard A. Tybout, *Government Contracting in Atomic Energy* (Ann Arbor: University of Michigan Press, 1956).

[143] The so-called Steelman Report noted, for example, that in 1947 government laboratories were

The military's research facilities continued to operate and, compared to their virtual starvation during the interwar period, to flourish. At the same time as they began grudgingly to abandon the actual manufacture of arms in their arsenals and shipyards, the Army and Navy both sought to preserve some in-house capacity for research and development work. Although few argued that government-owned and -operated laboratories should be abandoned altogether, Congress and the president were generally united in opposing any increase in the relative reliance placed on them. In a variety of ways (including slowing down authorization for the building of new federal facilities, placing limits on growth in civil service employment, and imposing caps on the salaries of government scientists) Congress acted during the 1950s to encourage the use of contracting instead of in-house research.[144] Civilian-run research establishments, it was widely agreed, were more efficient and more likely to be innovative than their government counterparts.[145] In any case, if tax dollars were to be spent on research, there were clear economic and political benefits to spending them in the private sector.[146]

As with arms manufacturing, ideological considerations also weighed heavily in favor of relying on industry and academia. In 1955 the second Hoover Commission, which also recommended increased privatization of arms production, concluded that "research and development . . . operations are, in general, best performed by civilian agencies." Every effort should therefore be made not only to avoid expanding the activities of the intramural labs but to constrict them and to shift much of their work toward "the civilian economy."[147] These recommendations, which accorded fully with the views of President Eisenhower and his top advisers, were soon echoed in declarations of executive branch policy.[148]

With the addition of a civilian space program to ongoing military research efforts, the extent of the government's reliance on private facilities and institutions took another large step forward. Federally funded private sector research was now absorbing an even larger portion of the nation's total pool of scientists and engineers. Meanwhile, thanks to the trend toward privatization, federally owned research facilities appeared to be dwindling in size and significance. Some critics began to worry that the government was losing the capacity even to monitor and control the vast research and development programs for which it was paying, still less to conduct its own research. Without their own in-house

---

performing only about a third of all federally funded research. The report concluded that there was "no reason to recommend any substantial change in this general pattern." President's Scientific Research Board, *Science and Public Policy*, p. 27.

[144] On the role of Congress see Danhof, *Government Contracting*, pp. 95–105.

[145] See, for example, an essay by the president of the California Institute of Technology, Lee A. Dubridge, "Science and Government," *Chemical and Engineering News* 31, no. 14 (April 6, 1953), p. 1384–90.

[146] On the political and budgetary benefits to the sponsoring agencies (and to Congress) of favoring private over public performance of research see Price, *Government and Science*, p. 79.

[147] See a Report to Congress by the Commission on Organization of the Executive Branch of Government (Hoover Commission), *Research and Development in the Government* (Washington, DC: U.S. Government Printing Office, May 1955), p. 16.

[148] Danhof, *Government Contracting*, p. 107.

expertise, federal agencies might be forced to place their trust in private actors whose interests did not necessarily coincide with those of the nation as a whole. In the late 1950s there were allegations of overly close, and possibly improper, relationships between companies advising the government on how to structure its missile and space programs and those actually doing the research, development, and manufacturing work.[149] Toward the end of Eisenhower's second term, his science advisers fretted publicly that government researchers had begun to "lose heart as the number of contract-operated laboratories has grown over the last decade." "Undue reliance on outside laboratories," they warned, "could greatly impair the morale and vitality of needed Government laboratories."[150]

These concerns ran counter to the Eisenhower administration's strong preference for privatization, and they consequently had little impact on policy. In 1961, noting that the federal government now had over a decade of experience in making "extensive use of contracts with private institutions and enterprises," President Kennedy ordered Budget Bureau Director David Bell to undertake a comprehensive review of past practices.[151] Although it offered a modest defense of the government labs (which permitted the preservation of a core of federal employees with the competence to oversee extramural research) and suggested some measures for strengthening them (primarily by increasing the salaries of government scientists), the so-called Bell Report did not offer a thoroughgoing critique of the contract system. To the contrary, it concluded that continued heavy reliance on contracting was in the national interest. The contract system afforded "the largest opportunity for initiative and the competition of ideas" while at the same time helping "to maintain and enlarge the long-term strength of the Nation's scientific resources."[152] Fundamental change was neither necessary nor desirable.

PERFORMANCE

Critics and enthusiasts alike agree that the American research and development system was highly productive of technological advances, that it tended over

[149] These issues are discussed at length in Hearings before a Subcommittee of the House Government Operations Committee, *Organization and Management of Missile Programs*, 86th Cong., 1st sess. (Washington, DC: U.S. Government Printing Office, 1959). For an analysis see Nieburg, *In the Name of Science*, pp. 200–217, 334–50.

[150] Report of the President's Science Advisory Committee, *Strengthening American Science* (Washington, DC: U.S. Government Printing Office, 1959), p. 16.

[151] For the text of the letter from President Kennedy ordering this study see Hearings before the Military Operations Subcommittee of the House Committee on Government Operations, *Systems Development and Management*, pt. 1, 87th Cong., 2d sess. (Washington, DC: U.S. Government Printing Office, 1962), pp. 250–51.

[152] The report is reprinted ibid., pp. 191–337, quotes from p. 192. Despite its soothing conclusion, the Bell Report was met with suspicion from industry and members of Congress, who subsequently watered down its proposals for salary increases. See the discussion in Nieburg, *In the Name of Science*, pp. 334–50.

time to outpace its Soviet counterpart, and that the superior performance of the American system was connected in some way to its structure. But how?

Political scientist Matthew Evangelista has argued persuasively that the comparative decentralization of the U.S. system helped to make it more innovative than its rigidly centralized and hierarchical rival. Where the United States has what Evangelista calls a "bottom up" system that "encourages the free flow of information and rewards low-level initiatives," the Soviets had a "top down" structure in which all important choices had ultimately to be made by high-level decision makers. The Soviet system tended to inhibit innovation, a failing for which it was able to compensate only in part by its capacity "to marshall resources behind new projects, once a decision to innovate" had been taken.[153] The stubborn American resistance to centralization, so often decried in the 1940s and 1950s, seems in retrospect to have been an important source of technological vitality.[154]

The fact that the great bulk of defense research in the United States was performed by private industry had similar stimulative effects. Advocates have praised "the flexibility, innovative nature, technical competence" and competitive spirit of industry, and applauded the way in which the pursuit of contracts (and profits) encouraged private defense firms to take risks and to push forward the technological frontier.[155] Critics, describing the same phenomena, deplored the way in which the use of "large private corporation[s], dependent on government orders, create[d] an 'industrial imperative' for rapid product improve-

---

[153] See the comparison of the U.S. and Soviet systems in Matthew Evangelista, *Innovation and the Arms Race: How the United States and the Soviet Union Develop New Military Technologies* (Ithaca: Cornell University Press, 1988), 30, and especially pp. 22–82. Evangelista also points to a number of other characteristics that favored the American system, including its complexity, relative informality, and high degree of interconnectedness.

[154] Some contemporary American observers did, of course, recognize the virtues of decentralization. Arguing against the post-Sputnik wave of enthusiasm for enhanced coordination and control, two RAND analysts pointed out: "Military research and development is being pilloried for precisely those characteristics that it has in common with research and development in the free enterprise economy. Research and development in the American economy is uncoordinated. There is no central planning or direction. There is a great deal of duplication, rivalry, and of course, viewed with the aid of hindsight, apparent waste. And yet the American economy is . . . the most progressive and advanced in the world. . . . Instead of striving for an extreme form of monopolistic bureaucracy in the management of research and development, we would do well to consider emulating part of the practices of our more progressive industries." Charles J. Hitch and Roland N. McKean, *The Economics of Defense in the Nuclear Age* (Cambridge: Harvard University Press, 1960), pp. 256–58.

[155] See the comparison of the U.S. and Soviet systems in Statement by William J. Perry, Undersecretary of Defense, Research, and Engineering, to the Congress of the United States, *The FY 1979 Department of Defense Program for Research, Development, and Acquisition*, 95th Cong., 2d sess. (Washington, DC: Department of Defense, February 1, 1978), pp. II-6, II-4 to II-6. For another sympathetic account (albeit one that urges government to ajdust incentives to make industry even *more* innovative) see Jacques S. Gansler, *The Defense Industry* (Cambridge: MIT Press, 1982), pp. 97–108. See also the discussion in Robert Perry, *Comparisons of Soviet and U.S. Technology*, R-827-PR (Santa Monica, CA: RAND, June 1973).

ment."[156] While the language differed, the fundamental conclusion remained the same: whether for good or ill, heavy reliance on private, profit-making enterprises (as compared to state-owned arsenals) helped make the United States more innovative than its rival.

In ways that the founding fathers of Cold War science and technology policy could not fully have anticipated, the *limitations* on the institutions they established may also have helped to contribute to their eventual strategic success. The constraints on the functional scope of the federal research system meant that the government could influence, but could not, and would not, seek ultimately to control the larger course of national technological development. The defense research establishment (and the closely related space and energy research and development efforts) were lodged within and connected, through the contract mechanism, to a civilian commercial and academic research system that tended to grow in size and independence as time wore on. If the federal science apparatus set up in the 1940s and 1950s had been granted greater authority and a broader directive scope, the evolution of science and technology in the postwar world might have been much different. It would, in any event, have been even more heavily shaped, and perhaps constrained and distorted, by the demands of the state than was in fact the case. Instead, the federal government's influence as the driving force of technological progress tended to diminish over time. In terms of their impact on the arms competition, the results were unintended, unanticipated, and, for the United States, highly beneficial.

During the first half of the Cold War, the federal government dominated the national scientific and technological enterprise, contributing between one-half and two thirds of the total dollars spent each year on research. The end of the space program's explosive growth phase and the continued, steady expansion in privately funded research combined, after the mid-1960s, to produce a steady decline in the government's share of national research and development spending. By the late 1970s, and for the first time since the onset of the Cold War, industry and academia had replaced government as the leading supplier of research dollars (see fig. 8.5).[157]

---

[156] Mary Kaldor, "The Weapons Succession Process," *World Politics* 38, no. 4 (July 1986), p. 595. Kaldor attributes the superior technological dynamism of the West to the behavior of the "supply institutions" (i.e., industry) rather than to the preferences of the "demand institutions (i.e., the military), which she regards as inherently conservative. She conludes that "in the East, the supply institutions are fundamentally bureaucratic organizations with the same inertial tendencies that are characteristic of the demand institutions; therefore there is not the same pressure for technological change." Ibid. See also Mary Kaldor, "Military R & D: Cause or Consequence of the Arms Race?" *International Social Science Journal* 35, no. 1 (1983), pp. 25–43. And Kaldor, *The Baroque Arsenal* (New York: Hill and Wang, 1981). Kaldor draws inspiration from an earlier article by James Kurth, "Why We Buy the Weapons We Do," *Foreign Policy*, no. 11 (Summer 1973), pp. 33–56.

[157] See tables in Mowery and Rosenberg, *Technology and the Pursuit of Economic Growth*, pp. 126–27. The rapid growth of research and development spending in other Western industrialized countries also meant that from the early 1960s onward, the U.S. defense establishment's share of total "free world" research tended to fall. In 1960 the Defense Department funded one-third of all

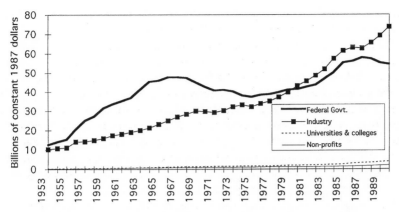

Figure 8.5. Sources of Funds for Research and Development, by Sector, 1953–1990

The relationship between the government-funded, largely defense-oriented research system and its increasingly vigorous, privately funded, mostly commercially oriented counterpart changed over time. From the 1940s to the 1960s most of the technologies being developed for defense purposes were either unrelated to or significantly more advanced than those being pursued primarily for commercial reasons. Intercontinental ballistic missiles and thermonuclear weapons had no obvious civilian applications, and government sponsors led the way in developing such things as jet engines and nuclear power plants. To the extent that there was a flow of ideas between the two, the balance of exchange appeared heavily to favor the civilian sector over its defense-driven counterpart.

Gradually at first, and then with increasing rapidity, this balance began to shift. In the 1960s and 1970s several technologies that had been nurtured initially by government agencies and whose early evolution had been shaped primarily by their needs entered a phase of accelerated, autonomous, commercially driven development. As their possible civilian applications became more obvious, innovations that had been launched by the defense and space programs were picked up and exploited by a private sector responding to commercial incentives and acting largely beyond the reach of governmental direction or control. The stimulus of unconstrained commercial competition forced technological development farther and faster than it would otherwise have gone.

In the closing two decades of the Cold War the presence of a large, vibrant, and independent civilian high-technology sector emerged as a decisive strategic advantage for the West. In contrast to the commercial research of the 1950s and 1960s, such exploration was now clearly producing substantial, tangible benefits for defense. Lacking a similar amplifier and accelerator for their own military research efforts, and able to gain access to Western technology only spo-

research conducted in the OECD countries; by 1990 the figure was only one-seventh. Alic et al., *Beyond Spinoff*, pp. 5–6.

radically, stealthily, and at great expense, the Soviets began, in a number of crucial respects, to fall farther and farther behind.

This pattern was most obvious and, from the strategic point of view, ultimately most important in the computer and semiconductor industries. In both, initial developments were supported by the U.S. government and, in particular, by the military. Federal agencies sponsored much early research, and by providing a guaranteed buyer for esoteric, experimental products, helped to encourage firms to enter new markets, acquire technological know-how, and invest in productive capacity. The demands of government customers also helped initially to drive the pace of technological advance, pushing industry to develop faster computers and smaller semiconductor devices than seemed necessary at the time for purely commercial purposes.[158]

By the mid-1960s, the importance and influence of the government as a funder of research and a consumer of new products had begun to decline, and the semiconductor and computer industries had started down a path of rapid, mutually reinforcing, and increasingly commercially driven growth and development.[159] The manifestations of this process included rising output, the perfection of mass production techniques, falling prices, growing reliability, and increasing performance.

The possible strategic implications of these trends were almost immediately apparent. In 1975, Malcolm Currie, the Director of Defense Research and Engineering, observed that an ongoing "transformation" in the "technology of conventional warfare" was bringing the world to "the threshold of a new era." The perfection of "precision guided ordnance, stand-off control of battlefield weapons, powerful new forms of surveillance, command and control, night vision and remotely piloted vehicles" could, together, have revolutionary effects.[160] Fortunately, it was precisely in the electronic technologies that underlay all of these systems that the United States appeared to be gaining ground on the

---

[158] For useful overviews of developments in these two closely related industries see Richard C. Levin, "The Semiconductor Industry," and Barbara Goody Katz and Almarin Phillips, "The Computer Industry," both in Richard R. Nelson, *Government and Technical Progress: A Cross-Industry Analysis* (New York: Pergamon Press, 1982), pp. 9–100 and 162–232.

[159] In 1960, for example, government agencies purchased almost half of all semiconductors manufactured in the United States; by 1970 the figure had dropped to 17 percent. Levin, "The Semiconductor Industry," p. 60. In 1962, having pressed hard for the development of integrated circuits, the missile and space programs consumed every one of the 4 million produced in that year. By 1968 total shipments of the miniature semiconductor devices had risen eighty times, but the government's share of industry output had dropped to over a third and was falling rapidly (p. 63). In the 1950s the military, and especially the Air Force, supported the development of computers that used transistors instead of more fragile, less reliable vacuum tubes. With the arrival after 1960 of these so-called second generation machines, the commercial market began to grow rapidly and the government's influence over the computer makers started to decline. Katz and Phillips, "The Computer Industry," p. 220.

[160] Statement before the House Armed Services Committee of Dr. Malcolm Currie, Director of Defense Research and Engineering, "The Department of Defense Program of Research, Development, Test, and Evaluation, FY 1976," (February 21, 1975), mimeo, pp. I-22–23.

Soviets. The driving force behind this advance, in turn, was the vitality of the commercial sector:

> Wherever we have leads of several years to a decade, and where our leads seem to be increasing, it is important to note that large civilian markets exist in the U.S. We should note also, however, that all these technologies had their roots in the U.S. military research and development program. Clearly the extent of these leads is due to a healthy relationship between the demand for civilian and military technologies and their combined impact on quality products.[161]

In contrast to the United States, the inability of "Soviet civilian R & D" to contribute "substantive benefits . . . to military programs" was "one of the great failures of the Soviet system." The task facing the American defense research establishment, Currie concluded, was how best to exploit its inherent advantages and, in particular, its proximity to a dynamic private sector.[162]

As the pace of the commercial electronics revolution continued to accelerate, the extent of the American edge became even more evident. By the mid-1980s U.S. intelligence analysts were reporting that much of the overall Soviet disadvantage in advanced military technologies could be traced to their failings in a handful of "underlying technologies," in particular, computers (where "the Soviets lag the United States by 5 to 15 years . . . and appear to be falling further behind"), microelectronics production techniques (where "the Soviets have been unable to achieve high-quality mass production both of electronics grade silicon and the micro-electronic devices themselves sufficient to their needs"), and precision instrumentation to monitor experiments and control production.[163] These, of course, were the areas in which Western civilian industry had been most active and innovative.[164]

---

[161] Ibid., II-10.

[162] Ibid., II-6.

[163] Statement by Rear Adm. Robert Schmitt, Deputy Director, Defense Intelligence Agency, in Hearing before the Subcommittee on Economic Resources, Competitiveness, and Security Economics of the Joint Economic Committee, *Allocation of Resources in the Soviet Union and China, 1985* 99th Cong., 2d sess. (Washington, DC: U.S. Government Printing Office, 1986), p. 115.

[164] Seeking to explain the apparent deterioration in the Soviet position, analyst David Holloway observed in 1985 that "Soviet military technology may be increasingly affected by the low technological level of Soviet industry as a whole, and particularly of the electronics industry. In the United States the civilian market has led the defence sector in . . . microelectronics, software, and instrumentation, and has thus generated new technological possibilities for military application; but this has not happened in the Soviet Union." If they did not develop some capacity for "indigenous innovation" in these areas, Holloway concluded, even a vigorous program of industrial espionage would not allow the Soviets to close the widening gap with the West. David Holloway, "Western Technology and Soviet Military Power," in Mark E. Schaffer, ed., *Technology Transfer and East-West Relations* (New York: St. Martin's Press, 1985), pp. 174–75.

Conclusions

Out of "Weakness," Strength

The arguments and evidence presented in the preceeding chapters can be briefly summarized:

- By the early 1960s the United States had forged a stable strategic synthesis, an outward-directed force posture and military strategy, and a supporting set of inward-directed power-creating mechanisms.
- The character of this synthesis was strongly shaped by anti-statist influences that were particularly potent during the opening stages of the Cold War, from the late 1940s to the closing years of the 1950s.
- Despite some relatively minor changes, the broad outlines of both the internal and the external aspects of U.S. policy would remain fixed for the remainder of the Cold War.

In closing I want to make the case that the American Cold War synthesis was functional as well as stable; it permitted the United States to achieve its goals of deterring, containing, and ultimately outlasting the Soviet Union, without at the same time transforming itself into a garrison state. Much of the credit for this fortuitous outcome must go to the constraints on governmental power imposed by the content of American ideology and by the basic structure of the nation's political institutions. These factors, often described as contributing to the "weakness" of the American state were, in the long run, sources of profound strength.

This point can be made most clearly by considering what would have happened if the anti-statist influences at work in the 1940s and 1950s had, in fact, been weaker. What seems most likely is not that the United States would have done *less* to gird itself for a possible war with the Soviet Union during the first, formative years of their confrontation, but that it would have done *more*, probably much more. And having started down this path when the Soviets were, in fact, comparatively weak, American policy makers would then likely have felt compelled to sustain an equivalent and perhaps even a higher level of effort as Soviet power grew (see table 9.1).

As compared to the most likely alternative, the synthesis that actually did emerge had a number of economic, political, and strategic advantages.[1]

---

[1] The most likely alternative synthesis for the United States bears a close resemblance, of course, to the one actually adopted by the Soviet Union. See the discussion at the close of chapter 3.

TABLE 9.1
Actual versus Most Likely Alternative Outcomes (circa Early 1960s)

	Actual Outcome	*Most Likely Alternative*
Strategy	flexible response	stalemate/warfighting
Money	< 10% GNP (and falling)	> 15% GNP?
Manpower	limited draft (then AVF)	UMT
Supporting industries	no central planning, procurement only, no dispersal	central planning, tariffs, subsidies, preferences, dispersal
Arms	privatization	large public production
Technology	decentralized, narrow, large private role	centralized, broad, large public role

Economic Advantages

Over the course of the Cold War, between 1948 and 1989, the United States expended an average of 7.5 percent of its gross domestic product each year on defense.[2] Had defense spending been lower, these resources could have been directed to other purposes: higher levels of personal consumption, more private investment, or bigger budgets for other, nonmilitary government programs. On the other hand, of course, if defense spending had been *higher*, the opposite would have been true. A larger share of national output devoted to defense would have meant smaller shares for consumption, investment, or government nondefense spending or, most likely, for all three combined.[3]

If the Cold War had never taken place or if it had been conducted at a substantially lower level of overall expense and financial extraction the average American would no doubt have been better off. In such a world, taxes would almost certainly have been lower than they actually were, the economy would have probably grown more quickly (stimulated by more private investment), and ordinary citizens could have enjoyed the benefits of a set of social welfare programs even more generous than those ultimately put into place. Depending on their structure, these programs might have been of particular benefit to the nation's poorest citizens.

The opposing possibility is less pleasing, but more plausible. Instead of

[2] Office of Management and Budget, *Budget of the U.S. Government, FY 98* (Washington, DC: U.S. Government Printing Office, 1997), table 6.1.

[3] These observations follow from the simple Keynesian national income identity: GNP = Consumption + Investment + Government Spending (Defense + Non-defense). For any given level of GNP, as one of the components increases its share, those of the others must decline. See the discussion in Aaron L. Friedberg, "The Political Economy of American National Strategy," *World Politics* 41, no. 3 (April 1989), pp. 381–406.

spending what it actually did on defense, the United States could easily have wound up spending a good deal more. Much bigger budgets were a very real possibility in the 1940s and especially the 1950s. Once set, a higher level of defense expenditure might have been sustained into the 1960s and beyond. Certainly there was considerable support in the late 1950s for up to 50 percent real increases in defense spending. The costs of such expenditures would have included higher taxes and some combination of lower consumption, less investment (and hence slower growth), and smaller social welfare programs. The most likely alternative to the Cold War America of historical fact was not a more prosperous and generous nation, but one that was certainly less comfortable and probably less equitable as well.

In addition to simply extracting more tax dollars and consuming a larger share of national output, a bigger, stronger Cold War state would have been more extensively and intensively involved in various directive activites. These would have had an array of direct and indirect costs. Instead of eschewing central planning, forgoing dispersal, and largely avoiding the use of national security tariffs, subsidies, and procurement preferences, the federal government might have become enmeshed in the coils of an aggressive, wide-ranging defense industrial policy. The immediate results would have included a bigger price tag for a given quantity of military power and higher prices for many commodities and consumer goods. Some portion of the additional cost of building and operating steel plants in remote locations, for example, would no doubt have been passed on to the buyers of automobiles (and tanks). And, to take another example, American watch manufacturers protected by tariff barriers justified on grounds of "defense essentiality" would have been able to charge higher prices for wrist watches as well as for artillery fuzes.

Over time, a national economy in which a substantial number of sectors were subject to the ministrations of government planners would likely have been less efficient, less flexible, and less capable of sustaining growth than one in which most business decisions were made primarily in response to market signals. Defense industrial planning might not have led directly to "serfdom," but over time it would probably have resulted in a less vibrant and vigorous economy. Nor would the consequences have been solely domestic. If the United States government had become more protectionist and more concerned with preserving defense autarky, it might have been less inclined and less able to promote freer trade among the advanced industrial democracies. In the long run, such a course would have been deeply damaging to the well-being of America's allies, to the cohesion of its alliances, and to the viability of its grand strategy.

What of the other directive activities of the American state? The most likely alternative to a big, private arms production base was not one that was significantly smaller, or that did not exist at all, but a mechanism for military manufacturing in which public actors played a much more substantial role. There is no reason to think that whatever the flaws and failings of their commercial counterparts, the public arsenals and shipyards would have been more efficient or innovative developers and manufacturers of weapons, and there is ample cause to expect that they would have been less so. A more heavily public arms production system would almost certainly have given less "bang for the buck"; it would have built weapons at higher cost, and it would probably also have been slower and less effective in introducing innovations than the privatized "military industrial complex."

In addition to relying more heavily on government researchers instead of private laboratories and scientists, the United States might have put in place a national research and development system that was both more tightly centralized in its administrative structure and broader in its directive scope. Such choices would probably also have contributed to stultification rather than to stimulating innovation. Maintaining several independent and at best loosely coordinated military and defense-related research and development programs was certainly costly, but it also allowed for competition and opened multiple avenues of technological advance. A more orderly "top-down" system, in which all decisions rested with a handful of scientific "wise men" might have been more focused, but it would also have been more prone to make mistakes, and perhaps less inclined to take risks.[4]

A system in which the state occupied the commanding heights of technological development and was empowered to allocate resources for civilian as well as defense purposes might well have ended up smothering strategically significant advances. We cannot know with certainty how American science and technology would have evolved if they had been placed more fully and firmly under the control of the federal government at the outset of the Cold War. What we do know is that over time, the government's ability to determine the overall rate and direction of technological progress tended to decline, that the pace of innovation in several key sectors that grew up largely beyond its reach tended to increase, and that the results, while unanticipated, were ultimately of great strategic benefit to the United States. Perhaps an economy in which government agencies played a greater role in supporting and directing every variety of research, and not just those of immediate concern to the military, could have produced the same results, but it seems unlikely.

Political Advantages

A power-creating program of constrained extraction and limited directive scope imposed fewer burdens, and hence provoked less resistance, than might otherwise have been the case. Heavy reliance on private entities to perform scientific research and to design and build new weapons also created sizable societal groups with a direct material interest in sustaining a strategic competition with

---

[4] One example may illustrate the point: Vannevar Bush, for all his practical wisdom, was slow to see the military potential of ballistic missiles. Had he been the nation's defense research "czar" in the 1940s and early 1950s, the United States would have been even slower than it actually was in making progress in this critical area. See the discussion in Stephen Peter Rosen, *Winning the Next War: Innovation and the Modern Military* (Ithaca: Cornell University Press, 1991), pp. 227–28.

the Soviet Union. These factors, taken together, contributed to the continuity of American policy during the Cold War.

Whatever their economic effects, significantly higher taxes would certainly have had political consequences. A much heavier defense burden in the 1940s and 1950s might have led to an early reconsideration, and perhaps to a partial or even a complete abandonment, of extended U.S. security commitments. If the costs of containment and internationalism had included a tax bill as high or even higher than that endured during the Second World War, Americans would no doubt have been more receptive to the lure of isolationism. Although the burden on taxpayers would have grown lighter as the economy expanded and incomes increased, this easing would have taken longer to manifest itself. In the meantime, American decision makers might have felt compelled to take drastic and potentially destabilizing actions designed to cut costs (such as actually withdrawing U.S. ground forces from Europe and transfering nuclear weapons to the NATO allies, steps contemplated and then abandoned by the Eisenhower administration).[5] On the other hand, in order to justify sustained, painful sacrifices, political leaders might have sought to stimulate an even greater sense of public alarm and to feed fears of an imminent "hot" war with the Soviet Union.

The early imposition of universal conscription would have reinforced the political effects of greater financial extraction. Whatever its true extent at the outset, public support for universal military training would almost certainly have diminished once such a scheme had actually been put in place. As the experience of war receded and war-fed patriotism faded, enthusiasm for shared sacrifice and communal effort would have dwindled along with it and traditional American individualism would have reasserted itself. With growing numbers of young men eager to get on with life and go about their business in the 1940s and 1950s, mandatory military service and the foreign policies that seemed to demand it might well have become a focal point for frustration. Instead of inculcating obedience and civic virtue, as its advocates hoped, or promoting "regimentation," as its opponents feared, universal training might instead have encouraged restlessness, resistance, and an increasingly widespread rejection of America's emerging Cold War role.

A broader, more active, and more intrusive industrial policy for defense-supporting industries might also have worked to prevent the formation of a solid domestic consensus on foreign affairs. Such a policy would no doubt have produced economic benefits for and generated political support from some commercial and regional interests. But the same directive policies would also have imposed burdens on the rest of the population and, in some cases, on other powerful interest groups. Higher levels of contention over power creation, strategy, and foreign policy would have been the inevitable result.

The controversy surrounding subsidies for industrial expansion and, even more, the industrial dispersal flaps of the late 1940s and early 1950s provide

---

[5] See Marc Trachtenberg, *A Constructed Peace: The Making of the European Settlement, 1945–1963* (Princeton: Princeton University Press, 1999).

vivid illustrations of this point. In the first case, individual firms and entire industrial sectors that did not qualify for government support complained that they were being placed at an unfair disadvantage. In the second, the allegedly more vulnerable coastal cities, states, and regions feared that they would lose out to the heartland and the South, where factories could be built at a greater distance from the Soviet Union. Bruising and potentially divisive battles over these issues were cut short by the termination of policies that seemed so clearly to transfer resources from one group to another.

In marked contrast, the use of tax dollars to procure research and arms from private entities produced many winners and, aside from the public institutions they displaced, no obvious losers. Such arrangements were not only ideologically acceptable to most Americans, they were also relatively painless. As the tax burden necessary to sustain them diminished, they grew even less so. While the Cold War was underway, a firm (or university) that did not get one government contract usually had others to help keep it going, or could count on getting them in the very near future. Although they competed vigorously and squabbled at times, the various participants in the contract system rarely questioned its legitimacy. To the contrary, most favored its continuation and, by extension, the continuation of the military and diplomatic policies that the system was intended to support.

In the conclusion to chapter 7, I suggested that the private arms producers could not fairly be blamed either for starting the Cold War or for perpetuating it beyond some point at which it might otherwise have been resolved. Larger ideological and geopolitical forces were what impelled the superpowers into conflict with one another, and kept them locked there for over forty years. It was only the collapse of one of the competitors that made it possible truly to bring their rivalry to a close.

This said, it must be noted also that the commercial arms makers and private research institutions, and the penumbra of employees, suppliers, and municipalities that grew up around them, were strongly inclined to favor increases in the scale and scope of the American defense effort and equally inclined to oppose reductions. Taken as a group, these individuals and institutions were a significant source of upward pressure on military spending against which other, countervailing influences had to be brought to bear; but they also provided a counterbalance or an anchor when, as in the 1970s, the forces favoring reduction, retrenchment, and a premature "settlement" with the Soviet Union might otherwise have been overwhelming. Perhaps after all, as they pursued their own interests, the much-reviled members of the "military industrial complex" did good by doing well.

With the partial exception of manpower policy, where a second round of pruning was necessary, the struggles of the 1940s and 1950s served to trim the rough edges off the American program of power creation, holding extraction to tolerable levels and eliminating those directive measures that generated the greatest opposition. The end result of this process was a strategic synthesis whose domestic components rested with relative ease on the nation's society and economy, and that could therefore be sustained until the Cold War had run its course. A state that extracted more money and manpower and which involved itself more directly in production and industrial planning would have found itself subject to much stronger pressures for contraction and retrenchment.

Strategic Advantages

There are at least three standards against which the external aspects of the American strategic synthesis must be judged: by their contribution to deterrence, by their adequacy for defense had deterrence failed, and by their impact on the dynamic development of the superpower arms competition.

The force posture and strategy adopted by the United States were clearly sufficient to deter overt Soviet aggression. Despite the anxieties of the military planners, no direct attack on the U.S. or its allies was ever forthcoming. Unless one is inclined to believe that the Soviets did not at any time harbor aggressive intentions toward the West, some part of the credit for this outcome must go to the military strength of the United States. At the same time, it is certainly possible that the Soviet inclination toward risk-taking was far lower than American strategists feared, and that the same result could have been achieved at a much lower level of military capability.[6]

Thankfully, what would have happened if deterrence had failed and conflict between the superpowers had actually broken out must remain forever a mystery. We cannot know with assurance whether American preparations for war with the Soviet Union would have been sufficient to achieve victory, or to avoid defeat, or even to prevent national disintegration. The outcome of a third world war would no doubt have been different depending on when it occurred. If the Soviets had themselves been able to generate the capacity for offensive operations, they might perhaps have been able to achieve quick victories during the period of comparative Western weakness that followed the end of the Second World War. The massive buildup that began during the Korean conflict, and especially the rapid accumulation of nuclear weapons that continued through the 1950s, might have permitted the United States to wreak terrible devastation on the Soviet Union while at the same time limiting damage to itself and perhaps to its allies as well. As Soviet power grew in the 1960s and 1970s, the likelihood that a superpower conflict could have been won in any meaningful sense of the word probably diminished. On the other hand, as American preparations for and thinking about actual large-scale warfighting dwindled in seriousness and intensity while Soviet capabilities continued to expand, it is at least conceivable that the United States and its allies could have suffered some stunning military setbacks. On these matters, the historian's puzzlement is the world's great good fortune.

---

[6] This is the implication, for example, of the line of analysis developed in Robert Jervis, *The Meaning of the Nuclear Revolution* (Ithaca: Cornell University Press, 1989).

What impact did the strategy and force posture into which the United States eventually settled have on the course and ultimate conclusion of its long-term competition with the Soviet Union? The answer to this question is knowable, at least in principle, although it cannot be said at this point to be known. A final judgment will depend not only on an analysis of American actions and intentions, but on an assessment of *Soviet* perceptions and behavior.

One aspect of American strategy deserves special attention: the persistent, deeply ingrained U.S. propensity for pursuing technological advantage gave the American defense effort a dynamism that it might otherwise have lacked and that seems, over time, to have imposed real and significant burdens on the Soviet Union. Even within the confines of the basic flexible response posture that it had adopted by the early 1960s, the United States continued to press ahead with qualitative improvements that the Soviets found increasingly difficult and costly to match or offset. The acceleration of progress in electronics and computing in the 1960s and the subsequent arrival of what Soviet analysts would label the "third revolution in military affairs" appear to have been particularly stressful in this regard. There is some evidence to suggest that in their efforts to keep pace with the West, Soviet planners felt compelled in the 1960s and 1970s to shift an even greater share of scarce scientific and technological resources from the civilian to the military sector, thereby contributing to a continuing slowdown in productivity growth and in national economic expansion. And there are reasons for believing also that in the 1980s it was anxiety over the prospect of falling technologically ever further behind that impelled the Soviet military to acquiesce in Mikhail Gorbachev's disastrous efforts at economic and political reform.[7]

The manner in which the Cold War ended suggests that the conventional wisdom about the qualitative arms race is badly in need of revision. The relentless American search for superiority was not as pointless or as dangerous as is commonly believed. To the contrary, it may be the well-intentioned efforts of Western diplomats and arms control experts to slow or stop the advance of military technology that were misguided and counterproductive. Perhaps if they had succeeded better at their task the Cold War would still be going on.

The United States applied continuing technological pressure to the USSR, but it did not adopt a strategic stance that was so aggressive and threatening as to make the Soviet leadership believe that war was imminent, or to fear at any point that "war now" might be preferable to "war later." In comparison to a relatively relaxed flexible response posture, ongoing preparations for all-out

---

[7] Regarding the impact of the high technology arms race on overall Soviet economic performance see Vladimir Kontorovich, "The Long-Run Decline in Soviet R & D Productivity," in Henry S. Rowen and Charles Wolf, Jr., eds., *The Impoverished Superpower: Perestroika and the Soviet Military Burden* (San Fransisco: Institute for Contemporary Studies, 1990), pp. 255–70. On the attitudes of the Soviet military toward technology and reform see Dale Herspring, *The Soviet High Command, 1967–1989* (Princeton: Princeton University Press, 1990), pp. 119–214. See also the discussion in Aaron L. Friedberg, "Science, the Cold War, and the American State," *Diplomatic History* 20, no. 1 (Winter 1996), pp. 107–18.

warfighting or for a massive conventional conflict would have appeared far more menacing. The consequences, while unintended, could nevertheless have been profoundly dangerous.

ON THE COMPETITIVE "FITNESS" OF LIBERAL DEMOCRACIES: PAST AND FUTURE[8]

Past

Democratic states have been aptly described as "powerful pacifists": they have tended to be remarkably peaceful in their relations with one another and strikingly successful in winning wars against nondemocratic regimes.[9] In recent years, scholars have devoted enormous energy to understanding the first of these phenomena (and to worrying about whether it will persist as democracy spreads), considerably less to analyzing the second.[10] Yet the two are clearly linked; if not for the past martial prowess of the democracies, there would today be no democratic "zone of peace."

What can explain the evolutionary advantage that democratic regimes appear to have enjoyed over their foes? A full answer to this question will no doubt have to take account of many factors, but one in particular stands out. The constraints that democracies (with their popularly elected leaders) and especially *liberal* democracies (with their additional protections for individual political and economic rights) place on their states have helped to make them surprisingly potent international competitors. In wartime, democracies have been able to summon up enormous reserves of societal strength and sacrifice. In peacetime and during periods of prolonged strategic competition the ideological

[8] On the question of the comparative "fitness" of regimes (which the D'Lugo and Rogowski define as "the degree to which a state's political and social constitution supports an optimal projection of military power") see an intriguing essay: David D'Lugo and Ronald Rogowski, "The Anglo-German Naval Race and Comparative Constitutional 'Fitness,'" in Richard Rosecrance and Arthur A. Stein, eds., *The Domestic Bases of Grand Strategy* (Ithaca: Cornell University Press, 1993), pp. 65, 65–95.

[9] See David A. Lake, "Powerful Pacifists: Democratic States and War," *American Political Science Review* 86, no. 1 (March 1992), pp. 24–37.

[10] For overviews of the vast literature on the "democratic peace," see Bruce Russett, *Grasping the Democratic Peace* (Princeton: Princeton University Press, 1993); James Lee Ray, *Democracy and International Conflict: An Evaluation of the Democratic Peace Proposition* (Columbia: University of South Carolina Press, 1995); Miriam Elman, ed., *Paths to Peace: Is Democracy the Answer?* (Cambridge: MIT Press, 1997). The question of whether, and if so why, democracies are, in fact, superior strategic competitors has recently begun to receive attention from political scientists. See Kenneth A. Schultz and Barry R. Weingast, "Limited Governments, Powerful States," in Randolph M. Siverson, ed., *Strategic Politicians, Institutions, and Foreign Policy* (Ann Arbor: University of Michigan Press, 1998), pp. 15–49; Scott D. Bennett and Allan C. Stam III, "The Declining Advantages of Democracy: A Combined Model of War Outcomes and Duration," *Journal of Conflict Resolution* 42, no. 3 (June 1998), pp. 344–66; Dan Reiter and Allan C. Stam III, "Democracy and Battlefield Military Effectiveness," ibid., pp. 259–77; *Journal of Conflict Resolution* 42, no. 3 (June 1998) Reiter and Stam, "Democracy, War Initiation, and Victory," *American Political Science Review* 92, no. 2 (June 1998), pp. 377–89.

and institutional limits on liberal democratic states appear to have contributed to the technological and overall economic dynamism of their societies.

Perhaps, in retrospect, the Cold War will come to be seen as one in a three-hundred-year series of contests between increasingly liberal, increasingly democratic states and a succession of autocratic, authoritarian, and totalitarian rivals. Future historians may date the beginning of this process to England's Glorious Revolution of 1688 which, by diminishing the authority of the king and giving Parliament the power of the purse, increased the state's revenue-raising capacity, permitted a sustained naval buildup, and cleared the way for England's eventual defeat of France and her emergence at the beginning of the nineteenth century as the world's preponderant power. What historian Lawrence Stone has described as the "metamorphosis of Britain between 1689 and 1815 . . . from a marginal player in the continental power-game into the major European and world imperial power" was marked by a seeming paradox: "on the one hand, the use of massive external military [power] to block a rival hegemonic power and to create a maritime trading [empire] and, on the other, the preservation of internal liberty and the rights of private property."[11] As Stone and others have pointed out, however, the contradiction in this case is more apparent than real.[12] For Britain as for America, and in the seventeenth and eighteenth centuries as in the nineteenth and twentieth, state weakness and national strength went hand in hand. Understanding exactly why this was so will be critical to explaining the survival and spread of democracy.

Future

It is tempting for Americans to believe that the collapse of the Soviet Union and the end of the Cold War mark the passing of the last serious challenge to liberal democracy as a system, and perhaps even to the United States as the preponderant global power. In the fullness of time, this may turn out to have been the case. But it is also possible that new challengers could arise, and that they could take forms quite different from any the world has previously seen.

The Soviet Union was, of course, neither liberal nor democratic, and it therefore labored under a double disadvantage. Lacking any reliable means of refreshing the sources of its popular support, the Soviet state tended over time to lose whatever legitimacy it may have had and was able to rule, in the end, only through coercion and by dint of the habitual subservience of its citizens. When the willingness of its leaders to coerce grew demonstrably weaker, the political system quickly collapsed. Meanwhile, the initial ideological commitments to

[11] Lawrence Stone, "Introduction," in Stone, ed., *An Imperial State at War: Britain from 1689 to 1815* (London: Routledge, 1994), p. 6. (The words *empire* and *power* are reversed in the original.)

[12] For further discussion see, in addition to the essays in Stone, John Brewer, *The Sinews of Power: War, Money and the English State, 1688–1783* (Cambridge: Harvard University Press, 1988); Douglass C. North and Barry R. Weingast, "Constitutions and Commitment: The Evolution of Institutions Governing Public Choice in Seventeenth-Century England," *Journal of Economic History* 49, no. 4 (December 1989), pp. 803–32.

central planning, public ownership, and virtual international autarky, the absence of any institutional or ideational constraints on state power, and the mounting pressures of a protracted competition with the United States combined to choke economic growth and stifle technological innovation. The Soviets could compensate for a time by extracting an ever greater share of societal resources and directing them toward military ends, but in the long run this only made their underlying problems worse. All of this is clearer now than it was at the time, but as we look back on it, the Soviet Union appears as a deeply, perhaps even a fatally flawed competitor.

Future challengers could have different internal characteristics and, consequently, different strategic strengths and weaknesses. A polity that was democratic without being liberal might be able to generate impressive popular energies and mobilize substantial resources, at least for a time. But the absence of protections for individual freedoms, and for property rights in particular, would probably have damaging long-term economic consequences.

More serious might be the challenge posed by a regime that was "liberal," at least in the limited sense of permitting private property, markets, and international trade, without being democratic. If it could suppress dissent while sustaining growth, such a state might be able to combine the tactical advantages that authoritarian regimes occasionally enjoy (including a capacity for secrecy, surprise, and diplomatic flexibility) with some of the deeper economic strength and technological vitality of a liberal democracy. Is such a balancing act possible? Could a "market authoritarian" regime maintain stability over time and, if so, how would its internal development effect its external behavior? China's rapid growth suggests that at the beginning of the twenty-first century, the answers to these questions will be of more than purely academic interest.

CLOSING THOUGHTS ON AMERICAN ANTI-STATISM

Powerful countervailing forces innoculated America against the worst extremes of statism during the critical opening stages of the Cold War. These protective, anti-statist influences had deep ideological and institutional sources, and they also drew strength from the specific circumstances of the late 1940s and early 1950s and from the events of the preceeding decade. In time, the intensity of the initial postwar anti-statist impulse grew weaker. Although by the early 1960s, the outlines of the nation's strategic synthesis were basically set, the way was cleared for a dramatic expansion in governmental activity at home and a stunningly ambitious application of national power abroad. With the elections of 1964, Lyndon Johnson had the support he needed to launch the Great Society while at the same time increasing the extraction of money and manpower necessary to escalate the war in Vietnam. After twenty years of working itself free, American statism was finally, if only briefly, unbound.

Suspicion of governmental power and institutionalized obstacles to its exercise have served the American people well over the past two hundred years.

When these constraints grow too weak, as they did in the 1960s, the results can be deeply damaging to the nation's foreign policy, economic performance, and social cohesion. It goes without saying, however, and so probably bears repeating, that nations, like people, can have too much of a good thing. Institutions that are perpetually deadlocked will be unable to generate workable solutions to the new problems and challenges that history inevitably presents. And a political culture in which *any* exercise of governmental power is regarded with distaste and fear and in which government itself becomes an object of hatred or scorn will eventually corrode the foundations of liberal democracy.

The proper balance between statist and anti-statist impulses can sometimes be attained in the American system through convergence and coolly reasoned compromise; more often it will be the product of heated debate and intense, often bitter struggle. This process is seldom pretty, its results are never perfect and rarely permanent, but it has proven its worth, time and again, in peace and in war. In the never-ending battle over the direction of the Republic, all parties have their part to play. America needs its Jeffersons, but it needs its Hamiltons too.

RECENT TITLES

In the Shadow of the Garrison State: America's Anti-Statism and Its Cold War Grand Strategy by Aaron L. Friedberg

States and Power in Africa: Comparative Lessons in Authority and Control by Jeffrey Herbst

The Moral Purpose of the State: Culture, Social Identity, and Institutional Rationality in International Relations by Christian Reus-Smit

Entangling Relations: American Foreign Policy in Its Century by David Lake

A Constructed Peace: The Making of the European Settlement, 1945–1963 by Marc Trachtenberg

Regional Orders at Century's Dawn: Global and Domestic Influences on Grand Strategy by Etel Solingen

From Wealth to Power: The Unusual Origins of America's World Role by Fareed Zakaria

Changing Course: Ideas, Politics, and the Soviet Withdrawal from Afghanistan by Sarah E. Mendelson

Disarming Strangers: Nuclear Diplomacy with North Korea by Leon V. Sigal

Imagining War: French and British Military Doctrine between the Wars by Elizabeth Kier

Roosevelt and the Munich Crisis: A Study of Political Decision-Making by Barbara Rearden Farnham

Useful Adversaries: Grand Strategy, Domestic Mobilization, and Sino-American Conflict, 1947–1958 by Thomas J. Christensen

Satellites and Commisars: Strategy and Conflict in the Politics of the Soviet-Bloc Trade by Randall W. Stone

Does Conquest Pay? The Exploitation of Occupied Industrial Societies by Peter Liberman

Cultural Realism: Strategic Culture and Grand Strategy in Chinese History by Alastair Iain Johnston

The Korean War: An International History by William W. Stueck

Cooperation among Democracies: The European Influence on U.S. Foreign Policy by Thomas Risse-Kappen

The Sovereign State and Its Competitors by Hendrik Spruyt

America's Mission: The United States and the Worldwide Struggle for Democracy in the Twentieth Century by Tony Smith

Who Adjusts? Domestic Sources of Foreign Economic Policy during the Interwar Years by Beth A. Simmons

PRINCETON STUDIES IN AMERICAN POLITICS: HISTORICAL,
INTERNATIONAL, AND COMPARATIVE PERSPECTIVES

SERIES EDITORS
Ira Katznelson, Martin Shefter, and Theda Skocpol

DATE DUE

The Library Store   #47-0106